ALPHABETICAL QUICK REFERENCE TO BIRD GROUPS

Akalats	328	Egrets	62	Mynas	384	Sheathbills	204
Albatrosses	32	Eremomelas	332	Nicators	312	Shelducks	76
Alethes	324	Fairy Flycatcher	342	Nightingales	328	Shrikes	372
Apalises	344	Falcons	122	Nightjars	244	Siskins	422
Avocets	162	Finches	414	Noddies	216	Skimmers	206
Babblers	308	Finfoots	146	Orioles	302	Skuas	204
Barbets	272	Firefinches	410	Ospreys	92	Snake-Eagles	94
Bat Hawk	124	Flamingoes	72	Ostriches	142	Snipes	186
Batises	360	Flufftails	152	Owls	240	Sparrowhawks	118
Bee-eaters	258	Flycatchers	354	Oxpeckers	384	Sparrowlarks	290
Bishops	402	Francolins	136	Oystercatchers	162	Sparrows	394
Bitterns	66	Frigatebirds	58	Painted-Snipes	186	Sparrow-Weavers	396
Boobies	54	Gallinules	148	Palm-Thrushes	328	Spinetails	250
Boubous	374	Gannets	54	Parakeets	228	Spoonbills	72
Boulder Chat	308	Geese	76	Parrots	226	Spurfowl	136
Broadbills	252	Giant Petrels	38	Partridges	140	Starlings	380
Brubru	378	Godwits	184	Peacock	142	Stilts	162
Brownbul	310	Goshawks	118	Pelicans	58	Storks	68
Buffalo-weavers	396	Grassbird	340	Penduline-Tits	332	Storm-Petrels	50
Bulbuls	310	Grebes	30	Penguins	28	Sugarbirds	386
Buntings	424	Greenbuls	312	Petrels	40	Sunbirds	386
Bush Blackcap	310	Ground-Hornbills	264	Phalaropes	188	Swallows	292
Bush-Shrikes	376	Guineafowl	142	Pigeons	220	Swamphens	148
Bustards	156	Gulls	206	Pipits	364	Swifts	248
Buttonquails	144	Hamerkop	72	Pittas	252	Tchagras	374
Buzzards	104	Harrier-Hawks	106	Plovers	164	Terns	210
Canaries	420	Harriers	108	Pratincoles	190	Thick-knees	202
Chanting Goshawks	112	Helmet-Shrikes	378	Prinias	352	Thrushes	314
Chats	318	Herons	60	Prions	48	Tinkerbirds	274
Cisticolas	346	Hobbies	124	Pytilias	416	Tit-Babblers	342
Coots	146	Honeybirds	270	Quails	144	Tits	306
Cormorants	56	Honeyguides	270	Queleas	402	Trogons	252
Coucals	238	Hoopoes	268	Rails	150	Tropicbirds	54
Coursers	202	Hornbills	264	Ravens	304	Turacos	230
Crab Plover	162	Hyliotas	358	Redstarts	322	Turnstones	186
Crakes	148	Ibises	74	Robin-Chats	324	Twinspots	418
Cranes	154	Indigobirds	408	Robins	328	Vultures	86
Creepers	306	Jacanas	148	Rock-Jumpers	316	Wagtails	362
Crimsonwings	418	Kestrels	126	Rockrunner	340	Warblers	330
Crombecs	342	Kingfishers	254	Rock-Thrushes	316	Wattle-eyes	360
Crows	304	Kites	112	Rollers	262	Waxbills	410
Cuckoo Finch	408	Kittiwakes	208	Ruff	174	Weavers	396
Cuckooshrikes	300	Korhaans	158	Sandgrouse	218	Wheatears	318
Cuckoos	232	Larks	280	Sandpipers	176	Whimbrels	184
Curlews	184	Longclaws	370	Saw-wings	296	White-eyes	358
Darters	56	Lovebirds	228	Scimitarbills	268	Whydahs	406
Doves	220	Mannikins	414	Secretarybird	154	Widowbirds	404
Drongos	300	Martins	298	Seedcrackers	418	Wood-Hoopoes	268
Ducks	76	Moorhens	146	Seed-eaters	422	Woodpeckers	276
Eagles	92	Mousebirds	252	Shearwaters	40	Wrynecks	276

QUICK COLOUR-CODED REFERENCE TO BIRD GROUPS

SEABIRDS: penguins, grebes, albatrosses, shearwaters, petrels, prions, storm-petrels, tropicbirds, gannets, boobies, cormorants, darters, frigatebirds, pelicans

LARGE WATERBIRDS: herons, egrets, bitterns, storks, flamingoes, spoonbills, Hamerkop, ibises, ducks, geese

BIRDS OF PREY: vultures, eagles, Osprey, buzzards, harrier-hawks, harriers, kites, hawks, falcons

Francolins, peacocks, guineafowl, ground-hornbills, Ostrich, quails, buttonquails, finfoots, coots, moorhens, gallinules, jacanas, rails, crakes, flufftails, cranes, bustards, korhaans

WADERS, SKUAS, GULLS AND TERNS: Crab Plover, oystercatchers, stilts, avocets, plovers, sandpipers and allies, painted-snipes, snipes, phalaropes, pratincoles, thick-knees, coursers, skuas, jaegers, sheathbills, gulls, terns

Sandgrouse, pigeons, doves, parrots, lovebirds

Turacos, cuckoos, coucals, owls, nightjars, swifts

Trogons, pittas, broadbills, mousebirds, kingfishers, bee-eaters, rollers, hornbills, hoopoes, wood-hoopoes, scimitarbills, honeyguides, barbets, wrynecks, woodpeckers, tinkerbirds

Larks, swallows, martins, drongos, cuckooshrikes, orioles, tits, creepers

BABBLERS, BULBULS, THRUSHES AND ALLIES: babblers, bulbuls, brownbuls, greenbuls, nica-tors, rock-jumpers, chats, robins, robin-chats, alethes, palm thrushes

Warblers, eremomelas, penduline-tits, Rockrunner, Grassbird, Fairy Flycatcher, titbabblers, crombecs, apalises

Cisticolas, prinias, flycatchers, white-eyes, batises, wagtails, pipits, longclaws

Shrikes, helmet-shrikes, starlings, oxpeckers, sugarbirds, sunbirds

Weavers, bishops, widowbirds, whydahs, indigobirds, finches, waxbills, canaries, buntings

sasol
BIRDS
of SOUTHERN AFRICA

**the region's most
comprehensively illustrated guide**

[handwritten inscription: 2006 — Happy Birthday, Mark, from Jim, en route, Johannesburg in fact, Brits, RSA, 5/9/2006]

Ian Sinclair • Phil Hockey • Warwick Tarboton

Illustrated by Peter Hayman & Norman Arlott

Struik Publishers
(a division of New Holland Publishing (South Africa) (Pty) Ltd)
Cornelis Struik House
80 McKenzie Street
Cape Town 8001

New Holland Publishing is a member of Johnnic Communications Ltd.
Visit us at **www.struik.co.za**

www.imagesofafrica.co.za

IMAGES OF AFRICA
PHOTO LIBRARY

First published in 1993
Second edition 1997
Third edition 2002

5 7 9 10 8 6 4

The plates were illustrated by Peter Hayman, with the exception of those on pages 271–279,
307–345, 353–363, 369–385 and 395–425, which were illustrated by Norman Arlott. The new images on pages
97(2), 101(2), 177(3), 205(6), 209(4) and 233(1) and the cover artwork were done by Norman Arlott.

Project manager: Pippa Parker
Managing editor: Helen de Villiers
Editor: Piera Abbott
Designer: Robin Cox
Cover design: Janice Evans, Robin Cox
Cartography: John Loubser, Ryan Africa, Elmari Kuyler
Reproduction by Hirt and Carter Cape (Pty) Ltd
Printed and bound by Times Offset (M) Sdn Bhd, Malaysia

ISBN 1 86872 721 1 (English softcover)
ISBN 1 86872 742 4 (English PVC cover)

Also available in Afrikaans as
Sasol Voëls van Suider-Afrika

ISBN 1 86872 722 X (Afrikaans softcover)
ISBN 1 86872 743 2 (Afrikaans PVC cover)

As always, for Jackie, Daryn and Kiera. **IAN SINCLAIR**

For Kim. **PHIL HOCKEY**

For Michèle. **WARWICK TARBOTEN**

CONTENTS

ACKNOWLEDGEMENTS

AUTHORS' ACKNOWLEDGMENTS
Our sincere thanks go to the Struik team – in particular Pippa Parker, Dominic Robson, Robin Cox and Piera Abbott – for their hard work and all the effort that went into this third edition.

The artist Norman Arlott did much more than was originally requested, and has improved this edition enormously by providing additional images. Our thanks also to Peter Hayman for the use of his images from the previous edition. To our generous sponsors, Sasol Limited, go our thanks.

Since the first Sasol guide was published in 1993, many friends and colleagues have contributed to improving the text, maps and illustrations. Their constructive criticism and readiness to give of their time is much appreciated. In particular, we are grateful to the late Richard Brooke, Rodney Cassidy, Alvin Cope, Adrian Craig, Richard Dean, Wayne Delport, John Graham, Trevor Hardaker, Rob Little, Alan Kemp, Rob Leslie, Morné du Plessis, Tony Harris, Joris Komen, Terry Oatley, Barrie Rose and Peter Ryan. Special thanks to Peter Ryan, who helped to revise thoroughly many species texts, especially those relating to the seabirds, for this third edition. Finally, without the understanding and patience of family and friends, who adapted to our frequent long absences in the field, this volume would still be in the making.

ARTIST'S ACKNOWLEDGEMENTS
My thanks go to the following for their help in supplying answers to queries that cropped up during the preparation of my artwork: Roger Mitchell of Papyrus Tows UK, Dr John Fanshawe, Dr Richard Liversidge, and the staff of the British Museum at Tring – especially Peter Colston, Michael Walters and Dr Robert Prys-Jones for allowing access to their skin collection. I also owe a great debt to John G Williams, who inspired my fanatic interest in Africa and its birds, and an unpayable debt to my wife, Marie, for managing a home and family while I spent days and weeks researching in museum and field.

Norman Arlott

I would like to acknowledge the help of the following people and institutions for their assistance in the compilation of this book: the staff of the British Museum (Natural History) at Tring, in particular Peter Colston, Michael Walters, Jo Bailey, Mark Adams and Mrs FE Warr for allowing reference to their skin, spirit and skeleton collection; Dr Alan Kemp, former curator of the Ornithology Department of the Transvaal Museum in Pretoria, for invaluable data and the loan of slides of captured birds of prey, for the skins sent to the UK and spirit specimens at Cape Town; Joris Komen, former curator of birds, State Museum of Namibia, for the loan of eagles in spirit to the British Museum and to me at the Percy FitzPatrick Institute of African Ornithology, University of Cape Town; Dr Clem Fisher, Liverpool Museum, for access to skins; the Library of BirdLife International (ICBP), Cambridge, for the loan of Bokmakierie; the South African Museum, Cape Town, for study skins; David Allan for providing dead bustards for measurement, and for his advice; Rob Hume of the Royal Society for the Protection of Birds, for checking a bookful of queries while on a visit to Kenya. Sally Michael and George Reynolds kindly provided accommodation and comfort during my many visits to the British Museum.

Peter Hayman

PUBLISHER'S ACKNOWLEDGEMENTS
The publisher would like to thank Sasol Limited for its continued generous sponsorship, without which the production of this book at a competitive price would not have been possible.

SPONSOR'S FOREWORD

In 1993 when Sasol first sponsored **Sasol Birds of Southern Africa**, little did we know that it would be the catalyst for an explosion of birding and birding-related activities in southern Africa and beyond.

The second edition, launched in 1997, with its significant improvements to both text and plates, allowed for easier bird identification by beginners and advanced birders alike.

We are delighted with the role that both these publications have played in popularising birding as a hobby and in promoting environmental education.

Over the last decade Sasol has been globalising its business interests and recently launched its new corporate identity, which features the positioning statement 'reaching new frontiers'. We are confident that this extensively updated third edition of **Sasol Birds of Southern Africa** will inspire twitchers, too, to reach new frontiers in their birding endeavours.

Pieter Cox
Deputy Chairman and Chief Executive
Sasol Limited

Sasol and the environment

'Protecting the environment is an obligation, not a choice'

We, the people of Sasol, striving for excellence in all we do, recognise the impact that our activities can have on people and the environment. Safety, health and protection of the environment will form an integral part of our planning and decision making. We will manage our company, wherever we do business, in an ethical way that strikes an appropriate and well-reasoned balance between economic, social and environmental needs.

Southern Africa's birds in perspective

Southern Africa is defined as the area south of the Kunene and Zambezi rivers, encompassing Namibia, Botswana, South Africa, Lesotho, Swaziland and southern and central Mozambique, as well as oceanic waters within 200 nautical miles of the coast. Mozambique north of the Zambezi River is excluded, as its avifauna has closer ties to that of east Africa than it does to that of the regions further south. Southern Africa covers a land area of approximately 3,5 million square kilometres and has a high bird diversity: more species breed here than in the United States and Canada combined. The region's bird list currently stands at 951 species, of which 144 are endemic (occurring or breeding only in the region) or near-endemic (having ranges which extend only slightly outside the region). The major centre of endemism is in the arid western regions of the Karoo and the Namib Desert.

One of the reasons for southern Africa's high bird diversity is the region's climatic and topographical diversity. The climate ranges from cool-temperate in the southwest to hot and tropical in the north. The southwest of the region experiences a winter rainfall regime, the north and east have summer rains and some of the central parts have aseasonal rainfall. Coupled with these seasonal differences, rainfall increases from west to east. Winter snows are regular on the higher mountains, which rise to 3 500 metres above sea level.

It has long been assumed that the avifauna of southern Africa is well known. However, since the last edition of this book, several new taxa have been described, with most 'splits' relying strongly on molecular data to support them. The splits include separation of Long-billed Lark into five species, and Clapper Lark into three species. Cape Parrot has been split from Grey-headed Parrot, Damara Hornbill from Red-billed Hornbill, Cape Gull from Kelp Gull and Damara Canary from Black-headed Canary. Black-backed Cisticola has been split into Rufous-winged and Luapula Cisticola and Wandering, Royal, Shy and Yellow-nosed Albatross are now recognised as containing multiple taxa. It is likely that other cryptic species remain to be discovered among the larks, pipits and cisticolas, and perhaps even the hornbills, so southern African ornithology is set on an exciting track for many years to come. Two species have been deleted from the region's list: the Bimaculated Lark's single specimen record from Namibia is untraceable, and the Mascarene Shearwater's validity as a full species is presently under review.

Aims of this book

Identification skills evolve constantly, and the quest for new knowledge about birds runs a parallel course. In this book, we have tried to keep abreast of these demands: illustrations have been improved and added to, and the maps reflect the most up-to-date information available to us at the time of going to press, greatly assisted by the recently published *Atlas of Southern African Birds*. Numbers appearing in brackets after species' names are those used in the 6th edition of *Roberts' Birds of Southern Africa* (1993). The book is geared primarily towards helping birders to identify birds in the field. The plumage and soft-part coloration of many species vary with age and season and we have illustrated this variation as far as possible. The text highlights the key identification features of each species and concentrates on the separation of potentially confusing species. The plates are colour-coded for ready reference, annotated for rapid reference to key features, and there are indexed and illustrated quick-reference guides, as well as a checklist. Where species differ considerably in abundance across their ranges, solid colour has been used to indicate where they are most common; hatching indicates where they are scarcer.

Bird classification and nomenclature

A new classification of the world's birds, based on molecular research, was published in 1990 (Sibley & Ahlquist 1990, Sibley & Monroe 1990). Evidence from several subsequent studies strongly suggests that this new classification is evolutionarily more correct than the arrangement currently used by most field guides and handbooks worldwide. However, one of the principal aims of any bird field guide is to be user friendly rather than to present a scientifically accurate treatise on the evolutionary and taxonomic relationships of birds. For this reason we have retained the old ordering system with which the majority of birders are familiar.

A problem that has dogged birders worldwide for decades relates to the common names of birds. Different regions of the world and different field guides have used a plethora of different names for many taxa, causing confusion and frustration. Over the past two years, the International Ornithological Committee (IOC) has addressed this problem by appointing a number of regional subcommittees which, collectively, will arrive at a standardised list of common names for all the world's birds – several of these names differ from the names currently in use in southern Africa. This task has largely been completed at the time of writing, and these new names now appear in this book. Change, however, is usually accompanied by some inconvenience. To make the transition as gentle as possible, we have included both the new names and the names as they appeared in the last edition. A species can thus be looked up in the index under either name. It was with some reluctance that the senior author of this book decided to use these new names, and only time will tell if they willl be adopted internationally and locally.

Bird habitats

A habitat is the particular environment in which an organism lives. Each species has a unique set of environmental requirements: some birds live at sea, but come ashore to breed, while others live in the air, settling only at nest sites; some are entirely terrestrial and have even lost the power of flight; some live in grasslands, and others in forests. Of the more than 950 species of birds occurring in southern Africa the majority (about 700 species) are land birds that depend on terrestrial ecosystems. The species dependent on aquatic ecosystems can be divided into those that live in the oceans (pelagic species, which number about 50) and those that don't.

Starting with land birds, which are by far the most diverse bird group in southern Africa, a glance at the individual species' maps in this field guide will show that the same distribution patterns are frequently repeated – these distributions tend to coincide with the position of the major biological regions, or biomes. There are eight such regions in southern Africa and these provide a useful basis for looking at the places where land birds live.

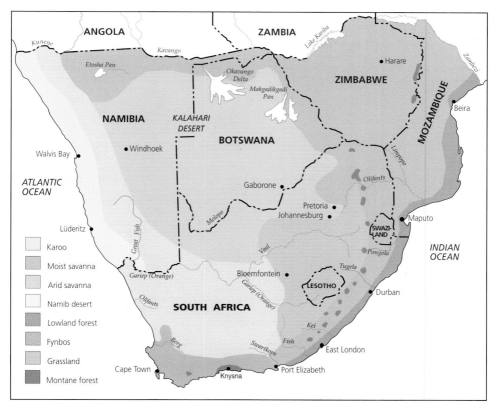

HABITAT MAP OF SOUTHERN AFRICA

11

Forests

The forest biome covers a tiny proportion of the southern African subregion and occurs as a series of scattered islands of varying size stretched along the eastern side of the subcontinent, where the rainfall is highest. Forests are formed by a variety of evergreen tree species that create a closed canopy. Two distinct types of forest occur in southern Africa, and many forest-living birds are found in either one or the other, but not in both. The first is the forest found at higher altitudes, termed Afromontane (or simply montane) forest. It extends as discontinuous islands from near sea level in the southern Cape, through KwaZulu-Natal, Mpumalanga and the Northern Province, into eastern Zimbabwe. The second forest type, lowland forest, is confined to low-lying areas along the eastern coastal plain, and occurs as fragmented remnants extending from the Eastern Cape Province northwards to Tanzania and Kenya. Lowland forests also penetrate westwards into the savanna as narrow ribbons along the larger rivers; these are referred to as riparian forests.

Savanna

The term 'savanna' embraces a range of wooded country from the tall, broad-leaved miombo woodland of Zimbabwe and northern Mozambique to the arid thornveld of the Kalahari. Its essential feature is deciduous trees with an understorey of grass, irrespective of the spacing between the trees or the type of trees. The term 'bushveld' is widely used in South Africa in reference to this biome. The term 'woodland' is used if the trees form a closed canopy, and 'parkland' if the trees are scattered. There are two distinct subdivisions in this biome, arid savanna and moist savanna, and many bird species are confined to one or the other. Arid savanna, centred in the western half of the savanna region, is usually dominated by Acacia species and is often called 'thornveld'; the trees are normally widely spaced and scrubby. By contrast, moist savanna forms the eastern and northern parts of the savanna region where the rainfall is higher, and is dominated by broad-leaved tree species.

Fynbos

The fynbos biome is confined to the extreme south and west of the subregion. Floristically it is an extremely rich biome in which an enormous variety of Protea, Erica, Restio and other characteristic species are found. These form shrublands of various types depending on the topography and underlying soil type; mountain fynbos, coastal fynbos, renosterveld and strandveld are examples. Despite its high plant diversity, the fynbos biome is poor in birds, both in numbers of species and individuals. It does, however support several localized endemics such as Cape Rockjumper, Victorin's Warbler and Protea Canary.

Grassland

The grassland biome is confined to South Africa and centres on the high-lying interior plateau known as the 'highveld'. It is a treeless region, varying greatly in topography, from flat plains to rugged mountainous areas, and from short grasslands on turf soils to tall grasslands elsewhere. The grasslands have been extensively modified by agriculture, and most arable areas are cultivated for crop production: only rocky, mountainous or high-lying, cold areas have escaped such changes. The highest altitudes in southern Africa are reached in this biome in the Maluti Mountains (above 3 000 metres), where an alpine grassland community is found. Several of southern Africa's endemic bird species occur in this biome and a disproportionately high number of South Africa's Red Data Book species are also found here.

Karoo

The two Karoo biomes cover a large part of the southwestern interior of the subcontinent where the annual rainfall is less than 400 millimetres. The succulent Karoo is located near the west coast in the winter-rainfall area, and the Nama-Karoo in the area of summer rainfall. Both are semi-desert shrublands with extensive areas of rocky outcrop and limited grass cover. There is little permanent surface water to be found in the Karoo, except for that in man-made dams. The Karoo is of special interest in that it supports a high proportion of southern Africa's endemic bird species.

Namib Desert

This desert, lying mainly in Namibia, runs north-south along the western seaboard of southern Africa. It is a region of extremely low rainfall (less than 50 millimetres per annum) and consists of gravel plains, sand dunes and rugged, rocky hills and mountains. The vegetation is sparse although it transforms briefly after the infrequent rains. Birdlife is likewise sparse but several of the species present are endemic to the biome.

Estuaries, lagoons, lakes, dams and pans

These water bodies differ in their origin and ecological functioning but they are all essentially bodies of open water with bare shorelines, and they all tend to support similar communities of waterbirds. Estuaries are shallow, open-water bays formed where rivers meet the sea, and they connect to the sea through a narrow mouth. There are many estuaries along the southern and eastern coasts, of which the largest is Lake St Lucia. Extensive mudflats are often found on estuaries, and these provide feeding areas for an array of waterbirds, especially waders. Lagoons, which are simply partly enclosed, protected arms of the sea, also provide mudflats of this nature. Apart from the coastal lakes that have developed from estuaries, there are virtually no natural lakes in southern Africa. There are, however, a great many (more than half a million) man-made dams on the subcontinent, which resemble lakes and offer open water that is attractive to a variety of waterbirds. Several species have undergone range expansions because of the construction of artificial water bodies. Pans are natural depressions that fill with water after periods of heavy rain. When filled, many pans support spectacular numbers of waterbirds.

Rivers

Southern Africa is poorly endowed with large, perennial rivers: many of its rivers cease flowing during the dry season, and some flow at even less frequent intervals. Two of the region's largest rivers, the Zambezi and the Kavango, are of interest in that they provide habitat for tropical river specialists such as African Skimmer, Rock Pratincole, Pel's Fishing-Owl and White-backed Night-Heron.

Marshlands

Vleis, sponges, bogs, swamps, flood plains and marshes are all wetlands dominated by emergent aquatic vegetation. Each of the terms used to describe a marshland has a particular connotation, for example, a bog is supported on a substratum of peat and a sponge is located at the headwaters of a river. The essential feature of marshlands is that they are wet underfoot and they provide dense cover in the form of reeds, sedges or grasses. The Okavango Delta contains the most extensive area of marshland in southern Africa but there are many other smaller marshland areas in Caprivi, Mozambique and northern KwaZulu-Natal.

Seashore

The interface between the ocean and the continent is a narrow strip of either sandy beach or rock that is subject to tidal action. The diversity of species found here is limited, but in some cases their numbers are spectacular. The endemic African Black Oystercatcher is confined to this area.

Ocean

Living on the open sea is a diverse and distinctive community of birds, mainly albatrosses, petrels and shearwaters. Most seldom come within sight of the coast except during severe storms. The waters off the southwestern tip of Africa are rated as offering some of the best seabird watching in the world. No fewer than 15 species of albatross have been seen here, and, especially during winter, petrels and shearwaters occur in huge numbers.

Additional aids to birding

The support and information available for birding in most of southern Africa are as good as or better than those available elsewhere on the continent. In addition to field guides, handbooks and locality guides that cover the entire region, there are several national or local guides, as well as an excellent network of local bird clubs and societies. Many bird species are best identified or located on the basis of call, and there are several excellent cassette tapes available. The most recent and comprehensive of these is Guy Gibbon's 'Southern African Bird Sounds', published by Southern African Birding (tapes released in 1991 and CDs in 1994). The names and addresses of the region's bird clubs are listed on the next page, and a list of other useful reference works is provided on page 426.

Bird societies and clubs

Societies and clubs play an important role in communication and co-ordination between birders. Most also hold regular meetings and outings, and many produce their own newsletters. Most bird clubs in South Africa and Namibia are affiliated to BirdLife South Africa.

South Africa
BirdLife South Africa, tel 011 789 1122, www.birdlife.org.za.
Cape Bird Club, tel 021 559 0726, ccohen@botzoo.uct.ac.za, PO Box 5022, Cape Town 8000.
BirdLife Eastern Cape, tel 041 581 5736, chakgh@upe.ac.za.
Diaz Cross Bird Club, tel 046 603 8525, 3 Florence Street, Grahamstown 6140.
Goldfields Bird Club, tel 057 733 8287, 14 Gencor Crescent, Marriesspruit, Virginia, 9430.
Free State Bird Club, tel 051 447 7195, PO Box 6614, Bloemfontein 9300.
Natal Bird Club, PO Box 1218, Durban 4000.
Natal Midlands Bird Club, tel 033 345 2570, mspain@glenrandmid.co.za, PO Box 2772,
    Pietermaritzburg 3200.
Lowveld Bird Club, tel 013 753 3238, nvpsvcs@cybertrade.co.za, PO Box 4113, Nelspruit 1200.
Northeastern Bird Club, PO Box 6007, Pietersburg Noord 0750.
Rand Barbet Bird Club, tel 011 803 1274, nwrexiln@mweb.co.za, 2 Flint Road, Parkwood 2193.
Sandton Bird Club, tel 011 883 4753, yvonnep@bac.org.za, PO Box 650890, Benmore 2010.
Vaal Reefs Bird Club, PO Box 5129, Vaal Reefs 2621.
Wesvaal Bird Club, PO Box 2413, Potchefstroom 2520.
Witwatersrand Bird Club, tel 011 884 0640, witsbc@mweb.co.za, PO Box 72091, Parkview 2122.
Zimbabwe: Ornithological Association of Zimbabwe, PO Box RV 100, Runiville, Zimbabwe.
Botswana: Botswana Bird Club, PO Box 71, Gaborone, Botswana.
Namibia: Namibian Bird Club, PO Box 67, Windhoek, Namibia.
Continental Africa: African Bird Club, c/o BirdLife International, Wellbrook Court, Girton Road,
Cambridge CB3 0NA, United Kingdom, www.africanbirdclub.org.

Abbreviations used in this book

		sub-ad.	subadult	non-br.	non-breeding
7	male (plates)	imm.	immature	h	height
6	female (plates)	juv.	juvenile	X	vagrant record (maps)
ad.	adult	br.	breeding	m	male

PROVINCIAL BOUNDARIES OF SOUTH AFRICA

FAMILY SUMMARIES

The family summaries below put the diversity of southern African birds into global and Afrotropical perspectives by comparing the numbers of species in the Afrotropics (Africa south of the Sahara but excluding Madagascar and its satellite islands) and southern Africa with the world totals. This helps to identify those families for which southern Africa is a 'special' region. Data on world diversity are based on Clements (2000).

Diversity data for each family are summarized as follows: World (W) and Afrotropical (A) data give the total number of species in the family. Southern African data (S) are given in the same format, but include the number of endemics. Thus, for penguins, S 6/1 means that within the southern African region there are six species recorded, one of which is endemic. At the end of the diversity data, a figure is given for the percentage of all species in the Afrotropical region that occur in southern Africa. Thus, 100% of the penguins that occur in the Afrotropics are found in southern Africa.

Ostrich • Struthionidae   p. 142
W 1, A 1, S 1/0, S/A=100%
Flightless; the world's largest bird.

Penguins • Spheniscidae   p. 28
W 18, A 6, S 6/1, S/A=100%
Flightless marine birds, the wings of which are rigid
flippers; predominantly sub-Antarctic in distribution.

Grebes • Podicipedidae   p. 30
W 19, A 3, S 3/0, S/A=100%
Aquatic diving birds with lobed, not webbed, toes.

Albatrosses • Diomedeidae   p. 32
W 21, A 15, S 15/0, S/A=100%
Huge, long-winged seabirds. Oceanic foragers,
breeding mainly on oceanic islands. Mostly southern
oceans.

**Petrels, shearwaters, storm-petrels, prions
• Procellariidae, Hydrobatidae**   p. 38
W 92, A 44, S 38/0, S/A=86%
Very small (storm-petrels) to very large (giant-petrels)
oceanic birds. Most species rarely seen from shore.

Tropicbirds • Phaethontidae   p. 54
W 3, A 3, S 3/0, S/A=100%
Predominantly white, long-tailed, plunge-diving
seabirds; distribution mostly tropical.

Pelicans • Pelecanidae   p. 58
W 8, A 2, S 2/0, S/A=100%
Huge, predominantly white waterbirds; long bill has a
distendable pouch used to catch fish.

Gannets, boobies • Sulidae   p. 54
W 9, A 6, S 4/1, S/A=67%
Large, plunge-diving seabirds; colonial breeders on
islands.

Cormorants, darters • Phalacrocoracidae, Anhingidae — p. 56
W 39, A 7, S 6/3, S/A=86%
Dark-plumaged, long-necked, surface-diving water-birds; coastal and/or freshwater.

Frigatebirds • Fregatidae — p. 58
W 5, A 4, S 2/0, S/A=50%
Large, long-winged seabirds with deeply forked tails; obtain much food by aerial piracy.

Bitterns, herons, egrets, Hamerkop • Ardeidae, Scopidae — p. 60
W 64, A 24, S 21/0, S/A=88%
Predominantly long-legged aquatic birds of variable size; most breed colonially.

Storks • Ciconiidae — p. 68
W 19, A 8, S 8/0, S/A=100%
Very large birds with long legs and wings and short tails. Mostly black and white. Forage in open habitats.

Ibises, spoonbills • Threskiornithidae — p. 72
W 33, A 11, S 5/1, S/A=45%
Large birds with long legs and elongate bills, either decurved or flattened. Forage mostly in aquatic or grassland habitats.

Flamingos • Phoenicopteridae — p. 72
W 5, A 2, S 2/0, S/A=100%
Extremely long-legged and long-necked pink aquatic birds; downcurved bill adapted for filter-feeding.

Ducks, geese • Anatidae — p. 76
W 157, A 36, S 20/2, S/A=56%
Short-legged swimming birds; forage by grazing, dabbling or diving. Fly fast with outstretched neck.

Secretarybird • Sagittariidae — p. 154
W 1, A 1, S 1/0, S/A=100%
Only species in its family. Large, long-legged bird of prey. Forages on ground, stamping on prey.

All raptors except Secretarybird, falcons • Accipitridae, Pandionidae (Osprey) — p. 86
W 237, A 74, S 54/4, S/A=73%
Small to very large predatory or scavenging birds; mostly broad- and/or long-winged and very aerial. Smaller species hunt by dash-and-seize techniques; scavengers are all vultures and kites. Unusual species include Palm-nut Vulture (a frugivore and scavenger), Bat Hawk and fish-eating species (African Fish Eagle and Osprey).

Falcons (includes kestrels) • Falconidae — p. 116
W 62, A 19, S 16/0, S/A=84%
All except Pygmy Falcon (*Polihierax*) belong to the genus *Falco*. Swift, agile fliers with pointed wings; pursue prey mostly in the air (except Pygmy Falcon). A few species roost communally.

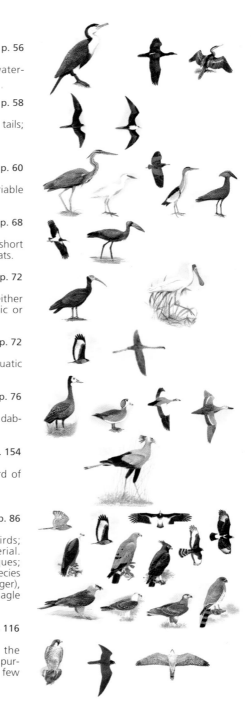

Francolins, partridges, spurfowl, quails, peafowl
• Phasianidae   p. 136
W 155, A 46, S 17/5, S/A=37%
Typical gamebirds; short-legged and heavy-bodied;
many cryptically coloured, some with leg spurs.

Guineafowl • Numididae   p. 142
W 6, A6, S 2/0, S/A=33%
Large-bodied, long-necked gamebirds with character-
istic casques or feather tufts on the crown.

Buttonquails • Turnicidae   p. 144
W 17, A 4, S 3/1, S/A=75%
Small, terrestrial, quail-like birds, cryptically patterned;
females brighter than males. All incubation and chick-
rearing done by males.

Rails, crakes, flufftails, gallinules (including moorhens
and coots) • Rallidae   p. 146
W 134, A 25, S 18/0, S/A=72%
Mostly ground-dwelling birds of wetlands and moist
grasslands. Small to medium-sized, with long legs and
toes. Many skulking and crepuscular. Short tails often
cocked or flicked.

Cranes • Gruidae   p. 154
W 15, A 6, S 3/1, S/A=50%
Very large, long-legged terrestrial birds with relatively
short bills. Favour wetlands and grasslands; courtship
displays include elaborate dances.

Finfoots • Heliornithidae   p. 146
W 3, A1, S 1/0, S/A=100%
Skulking cormorant-like birds of wooded rivers. Bill
pointed, not hooked. Toes lobed, not webbed. Sexually
dimorphic.

Bustards (including korhaans) • Otididae   p. 156
W 26, A 19, S 11/8, S/A=58%
Large, terrestrial birds; long and sometimes very slender
necks, and long legs. Habitat from woodland to desert.
Males of most species have elaborate courtship rituals.

Sheathbills • Chionididae   p. 204
W 2, A 1, S 1/0, S/A=100%
White, bantam-like coastal birds; scavenge around
seabird colonies and along driftline.

Jacanas • Jacanidae   p. 148
W 8, A 2, S 2/0, S/A=100%
Small to medium-sized waterbirds with extraordinarily
long toes and toenails, enabling them to walk on floating vegetation. Male incubation and parental care is the
norm (except for Lesser Jacana).

Painted-snipes • Rostratulidae   p. 186
W 2, A 1, S 1/0, S/A=100%
Snipe-like waders of freshwater and brackish wetlands;
female more brightly coloured than male. Male incu-
bates eggs and raises chicks alone.

Oystercatchers • Haematopodidae p. 162
W 11, A 2, S 2/1, S/A=100%
Large black or black-and-white waders, all with long, straight, orange-red bills and pinkish legs. Mostly coastal shellfish-eaters. Chicks are fed by the parents until after fledging.

Avocets, stilts • Recurvirostridae p. 162
W 10, A 2, S 2/0, S/A=100%
Long-legged, mostly black-and-white birds with long, fine bills (recurved in avocets). Favour freshwater wetlands, also estuaries and saltpans. Often breed at ephemeral wetlands.

Crab Plover • Dromadidae p. 162
W 1, A 1, S 1/0, S/A=100%
Monotypic family. Large black-and-white wader with heavy bill adapted for catching crabs. Unique among waders in breeding colonially underground. Endemic to Indian Ocean coasts.

Plovers • Charadriidae p. 164
W 66, A 30, S 21/0, S/A=66%
Small to medium-sized waders; all have short bills and hunt in a stereotypical 'walk-stop-search' manner. Most found in wetlands (including open coast), grasslands or arid savannas.

Snipes, godwits, sandpipers, stints, curlews, turnstones, Ruff, phalaropes • Scolopacidae p. 176
W 87, A 40, S 35/0, S/A=88%
Largely aquatic waders, varying greatly in size and morphology. All southern African species except African Snipe are Holarctic-breeding migrants. Most are coastal and wetland species, and many are typically found in flocks. Red Phalarope is exclusively pelagic outside the breeding season.

Thick-knees • Burhinidae p. 202
W 9, A 4, S 2/0, S/A=50%
Large, predominantly nocturnal waders. Cryptically coloured; large heads and eyes and long legs. Highly vocal at night.

Coursers, pratincoles • Glareolidae p. 190
W 17, A 13, S 8/1, S/A=62%
Coursers are lightly built, long-legged dryland waders; some nocturnal. Pratincoles are short-legged, long-winged, swallow-like birds, most of which breed colonially close to water.

Skuas, gulls, terns (including skimmers) • Stercoraridae, Laridae, Sternidae, Rhynchopidae p. 204
W 106, A 50, S 38/3, S/A=76%
Skuas are gull-like migratory seabirds, partially or totally dependent on piracy for food. Gulls and terns are generally water-associated, from open ocean to inland wetlands: most species breed colonially. Skimmers have unique foraging behaviour and bill structure.

Sandgrouse • Pteroclidae   p. 218
W 16, A 10, S 4/2, S/A=40%
Ground-dwelling birds with very short legs and pointed tails; mostly found in open arid and semi-arid habitats. Drink daily, often in large flocks; moisture carried to chicks on belly feathers.

Pigeons, doves • Columbidae   p. 220
W 308, A 34, S 15/0, S/A=44%
Pigeons generally larger than doves; found in all terrestrial habitats. Frugivorous and/or granivorous; unusual in feeding chicks with gastric secretion (pigeon's milk).

Parrots, lovebirds • Psittacidae   p. 226
W 331, A 21, S 9/3, S/A=43%
Small to medium-sized birds; brightly coloured and noisy with short, heavy, hooked bills. Mostly frugivorous and exclusively hole- or crevice-nesting.

Turacos • Musophagidae   p. 230
W 23, A 23, S 6/1, S/A=26%
Medium-sized, long-tailed arboreal birds: in southern Africa, all except Grey Go-away-bird have predominantly green or blue plumage with large, red wing patches. Frequently bound and clamber through trees rather than flying. Mostly frugivorous.

Cuckoos, coucals, malkohas • Cuculidae   p. 232
W 138, A 27, S 20/1, S/A=74%
All cuckoos are brood-parasites on either a single host or a range of hosts. Coucals and malkohas are not parasitic; all three groups are unusual in having zygodactylous feet (two toes pointing forwards and two backwards).

Owls • Tytonidae, Strigidae   p. 240
W 204, A 33, S 12/0, S/A=36%
Predominantly nocturnal, predatory birds. Tytonidae (Barn and Grass owls) differ from others in having a heart-shaped facial disc. Plumage soft and fluffy, allowing silent flight. Sight and hearing acute.

Nightjars • Caprimulgidae   p. 244
W 89, A 25, S 7/0, S/A=28%
Nocturnal, aerial insectivores with exceptionally wide gapes and prominent rictal bristles. Most have far-carrying, diagnostic calls. One of the most cryptically coloured of all bird families.

Swifts • Apodidae   p. 248
W 98, A 23, S 13/1, S/A=57%
Fast-flying, diurnal, aerial insectivores. Forage and sleep on the wing. All four toes point forwards, precluding perching.

Mousebirds • Coliidae   p. 252
W 6, A 6, S 3/1, S/A=50%
Small-bodied frugivores with long, stiff tails, crests and bare faces. Usually in small flocks; roost huddled together.

Trogons • Trogonidae   p. 252
W 39, A 3, S 1/0, S/A=33%
Brilliantly coloured, slow-moving, forest-dwelling birds.
Perch upright like flycatchers; hawk insects and also eat
fruit.

Kingfishers • Alcedinidae   p. 254
W 93, A 19, S 10/0, S/A=53%
Small to medium-sized hole-nesting birds, with heavy,
often brightly coloured bills. Frequent aquatic and
wooded or forested habitats, feeding on fish, insects
and small land vertebrates.

Bee-eaters • Meropidae   p. 258
W 26, A 19, S 9/0, S/A=47%
Brilliantly coloured aerial insectivores; usually in flocks.
Most breed colonially, sometimes cooperatively, exca-
vating their own burrows, usually in steep sandbanks or
roadside cuttings.

Rollers • Coraciidae   p. 262
W 12, A 8, S 5/0, S/A=63%
Conspicuous, stocky perching birds with elaborate and
noisy aerial display flights from which their name is
derived. Most are predominantly blue or purple in
colour.

Wood-hoopoes, scimitarbills, hoopoes •
Phoeniculidae, Upupidae   p. 268
W 12, A 11, S 4/1, S/A=40%
Woodhoopoes and scimitarbills are arboreal and long-
tailed, and have decurved bills. Both are hole-nesters
using natural cavities and abandoned nests of other
species; woodhoopoes are gregarious and breed cooperatively. Hoopoes are largely terrestrial. All produce a
pungent smell from the preen gland.

Hornbills • Bucerotidae   p. 264
W 58, A 26, S 10/1, S/A=38%
Characterized by long, heavy, slightly decurved bills,
some with a casque on the upper mandible, especially
in males. During incubation female is sealed into the
nest cavity and moults (except for ground hornbills).

Honeyguides, honeybirds • Indicatoridae   p. 270
W17, A 15, S 6/0, S/A=40%
Small, short-legged, drably coloured birds, unique in
that they can digest beeswax. All are brood parasites,
mostly of barbets and woodpeckers. Only one species,
Greater Honeyguide, is known to guide mammals,
especially Honey Badgers *Mellivora capensis*, to bees'
nests.

Barbets • Capitonidae   p. 272
W 83, A 42, S 10/0, S/A=24%
Small, stout-bodied birds with large heads and powerful bills. Mostly frugivorous; excavate their own nest
holes in trees; some species are regularly parasitized by
honeyguides.

Woodpeckers, wrynecks • Picidae   p. 276
W 217, A 31, S 10/2, S/A=32%
Woodpeckers are unusual in having specially adapted skull architecture that allows them to hammer at wood when feeding and building nests. Also have stiff tail feathers that are used to brace the climbing bird. Wrynecks are cryptically coloured; feign death when handled.

Broadbills • Eurylaimidae   p. 252
W 15, A 4, S 1/0, S/A=25%
Small, forest-dwelling birds with dorsally flattened bills; all have elaborate, aerial courtship displays.

Pittas • Pittidae   p. 252
W 32, A 2, S 1/0, S/A=50%
Brightly coloured and secretive ground-dwelling birds. Highly cryptic; 'freeze' when alarmed. Males have distinctive calls and displays.

Larks, sparrowlarks • Alaudidae   p. 280
W 93, A 75, S 32/23, S/A=43%
Drably coloured terrestrial birds, most with aerial displays. Taxonomy in flux: there are possibly still some undescribed species in southern Africa.

Swallows, martins • Hirundinidae   p. 292
W 90, A 38, S 22/2, S/A=58%
Small, aerial insectivores, often seen in flocks. Have wide, flattened bills and a wide gape. Regularly perch on telephone wires. Some build elaborate mud nests, frequently on man-made structures. Most are seasonal visitors.

Cuckooshrikes • Campephagidae   p. 300
W 82, A 10, S 3/0, S/A=30%
Slow-moving, arboreal birds, superficially resembling cuckoos but most closely related to orioles. Not parasitic. Slight sexual dimorphism, except in the Black Cuckooshrike, where dimorphism is extreme.

Drongos • Dicruridae   p. 300
W 23, A 5, S 2/0, S/A=40%
Black, arboreal birds with stout, slightly hooked bills and prominent rictal bristles; hawk insects like flycatchers. Bold and aggressive, they are also excellent mimics.

Orioles • Oriolidae   p. 302
W 29, A 9, S 4/0, S/A=44%
Brightly coloured, frugivorous, forest and bushveld birds; males of all African species predominantly yellow. All have very similar clear, liquid calls.

Crows, ravens • Corvidae   p. 304
W 117, A 11, S 4/0, S/A=36%
Large, iridescent, black or black-and-white birds. Pied and House Crows have successfully adapted to human habitation.

Tits, penduline-tits • Paridae, Remizidae   p. 306
W 69, A 22, S 9/4, S/A=41%

Small, active, arboreal species with short, robust bills. Tits are prominent and noisy members of bird parties. Penduline-tits build elaborate suspended nests, those of African species being characterized by a false entrance.

Creepers • Certhiidae   p. 306
W 7, A 1, S 1/0, S/A=100%

Small, cryptically coloured birds with long, decurved bills. Foraging behaviour similar to that of woodpeckers, working along tree trunks and branches with stiffened tail feathers acting as a brace.

Babblers and allies • Timaliidae   p. 308
W 265, A 35, S 6/3, S/A=17%

True babblers (*Turdoides*) are noisy, group-living species, most or all of which breed cooperatively. Bush Blackcaps are solitary or in pairs, and are secretive forest-dwellers; may have close affiliations with Asian bulbuls.

Bulbuls, greenbuls, brownbuls • Pycnonotidae p. 310
W 130, A 68, S 10/2, S/A=15%

One of Africa's most ubiquitous bird families, occurring in habitats ranging from forest to semi-desert: predominantly tropical in distribution. Feed on fruit and insects.

Thrushes, alethes, robins, robin-chats, chats, rock-jumpers, flycatchers • Turdidae, Muscicapidae   p. 314
W 445, A 162, S 56/18, S/A=35%

A highly diverse family; predominantly ground-dwelling. Thrushes, alethes and some robins are mostly forest species; some robin species are accomplished mimics. Chats inhabit open areas from deserts to savannas; less frequently in woodland. Rockjumpers, whose taxonomic affinities are unclear, inhabit montane grasslands and fynbos. Flycatchers hunt by hawking from a perch, whereas batises mostly glean food from leaf surfaces.

Titbabblers, hyliotas, warblers, apalises, crombecs, eremomelas, Grassbird, Rockrunner, cisticolas, prinias • Sylviidae, Cisticolidae   p. 330
W 390, A 251, S 68/15, S/A=27%

A highly diverse group of small, mostly drably coloured, insectivorous species that lack marked sexual dimorphism. The cisticolas in particular are notoriously difficult to identify and it is likely that undescribed species remain (Luapula and Rufous-winged Cisticolas have only very recently been recognized as full species).

Wattle-eyes, batises • Platysteiridae   p. 360
W 32, A 32, S 7/2, S/A=22%

Predominantly arboreal insectivores.

Wagtails, pipits, longclaws • Motacillidae   p. 362
W 56, A 34, S 24/4, S/A=71%

Ground-dwelling insectivorous birds, mostly found in open country or associated with water. Wagtails and pipits actively wag their tails while foraging. Longclaws exhibit remarkable convergence with American meadowlarks. The taxonomy of African pipits is not well known and there may be several undescribed species.

Shrikes • Laniidae   p. 372
W 30, A 21, S 6/0, S/A=29%

Aggressive, predatory birds with stout, hooked bills and medium to long tails. Feet are disproportionately large. Many species impale prey on thorns, forming characteristic 'larders'.

Bush shrikes, boubous, tchagras, Brubru, puffbacks, White-tailed Shrike • Malaconotidae   p. 374
W 49, A 49, S 17/6, S/A=35%

Bush shrikes, boubous and tchagras are mostly secretive birds with loud, ringing calls: the bush shrikes are brightly coloured, and boubous, with one exception, are predominantly black and white. Brubru, puffbacks and White-tailed Shrike are smaller than other species in the family.

Helmet-shrikes • Prionopidae   p. 378
W 11, A 8, S 3/0, S/A=38%.

Characterized by bristled foreheads, these are group-living birds of savannas and forests. They breed co-operatively. Retz's Helmet-Shrike is host to Thick-billed Cuckoo and White-crested Helmet-Shrike may be parasitized by Black Cuckoo.

Starlings, mynas, oxpeckers • Sturnidae, Buphagidae   p. 380
W 114, A 49, S 16/2, S/A=33%

Mostly noisy, social species, some of which breed communally. Several of the starlings have glossy, iridescent plumage. Oxpeckers are highly specialized foragers, removing parasites from the skin of large mammals.

Sugarbirds • Promeropidae   p. 386
W 2, A 2, S 2/2, S/A=100%

Superficially resemble large, long-tailed sunbirds, but lack iridescent plumage. Endemic to southern Africa: taxonomic affiliations uncertain. Closely associated with proteas for both feeding and breeding.

Sunbirds • Nectariniidae   p. 386
W 130, A 81, S 21/5, S/A=26%

Small, nectarivorous and insectivorous birds with thin, mostly decurved, bills. Typically sexually dimorphic with males being iridescently coloured and frequently having elongated central tail feathers. Although superficially resembling hummingbirds, the two groups are not closely related; sunbirds do not habitually hover.

White-eyes • Zosteropidae p. 358
W 96, A 14, S 3/2, S/A=14%
Small, warbler-like arboreal birds with short, pointed bills, grey, yellow and green plumage, and a white eye-ring around a dark eye. Gregarious and vocal when foraging.

Sparrows, weavers, bishops, queleas, widowbirds, Cuckoo Finch • Passeridae, Ploceidae p. 394
W 149, A 123, S 36/3, S/A=29%
Small, predominantly social, seed-eating birds, many of which breed colonially and are associated with water. Sparrows are often classified in a different family, Passeridae, and differ from others in being mono-gamous, not polygamous. Several species are parasitized by cuckoos, but the Cuckoo Finch is unique in the family in itself being a parasite (of cisticolas and prinias).

Pytilias, twinspots, crimsonwings, seedcrackers, fire-finches, waxbills, mannikins • Estrildidae p. 410
W 140, A 74, S 27/3, S/A=36%
A diverse group of small, mostly brightly coloured, granivorous birds, most of which are sexually di-morphic. All have short, conical bills. Many species are parasitized by whydahs and indigobirds.

Whydahs, indigobirds • Viduidae p. 406
W 20, A 20, S 8/0, S/A=40%
All highly sexually dimorphic, but males resemble females outside the breeding season. Male whydahs develop elaborate central tail feathers during the breeding sea-son. All are parasitic and most are highly host-specific; several species have been described on this basis. Whydahs and indigobirds occasionally hybridize: male hybrid offspring structurally resemble whydahs and have erroneously been ascribed to new species in the past.

Finches, siskins, seed-eaters, canaries • Fringillidae p. 414
W 134, A 45, S 16/8, S/A=36%
Small, arboreal or ground-dwelling, predominantly granivorous birds. Frequently in mixed-species foraging flocks, but solitary breeders. Popular cage-birds world-wide. This family previously included the buntings.

Buntings • Emberizidae (includes New World sparrows and allies) p. 424
W 321, A 13, S 5/1, S/A=38%
Mostly well-marked, ground-dwelling species, although some also perch in trees (e.g. Golden-breasted Bunting). Granivorous, sometimes forming foraging flocks in semi-desert areas (Lark-like Bunting).

References
Clements, J.F. 2000. *Birds of the World: a Checklist*. Vista, California: Ibis Publishing Company.
Harrrison, J.A. et al. 1997. *The Atlas of Southern African Birds*. (2 vols). Johannesburg: BirdLife South Africa.
Sibley, C.G. & Ahlquist, J.E. 1990. *Phylogeny and Classification of Birds*. New Haven: Yale University Press.
Sibley, C.G. & Monroe, B.L. 1990. *Distribution and Taxonomy of Birds of the World*. New Haven: Yale University Press.

GLOSSARY

Accidental. A vagrant or stray species not normally found within the region.
Arboreal. Tree dwelling.
Colonial. Associating in close proximity while roosting, feeding or nesting.
Commensal. Living with or near another species, without being interdependent.
Crepuscular. Active at dawn and dusk.
Cryptic. Pertaining to camouflage coloration.
Diurnal. Active during daylight hours.
Eclipse plumage. Dull plumage attained by male ducks and sunbirds during a transitional moult, after the breeding season and before they acquire brighter plumage.
Endemic. A species whose breeding and non-breeding ranges are confined to a particular region.
Near-endemic. A species whose range is largely restricted to a region but extends slightly outside the region's borders. (In southern Africa, this category includes mostly species whose ranges extend into the arid regions of southwestern Angola.)
Breeding endemic. A species that breeds only in a particular region but undertakes movements or migrations during the non-breeding season such that a measurable proportion of the population leaves the region.
Feral. Species that have escaped from captivity and now live in the wild.
Flight feathers. The longest feathers on the wings and tail.
Flush. Put to flight.
Form. A colour variant within a species; the colour variation may or may not be linked to sub-specific status.
Frons. Forehead.
Fulvous. Reddish yellow or tawny.
Gorget. A band of distinctive colour on the throat.
Immature. A bird that has moulted from juvenile plumage but has not attained adult plumage; can also include juvenile plumage.
Irruption. A rapid expansion of a species' normal range.
Jizz. A general impression of size, shape and behaviour.
Juvenile. The first fully feathered plumage of a young bird.
Melanistic. Describes a dark form of a particular species, the colour resulting from high levels of a pigment, melanin. In southern Africa most frequently encountered among raptors, especially hawks.
Migrant. A species that undertakes (usually) long-distance flights between its breeding and non-breeding areas.
Mirrors. The white spots on the primaries of gulls.
Montane. Pertaining to mountains.
Nocturnal. Active at night.
Nuchal. Describes the back or nape of the neck.
Overwintering. A bird that remains in the subregion instead of migrating to its breeding grounds.
Palearctic. North Africa, Greenland, Europe, Asia north of the Himalayas and southern China.
Pelagic. Ocean dwelling.
Race. A geographical population of a species; a subspecies.
Range. A bird's distribution.
Raptor. A bird of prey.
Rectrices. Tail feathers.
Remiges. Flight feathers of the wing.
Resident. A species not prone to migration, remaining in the same area all year.
Rufous. Reddish brown.
Speculum. A patch of distinctive colour on a bird's wing.
Sub-adult. A bird intermediate in age and plumage between immature and adult.
Territory. The area a bird establishes and then defends against others for breeding, feeding, or both.
Vagrant. Rare and accidental to the region.

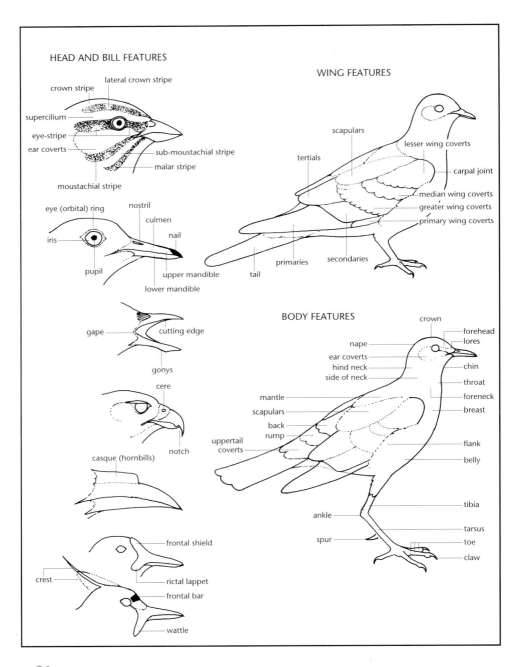

HEAD AND BILL FEATURES

crown stripe
lateral crown stripe
supercilium
eye-stripe
ear coverts
sub-moustachial stripe
malar stripe
moustachial stripe

eye (orbital) ring
nostril
culmen
iris
nail
pupil
upper mandible
lower mandible
tail

gape
cutting edge
gonys

cere
notch
casque (hornbills)

frontal shield
crest
rictal lappet
frontal bar
wattle

WING FEATURES

scapulars
lesser wing coverts
tertials
carpal joint
median wing coverts
greater wing coverts
primary wing coverts
primaries
secondaries

BODY FEATURES

crown
forehead
lores
nape
ear coverts
hind neck
side of neck
chin
mantle
throat
scapulars
foreneck
back
breast
rump
uppertail
coverts
flank
belly
ankle
spur
tibia
tarsus
toe
claw

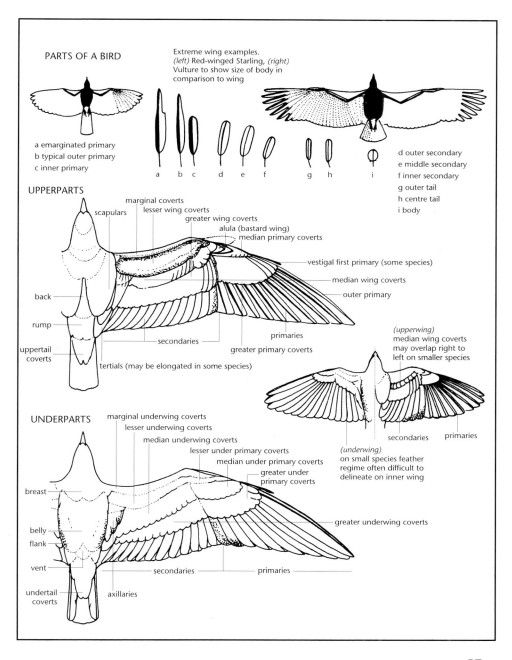

PARTS OF A BIRD

Extreme wing examples.
(left) Red-winged Starling, *(right)*
Vulture to show size of body in
comparison to wing

a emarginated primary
b typical outer primary
c inner primary

a   b   c   d   e   f   g   h   i

d outer secondary
e middle secondary
f inner secondary
g outer tail
h centre tail
i body

UPPERPARTS

marginal coverts
lesser wing coverts
scapulars
greater wing coverts
alula (bastard wing)
median primary coverts

vestigal first primary (some species)

median wing coverts

back

outer primary

rump

primaries

uppertail
coverts

secondaries

greater primary coverts

tertials (may be elongated in some species)

(upperwing)
median wing coverts
may overlap right to
left on smaller species

secondaries   primaries

UNDERPARTS

marginal underwing coverts
lesser underwing coverts
median underwing coverts
lesser under primary coverts
median under primary coverts
greater under
primary coverts

(underwing)
on small species feather
regime often difficult to
delineate on inner wing

breast

greater underwing coverts

belly
flank

vent

secondaries   primaries

undertail
coverts

axillaries

1. KING PENGUIN *Aptenodytes patagonicus* (2)   94 cm
The long, pointed bill, large size and bright orange ear patches are distinctive.
Sexes alike but male is larger. **Juv.** is a paler version of ad. **Habitat.** Pelagic; ranges throughout the southern oceans south of 40°S. **Status.** Vagrant; two records from the southern Cape. **Call.** On breeding grounds a loud trumpeting, given during display. (Koningspikkewyn)

2. GENTOO PENGUIN *Pygoscelis papua* (926)   76-81 cm
Much larger than the local African Penguin, and instantly recognisable by the red bill and white patch behind the eye. When swimming, the head pattern is very obvious. **Juv.** lacks the white blaze behind the eye. **Habitat.** Open oceans and Antarctic islands. **Status.** Only one, beach-stranded record from the Western Cape. **Call.** Grunts, hisses and trumpetings given at the breeding colony, but probably silent away from colonies. (Witoorpikkewyn)

3. MACARONI PENGUIN *Eudyptes chrysolophus* (5)   70 cm
Distinguished from Rockhopper Penguin by its more robust bill, larger size, and orange-yellow eyebrows that meet on the forehead; at sea, differentiated from Rockhopper Penguin by pale pink patch on sides of gape and white spot on rump. **Juv.** differs from juv. Rockhopper Penguin in having the yellow eyebrow starting above the eye. **Habitat.** Sea and sub-Antarctic islands. **Status.** Rare vagrant. **Call.** A loud trumpeting in display; at sea, a harsh 'aaark'. (Langkuifpikkewyn)

4. ROCKHOPPER PENGUIN *Eudyptes chrysocome* (4)   55-61 cm
Has a short, stubby, red bill and a pale yellow stripe extending from in front of the eye to the nape, where it ends in a golden, shaggy crest. The eyebrow stripe does not meet on the forehead as it does in Macaroni Penguin.
Juv. told from juv. Macaroni Penguin by conspicuous yellow eyebrow stripe starting well before the eye. **Habitat.** Breeds on sub-Antarctic islands; pelagic south of 30°S when not breeding. **Status.** Rare visitor, mostly in summer. Many records of birds ashore are of moulting juveniles. **Call.** In display, a trumpeting 'wada, wada, wada'. (Geelkuifpikkewyn)

5. AFRICAN (JACKASS) PENGUIN *Spheniscus demersus* (3)   60-70 cm
The region's only resident penguin, it has a diagnostic black and white facial pattern. Some birds show a double bar on the throat and chest – this is diagnostic of the Magellanic Penguin, from which it is not likely to be differentiated in the field. **Male** has a heavier bill than female. **Juv.** is dark greyish blue with grey cheeks, and lacks the breast band. **Habitat.** Occurs within 50 km of the shore; breeds mostly on offshore islands, with three mainland colonies. **Status.** Resident; endemic. Locally common but decreasing in numbers. **Call.** Loud, donkey-like braying, especially at night. (Brilpikkewyn)

6. MAGELLANIC PENGUIN *Spheniscus magellanicus* (927)   70-76 cm
Shows a broad double black band across breast as do some African Penguins. A thin, white line extends from below the eye towards the chin. Not reliably separated from African Penguin in the field (especially juvs) unless seen at very close range or caught and measured.
Habitat. Coastal areas and offshore. **Status.** Vagrant; one record, probably ship-assisted, from Cape Town docks. **Call.** Not recorded in SA. (Magellaanse Pikkewyn)

white ear patch

1

imm.

orange ear patch

large size

ad.

imm.

2

3

large bill

fleshy gape

juv.

ad.

yellow extends to front of eye

small bill

juv.

ad.

4

black & white face

juv.

imm.

ad.

ad. moulting

5

white line

6

1. GREAT CRESTED GREBE *Podiceps cristatus* (6) 45-56 cm
Breeding ad. unmistakable, having a dark double crest and a rufous-edged ruff ringing the sides of the head; ruff of female is paler. Shows white secondaries and leading edge to upperwing in flight.
Juv. has black-and-white striping on head. **Habitat.** Large stretches of fresh water, rarely in sheltered coastal embayments. **Status.** Locally common resident. **Call.** A barking 'rah-rah-rah'; various growls and snarls. (Kuifkopdobbertjie)

2. BLACK-NECKED GREBE *Podiceps nigricollis* (7) 28-33 cm
Breeding ad. has black head and throat, and conspicuous orange ear tufts. Non-breeding ad. distinguished from Little Grebe by its white cheeks and throat, and distinctive head and bill shape; at close range the cherry-red eye is obvious.
Juv. resembles non-breeding ad. **Habitat.** Open stretches of water, especially saline pans; also sheltered embayments on the Namibian coast. **Status.** Resident, with local movements. **Call.** A mellow trill during display. (Swartnekdobbertjie)

3. LITTLE GREBE (DABCHICK) *Tachybaptus ruficollis* (8) 23-29 cm
When breeding, this very small, dark grebe has chestnut sides to the neck and a diagnostic pale, creamy spot at the base of the bill. Non-breeding ad. can be distinguished from Black-necked Grebe by its smaller size and dusky cheeks and throat. In flight, shows extensive white trailing edge to upperwing.
Juv. similar to non-breeding ad. but has black-and-white striping on the cheeks. **Habitat.** Virtually any open stretch of fresh water. **Status.** Common resident. **Call.** Noisy; a distinctive, whinnying trill. (Kleindobbertjie)

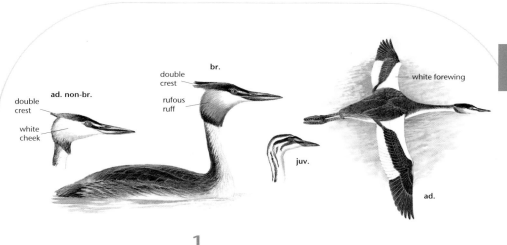

br.

double
crest

rufous
ruff

ad. non-br.

double
crest

white
cheek

white forewing

juv.

ad.

1

ad. non-br.

white

orange
ears

br.

ad. non-br.

2

ad. non-br.

pale spot

ad. non-br.

chestnut
neck

br.

ad. non-br.

3

1. WANDERING ALBATROSS *Diomedea exulans* (10)   107-130 cm

A huge, hump-backed albatross with a pink bill. At all ages has a white underwing with a narrow black trailing edge, tip and leading edge to carpal joint.

Juv. is dark, chocolate-brown with a white face and underwings. As birds age, they become progressively whiter. The body becomes mottled ('leopard' stage), then all white with fine vermiculations concentrated on back and breast, forming a shadow breast band. Upperwing then starts to whiten, initially from the centre of the wing over the elbow (not the leading edge as in Southern Royal Albatross). Throughout these stages has a black tail tip (mostly white in royal albatrosses). **Males** whiten faster than females, and eventually, after 20–25 years, become all white apart from black flight feathers. These very old males differ from old Southern Royal Albatrosses by having a pinker bill with no dark cutting edge. Feathering doesn't extend far onto the lower mandible (cf. Royal Albatross), making the forehead appear steeper. **Habitat.** Open ocean, breeding at sub-Antarctic islands. Occasionally visits trawlers. **Status.** Vulnerable. Rare inshore, but more common seaward of the continental shelf. **Call.** A harsh, nasal 'waaaak', seldom heard at sea. (Grootalbatros)

2. TRISTAN ALBATROSS *Diomedea dabbenena*   100-120 cm

(Not illustrated) Very difficult to distinguish from the slightly larger Wandering Albatross. It is unlikely, with present knowledge, that these two species could reliably be distinguished at sea.

Habitat. Open ocean, breeding on the Tristan Archipelago. **Status.** Unknown in our waters; only a few ringing recoveries to date. **Call.** Similar to Wandering Albatross. (Tristangrootalbatros)

3. NORTHERN ROYAL ALBATROSS *Diomedea sanfordi*   107-122 cm

Same size and shape as Wandering Albatross. Totally black upperwing, contrasting with white body and tail, is diagnostic. Underwing like Wandering Albatross but has a broader black leading edge from the carpal joint to the wing tips. Bill slightly yellower than Wandering Albatross; black cutting edge is visible only at close range.

Juv. has some black in outer tail and slight scalloping on back, but the body is white (not brown as in Wandering Albatross). The upperwings are dark, with a pale back; has much less black in the tail than Wandering Albatross. Black carpal leading edge narrower than in adult. **Habitat.** Open ocean, mostly at shelf break. **Status.** Endangered. Rare visitor to southern Africa. **Call.** Silent at sea. (Swartvlerkkoningalbatros)

4. SOUTHERN ROYAL ALBATROSS *Diomedea epomophora* (9)   107-122 cm

Can be confused with both Wandering and Northern Royal albatrosses. Differs chiefly from Wandering Albatross by upperwing whitening with age from the leading edge (not from the centre of the wing), and having a black cutting edge to bill and black eyelids. Also, white tail separates it from Wandering Albatross, except for very old birds. Some female Southern Royal Albatrosses in breeding plumage show a dusky subterminal band on the tail.

Juv. similar to juv. Northern Royal Albatross. **Habitat.** Open ocean. **Status.** Rare visitor to southern Africa. **Call.** Mostly silent at sea. (Witvlerkkoningalbatros)

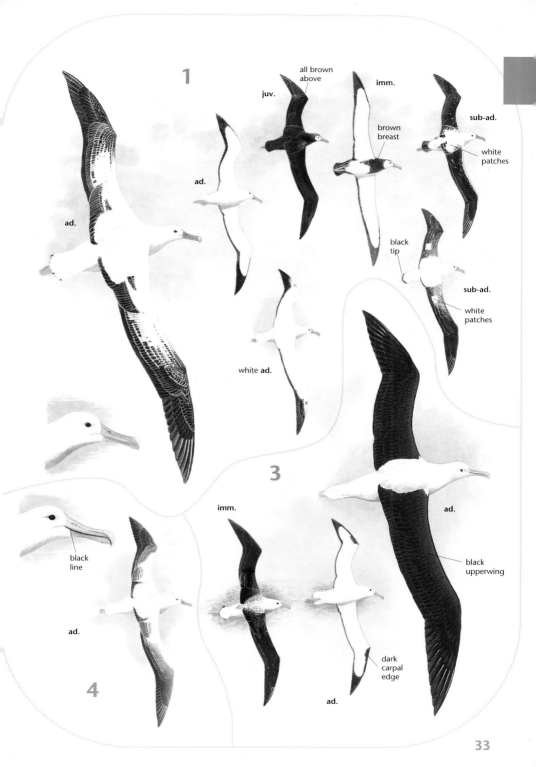

1

juv.

all brown above

imm.

brown breast

sub-ad.

white patches

ad.

ad.

black tip

sub-ad.

white patches

white ad.

3

black line

imm.

ad.

black upperwing

ad.

dark carpal edge

ad.

4

ad.

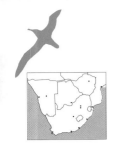

1. SHY ALBATROSS *Thalassarche cauta* (11) 92-100 cm

Largest of the 'dark-backed' albatrosses. At all ages, underwing pattern distinguishes it from all except Salvin's and Chatham Albatrosses. It is mostly white, with a narrow black border and a diagnostic black 'thumb-print' on the leading edge near the body. Ad. has pale grey cheeks and a white crown; the bill is pale olive-grey with a yellow tip. Rarely, individuals can appear unusually large and show a very pale grey or white back, sometimes mottled. They differ from all `great' albatrosses in this plumage by their smaller grey bill and lack of hump-backed shape.

Juv. and imm. have grey-washed heads, often with an incomplete grey breast band; bill is grey with a black tip. Habitat. Open ocean; mostly over the continental shelf. Large numbers scavenge at trawlers. Generally occurs closer to land than other albatrosses. Status. Common year round; adults most abundant May–Aug. Call. A loud, raucous 'waak' when squabbling over food. (Bloubekalbatros)

2. SALVIN'S ALBATROSS *Thalassarche salvini* 85-90 cm

Smaller and with a much paler back than either Shy or Chatham Albatrosses, back sometimes appearing white at a distance. The head is a deeper grey than Shy but not nearly as dark grey as Chatham. Ad. has grey-sided bill with a paler, yellowish ridge along the upper and lower mandible, and a dark spot on the lower mandible tip. Head and neck washed grey, merging onto mantle; crown paler.

Juv. and imm. virtually identical to Shy Albatross, but black primary tips on underwing slightly more extensive. Habitat. Open ocean and around trawlers. Status. Poorly known; a few records of ads and sub-ads from southern Africa. (Salvinalbatros)

3. CHATHAM ALBATROSS *Thalassarche eremita* 85-90 cm

Smaller than Shy Albatross and easily distinguished from Salvin's and Shy Albatrosses by its very dark, uniform grey head and bright yellow bill with a dark tip to lower mandible.

Juv. inadequately described so not known if distinguishable in the field from juv. Shy or Salvin's Albatrosses. Habitat. Open ocean and around trawlers. Status. Vagrant; two records, both at trawlers. Call. Not recorded in the region. (Chathamalbatros)

4. BLACK-BROWED ALBATROSS *Thalassarche melanophris* (12) 81-95 cm

Ad. has a yellow bill with a reddish tip.

Juv. and imm. have a grey bill with a black tip, and varying amounts of grey on the head and sides of the neck that sometimes join to form a collar. Underwing in juv. plumage is all dark but lightens with age. Underwing of juv. Grey-headed Albatross is also dark but Grey-headed Albatross has an all-dark bill. Juv. and imm. Shy and Yellow-nosed Albatrosses have mostly white underwings with black borders. Habitat. Southern oceans. Status. Visitor along the coast throughout the year but most abundant in winter, especially in association with fishing boats; the most common albatross in Cape waters. Call. Grunts and squawks when squabbling over food. (Swartrugalbatros)

5. LAYSAN ALBATROSS *Phoebastria immutabilis* (905) 79-81 cm

This is the only small albatross in our region in which the feet project beyond the tail tip in flight. The upperwing is dark, except for the white flash in the primaries. The pale underwing has a dark leading and trailing edge and shows a variable amount of black streaking in the centre, especially towards the inner secondaries.

Juv. resembles ad. but has a slightly greyer bill. Habitat. North Pacific Ocean. Status. Very rare vagrant, recorded only once. Call. Not recorded in the region. (Swartwangalbatros)

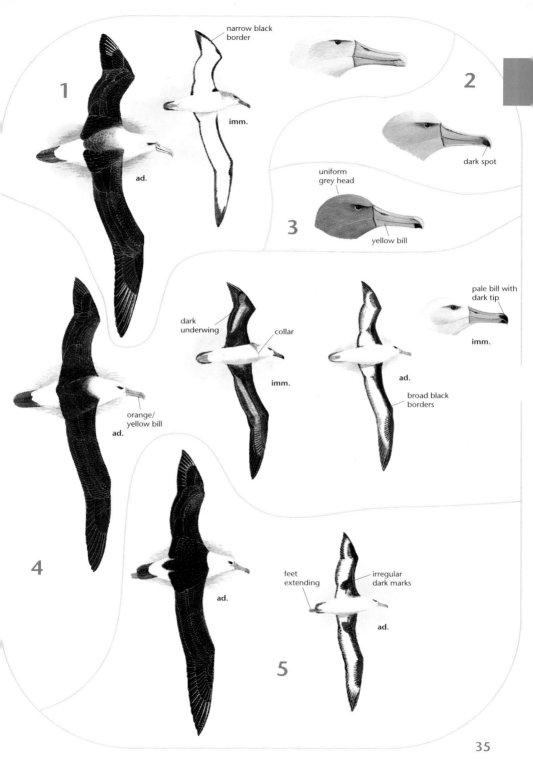

1

narrow black border

imm.

ad.

2

dark spot

3

uniform grey head

yellow bill

4

dark underwing

collar

imm.

ad.

broad black borders

pale bill with dark tip

imm.

orange/ yellow bill

ad.

ad.

5

feet extending

irregular dark marks

ad.

1. GREY-HEADED ALBATROSS *Thalassarche chrysostoma* (13)   89 cm
This albatross is similar in size to Black-browed Albatross but differs in having a grey head and a black bill with a yellow ridge along the upper and lower mandibles.
Juv. has a darker grey head than ad. but the cheeks may become almost white in the second and third years, attaining the pale grey head of ad. in the fifth year. Juv. and imm. are best separated from juv. and imm. Black-browed Albatross by the all-dark (not grey, black-tipped) bill. **Habitat.** Southern oceans, breeding during summer on sub-Antarctic islands. **Status.** Rare, mostly juv. birds, Jun–Sept. **Call.** Grunts and squawks when fighting over food. (Gryskopalbatros)

2. INDIAN YELLOW-NOSED ALBATROSS *Thalassarche carteri*   72-80 cm
Ad. differs from Atlantic Yellow-nosed Albatross by having a mostly white head, with only a faint grey wash on the cheek. At close range, the yellow bill stripe on the upper mandible has a pointed base (not rounded).
Juv. has all-black bill and white head; indistinguishable from juv. Atlantic Yellow-nosed Albatross. **Habitat.** Open ocean, breeding at islands in the Indian Ocean. **Status.** Vulnerable. Fairly common, year-round, but mostly May–Sept and the most abundant albatross in the warmer waters of the east coast. **Call.** Similar to Atlantic Yellow-nosed Albatross. (Indiese Geelneusalbatros)

3. ATLANTIC YELLOW-NOSED ALBATROSS *Thalassarche chlororhynchos* (14) 72-80 cm
A small, slender albatross with a relatively long bill. Underwing has crisp black margin, with leading edge roughly twice as broad as trailing edge. Ad. has a black bill with yellow stripe along the upper mandible, becoming reddish towards the tip. Differs from Indian Yellow-nosed Albatross by having a grey wash on the head and nape (slightly paler on forecrown). At close range, the base of the yellow stripe on the upper mandible is broad and rounded (not pointed).
Juv. has all-black bill and white head; indistinguishable from juv. Indian Yellow-nosed Albatross. **Habitat.** Open ocean, breeding at Tristan and Gough islands. **Status.** Fairly common year-round, but mostly May–Sept and most frequent in the southwestern Cape and Namibian waters. **Call.** Throaty 'waah' and 'weeeeh' notes when squabbling over food. (Atlantiese Geelneusalbatros)

4. BULLER'S ALBATROSS *Thalassarche bulleri* (928)   79-85 cm
In the region, can be confused with Atlantic Yellow-nosed Albatross. Differs in being larger and bulkier, having more extensive and darker grey coloration on the head with an obvious and contrasting pale grey crown, and by the yellow upper- and underside of the black bill. (In both yellow-nosed albatrosses, the yellow on the bill is confined to the upperside.) Differs from similar Grey-headed Albatross by its pale grey crown and white underwing with narrower black borders.
Juv. has a dark grey head, as in juv. Grey-headed Albatross, but unlike the latter, juv. Buller's Albatross has white, not dark, underwings. **Habitat.** Southern oceans. **Status.** Vagrant; one record off the Cape Peninsula. **Call.** Not recorded in the region. (Witkroonalbatros)

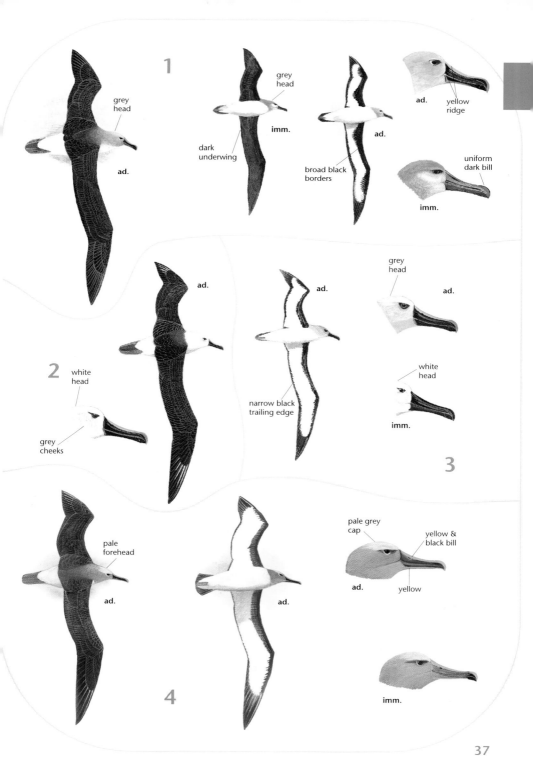

1

grey head

grey head

imm.

dark underwing

ad.

broad black borders

ad.

yellow ridge

uniform dark bill

imm.

2

white head

grey cheeks

ad.

ad.

narrow black trailing edge

grey head

ad.

white head

imm.

3

pale forehead

ad.

ad.

pale grey cap

yellow & black bill

ad.

yellow

imm.

4

1. SOUTHERN GIANT-PETREL *Macronectes giganteus* (17)   86-99 cm
This species has an all-white form that is unknown in Northern Giant-Petrel; otherwise these two species are very similar and can be identified with certainty only at close range. They are both large (the size of a small albatross), with heavy, pale-coloured bills (Southern Giant-Petrel has a fleshy green bill with a darker green tip). The flight is less graceful than that of the albatrosses – a heavy-bodied, hunch-backed, stiff-winged, clumsy, flapping motion.
Juv. is dark brown to black, becoming lighter with age; the all-white form fledges white and remains so. **Habitat.** Southern oceans; scavenges around seal colonies off the Cape and Namibian coasts. **Status.** Common visitor to coastal waters. **Call.** Harsh grunts when squabbling over food. (Reusenellie)

2. NORTHERN GIANT-PETREL *Macronectes halli* (18)   81-94 cm
The flesh-coloured, green-tinged bill with a reddish brown tip distinguishes this species from Southern Giant-Petrel. The dark plumage is very variable in both species but tends more to grey in Northern Giant-Petrel.
Juv. is uniformly very dark brown, lightening with age. **Habitat.** Southern oceans; occurs at seal colonies more frequently than Southern Giant-Petrel. **Status.** Common visitor, chiefly to the west coast. **Call.** Similar to that of Southern Giant-Petrel but slightly higher pitched. (Grootnellie)

3. LIGHT-MANTLED SOOTY ALBATROSS *Phoebetria palpebrata* (16)   79-87 cm
Differs from Dark-mantled Sooty Albatross in having an ashy-grey mantle, back and rump, which contrast with the darker head, wings and tail. The dark bill has a pale blue stripe on the lower mandible.
Juv. and **imm.** are paler than juv. and imm. Dark-mantled Sooty Albatross, and the mottling on the back extends onto the lower back and rump. **Habitat.** Southern oceans; has a more southerly distribution than Dark-mantled Sooty Albatross, rarely straying north of 45°S. **Status.** Very rare vagrant. **Call.** Silent at sea. (Swartkopalbatros)

4. DARK-MANTLED SOOTY ALBATROSS *Phoebetria fusca* (15)   84-89 cm
An all-dark, very slender albatross with long, narrow wings and an elongated, wedge-shaped tail that is usually held closed and appears pointed. The back is usually uniformly dark, matching the upperwings. The upper back can be pale but the pale coloration does not extend to the rump as it does in Light-mantled Sooty Albatross. At close range the dark bill shows a cream to yellow stripe on the lower mandible.
Juv. and **imm.** of both *Phoebetria* albatrosses are difficult to tell apart but this species has a conspicuous buff collar and mottling on the back. It might be mistaken for a giant petrel, but those species have a short, rounded tail, much shorter wings and a heavy-bodied appearance. **Habitat.** Southern oceans, seldom north of 40°S. **Status.** Rare winter vagrant. **Call.** Silent at sea. (Bruinalbatros)

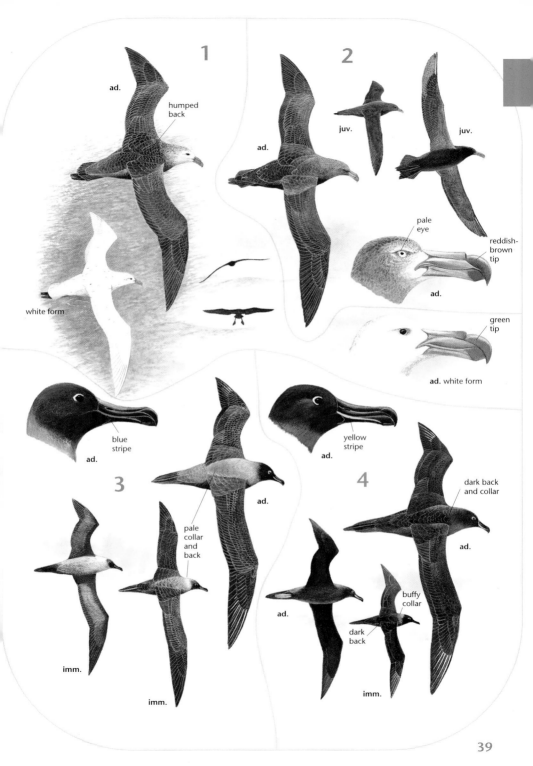

1

ad.

humped back

white form

2

ad.

juv.

juv.

pale eye

reddish-brown tip

ad.

green tip

ad. white form

3

ad.

blue stripe

ad.

yellow stripe

ad.

pale collar and back

imm.

imm.

4

dark back and collar

ad.

ad.

buffy collar

dark back

imm.

1. WHITE-CHINNED PETREL *Procellaria aequinoctialis* (32) 51-58 cm
Differs from all other dark brown petrels by its large size and long, robust, pale greenish white bill with black saddle. The white chin varies in extent: it may encompass the whole throat and cheeks or may be absent. At long range resembles most other all-dark shearwaters and petrels, but is darker brown in colour and the bill is always pale, sometimes showing as white. Spectacled Petrel has more extensive white on the sides of the head and a dark tip to the bill.
Habitat. Southern oceans, breeding on sub-Antarctic islands. **Status.** Common visitor, exceptionally abundant over the trawling grounds of the Western Cape. **Call.** A screaming 'tititititititi' when squabbling over food. (Bassiaan)

2. SPECTACLED PETREL *Procellaria conspicillata* (932) 50-56 cm
Very similar to White-chinned Petrel, but has diagnostic white spectacles. Size of spectacles varies; incomplete in some birds, but when the spectacles are narrow, they are not connected to the white throat. Pale bill has a slightly darker tip. Note that some White-chinned Petrels have a large white throat, and aberrant birds may have white head markings (often on nape).
Habitat. Open ocean; breeds only at Inaccessible Island, Tristan da Cunha. Attends trawlers. **Status.** Critically endangered. Rare, mostly Oct–Apr, but some records year-round. **Call.** Deeper than White-chinned Petrel; seldom heard at sea. (Brilbassiaan)

3. FLESH-FOOTED SHEARWATER *Puffinus carneipes* (36) 41-45 cm
Dark brown with a dark-tipped, flesh-coloured bill and flesh-coloured legs and feet. Its larger size and dark underwing distinguish it from Sooty Shearwater, while its bill and leg coloration, larger size, and rounded tail differentiate it from Wedge-tailed Shearwater (p. 50). At long range, if the feet are visible they appear as a pale area on the vent.
Habitat. Coastal waters, mainly from Eastern Cape and KwaZulu-Natal northwards. **Status.** Small numbers present year-round. **Call.** Silent at sea. (Bruinpylstormvoël)

4. SOOTY SHEARWATER *Puffinus griseus* (37) 40-46 cm
Differentiated from all other shearwaters by the silvery lining to the underwing. Wing beats are rapid, interspersed with short glides.
Habitat. Most abundant in Cape coastal waters, where it forages on small shoaling fish. **Status.** Common throughout the year; most abundant in early spring, often in large flocks. **Call.** Silent at sea. (Malbaartjie)

5. GREAT-WINGED PETREL *Pterodroma macroptera* (23) 40-42 cm
A dark brown petrel that differs from the similarly sized Sooty Shearwater in having a dark (not silvery) underwing, and from the much larger White-chinned Petrel by its short, black (not long, pale) bill. In flight, the wings are held at a sharp angle at the wrist and the head appears large, heavy and downward pointing on a short neck. Flight action in strong winds is fast and dynamic, the bird twisting, turning and wheeling in high arcs over the sea.
Habitat. Southern oceans; breeds on sub-Antarctic islands. **Status.** Common visitor, mainly Oct–Apr. **Call.** Silent at sea. (Langvlerkstormvoël)

6. KERGUELEN PETREL *Aphodroma brevirostris* (27) 34-36 cm
A small, compact petrel. Shape recalls *Pterodroma* petrels, but has characteristic 'bull-neck' and large head with a large, dark eye; often appears hooded. Smaller and greyer than Great-winged Petrel, with silvery highlights, especially on the leading edge of the forewing. Often towers up to 50 m above sea, hanging motionless or even hovering kestrel-like on rapid, shallow wingbeats. Flight very rapid and erratic.
Habitat. Open ocean, breeds on sub-Antarctic islands. **Status.** Vagrant, mostly Jun–Sept. Irrupts in large numbers in some years. **Call.** Silent at sea. (Kerguelense Stormvoël)

irruptive range

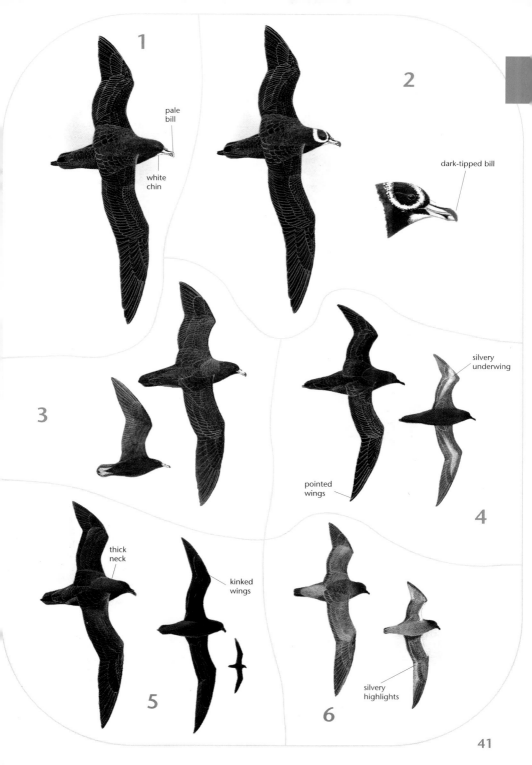

1

pale
bill

white
chin

2

dark-tipped bill

3

4

silvery
underwing

pointed
wings

5

thick
neck

kinked
wings

6

silvery
highlights

41

1. GREY PETREL *Procellaria cinerea* (33) 98 cm

This petrel superficially resembles Cory's Shearwater, from which it can be told by its dark underwing and undertail. The grey-brown of the head extends very low on the cheeks, leaving only a narrow, white throat patch; at long range this species can appear dark-headed. It has unusual shallow, stiff wing beats and a more direct flight action than other shearwaters, with less banking and shearing.
Habitat. Open oceans, breeding on the sub-Antarctic islands. **Status.** Rare summer vagrant. **Call.** Silent at sea. (Pediunker)

2. GREAT SHEARWATER *Puffinus gravis* (35) 46-53 cm

Similar in size to Cory's Shearwater but distinguished by its distinctive dark cap, dark, not yellow, bill, overall darker upperparts, barred brown-and-buff back, dark patch on the lower belly, dark shoulder smudge and indistinct black lines on underwing. The flight action is more dynamic than that of Cory's Shearwater, flying higher over the waves with more rapid wing beats on straighter wings.
Habitat. Open ocean, seldom close inshore. **Status.** Breeds on Tristan Archipelago. Common in south and western Cape waters in Aug–Oct and Apr–May and fairly common in Nov–Mar. Scarce Jun–Jul. **Call.** Silent at sea. (Grootpylstormvoël)

3. STREAKED SHEARWATER *Calonectris leucomelas* (933) 45-48 cm

Can be confused only with very similar Cory's Shearwater. It differs in having greyish (not warm brown) upperparts, much whiter underwings and a white face heavily streaked with brown. At long range, the head appears much paler than Cory's Shearwater.
Habitat. Eastern Indian and Pacific oceans. **Status.** Only two records in our region, both off KwaZulu-Natal; possibly more frequent but overlooked. **Call.** Not recorded within the region; probably silent at sea. (Gestreepte Pylstormvoël)

4. CORY'S SHEARWATER *Calonectris diomedea* (34) 45-53 cm

The ashy brown upperparts and lack of a dark-capped effect or pale collar differentiate this large, heavy-bodied species from Great Shearwater. At close range, it shows a yellow, not dark, bill, and individuals display varying amounts of white on the rump. It has a slower, more laboured flight than Great Shearwater and flies lower over the sea, not shearing and banking as much as other shearwaters. Browner and darker-headed than very similar Streaked Shearwater. In worn plumage can show vague pale streaking on forehead and crown, but this is never as obvious as in Streaked Shearwater. The Atlantic race *borealis* has a more robust bill and more extensive dark flight feathers on underwing.
Habitat. Open oceans, breeding on islands in the north Atlantic (*borealis*) and Mediterranean ('Scopoli's Shearwater' *diomedea*); sometimes forages close inshore on schooling fish, following tuna and dolphins. **Status.** Common summer visitor to all coasts. **Call.** Silent at sea. (Geelbekpylstormvoël)

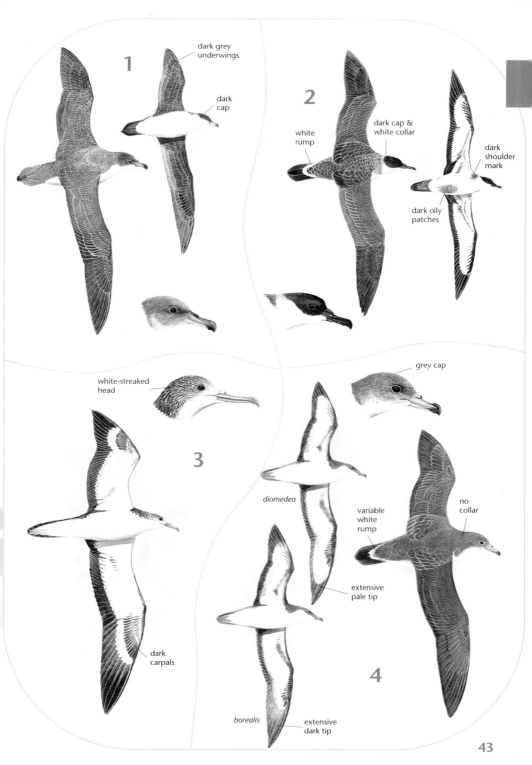

1

dark grey underwings

dark cap

2

white rump

dark cap & white collar

dark shoulder mark

dark oily patches

3

white-streaked head

dark carpals

grey cap

diomedea

variable white rump

no collar

extensive pale tip

4

borealis

extensive dark tip

1. BALEARIC (YELKOUAN) SHEARWATER *Puffinus mauretanicus* (934)   32-38 cm
Previously treated as a race of Manx Shearwater, and very difficult to tell from that species in the field. It is proportionally larger, evident only if a direct comparison is made. It is not as contrastingly black and white as Manx Shearwater, and has brown (not black) upperparts and dusky underparts and underwings, although this is variable. It does show a dark vent (not white as in Manx Shearwater) and dark axillaries. Two birds collected off the Western Cape were ascribed to the nominate race *mauretanicus*.
Habitat. Open seas. **Status.** Vagrant to the Western Cape, with two specimens and several sight records. **Call.** Not recorded in the region. (Baleariese Pylstormvoël)

2. MANX SHEARWATER *Puffinus puffinus* (38)   30-38 cm
This species is larger than Little Shearwater and has a more extensive black cap that extends below the eye, a broader black trailing edge to the underwing and a less fluttering flight. The flight action consists of long glides interspersed with a series of rapid wing beats. Differs from similar Balearic Shearwater in being obviously black and white, not brown and off-white, and in having a clear white, not dark, vent.
Habitat. Open seas; mainly coastal in the region. **Status.** Uncommon Palearctic visitor from Oct–Apr. Irruptive in some years. **Call.** Silent at sea. (Swartbekpylstormvoël)

3. AUDUBON'S SHEARWATER *Puffinus lherminieri* (40)   30 cm
Difficult to distinguish from Little Shearwater. It is slightly larger and in good light, this species' dark (not white) undertail coverts can be seen. The sub-Antarctic race of Little Shearwater is dark grey above and can appear brownish: it is doubtful if this race and Audubon's Shearwater can be distinguished reliably in the field unless the undertail is seen. However, their ranges are not known to overlap.
Habitat. Tropical and subtropical oceans. **Status.** Regular in small numbers off Mozambique; rare visitor to KwaZulu-Natal, especially in late summer during cyclonic conditions. **Call.** Silent at sea. (Swartkroonpylstormvoël)

4. LITTLE SHEARWATER *Puffinus assimilis* (39)   25-30 cm
A tiny, black-and-white shearwater. Appreciably smaller than Manx Shearwater, with short, rounded wings and narrow black trailing edge to the underwing (similar in width to leading edge, not twice as wide as in Manx Shearwater). Flight action distinctive: very rapid wing beats punctuated by short glides. Audubon's Shearwater is browner above, with dark vent and flight feathers. Both white-faced *tunneyi* (Indian Ocean and Australia) and dark-faced, silvery-grey *elegans* (sub-Antarctic islands) occur in southern African waters.
Habitat. Open ocean. In coastal waters, often joins flocks of Sooty Shearwaters. **Status.** Uncommon in northwest; rare in south, mostly May–Sept. **Call.** Silent at sea. (Kleinpylstormvoël)

1

dusky
underwing

dark
vent

dusky
under-
parts

brown
upperparts

white
vent

2

dark
vent

darker
underwing

3

white
vent

white
face

4

elegans

tunneyi

paler
underwing

1. SOUTHERN (ANTARCTIC) FULMAR *Fulmarus glacialoides* (19)   45-51 cm

A very pale grey, gull-sized petrel, with white underparts and white wing flashes at the base of the primaries. At close range, the dark-tipped pink bill is diagnostic. Unlikely to be confused with any other petrel in the region.
Habitat. Southern oceans, breeding in the far south on Antarctic islands and mainland.
Status. Uncommon winter visitor; most frequently seen in the Western Cape trawling grounds where it scavenges offal. **Call.** A high-pitched cackle when squabbling over food. (Silwerstormvoël)

2. ANTARCTIC PETREL *Thalassoica antarctica* (20)   40-46 cm

Vaguely resembles Pintado Petrel but lacks the chequered back and has a broad white stripe on each wing. The head is dark and the white tail narrowly tipped with black. The underparts are white. During the 24-hour sunlight of the Antarctic summer, the dark brown coloration bleaches to pale brown.
Habitat. Antarctica, rarely north of the pack ice. **Status.** Vagrant during winter. **Call.** Usually silent at sea and at the pack ice. (Antarktiese Stormvoël)

3. PINTADO PETREL *Daption capense* (21)   38-40 cm

A small, black-and-white petrel with chequering on the back and two white patches on each upperwing. The head is black and the tail white with a black tip. The underparts are white, with a black throat that is sometimes grizzled. The underwing is white, narrowly bordered with black.
Habitat. Southern oceans; breeds on islands in the Antarctic and sub-Antarctic. **Status.** Common winter visitor, May–Nov; extremely abundant on Western Cape trawling grounds. **Call.** When feeding, a high-pitched 'chee-chee-chee-chee'. (Seeduifstormvoël)

4. ATLANTIC PETREL *Pterodroma incerta* (26)   44 cm

A large, dark brown petrel with a conspicuous white lower breast and belly. In worn plumage, the breast and throat can appear mottled brown but never pure white. Much larger than Soft-plumaged Petrel and is brown, not grey. The upperparts are uniformly dark brown with no suggestion of an open 'M' on the upperwings.
Habitat. Open ocean; breeds only on the Tristan Archipelago. **Status.** Rare vagrant, mostly May–Sept. **Call.** Silent at sea. (Bruinvlerkstormvoël)

5. WHITE-HEADED PETREL *Pterodroma lessonii* (25)   40-46 cm

The white head has distinctive black, lozenge-shaped patches around the eyes. Underparts are white, contrasting with dark grey underwings. Distinguished from the much larger but similarly patterned Grey Petrel (p. 42) by its white head and undertail. The upperwings are greyish brown with a faint, darker, open 'M' pattern across the wings. An easily identified petrel with a fast, high-arcing flight action. Rarely attracted to ships.
Habitat. Southern oceans; does not breed near the region. Rarely ventures north of 40°S. **Status.** Winter vagrant. **Call.** Silent at sea. (Witkopstormvoël)

6. SOFT-PLUMAGED PETREL *Pterodroma mollis* (24)   32-37 cm

Resembles Atlantic Petrel but is much smaller and has a white throat. Dark brown smudges on sides of breast form a complete breast band. The white underparts contrast strongly with the dark underwings. The upperparts are dark, with a faint, darker, open 'M' pattern across the upperwings. The rare dark morph resembles Kerguelen Petrel (p. 40) but has broader, more rounded wings and is mottled on the belly and lacks silvery reflections. Does not have the same high-flying action as Kerguelen Petrel.
Habitat. Southern oceans, breeding on sub-Antarctic islands. **Status.** The most common *Pterodroma* petrel in Cape and KwaZulu-Natal coastal waters, chiefly in winter and spring. **Call.** Silent at sea. (Donsveerstormvoël)

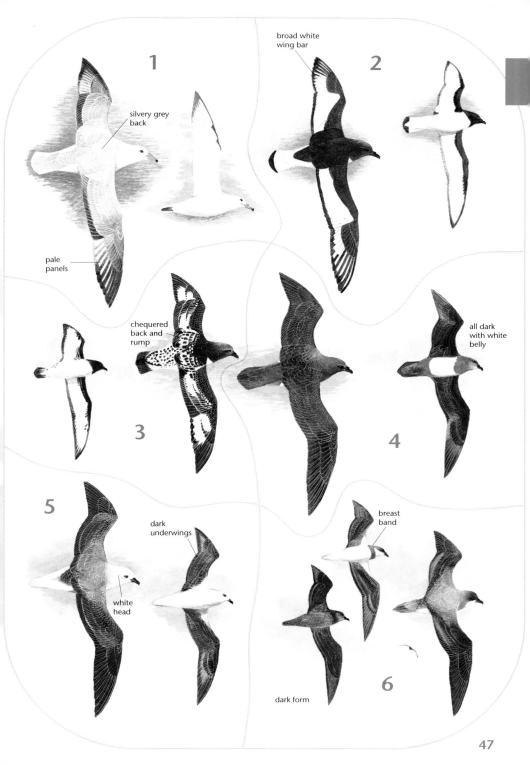

1

silvery grey back

pale panels

2

broad white wing bar

3

chequered back and rump

4

all dark with white belly

5

dark underwings

white head

6

breast band

dark form

1. BROAD-BILLED PRION *Pachyptila vittata* (29)   25-30 cm
The largest of the prions, identifiable at sea only if seen at very close range, when the broad, flattened, black (rather than blue) bill is diagnostic. Other characteristics are the unusually large head and the broad grey smudges on the sides of the breast. It is doubtful whether this species can be distinguished from Salvin's Prion at sea away from breeding islands.
Habitat. Open oceans, breeding on sub-Antarctic islands. **Status.** Uncertain, apparently rare winter visitor. **Call.** Silent at sea. (Breëbekwalvisvoël)

2. ANTARCTIC PRION *Pachyptila desolata*   25-28 cm
A small, blue-grey prion with a well-defined, dark 'M' across the upperwing. Underparts and underwings white. Like all prions, flight fluttery and erratic. Prion identification is very tricky; but this particular species is by far the most abundant species in African waters. Black tail tip relatively narrow, with a dark central stripe on the undertail (T-bar). Bill relatively narrow and bluish, and tends to have smaller breast smudges than larger Salvin's and Broad-billed Prions.
Habitat. Open ocean, breeding at sub-Antarctic islands and Antarctica. **Status.** Common, mostly late May–Aug, occurring in large flocks. Subject to 'wrecks', when large numbers of dead and dying birds come ashore. **Call.** Silent at sea. (Antarktiese Walvisvoël)

irruptive range

3. BLUE PETREL *Halobaena caerulea* (28)   28-30 cm
A small, blue-grey petrel with white underparts and underwings. Diagnostic features are the black markings on the crown and nape, and the square-ended, white-tipped tail. The open 'M' pattern on the upperwings is less distinct than in the prions. This species flies faster and arcs higher over the waves than the prions.
Habitat. Open ocean, seldom straying north of 40°S. **Status.** Irruptive winter vagrant, most records being of beach-wrecked birds. **Call.** Silent at sea. (Bloustormvoël)

4. SALVIN'S PRION *Pachyptila salvini*   27-29 cm
Bill width and length are the key to identifying this species and it is highly unlikely that this can be accomplished in the field. Dubious subtle differences in plumage have been suggested for telling this species apart from Broad-billed and Antarctic Prions, but have not been critically tested.
Habitat. Open oceans; with occasional wrecks around the coast. **Status.** Uncertain but apparently rare. No positive sight records; most specimens found during winter. **Call.** Silent at sea. (Salvinse Walvisvoël)

5. SLENDER-BILLED PRION *Pachyptila belcheri* (30)   25-27 cm
Similar to Antarctic Prion, but paler, especially on the head. Tends to have a longer white eye-stripe than other prions. Grey breast smudges reduced. Black tail tip is reduced, with outer 2–3 tail feathers white (cf. Antarctic Prion, with only outermost tail feather white). Flight rather more like that of shearwater than other prions: wings stiffer, with rapid bursts of flapping. At very close range the thin bill is diagnostic.
Habitat. Open ocean, breeding at sub-Antarctic islands. **Status.** Poorly known; apparently rare in shelf waters, but large numbers irrupting in some years. **Call.** Silent at sea. (Dunbekwalvisvoël)

6. FAIRY PRION *Pachyptila turtur* (31)   25-28 cm
This is the most easily identifiable prion in the region. Its coloration is more blue and less grey than that of other prions, with a very pale, unmarked head, short bill, diagnostic broad, black tip to the tail and lack of a broad central stripe to undertail. All other prions have narrow black tail bands.
Habitat. Open ocean, breeding on sub-Antarctic islands. **Status.** Vagrant, most records of beached birds May–Sept. **Call.** Silent at sea. (Swartstertwalvisvoël)

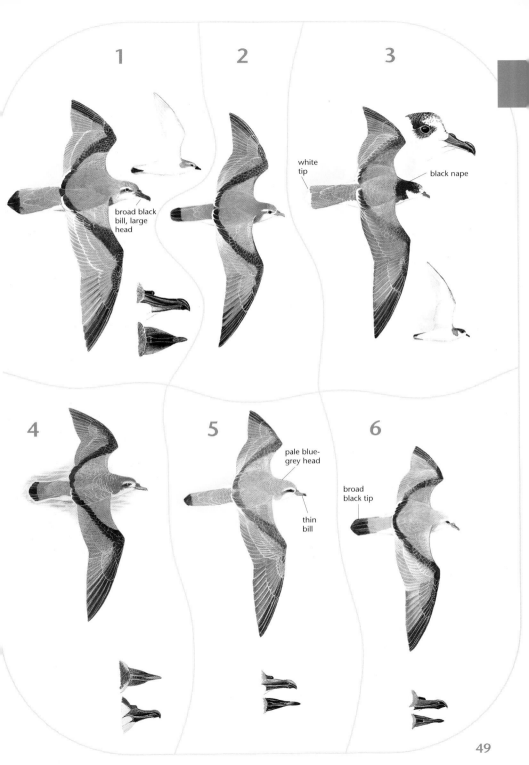

1

broad black
bill, large
head

2

3

white
tip

black nape

4

5

pale blue-
grey head

thin
bill

6

broad
black tip

1. MATSUDAIRA'S STORM-PETREL *Oceanodroma matsudairae* (918) 25 cm
In the region, this large, dark storm-petrel could be mistaken only for Bulwer's Petrel. Matsudaira's Storm-Petrel is slightly smaller and has a deeply forked tail, not the pointed tail of Bulwer's Petrel. Sometimes in flight it shows a noticeable white, crescent-shaped, jaeger-like flash at the base of the outer primaries.
Habitat. Open ocean. **Status.** Vagrant to the east coast, recorded only once. **Call.** Probably silent at sea. (Matsudairase Stormvoël)

2. BULWER'S PETREL *Bulweria bulwerii* (22) 26-27 cm
A small, prion-sized petrel that is uniformly dark brown and has a diagnostic, long, wedge-shaped tail that is usually held closed and appears pointed. A pale grey-brown stripe runs across each upperwing on the edges of the secondary coverts. The flight is buoyant and graceful, with the bird swooping over the wave tops, then dipping into the next trough.
Habitat. Open ocean, seldom close to shore. Breeds on islands in the North Atlantic Ocean. **Status.** Vagrant to the west coast. **Call.** Silent at sea. (Bulwerse Stormvoël)

3. JOUANIN'S PETREL *Bulweria fallax* 30-32 cm
Very similar to Bulwer's Petrel but is larger and has a different flight action. It gives the impression of having a long, pointed tail in the field, and could be confused with a noddy. It is usually seen in calm, tropical oceans, where it flies low over the water with long glides interspersed with shallow, rapid flicks of the wings. In windy conditions, it arcs and wheels high over the waves with a dynamic, *Pterodroma*-like flight.
Habitat. Open tropical oceans and seen regularly in western Indian Ocean south of the equator. **Status.** Recorded twice only in the region, in offshore Mozambican waters. **Call.** Unknown. (Jouaninse Stormvoël)

4. WEDGE-TAILED SHEARWATER *Puffinus pacificus* (41) 41-46 cm
Similar to Flesh-footed Shearwater (p. 40) in colour and size but lacks that species' flesh-coloured bill and feet. The tail is wedge-shaped but appears pointed in flight. Sooty Shearwater (p. 40) is larger, has silvery underwings and lacks the pointed tail. The rare pale morph most likely to be confused with Great Shearwater (p. 42), but lacks pale rump and nape and heavy brown mottling on underwing coverts.
Habitat. Tropical and subtropical oceans. **Status.** Regular off Mozambique; rare vagrant to KwaZulu-Natal and the Eastern Cape. **Call.** Silent at sea. (Keilstertpylstormvoël)

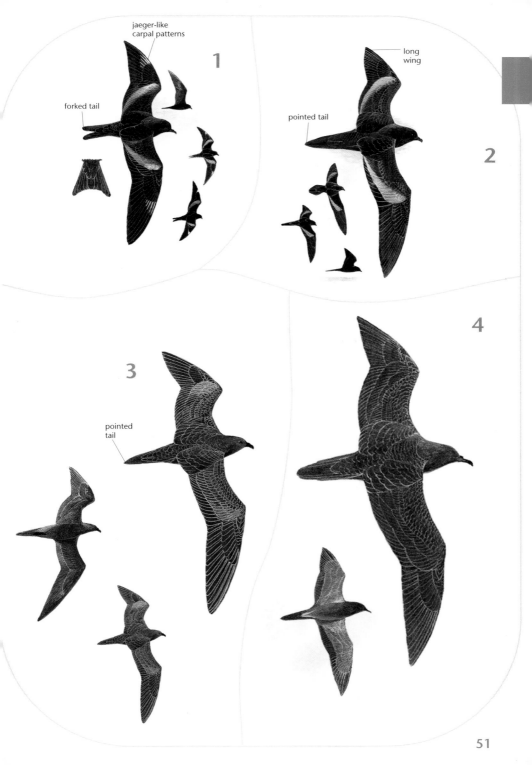

jaeger-like
carpal patterns

1

forked tail

long
wing

pointed tail

2

3

pointed
tail

4

1. WILSON'S STORM-PETREL *Oceanites oceanicus* (44)   15-19 cm
Differs from all other storm-petrels in wing shape and flight action. Larger than European Storm-Petrel, it has broader, more rounded and flattened wings, and long, spindly legs that usually project beyond the end of the tail. Lacks the conspicuous white underwing flash of European Storm-Petrel. The yellow webbing on the feet is difficult to see when the bird is in flight. The flight is swallow-like and direct, with frequent glides. The long legs dangle in and patter over the water when the bird is feeding.
Habitat. Open oceans, breeding in Antarctica and on sub-Antarctic islands. Status. Abundant visitor along the coast throughout the year but chiefly during winter. Call. Silent at sea. (Geelpootstormswael)

2. WHITE-FACED STORM-PETREL *Pelagodroma marina* (937)   19-20 cm
Cannot be confused with any other storm-petrel in the region. The all-white underparts and underwing coverts and the noticeable white eyebrow stripe are diagnostic. The flight is direct and buoyantly light, with regular side-to-side sweeps with the long legs trailing through the water.
Habitat. Open seas; rarely inshore. Status. Rare in Cape and Mozambican waters. Call. Silent at sea. (Witgesigstormswael)

3. LEACH'S STORM-PETREL *Oceanodroma leucorhoa* (43)   19-22 cm
Larger than European Storm-Petrel. Best identified by its long, narrow wings and distinctive flight action: it bounds low over the waves with quick, jerky movements and sudden directional changes. When the bird spreads its tail, a clear fork can be seen. The small white rump has a narrow dusky centre, but this is not easily seen.
Habitat. Open oceans. Status. Uncommon summer visitor to oceanic waters, mainly off the west coast; breeds in small numbers on islands off the Western Cape. Call. Musical chattering and trilling at breeding sites. (Swaelstertstormswael)

4. EUROPEAN STORM-PETREL *Hydrobates pelagicus* (42)   14-17 cm
The smallest seabird in the region. It commonly occurs in large flocks, and the combination of black plumage, white rump and conspicuous white flash on the underwing distinguishes it from other local storm-petrels. The feet do not project beyond the end of the tail in flight, which is bat-like and direct. The bird some-times hovers, pattering its feet over the water when feeding.
Habitat. Open ocean; common around trawlers. Status. Common summer visitor to Cape and KwaZulu-Natal coastal waters. Call. Silent in the region. (Swartpootstormswael)

5. BLACK-BELLIED STORM-PETREL *Fregetta tropica* (46)   20 cm
Larger than Wilson's Storm-Petrel, from which it differs in having extensive white on the underwings and a white belly with a black line down the centre. The black line is only obvious when the bird banks. Distinguished from White-bellied Storm-Petrel by its much darker appearance and by the black line down its belly; the two species share similar flight characteristics, bounding over the waves and, when feeding, appearing to bounce off waves on their breasts.
Habitat. Southern oceans. Status. A fairly common passage migrant off the Western Cape during Apr–May and Sept–Oct; rare elsewhere. Call. Silent at sea. (Swart-streepstormswael)

6. WHITE-BELLIED STORM-PETREL *Fregetta grallaria* (45)   20 cm
Very difficult to distinguish from Black-bellied Storm-Petrel but always appears much paler, and has the back feathers edged with grey and a totally white belly extending onto the vent and undertail coverts. Sometimes accompanies ships, where it is seen more often in the bow waves and in front of the vessel than in the wake.
Habitat. Open oceans. Status. Rare visitor to Cape and KwaZulu-Natal seas. Perhaps more regular seaward of the continental shelf. Call. Silent at sea. (Witpensstormswael)

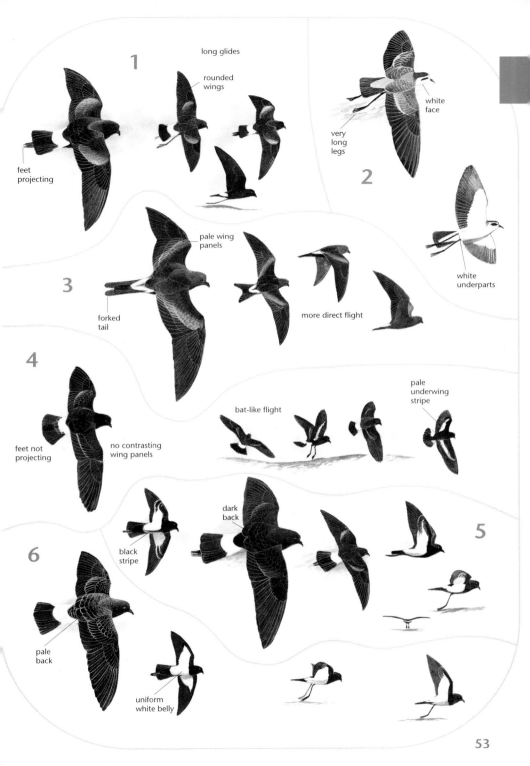

1

long glides

rounded wings

feet projecting

2

very long legs

white face

white underparts

3

pale wing panels

forked tail

more direct flight

4

feet not projecting

no contrasting wing panels

bat-like flight

pale underwing stripe

6

pale back

black stripe

dark back

uniform white belly

5

1. RED-TAILED TROPICBIRD *Phaethon rubricauda* (47)   50 cm

Ad. is almost pure white (tinged with pink when breeding) with a stout, red bill and two extremely long, wispy, red central tail feathers.
Juv. lacks nuchal collar of Red-billed Tropicbird and solid black primary patch of White-tailed Tropicbird, and has a dark bill. **Habitat.** Tropical oceans and Indian Ocean islands. **Status.** Rare summer visitor to southern coastal waters; regular off northern KwaZulu-Natal and Mozambique. **Call.** Various grunts and cackles, and a deep 'kraak'. (Rooipylstert)

2. RED-BILLED TROPICBIRD *Phaethon aethereus* (910)   46-50 cm

Ad. distinguished from ad. Red-tailed Tropicbird by its finely barred back, which appears grey at a distance, and by its long, white (not red) tail streamers.
Juv. is the only juv. tropicbird to have a broad, dark stripe through the eye that extends back to form a nuchal collar. **Habitat.** Oceanic islands and open sea. **Status.** Vagrant. **Call.** Largely silent at sea. (Rooibekpylstert)

3. WHITE-TAILED TROPICBIRD *Phaethon lepturus* (48)   44 cm

Ad. has two black patches on each wing and two conspicuous, elongated, white central tail feathers. The bill is orange-yellow in both ad. and imm.
Juv. is much smaller than other juv. tropicbirds, lacks a nuchal collar, has a black patch in outer primaries and a dull yellow bill with a dark tip. **Habitat.** Tropical oceans and islands. **Status.** Rare visitor to Mozambican waters; vagrant elsewhere. **Call.** Silent in the region. (Witpylstert)

4. BROWN BOOBY *Sula leucogaster* (52)   64-74 cm

Ad. is brown with a white lower breast and belly, and a broad white stripe on the otherwise brown underwings extending from the body to the carpal region. Similar to juv. Cape Gannet, it has a long, cigar-shaped body outline, and a pointed bill and tail. The border between the brown and white on the breast is clearly defined.
Juv. and imm. are paler versions of ad. and have white bellies flecked with brown; they lack the white speckling of juv. Cape Gannet. **Habitat.** Tropical oceans and islands. **Status.** Vagrant. **Call.** Usually silent at sea. (Bruinmalgas)

5. RED-FOOTED BOOBY *Sula sula* (921)   66-77 cm

Brown morph confusable only with juv. Cape Gannet but is smaller and slimmer, has a much longer, pointed tail, and at close range shows vermilion feet and a blue bill. White morph very similar to ad. Cape Gannet but has the same structural differences as the brown morph and an all-white (not black) tail. In flight, white morph shows a black carpal patch on the underwing, and vermilion feet.
Juv. and imm. have greyish yellow feet and a pinkish blue bill. **Habitat.** Tropical oceans. **Status.** Uncommon in tropical Mozambican waters, vagrant elsewhere. **Call.** Not recorded in the region. (Rooipootmalgas)

6. CAPE GANNET *Morus capensis* (53)   87-100 cm

Ad. is white with black flight feathers and a black, pointed tail: a variable number of outer-tail feathers may be white. The bill is heavy, long, pointed and pale grey, while the nape and sides of the neck are straw-yellow.
Juv. and imm. progress through mottled brown and white stages, when they could be confused with Brown Booby, which is smaller and always shows a well-defined brown bib and white belly. **Habitat.** Coastal. Breeds on islands off the Cape and Namibia. **Status.** Common breeding endemic. **Call.** 'Warrra-warrra-warrra' when feeding in flocks at sea. (Witmalgas)

7. AUSTRALIAN GANNET *Morus serrator* (54)   83-95 cm

Almost identical to Cape Gannet but has a higher-pitched call, a darker blue eye and a gular stripe only one third the length of that of Cape Gannet.
Juv. and imm. indistinguishable from juv. and imm. Cape Gannet except by length of gular stripe. **Habitat.** Coastal. **Status.** Vagrant, occurs annually in Cape Gannet colonies. **Call.** Higher in pitch than that of Cape Gannet. (Australiese Malgas)

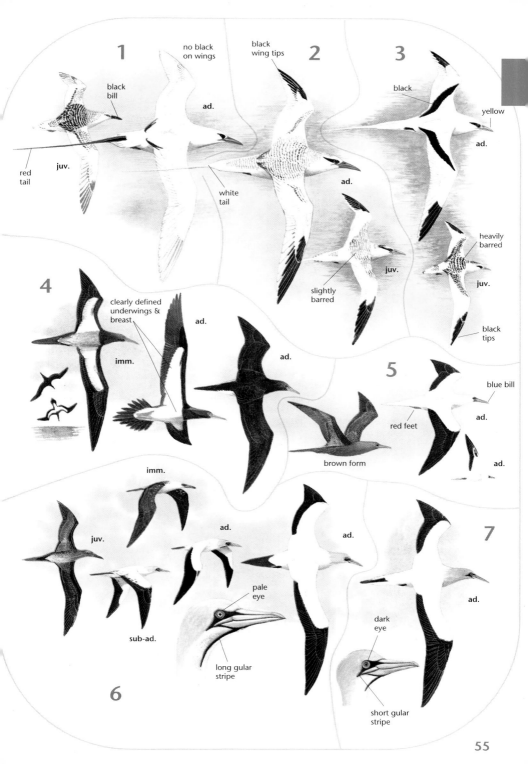

1

no black
on wings

black
bill

ad.

red
tail

juv.

white
tail

2

black
wing tips

ad.

ad.

juv.

slightly
barred

3

black

yellow

ad.

heavily
barred

juv.

black
tips

4

clearly defined
underwings &
breast

ad.

imm.

ad.

ad.

brown form

5

blue bill

red feet

ad.

ad.

6

imm.

juv.

ad.

ad.

ad.

sub-ad.

pale
eye

long gular
stripe

7

ad.

dark
eye

short gular
stripe

1. WHITE-BREASTED CORMORANT *Phalacrocorax lucidus* (55) 80-100 cm
The largest cormorant of the region. Ad. is glossy black with a white throat and breast, and a bright yellow patch at the base of the bill. During the breeding season, it has white flank patches.
Juv. and imm. are dark brown with white underparts. **Habitat.** Coastal and fresh waters. **Status.** Locally common resident. **Call.** Silent except at breeding colonies when grunts and squeals are uttered. (Witborsduiker)

2. BANK CORMORANT *Phalacrocorax neglectus* (57) 76 cm
Larger and more robust than Cape Cormorant, from which it also differs by its dull black plumage and thick, woolly-textured neck, and by the lack of yellow facial skin. The eye and bill are dark. In breeding plumage it shows white flecks on the head and a diagnostic white rump. A small tuft of feathers on the forehead is erectile, giving the appearance of a small, rounded crest.
Juv. and imm. lack white plumage flecks and have dull-coloured eyes. **Habitat.** Rocky shores and islands off the west coast. **Status.** Locally common resident; endemic. **Call.** Normally silent except at colonies; when bird alights near nest, a wheezy 'wheeee' is given. (Bankduiker)

3. CAPE CORMORANT *Phalacrocorax capensis* (56) 61-65 cm
Intermediate in size between Bank and Crowned Cormorants. Ad. has glossy blue-black plumage with a bright yellow-orange patch at the base of the bill; the patch brightens during the breeding season. The eye is bright turquoise.
Juv. and imm. are dark brown with slightly paler underparts than ad. **Habitat.** A flock-feeding marine cormorant that enters harbours and estuaries. **Status.** Common resident; breeding endemic. **Call.** Silent except during the breeding season, when various 'gaaaa' and 'geeee' noises are uttered. (Trekduiker)

4. REED CORMORANT *Phalacrocorax africanus* (58) 50-55 cm
A small, black cormorant with pale spotting on the back, and a long, unmarked tail. In breeding plumage, ad. has a yellow-orange face patch and throat, and a small crest on the forehead. A freshwater cormorant rarely seen at the coast.
Juv. and imm. are dark brown above and white below. **Habitat.** Freshwater dams, lakes and rivers. Roosts and breeds colonially. **Status.** Common resident. **Call.** Silent except for cackling and hissing at breeding colonies. (Rietduiker)

5. CROWNED CORMORANT *Phalacrocorax coronatus* (59) 50-55 cm
Differs from Reed Cormorant by its orange-red face and throat patch (breeding plumage), longer and more pronounced erectile forehead crest, and shorter tail.
Juv. and imm. are dark brown above and differ from juv. and imm. Reed Cormorant by their shorter tail and brown (not white) underparts. **Habitat.** Almost entirely marine, on islands off west coast and in estuaries and lagoons in the Western Cape. **Status.** Locally common resident; endemic. **Call.** Silent except for croaking sounds at breeding colonies. (Kuifkopduiker)

6. AFRICAN DARTER *Anhinga rufa* (60) 80 cm
The long, egret-like neck, slender head and long, pointed bill should prevent confusion with cormorants. When swimming it sometimes totally submerges its body, leaving only its long neck and head showing.
Breeding male has a rufous head and neck, with a long, white stripe running from the eye onto the neck. Female and non-breeding male are pale brown on the face and throat. **Juv.** and imm. have a buffy neck, more streaking on the head and neck, and lack streaking on the back. **Habitat.** Freshwater dams, lakes and slow-moving streams; less often coastal lagoons and estuaries. **Status.** Common resident. **Call.** A distinctive croaking. (Afrikaanse Slanghalsvoël)

1

imm.

br.

ad.

2

white
rump

rounded
crest

yellow
gular patch

3

no gular
patch

imm.

pale
pattern

ad.

imm.

pale
under-
parts

ad.

crest

pointed
bill

juv.

thin
neck

4

imm.

dark
underparts

5

♂ br.

6

1. GREATER FRIGATEBIRD *Fregata minor* (61)   86-100 cm

A large, black bird with very long, pointed wings. The elongated, forked tail appears pointed when held closed.

Male is all-black with a red throat pouch, and lacks the white 'armpits' of male Lesser Frigatebird. Female shows a white breast and throat, and a grey chin. **Juv.** and imm. have a whitish or tawny head and a white breast (cf. Lesser Frigatebird). **Habitat.** Tropical seas and islands. **Status.** Regular off the Mozambique coast, otherwise vagrants recorded in late summer on south and east coasts during or after cyclonic conditions. **Call.** Silent at sea. (Groot Fregatvoël)

2. LESSER FRIGATEBIRD *Fregata ariel* (922)   71-81cm

Male is readily identified by the all-black plumage with diagnostic white 'armpits' extending from the axillaries to the sides of the breast. Female is distinguished from female Greater Frigatebird by the black chin and throat, noticeable white collar, and the white on the breast extending to the 'armpits'. **Juv.** and imm. are distinguished from juv. and imm. Greater Frigatebird by having more extensive black on the belly, and the white on the breast extending to the white 'armpits'. Although this species is smaller and more angular than Greater Frigatebird, size-based identification requires direct comparison. **Habitat.** Open ocean. **Status.** Vagrant to Mozambican waters, particularly following summer cyclones. **Call.** Silent at sea. (Klein Fregatvoël)

3. GREAT (EASTERN) WHITE PELICAN *Pelecanus onocrotalus* (49)   140-178 cm

A very large, white bird that assumes a pinkish flush in the breeding season. In flight, the black primaries and secondaries contrast with the white coverts. The orbital skin is pink, the bill pink and yellow and the pouch yellow. Larger than Pink-backed Pelican, which also has less strongly contrasting underwings in flight and, outside breeding season, is greyer-coloured.

Juv. is dark brown and whitens progressively with age. **Habitat.** Habitually fishes in groups on open, freshwater lakes. Also preys on eggs and young of gulls and cormorants. Frequents estuaries in the Western Cape, Namibia and KwaZulu-Natal. Nests on the ground, usually on flat islands, in colonies. **Status.** Locally common resident. **Call.** Usually silent; a deep 'mooo' is given at breeding colonies. (Witpelikaan)

4. PINK-BACKED PELICAN *Pelecanus rufescens* (50)   135-152 cm

Considerably smaller than Great White Pelican, this species differs in being greyer, with a pink back, and, in breeding plumage, having an all-yellow bill, pouch and orbital skin. In flight the primaries and secondaries do not contrast strongly with the coverts, appearing more uniform. It has a grey crest when breeding. Non-breeding ads have a pinkish bill and pouch and whitish orbital skin.

Juv. is dark brown at first and becomes greyer with age. Best distinguished from Great White Pelican by smaller size. **Habitat.** Coastal estuaries, less often on fresh water. Nests in colonies in trees. Feeds solitarily. **Status.** Resident from KwaZulu-Natal northwards; vagrant elsewhere. **Call.** Usually silent; guttural calls uttered at breeding colonies. (Kleinpelikaan)

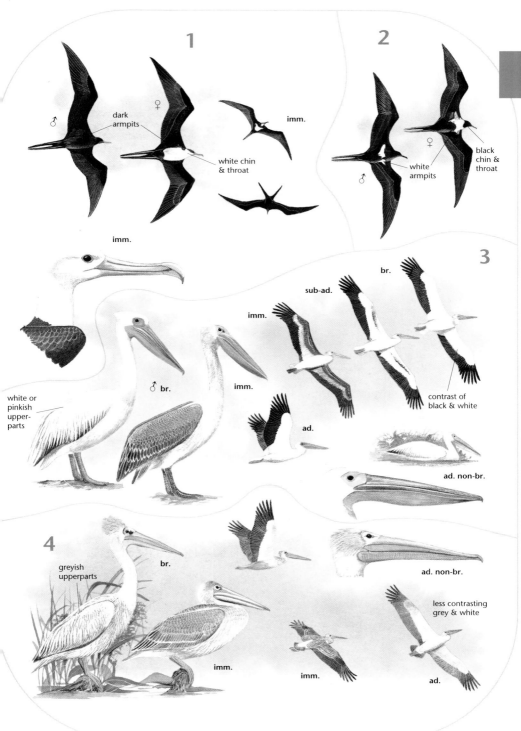

1

♂

dark
armpits

♀

imm.

white chin
& throat

imm.

2

♀

black
chin &
throat

white
armpits

♂

3

br.

sub-ad.

imm.

contrast of
black & white

white or
pinkish
upper-
parts

♂ br.

imm.

ad.

ad. non-br.

4

greyish
upperparts

br.

ad. non-br.

less contrasting
grey & white

imm.

imm.

ad.

1. GOLIATH HERON *Ardea goliath* (64)   120-152 cm

Its large size is diagnostic: it is the world's largest heron. In colour it most closely resembles the smaller Purple Heron, but Goliath Heron has an unstriped head and neck and dark legs.

Juv. and imm. less rufous than adult, with chest, belly and underwing coverts white, streaked with black. **Habitat.** Freshwater dams, lakes, large rivers and sometimes estuaries. **Status.** Locally common resident in the north and east. Usually solitary or in pairs. **Call.** A loud, low-pitched 'kwaaark'. (Reusereier)

2. PURPLE HERON *Ardea purpurea* (65)   79-84 cm

The rufous head and neck and dark grey wings are distinctive; much smaller than Goliath Heron, and marked on the crown and neck with black stripes.

Juv. and imm. lack the grey nape and mantle of ad., are less streaked on the neck and have far less black on the crown. **Habitat.** Aquatic, favouring sedges and reeds in freshwater and estuarine habitats. Reluctant to feed in the open. **Status.** Common resident. **Call.** Similar to Grey Heron's 'kraaark'. (Rooireier)

3. GREY HERON *Ardea cinerea* (62)   90-100 cm

A large, greyish heron distinguished from others by its white head and neck and the wide black eyebrow, which ends on the nape in a wispy black plume. The bill is yellow. In flight, can be distinguished from Black-headed Heron by its uniformly grey underwings.

Juv. and imm. easily confused with juv. and imm. Black-headed Heron but have light flanks and yellow (not dark) upper legs and white, not black, ear coverts. **Habitat.** Pans, dams, slow-flowing rivers, lagoons and estuaries. **Status.** Common resident. **Call.** A harsh 'kraaunk', given in flight. (Bloureier)

4. BLACK-HEADED HERON *Ardea melanocephala* (63)   84-92 cm

Slightly smaller than Grey Heron. The black-topped head and hind neck contrast with the white throat. In flight, the contrasting dark and pale underwing differentiates it from Grey Heron, which has a uniformly grey underwing. Eye yellow most of the year, but becomes red when breeding.

Juv. and imm. have grey (not black) on the head and neck. Distinguished from juv. and imm. Grey Heron by the dark legs and thighs, dark ear coverts and underwing pattern. **Habitat.** More often seen stalking through open grasslands than around water. **Status.** Common resident. **Call.** A loud 'aaaaark', and various hoarse cackles and bill clapping at the nest. (Swartkopreier)

1

chestnut crown

slow, laboured flight

br.

imm.

ad.

enormous size

2

striped face

juv.

ad.

juv.

juv.

br.

juv.

black crown & neck

ad.

juv.

uniformly grey underwing

contrasting underwing pattern

ad.

3

4

1. YELLOW-BILLED EGRET *Egretta intermedia* (68) 61-69 cm

Differentiated from larger Great Egret by its noticeably shorter neck, which is not held in such a pronounced S-shape, and by the shorter bill. The gape does not extend behind the eye but ends just below it. Although not easily seen, the yellowish upper legs are diagnostic. Differs from Cattle Egret by its larger size, longer bill and more slender appearance. When breeding, it has long plumes on the back and chest, a reddish bill and upper legs, and lime-green lores.
Juv. and imm. resemble ad. Habitat. Flooded veld and marshes and any damp, grassy areas, but infrequently near open water. Status. Common resident. Call. Typical, heron-like 'waaaark'. (Geelbekwitreier)

2. GREAT (WHITE) EGRET *Egretta alba* (66) 85-92 cm

The largest white heron of the region. Legs and feet are black at all times. Breeding bird has elaborate plumes, a black bill and lime-green lores; in non-breeding plumage lacks plumes and has a yellow bill. Differs from Yellow-billed Egret by its larger size, longer and heavier bill with gape extending behind the eye, and much longer, thinner neck, which is usually held kinked in an 'S' shape. Distinguished from Little Egret by its much larger size and black (not yellow) toes.
Juv. and imm. resemble non-breeding ad. Habitat. Freshwater dams, lakes, flooded meadows, estuaries and lagoons. Status. Common resident. Call. A low, heron-like 'waaaark'. (Grootwitreier)

3. LITTLE EGRET *Egretta garzetta* (67) 55-65 cm

The black legs and contrasting yellow toes differentiate this species from any other white heron in the region. The bill is slender and black. It feeds by dashing to and fro in shallow water in pursuit of prey. It usually forages alone, and is only gregarious when breeding. Breeding birds have mauve lores and black eyes.
Juv. and imm. lack the head plumes and aigrettes (plumes on the back) of ad. Toes are a duller yellow. Habitat. Most freshwater situations; also along rocky coastlines and estuaries. Status. Common resident. Call. A harsh 'waaark'. (Kleinwitreier)

4. CATTLE EGRET *Bubulcus ibis* (71) 50-56 cm

Breeding bird has a red bill, and buff plumes on the head, breast and mantle, but is never as dark as Squacco Heron. The bill is shorter and more robust than in other white herons, and there is a noticeable shaggy bib and throat that give this species a distinct jowl. The legs are never black, but vary from dark brown to yellowish green, and are red at the start of the breeding season.
Juv. and imm. resemble non-breeding ad. Habitat. Essentially non-aquatic; most often found in association with cattle or game. Highly gregarious. Status. Common resident. Call. Typical, heron-like 'aaaark' or 'pok-pok'. (Veereier)

5. (COMMON) SQUACCO HERON *Ardeola ralloides* (72) 40-46 cm

The smallest white heron in the region. At rest, it looks bittern-like but in flight shows all-white wings.
Juv. and imm. are browner on the mantle and more streaked below than ad., but not as heavily streaked as non-breeding/juv. Malagasy Pond-Heron. Habitat. Vegetated margins of freshwater lakes, pans and slow-moving rivers. Skulks in long grass, sitting motionless for long periods. Status. Common resident. Call. Low-pitched, rattling 'kek-kek-kek'. (Ralreier)

6. MALAGASY (MADAGASCAR SQUACCO) POND-HERON *Ardeola idae* (73) 45-48 cm

Breeding plumage is completely white. In non-breeding dress, very difficult to distinguish from Squacco Heron but is slightly larger, and has a noticeably heavier bill and much broader streaking on the throat and breast.
Juv. and imm. resemble non-breeding ad. Habitat. Like that of Squacco Heron but includes open situations more often. Status. Vagrant to the region; recorded only from Zimbabwe and Mozambique. Call. Usually silent. (Madagaskar-ralreier)

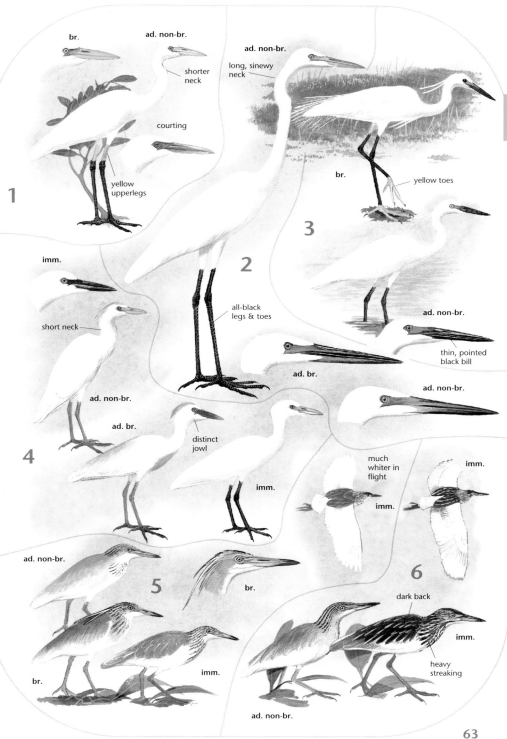

1

br.

ad. non-br.

shorter neck

courting

yellow upperlegs

2

all-black legs & toes

3

ad. non-br.

long, sinewy neck

br.

yellow toes

ad. non-br.

thin, pointed black bill

ad. non-br.

4

imm.

short neck

ad. non-br.

ad. br.

distinct jowl

ad. br.

imm.

5

ad. non-br.

br.

br.

imm.

much whiter in flight

imm.

imm.

6

dark back

imm.

heavy streaking

ad. non-br.

1. BLACK HERON (EGRET) *Egretta ardesiaca* (69)   48-50 cm
A small, slate-black version of Little Egret (p. 62), with black legs and yellow toes. Lacks the rufous throat of Slaty Egret. Diagnostic feeding behaviour involves forming an 'umbrella' over the head, with the wings held forward and outstretched. Has long nape and breast plumes. **Juv.** and **imm.** are slightly paler than ad. and lack long plumes on the head, back and breast. **Habitat.** Freshwater lakes and dams; occasionally estuaries. **Status.** Resident, with local movements; rare to locally common. **Call.** Seldom calls; a deep 'kraak'. (Swartreier)

2. SLATY EGRET *Egretta vinaceigula* (70)   60 cm
Very similar to Little Egret (p. 62) in shape and behaviour. In colour resembles Black Heron but differs in having greenish yellow legs and feet and a rufous throat, and in lacking the wing-canopy feeding action. Breeding bird has black eye. **Juv.** and **imm.** resemble ad. but lack the long head and breast plumes. **Habitat.** Tropical wetlands. **Status.** Uncommon resident, confined to upper reaches of Zambezi River and the Okavango swamps; vagrant to Zimbabwe and the Northern Province. **Call.** Unknown. (Rooikeelreier)

3. RUFOUS-BELLIED HERON *Ardeola rufiventris* (75)   38-40 cm
A small heron with a sooty black head, breast and back and a rufous belly, wings and tail. In flight, the bright yellow legs and feet contrast strongly with the dark underparts. **Female** is duller than male. **Juv.** and **imm.** have dull brown (not blackish) upperparts, becoming darker with age. **Habitat.** Seasonal wetlands with sedges or grasses. Easily overlooked and often seen only when put to flight. **Status.** Uncommon summer visitor in the east but resident farther north. **Call.** Typically heron-like 'waaaaak'. (Rooipensreier)

4. LITTLE BLUE HERON *Egretta caerulea*   72 cm
Because of its similarities to Little Egret (p. 62), this species is easily overlooked in juv. plumage, but may be distinguished by its all-yellowish legs and toes, and its dark-tipped (not all-black) bill. Ad. could be confused with Black Heron but shows an overall greyer cast and has a deep maroon head and neck, dark feet and a heavy, dark-tipped, blue bill. **Imm.** is mottled grey and white, unlike any other heron in Africa. **Habitat.** Freshwater lagoons and coastal estuaries. **Status.** Vagrant. **Call.** Usually quiet when not breeding, but gives a 'girr-girr-girr' alarm call. (Kleinbloureier)

5. WHITE-BACKED NIGHT-HERON *Gorsachius leuconotus* (77)   50-56 cm
The large, dark head with its conspicuous pale eye patch, dark back and wings and dull chestnut neck render this species unmistakable. The small white patch on the back is visible in flight and during display. **Juv.** may be distinguished from juv. Black-crowned Night-Heron (p. 66) by its extensive dark cap and the lack of white spotting on the mantle and back, and from Eurasian Bittern (p. 66) by its much smaller size and lack of black moustachial stripes. **Habitat.** Slow-moving streams and rivers overhung with thick tangles of reeds and trees. **Status.** Uncommon resident, easily overlooked, confined to the east and north. **Call.** When disturbed gives a sharp 'kaaark'. (Witrugnagreier)

6. WESTERN REEF HERON *Egretta gularis*   56-66 cm
Occurs in dark and white morphs. Dark morph differs from Black Egret in being grey, not black and has a white throat and pale, not dark legs. White morph differs from Little Egret in having greenish, not black legs and from imm. Little Blue Heron in lacking a dark tipped grey bill. **Habitat.** Coastal rocky beaches. **Status.** Vagrant from west Africa. **Call.** Harsh 'gaaar'. (Westelike Kusreier)

1

foraging 'umbrella'

dark plumage

yellow toes only

2

chestnut throat

yellow legs & feet

ad.

ad.

juv.

rufous belly

rufous wing patches

imm.

imm.

ad.

3

bi-coloured bill

juv.

dark legs & feet

ad.

imm.

4

dark head

ad.

juv.

white patch

ad.

5

juv.

ad.

dark morph

6

1. EURASIAN (GREAT) BITTERN *Botaurus stellaris* (80)   64 cm

The largest bittern, this species is more often heard than seen. The upperparts are streaked buff-brown and black, with a black crown and broad, conspicuous, moustachial stripes. The underparts are buff, heavily streaked with dark brown. The black moustachial stripes and tawny (not grey) overall colour should prevent confusion with juv. Black-crowned Night-Heron. **Habitat.** Reedbeds, sedge beds and flooded grassland. **Status.** Rare, movements poorly understood. **Call.** Deep, resonant three- to five-syllable booming, reminiscent of the grunting of a distant lion. (Grootrietreier)

2. BLACK-CROWNED NIGHT-HERON *Nycticorax nycticorax* (76)   56-61 cm

The black crown, nape and back contrast distinctly with the grey wings and tail, and the white underparts. **Juv.** superficially resembles Eurasian Bittern but is grey-brown (not tawny), and lacks the black crown and moustachial stripes. Distinguished from juv. White-backed Night-Heron (p. 64) by its paler cheeks and extensive white spotting on the mantle and back. **Habitat.** Freshwater dams, streams and lagoons. Flocks roost in reedbeds and trees during the day, and venture out at dusk to feed. **Status.** Common resident. **Call.** A characteristic, harsh 'kwok' when flying to and from roosts. (Gewone Nagreier)

3. GREEN-BACKED HERON *Butorides striata* (74)   40 cm

A small, dark grey heron with a black crown, dark green back and paler grey underparts. The legs and feet are bright orange-yellow. From behind easily confused with Dwarf Bittern, but the latter has more uniformly dark grey upperparts. The black, wispy nape plume is not usually seen except when the bird alights. **Juv.** is streaked brown and buff and has dull orange legs. **Habitat.** Frequents mangrove stands and coral reefs at low tide, as well as freshwater dams, lakes and sluggish rivers overhung with trees. **Status.** Fairly common resident. **Call.** A characteristic, sharp 'baaek' when the bird takes to flight. (Groenrugreier)

4. DWARF BITTERN *Ixobrychus sturmii* (79)   25-30 cm

This bittern is uniformly dark slaty blue above, and buff below overlaid with blackish vertical stripes running from the throat down onto the breast. The smallest heron in the region, it appears more like a large rail in the field. Most easily confused with juv. Green-backed Heron. **Juv.** is similar to ad. but the head and back feathers are scalloped with buff, and the breast is more rufous. **Habitat.** Freshwater ponds and lakes surrounded by trees, and especially flooded woodlands. **Status.** Locally common summer visitor. **Call.** A barking 'ra-ra-ra-ra-ra' at the start of breeding, otherwise silent. (Dwergrietreier)

5. LITTLE BITTERN *Ixobrychus minutus* (78)   27-38 cm

Differs from smaller Dwarf Bittern in having conspicuous pale buff wing panels and less striping on the throat and breast. **Female** is browner and more streaked than male. **Juv.** resembles female but is much more heavily streaked below; distinguished from Green-backed Heron by its smaller size and green (not orange) legs. **Habitat.** Thick reedbeds. **Status.** Uncommon resident (*I. m. payesii*) and locally common non-breeding summer visitor (paler faced *I. m. minutus*). Solitary breeder. **Call.** A short bark, 'rao', uttered at intervals of a few seconds, at the start of breeding. (Kleinrietreier (Woudapie))

1

black crown

black crown, hind neck & back

br.

juv.

2

white spotting

juv.

juv.

ad.

ad.

blue-grey underparts

yellow legs

juv.

ad.

3

heavy streaking

4

very dark upperparts

ad.

ad.

♂ ad. *minutus*

♂ ad. *payesii*

♀ ad.

5

buff wing panels

juv.

♂ ad.

♀ ad.

imm.

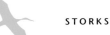

1. BLACK STORK *Ciconia nigra* (84)   95-100 cm

A large, glossy, black stork with a white lower breast, belly and undertail. Distinguished from the smaller Abdim's Stork by the black (not white) rump and lower back, and by the red (not greenish) bill and legs.

Juv. is a browner version of ad. and has a yellowish green bill and legs (bill of juv. Abdim's Stork is grey). **Habitat.** Feeds in streams and ponds, usually solitarily. Also occurs along the coast in estuaries and lagoons. **Status.** Uncommon to rare resident. Nests solitarily on cliff ledges. **Call.** Silent except on the nest, when loud whining and bill-clapping are given. (Grootswartooievaar)

2. ABDIM'S STORK *Ciconia abdimii* (85)   76-81 cm

Distinguished from the larger Black Stork by its smaller size, white (not black) lower back and rump, greyish (not red) legs with pink ankles, and greyish (not red) bill. In flight, legs do not project as far beyond the end of the tail as they do in Black Stork.

Juv. is duller than ad. **Habitat.** Open fields and agricultural lands, often in the company of White Storks. **Status.** Common summer visitor, usually in large flocks. **Call.** Usually silent in the region; a weak, two-note whistle is given at roosts. (Kleinswartooievaar)

3. WHITE STORK *Ciconia ciconia* (83)   102-120 cm

Most closely resembles Yellow-billed Stork but differs in having a red (not yellow) bill and legs, and an all-white tail. The legs often appear white because the birds excrete on them to lose body heat.

Juv. has a darker bill and legs, and the white plumage is tinged with brown. **Habitat.** Grassland, vleis, cultivated lands and pastures. **Status.** Common summer visitor. Small breeding population in the Western Cape. **Call.** Silent except on the nest, when loud whining and bill-clapping are given. (Witooievaar)

4. YELLOW-BILLED STORK *Mycteria ibis* (90)   95-105 cm

The very long, slightly decurved, yellow bill is diagnostic. During the breeding season the naked facial skin is red and the wing coverts and back are tinged with pink. In flight it appears similar to White Stork but differs in having a black tail.

Juv. is brownish above and washed with grey-brown below, becoming whiter with age. The facial skin, bill and legs are duller than those of ad. **Habitat.** Lakes, large rivers and estuaries. **Status.** Common resident in the north; rare summer visitor further south. **Call.** Normally silent except during the breeding season, when it gives loud squeaks and hisses. (Nimmersat)

1

red bill

ad.

black rump

ad.

red legs

yellowish-green bill

juv.

2

white rump

grey bill

ad.

juv.

blue & red legs

black tail

ad.

white tail

ad.

3

imm.

ad.

4

red face & yellow bill

juv.

br.

1. MARABOU STORK *Leptoptilos crumeniferus* (89)   150-155 cm
The huge size, unfeathered head and neck, and massive bill render this species unmistakable. In flight, the black wings contrast with the white body, and the head is tucked into the shoulders.
Juv. like ad. but has the head and neck covered with a sparse, woolly down. **Habitat.** Not often seen outside major game reserves, where it scavenges at game kills, refuse dumps and abattoirs. **Status.** Uncommon resident, usually in flocks. **Call.** A low, hoarse, croak given when alarmed; claps bill when displaying. (Maraboe)

2. SADDLE-BILLED STORK *Ephippiorhynchus senegalensis* (88)   145 cm
Unlikely to be confused with any other stork species because of its large size, unusual, red-and-black-banded bill, and the yellow 'saddle' at the bill base.
Male has brown eyes and a small, yellow wattle. Female has yellow eyes and lacks the wattle. **Juv.** and imm. are grey (not black), the neck and head are brown, and they lack the yellow 'saddle' at the bill base. **Habitat.** Dams, pans, rivers and flood plains. **Status.** Uncommon resident; usually solitary or in pairs. **Call.** Normally silent except for bill-clapping during display. (Saalbekooievaar)

3. AFRICAN OPENBILL (OPENBILLED STORK)
Anastomus lamelligerus (87)   81-94 cm
A large, black stork with a large bill that has a diagnostic wide, nutcracker-like gap between the mandibles. The bill is usually dark towards the tip, paling to ivory at the base.
Juv. and imm. are duller versions of ad. and lack the bill gap, which develops with maturity. **Habitat.** Freshwater lakes and dams. **Status.** Uncommon visitor, mainly in summer. **Call.** Seldom heard; a croaking 'honk'. (Oopbekooievaar)

4. WOOLLY-NECKED STORK *Ciconia episcopus* (86)   85 cm
The combination of the glossy black plumage, white woolly neck, and white belly and undertail is distinctive.
Juv. and imm. are like ad. but the glossy black is replaced by brown and the black forehead extends further back on the crown. **Habitat.** Usually near fresh water: lagoons, ponds and rivers. **Status.** Uncommon resident. Solitary, in pairs, and occasionally in flocks. **Call.** Seldom heard; a harsh croak. (Wolnekooievaar)

1

ad.

soaring

♀

♂

2

♂

♀

juv.

3

ad.

huge,
mostly
dark bill

imm.

white
neck

imm.

ad.

4

1. GREATER FLAMINGO *Phoenicopterus ruber* (96) 127-140 cm

The very long legs and long neck are characteristic. In flight, shows brilliant red patches in the forewings. It differs from Lesser Flamingo in being larger and paler pink, and in having a pink (not dark red) bill with a black tip.

Juv. is dull brown, becoming paler with age. Juv. and imm. are readily distinguished from juv. and imm. Lesser Flamingo by the black-tipped grey bill. **Habitat.** Shallow, freshwater lakes, salt pans, estuaries and open coast. **Status.** Common but nomadic resident; sometimes occurs in huge concentrations. **Call.** 'Honk, honk', sounding not unlike a farmyard goose. (Grootflamink)

2. LESSER FLAMINGO *Phoenicopterus minor* (97) 81-90 cm

Distinguished from Greater Flamingo by its much smaller size and by its dark red (not pink) bill, which appears black when seen at a distance. The head, neck and body plumage are very variable, but are normally far redder than those of Greater Flamingo, with a larger expanse of crimson in the wings.

Juv. is brown, becoming paler with age. Juv. and imm. are readily distinguished from juv. and imm. Greater Flamingo by their all-dark bill. **Habitat.** Freshwater lakes, salt pans and estuaries, usually in the company of Greater Flamingo. **Status.** Common but nomadic resident. **Call.** A goose-like honking. (Kleinflamink)

3. AFRICAN SPOONBILL *Platalea alba* (95) 90 cm

The long, flattened, spoon-shaped, grey-and-red bill is diagnostic. In flight it differs from the similarly sized white egrets by the way in which it holds its neck outstretched (not tucked into the shoulders). It feeds with a characteristic side-to-side sweeping motion of the bill.

Male has a longer bill than female. **Juv.** and imm. have a yellowish horn-coloured bill and dark-tipped flight feathers. Juv. has a markedly shorter bill than ad. **Habitat.** Freshwater lakes, flood plains and estuaries. **Status.** Fairly common resident with local movements. **Call.** A low 'kaark'. In breeding colonies emits various grunts and claps bill. (Lepelaar)

4. HAMERKOP *Scopus umbretta* (81) 48-56 cm

A dark brown, long-legged bird with a heavy crest and a flattened bill. The hammer-shaped profile of the head renders this bird unmistakable. In flight, its shape and barred tail lend it a hawk-like appearance, but the long bill and legs rule out confusion with any bird of prey.

Juv. and imm. like ad. **Habitat.** Freshwater dams, lakes and rivers. Nest is a characteristic huge, domed structure of sticks, with small side entrance, usually in a sturdy tree or on a cliff ledge. **Status.** Common resident. **Call.** A sharp 'kiep' in flight; a jumbled mixture of querulous squawks and frog-like croaks during courtship. (Hamerkop)

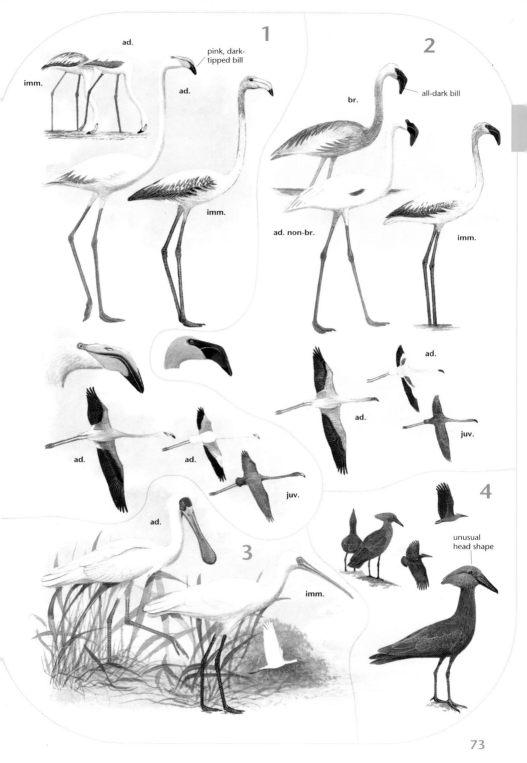

1

imm.

ad.

ad.

pink, dark-tipped bill

ad.

imm.

2

br.

all-dark bill

ad. non-br.

imm.

ad.

ad.

juv.

ad.

ad.

ad.

juv.

ad.

3

imm.

4

unusual head shape

1. HADEDA IBIS *Bostrychia hagedash* (94)   76-89 cm

A drab, greyish brown bird which at close range shows glossy, bronze wing coverts. The face is grey, and a white stripe runs from the bill base to below and behind the eye. The long, dark, decurved bill has a red ridge on the upper mandible.

Juv. and imm. lack the red on the bill and the bronze on the wings. **Habitat.** Diverse: forest clearings, woodland, savanna, open grassland, farmland and suburban gardens. **Status.** Common resident; has expanded its range westwards in past 30 years. Usually in small parties. **Call.** One of the most familiar calls in parts of Africa. Noisy in flight, uttering a loud 'ha-ha-ha-dah-da'. (Hadeda)

2. SOUTHERN BALD IBIS *Geronticus calvus* (92)   78 cm

Differs from the smaller Glossy Ibis by having a bald red (not dark chestnut) head with a white face, a long, decurved, red bill, and red legs and feet. General colour is glossy blue-black, with coppery patches on the forewings.

Sexes alike but male has a longer bill. **Juv.** and imm. have duller plumage, with the head covered in short, light brown feathers, and have the red on the bill confined to the base. The legs are brown (not red as in ad.) and the coppery patches on the forewings are absent. **Habitat.** Short-grazed or burnt upland grassland. Breeds on cliffs. **Status.** Locally common resident; endemic. Found in flocks. **Call.** A high-pitched, wheezing call. (Kalkoenibis)

3. GLOSSY IBIS *Plegadis falcinellus* (93)   55-65 cm

The smallest ibis of the region, it appears black when seen at a distance, but closer views show the head, neck and body to be a dark chestnut and the wings, back and tail a dark, glossy green with bronze and purple highlights. Breeding bird has white line at base of upper and lower mandibles.

Juv. and imm. have the glossy areas of ad. but the remainder of the body plumage is a dull, sooty brown; they may show a pale spot at the base of the bill. **Habitat.** Invariably associated with water: dams, pans, vleis and flooded grassland. **Status.** Locally common resident; range has expanded westwards in the last 30 years. **Call.** Normally silent; a low, guttural 'kok-kok-kok' is given in breeding colonies. (Glansibis)

4. AFRICAN SACRED IBIS *Threskiornis aethiopicus* (91)   64-82 cm

A white bird with an unfeathered black head and neck, and a long, decurved, black bill. The scapular feathers are blue-black and the flight feathers are black-tipped, giving a narrow black edge to the wing. Groups of birds often fly in a 'V' formation. During breeding, the naked skin on the underwing turns scarlet and the flank feathers become yellow.

Sexes alike but male is longer-billed. **Juv.** and imm. differ from ad. by having off-white feathering on the neck. Juv. has a greyish cast to the feathers. **Habitat.** Ranges from offshore islands and estuaries to grassland and vleis. Regular at man-made wetlands and croplands. **Status.** Common resident. **Call.** A loud croaking given at breeding colonies. (Skoorsteenveër)

1

greyish head

dark, uniform back

ad.

sub-ad.

2

ad.

red & white face

imm.

3

thin, long neck

ad.

thin, dark neck

imm.

4

black tips

br.

br.

black unfeathered neck & head

imm.

1. SPUR-WINGED GOOSE *Plectropterus gambensis* (116)   75-100 cm

A large, mostly black goose with variable amounts of white on the throat, neck and belly. In flight, its huge size and the large white area in the forewing distinguish this species from Comb Duck.

Male is much larger than female, and its facial skin extends behind the eye. **Juv.** and **imm.** are like ad. but browner. **Habitat.** Frequents water bordered by grassland and agricultural areas. Feeds ashore, often at night, on grasses and other vegetable matter. **Status.** Common resident. **Call.** A feeble, wheezy whistle given in flight. (Wildemakou)

2. EGYPTIAN GOOSE *Alopochen aegyptiaca* (102)   63-73 cm

This large, brown bird has a dark brown mask around the eye, and a brown patch on the breast that is distinctive in flight. Compared with South African Shelduck it has a longer neck and legs, and a thin, dark line running through the white forewing is visible in flight.

Juv. lacks the brown mask and breast patch, and the forewing is not pure white. **Habitat.** Almost any freshwater habitat but frequently feeds in fields. **Status.** Very common resident. **Call.** Male hisses, female utters a grunting honk; both give rapidly repeated honks at take-off. (Kolgans)

3. SOUTH AFRICAN SHELDUCK *Tadorna cana* (103)   64 cm

A large, russet-coloured duck with a black bill and legs.

Male has a diagnostic grey head. Female has a variable white-and-grey head, whereas White-faced Duck (p. 78) has a white-and-black head. In flight, both sexes show white forewings but lack the black dividing line of Egyptian Goose. **Juv.** is like male but duller, and the head is suffused with brown. **Habitat.** Freshwater lakes and dams in drier areas. Nests underground in mammal burrows. **Status.** Common resident and local nomad; endemic. **Call.** Various honks and hisses. (Kopereend)

4. COMB (KNOB-BILLED) DUCK *Sarkidiornis melanotos* (115)   56-76 cm

This large duck with its grey-speckled head and contrasting blue-black and white plumage is unmistakable. In flight, the wings are black and unmarked; female shows a little white on the lower back.

Male is larger than female and has a rounded protuberance on the bill that enlarges conspicuously during the breeding season. Female lacks the bill development of breeding male and is smaller. **Juv.** and **imm.** resemble female but are duller, and have dark speckling on the breast, belly and flanks. **Habitat.** Mainly on pans and dams in woodland and along larger rivers in the north. Nests in a large hole in a tree. **Status.** Mainly a summer visitor, more common to the north; widely distributed but nomadic. **Call.** Whistles, but usually silent. (Knobbeleend)

See also page 84

1

black
neck

northern race

2

dark eye
patch

juv.

ad.

brown
chest
patch

grey
flanks

3

grey
head

♂

chestnut
flanks

white face,
dark neck

♀

speckled head,
white neck

♂ br.

4

1. WHITE-FACED DUCK *Dendrocygna viduata* (99)　　　　43-48 cm
A distinctive, long-necked duck with a diagnostic white face. It differs from the larger South African Shelduck (p. 76) by lacking grey on the head. Like Fulvous Duck it stands very erect and is highly gregarious, but it can be distinguished from that species in flight by the lack of white on the uppertail coverts. At times the white face can be stained a muddy brown.
Juv. has a dirty brown face. **Habitat.** Almost any expanse of water but spends much time ashore. **Status.** Common resident. **Call.** A characteristic, three-noted whistle, the last two notes being closer together. (Nonnetjie-eend)

2. FULVOUS DUCK *Dendrocygna bicolor* (100)　　　　43-53 cm
Similar in shape to White-faced Duck but has a golden brown, not white, head. It shows a dark line down the centre of the nape and neck, and has conspicuous white flank stripes. In flight, it may be distinguished from White-faced Duck by its white uppertail coverts, which form a horseshoe and contrast with the dark upperparts. Juv. may be distinguished from juv. White-faced Duck by having white on the flanks and rump.
Habitat. Freshwater lakes and dams. **Status.** Locally common resident; less abundant than White-faced Duck. **Call.** A soft, disyllabic whistle. (Fluiteend)

3. WHITE-BACKED DUCK *Thalassornis leuconotus* (101)　　　　38-40 cm
A mottled brown, hump-backed, large-headed duck. When swimming, the most diagnostic feature of this species is the pale patch at the base of the bill. Only in flight is the white back visible.
Male, female and juv. are similar. **Habitat.** Fresh water, typically among floating vegetation. **Status.** Locally common resident. **Call.** A low-pitched whistle, rising on the second syllable. (Witrugeend)

4. AFRICAN PYGMY-GOOSE *Nettapus auritus* (114)　　　　30-33 cm
The orange body, white face and dark green upperparts are diagnostic. In flight the white secondaries are distinctive. Often sits motionless among floating vegetation.
Male has highly contrasting head markings and a vertical black ear-stripe. Female's head tends to be more speckled, and lacks the ear-stripe. Juv. resembles female. **Habitat.** Prefers freshwater areas with floating vegetation, especially *Nymphaea*. Nests in a hole in a tree. **Status.** Locally common resident. **Call.** A soft, repeated 'tsui-tsui'. (Dwerggans)

5. SOUTHERN POCHARD *Netta erythrophthalma* (113)　　　　48-51 cm
A dark brown duck. In flight, both sexes show a distinct white wing bar along the base of the flight feathers but lack a coloured speculum. Sits low in the water with its tail submerged.
Male is superficially similar to male Maccoa Duck but has uniformly blackish brown plumage with a glossy sheen, a pale blue bill with a dark nail and bright red eyes. Female is dark brown with a pale patch at the bill base and a pale crescent extending down from the eye. Juv. resembles female but lacks the white facial crescent. **Habitat.** Lakes, dams and vleis. **Status.** Common resident. **Call.** Male makes a whining sound; female quacks. (Bruineend)

6. MACCOA DUCK *Oxyura maccoa* (117)　　　　48-51 cm
Male has a chestnut body, a large, black head and a bright, cobalt-blue bill. In eclipse plumage male resembles female. It sits very low in the water, with its stiff tail often cocked at a 45° angle. In flight, the upperwing is a uniform dark brown.
Female is dark brown with a pale cheek stripe, under which is a dark line. This gives the impression of a pale stripe running from the bill beyond the eye; in comparison, female Southern Pochard has a pale vertical crescent behind the eye. Juv. resembles female. **Habitat.** A diving species of quieter waters with surface vegetation. **Status.** Localised resident, thinly distributed. **Call.** A peculiar, nasal trill. (Bloubekeend)

　　　　　　　　　　　　　　　　　　　　See also pages 84–85

white
face

ad.

barred
flanks

1

juv.

golden-
brown head

2

3

white spot at
bill base

white flank
plumes

red
eye

green
back

♂

tiny
bill

♀

4

uniformly dark
upperparts

♂

pale
bill

juv.

white crescent

♀

white at
bill base

all-dark
head

♂

blue
bill

pointed,
cocked tail

cheek
stripe

♀

5

6

1. YELLOW-BILLED DUCK *Anas undulata* (104) 51-58 cm
The rich yellow bill with a black saddle on the upper mandible is distinctive. From a distance the plumage appears dark, but less so than that of African Black Duck. In flight, it shows a blue-green speculum narrowly edged with white.
Juv. is duller than ad. **Habitat.** Virtually any area of open fresh water, as well as estuaries; often in flocks. **Status.** Common resident. **Call.** Male gives a rasping hiss; female quacks. (Geelbekeend)

2. AFRICAN BLACK DUCK *Anas sparsa* (105) 48-57 cm
A dark-billed, dark-plumaged duck with white speckles on the back, and bright orange legs and feet. In flight, might be confused with Yellow-billed Duck as it also has a blue-green speculum edged with white, but the underwing is whitish (not grey). When sitting in the water, it appears long bodied.
Sexes alike but female is smaller. **Juv.** is paler, with a whitish belly. **Habitat.** Prefers fast-flowing streams and rivers; less frequent on dams and at sewage works. **Status.** Widespread resident. **Call.** 'Quack', especially in flight. Male gives a high-pitched, weak whistle. (Swarteend)

3. MALLARD *Anas platyrhynchos* (923) 50-65 cm
Male is unmistakable with a bottle-green, glossy head, white ring around the neck and a chestnut breast. When in eclipse plumage, male resembles female. Domesticated form of Mallard is the Khaki Campbell, which looks very similar but is much larger and has a khaki (not grey) back.
Female is very similar to Yellow-billed Duck but has a grey, not yellow bill. **Juv.** resembles female. **Habitat.** Any area of open water. **Status.** Resident; feral populations in Gauteng and in the Western Cape, where there is some hybridisation with Yellow-billed Duck. **Call.** Male and female call similar to that of Yellow-billed Duck. (Groenkopeend)

4. CAPE SHOVELER *Anas smithii* (112) 53 cm
Both sexes can be distinguished from all ducks except Northern Shoveler by the long, black, spatulate bill. The plumage is finely speckled grey-brown and the legs are a rich orange in colour.
Male has a paler head and yellower eyes than female. Female is darker and greyer than Northern Shoveler, especially around the head and neck, and lacks white edges to the tail. **Juv.** resembles female. **Habitat.** Fresh water, preferably with surface vegetation. **Status.** Common resident; endemic. **Call.** 'Quack', and a continuous rasping. (Kaapse Slopeend)

5. NORTHERN (EUROPEAN) SHOVELER *Anas clypeata* (111) 44-52 cm
Breeding plumage of male is unmistakable: green head, white breast and chestnut belly. The very rapid, direct flight shows the powder-blue forewing similar to that of Cape Shoveler and (smaller) Garganey (p. 82), but differs in having a black back rimmed with white. In both sexes, European Shoveler has a heavier, longer and more spatulate bill than Cape Shoveler.
Male in eclipse plumage resembles female. Female differs from Cape Shoveler in being speckled brown and much paler overall, especially around the head and neck, and in having white edges to tail. **Juv.** resembles female. **Habitat.** Inland water bodies. **Status.** Most records are probably of escaped aviary birds, but genuine vagrants may occasionally occur in Zimbabwe, Namibia, Mozambique and the northeastern parts of South Africa. **Call.** Male gives a nasal 'crook, crook'; female quacks. (Europese Slopeend)

See also pages 84–85

yellow bill, black saddle

1

black head

white-spotted uppers

black below

2

green head, yellow bill

♂

grey bill

dark blue speculum

♀

orange legs

3

♀

dark tail edges

yellow eye

♂

spatulate bill

4

green head

♂

large white collar

5

♀

white tail edges

1. NORTHERN PINTAIL *Anas acuta* (109)   51-65 cm

Breeding male is striking, with a dark, chocolate-brown head, a white stripe running down the side of the neck to the white breast and a dark, pointed tail. In eclipse plumage, male resembles female.

Female is similar to Yellow-billed Duck (p. 80) but has a dark grey bill, paler plumage, a brown speculum with a white trailing edge, a long, slender neck and body and a pointed tail (shorter than the male's). **Juv.** resembles female. **Habitat.** Inland water bodies. **Status.** Most sightings are probably of escaped aviary birds, but vagrants occasionally occur in the northern parts of the subregion. **Call.** Male's call is a soft, nasal honk; female quacks. (Pylsterteend)

2. GARGANEY *Anas querquedula* (110)   37-41 cm

Male has an obvious white eyebrow stripe on a dark brown head. The brown breast is sharply demarcated by the white belly and pale grey flanks; the elongated black-and-white scapulars are conspicuous.

Male in eclipse plumage resembles female but has a more pronounced eyebrow stripe. Female is mid-brown with obviously pale feather margins, and has a dark stripe through the eye, bordered above and below by a pale stripe; the head is more boldly marked than that of female Maccoa Duck (p. 78). In flight, both sexes show the pale blue forewings and green speculum also found in Cape and Northern Shovelers (p. 80), but lack their heavy bills. **Juv.** resembles female. **Habitat.** Inland water bodies. **Status.** Rare summer vagrant. **Call.** A nasal 'quack' and harsh rattles. (Somereend)

3. CAPE TEAL *Anas capensis* (106)   44-48 cm

The palest duck of the region. At close range, the combination of a speckled head and pink bill is diagnostic. Can be distinguished from Red-billed Teal by the uniformly coloured head and lack of a dark cap. In flight it shows a dark greenish speculum surrounded by white. Usually occurs in mixed flocks.

Juv. is paler grey than ad. **Habitat.** Any open area of fresh or saline water. **Status.** Common resident. Most abundant in the dry west. **Call.** A thin whistle, usually given in flight. (Teeleend)

4. RED-BILLED TEAL *Anas erythrorhyncha* (108)   43-48 cm

The combination of a dark cap, pale buffy cheeks and red bill is diagnostic. Larger than Hottentot Teal, which has a blue (not red) bill. The dark cap distinguishes it from Cape Teal. In flight, the secondaries are pale and the lack of a dark green speculum precludes confusion with Hottentot Teal.

Female has less black on bill than male. **Juv.** is duller than ad. **Habitat.** Occurs in mixed flocks on fresh water. **Status.** Very common resident. **Call.** Male gives a soft, nasal whistle; female quacks. (Rooibekeend)

5. HOTTENTOT TEAL *Anas hottentota* (107)   30-35 cm

A diminutive species resembling Red-billed Teal, from which it differs by its blue (not red) bill and the dark smudge on its creamy cheeks.

In flight, **male** has a green speculum with white secondaries, and a black and white underwing. Female lacks the green speculum. **Juv.** is duller than ad. **Habitat.** Mainly inland on small water bodies, often close to floating vegetation. **Status.** Locally common resident but rare in the southwest of its range. **Call.** Soft quacks. (Gevlekte Eend)

See also pages 84–85

long tail

white neck stripe

1

plain head

pointed tail

brown face

♂

♀

long white supercilium

♂

2

brown breast

short tail

pale parallel head stripes

eclipse plumage

♂

♀

pale speckled head

3

red eye

pink bill

buffy cheeks

4

dark cap

red bill

dark cap & cheek patch

blue bill

5

EGYPTIAN GOOSE

SOUTH AFRICAN
SHELDUCK

brown
head

white
face

♀

♂ non-**br.**

♀

COMB DUCK

white leading
edge

♂ grey
head

white back
& rump

SPUR-WINGED
GOOSE

WHITE-FACED
DUCK

dark upper
tail coverts

FULVOUS DUCK

no coloured
speculum

white
crescent

RED-BILLED
TEAL

HOTTENTOT TEAL

♂

CAPE TEAL

♂

♀

♀

blue
speculum

white
back

trailing
feet

MALLARD

WHITE-BACKED
DUCK

GARGANEY

NORTHERN SHOVELER

pale grey
forewing

♂

♀

juv.

long
speculum

♂

♀

white-edged
tail

♂

long, pointed
tail

NORTHERN PINTAIL

YELLOW-BILLED
DUCK

AFRICAN
BLACK DUCK

♂

powder-blue
forewing

CAPE SHOVELER

♀

AFRICAN
PYGMY-
GOOSE

♂

♀

white
speculum

♂

♀

♂
plain
back

♀

long white
wing bar

♂

SOUTHERN POCHARD

no wing bar
or speculum

MACCOA DUCK

1. LAPPET-FACED VULTURE *Torgos tracheliotus* (124) 78-115 cm

At close range, the bare red skin on the face and throat is diagnostic. In flight, the white thighs and the white bar running along the forepart of the underwing, from the body to the carpal joint, contrast with the otherwise black underside.

Juv. and imm. are dark brown all over and most closely resemble Hooded Vulture (p. 88) but are almost twice the size. Juv. has conspicuous white streaks on the mantle. **Habitat.** Thornveld; mainly in drier regions. Nests on tree-tops, solitarily or in small, scattered colonies. **Status.** Resident; rare outside major game reserves. Threatened. **Call.** High-pitched whistles during display. (Swartaasvoël)

2. WHITE-HEADED VULTURE *Trigonoceps occipitalis* (125) 78-84 cm

The only dark vulture in the region with a dark upper breast and white lower breast and belly. Inner secondaries of female are white, forming a white, rectangular patch on the inner wing. Male has dark secondaries, separated from the underwing coverts by a thin white line. The triangular-looking head and the neck are white, the naked face is pink, and the bill is orange with a blue base.

Juv. is dark brown and distinguishable in flight from juv. Lappet-faced Vulture and juv. Hooded Vulture (p. 88) by having a narrow white line between the flight feathers and the wing coverts. **Habitat.** Thornveld and savanna. Nests solitarily on tree-tops; solitary. **Status.** Uncommon resident; rare outside major game reserves. **Call.** High-pitched chittering when feeding. (Witkopaasvoël)

3. RÜPPELL'S VULTURE *Gyps rueppellii* 95-107 cm

Intermediate in size between Cape and White-backed vultures, this species is readily identified by its 'scaly' feather pattern, the result of the dark feathers on body and wing coverts being broadly edged with buff. The yellow bill is also diagnostic. In flight from below, confusion is likely only with juv. White-backed Vulture, but the underbody of the latter is streaked, not speckled.

Juv. resembles juv. Cape Vulture, but is darker with broadly streaked body feathers. Juvs of these two species probably very difficult to separate in the field. The bill is black and the neck reddish pink. **Habitat.** Open Acacia savannas and mountains. **Status.** Vagrant; associates with Cape Vultures both at cliff colonies and at carcasses. **Call.** Noisy hissing and cackling when feeding at carcasses. (Rüppelse Aasvoël)

4. CAPE VULTURE *Gyps coprotheres* (122) 100-115 cm

Difficult to distinguish from White-backed Vulture. When seen together, Cape Vulture is much larger and (in ad.) much paler in appearance and has a honey-coloured, not dark, eye. Under ideal viewing conditions, the two bare patches of blue skin at the base of the neck are diagnostic.

Juv. very like juv. White-backed Vulture but is much larger and (in flight) best distinguished by absence of white line along underwing coverts. **Habitat.** Grassland, savanna and semi-desert. Nests colonially on cliff ledges. **Status.** Endemic. Threatened. The most common vulture in the Drakensberg and the Eastern Cape. **Call.** Cackling and hissing noises given when feeding and at the nest. (Kransaasvoël)

5. (AFRICAN) WHITE-BACKED VULTURE *Gyps africanus* (123) 95 cm

If seen from above, ad. has a white lower back that contrasts with the dark upperwings. Smaller than Cape Vulture, in flight from below shows a strong contrast between dark flight feathers and whitish underwing coverts (contrast less marked in Cape Vulture).

Juv.'s smaller size and dark underwing coverts lined with white differentiate it from juv. Cape Vulture. Distinguished from Rüppell's Vulture in flight from below by streaked, not speckled, underbody. **Habitat.** Savanna. Nests on tree-tops in small colonies. **Status.** Resident. The commonest vulture in bushveld game reserves. **Call.** Harsh cackles and hisses when feeding and at the nest. (Witrugaasvoël)

See also pages 90–91

juv.

bare red skin

ad.

1

angular white head

♀

♂

2

♂

yellow bill

scaly appearance

3

pale eye

4

ad.

juv.

line of spots

dark eye

ad.

5

white back

ad.

ad.

juv.

1. LAMMERGEIER (BEARDED VULTURE) *Gypaetus barbatus* (119) 110 cm
Shape in flight is unlike that of any other vulture in the region: the long, narrow, pointed wings and long, wedge-shaped tail impart a falcon-like silhouette. Ad. is mainly dark above with rufous underbody, and has a black mask across the face, terminating in a black 'beard'. (The 'beard' is only visible at close quarters.)
Juv. is dark brown all over, with the underparts lightening with age. **Habitat.** Remote high mountains; usually above 2 000 m. Confined to the Drakensberg. Nests on cliff ledges; solitary. **Status.** Scarce resident. **Call.** Silent except for high-pitched whistling during display. (Baardaasvoël)

2. PALM-NUT VULTURE *Gypohierax angolensis* (147) 60 cm
This small, black-and-white vulture is likely to be confused only with Egyptian Vulture, from which it differs by the extensive white in the primaries (all black in Egyptian Vulture), and by its much shorter tail, which is black, tipped with white, and slightly rounded (not white and wedge-shaped).
Juv. resembles Hooded Vulture but is smaller and has a feathered (not bare) throat and neck. **Habitat.** Coastal forests in the vicinity of raffia palms; occasional along large rivers with riparian forest in the north. **Status.** Rare and localised, restricted as a resident to northern KwaZulu-Natal and farther north. Vagrant elsewhere. **Call.** In flight, sometimes utters a 'kok-kok-kok'. (Witaasvoël)

3. EGYPTIAN VULTURE *Neophron percnopterus* (120) 58-71 cm
Ad. could be confused with similar black-and-white Palm-nut Vulture, but has all-black primaries and an all-white, wedge-shaped tail.
Juv. in flight looks like diminutive juv. Lammergeier, but has a bare face and a long, thin bill. Differs from juv. Palm-nut and Hooded Vultures by its long, wedge-shaped tail. **Habitat.** Grassland, savanna, semi-desert; usually found at kills in game reserves. **Status.** Formerly a localised breeding resident, now mostly a rare vagrant. One or two pairs may still breed in northern Namibia and in mountainous regions of the Eastern Cape. **Call.** Soft grunts and hisses when excited. (Egiptiese Aasvoël)

4. HOODED VULTURE *Necrosyrtes monachus* (121) 65-75 cm
This small, brown vulture could be confused with juv. Palm-nut and Egyptian Vultures. It may be distinguished from Palm-nut Vulture by its larger size, and by the down (not feathers) on the head and neck. Unlike this species, juv. Egyptian Vulture has a long, wedge-shaped tail and elongated nape feathers. Hooded Vulture resembles juv. and imm. Lappet-faced Vulture, but is much smaller.
Juv. is darker, with a blackish brown head. **Habitat.** Savanna; found mostly in game reserves in the north. **Status.** Uncommon resident. **Call.** Normally silent; emits soft whistling calls at the nest. (Monnikaasvoël)

See also pages 90–91

1

ad.

long tail

long tail

imm.

2

short, heavy bill

ad.

black tail, tipped white

short, heavy bill

juv.

3

ad.

long thin bill

all-white tail

long nape feathers

long thin bill

juv.

4

ad.

rounded tail

juv.

HOODED VULTURE

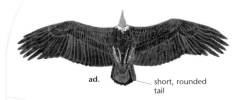

ad. — short, rounded tail

juv.

black primaries

ad.

long, wedge-shaped tail

ad.

imm.

juv.

EGYPTIAN VULTURE

ad.

mostly white primaries — short, square tail

PALM-NUT VULTURE

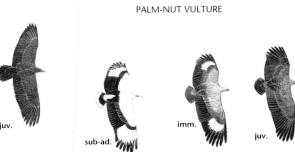

sub-ad.

imm.

juv.

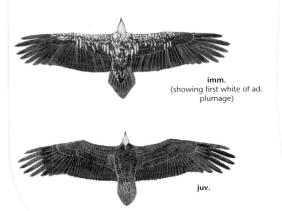

imm.
(showing first white of ad. plumage)

juv.

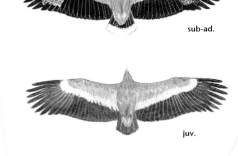

sub-ad.

juv.

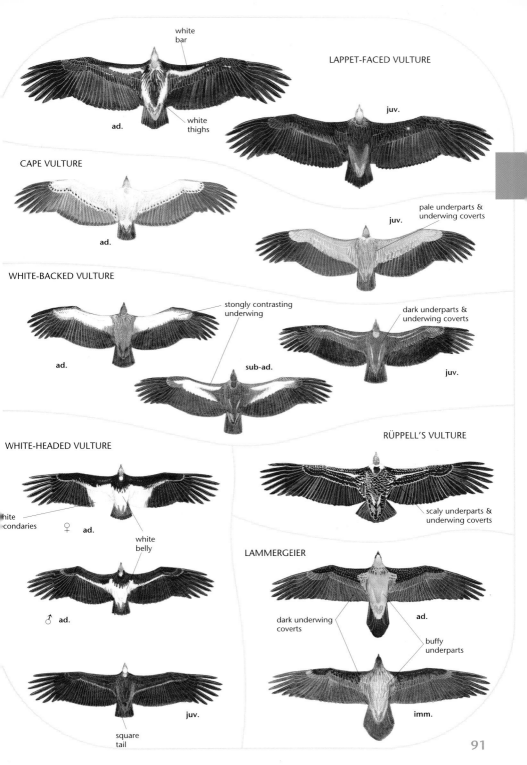

LAPPET-FACED VULTURE

white bar

white thighs

ad.

juv.

CAPE VULTURE

ad.

pale underparts & underwing coverts

juv.

WHITE-BACKED VULTURE

stongly contrasting underwing

dark underparts & underwing coverts

ad.

sub-ad.

juv.

WHITE-HEADED VULTURE

RÜPPELL'S VULTURE

white secondaries

♀ ad.

white belly

scaly underparts & underwing coverts

LAMMERGEIER

♂ ad.

dark underwing coverts

ad.

buffy underparts

juv.

square tail

imm.

1. AFRICAN FISH-EAGLE *Haliaeetus vocifer* (148) 63-73 cm

In addition to having a diagnostic call, ad. African Fish-Eagle is unmistakable with its white head and breast, chestnut belly and forewings, black-and-chestnut under-wings and white tail. Overall impression in flight is of a large, broad-winged eagle with a short tail.

Sexes alike but female is larger. **Juv.** and imm. are identifiable by their generally dark brown coloration with white streaks on the head and throat, white patches in the flight feathers, and the diagnostic white tail with a dark terminal band. **Habitat.** Aquatic: large rivers, lakes and dams; coastal in some regions, where it frequents estuaries and lagoons. Found throughout except in the extreme dry west. **Status.** Locally common resident. **Call.** A characteristic, ringing 'kyow-kow-kow', male's higher pitched; often in duet. (Visarend)

2. OSPREY *Pandion haliaetus* (170) 51-68 cm

Flight outline resembles that of a huge gull with pale underwings, black patches at the carpal joints and a diagnostic black mask on a white head. Might be confused with imm. African Fish-Eagle found in similar habitat but the latter is a larger bird with broad wings and a very short tail.

Juv. and imm. resemble ad. **Habitat.** Inland freshwater bodies, and coastal lagoons, occa-sionally fishing over open sea. **Status.** Regular but scarce visitor, chiefly in summer; rare in the west of its range. **Call.** Usually silent. (Visvalk)

3. BATELEUR *Terathopius ecaudatus* (146) 55-70 cm

The most easily identified eagle of the region: the black, white and chestnut plumage, combined with the diagnostic wing shape and very short tail, render this bird unmistakable. The flight action is also diagnostic, with the long wings held slightly angled upwards, rarely flapping; it flies direct, canting from side to side. The black trailing edge to the wing is broad in the male and narrow in the female.

Juv. and imm. are uniform brown; may be distinguished from all other brown eagles by the flight action and very short tail. Sex of juvs and imms can be determined by the extent of brown on the trailing edge of the underwing, as in ad. **Habitat.** Savanna. **Status.** Resident; in the north and east, most often encountered in large game reserves. Often seen on the ground at waterholes, sometimes in groups. **Call.** A loud bark, 'kow-wah'. (Berghaan)

ad.

dark
crown

dark-tipped,
white tail

imm.

imm.

1

♀

♂

dark carpal
patch

2

black mask below
white crown

juv.

very
short tail

♀

3

♂

♂

♀

bulging
secondaries

♀ juv.

toes extend
beyond tail

93

1. BROWN SNAKE-EAGLE *Circaetus cinereus* (142)   66-71 cm

Ad. distinguished from all other dark brown eagles by its unfeathered, creamy white legs. At rest it appears to have an unusually large head with big yellow eyes. In flight the dark brown underwing coverts contrast with almost white primaries and secondaries.

Juv. resembles ad. and differs from juv. Black-chested Snake-Eagle by its darker brown coloration, but differentiation can be difficult. **Habitat.** Savanna, avoiding open grassland and forests. **Status.** Locally common to rare resident; nomadic within subregion. **Call.** Rarely calls. A croaking 'hok-hok-hok-hok' is uttered in flight. (Bruinslangarend)

2. BLACK-CHESTED (BLACK-BREASTED) SNAKE-EAGLE

Circaetus pectoralis (143)   63-68 cm

In flight, ad. most closely resembles ad. Martial Eagle (p. 100) but differs in having white underwings, with the inner primaries and secondaries barred with black. At rest, the exceptionally large, bright yellow eyes contrast with the dark head. It lacks the black spots of Martial Eagle on the lower breast and belly.

Sexes alike but female is larger. **Juv.** differs from ad. and juv. Brown Snake-Eagle by being warm rufous when recently fledged, becoming pale brown below, with a pale underwing and undertail, both lightly barred. **Habitat.** Frequents a wide range of habitats, from desert to savanna. **Status.** Locally common to scarce resident; nomadic within the subregion. **Call.** Rarely calls; a melodious whistle, 'kwo-kwo-kwo-kweeu'. (Swartborsslangarend)

3. SOUTHERN BANDED SNAKE-EAGLE *Circaetus fasciolatus* (144)   55-60 cm

Ad. resembles ad. African Cuckoo Hawk (p. 116) but is much larger, with a large, rounded head and relatively short tail. In flight it may be distinguished from Western Banded Snake-Eagle by its darker underwings and the three (not two) black bars on the tail: the ranges of these two species are not known to overlap.

Juv. is dark brown above, and pale below, with dark streaks on the face, throat and upper breast. **Habitat.** Coastal evergreen forest, riverine forest and open woodland in marshy areas. **Status.** Uncommon resident. **Call.** A harsh 'crok-crok-crok' and high-pitched 'ko-ko-ko-ko-keear'. (Dubbelbandslangarend)

4. WESTERN BANDED SNAKE-EAGLE *Circaetus cinerascens* (145)   55-60 cm

Differs from the similar Southern Banded Snake-Eagle by being stockier and less heavily barred below, and by having a shorter, dark tail with a diagnostic broad, white bar across the middle, visible both in flight and at rest.

Juv. is paler below than ad. and is not easily distinguishable from juv. Southern Banded Snake-Eagle; the ranges of the two species do not overlap. **Habitat.** Woodland fringing large tropical rivers. **Status.** Uncommon resident. **Call.** A high-pitched 'kok-kok-kok-kok-kok'. (Enkelbandslangarend)

large
head

ad.

white
legs

ad.

ad.

unmarked, pale
flight feathers

1

juv.

dark brown
underparts

yellow
eye

white
coverts

dark
head

ad.

ad.

2

barred flight
feathers

ad.

juv.

juv.

large
head

ad.

3

juv.

juv.

rufous
underparts

heavily barred
underwings

ad.

three dark
tail bars

ad.

three
dark bars

large
head

ad.

ad.

broad white
band

4

single broad
white bar

ad.

1. STEPPE EAGLE *Aquila nipalensis* (133)   65-80 cm

Plumage is variable but ad. is usually a uniform dark brown, and the tail of ad. is always strongly barred.

Juv. and imm, which are much more common in the subregion, are lighter brown, with two prominent, light bars along the wing, a white, U-shaped crescent formed by the uppertail coverts and pale panels in the outer wing. The yellow gape is long and extends behind the eye in the race *A.n. nipalensis*, whereas the gape of the race *A.n. orientalis* (the commonest race in the subregion) extends behind the middle of the eye, but not to the back of the eye. The gape of Tawny Eagle extends only to the middle of the eye. Although similar in plumage, *A.n. nipalensis* is larger than *A.n. orientalis* and appears longer-winged in flight. (Note: some authorities do not recognise these subspecies and consider them to be the extremes of a west-east cline of increasing size.) **Habitat.** Thornveld and semi-desert regions. **Status.** An erratic but sometimes common summer visitor to the north. Often gregarious. **Call.** Silent in the region. (Steppe-arend)

2. LESSER SPOTTED EAGLE *Aquila pomarina* (134)   61-66 cm

A small, dark eagle of buzzard-like proportions. Differs from Wahlberg's Eagle (p. 106) in having a short, rounded tail. At rest, the tightly feathered legs appear unusually thin (cf. Greater Spotted Eagle). Yellow eye.

Juv. and imm. from above are very similar to juv. and imm. Steppe Eagle, showing white bases to primaries, white edging to coverts and secondaries, a white, U-shaped crescent formed by the uppertail coverts; sometimes have a white patch on the back. **Habitat.** Often with Steppe Eagles in savanna. **Status.** Uncommon summer visitor. **Call.** Silent in the region. (Gevlekte Arend)

3. TAWNY EAGLE *Aquila rapax* (132)   66-73 cm

Easily confused with migrant Steppe Eagle, which is similar in size and shape. At close range, the gape length is diagnostic; in Tawny Eagle it extends only to below the middle of the eye. Confusion is possible in the gape length of Steppe Eagle race *A.n. orientalis*. The unbarred to faintly barred tail is diagnostic. The plumage is variable: most birds are uniformly tawny, but they range from streaked dark brown to pale buff in colour.

Ad. has a pale yellow eye. **Female** is usually darker than male. **Juv.** is rufous brown, fading to buff as sub-ad. **Habitat.** Thornveld and semi-desert areas. **Status.** Resident and local migrant; common in the major game reserves but thinly distributed elsewhere. **Call.** Seldom calls; a sharp bark, 'kyow'. (Roofarend)

4. GREATER SPOTTED EAGLE *Aquila clanga*   65-72 cm

A broad-winged, relatively long-legged eagle, with tightly feathered tarsi. Darker than other brown eagles. In flight, upperwings, back and tail appear uniformly blackish brown with a narrow white crescent on uppertail coverts; underwing has dark lining contrasting with paler flight feathers, the opposite of Lesser Spotted, Steppe, and Tawny Eagles. Gape extends to below middle, not rear, of eye (cf. Lesser Spotted and Steppe Eagles). Ad. has dark brown eye (yellow in ad. Lesser Spotted Eagle).

Juv. is heavily spotted creamy buff above; underparts streaked buff. **Habitat.** Savanna and open woodland. **Status.** Vagrant from the Palearctic, with only one record; possibly under-recorded; (one satellite-tracked bird in Zambia was never seen!). **Call.** Silent in the region. (Groot Gevlekte Arend)

See also page 98-99

gape extends
beyond eye

gape reaches
below eye

gape reaches
below eye

A.n. nipalensis
ad.

A.n. orientalis
ad.

ad.

1

thin
leggings

barred
tail

A.n. nipalensis
juv.

A.n. orientalis
juv.

2

juv.

dark form

A.n. nipalensis

no crest

medium
pale form

A.n. orientalis

3

gape to
below
mid-eye

4

juv.

spotted
above

blackish-brown
upperparts

rufous form **juv.**

streaked form

gape to
middle of
dark eye

pale form **juv.**

ad.

STEPPE EAGLE

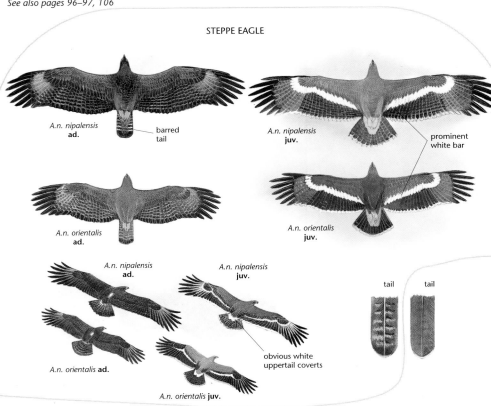

A.n. nipalensis **ad.** — barred tail

A.n. nipalensis **juv.** — prominent white bar

A.n. orientalis **ad.**

A.n. orientalis **juv.**

A.n. nipalensis **ad.**

A.n. nipalensis **juv.**

A.n. orientalis **ad.**

obvious white uppertail coverts

A.n. orientalis **juv.**

tail   tail

dark form

medium pale form

tail unbarred, or very faintly barred — very pale form

juv.

ad.

TAWNY EAGLE   ad.

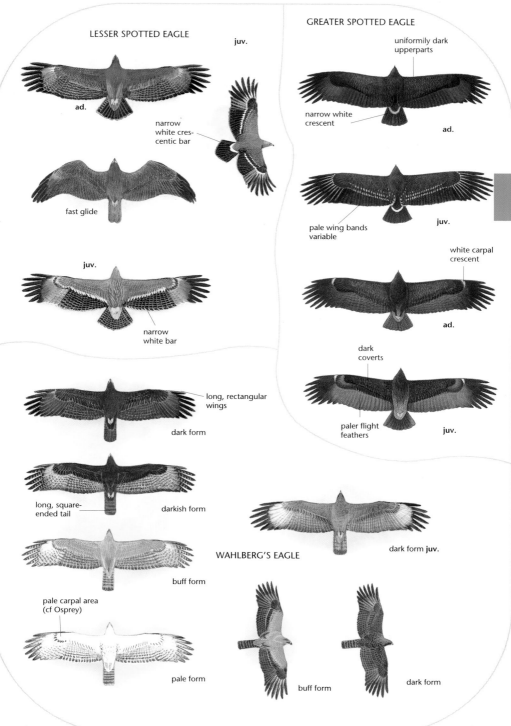

LESSER SPOTTED EAGLE

juv.

ad.

narrow white crescentic bar

fast glide

juv.

narrow white bar

long, rectangular wings

dark form

long, square-ended tail

darkish form

buff form

pale carpal area (cf Osprey)

pale form

GREATER SPOTTED EAGLE

uniformily dark upperparts

narrow white crescent

ad.

pale wing bands variable

juv.

white carpal crescent

ad.

dark coverts

paler flight feathers

juv.

dark form juv.

WAHLBERG'S EAGLE

buff form

dark form

1. VERREAUX'S EAGLE *Aquila verreauxii* (131)   82-96 cm

Ad. unmistakable. In flight the wings are narrow at the base, broadening in the middle, and the white back and wing panels contrasting with the black plumage are characteristic.

Sexes similar, but female is larger with more white on the back. **Juv.** is best recognised by its characteristic flight shape, as well as by the mottled light and dark brown plumage. Has a diagnostic rufous crown and nape contrasting with the darker face and throat. **Habitat.** Mountainous regions where there are cliffs and where dassies (rock hyraxes), its major prey, are common. **Status.** Locally common to scarce resident. **Call.** Rarely calls; a melodious 'keee-uup'. (Witkruisarend)

2. MARTIAL EAGLE *Polemaetus bellicosus* (140)   78-83 cm

The dark head, throat and upper breast, combined with the white, lightly spotted breast and belly and very dark underwings are diagnostic in this eagle. From below, ad. Black-chested Snake-Eagle (p. 94) resembles this species, but it has a white underwing barred with black on the inner primaries and secondaries.

Sexes alike but female is larger. **Juv.** and imm. differ from juv. and imm. African Crowned Eagle in being longer-winged and whiter, and in having unspotted flanks and the underwings finely (not broadly) barred. **Habitat.** Primarily savannas, but frequents a wide range of habitats, from desert to forest edge. **Status.** Uncommon resident; scarce outside large reserves. **Call.** In display, a rapid 'klooee-klooee-klooee'. (Breëkoparend)

3. AFRICAN CROWNED EAGLE *Stephanoaetus coronatus* (141)   82-92 cm

The combination of the large size and hawk-like appearance (especially in flight) along with the dark coloration, characterise this species. Ad. is dark grey above and rufous below, with the breast and belly heavily mottled with black. In flight, has well-rounded wings and a long, barred tail. The underwing coverts are rufous, with the primaries and secondaries white, heavily barred with black.

Female is larger and underwing barring less extensive than on male. **Juv.** and imm. are similar to juv. and imm. Martial Eagle, but they differ in shape, are creamy white in front with pale buff underwing coverts, and have dark speckling on the flanks and legs and a heavily barred tail and underwing. **Habitat.** Evergreen and riverine gallery forest. **Status.** Locally common resident. **Call.** A very vocal species: utters a ringing 'kewee-kewee-kewee' call in flight. Male's call is higher pitched than female's. (Kroonarend)

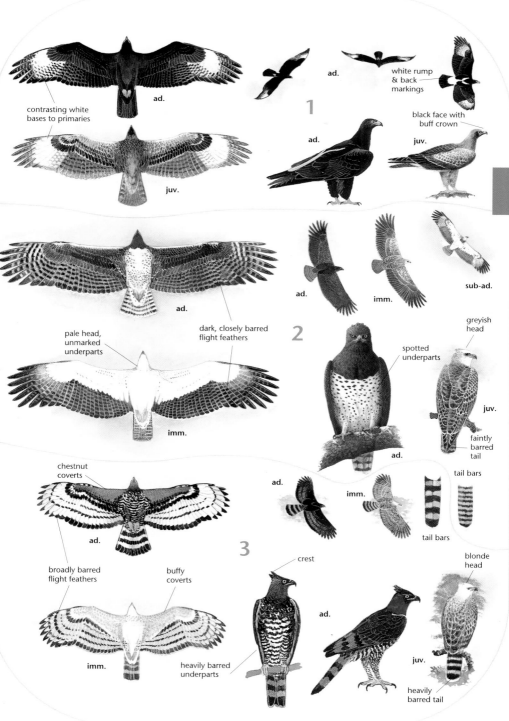

contrasting white bases to primaries

ad.

juv.

ad.

white rump & back markings

1

black face with buff crown

ad.

juv.

ad.

imm.

sub-ad.

2

pale head, unmarked underparts

dark, closely barred flight feathers

ad.

greyish head

spotted underparts

juv.

imm.

faintly barred tail

ad.

chestnut coverts

ad.

ad.

imm.

tail bars

3

broadly barred flight feathers

buffy coverts

tail bars

crest

imm.

blonde head

heavily barred underparts

ad.

juv.

heavily barred tail

1. LONG-CRESTED EAGLE *Lophaetus occipitalis* (139)   52-58 cm

The combination of the dull black plumage and the long, wispy crest renders this eagle unmistakable. In flight, shows conspicuous white bases to the primaries, and a black-and-white barred tail. The flight action is fast and direct, on stiffly held wings, with shallow wing beats.

Male has white leggings and a longer crest than female, which has brown or brown-and-white mottled leggings. **Juv.** is very like ad. but has a short crest and grey (not yellow) eyes. **Habitat.** Well-wooded country (including plantations) and forest edges, especially where it is marshy. **Status.** Common resident. **Call.** High-pitched, screaming 'kee-ah', given during display flight or when perched. (Langkuifarend)

2. AFRICAN HAWK-EAGLE *Aquila fasciatus* (137)   60-65 cm

Ad. likely to be confused only with smaller Ayres's Hawk-Eagle but is less boldly marked below and has white, unspotted thighs; in flight, the underwing is mainly white (it is dark and heavily barred in Ayres's Hawk-Eagle), and the upperwing is dark brown, with distinctive white panels at the base of the primaries (Ayres's Hawk-Eagle has a uniformly dark upperwing).

Female is larger and more heavily streaked in front than male. **Juv.** has the underwing coverts and underbody pale rufous, becoming more black-streaked with age; above, it is browner than ad. and it lacks the conspicuous terminal tail bar. It is easily confused with juv. Black Sparrowhawk (p. 120) but has feathered (not bare) legs. **Habitat.** Woodland and savanna. **Status.** Locally common resident. **Call.** Seldom calls; a whistled, musical 'klee-klee-klee'. (Afrikaanse Jagarend)

3. AYRES'S HAWK-EAGLE *Aquila ayresii* (138)   46-56 cm

The bold, black spotting on the white underparts, extending onto the belly and legs, helps differentiate this species from the larger African Hawk-Eagle. The underwing is heavily barred and the underwing coverts are heavily blotched. The upperwing is uniformly dark brown, in contrast to African Hawk-Eagle, which shows pale panels in the outer wing. The head is usually dark brown, but the colour is variable, grading all the way to white.

Sexes alike but female is larger than male. **Juv.** has a more heavily barred underwing than juv. African Hawk-Eagle. **Habitat.** Well-wooded country. **Status.** Uncommon to rare resident in north; uncommon to rare summer visitor in south. **Call.** Normally silent; when displaying, utters a shrill 'pueep-pip-pip-pueep'. (Kleinjagarend)

4. BOOTED EAGLE *Aquila pennatus* (136)   48-51 cm

This small, buzzard-sized eagle has pale and dark colour forms: in both of these it differs from Wahlberg's Eagle (p. 106) by its shorter, broader tail and broader wings. The underparts and underwing coverts are whitish in the pale colour form; the dark form is uniformly dark brown below, with a paler brown tail. From above, a small white patch is visible at the base of the forewing, giving the impression of a pair of white 'braces'. The dark brown on the head and face of the pale form extends well below the eyes and contrasts with the small, white throat.

Juv. resembles ad. **Habitat.** Fynbos, Karoo, semi-desert, savanna; usually in mountainous country. **Status.** Uncommon resident and summer visitor; a small number breed in the south and west. **Call.** High-pitched 'kee-keeee' or 'pee-pee-pee-pee'. (Dwergarend)

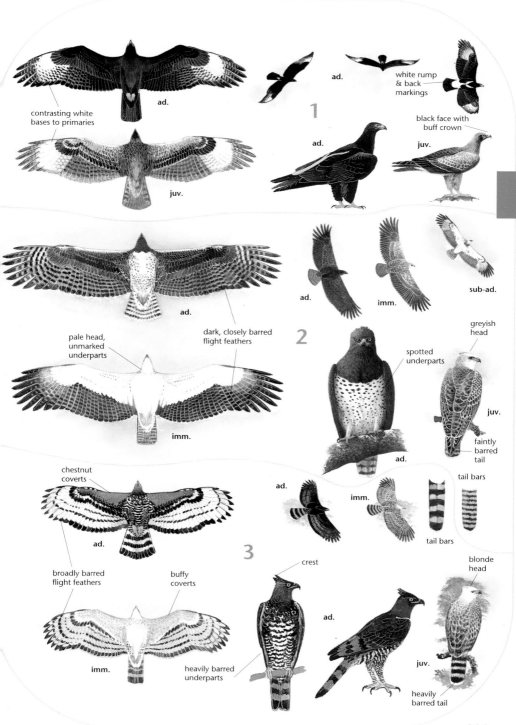

1

contrasting white bases to primaries

ad.

juv.

ad.

white rump & back markings

ad.

juv.

black face with buff crown

2

ad.

pale head, unmarked underparts

dark, closely barred flight feathers

imm.

ad.

imm.

sub-ad.

greyish head

spotted underparts

juv.

faintly barred tail

ad.

3

chestnut coverts

ad.

broadly barred flight feathers

buffy coverts

imm.

heavily barred underparts

crest

ad.

ad.

imm.

tail bars

tail bars

blonde head

juv.

heavily barred tail

101

1. LONG-CRESTED EAGLE *Lophaetus occipitalis* (139) 52-58 cm
The combination of the dull black plumage and the long, wispy crest renders this eagle unmistakable. In flight, shows conspicuous white bases to the primaries, and a black-and-white barred tail. The flight action is fast and direct, on stiffly held wings, with shallow wing beats.
Male has white leggings and a longer crest than female, which has brown or brown-and-white mottled leggings. **Juv.** is very like ad. but has a short crest and grey (not yellow) eyes. **Habitat.** Well-wooded country (including plantations) and forest edges, especially where it is marshy. **Status.** Common resident. **Call.** High-pitched, screaming 'kee-ah', given during display flight or when perched. (Langkuifarend)

2. AFRICAN HAWK-EAGLE *Aquila fasciatus* (137) 60-65 cm
Ad. likely to be confused only with smaller Ayres's Hawk-Eagle but is less boldly marked below and has white, unspotted thighs; in flight, the underwing is mainly white (it is dark and heavily barred in Ayres's Hawk-Eagle), and the upperwing is dark brown, with distinctive white panels at the base of the primaries (Ayres's Hawk-Eagle has a uniformly dark upperwing).
Female is larger and more heavily streaked in front than male. **Juv.** has the underwing coverts and underbody pale rufous, becoming more black-streaked with age; above, it is browner than ad. and it lacks the conspicuous terminal tail bar. It is easily confused with juv. Black Sparrowhawk (p. 120) but has feathered (not bare) legs. **Habitat.** Woodland and savanna. **Status.** Locally common resident. **Call.** Seldom calls; a whistled, musical 'klee-klee-klee'. (Afrikaanse Jagarend)

3. AYRES'S HAWK-EAGLE *Aquila ayresii* (138) 46-56 cm
The bold, black spotting on the white underparts, extending onto the belly and legs, helps differentiate this species from the larger African Hawk-Eagle. The underwing is heavily barred and the underwing coverts are heavily blotched. The upperwing is uniformly dark brown, in contrast to African Hawk-Eagle, which shows pale panels in the outer wing. The head is usually dark brown, but the colour is variable, grading all the way to white.
Sexes alike but female is larger than male. **Juv.** has a more heavily barred underwing than juv. African Hawk-Eagle. **Habitat.** Well-wooded country. **Status.** Uncommon to rare resident in north; uncommon to rare summer visitor in south. **Call.** Normally silent; when displaying, utters a shrill 'pueep-pip-pip-pueep'. (Kleinjagarend)

4. BOOTED EAGLE *Aquila pennatus* (136) 48-51 cm
This small, buzzard-sized eagle has pale and dark colour forms: in both of these it differs from Wahlberg's Eagle (p. 106) by its shorter, broader tail and broader wings. The underparts and underwing coverts are whitish in the pale colour form; the dark form is uniformly dark brown below, with a paler brown tail. From above, a small white patch is visible at the base of the forewing, giving the impression of a pair of white 'braces'. The dark brown on the head and face of the pale form extends well below the eyes and contrasts with the small, white throat.
Juv. resembles ad. **Habitat.** Fynbos, Karoo, semi-desert, savanna; usually in mountainous country. **Status.** Uncommon resident and summer visitor; a small number breed in the south and west. **Call.** High-pitched 'kee-keeee' or 'pee-pee-pee-pee'. (Dwergarend)

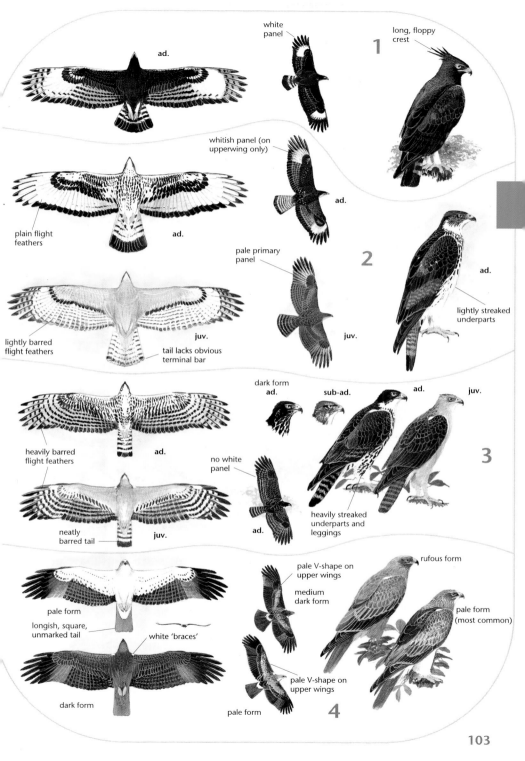

1

long, floppy crest

white panel

ad.

ad.

plain flight feathers

ad.

lightly barred flight feathers

juv.

tail lacks obvious terminal bar

2

whitish panel (on upperwing only)

ad.

pale primary panel

juv.

ad.

lightly streaked underparts

3

heavily barred flight feathers

ad.

neatly barred tail

juv.

no white panel

ad.

dark form
ad.

sub-ad.

ad.

juv.

heavily streaked underparts and leggings

4

pale form

longish, square, unmarked tail

white 'braces'

dark form

pale V-shape on upper wings

medium dark form

pale V-shape on upper wings

pale form

rufous form

pale form (most common)

1. EUROPEAN HONEY-BUZZARD *Pernis apivorus* (130)   52-60 cm
Like Steppe Buzzard (p. 106), which it resembles, this species is very variable in colour, but differs in having two broad, black bars (not easily seen) at the base of its tail and a broad, dark terminal tail band. It is more slender in appearance than Steppe Buzzard, and has a smaller, more compact head. At close range, the scaly feathering that covers the face is diagnostic.
Juv. has an indistinctly barred tail, lacking the diagnostic tail pattern of ad.; the general shape and small head should help one to distinguish it from Steppe Buzzard. **Habitat.** Found mostly in woodland. **Status.** An annual but rare summer visitor. **Call.** 'Meeuuw', a higher pitched call than that of Steppe Buzzard. (Wespedief)

2. JACKAL BUZZARD *Buteo rufofuscus* (152)   55-60 cm
Ad. has blackish upperparts with a bright chestnut breast, a black-and-white barred belly and a short, rufous tail. In flight, it vaguely resembles ad. Bateleur (p. 92) but the longer tail, broader wing tips and more flapping flight action eliminate confusion. Jackal Buzzards with white breasts (found mainly in the northwest of the range) can be distinguished from Augur Buzzard by their black, not white, underwing coverts.
Juv. is easily mistaken for Steppe Buzzard (p. 106) but has larger, broader wings and a pale, unbarred undertail. **Habitat.** Generally confined to mountain ranges and adjacent grassland. **Status.** Locally common resident; endemic. **Call.** A loud, drawn-out 'weeaah-ka-ka-ka', much like the yelp of Black-backed Jackal. Male's call higher-pitched than female's. (Rooiborsjakkalsvoël)

3. AUGUR BUZZARD *Buteo augur* (153)   55-60 cm
This species is similar in shape and overall structure to Jackal Buzzard but differs in having a white throat, breast and belly, and white, not black, underwing coverts. Some Jackal Buzzards show white breasts, but their dark underwing coverts should eliminate confusion with Augur Buzzard.
Female has black on the lower throat. **Juv.** is brown above and buffy below, with dark streaking on the sides of the breast. **Imm.** is predominantly white below and brown above. **Habitat.** Mountain ranges and hilly country in woodland, savanna and desert. **Status.** Common resident in the east, uncommon resident in the west. **Call.** A harsh 'kow-kow-kow-kow' given during display. Male's call higher pitched than female's. (Witbors-jakkalsvoël)

4. LONG-LEGGED BUZZARD *Buteo rufinus* (151)   55-65 cm
As with other buzzards, the plumage is very variable. However, this species is large and bulky, and occasionally hovers in flight. The combination of the dark belly, pale head and longer, broader wings also distinguishes this species from Steppe and Forest Buzzards (p. 106). Other useful identification characters are the white, unmarked primaries with the black wing tips, dark trailing edge to the wing, and the pale, almost translucent tail in the typical ad.
Juv. and imm. are indistinguishable from other juv. and imm. buzzards unless a direct comparison of size and shape is made. **Habitat.** Open grassland and semi-desert. **Status.** Vagrant. **Call.** Typically buzzard-like 'pee-ooo'. (Langbeenjakkalsvoël)

1

imm. pale form

ad. dark form

juv. dark form

small head

pale form

ad. pale form

imm. pale form

diagnostic barring

long tail

pale form

juv. undertail

ad. undertail

ad.

2

ad.

juv.

ad.

dark coverts

ad.

ad.

rufous tail

buffy brown underparts

3

♀ ad.

imm.

white underparts

♀ ad.

black carpal 'comma'

pale coverts

♂ ad.

♂ ad.

4

juv.

ad.

pale head

light-coloured tail

dark belly, leggings

1. WAHLBERG'S EAGLE *Aquila wahlbergi* (135) 55-60 cm

Very variable in colour, from buff to dark brown, occasionally all-white or having mixed light and dark plumage. The flight shape is diagnostic, with long, straight-edged wings and a long, narrow, square-ended tail. Pale-form birds could be confused with pale-form Booted Eagle (p. 102) but differ in flight shape and by the long, pencil-thin tail, as well as in having more white on the head. At rest it shows a small, pointed crest.
Female larger and usually darker than male. **Juv.** resembles ad. **Habitat.** Woodland and savanna. **Status.** Common summer visitor to the north and east from central Africa. **Call.** A drawn-out whistle while soaring, and yelping 'kop-yop-yip-yip-yip' when perched. (Bruinarend)

2. FOREST BUZZARD *Buteo trizonatus* (150) 45-50 cm

Very similar to Steppe Buzzard in size and plumage; the two are not easily distinguished in the field. Forest Buzzard typically lacks the barring on the flanks and is normally whiter below than Steppe Buzzard.
Juv. is distinguished from juv. Common Buzzard by its mostly white front and the tear-shaped flank streaks. **Habitat.** Evergreen forests and forest edges; has adapted to exotic eucalyptus and pine plantations and is largely confined to these habitats in the extreme west of its range. **Status.** Locally common resident. Endemic. **Call.** A gull-like 'pee-ooo'. (Bosjakkalsvoël)

3. STEPPE BUZZARD *Buteo vulpinus* (149) 45-50 cm

The plumage varies from pale brown to almost black. It is generally darker below than Forest Buzzard, and occurs mostly in different habitats. Unlike in Forest Buzzard, the flanks are usually conspicuously barred. It is frequently seen perched on roadside telephone poles.
Juv. resembles ad. but has yellow (not brown) eyes, streaked underparts and a narrower terminal tail bar. **Habitat.** Open country, avoiding desert and well-wooded regions. **Status.** Common summer visitor; some overwinter. **Call.** A gull-like 'pee-ooo'. (Bruinjakkalsvoël)

4. AFRICAN HARRIER-HAWK (GYMNOGENE)
Polyboroides typus (169) 60-66 cm

Ad. could be confused with chanting goshawks (p. 112) but the broad, floppy wings and the single central white tail bar are distinctive. The legs are yellow (not red). Close view reveals the bare yellow facial skin and the elongated nape feathers.
Juv. and imm. are easily confused with many other brown-plumaged raptors as they have variable brown plumage with no diagnostic markings, but the small head and broad wings, combined with the lazy manner of flight, aid identification. At close range, juv. shows bare, greyish facial skin. **Habitat.** Forests, riverine forests and open, broad-leaved woodland. **Status.** Common to scarce resident. **Call.** During the breeding season, a whistled 'suuu-eeee-ooo'. (Kaalwangvalk)

See also pages 99, 131

1

dark form

long wings
& tail

crested
appearance

pale form

long,
thin tail

dark-
headed
form

ad.

imm.

buff
form

imm.

2

spotted
underparts

ad.

imm.

ad.

imm.

ad.

imm.

pale greater &
median coverts

3

well-
marked
greater &
median
coverts

juv.

imm.

ad. rufous form

imm. grey form

ad. grey form

barred
flanks

barred
flanks

ad.

colour of underparts
variable

sub-ad.

juv.

pale inner
coverts

barred
tail

4

bare skin
around eye

juv.

small
head

ad.

sub-ad.

imm.

broad white
tail bar

display

ad.

1. AFRICAN MARSH-HARRIER *Circus ranivorus* (165)   45-50 cm
Ad. differs from female Western Marsh-Harrier by the lack of a well-demarcated white crown and throat, and by the barring on the flight feathers and tail. Distinguished from female Pallid and Montagu's Harriers by its larger size and broader wings, and by the lack of a white rump.

Juv. has a pale, creamy head and a creamy leading edge to the upperwing. Could be confused with female Western Marsh-Harrier, but shows a pale bar across the breast and has barred flight feathers and tail. Barring is not always easily seen. **Habitat.** Marshland, flooded grassland and adjacent areas. **Status.** Locally common to scarce resident. **Call.** Mainly silent except in breeding season, when a variety of chattering notes are uttered. (Afrikaanse Vleivalk)

2. WESTERN MARSH-HARRIER *Circus aeruginosus* (164)   48-56 cm
Male is easily identifiable by its brownish body contrasting with the grey on the wings and the unbarred grey tail. Female is dark brown with a creamy white cap and throat, white-edged forewings, and an unbarred brown tail. Juv. African Marsh-Harrier, in worn and abraded plumage, can also show a pale forehead and leading edge to the wings but has barred flight feathers and tail and a pale band across the breast.

Juv. resembles female, or can lack the white on the crown and forewings. **Habitat.** Confined to marshy areas and adjoining fields. **Status.** Uncommon summer visitor. **Call.** Silent in the region. (Europese Vleivalk)

3. BLACK HARRIER *Circus maurus* (168)   48-53 cm
The pied plumage of ad. renders this harrier unmistakable.

Juv. resembles imm. and female Pallid and Montagu's Harriers but differs in having white undersides to the secondaries, the primaries barred with brown, and the tail barred white and brown; imm. has tail barred with black and grey. **Habitat.** Open grassland, scrub, semi-desert and mountainous regions. **Status.** Uncommon resident in the southwestern parts of its range, but outside the breeding season it wanders to the northern and central regions. Endemic. **Call.** A 'pee-pee-pee-pee' call, given during display; a harsh 'chak-chak-chak' when alarmed. (Witkruisvleivalk)

4. PALLID HARRIER *Circus macrourus* (167)   40-48 cm
Male has a very pale grey body and plain grey upperwings with a wedge-shaped black patch at the wing tips. Can be distinguished from male Montagu's Harrier by the lack of streaking on the belly and flanks and the lack of a black bar on the secondaries.

Female, juv. and imm. Pallid and Montagu's Harriers are not easily distinguishable in the field unless a close view is obtained. Female, juv. and imm. Pallid Harrier show whitish cheeks with a dark line through the eye and a black crescent behind the ear, a pattern lacking in female, juv. and imm. Montagu's Harrier. Juv. and imm. have five tail bars (cf. four in juv. and imm. Montagu's Harrier). Pallid Harrier typically shows a pale collar, lacking in Montagu's Harrier. **Habitat.** Grassland and savanna. **Status.** Uncommon to rare summer visitor. **Call.** Silent in the region. (Witborsvleivalk)

5. MONTAGU'S HARRIER *Circus pygargus* (166)   43-47 cm
Male differs from male Pallid Harrier by its larger size, bulkier shape, grey throat and upper breast, streaks on the belly and flanks, and the conspicuous black bar on the secondaries visible in flight from above. Secondaries are lightly barred below.

Female, juv. and imm. are virtually inseparable except at close quarters from female, juv. and imm. Pallid Harrier. However, juv. and imm. Pallid Harrier have five tail bars compared to juv. and imm. Montagu's Harrier, which have four. The dark markings on the head are restricted to the crescent on the ear coverts and the very small, dark eye-stripe. Juv. and imm. lack a pale collar behind the ear covert crescent. **Habitat.** Grassland and savanna. **Status.** Uncommon summer visitor. **Call.** Silent in the region. (Blouvleivalk)

See also pages 110–111

barred tail

ad.

barred tail

juv.

1

juv.

2

unbarred tail

♀

♂

3

ad.

♂

plain belly

♀

juv.

4

♀

juv.

5

♂

black line

streaked belly

♀

juv.

♀

juv.

AFRICAN MARSH-HARRIER

extensively barred underwing

ad.

juv.

banded tail

ad.

ad.

juv.

WESTERN MARSH-HARRIER

♀

unbarred underwing

♂ ad.

♀

♂ juv.

♂ ad.

unbarred tail

♂ ad.

♀ ad.

imm.

extensive white on primary bases

imm.

imm.

ad.

ad.

BLACK HARRIER

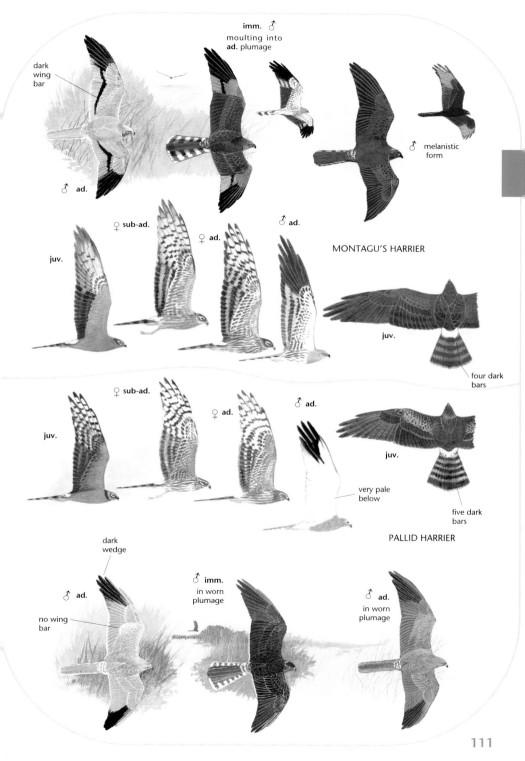

imm. ♂
moulting into
ad. plumage

dark
wing
bar

♂ ad.

♂ melanistic
form

♀ sub-ad.

♀ ad.

♂ ad.

juv.

MONTAGU'S HARRIER

juv.

four dark
bars

♀ sub-ad.

♀ ad.

♂ ad.

juv.

very pale
below

five dark
bars

PALLID HARRIER

dark
wedge

♂ ad.

no wing
bar

♂ imm.
in worn
plumage

♂ ad.
in worn
plumage

1. SOUTHERN PALE CHANTING GOSHAWK *Melierax canorus* (162)   48-63 cm
This species is paler grey than Dark Chanting Goshawk, especially on the forewings, and has a white rump and white secondaries.
Juv. is paler than juv. Dark Chanting Goshawk and has a white (not barred) rump. Superficially it resembles a female harrier, but the broader wings, flight action and long legs should eliminate confusion. **Habitat.** Common along the roadside in arid areas. The northeastern part of its range overlaps with the range of Dark Chanting Goshawk. **Status.** Common resident; near-endemic. **Call.** A melodious, piping 'kleeuu-kleeuu-klu-klu-klu', usually uttered at dawn. (Bleeksingvalk)

2. DARK CHANTING GOSHAWK *Melierax metabates* (163)   43-56 cm
Darker grey than Southern Pale Chanting Goshawk. At rest, the grey forewing does not contrast with the rest of the wing as it does in Southern Pale Chanting Goshawk. The rump and secondaries are grey (not white).
Juv. has a darker brown breast band than juv. Southern Pale Chanting Goshawk, and has a barred, grey-brown rump. **Habitat.** Thornveld and open, broad-leaved woodland. Range overlaps narrowly with that of Southern Pale Chanting Goshawk. **Status.** Scarce resident. **Call.** Piping call, similar to that of Southern Pale Chanting Goshawk: 'kleeu-kleeu-klu-klu'. (Donkersingvalk)

3. BLACK KITE *Milvus migrans* (126)   51-60 cm
Differs from smaller Common Buzzard (p. 106) by the longer, forked tail and the narrower wings, which are more acutely angled backwards in flight. Although much the same size, African Marsh-Harrier (p. 108) has a longer, square-ended tail and flies with the wings canted up; Black Kite has a floppy flight action and twists its long tail for steering. It differs from Yellow-billed Kite in having a black bill (but a yellowish cere), a paler, greyer head and a less deeply forked tail.
Juv. has buffy feather margins. **Habitat.** Diverse; from forest edge to savanna and semi-desert. Often found in flocks at termite emergences. **Status.** Locally common non-breeding summer visitor. **Call.** A high-pitched, shrill whinnying. (Swartwou)

4. YELLOW-BILLED KITE *Milvus parasitus*   51-60 cm
The same size and shape as Black Kite, with much the same jizz. It differs from Black Kite in ad. plumage by its bright yellow bill, more deeply forked tail and paler, greyer head.
Juv.. has a black bill and buffy feather margins. **Habitat.** Diverse; commonly seen around human habitation. **Status.** Locally abundant breeding summer visitor. **Call.** Similar to that of Black Kite. (Geelbekwou)

5. BLACK-SHOULDERED KITE *Elanus caeruleus* (127)   33 cm
A small, easily identified, grey-and-white raptor with diagnostic black shoulder patches. It has a characteristic habit of hovering and, when perched, often wags its white tail up and down.
Juv. is more buffy than ad., with a scalloped, brown-washed back, grey tail and dark shoulders. **Habitat.** A wide range of open habitats, but most common in agricultural areas; often seen perched on telephone poles and lines. **Status.** Common resident with local movements. **Call.** A high-pitched, whistled 'peeeu', a soft 'weep' and a rasping 'wee-ah'. (Blouvalk)

See also pages 114–115

1

ad.

pale panel in closed wing

juv.

2

ad.

no wing contrast

juv.

3

greyish head

ad.

mainly black bill

less deeply forked tail than Yellow-billed Kite

juv.

4

brown head

all-yellow bill

deeply forked tail

5

juv.

ad.

dark shoulder

113

See also pages 109, 112–113

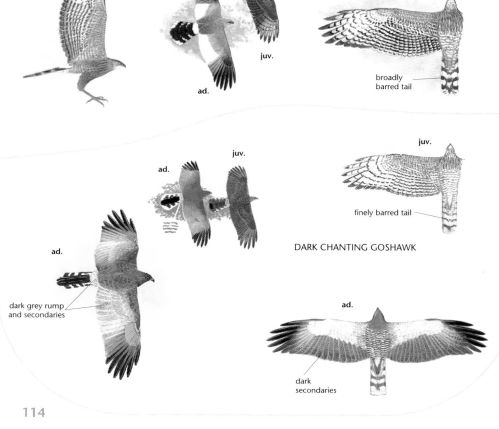

ad.

white rump
and secondaries

pale
secondaries

ad.

extensive
dark tips

SOUTHERN PALE CHANTING GOSHAWK

juv.

juv.

juv.

juv.

ad.

broadly
barred tail

juv.

ad.

finely barred tail

DARK CHANTING GOSHAWK

ad.

dark grey rump
and secondaries

ad.

dark
secondaries

juv.

brown
head

YELLOW-BILLED KITE

ad.

greyish
head

BLACK KITE

ad.

ad.

juv.

BLACK-SHOULDERED KITE

plain white tail

ad.

often
hovers

ad.

juv.

dark
shoulders

1. AFRICAN CUCKOO HAWK *Aviceda cuculoides* (128)   40 cm
Superficially resembles male African Goshawk (p. 120), but has a crest, a grey throat and upper breast that form a clearly defined bib, a heavily rufous-barred breast and belly, and short legs. In flight, it has long wings (not short and rounded as in African Goshawk) with the underwing coverts barred rufous and white.
Sexes alike except in eye colour: Female's are yellow and male's red or brown. **Juv.** resembles juv. African Goshawk and juv. Little Sparrowhawk (p. 118) but is larger, and has shorter legs, a small crest and, in flight, pointed (not rounded) wings. **Habitat.** Mature woodland, riparian forest and evergreen forest fringes. **Status.** Uncommon resident. **Call.** A loud, far-carrying 'teee-oooo' whistle and a shorter 'tittit-eooo'. (Koekoekvalk)

2. LIZARD BUZZARD *Kaupifalco monogrammicus* (154)   35-37 cm
Larger and bulkier than the similar Gabar Goshawk (p. 118), this bird has a white throat with a black line down the centre, a white rump and a broad white tail bar (or, rarely, two tail bars).
Juv. similar to ad. but has a paler cere and legs. **Habitat.** Open, broad-leaved woodland and thornveld in the east and north. **Status.** Common to scarce resident and local migrant. **Call.** Noisy in the breeding season: a whistled 'peoo-peoo' and a melodious 'klioo-klu-klu-klu-klu'. (Akkedisvalk)

3. PYGMY FALCON *Polihierax semitorquatus* (186)   18-20 cm
A shrike-like and shrike-sized raptor that sits very upright on an exposed perch from which it hawks lizards and insects. Flight is undulating.
Male is grey above and white below. Female has a chestnut back. **Juv.** resembles female but has a dull brown back and is washed rufous below. **Habitat.** Dry thornveld and semi-desert regions. Breeds in a chamber of Sociable Weaver nests, leaving a telltale, white-washed rim around the nest entrance. Also found around Red-billed Buffalo-Weaver nests. **Status.** Uncommon to locally common resident. **Call.** Noisy; a 'chip-chip' and a 'kik-kik-kik-kik' call. (Dwergvalk)

See also page 132

rufous 'armpits'

long wings

ad.

small crest

1

juv.

no white on rump

broad bars on belly

ad.

short legs

ad.

2

ad.

black line down throat

white rump

juv.

two-banded tail

normal tail

ad.

narrow white tail bar (sometimes two)

white rump

3

♀

♂

♀

♂

shrike-like size & posture

♂

white underwing coverts

1. OVAMBO SPARROWHAWK *Accipiter ovampensis* (156)   33-40 cm
Distinguished from similar, but smaller, Shikra by its brown (not red) eye, the grey (not rufous) barring on the front, and the white vertical flecks on the black-and-grey barred tail. The cere and legs are usually yellow, but can be orange or red. A rare melanistic form differs from the melanistic form of Gabar Goshawk in having orange, not red cere and legs and white vertical flecks in the tail and no white webbing in the tail.
Sexes alike, but female is larger. **Juv.** has two forms: the dark form differs from ad. Rufous-chested Sparrowhawk (p. 120) by its rufous (not dark grey) head, and by its pale eyebrow. The pale form is much whiter below and around the head, and has streaked underparts. The uppertail of both is as in ad. **Habitat.** Tall woodland, avoiding forests and desert areas; has adapted to exotic plantations, favouring poplars. **Status.** Locally common to rare resident. **Call.** A soft 'keeep-keeep-keeep', given when breeding. (Ovambosperwer)

2. GABAR GOSHAWK *Melierax gabar* (161)   28-36 cm
Distinguished by its grey throat and breast, and red cere and legs. Could be confused with Lizard Buzzard (p. 116), but that species has a white throat with a central stripe and a broad, white tail band. The larger Ovambo Sparrowhawk has a dark rump and barred, not uniform, grey throat and breast. The melanistic form of Gabar Goshawk differs from the melanistic form of Ovambo Sparrowhawk in having white webbing in the rectrices and black markings on the scales on the front of the legs, and in lacking white vertical flecks in the tail.
Sexes alike, but female is larger. **Juv.** differs from other juv. hawks by its white rump. **Habitat.** Savanna, especially thornveld and semi-arid habitats. **Status.** Locally common to scarce resident. **Call.** A high-pitched, whistling 'kik-kik-kik-kik-kik'. (Kleinsingvalk)

3. SHIKRA (LITTLE BANDED GOSHAWK) *Accipiter badius* (159)   28-30 cm
This species lacks the white rump and tail spots of Little Sparrowhawk. It differs from Ovambo Sparrowhawk by its rufous (not grey) barring below, the cherry-red (not brown) eye, and the unbarred tail (when seen closed).
Juv. most like juv. Gabar Goshawk (both are brown with a streaked breast and barred belly) but lacks the white rump. **Habitat.** Savanna and tall woodland. **Status.** Common to scarce resident, with local movements. **Call.** Male's call is a high-pitched 'keewik-keewik-keewik'; female's is a softer 'kee-uuu'. (Gebande Sperwer)

4. LITTLE SPARROWHAWK *Accipiter minullus* (157)   23-28 cm
Ad. is distinguished from Shikra by its white rump and the two white spots on the uppertail. Most like male African Goshawk (p. 120) but much smaller; it also has a white rump and a yellow, not grey, cere.
Sexes alike, but female is larger. **Juv.** lacks the white rump of ad.; it is similar to juv. male African Goshawk in colour but is smaller, has a yellow eye, and lacks the grey cere. **Habitat.** Diverse; frequents forests, woodland, savanna and has adapted to exotic plantations. Secretive. **Status.** Common to scarce resident. **Call.** A high-pitched 'tu-tu-tu-tu-tu', uttered by male during the breeding season; female gives a softer 'kew-kew-kew'. (Kleinsperwer)

See also pages 132–133

1

♂ juv.
pale form

white streaks on
barred uppertail

red-brown eye

♂ juv.
dark form

♀ ad.

finely barred from
throat to tail

2

♀ juv.

two-tone
underparts

♂ ad.

red
cere

red
legs

♂ ad.
melanistic
form

broad white
rump

broad
white
rump

3

cherry-red
eye

plain
uppertail

no white
on rump

♂ ad.

♀ juv.

dark
rump

4

yellow eye
and eye-ring

yellow
cere

♂ ad.

tail
spots

narrow
white rump

♂ juv.

dark
rump

♀ juv.

1. BLACK SPARROWHAWK *Accipiter melanoleucus* (158)   46-58 cm

This is the largest accipiter of the region. The black and white plumage and large size render the pale form of this species unmistakable. A melanistic form occurs and is the commonest form in the south west of the species' range (about 80% of birds). Melanistic birds vary from having a white throat and sparse white blotching on the breast and vent area (as illustrated) to being entirely black from chin to vent. Melanistic Gabar Goshawk is much smaller and has red legs and cere. In the north of its range, confusion is possible with (rare) melanistic form of Ovambo Sparrowhawk. Latter is much smaller (less than half the weight and with wingspan 65-70 cm vs about 100 cm for Black Sparrowhawk). The eye of Black Sparrowhawk is deep blood red, of Ovambo Sparrowhawk is dark brown.

Male is smaller than female. **Juv.** has both pale and rufous forms. The pale form may be confused with juv. African Goshawk but is much larger. The rufous form resembles juv. African Hawk-Eagle (p.102) but has more heavily streaked underparts, unfeathered tarsi and a different shape and flight action. **Habitat.** Forests and kloofs; has adapted to exotic plantations. **Status.** Locally common resident. **Call.** Normally silent except when breeding. Male's call is a 'keeyp'; female's is a repeated, short 'kek'. (Swartsperwer)

2. AFRICAN GOSHAWK *Accipiter tachiro* (160)   36-46 cm

This species is wholly barred on the front, has no white on the rump, and its yellow eye and grey cere distinguish ad. from other similar-looking hawks.

Sexes are highly dimorphic; the small males are bluish grey above and barred rufous below, and have two white spots in the tail (like Little Sparrowhawk, p. 118); the large females are brown above and barred brown below, and lack the tail spots. **Juv.** is boldly spotted on the front, and is distinguished from juv. Little Sparrowhawk by the grey cere and from juv. African Cuckoo Hawk (p. 116) by its smaller size, longer legs and the lack of a crest. **Habitat.** Evergreen and riverine forests, tall mature woodland and well-wooded suburbia. **Status.** Common resident. **Call.** Noisy; usually detected by a short 'whit' or 'chip' uttered on the wing or while perched. Female has mewing 'keeuuu' call. (Afrikaanse Sperwer)

3. RUFOUS-CHESTED (REDBREASTED) SPARROWHAWK

Accipiter rufiventris (155)   33-40 cm

Ad. is identified by its uniformly rufous underparts, slate-grey upperparts, and the lack of white on the rump.

Sexes alike, but female is larger. **Juv.** has variable plumage; it is generally darker above and more mottled below than juv. Ovambo Sparrowhawk (p. 118), which lacks the uniform dark cap, showing only a dark spot behind the eye. **Habitat.** Montane grassland/forest mosaics; adapted to exotic plantations and has extended its range in the Karoo and on the highveld where these occur. **Status.** Locally common to rare resident. **Call.** A sharp, staccato 'kee-kee-kee-kee-kee', given during display. (Rooiborssperwer)

See also page 133

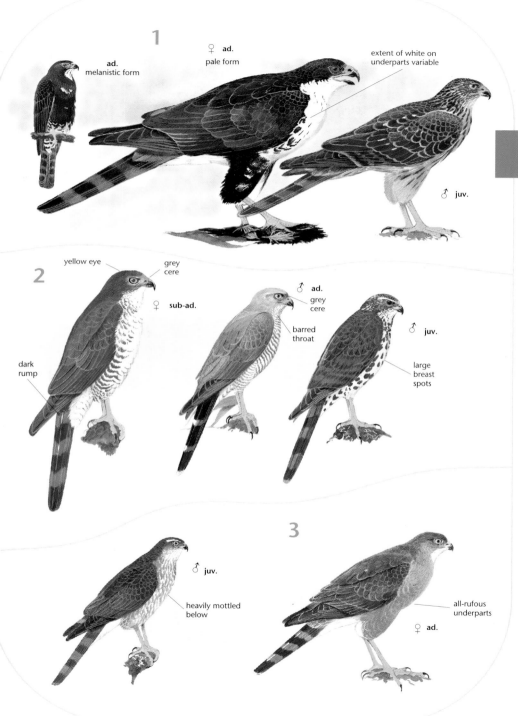

1

ad.
melanistic form

♀ **ad.**
pale form

extent of white on
underparts variable

♂ **juv.**

2

yellow eye

grey
cere

♀ **sub-ad.**

♂ **ad.**
grey
cere

barred
throat

♂ **juv.**

dark
rump

large
breast
spots

3

♂ **juv.**

heavily mottled
below

all-rufous
underparts

♀ **ad.**

1. LANNER FALCON *Falco biarmicus* (172)   38-45 cm

The rufous forehead and crown and pinkish, unmarked underparts distinguish this species from Peregrine Falcon. It also has broader, more rounded wings, a longer tail and a floppier, less dynamic flight action than Peregrine Falcon.

Sexes alike except in size – female is larger. **Juv.** is much paler than juv. Peregrine Falcon, with less streaking on the underparts and a pale creamy or rufous crown. **Habitat.** A wide range of habitats, from mountainous terrain to deserts and open grassland. Avoids forests. **Status.** Common to scarce resident. **Call.** A harsh 'kak-kak-kak-kak-kak', similar to call of Peregrine Falcon; also gives whining and chopping notes. (Edelvalk)

2. PEREGRINE FALCON *Falco peregrinus* (171)   34-38 cm

Can be confused with Lanner and Taita falcons. It differs from Lanner Falcon by its smaller size, black forehead and crown, and white breast with the underparts finely barred with black. It is swifter and more agile than Lanner Falcon, and has more pointed wings and a relatively short tail. Taita Falcon is smaller, and has rufous underparts and two rufous patches on the nape.

Sexes alike except for size – female is larger. **Juv.** is darker than juv. Lanner Falcon and has the forehead and crown dark brown (not rufous). **Habitat.** High cliffs and gorges, both coastal and inland. **Status.** Scarce or rare resident and summer visitor. The larger and paler northern-hemisphere race *calidus* visits in summer and may occur anywhere, but is scarce. **Call.** A raucous 'kak-kak-kak-kak-kak', uttered around nesting cliff; also gives whining and chopping notes. (Swerfvalk)

3. TAITA FALCON *Falco fasciinucha* (176)   28-30 cm

This small, robust falcon is shaped like Peregrine Falcon and, in flight, shows the dash and speed of that species. In coloration it resembles African Hobby (p. 124) but differs in having rufous patches on the nape, and a white throat that contrasts with the black moustachial stripes.

Juv. resembles ad. but has buff edges to the back feathers. **Habitat.** High cliffs and gorges. **Status.** Rare resident. **Call.** A high-pitched 'kree-kree-kree' and 'kek-kek-kek'. (Taitavalk)

4. RED-NECKED FALCON *Falco chicquera* (178)   30-36 cm

Ad. is unmistakable with its chestnut crown and nape, and dark brown moustachial stripes on white cheeks.

Juv. has a dark brown head, two buff patches on the nape, and pale rufous underparts finely barred with brown. **Habitat.** Palm savanna and arid thornveld. **Status.** Uncommon resident. **Call.** A shrill 'ki-ki-ki-ki-ki', given during the breeding season. (Rooinekvalk)

See also page 134

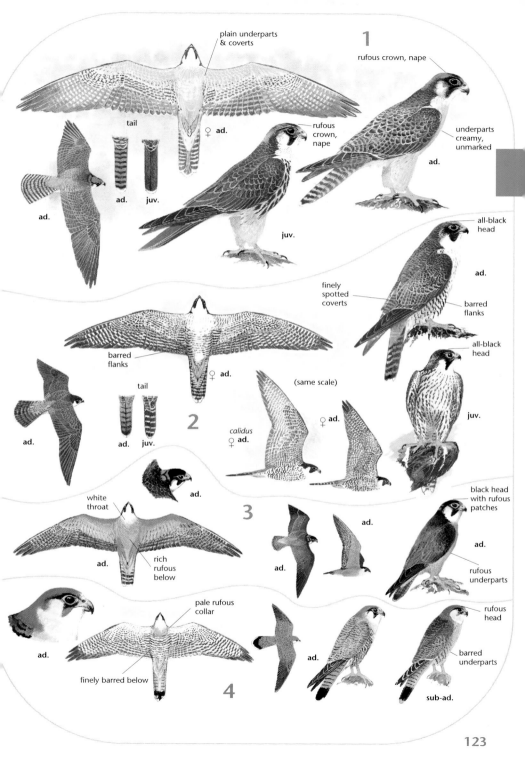

1

plain underparts & coverts

rufous crown, nape

tail

♀ **ad.**

ad. **juv.**

ad.

rufous crown, nape

underparts creamy, unmarked

ad.

juv.

all-black head

ad.

finely spotted coverts

barred flanks

all-black head

2

barred flanks

tail

♀ **ad.**

(same scale)

ad. **juv.**

calidus ♀ **ad.**

♀ **ad.**

juv.

ad.

3

ad.

black head with rufous patches

ad.

white throat

rich rufous below

ad.

ad.

ad.

rufous underparts

pale rufous collar

rufous head

ad.

ad.

barred underparts

finely barred below

ad.

4

sub-ad.

1. ELEONORA'S FALCON *Falco eleonorae* (177)   36-40 cm
The pale form is distinguished from juv. Peregrine Falcon (p. 122) by its heavily streaked, rufous underparts, and longer wings and tail. It differs from Eurasian Hobby by its larger size, the rufous underparts and the dark underwing. The dark form is most likely to be confused with Sooty Falcon (p. 126) but is larger and darker and has a longer tail, darker underwing coverts and greenish (not chrome yellow) legs and feet.
Sexes alike except that male's cere is yellow and female's is blue. **Juv.** differs from juv. Peregrine Falcon in having a rufous wash and darker underwing. **Habitat.** Open, broad-leaved woodland and adjoining grassland. **Status.** Rare vagrant during late summer. **Call.** Silent in the region. (Eleonoravalk)

2. EURASIAN (EUROPEAN) HOBBY *Falco subbuteo* (173)   28-35 cm
In flight, the long, pointed wings and relatively short tail give this species a swift-like appearance. It has the breast heavily streaked and has conspicuous rufous leggings and vent. Distinguished from similarly shaped African Hobby by the rufous front of that species. Larger, darker-backed and more heavily streaked in front than female and juv. Amur Falcon (p. 128). The flight shape is like that of Sooty Falcon, but the wings are shorter.
Juv. lacks the rufous vent and leggings of ad. **Habitat.** Broad-leaved woodland and savanna; avoids forests and deserts. Often found near open water. **Status.** Uncommon summer visitor. **Call.** Silent in the region. (Europese Boomvalk)

3. AFRICAN HOBBY *Falco cuvierii* (174)   28-30 cm
Resembles Eurasian Hobby but is smaller and has an unstreaked, rufous breast and underparts. Might be mistaken for Taita Falcon (p. 122), which is more robust and has rufous nape markings and a white throat.
Juv. has a streaked front. The head and throat coloration is variable but is often paler than that of ad. **Habitat.** Open, broad-leaved woodland, forests and adjoining open country. **Status.** Rare. **Call.** A high-pitched 'kik-kik-kik-kik', given in display. (Afrikaanse Boomvalk)

4. BAT HAWK *Macheiramphus alcinus* (129)   45 cm
A dark brown bird, appearing black in the field, with a varying amount of white visible on the throat and abdomen. Falcon-shaped in flight, it could easily be mistaken for a Lanner or Peregrine Falcon (p. 122) if seen in twilight when the colours are not discernible, but it has a thinner body and longer wings. At close quarters, the white legs, eyelids and nape patches are distinctive.
Juv. shows more white on the underparts. **Habitat.** Woodland, including plantations, and savanna. Crepuscular and nocturnal, roosts in thick foliage during the day; easily overlooked. **Status.** Rare resident. **Call.** A high-pitched whistling, reminiscent of that of a thick-knee (p. 202). (Vlermuisvalk)

124   *See also page 134*

1

dark underwing

♂ ad.

ad.

juv.

ad.

ad. dark form

very long wings & tail

underparts vary from cream to rufous, rarely grey-black

juv.

2

ad.

spotted underwing

black & white streaked breast

rufous vent

ad.

ad.

juv.

rufous vent, leggings

3

plain rufous breast

ad.

imm.

ad.

juv.

underparts entirely rufous

underparts rufous, streaked black

4

small crest

ad.

juv. pale form

white eyelids

white legs & feet

1. SOOTY FALCON *Falco concolor* (175)   32-36 cm

Most like Grey Kestrel, which is squatter and shorter-winged (the wings do not extend beyond the tail when the bird is perched), and Dickinson's Kestrel, which has a paler head and rump. Differs from ad. male Red-footed Falcon (p. 128) by the lack of a chestnut vent and by the chrome yellow (not red) legs and cere. The flight shape is like that of Eurasian Hobby (p. 124) but the wings are longer.
Juv. has the shape of ad. but is buffy below, heavily streaked with grey. The moustachial streak is less pronounced than in Eurasian Hobby. **Habitat.** Well-wooded coastal areas. **Status.** Rare summer visitor to east coast; vagrant elsewhere. **Call.** Silent in southern Africa. (Roetvalk)

2. GREY KESTREL *Falco ardosiaceus* (184)   36 cm

Distinguished from Sooty Falcon by the shorter, broader wings, and the stockier, more robust build. At rest, the wings do not reach the tip of the square tail. An entirely grey falcon, it lacks the pale head and rump of Dickinson's Kestrel.
Juv. resembles ad. but is lightly suffused with brown. **Habitat.** Savanna, especially where there are palms present. **Status.** Rare and localised in the extreme northwest. **Call.** A high-pitched, rasping trill. (Donkergrysvalk)

3. DICKINSON'S KESTREL *Falco dickinsoni* (185)   28-30 cm

The combination of a grey body contrasting with a very pale grey head and pale grey rump should rule out confusion with any other greyish falcon in the region.
Juv. resembles ad. but has white barring on the flanks. **Habitat.** Open palm and woodland savanna, often in the vicinity of baobab trees. **Status.** Scarce resident. **Call.** A high-pitched 'keee-keee-keee'. (Dickinsonse Valk)

See also page 135

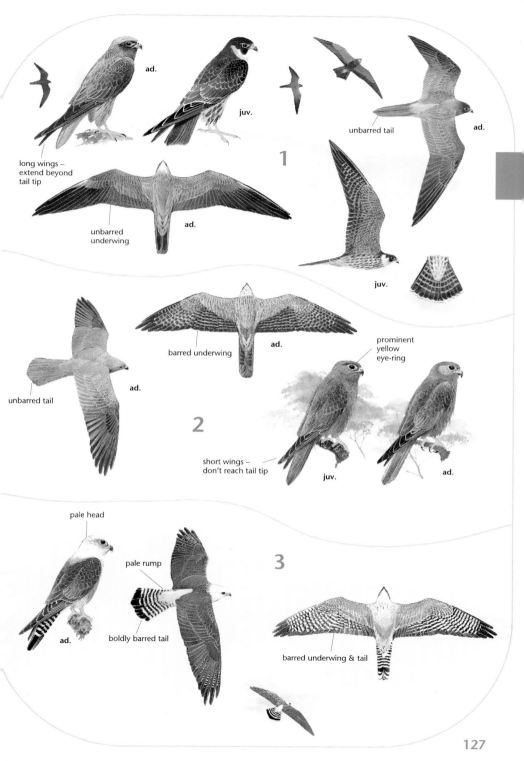

1

ad.

juv.

long wings – extend beyond tail tip

unbarred underwing

ad.

unbarred tail

ad.

juv.

2

unbarred tail

ad.

barred underwing

ad.

prominent yellow eye-ring

short wings – don't reach tail tip

juv.

ad.

3

pale head

pale rump

boldly barred tail

ad.

barred underwing & tail

1. AMUR (EASTERN RED-FOOTED) FALCON *Falco amurensis* (180)   30 cm

Female and juv. resemble Eurasian Hobby (p. 124) but have a small white forehead patch, a pale grey crown and paler underwing coverts. Female lacks the rufous crown, nape and underparts of female Red-footed Falcon.

Juv. resembles female but is streaked below and has buffy edges to the upperpart feathers. **Habitat.** Open grassland. Roosts communally in tall trees in towns. **Status.** Common summer visitor. **Call.** A shrill chattering at roosts. (Oostelike Rooipootvalk)

2. (WESTERN) RED-FOOTED FALCON *Falco vespertinus* (179)   29-31 cm

The combination of the slate-grey plumage and chestnut vent is diagnostic in male. It lacks the white underwing coverts of Amur Falcon.

Female differs from female Amur Falcon in having a rufous crown and nape, and buffy underparts. **Juv.** might be confused with Eurasian Hobby (p. 124) but differs in having a pale crown, paler underparts and a much paler underwing with a dark trailing edge. **Habitat.** Open grassland and savanna. **Status.** Common to rare summer visitor. **Call.** A shrill chattering at roosts. (Westelike Rooipootvalk)

3. LESSER KESTREL *Falco naumanni* (183)   29-33 cm

Male differs from ad. Rock Kestrel by its unspotted, chestnut back, grey secondary coverts and lightly spotted, buff-coloured front.

Female and juv. are similar to juv. Rock Kestrel but are paler below, especially on the underwing. **Habitat.** Open grassland and agricultural areas. Roosts communally in tall trees in towns. **Status.** Common summer visitor. **Call.** Silent in the region. (Kleinrooivalk)

4. ROCK KESTREL *Falco [tinnunculus] rupicolis* (181)   30-33 cm

This species differs from male Lesser Kestrel in having a spotted chestnut back and wings, lacking grey on the secondary coverts and in having the underwing spotted and barred (not silvery white). It differs from Greater Kestrel by its grey head, more rufous colour, smaller size, spotted (not barred) back, and more heavily marked underwing.

Sexes alike except on the tail, where female has narrow dark bars that male lacks. **Juv.** differs from female and juv. Lesser Kestrels by being slimmer and darker below, especially on the underwing. **Habitat.** Diverse, but usually in mountainous or rocky terrain. **Status.** Common resident with local movements, near-endemic. **Call.** A high-pitched 'kik-kik-kik'. (Kransvalk)

5. GREATER KESTREL *Falco rupicoloides* (182)   36-40 cm

At close range the diagnostic whitish eye is obvious. This kestrel is larger and paler brown than Rock Kestrel, and has a whitish underwing; it is distinguished from female Lesser Kestrel by its grey, barred tail, and the lack of moustachial stripes.

Juv. has a rufous, barred tail, a dark eye and streaked (not barred) flanks. **Habitat.** Dry areas, ranging from open grasslands and arid savanna to desert. **Status.** Locally common resident. **Call.** A shrill, repeated 'kee-ker-rik', given during display. (Grootrooivalk)

See also page 135

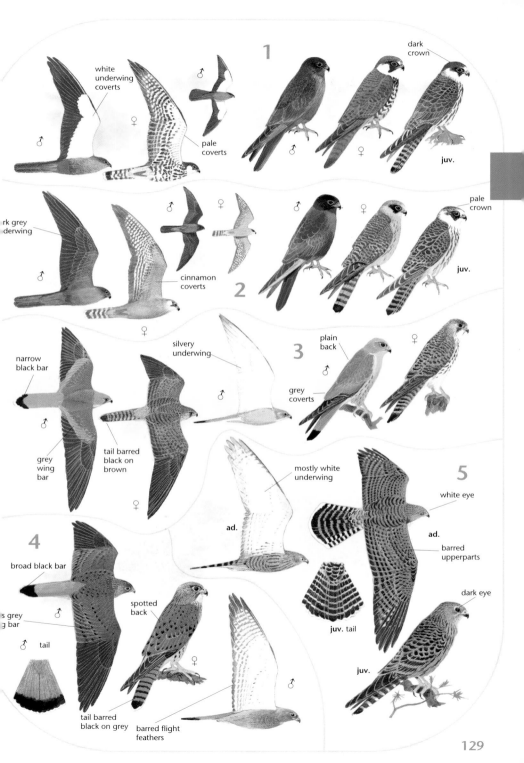

1

white underwing coverts

♀

♂

pale coverts

♂

dark crown

♂

♀

juv.

2

rk grey derwing

♂

cinnamon coverts

♀

♂

♀

pale crown

juv.

3

narrow black bar

♂

grey wing bar

tail barred black on brown

silvery underwing

♂

♀

plain back

♂

grey coverts

♀

mostly white underwing

ad.

5

white eye

ad.

barred upperparts

4

broad black bar

s grey g bar

♂

♂ tail

spotted back

♀

tail barred black on grey

barred flight feathers

♂

juv. tail

dark eye

juv.

See also pages 104–107

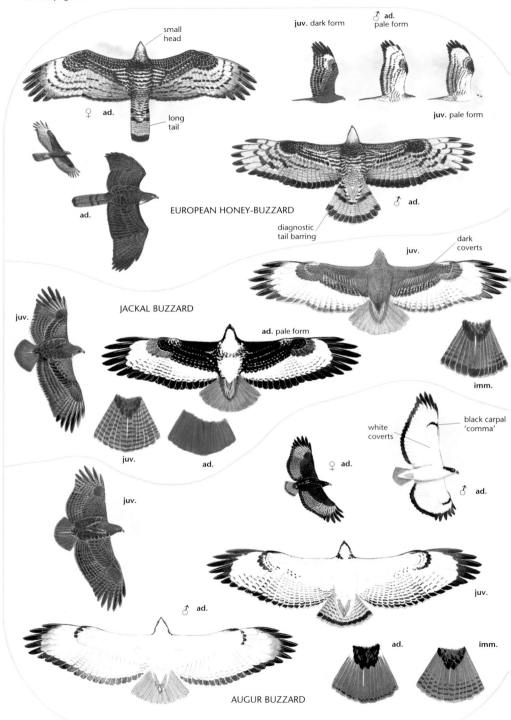

juv. dark form

♂ ad.
pale form

small head

juv. pale form

♀ ad.

long tail

ad.

EUROPEAN HONEY-BUZZARD

diagnostic tail barring

♂ ad.

juv.

dark coverts

JACKAL BUZZARD

juv.

ad. pale form

imm.

juv.

ad.

black carpal 'comma'

white coverts

♀ ad.

♂ ad.

juv.

juv.

♂ ad.

ad.

imm.

AUGUR BUZZARD

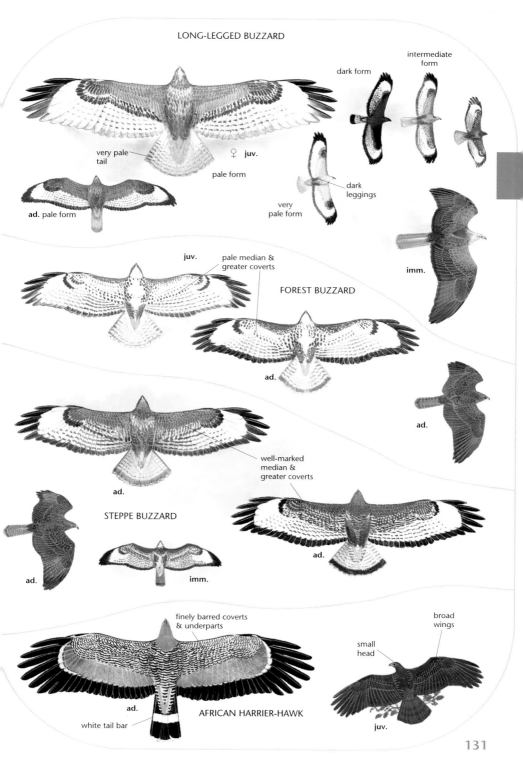

LONG-LEGGED BUZZARD

intermediate
form

dark form

very pale
tail

♀ juv.

pale form

dark
leggings

ad. pale form

very
pale form

imm.

juv. pale median &
greater coverts

FOREST BUZZARD

ad.

ad.

well-marked
median &
greater coverts

ad.

STEPPE BUZZARD

ad.

imm.

ad.

finely barred coverts
& underparts

broad
wings

small
head

ad.

white tail bar

AFRICAN HARRIER-HAWK

juv.

131

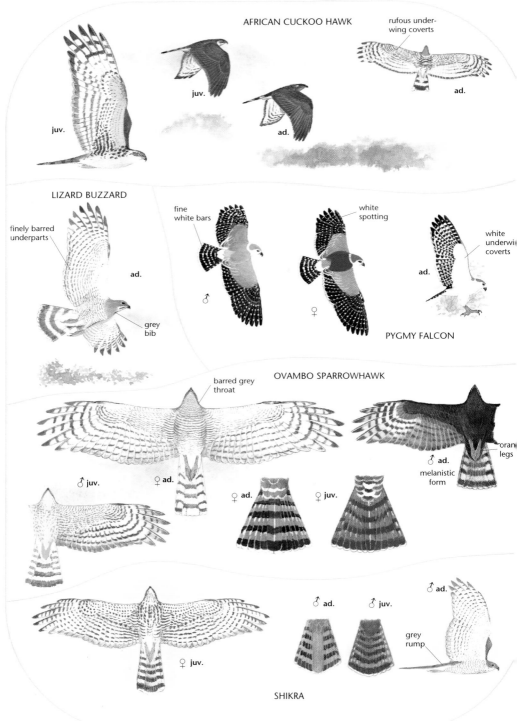

AFRICAN CUCKOO HAWK

rufous under-wing coverts

juv.

juv.

ad.

ad.

LIZARD BUZZARD

finely barred underparts

ad.

grey bib

fine white bars

white spotting

white underwing coverts

♂

♀

ad.

PYGMY FALCON

OVAMBO SPARROWHAWK

barred grey throat

♂ juv.

♀ ad.

♀ ad.

♀ juv.

♂ ad.
melanistic form

oran legs

♂ ad.

♂ juv.

♂ ad.

grey rump

♀ juv.

SHIKRA

LITTLE SPARROWHAWK

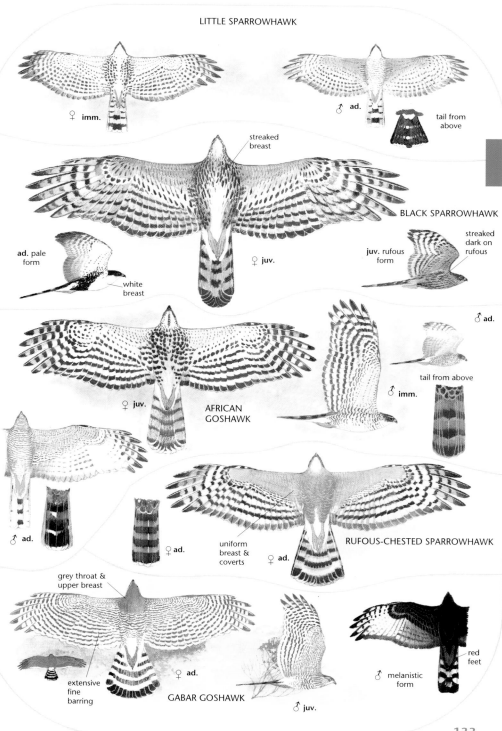

♀ imm.

♂ ad.

tail from above

streaked breast

BLACK SPARROWHAWK

streaked dark on rufous

ad. pale form

white breast

♀ juv.

juv. rufous form

♂ ad.

♀ juv.

AFRICAN GOSHAWK

♂ imm.

tail from above

♂ ad.

♀ ad.

uniform breast & coverts

♀ ad.

RUFOUS-CHESTED SPARROWHAWK

grey throat & upper breast

♀ ad.

extensive fine barring

GABAR GOSHAWK

♂ juv.

red feet

♂ melanistic form

See also pages 122–129

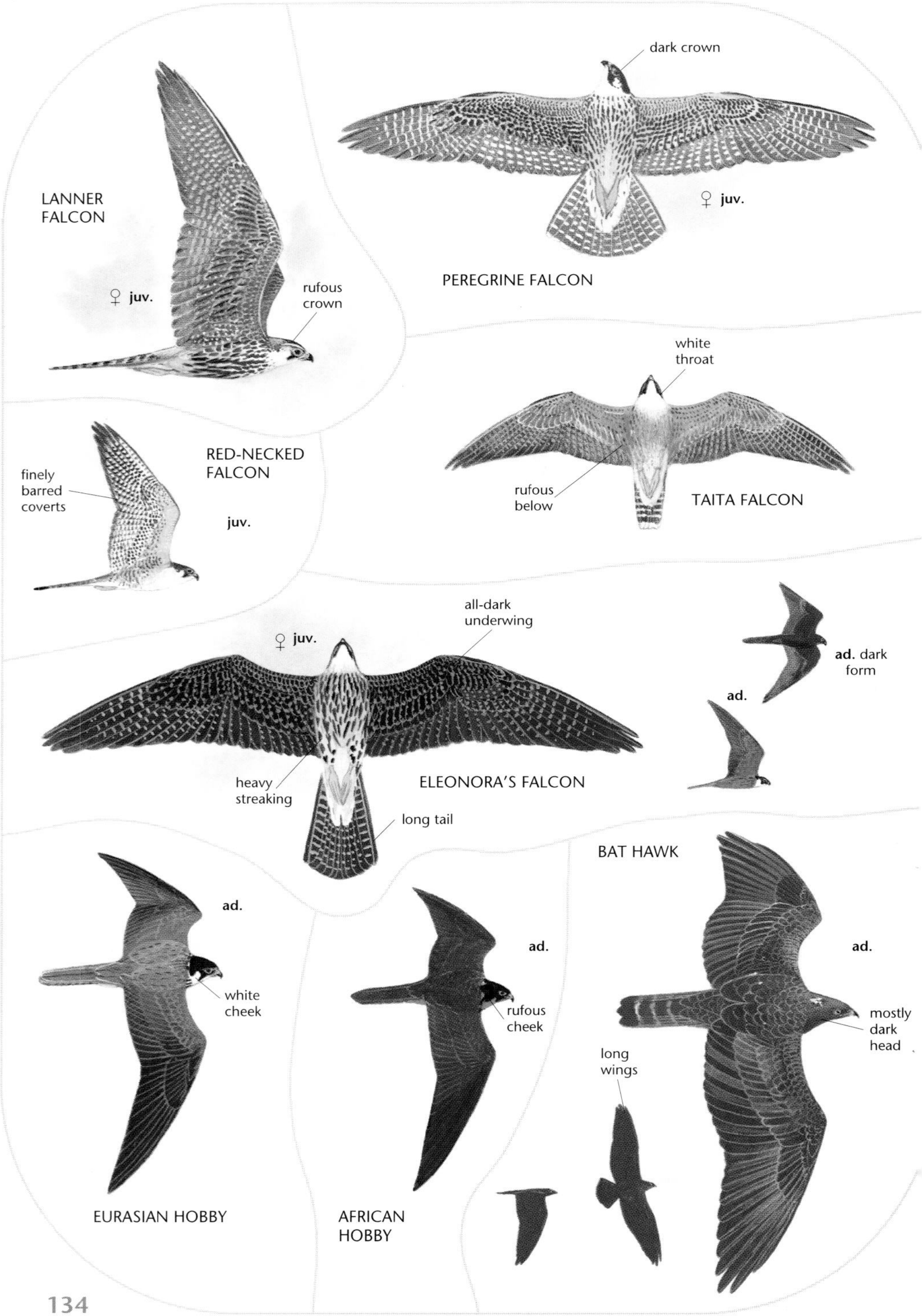
LANNER FALCON
♀ juv.
rufous crown
dark crown
♀ juv.
PEREGRINE FALCON
white throat
rufous below
TAITA FALCON
RED-NECKED FALCON
finely barred coverts
juv.
all-dark underwing
♀ juv.
heavy streaking
long tail
ELEONORA'S FALCON
ad. dark form
ad.
BAT HAWK
ad.
white cheek
EURASIAN HOBBY
ad.
rufous cheek
AFRICAN HOBBY
ad.
mostly dark head
long wings

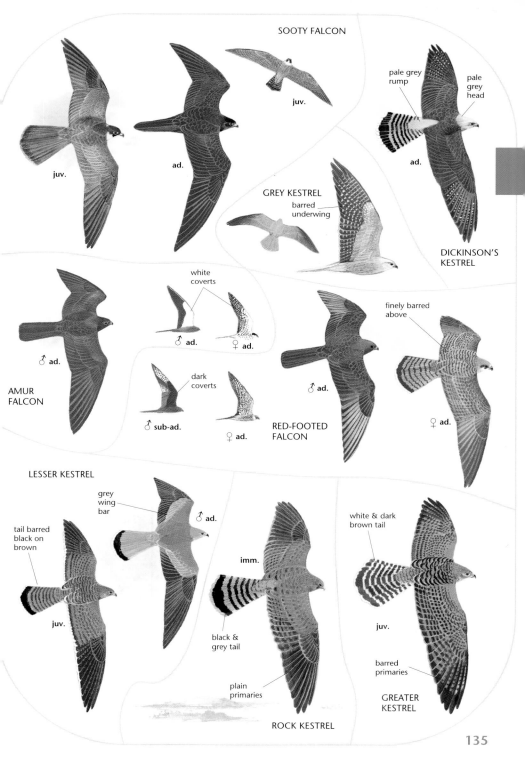

SOOTY FALCON

juv.

juv.

ad.

pale grey rump

pale grey head

ad.

DICKINSON'S KESTREL

GREY KESTREL

barred underwing

white coverts

♂ ad.

♀ ad.

dark coverts

♂ sub-ad.

♀ ad.

RED-FOOTED FALCON

♂ ad.

finely barred above

♂ ad.

♀ ad.

AMUR FALCON

LESSER KESTREL

grey wing bar

♂ ad.

tail barred black on brown

juv.

white & dark brown tail

imm.

black & grey tail

plain primaries

juv.

barred primaries

GREATER KESTREL

ROCK KESTREL

135

1. RED-BILLED FRANCOLIN *Pternistes adspersus* (194) 35-38 cm
The combination of the dull red bill and legs and the yellow eye-ring is diagnostic.
Female lacks the spurs of male. **Juv.** lacks the yellow around the eye. **Habitat.** Dry thorn-veld and open, broad-leaved woodland. In the dry northwest it is the common spurfowl of seasonal riverbeds and associated riverine vegetation. Feeds freely in the open and is less skulking than other francolins. **Status.** Locally common resident; near-endemic. **Call.** A loud, harsh 'chaa-chaa-chek-chek', uttered at dawn and dusk. (Rooibekfisant)

2. SWAINSON'S SPURFOWL (FRANCOLIN) *Pternistes swainsonii* (199) 38 cm
The combination of bare red face and throat, black bill and blackish brown legs differentiates this species from all other spurfowl and francolins in the region.
Female lacks the spurs of male. The red on face of **juv.** is less extensive and paler than in ad. **Habitat.** Dry thornveld and agricultural lands, usually in groups of three to five. **Status.** Common, near-endemic. **Call.** A raucous 'krraae-krraae-krraae', given by males at dawn and dusk. (Bosveldfisant)

3. RED-NECKED SPURFOWL (FRANCOLIN) *Pternistes afer* (198) 36 cm
Similar to Swainson's Spurfowl in having bare red skin on the throat and around the eyes, but this species has red (not black) legs and bill, and conspicuous white striping on the flanks. Different races vary in the amount of white on the face and underparts.
Juv. resembles ad. but is duller. **Habitat.** Evergreen and riverine forests, their edges and adjoining grassland. **Status.** Common resident. **Call.** A loud 'kwoor-kwoor-kwoor-kwaaa', given at dusk and dawn. (Rooikeelfisant)

4. CAPE FRANCOLIN *Pternistes capensis* (195) 42 cm
Can be distinguished from all other large, dark francolins and spurfowl by the pale cheeks that contrast with the dark cap (but co-occurs only with Red-necked Spurfowl). It has no red on the throat or around the eyes. Ad. has a greyish horn-coloured bill and diffuse white streaking on the lower belly.
Male has a spur, female has only a reduced spur. **Juv.** resembles ad. **Habitat.** The common francolin of fynbos; also regular on pastures and croplands. **Status.** Common resident; endemic. **Call.** A loud, screeching 'cackalac-cackalac-cackalac'. (Kaapse Fisant)

5. NATAL FRANCOLIN *Pternistes natalensis* (196) 35 cm
Similar to the larger Red-necked Spurfowl but lacks bare red skin around the eyes and on the throat. Generally brown above and barred and speckled black and white below.
Juv. resembles ad. but has less speckling below and is darker brown on the breast and back. **Habitat.** Wooded areas, especially bush thickets along rivers and on hill slopes. **Status.** Common resident; near-endemic. **Call.** A raucous, unmusical screeching. (Natalse Fisant)

1

♂ ad.

yellow
eye-ring

juv.

2

ad.

juv.

red
face

♂ ad.

brown
legs

castaneiventer
♂ ad.

notatus
♀ ad.

lehmanni
♀ ad.

swynnertoni
♂ ad.

red
legs

3

all races
streaked
black &
white
below

cunensis
♂ ad.

dark
cap

unpatterned
breast

orange
bill

no red
skin

scaly
breast

♂ ad.

5

♂ ad.

4

1. ORANGE RIVER FRANCOLIN *Scleroptila levaillantoides* (193)　　　35 cm
This species is slightly smaller than the very similar Red-winged Francolin: it differs in having a thin, dark necklace that never broadens to form a dark breast band. There are many races, which vary greatly in coloration. It is distinguished from Shelley's Francolin by the lack of black markings on the belly, and from Grey-winged Francolin by the white (not grey-freckled) throat.
Juv. resembles ad. **Habitat.** Open grassland to bush or shrub savanna. **Status.** Locally common resident; near-endemic. **Call.** A melodious, often-repeated 'kibitele', given mostly at dawn. (Kalaharipatrys)

2. GREY-WINGED FRANCOLIN *Scleroptila africanus* (190)　　　33 cm
A mainly grey francolin, easily identified by its throat, which is grey and freckled, not white or buff as in other grassland francolins.
Juv. is a duller version of ad. but still displays the throat character. **Habitat.** Upland grassland and fynbos. **Status.** Common resident; endemic. **Call.** A multi-syllabic, whistling call, starting with a series of 'pi' notes and ending with an explosive 'wip, ki-peeo'. (Bergpatrys)

3. RED-WINGED FRANCOLIN *Scleroptila levaillantii* (192)　　　36-38 cm
The black-flecked necklace on the breast is much broader than that of any other francolin. It forms a distinct breast band, which differentiates this species from Orange River Francolin. The rufous on the head is variable but at times is very rich and extensive.
Juv. is paler than ad. but still shows the dark breast band. **Habitat.** Grassland and fields in mountainous terrain, usually on lower slopes and in valleys. **Status.** Locally common resident. **Call.** A melodious, piping 'too-queequee', sometimes preceded by several short 'tok' notes. (Rooivlerkpatrys)

4. SHELLEY'S FRANCOLIN *Scleroptila shelleyi* (191)　　　28-31 cm
The chestnut-striped upper breast and flanks and the boldly marked black-and-white lower breast and belly are diagnostic. The throat is white, edged with black.
Juv. resembles ad. but the throat is streaked with brown. **Habitat.** Savanna, especially associated with rocky ground. **Status.** Locally common resident. **Call.** A rhythmic 'tili-tileeo', repeated many times at dawn and dusk. (Laeveldpatrys)

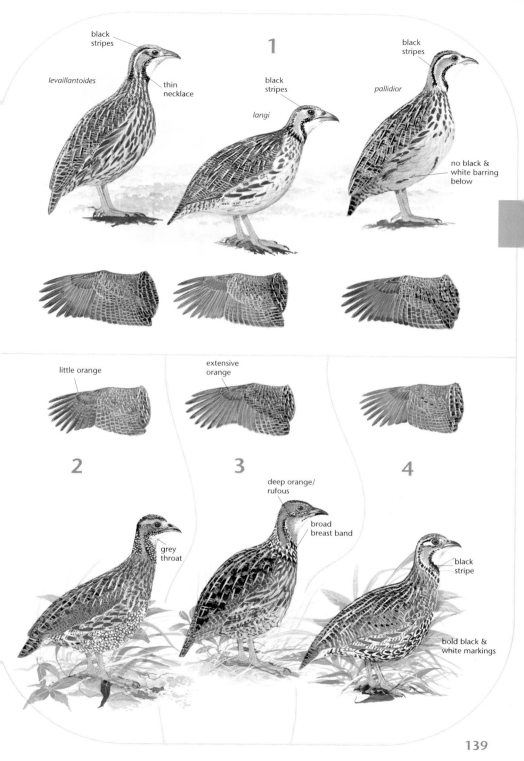

black stripes

levaillantoides

thin necklace

1

black stripes

langi

black stripes

pallidior

no black & white barring below

little orange

extensive orange

2

3

4

grey throat

deep orange/ rufous

broad breast band

black stripe

bold black & white markings

1. CHUKAR PARTRIDGE *Alectoris chukar* (187)   33 cm
Totally unlike any francolin or spurfowl in the region. The creamy white throat with its broad, black border and the barred chestnut, black and white flanks are diagnostic.
Juv. is a duller version of ad. **Habitat.** Dense thickets, open clearings and grassy areas. **Status.** Common, introduced resident on Robben Island, usually in small groups. **Call.** A distinctive 'chuk-chuk-chuk-chukar'. (Asiatiese Patrys)

2. CRESTED FRANCOLIN *Peliperdix sephaena* (189)   33-35 cm
The dark cap with the contrasting, broad, white eyebrow stripe and dark-striped chest are diagnostic in all races. The tail is frequently held cocked at a 45° angle, imparting a bantam-like appearance.
Female is less boldly marked than male. **Juv.** resembles female but is paler. **Habitat.** Woodland and savanna, especially in thornveld. **Status.** Common resident, usually in pairs or small groups. **Call.** A rattling 'chee-chakla, chee-chakla', given by birds calling in duet. (Bospatrys)

3. COQUI FRANCOLIN *Peliperdix coqui* (188)   21-26 cm
Male is the only francolin in the region to have a plain buffy head with a contrasting darker crown. The collar and underparts are barred black, white and buff. This species is smaller than all other francolins except Hartlaub's Francolin.
Female resembles Shelley's Francolin (p. 138) but is smaller, has a broad white eye-stripe that runs behind the eye and onto the neck, lacks the chestnut striping on the breast and flanks and has a rufous tail, barred black. **Juv.** resembles ad. of the respective sex. **Habitat.** Woodland, savanna and fringing open areas; favours sandy soils. **Status.** Common resident. **Call.** The common call is a disyllabic 'co-qui'; less frequently heard is 'kraak, kara-ka ka'. (Swempie)

4. HARTLAUB'S FRANCOLIN *Pternistes hartlaubi* (197)   26 cm
Male is easily identified by the dark cap, which contrasts with a distinct white eyebrow, also by the large decurved bill and the pale underparts, which are heavily streaked with brown.
Female is a dull orange-brown bird lacking distinguishing features other than the large bill. **Juv.** female is a drab version of ad. female, while juv. male shows a white eyebrow. **Habitat.** Boulder-strewn slopes and rocky outcrops in hilly and mountainous regions in arid areas. Often seen in small groups scurrying over rocks. **Status.** Uncommon, localised resident; near-endemic. **Call.** A 'wa-ak-ak-ak-ak' alarm call; a very distinct duet and rapidly repeated 'wiich ter wideo' is uttered at dawn. (Klipfisant)

1

piebald face

boldly barred flanks

dark cap

rovuma

♂ **ad.**

2

pale supercilium

♂ **ad.**

sephaena

juv.

cocked tail

3

dark crown, buff head

broad white eye-stripe

small size

small size

heavily barred below

♀

4

prominent eyebrow

long bill

♂

no distinctive head markings

♀

uniform patterning

heavily streaked below

1. COMMON PEACOCK (PEAFOWL) *Pavo cristatus* (924) m = 120 cm
Both male and female are unmistakable. The species is included here on the admission to the subregion list of a feral population on Robben Island, Western Cape. (Pou)

2. HELMETED GUINEAFOWL *Numida meleagris* (203) 58-64 cm
The dark grey body flecked with white, naked blue-and-red head and bare casque on the crown render this large gamebird unmistakable.
Male has a longer casque than female (casque size varies regionally). **Juv.** resembles ad. but has a less developed casque on the crown, and browner body coloration with the white flecking enlarged on the neck feathering. **Habitat.** Grassland, broad-leaved woodland, thornveld and agricultural land. **Status.** Common resident. May flock in hundreds. **Call.** A loud, repeated 'krrdii-krrdii-krrdii-krrdii' and a 'kek-kek-kek-kek' alarm note. (Gewone Tarentaal)

3. CRESTED GUINEAFOWL *Guttera edouardi* (204) 46-51 cm
A black guineafowl finely spotted with white, and with a tuft of curly black feathers on the crown. The naked face is blue-grey. The neck is all black. In flight, it shows a white stripe on the outer secondaries and inner primaries.
Juv. is mottled and barred above and below. **Habitat.** Montane, riparian, dune and coastal forests. **Status.** Uncommon and localised resident. **Call.** A 'chik-chik-chil-chrrrrr', given by males; a soft 'keet-keet-keet' contact call, uttered by groups foraging on the forest floor. (Kuifkoptarentaal)

4. COMMON OSTRICH *Struthio camelus* (1) h = 2 m
By far the largest bird of the region; flightless. Male is black with a grey neck, predominantly white wings and a pale chestnut tail. In female, the body feathering and tail are brown and the wings off-white.
Juv. resembles a small female; chick resembles a korhaan (pp. 158, 160) but has a flattened bill and thick legs. **Habitat.** Feral stock found on farms virtually throughout the region. **Status.** The only genuine wild ostriches occur in northern Namibia and the Kalahari. All others are descended from captive stock bred for the feather trade. **Call.** Nocturnal; a booming, leonine roar. (Volstruis)

1

♂

♀

not to scale

2

unfeathered casque

blue & red head

ad.

imm.

3

narrow white stripe

curly tuft

blue-grey face

ad.

imm.

all-black neck

4

♀

very large size

♂

chick

not to scale

143

1. BLUE QUAIL *Coturnix adansonii* (202)   12,5-13,5 cm
The smallest quail of the region, similar in size to the buttonquails.
Male is unmistakable, with its black-and-white face and throat pattern, lacking a white eyebrow stripe, rufous upperparts, and blue underparts that appear black in flight and contrast strongly with the rufous forewings. On the ground, female and **juv.** can be distinguished from other quails by their barred underparts. **Habitat.** Damp and flooded grassland in lightly wooded areas. **Status.** Rare resident; summer visitor to some areas. **Call.** Described as a high-pitched whistle, 'teee-ti-ti'. (Bloukwartel)

2. HARLEQUIN QUAIL *Coturnix delegorguei* (201)   14-15 cm
Male is much darker in appearance than Common Quail, and differs from Common and Blue Quails by its chestnut-and-black underparts.
Female and **juv.** are pale versions of male but are almost indistinguishable from Common Quail in flight. **Habitat.** Grassland, damp fields and open savanna. **Status.** Sporadic summer visitor, locally abundant in some years. **Call.** A high-pitched 'wit, wit-wit', similar to that of Common Quail but more metallic in tone; a squeaky 'kree-kree', given in flight. (Bontkwartel)

3. COMMON QUAIL *Coturnix coturnix* (200)   17-20 cm
A small, dumpy gamebird usually flushed into flight on rapidly whirring wings. On the ground, it runs swiftly, rodent-like, through the grass with its head hunched into its body
Male has a black or russet throat and lacks the chestnut and black underparts of male Harlequin Quail. Female and **juv.** are much paler below than female Harlequin Quail. **Habitat.** Grassland, fields and croplands. **Status.** Locally abundant summer visitor. **Call.** A high-pitched 'whit wit-wit', repeated at intervals, more mellow than that of Harlequin Quail; also a 'crwee-crwee', given in flight. (Afrikaanse Kwartel)

4. SMALL (KURRICHANE) BUTTONQUAIL *Turnix sylvaticus* (205)   14-15 cm
In flight, the lack of a dark rump and back distinguishes this species from Black-rumped Buttonquail. On the ground, the black flecks on the sides of the breast and flanks, the pale eye, and the absence of chestnut on the face are diagnostic.
Female is larger and more boldly marked than male. **Juv.** is similar to male. **Habitat.** Open grassland, old fields and open savanna. **Status.** Resident, with local movements. The most frequently encountered buttonquail throughout the region, except in the south and southwest. **Call.** A low-pitched hoot, 'hmmmmmm', repeated at intervals. (Bosveldkwarteltjie)

5. BLACK-RUMPED BUTTONQUAIL *Turnix nanus*   14-15,5 cm
This and Small Buttonquail, unless clearly seen, are difficult to distinguish. In flight, this species shows a diagnostic dark back and rump that contrast with the paler wings. At rest, the ginger face and throat and dark eye distinguish it from Small Buttonquail. Both species are noticeably smaller than the similar *Coturnix* quails, and appear to buzz through the air when put to flight.
Female resembles male but has less pronounced barring on breast and flanks. **Juv.** is spotted across the breast. **Habitat.** Edges of vleis and moist grassland in hilly and mountainous areas. **Status.** Rare resident and summer visitor. **Call.** A flufftail-like 'ooooop-oooooop'. (Swartrugkwarteltjie)

6. HOTTENTOT BUTTONQUAIL *Turnix hottentottus* (206)   14-16 cm
Confusion with both Black-rumped and Small Buttonquails unlikely because their ranges do not overlap. In flight the dark rump contrasts only slightly with pale buffy wing panels. The legs and feet are bright yellow.
Habitat. Coastal and mountain fynbos and damp grassy and short restio patches. **Status.** Locally common. **Call.** Not known to differ from Black-rumped Buttonquail. (Kaapse Kwarteltjie)

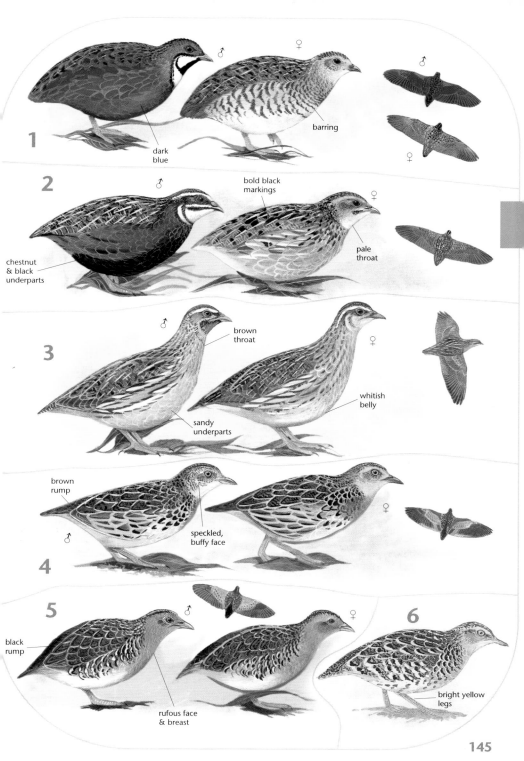

1

♂
dark
blue

♀
barring

2

♂
chestnut
& black
underparts

bold black
markings

♀
pale
throat

3

♂
brown
throat

♀
whitish
belly

sandy
underparts

4

brown
rump

♂
speckled,
buffy face

♀

5

black
rump

♂
rufous face
& breast

♀

6

bright yellow
legs

1. AFRICAN FINFOOT *Podica senegalensis* (229)   52-65 cm

When swimming, the head shape and submerged body suggest an African Darter (p. 56), but this species differs in having a much shorter, stouter neck and a red bill. Out of the water, the bright reddish orange feet and legs are conspicuous.

Male is greyer and darker headed than female and has a grey, not white, throat. **Juv.** resembles female but has a dark bill and has reduced barring below. **Habitat.** Densely vegetated rivers with overgrown banks. A shy, furtive species. **Status.** Uncommon resident. **Call.** Normally silent except for a short, frog-like 'krork'. (Watertrapper)

2. RED-KNOBBED COOT *Fulica cristata* (228)   41-46 cm

A black, duck-like bird with a white bill and white, unfeathered forehead. The two red knobs on the forehead swell and become more noticeable during the breeding season.

Juv. is dull grey-brown and differs from the smaller juv. Common Moorhen in lacking the white undertail coverts. **Habitat.** Dams, pans and lakes; virtually any stretch of fresh water except fast-flowing rivers. **Status.** Common to abundant resident. **Call.** A harsh, metallic 'claak'. (Bleshoender)

3. COMMON MOORHEN *Gallinula chloropus* (226)   30-36 cm

Unlike the glossy purple and green Allen's and American Purple Gallinules (p. 148), Common Moorhen is a dull, sooty black, and also differs in having greenish yellow legs and a red frontal shield. Bolder than Lesser Moorhen and the gallinules, it swims freely in patches of open water.

Juv. may be distinguished from juv. Lesser Moorhen by its larger size, dark bill and greyer colour. **Habitat.** Virtually any stretch of fresh water surrounded by reeds and tall grasses. **Status.** Common resident. **Call.** A sharp 'krrik'. (Grootwaterhoender)

4. LESSER MOORHEN *Gallinula angulata* (227)   23-27 cm

Similar to Common Moorhen but is smaller, with less conspicuous white flank feathers, and has a mainly yellow (not red) bill. Far more secretive than Common Moorhen and in flight is thinner and more elongate.

Juv. is sandy buff with a dull, yellowish green bill and legs. Juv. Common Moorhen is greyer and has a dark bill. **Habitat.** Flooded grassland and small, secluded ponds. Skulking, and usually heard rather than seen. **Status.** Locally common but erratic summer visitor. **Call.** A series of hollow notes, 'do do do do do do do'. (Kleinwaterhoender)

1

juv.

red legs & feet

short neck

♀

'flat' silhouette

♂

red bill

2

uniform upperparts

chick

white shield

ad.

imm.

3

ad.

red shield

red bill tipped yellow

juv.

dark bill

dusky below

ad.

4

mostly yellow bill

pale bill

ad.

juv.

imm.

buffy & whitish below

1. AFRICAN PURPLE SWAMPHEN (PURPLE GALLINULE)
Porphyrio madagascariensis (223)   38-46 cm
The large size, massive red bill and frontal shield, red legs and toes, general pur-
plish coloration and turquoise neck and breast, are unmistakable. Allen's Gallinule
is much smaller and daintier and has a green or blue (not red) frontal shield.
Juv. is dull brown above and grey below, and has a massive, dull, reddish brown bill.
Habitat. Reedbeds, sedge marshes and flooded grassland. **Status.** Common resident. **Call.**
A variety of harsh shrieks, wails and booming notes. (Grootkoningriethaan)

2. ALLEN'S (LESSER) GALLINULE *Porphyrio alleni* (224)   26-30 cm
Easily distinguished from African Purple Swamphen by its smaller size, dark colour,
and green or blue shield, and from American Purple Gallinule by its red (not yellow) legs and the lack of a yellow tip to the bill.
Male in breeding condition has a blue frontal shield; the female's is lime-green. Non-breeding
birds of both sexes have dull brown shields. **Juv.** is differentiated from juv. Common Moorhen
(p. 146) by its pale, fleshy coloured (not greenish brown) legs, and by lacking the white stripes
along the flanks. Very similar to juv. American Purple Gallinule but that species has olive (not
pale fleshy) legs. **Habitat.** Flooded grassland. **Status.** Locally common summer visitor. **Call.**
Six or more rapidly uttered, sharp clicks, 'duk duk duk duk duk duk'. (Kleinkoningriethaan)

3. AMERICAN PURPLE GALLINULE *Porphyrio martinicus* (225)   33 cm
Similar to African Purple Swamphen but smaller, and with bright yellowish green
(not red) legs and a yellow tip to its bill. The yellow legs and bill colour distinguish
ad. from Allen's Gallinule. The frontal shield is a pale chalky blue.
Juv. differs from juv. Common Moorhen (p. 146) by the lack of white stripes on the flanks,
and has olive (not green) legs. Juv. Allen's Gallinule is very similar but that species has more
scalloped upperparts and flesh-coloured legs. **Habitat.** Usually thick reedbeds but virtually
anywhere, some having been found walking along roads in an exhausted state. **Status.**
Vagrant, mostly Apr–July. **Call.** Silent in southern Africa. (Amerikaanse Koningriethaan)

4. BLACK CRAKE *Amaurornis flavirostris* (213)   18-20 cm
Ad. has jet-black coloration, a bright yellow bill, and red eyes and legs.
Sexes alike but male is slightly larger. **Juv.** is a grey version of ad. and has a black bill, pale
throat and dull red to black legs. **Habitat.** Marshes with a thick cover of reeds and other
aquatic vegetation. **Status.** Common resident. **Call.** A throaty 'chrrooo' and a rippling trill,
'weet-eet-eet-eet', uttered in duet. (Swartriethaan)

5. AFRICAN JACANA *Actophilornis africanus* (240)   28-31 cm
Unmistakable. A rufous bird with a white neck and yellow upper breast, and a contrasting black-and-white head that highlights the blue frontal shield. The extremely
long toes and nails, which enable it to walk over floating vegetation, are diagnostic.
Sexes alike but female is larger. **Juv.** is paler than ad., lacks the frontal shield and has a
white belly. Might be confused with Lesser Jacana, but is very much larger, lacks the white
trailing edge to the secondaries, and has dark upperwing coverts. **Habitat.** Wetlands with
floating vegetation, especially water lilies. **Status.** Locally common resident. **Call.** Noisy; a
sharp, ringing 'krrrek', rasping 'krrrrrrk' and barking 'yowk-yowk'. (Grootlangtoon)

6. LESSER JACANA *Microparra capensis* (241)   15-16,5 cm
Much smaller than African Jacana, it has a white belly, breast and throat; otherwise is pale brown. Resembles juv. African Jacana but is very much smaller and in
flight shows white on the trailing edges of the secondaries. Black flight feathers
contrast with the pale upperwing coverts.
Juv. lacks the rusty coloration of ad. **Habitat.** River flood plains, and lagoons and bays in
wetlands with emergent grass and sedge. **Status.** Uncommon resident with local movements. **Call.** A soft, flufftail-like 'poop-oop-oop-oop'; a scolding 'ksh-ksh-ksh'; and a high-
pitched 'tititititititi'. (Dwerglangtoon)

1

red bill & shield

sub-ad.

ad.

ad.

imm.

juv.

2

red bill, blue shield

scaled upperparts

juv.

juv.

ad.

br. ad.

red legs

flesh-coloured legs

3

red & yellow bill, pale blue shield

juv.

juv.

ad.

yellow bill

ad.

imm.

yellow legs

olive legs

red legs

ad.

4

5

chestnut body

black hindneck

blue bill & shield

ad.

pale upperwing coverts

6

grey bill

ad.

white neck

white trailing edge

ad.

ad.

juv.

juv.

149

1. AFRICAN RAIL *Rallus caerulescens* (210)   28-30 cm

A distinctive species with a long, slightly decurved, dull red bill and legs, a white chin, blue-grey foreneck and breast, black-and-white barred flanks and undertail, and dull chestnut upperparts. More frequently seen than other rails and crakes, it readily ventures out into the open, especially in the early morning.

Sexes alike but male is longer billed. **Juv.** has a brown bill and a buff throat and breast. **Habitat.** Marshes, thick reedbeds and flooded grassland. **Status.** Common resident. **Call.** A high-pitched, trilling whistle, 'trrreee-tee-tee-tee-tee-tee'. (Grootriethaan)

2. CORN CRAKE *Crex crex* (211)   25-30 cm

Much paler and more sandy coloured than the smaller African Crake. Rarely seen except when flushed, when it flies away on whirring wings, legs dangling, showing its diagnostic, conspicuous, chestnut-orange wing coverts.

Juv. resembles ad. **Habitat.** Rank grassland, lightly wooded, grassy areas, and vlei margins. **Status.** Uncommon summer visitor. **Call.** Silent in the region. (Kwartelkoning)

3. SPOTTED CRAKE *Porzana porzana* (214)   21-24 cm

Most likely to be confused with African Crake but has a predominantly yellow bill, and obvious white spots and stripes on the upperparts. When flushed, it shows a distinctive white leading edge to the wing, and the diagnostic greenish legs and barring on the flanks (less bold than in African Crake) can be seen. When on the ground, the bird flicks its tail, showing the buffy undertail coverts.

Juv. resembles ad. **Habitat.** Flooded grassland. **Status.** Rare summer visitor. A secretive species, easily overlooked. **Call.** Silent in the region. (Gevlekte Riethaan)

4. AFRICAN CRAKE *Crecopsis egregia* (212)   19-23 cm

Distinguished from African Rail by its short, stubby bill, and from Spotted Crake by its unmarked breast and neck and more boldly barred flanks and belly. When flushed the bird flies a short distance, legs dangling, showing clearly the brown, mottled upperparts and black-and-white barred flanks.

Juv. resembles ad. and, although browner in appearance, still shows the black-and-white barred flanks. **Habitat.** Damp grassland and vleis. Has adapted to sugar-cane plantations bordering rivers and dams. **Status.** Uncommon to locally common summer visitor. **Call.** A monotonous, hollow-sounding series of notes, 'krrr-krrr-krrr'. (Afrikaanse Riethaan)

5. STRIPED CRAKE *Aenigmatolimnas marginalis* (216)   20-22 cm

The rich brown upperparts with long white stripes on the back and wings are obvious characters in male. The undertail and flanks are russet; the flanks are not barred.

Female differs markedly from male in having a blue-grey breast and belly, but still shows the rich russet flanks and undertail. **Juv.** resembles male. **Habitat.** Seasonally flooded grassland and marshes. **Status.** An erratic and localised summer visitor. **Call.** A rapid 'tik-tik-tik-tik-tik...' which may continue for a minute or more. (Gestreepte Riethaan)

6. BAILLON'S CRAKE *Porzana pusilla* (215)   16-18 cm

The smallest crake in the region, similar to a flufftail in size. Resembling a diminutive African Crake, it differs in having warm brown upperparts flecked and spotted with black and white, and less contrasting black-and-white barring on the flanks and undertail.

Juv. resembles ad. but is paler, and is mottled and barred with white below. **Habitat.** Vlei margins, thick reedbeds, flooded grassland and flooded broad-leaved woodland with tall grass. Rarely seen in the open except at dawn or dusk. **Status.** Uncommon to locally common resident with local movements. **Call.** A soft 'qurrr-qurrr' and various frog-like croaks. (Kleinriethaan)

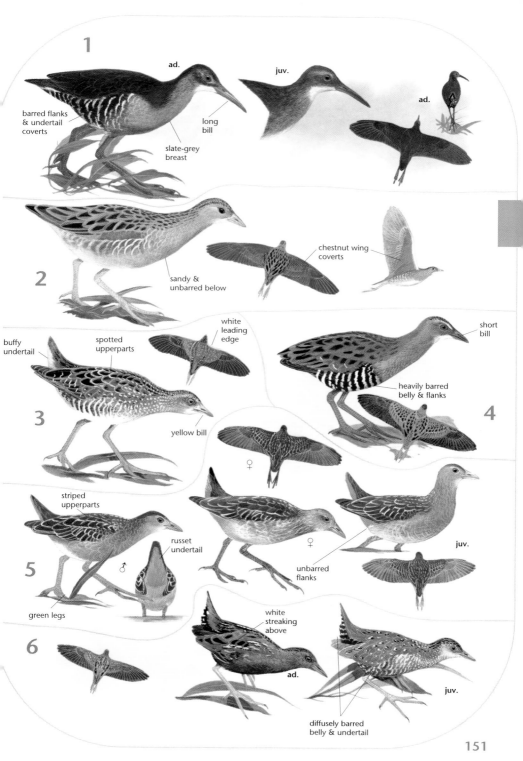

1

ad.

barred flanks
& undertail
coverts

long
bill

slate-grey
breast

juv.

ad.

2

sandy &
unbarred below

chestnut wing
coverts

3

buffy
undertail

spotted
upperparts

white
leading
edge

yellow bill

4

short
bill

heavily barred
belly & flanks

♀

5

striped
upperparts

russet
undertail

♂

green legs

♀

unbarred
flanks

juv.

6

white
streaking
above

ad.

diffusely barred
belly & undertail

juv.

1. RED-CHESTED FLUFFTAIL *Sarothrura rufa* (217)   15-17 cm
Male is the only flufftail in the region in which the rufous head colour extends to the lower breast. In flight it is distinguished from Striped Flufftail by its black (not red) tail.
Female is distinguished from female Striped Flufftail by appearing much blacker and larger, with a floppier, less deliberate flight and a dark brown, not russet, tail. Darker than female Streaky-breasted Flufftail, especially below. **Juv.** resembles female. **Habitat.** Thick stands of reeds and tall water grasses, marshes and small vleis. **Status.** Common resident. **Call.** A low hoot, 'woop', repeated at intervals of about one second; a more rapid 'gu-duk, gu-duk, gu-duk'; and a ringing 'tuwi-tuwi-tuwi'. (Rooiborsvleikuiken)

2. STRIPED FLUFFTAIL *Sarothrura affinis* (221)   14-15 cm
On the ground, the plain chestnut tail is diagnostic and distinguishes it from male White-winged Flufftail, which has a barred chestnut-and-black tail.
Female differs from female Red-chested Flufftail in being smaller and much swifter on the wing, and by having the plain tail suffused with chestnut. **Juv.** resembles female. **Habitat.** Upland grassland and fynbos in mountainous regions; often in damp areas and sometimes associated with vleis. **Status.** Locally common resident. **Call.** A low, long hoot, 'oooooop', lasting about a second and repeated at two-second intervals. (Gestreepte Vleikuiken)

3. STREAKY-BREASTED FLUFFTAIL *Sarothrura boehmi* (219)   16-17 cm
In male, the chestnut head and neck contrasting with the very pale throat, along with the all-dark tail, are diagnostic. Most likely to be confused with Red-chested Flufftail, but when flushed it appears much paler and it can be seen that the paler chestnut on the head does not extend onto the lower breast.
Female and juv. are much paler below than female Red-chested Flufftail. **Habitat.** Seasonally flooded grassland. A rarely seen species; usually detected by its call. **Status.** Uncommon and localised summer visitor to Zimbabwe; vagrant elsewhere. **Call.** Low hoot, 'gawooo', repeated at half-second intervals 20–30 times. (Streepborsvleikuiken)

4. WHITE-WINGED FLUFFTAIL *Sarothrura ayresi* (222)   14 cm
When flushed, both sexes show diagnostic, square, white panels on the secondaries. The flight is very fast and direct, with whirring wing beats, ending with a plunge into the vegetation. On the ground, a thin white line is noticeable on the outer web of the first primary. Distinguished from Striped Flufftail by this white line, tail barred black-and-chestnut (not plain chestnut), whitish belly and chestnut upper breast .
Female and **juv.** distinguished from all other female and juv. flufftails by the white wing panel. **Habitat.** Upland marshes and vleis, where sedges and aquatic grasses grow in shallow water. **Status.** Rare, erratic and localised in occurrence. **Call.** A low, deep hoot, repeated in duet. (Witvlerkvleikuiken)

5. BUFF-SPOTTED FLUFFTAIL *Sarothrura elegans* (218)   16-17 cm
In male, the dark body has more pale speckling than that of other flufftails and the chestnut extends only to the mid-breast, not onto the lower breast and back as in Red-chested Flufftail.
Male, if seen on the forest floor, gives the impression of a small, plump, chestnut-headed bird, heavily spotted with golden buff. **Juv.** and female are buff breasted, barred brown, and earth brown above. **Habitat.** Evergreen forests, coastal scrub, and well-wooded gardens. **Status.** Common resident. **Call.** A long, low, foghorn-like 'dooooooo', given mainly at night and on overcast days. (Gevlekte Vleikuiken)

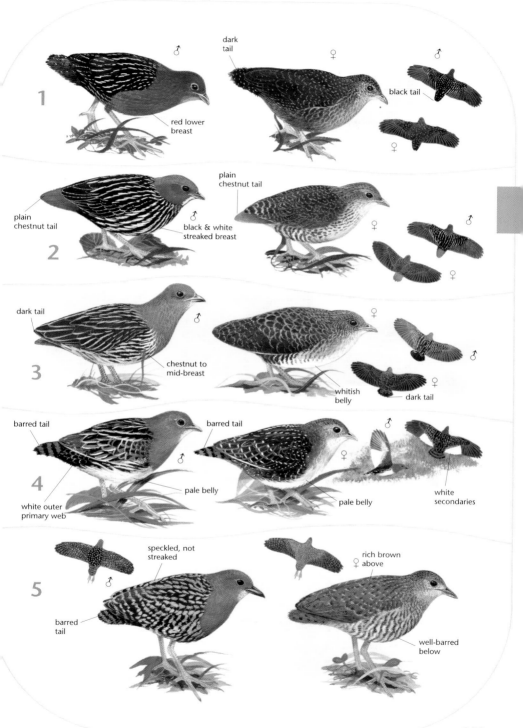

1 ♂ red lower breast — ♀ dark tail — ♂ black tail — ♀

2 plain chestnut tail — ♂ black & white streaked breast — plain chestnut tail — ♀ — ♂ — ♀

3 dark tail — ♂ chestnut to mid-breast — ♀ — whitish belly — ♂ — ♀ dark tail

4 barred tail — ♂ — barred tail — ♀ — white outer primary web — pale belly — pale belly — white secondaries

5 ♂ speckled, not streaked — barred tail — rich brown ♀ above — well-barred below

1. GREY (SOUTHERN) CROWNED CRANE *Balearica regulorum* (209)   105-112 cm
Unlikely to be confused with any other species. In flight, the white upper- and underwing coverts are diagnostic. During the non-breeding season it may be found in mixed flocks with Blue Cranes.
Juv. lacks the large, white, unfeathered face patch, and the bristly crown is less well developed. **Habitat.** Marshes, dams and adjoining grassland; agricultural lands. **Status.** Common but localised resident. **Call.** A trumpeting flight call, 'may hem', and a deep 'huum huum', given when breeding. (Mahem)

2. WATTLED CRANE *Grus carunculatus* (207)   120 cm
This enormous crane with its long, white, feathered wattles is unmistakable. Even at a great distance, it can easily be identified by its dark face and crown, and by the white head and neck contrasting with the black underparts.
Juv. has a white (not grey) crown until a year old. **Habitat.** Upland vleis and marshes and adjoining grassland in the south of its range, extensive wetlands (Okavango, Zambezi Delta) in more tropical regions. Usually found in pairs or small groups, but non-breeding birds sometimes gather in flocks of 50 or more. **Status.** Rare and patchily distributed resident; endangered. **Call.** Seldom calls; a loud 'kwaarnk'. (Lelkraanvoël)

3. BLUE CRANE *Anthropoides paradiseus* (208)   100 cm
The large head, long, slender neck and elongated, trailing tertials are diagnostic of this species.
Juv. lacks the long inner tertials and is paler grey, especially on the head, which is almost white. **Habitat.** Vleis, grassland, Karoo scrub and agricultural lands. Found in small groups or in pairs, but non-breeding birds gather in large flocks that sometimes contain several hundred birds. **Status.** Common resident; endemic. **Call.** A loud, nasal 'kraaaank'. (Bloukraanvoël)

4. SECRETARYBIRD *Sagittarius serpentarius* (118)   140 cm
This bird's peculiar shape and long legs render it likely to be confused only with a crane at a distance. Very crane-like in flight; the two elongated central tail feathers project well beyond the remainder of the tail and the legs, producing an unmistakable flight shape. The black leggings are conspicuous.
Juv. resembles ad. but has a shorter tail and yellow (not red), bare facial skin. **Habitat.** Savanna and open grassland from coastal regions to high altitudes. Avoids thick bush and forests. **Status.** Uncommon to locally common resident, now absent from many settled areas. **Call.** Normally silent but during aerial display utters a deep croak. (Sekretarisvoël)

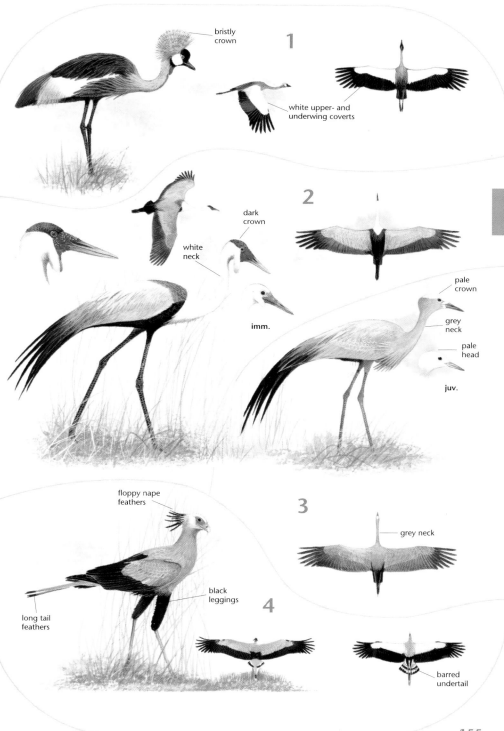

1

bristly crown

white upper- and underwing coverts

2

dark crown

white neck

imm.

pale crown

grey neck

pale head

juv.

floppy nape feathers

3

grey neck

black leggings

4

long tail feathers

barred undertail

1. KORI BUSTARD *Ardeotis kori* (230)　　　　　　　105-135 cm

The largest bustard of the region. The size, dark crest and lack of any rufous on the hind neck and upper mantle are diagnostic. In flight, it may be distinguished from Denham's and Ludwig's Bustards by its uniformly speckled, grey upperwing, which lacks conspicuous white markings.

Displaying **male** balloons out the breast feathers. Female resembles male but is noticeably smaller. **Juv.** resembles female. **Habitat.** Dry thornveld, grassland and semi-desert, usually near the cover of trees. **Status.** Resident but with nomadic local movements. Numbers much reduced by habitat destruction and now uncommon in many regions outside major game reserves. **Call.** A deep, resonant 'oom-oom-oom', given by male during the breeding season. (Gompou)

2. DENHAM'S (STANLEY'S) BUSTARD *Neotis denhami* (231)　　　　84-116 cm

The pale crown stripe, throat and pale grey foreneck are diagnostic in the male. The similar Ludwig's Bustard has a dark throat and foreneck, and has less white in the wing.

Male is considerably larger than female, with a darker, plainer back. Displaying male inflates the throat and forms a conspicuous balloon of white feathers. **Juv.** and female have less white in the wings and have brown speckling on the neck. **Habitat.** Recently burnt fynbos, open grassland and agricultural land. **Status.** Uncommon resident at the coast; inland populations tend to move to lower altitudes during winter. **Call.** Largely silent. (Veldpou)

3. LUDWIG'S BUSTARD *Neotis ludwigii* (232)　　　　　　85-100 cm

This species is most likely to be confused with Denham's Bustard but differs in having a dark brown throat and foreneck, lacking a pale central crown stripe and normally showing far less white in the wings. The amount of white on the wings of both Denham's and Ludwig's Bustards is variable.

Br. male has a similar display to Denham's Bustard, but the balloon is grey (not white). Female is noticeably smaller than male and is paler on the foreneck. **Juv.** is paler on the head and neck than ad. **Habitat.** Karoo scrub and arid savannas; frequents drier areas than Denham's Bustard but their ranges overlap in the Eastern Cape. **Status.** Nomadic near-endemic, uncommon to locally common. **Call.** In display, male gives an explosive, far-carrying 'woodoomp', repeated every 15–30 seconds. (Ludwigse Pou)

1

dark crest

barred grey neck

display

largely grey upperwing

2

striped crown ♂

♀

♀ nape

pale grey foreneck

dark crown

♂ nape

dark brown foreneck

♀

3

upperwing

♂

♀

white carpals

upperwing

1. RÜPPELL'S KORHAAN *Eupodotis rueppellii* (236) 58 cm

This species could be confused only with Karoo Korhaan, from which it differs by the much paler coloration on the back, by the conspicuous black line which runs down the centre of the foreneck and onto the breast, and by the contrasting black-and-white facial markings. Ranges of the two species overlap marginally in southern Namibia.

Male is more boldly marked than female on the head and throat. Female has dark markings on upperparts, reduced black-and-white patterning on the hindneck and a pale, not dark, eye. **Juv.** resembles female. **Habitat.** Gravel plains and scrub desert of Namibia. **Status.** Common resident; near-endemic. Usually encountered in small groups. **Call.** Similar to that of Karoo Korhaan but slightly higher pitched. (Woestynkorhaan)

2. KAROO KORHAAN *Eupodotis vigorsii* (235) 58 cm

The plumage is variable but is generally greyish brown on the back, with a greyer head and neck and a black throat patch. It is similar to Rüppell's Korhaan but is darker on the back and lacks the black line down the centre of the foreneck from the throat to the breast and the contrasting black-and-white facial markings.

Female has a less well-developed throat patch and more mottled wing coverts. **Juv.** resembles female. **Habitat.** Desert and semi-desert of the Karoo, and wheatfields and pastures in the southern Cape. **Status.** Common resident; endemic. Usually found in groups of two or three. **Call.** A deep, rhythmical, frog-like, two- or three-syllabled 'kraak-rak' or 'crrok-rak-rak', with the accent on the deeper first syllable, given repeatedly at dawn and dusk. Pairs call in duet. (Vaalkorhaan)

3. BLUE KORHAAN *Eupodotis caerulescens* (234) 56 cm

The blue underparts of this species are diagnostic; it is the only korhaan to show blue in the wings in flight.

Male has extensive white ear coverts. Female has brown ear coverts and a pale supercilium. **Juv.** has blackish ear coverts. **Habitat.** Open, short grassland, extending marginally into the semi-desert eastern Karoo. **Status.** Locally common resident; endemic. Usually located early in the morning when males call. Very wary, running off at close approach before finally taking flight, calling loudly. **Call.** A deep, discordant 'krok-kaa-krow', given repeatedly at dawn and dusk. (Bloukorhaan)

4. BARROW'S (SOUTHERN WHITEBELLIED) KORHAAN
Eupodotis barrowii (233) 52-61 cm

In male, the combination of the blue foreneck and white belly is diagnostic.

Female and **juv.** have brown necks and resemble female Black-bellied Bustard (p. 160), as both species have white underparts, but Barrow's Korhaan has a shorter neck and legs, and lacks the black underwing coverts of Black-bellied Bustard. **Habitat.** Open grassland or lightly wooded savanna; requires taller grass than most other korhaans. **Status.** Uncommon resident; endemic. **Call.** A rhythmic, crowing 'takwarat', given repeatedly at dawn and dusk. (Witpenskorhaan)

1

pale coverts

upperwing

contrasting face

♂

sandy back

♀

thin black stripe

black foreneck stripe

♂

2

plain face

black throat

♀

plain foreneck

grey-brown back

ad.

dark coverts

upperwing

♂

blue breast & belly

3

upperwing

black chin

♀

upperwing

blue in wings

4

upperwing

white throat

♀

buffy primary patch

♂

blue-grey foreneck & breast

pale underwing coverts

white belly

♂

fairly short legs

1. BLACK-BELLIED BUSTARD (KORHAAN) *Eupodotis melanogaster* (238)   58-63 cm
The long, thin neck and legs are diagnostic. The back of both sexes is spotted and barred. Male has a dusky throat with a black line extending down the centre of the foreneck to join the black breast and belly; the underwings are predominantly black.
Male, in its slow display flight, shows the striking and diagnostic large, white patches in the primaries, visible from above and below. There is extensive white in the upperwing coverts, but underwing coverts are wholly black. Female is plainer, with a brown head and neck, and white underparts. Female can be distinguished from other bustards and korhaans in flight by its combination of white underparts and black underwing coverts. **Juv.** resembles female. **Habitat.** Woodland and tall open grassland. **Status.** Uncommon and easily overlooked resident. **Call.** A short, sharp 'chikk', followed by a 'pop'. (Langbeenkorhaan)

2. RED-CRESTED KORHAAN *Eupodotis ruficrista* (237)   50 cm
The red crest is rarely visible except on displaying male, when the elongated, rufous feathers are erected to form a crest resembling that of Grey Crowned Crane (p. 154). Both sexes have a black belly.
Male, in courtship display, flies straight up, then suddenly tumbles and plummets towards the ground before gliding off and settling. Female has a mottled brown crown and neck. It is readily distinguished from female Northern Black Korhaan by the chevron-shaped markings (not barring) on the back. **Juv.** resembles female. **Habitat.** Dry woodland and semi-desert Kalahari grassland and thornveld. **Status.** Common resident. **Call.** Male's protracted call is a characteristic sound of the bushveld in summer. It starts with a series of clicks, 'tic-tic-tic', which builds into an extended series of loud, piping whistles, 'pi-pi-pi ... pipity-pipity'. (Boskorhaan)

3. NORTHERN BLACK KORHAAN *Eupodotis afraoides* (239b)   52 cm
This species differs from Southern Black Korhaan in showing conspicuous white flashes in the primaries in flight. Illustrated race, *etoshae*, is more boldly barred above than other races. Confusion with Southern Black Korhaan is unlikely as their ranges do not overlap.
Female resembles female Southern Black Korhaan but is easily distinguished in flight by the extensive white in the primaries. It may be distinguished from female Red-crested Korhaan by the barring (not chevron-shaped markings) on the upperparts. **Juv.** resembles female. **Habitat.** Open grassland and scrub. **Status.** Common resident; near-endemic. **Call.** Similar to that of Southern Black Korhaan. (Witvlerkkorhaan)

4. SOUTHERN BLACK KORHAAN *Eupodotis afra* (239a)   52 cm
At rest almost indistinguishable from Northern Black Korhaan: easily identified in flight, however, by the lack of extensive white in the primaries. Ranges of the two species do not overlap.
Male, in display flight, dangles the legs as the bird 'parachutes' slowly to the ground, continually giving its harsh call. Female resembles female Northern Black Korhaan but lacks the extensive white patch in the primaries. **Juv.** resembles female. **Habitat.** Coastal and strandveld fynbos. **Status.** Common resident; endemic. **Call.** Male gives a raucous and repeated 'kerrrak-kerrrak-kerrrak', both in flight and on the ground. (Swartvlerkkorhaan)

1

upperwing ♂

extensive white in upper wing

♀

long, plain neck

white below

long legs

mostly black underwings

♂

♂

white cheek

black foreneck stripe

black below

♂

2

♂

♂

upperwing

♀

chevrons on back

♂

♂ display

3

mostly white primaries

barred back

♀

all-black neck

♀

♂

wing all-black below

♀

barred back

all-black neck

♂

4

♀

extensive white in primaries

upperwing ♂

♂ upperwing

all-black flight feathers

161

1. CRAB PLOVER *Dromas ardeola* (296) 38-41 cm
A large, predominantly white wader with extensive black patches on its back and upperwings. The black, dagger-shaped bill is proportionally very heavy and thick for a bird of this size. The long, greyish legs extend well beyond the tail in flight.
Juv. and imm. are greyer than ad. on the upperwings and tail; they have a grey back and streaking on the crown and hindneck. Birds with brown suffusion on the upperparts are juvs. **Habitat.** Coastal areas and estuaries, especially muddy mangrove stands that are rich in crabs. **Status.** Non-breeding summer visitor; regular only in Mozambique from Maputo northwards, uncommon and erratic in KwaZulu-Natal, several records from the Eastern Cape. **Call.** A variety of metallic calls while foraging: 'kwa-daaa-dak', 'kwa-da-dak' or 'grr-kwo-kwo-kwo-kwo'. Flight call a two-noted 'kwa-da'. (Krapvreter)

2. AFRICAN BLACK OYSTERCATCHER *Haematopus moquini* (244) 44 cm
Easily identified, this large, all-black wader has a bright orange bill and eye-ring and dull pink legs. Some ads. have small white patches on the underparts.
Juv. is duller, appearing faintly buff-scaled, with a duller orange bill tipped with brown. The legs are grey or greyish pink. **Habitat.** Strictly coastal; may be encountered along any shoreline, estuary or lagoon from northern Namibia to southern KwaZulu-Natal. Usually in pairs or small flocks. **Status.** Common on rocky islands and adjacent mainland; vagrant to central coast of KwaZulu-Natal and Mozambique (Inhaca Island). Endemic. **Call.** A 'klee-kleeep', similar to that of Eurasian Oystercatcher, and a fast 'peeka-peeka-peeka' alarm call. Display calls more complex, including rapid trilling. (Swarttobie)

3. EURASIAN (EUROPEAN) OYSTERCATCHER
Haematopus ostralegus (243) 40-43 cm
Smaller and more slender than African Black Oystercatcher, this large, pied wader has white underparts and a bold, white wing bar. The bill is orange and the legs are pink. The broad, white wing bar, white rump and base of the tail are visible in flight.
Juv. and most non-breeding ads have a white throat crescent. The bill and legs are duller than those of ad., and the black feathering is tinged with brown. **Habitat.** Open coast, estuaries and coastal lagoons. **Status.** Rare, chiefly summer visitor to all coasts. **Call.** A sharp, high-pitched 'klee-kleep'. (Bonttobie)

4. BLACK-WINGED STILT *Himantopus himantopus* (295) 38 cm
A large, black-and-white wader with very long, red legs and a thin, pointed, black bill. In flight, the black underwings contrast with the white underparts, and the long red legs trail conspicuously.
Sexes alike except that female is duller on the wings. The head and neck markings are variable in both sexes, from pure white to predominantly dusky. Juv. and imm. have some grey on the nape, dull wings and greyish pink legs. **Habitat.** Estuaries, marshes, vleis, saltpans and flooded ground. **Status.** Common resident and local nomad. **Call.** A harsh, short 'kik-kik', especially when alarmed. Very vocal in defence of nest and young. (Rooipootelsie)

5. PIED AVOCET *Recurvirostra avosetta* (294) 43 cm
An unmistakable black-and-white wading bird with a long, very thin, upturned bill and a black cap and hindneck. In flight, the pied pattern is striking, with three black patches on each upperwing. The underwing is black only at the tip. The long, bluish grey legs extend beyond the tail in flight.
Juv. has the black replaced by mottled brown. **Habitat.** Lakes, estuaries, vleis, saltpans and temporary pools, both coastal and inland. Feeds in water, using a sweeping, side-to-side bill movement or by upending, duck-style, in deeper water. Usually in small flocks. **Status.** Common and widespread resident and local nomad. **Call.** A clear 'kooit'; also a 'kik-kik' alarm call. (Bontelsie)

See also page 192

1

thick bill

ad.

imm.

2

ad.

dark tip

imm.

3

ad. non-br.

very thin bill

4

ad.

imm.

juv.

extremely long legs

black cap & hindneck

juv.

bill strongly upcurved

ad.

5

1. COMMON RINGED PLOVER *Charadrius hiaticula* (245) 18-20 cm

A small, short-legged, dark plover with a white collar above a blackish brown breast band that is often incomplete in non-breeding plumage. This species may be distinguished from Greater and Lesser Sand Plovers (p. 166) by the combination of the collar, the smaller size, the slighter bill, which is usually orange at the base, and the orange-yellow legs. In flight, the narrow, white wing bar and collar are conspicuous.

Juv. has duller plumage overall; the breast band is incomplete. **Habitat.** Coastal and inland wetlands, preferring patches of soft, fine mud. **Status.** Common summer visitor; some overwinter. **Call.** A fluty 'tooi'. (Ringnekstrandkiewiet)

2. LITTLE RINGED PLOVER *Charadrius dubius* 15-17 cm

Smaller than Common Ringed Plover, with a conspicuous yellow eye-ring, pinkish grey (not orange) legs and no obvious white wing bar.

Juv differs from other small plovers by its uniform upperwings. Habitat. Usually close to fresh water, favouring shores of lakes and rivers; occasionally on the coast. Status. Palearctic vagrant with one record from Zimbabwe. **Call.** Descending 'pee-oo'. (Kleinringnekstrandkiewiet)

3. THREE-BANDED PLOVER *Charadrius tricollaris* (249) 18 cm

The black double breast band, grey cheeks and conspicuous red eye-ring and base to the bill are distinctive. In flight, the tail shows white outer tips and edges; it has a very narrow, white wing bar. The rump and tail appear elongate in flight, resembling Common Ringed Plover.

Juv. is a duller version of ad. but lacks the red eye-ring. **Habitat.** On most water bodies with sandy or pebbly margins. Rare on the open coast. **Status.** Widespread and common resident. **Call.** A penetrating, high-pitched 'weee-weet' whistle. (Driebandstrandkiewiet)

4. KITTLITZ'S PLOVER *Charadrius pecuarius* (248) 14-15 cm

The black forehead line that extends behind the eye to the nape is distinctive when this species is breeding. The breast is variably creamy buff to chestnut, and there is a dark shoulder patch. The head is less well marked in non-breeding plumage, with the pale buffy ring around the crown extending to the nape. There is a dark eye patch at all times.

Juv. may be distinguished from juv. White-fronted Plover (p. 166) by the broad, buffy eyebrow stripe extending onto the buffy (not white) nape. **Habitat.** Found throughout in dried muddy or short grassy areas near water; also on mudflats in estuaries and coastal lagoons. **Status.** Common resident and local nomad. **Call.** A short, clipped trill, 'kittip'. (Geelborsstrandkiewiet)

5. CASPIAN PLOVER *Charadrius asiaticus* (252) 18-22 cm

In breeding plumage this species differs from Greater and Lesser sand plovers (p. 166) in having a black lower border to the chestnut breast band and an obvious pale eyebrow stripe, and in lacking an extensive dark eye patch. In all other plumages, it has a complete (or virtually complete) grey-brown wash across the breast, and a broad, buffy eyebrow stripe. The bill is thin. In flight, it lacks distinct white areas on the upperparts, but the pale bases to the inner primaries are usually visible. It may be distinguished from non-breeding American and Pacific Golden Plovers (p. 174) by the uniform upperwings and smaller size.

Male is brighter than female in breeding dress. **Juv.** is similar to non-breeding ad. but buffy tips to the mantle feathers give it a scaled appearance. **Habitat.** Sparsely grassed areas and wetland fringes. **Status.** Uncommon summer visitor; patchily distributed, mainly in the north. Usually in flocks. **Call.** A clear, whistled 'tooeet'. (Asiatiese Strandkiewiet)

See also page 193

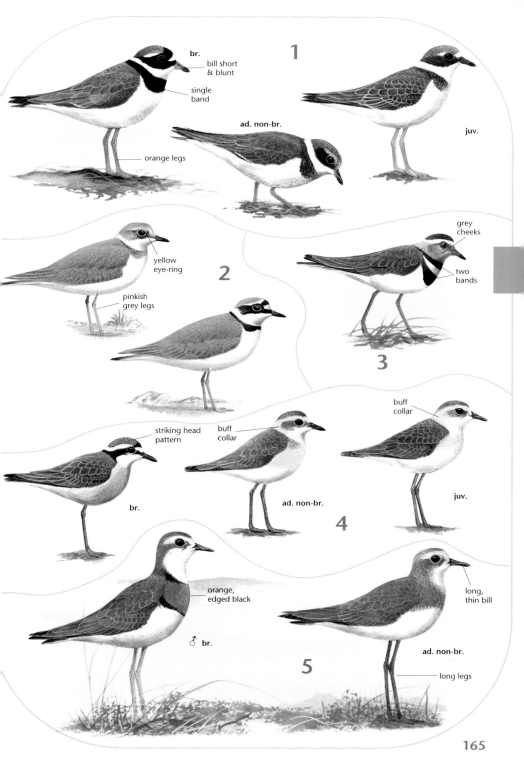

1

br.

bill short
& blunt

single
band

orange legs

ad. non-br.

juv.

2

yellow
eye-ring

pinkish
grey legs

3

grey
cheeks

two
bands

striking head
pattern

buff
collar

buff
collar

br.

ad. non-br.

juv.

4

orange,
edged black

♂ br.

5

long,
thin bill

ad. non-br.

long legs

1. CHESTNUT-BANDED PLOVER *Charadrius pallidus* (247)   15 cm
The smallest, palest plover of the region. Ad. has a thin, chestnut breast band that extends onto the crown in male.
Male has neat black markings on the forehead and lores. It is distinguished from larger White-fronted Plover by the breast band and the lack of a white hindneck collar. **Female** has grey in place of the neat markings on the forehead and lores and has a paler breast band. **Juv.** lacks the black-and-chestnut coloration; the breast band is pale grey and usually incomplete. **Habitat.** Predominantly salt pans in summer, some moving to estuaries and coastal wetlands in winter. **Status.** Generally an uncommon, localised resident and partial migrant, but several thousand present at Walvis Bay and Sandwich Harbour in winter. **Call.** A single 'prrp' or 'tooit'. (Rooibandstrandkiewiet)

2. KENTISH PLOVER *Charadrius alexandrinus* (908)   15-17 cm
Ad. in breeding plumage may be distinguished from the closely related White-fronted Plover by the chestnut crown and nape, and the small black patch extending from the shoulder to the sides of the breast. Non-breeding birds and juv. are virtually impossible to distinguish from juv. White-fronted Plover but appear more slender and attenuated in the body.
Habitat. Coastal wetlands and sandy beaches. **Status.** Very rare vagrant. Occurrence in the region based on a single beached specimen from Namibia. **Call.** A short, sharp 'wiiit', similar to that of White-fronted Plover. (Kenste Strandkiewiet)

3. WHITE-FRONTED PLOVER *Charadrius marginatus* (246)   16 cm
A pale plover that superficially resembles Chestnut-banded Plover but is slightly larger, with a white collar and lacking a complete breast band. Paler than Kittlitz's Plover (p. 164), it also lacks the dark head markings, but may have a thin, black line through the eye and across the forehead. It is also lighter coloured and smaller than Lesser Sand Plover. Underpart colour varies regionally from white to a rich salmon. Non-breeding birds and juv. are greyer and lack black markings on the head. The breast is usually white with small, dusky, lateral patches.
Habitat. Sandy and rocky shores, muddy coastal areas and larger inland rivers and pans. **Status.** Common resident. **Call.** A clear 'wiiit'; also a 'tukut' alarm call. (Vaalstrandkiewiet)

4. GREATER SAND PLOVER *Charadrius leschenaultii* (251)   22-25 cm
Very similar to Lesser Sand Plover, but this species stands taller and has a bigger body and a longer, more robust bill. It differs from White-fronted Plover in being much larger and in lacking a white collar. Caspian Plover (p. 164) has a smaller bill and lacks the extensive white on the sides of the rump.
Sexes alike in non-breeding plumage. In breeding plumage, the brown shoulder patches become rufous and extend across the breast, but not as extensively as in Lesser Sand Plover. The leg colour is variable: usually greyish green and very rarely black (legs of Lesser Sand Plover are almost invariably black). In flight, the more extensive white on the sides of the rump and the dark subterminal tail band aid distinction from Lesser Sand Plover. **Juv.** has the upperparts fringed with buff. **Habitat.** Coastal wetlands. **Status.** Uncommon to locally common summer visitor, most regular in the east. **Call.** A short, musical trill. (Grootstrandkiewiet)

5. LESSER SAND (MONGOLIAN) PLOVER *Charadrius mongolus* (250)   19-21 cm
Confusion with Greater Sand Plover is possible, but this species has shorter legs, a smaller body and a shorter, less robust bill. Both ad. White fronted Plover and Kittlitz's Plover (p. 164) are smaller and have a pale collar. In breeding plumage, the rufous breast band is more extensive than that of Greater Sand Plover. The legs are almost always black or very dark grey. In flight, there is little colour contrast between the tail, rump and back.
Sexes alike in non-breeding plumage. **Juv.** has the upperparts fringed with buff. **Habitat.** Coastal wetlands. **Status.** Fairly common summer visitor to coasts of Mozambique and northern KwaZulu-Natal; vagrant elsewhere. **Call.** 'Chittick'. (Mongoolse Strandkiewiet)

See also page 193

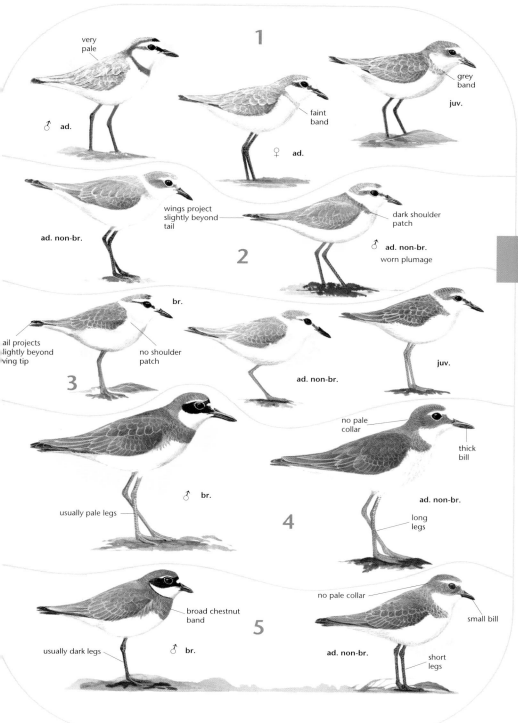

1

very pale

♂ ad.

faint band

grey band

juv.

♀ ad.

2

ad. non-br.

wings project slightly beyond tail

dark shoulder patch

♂ ad. non-br.
worn plumage

3

tail projects slightly beyond wing tip

br.

no shoulder patch

ad. non-br.

juv.

♂ br.

usually pale legs

4

no pale collar

thick bill

ad. non-br.

long legs

5

broad chestnut band

usually dark legs

♂ br.

no pale collar

ad. non-br.

small bill

short legs

1. CROWNED LAPWING (PLOVER) *Vanellus coronatus (255)* 30-31cm

A large, unmistakable plover, with its black cap surrounded by a white 'halo'. The legs and basal part of the bill are red. The sandy brown breast is separated from the white belly by a black band.

Juv. is much like ad. but is less strikingly marked. The upperparts are more scalloped, the legs are paler and the crown is barred with buff. **Habitat.** Short grassland (either grazed or burnt); also on golf courses, playing fields and fallow land. Aggregates in small flocks, especially when not breeding. Regularly associates with Black-winged Lapwings. **Status.** Common resident. **Call.** A noisy species, uttering a loud, grating 'kreep', day and night. (Kroonkiewiet)

2. BLACK-WINGED LAPWING (PLOVER) *Vanellus melanopterus* (257) 26-27 cm

Similar to Senegal Lapwing, but larger and more heavily built, with more white on the forehead (extending back almost to the eye) and a broader black border separating the breast from the belly, especially in male. The black breast band of female is less obvious. In flight from above, it may be distinguished from Senegal Lapwing by the broad, white wing bar and the black trailing edge to the secondaries, and from below by the black (not white) trailing edge to the secondaries.

Female has narrower breast band and a browner head and neck than male and the facial patch is reduced and off-white. **Juv.** is browner, with buff edges to the back and wing feathers. **Habitat.** Short grassland, both coastal and upland; frequently associates with Crowned Lapwings. **Status.** Uncommon resident and local migrant, with movements between uplands and the coast. **Call.** A shrill, piping 'ti-tirree', higher pitched than that of Senegal Lapwing. (Grootswartvlerkkiewiet)

3. SENEGAL LAPWING (LESSER BLACKWINGED PLOVER)
Vanellus lugubris (256) 22-26 cm

This species closely resembles Black-winged Lapwing but is smaller, has a narrow, black border to the breast, less white on the forehead and a slight greenish tinge to the upperparts. In flight both the upperwings and the underwings show completely white secondaries.

Juv. is less clearly marked than ad. and has the upperparts spotted with buff. **Habitat.** Dry, open, short-grass areas in savanna, especially where these have been recently burnt. **Status.** Uncommon resident and local migrant. **Call.** A clear, double-noted 'teeyoo, teeyoo'. (Kleinswartvlerkkiewiet)

See also pages 172–173

1

white
stripe

ad.

red
legs

juv.

2

buffy
supercilium

broad white
forehead

broad black
band

♂ ad.

reddish
legs

juv.

3

small white
forehead

plain
face

ad.

narrow black
band

juv.

dark
legs

169

1. LONG-TOED LAPWING (PLOVER) *Vanellus crassirostris* (261)   31 cm
The only lapwing in the region to have a white face, throat and foreneck. The black nape extends down the sides of the neck to form a broad breast band. This species is very striking in flight, with a grey back and all-white wings except for the black outer primaries. The tail is black and the rump is white. The legs and basal portion of the bill are reddish.
Juv. resembles ad. but has buffy mottling on the upperparts. **Habitat.** Well-vegetated vleis, marshes and river flood plains. **Status.** Locally common resident. **Call.** A repeated, high-pitched 'pink-pink'. (Witvlerkkiewiet)

2. WHITE-CROWNED LAPWING (PLOVER) *Vanellus albiceps* (259)   30 cm
This large lapwing, with its distinctive pendulous, yellow wattles, might be con-fused with African Wattled Lapwing, but the latter species has a dark (not white) breast. White-crowned Lapwing is also identified by a white stripe running from the forehead to the nape. In flight, the upperwings appear very white, with only the outermost primaries and inner coverts being black. The underwings are white except for the outer primaries. The tail is predominantly black.
Juv. is similar to ad. but has a brownish crown and barring on the upperparts. Its wattles are smaller than those of ad. **Habitat.** Sandbanks and sandbars of major rivers. **Status.** Locally common resident. **Call.** A repeated, ringing 'peek-peek'. (Witkopkiewiet)

3. SPUR-WINGED LAPWING (PLOVER) *Vanellus spinosus* (920)   25-28 cm
The combination of a buff back and upperwing coverts and a black breast and crown renders this large wader unmistakable.
Juv. Blacksmith Lapwing is often confused with many waders but is easily told from this species by its dark (not pale) back and more extensive dark markings on the foreneck. **Habitat.** Frequents wetland margins and adjoining grassy areas. **Status.** Only two records from our region, Botswana and northeastern Namibia. Other recent sightings from Malawi and Zambia suggest a southward extension of its range. **Call.** A loud, screeching 'ti-ti-tirri-ti' of either three or four notes. (Spoorvlerkkiewiet)

4. AFRICAN WATTLED LAPWING (PLOVER) *Vanellus senegallus* (260)   35 cm
The largest lapwing of the region. It has smaller yellow wattles than does White-crowned Lapwing, from which it also differs in having a dark breast bordered by a black line on the belly, and streaked (not grey) sides to the head and upper neck. The white on the head is restricted to the forecrown and forehead, unlike White-crowned Lapwing, in which the white stripe extends to the nape. In flight this species does not have the startling white-winged appearance of White-crowned Lapwing, but does have an obvious pale wing bar.
Juv. resembles ad. but has much reduced wattles and less distinct head markings. **Habitat.** Damp grassland and wetland fringes. **Status.** Fairly common resident. **Call.** A high-pitched, ringing 'keep-keep'; regularly calls at night. (Lelkiewiet)

5. BLACKSMITH LAPWING (PLOVER) *Vanellus armatus* (258)   31 cm
This large, black, white and grey bird is the easiest lapwing to identify in the region, and its bold pattern makes it easily distinguishable in flight.
Juv. is duller than ad. and has greyish brown feathering replacing the black-and-brown streaking on the crown. **Habitat.** Damp areas of wetland margins and adjoining grassland and fields. Often in flocks when not breeding. **Status.** Common resident. **Call.** Very vocal, with a loud, ringing 'tink, tink, tink' alarm call. (Bontkiewiet)

See also pages 172–173

1

white face

broad black breast band

2

white crown

long yellow wattles

white underparts

white wings

3

black cap

4

grey-streaked neck

short yellow wattles

black belly

5

white forehead

grey & black upperparts

ad.

white hind neck

juv.

171

See also pages 168–171

AFRICAN WATTLED LAPWING

black
cap

white
crown

pale base
to bill

CROWNED LAPWING

dark
cap

black
belly

SPUR-WINGED LAPWING

no white

ad.

imm.

BLACKSMITH LAPWING

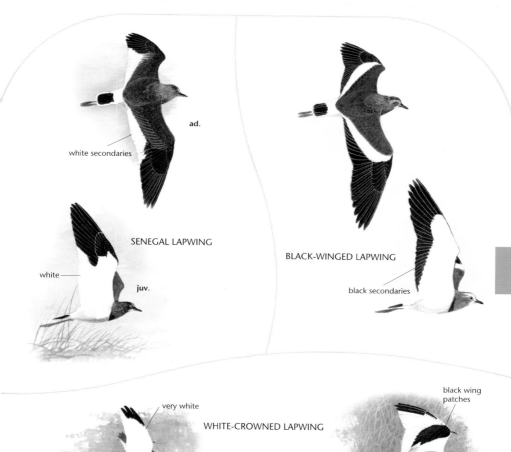

white secondaries

ad.

SENEGAL LAPWING

white

juv.

BLACK-WINGED LAPWING

black secondaries

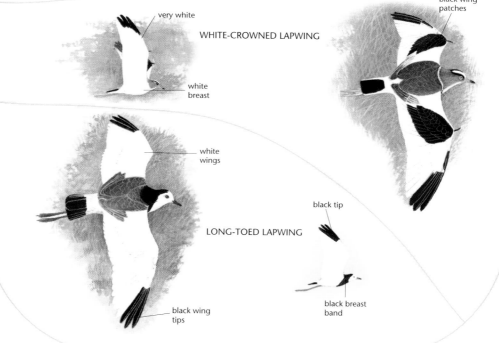

very white

WHITE-CROWNED LAPWING

white
breast

black wing
patches

white
wings

black tip

LONG-TOED LAPWING

black breast
band

black wing
tips

1. GREY PLOVER *Pluvialis squatarola* (254)   28-31 cm
In flight, the whitish underwings, black axillaries and pale rump distinguish it from both American and Pacific Golden Plovers. At rest it has grey (not buff) speckling on the back and wing coverts. In breeding plumage it has whitish (not golden) speckling on the back and wings. In breeding plumage, the breast, foreneck and sides of the face are black, and there is a wide white forecrown and eyebrow stripe that extends to the sides of the upper breast.
Juv. has buffy yellow markings on the upperparts. **Habitat.** Open shore and coastal wetlands. Occurs inland only during migration. **Status.** Common summer visitor; many overwinter. **Call.** A clear 'tluui', lower in pitch in the middle. (Grysstrandkiewiet)

2. AMERICAN GOLDEN PLOVER *Pluvialis dominica* (253a)   26 cm
Both Golden Plovers are easily told from Grey Plover by their dark, not pale rumps and grey, not black 'armpits'. Best told from Pacific Golden Plover by its heavier build, less yellowish speckling on mantle, bolder eyebrow stripe and tertials not extending to tail tip.
In br. plumage it can be distinguished from Pacific Golden Plover by its black, not white vent and lack of a white flank stripe. **Habitat.** Short grasslands, more often inland than coastal. **Status.** Summer vagrant. **Call.** A whistled 'oodle-oo'. (Amerikaanse Goue Strandkiewiet)

3. PACIFIC GOLDEN PLOVER *Pluvialis fulva* (253b)   23-26 cm
Smaller, more slightly built and more 'leggy' than American Golden Plover. Further distinguished from American Golden Plover by tertials extending almost to the tail tip and by having more yellow spangling on the mantle. Has white, not black vent and has bold white flank stripe in br. plumage.
Habitat. Chiefly coastal estuaries and less commonly inland. **Status.** Summer vagrant. **Call.** Similar to that of American Golden Plover. (Asiatiese Goue Strandkiewiet)

4. RUFF *Philomachus pugnax* (284)   m = 30 cm, f = 24 cm
The scaling on the upperparts is conspicuous. The black bill may show an orange or reddish base. Leg colour is variable, often orange or reddish. Common Redshank (p. 180) lacks the scaled upperparts and has striking white secondaries. In flight the white, oval patch on either side of the dark rump is diagnostic.
Male sometimes has a white head and neck during the non-breeding season. **Juv.** resembles non-breeding ad. but is buffier. **Habitat.** Vleis, lakes, estuaries and adjacent grassy areas. **Status.** Common summer visitor throughout, often in large flocks; some overwinter. **Call.** Largely silent in the region. (Kemphaan)

5. BUFF-BREASTED SANDPIPER *Tryngites subruficollis* (282)   18-19 cm
Coloration most closely resembles that of juv. female Ruff, but it is smaller and proportionally shorter-legged. The crown is spotted. It has a short, straight bill, yellow legs, and a white eye-ring. The underwing is predominantly white, with a small, dark crescent between the carpal joint and outer primary tips.
Juv. has a paler lower belly. **Habitat.** Short grassy areas and wetlands. **Status.** Summer vagrant. **Call.** Not recorded in the region. (Taanborsstrandloper) cut 1 line

6. PECTORAL SANDPIPER *Calidris melanotos* (279)   19-23 cm
The abrupt division between the streaked breast and the white underparts is distinctive. It is longer-necked than the stints, with a dark-capped appearance and darker upperparts. The legs are yellowish or greenish. Smaller Baird's Sandpiper (p. 178) has a black bill and legs, and larger Ruff (p. 174) lacks the distinctive bib.
Juv. resembles ad. but is brighter. **Habitat.** Margins of estuaries and wetlands. **Status.** Rare summer visitor. **Call.** A low trill, 'prrt'. (Geelpootstrandloper)

1

ad. non-br.

br.

brownish
above

ad. non-br.

white
stripe

br.

2

greyish
upperparts

long
wings

ad. non-br.

black
below

br.

3

pale bill
base

♂ colour variant

scaled
upperparts

♂ ad. non-br.

usually
orange
legs

♂ juv.

4

scalloped
upperparts

♀ juv.

5

spotted
crown

ad.

short
bill

golden
buff

freckled
sides

yellow
legs

6

dark
cap

short
bill

abrupt
demarcation

ad. non-br.

yellow
legs

1. GREAT KNOT *Calidris tenuirostris* 26-28 cm

Differs from Red Knot by its larger size and longer, more robust bill, especially at base. Overall slightly paler with marked speckling on breast and streaking on flanks. Br. plumage has spangled rufous on mantle with heavy black mottling and streaking on underparts.
Habitat. Coastal estuaries. **Status.** Vagrant, (one record). **Call.** Usually silent, but call similar to that of Red Knot. (Groot Knoet)

2. RED KNOT *Calidris canutus* (271) 23-25 cm

This short-legged, dumpy and rather plain wader differs from the smaller Curlew Sandpiper by its shorter, straight bill and greenish (not grey) legs. It is much smaller than Grey Plover (p. 174), which has a speckled (not uniformly grey) back and a short bill. In flight a pale wing bar is visible and the rump is flecked with pale grey.
Male is brighter than female in breeding dress. In breeding plumage all underparts, except for the underwing, are deep chestnut and the upperparts are spangled gold and black.
Habitat. Gregarious at estuaries and coastal lagoons; occasionally inland. **Status.** Locally common summer visitor; regularly overwinters. **Call.** A nondescript 'knut'. (Knoet)

3. CURLEW SANDPIPER *Calidris ferruginea* (272) 18-23 cm

The only small, plain, greyish wader with an obviously decurved bill. In flight it has a squarish white rump, variably scalloped with pale grey.
In breeding plumage the rump becomes blotched and the underparts and face rufous; **male** is brighter than female. **Juv.** has buffy edgings to the mantle feathers. **Habitat.** Coastal and freshwater wetlands, usually in flocks. **Status.** Very common summer visitor; regularly overwinters. **Call.** A short trill, 'chirrup'. (Krombekstrandloper)

4. DUNLIN *Calidris alpina* (273) 15-22 cm

The bill is less evenly curved than that of Curlew Sandpiper, from which it differs by its less conspicuous eyebrow stripe and the dark rump with white edges. Broad-billed Sandpiper has paler, shorter legs, a striped head and a flattened bill tip. In breeding and transitional plumage it has a black patch on the belly and chestnut feathering on the back.
Juv. is similar to non-breeding ad. **Habitat.** Coastal wetlands. **Status.** Vagrant. **Call.** A weak 'treep'. (Bontstrandloper)

5. SANDERLING *Calidris alba* (281) 19-21 cm

In non-breeding plumage this is the palest sandpiper of the region. It has a rather short, stubby, black bill and a dark shoulder patch. It is similar to the dark-shouldered Broad-billed Sandpiper, but is larger, has a shorter, straighter bill, and lacks the head stripes. In breeding plumage the wing and back feathers are black with chestnut centres, and there is a broad, diffuse, chestnut breast band streaked with black. In flight it shows a distinct white wing bar and a dark centre line through the white rump and tail.
Juv. resembles non-breeding ad. **Habitat.** Mainly sandy beaches; also rocky coasts, estuaries and lagoons. Sometimes inland, especially during migration. **Status.** Common summer visitor. **Call.** A single, decisive 'wick'. (Drietoonstrandloper)

6. BROAD-BILLED SANDPIPER *Limicola falcinellus* (283) 17 cm

A small, markedly short-legged wader, distinguished from Little Stint (p. 178) by its relatively long bill, which droops slightly at the flattened tip. The legs are dark grey, sometimes greenish. It has a dark shoulder patch that is less pronounced than in Sanderling. The whitish double eyebrow stripe is diagnostic. In breeding plumage the upperparts become blackish, with narrow, buffy feather margins.
Juv. has warmer-coloured upperparts than non-breeding ad. **Habitat.** Vleis, lakes and estuaries. **Status.** Rare but regular summer visitor. **Call.** A low-pitched, short trill, 'drrrt'. (Breëbekstrandloper)

See also pages 194–195, 198

robust bill

rufous spangling

speckled breast

1

br.

dumpy body

ad. non-br.

short, greenish legs

br.

2

3

ad. non-br.

long bill

br.

plain crown

ad. non-br.

4

br.

black belly patch

dark shoulder patch

pale grey upperparts

ad. non-br.

short, stout bill

5

br.

grey upperparts

dark shoulder

juv.

streaked breast

ad. non-br.

short legs

6

from above

striped head

177

1. WHITE-RUMPED SANDPIPER *Calidris fuscicollis* (277)   15-17 cm
This small, rather plain sandpiper has a white rump like that of Curlew Sandpiper (p. 176), but is smaller and has a shorter, straighter bill. Its elongated shape (wings extending beyond tail tip at rest) and posture resemble Baird's Sandpiper, but it is easily distinguished in flight by its white rump.
Juv. resembles ad. but the crown is chestnut and the dark back feathers are broadly fringed with chestnut. **Habitat.** Wetlands. **Status.** Summer vagrant. **Call.** A thin, mouse-like 'jeep'. (Witrugstrandloper)

2. BAIRD'S SANDPIPER *Calidris bairdii* (278)   14-16 cm
The long wings extend well beyond the tail at rest, giving an elongated appearance. It is distinguished by its scaled, essentially brown, rarely grey, upperparts, and by the light vertical streaking on the breast. The legs are black, sometimes tinged with green. Most likely to be confused with White-rumped Sandpiper, but easily distinguished in flight by the black line down the centre of the white rump.
Juv. resembles non-breeding ad. **Habitat.** Open shore and wetland margins. **Status.** Very rare vagrant. **Call.** A short trill, 'kreep'. (Bairdse Strandloper)

3. LITTLE STINT *Calidris minuta* (274)   13-15 cm
Very similar to Red-necked Stint, but with a longer, less stubby bill; in breeding plumage it lacks the rufous chin of that species. Temminck's Stint has olive, not black, legs, plainer upperparts and white, not grey, outer tail feathers. Long-toed Stint has darker upperparts, a thinner bill and greenish yellow legs. Broad-billed Sandpiper and Dunlin (p. 176) have longer bills that droop very slightly at the tip; the former shows a dark shoulder at rest. The narrow white wing bar and the white sides to the rump are obvious in flight
Juv. resembles non-breeding ad. but colouring above is warmer. **Habitat.** Coastal and freshwater wetlands; typically forages in flocks and has a very rapid feeding action. **Status.** Common summer visitor; very few overwinter. **Call.** A short, sharp 'schit'. (Kleinstrandloper)

4. RED-NECKED STINT *Calidris ruficollis* (276)   13-16 cm
Extremely difficult to distinguish from Little Stint, except in breeding plumage when the throat, neck and cheeks become rufous. In all other plumages, Red-necked Stint's bill is shorter and stubbier. Appears slightly heavier bellied and shorter legged than Little Stint. In non-breeding plumage it is very pale, with wing coverts and back feathers a uniformly pale grey with dark feather shafts. May be distinguished from Temminck's and Long-toed Stints by its black (not greenish or yellowish) legs.
Juv. resembles non-breeding ad. **Habitat.** Usually with Little Stints or Curlew Sandpipers at vleis, dams, estuaries or bays. **Status.** Rare summer visitor; may be more regular and widespread than presumed. **Call.** A short 'chit' or 'prrp'. (Rooinekstrandloper)

5. TEMMINCK'S STINT *Calidris temminckii* (280)   13-15 cm
More elongate in appearance than Little Stint. It is distinguished by its greenish legs, white outer tail feathers and uniform grey-brown upperparts. Long-toed Stint generally has yellow legs and is much darker and browner above.
Juv. resembles ad. but upperparts are scaled with buff. **Habitat.** Wetland margins with short grass or reeds. Could occur on any vlei, estuary or dam. **Status.** Summer vagrant. **Call.** A shrill 'prrrrtt'. (Temminckse Strandloper)

6. LONG-TOED STINT *Calidris subminuta* (275)   13-15 cm
Distinguished from Little and Red-necked Stints by its darker brown and more scalloped upperparts, yellow (not black) legs and more slender bill. Some Temminck's Stints have yellow legs but they have plainer, paler upperparts and white (not greyish) edges to the tail. Only at very close range can the long toes be seen.
Juv. is more brightly patterned than ad. **Habitat.** Liable to occur on any water body. **Status.** Summer vagrant. **Call.** Not recorded in the region. (Langtoonstrandloper)

See also pages 194–195, 198

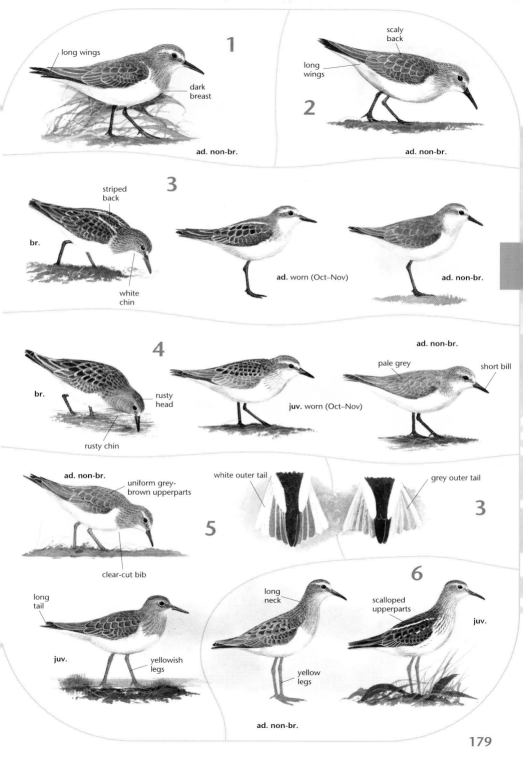

1

long wings

dark breast

ad. non-br.

2

scaly back

long wings

ad. non-br.

3

striped back

br.

white chin

ad. worn (Oct–Nov)

ad. non-br.

4

br.

rusty head

rusty chin

juv. worn (Oct–Nov)

ad. non-br.

pale grey

short bill

5

ad. non-br.

uniform grey-brown upperparts

clear-cut bib

white outer tail

grey outer tail

3

long tail

juv.

yellowish legs

6

long neck

scalloped upperparts

juv.

yellow legs

ad. non-br.

179

SANDPIPERS

1. COMMON SANDPIPER *Actitis hypoleucos* (264)   19-21 cm
This species shows an obvious white shoulder in front of the closed wing. The legs are dull green. Wood Sandpiper is larger and longer-legged, and has pale spotting on the upperparts and a white rump. Green Sandpiper is larger and has a white rump and black underwings. The flight comprises bursts of shallow wing beats on slightly bowed wings, interspersed with short glides. It has a prominent pale wing bar, brown rump and barred sides to the dark tail. Continually bobs rear end, much more so than *Tringa* waders.
Juv. resembles ad. **Habitat.** Wide range of wetland types, including rivers. **Status.** Common summer visitor. **Call.** A very shrill 'ti-ti-ti'. (Gewone Ruiter)

2. GREEN SANDPIPER *Tringa ochropus* (265)   21-24 cm
Resembles Wood and Common Sandpipers but is larger, has darker upperparts that contrast with its square white rump, and blackish underwings. It has less extensive and broader barring on the upper tail than does Wood Sandpiper. Common Greenshank and Marsh Sandpiper (p. 182) are paler, have much longer legs and bill and the white of the rump extends onto the back; both lack the black underwings.
Juv. resembles ad. but is browner. **Habitat.** Freshwater wetlands, principally along tropical rivers and at small waterbodies such as sewage ponds. **Status.** Uncommon to rare summer visitor to the north and east; vagrant elsewhere. **Call.** A three-noted whistle, 'tew-a-tew'. (Witgatruiter)

3. WOOD SANDPIPER *Tringa glareola* (266)   19-21 cm
Intermediate in size between Common and Green Sandpipers, which it superficially resembles. Distinguished from Green Sandpiper by the paler upperparts with pale flecking, the grey (not black) underwings and the yellower legs, and by its less streaked breast. Lacks the white shoulder patch, dark rump and tail and the wing bar of Common Sandpiper, and has a different flight action. Darker and browner than Common Greenshank or Marsh Sandpiper (p. 182), and has a square white rump. Distinguished from Lesser Yellowlegs (p. 182) by its smaller size, longer white eye-stripe, less streaked breast, and by the wings not projecting beyond the tail at rest.
Juv. resembles ad. but is warmer brown above. **Habitat.** Occurs at a wide range of wetland types throughout the region, but is rare on the coast. **Status.** Common summer visitor, singly or in small flocks. **Call.** A very vocal species, with a high-pitched, slightly descending 'chiff-iff-iff'. (Bosruiter)

4. TEREK SANDPIPER *Xenus cinereus* (263)   22-25 cm
The only small wader with yellow-orange legs and a long, upturned, dark brown bill with an orange base. At a distance it appears pale with a dark shoulder. The white trailing edge to the secondaries is clearly visible in flight.
Juv. resembles ad. but is buffier above. **Habitat.** Muddy estuaries and coastal lagoons, especially near mangroves and in areas covered by eel-grass (*Zostera*). **Status.** Locally common summer visitor; a few overwinter. **Call.** A series of fluty, uniformly pitched 'weet-weet-weet' notes. (Terekruiter)

5. COMMON REDSHANK *Tringa totanus* (268)   27-29 cm
The red base of the bill and the bright orange-red legs differentiate this species from all other waders except Ruff (p. 174) and Spotted Redshank (p. 182). Ruff lacks the triangular white rump and finely barred white tail. Spotted Redshank is paler and longer billed. Both Ruff and Spotted Redshank lack the striking white secondaries. At rest, Common Redshank's wings and back appear plain brownish grey, unlike Ruff's scaled and mottled upperparts.
Juv. is generally browner than ad., with the legs and the base of the bill duller red. **Habitat.** Freshwater and coastal wetland margins. **Status.** Rare summer visitor, mainly to the coast and northern wetlands. **Call.** 'Tiw-hu-hu', the first syllable being a tone above the others. (Rooipootruiter)

See also page 196

1
white shoulder patch

dark upperparts
broad bars

2
dark upperparts
greenish legs
ad. non-br.
long bill

narrow bars
ad. non-br.
yellowish legs
3
juv.

4
pale grey upperparts
upturned bill
short, orange-yellow legs
white trailing edge
ad. non-br.
fairly long, straight bill

br.
broad white edge

♂ br.
red base
uniform upperparts
ad. non-br.
red legs

5

1. COMMON GREENSHANK *Tringa nebularia* (270)   30-35 cm
Resembles a large Marsh Sandpiper, but has a heavier, slightly upturned, black bill, usually with a grey or greenish base. Bar-tailed Godwit (p. 184) is larger, browner and heavier, and has relatively short legs and an upturned bill with a pinkish base. Common Greenshank may be differentiated from Greater Yellowlegs by its green (not orange-yellow) legs and by its flight pattern (white rump extending onto back). Juv. resembles ad. but is darker above. **Habitat.** Coastal and freshwater wetlands. **Status.** Common summer visitor; regularly overwinters. **Call.** A loud, rasping 'chew-chew-chew'. (Groenpootruiter)

2. LESSER YELLOWLEGS *Tringa flavipes* (902)   23-25 cm
Closely resembles Wood Sandpiper (p. 180) but is larger and has a more streaked breast. Unlike Wood Sandpiper, the wings of this species project noticeably beyond the tail at rest. The legs are yellower than those of any other similar-sized wader of the region. It may be distinguished from Marsh Sandpiper in transitional plumage (when the legs can become fairly bright yellow) by its relatively short bill and, in flight, by its square white rump, which does not extend onto the back. Juv. has the upperparts brown, spotted with buff; the breast is greyish. **Habitat.** Small vleis and pans, bays and estuaries; forages on mud and in waterside vegetation. **Status.** Summer vagrant. **Call.** A repeated, ringing 'chew', softer than that of Greater Yellowlegs. (Kleingeelpootruiter)

3. GREATER YELLOWLEGS *Tringa melanoleuca* (906)   29-33 cm
Slightly smaller than Common Greenshank, it has orange-yellow (not yellow or greenish yellow) legs and a square white rump that does not extend up the back. The upperparts are more obviously spotted than those of Common Greenshank. Juv. resembles ad. **Habitat.** Freshwater habitats and estuaries; regularly wades in deep water. **Status.** Summer vagrant (one record). **Call.** A loud 'tew-tew-tew-tew', similar to that of Common Greenshank. (Grootgeelpootruiter)

4. MARSH SANDPIPER *Tringa stagnatilis* (269)   22-25 cm
This pale grey sandpiper resembles Common Greenshank but is much smaller, has a much thinner, straight, black bill, a slighter build and proportionally longer legs. Non-breeding Wilson's Phalarope (p. 188) is smaller, and has much shorter, yellow (not grey-green) legs and a square (not triangular), white rump. Juv. resembles non-breeding ad. **Habitat.** Estuaries, coastal lagoons and larger inland waterbodies. **Status.** Common summer visitor. **Call.** A high-pitched 'yeup', often repeated rapidly. Superficially resembles that of Common Greenshank, but is higher-pitched and less strident. Also a single 'tchuk'. (Moerasruiter)

5. SPOTTED REDSHANK *Tringa erythropus* (267)   29-32 cm
Similar to Common Redshank (p. 180) but is larger, paler and much longer-billed, and lacks the white secondaries. The legs and the base of the lower mandible are dark reddish, distinguishing it from other waders, except Ruff (p. 174). Ruff lacks the white rump and the prominent white stripe between the bill and the eye. In breeding plumage Spotted Redshank is black, finely spotted and scalloped with white. Juv. resembles non-breeding ad. but has more extensive grey barring on the underparts. **Habitat.** Vleis, lakes, estuaries, bays and lagoons. **Status.** Summer vagrant. **Call.** A clear, double-noted 'tu wik'. (Gevlekte Rooipootruiter)

182

See also pages 196–197

1

ad. non-br.

greenish legs

stout base

slightly upturned bill

ad. non-br.

juv.

2

wings project beyond tail

straight bill

ad. non-br.

yellow legs

spotted upperparts

thick base

slightly upturned bill

ad. non-br.

orange-yellow legs

3

4

pale grey upperparts

long, thin bill

ad. non-br.

br.

very long legs

5

grey rump

long, thin bill

red base

unmarked white underparts

ad. non-br.

red legs

1. BAR-TAILED GODWIT *Limosa lapponica* (288)   38 cm

At rest this species resembles Black-tailed Godwit, but its bill is shorter and slightly upturned, its legs much shorter and its upperparts browner and more distinctly marked. In flight it lacks Black-tailed Godwit's white wing bar and has thinly brown-barred, not broadly black-tipped tail. The white, V-shaped (not square) rump extends up the back. It is best told from Hudsonian Godwit by its flight pattern; difficult to distinguish on the ground.

Sexes alike, but female has a longer bill. In breeding plumage, the head, neck and underparts are deep chestnut. **Juv.** resembles non-breeding ad. but is extensively buffy below. **Habitat.** Mainly larger estuaries and coastal lagoons; rare inland. **Status.** Fairly common summer visitor to all coasts; regularly overwinters. **Call.** Generally silent, but utters a 'wik-wik' or 'kirrik' call. (Bandstertgriet)

2. HUDSONIAN GODWIT *Limosa haemastica* (914)   39 cm

In non-breeding plumage at rest, confusion is most likely with Bar-tailed Godwit due to the generally brown coloration; it can safely be told from this species only if the subterminal black band on the tail is seen or if the two species are side by side. In all age classes, it may be distinguished from Black-tailed Godwit in flight by its smaller white wing bar and the conspicuous black underwing coverts, which are diagnostic. Differs in breeding plumage from Black-tailed Godwit in being dark chestnut below, and having black underwing coverts.

Juv. resembles non-breeding ad. but is buffy below. **Habitat.** Estuaries and coastal lagoons. **Status.** Summer vagrant to the Western and Eastern Cape provinces. **Call.** A sharp 'keeewek-keeewek'. (Hudsonbaaigriet).

3. BLACK-TAILED GODWIT *Limosa limosa* (287)   40 cm

Superficially resembles Bar-tailed and Hudsonian Godwits, but is markedly larger and has noticeably longer legs, a greyer, unmottled back, and a relatively long, almost straight, pink-based bill. In flight the broad, white wing bar and white, black-tipped tail are conspicuous. In all age classes it may be distinguished in flight from Hudsonian Godwit by its larger wing bar and the white (not black) underwing coverts. In breeding plumage, the neck and upper breast are chestnut and the belly is white, barred with black.

Juv. has buffy-orange neck and upper breast. **Habitat.** Large lakes, estuaries and coastal lagoons. Forages in deeper water more regularly than does Bar-tailed Godwit. **Status.** Rare summer visitor. **Call.** A repeated 'weeka-weeka', given especially in flight. (Swartstertgriet)

4. COMMON WHIMBREL *Numenius phaeopus* (290)   40-43 cm

Apart from Eurasian Curlew, this is the only large wader in the region with a decurved bill. The bill is decurved along its full length. Common Whimbrel is shorter-billed and darker than Eurasian Curlew, and has parallel pale and dark stripes on the head, with an obvious pale eyebrow stripe.

Sexes alike but female is larger. **Juv.** resembles ad. but has the upperparts more scalloped. **Habitat.** Mainly estuaries, coastal lagoons and, to a lesser extent, open shores. **Status.** Common summer visitor to all coasts; regularly overwinters. **Call.** An evenly pitched, bubbling call of about seven syllables; highly vocal in the non-breeding season. (Kleinwulp)

5. EURASIAN CURLEW *Numenius arquata* (289)   53-59 cm

A very large wader with a long, decurved bill, proportionally much longer than that of Common Whimbrel. Eurasian Curlew is paler overall and lacks Common Whimbrel's head stripes, although a faint eyebrow stripe may be visible. In flight, it shows a conspicuous white rump that extends up the back as a white triangle.

Sexes alike but female is larger and has a longer bill. **Juv.** has a relatively short bill and lacks the head stripes of Common Whimbrel and is paler. **Habitat.** Large estuaries and lagoons; a few birds wander inland. **Status.** Locally common but decreasing summer visitor, rare in the east. **Call.** A loud 'cur-lew'. (Grootwulp)

See also pages 198–199

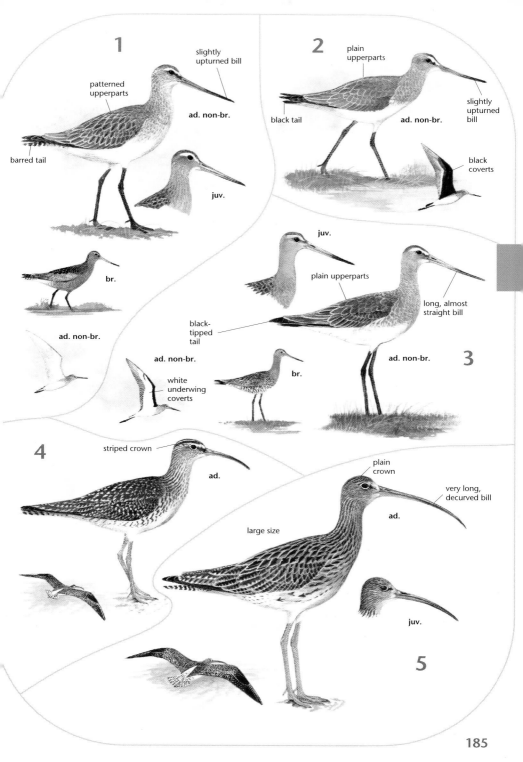

1

patterned
upperparts

slightly
upturned bill

ad. non-br.

barred tail

juv.

br.

ad. non-br.

2

plain
upperparts

slightly
upturned
bill

black tail

ad. non-br.

black
coverts

juv.

plain upperparts

long, almost
straight bill

black-
tipped
tail

ad. non-br.

white
underwing
coverts

br.

ad. non-br.

3

4

striped crown

ad.

plain
crown

very long,
decurved bill

ad.

large size

juv.

5

185

1. GREATER PAINTED-SNIPE *Rostratula benghalensis* (242)　　　　　23-26 cm
Male distinguished from African and Great snipes by its breast pattern, longer legs, and shorter, slightly decurved, pale bill. It has a laboured flight action on broad wings.
Female is more striking than male, with a chestnut neck and breast and a white eye patch. Both sexes have a conspicuous pale harness extending upwards from the breast. **Juv.** resembles male. **Habitat.** Skulks among reeds in marshes and on the edges of lakes, vleis, dams and seasonally inundated ponds and river flood plains. **Status.** Scarce resident, with local movements. **Call.** Male utters a trill; female gives a distinctive, soft, disyllabic 'wuk-oooooo', repeated monotonously, often after dark. (Goudsnip)

2. AFRICAN (ETHIOPIAN) SNIPE *Gallinago nigripennis* (286)　　　　30-32 cm
The long, straight bill and striped head markings distinguish this species from all except Great Snipe, from which it is differentiated by the longer bill, barred outer tail feathers at all ages (juv. only in Great Snipe) and the plain white belly, with dark barring restricted to the flanks. The flight is faster and more zigzagging than that of Great Snipe; it generally flies farther than Great Snipe when flushed.
Juv. is duller than ad.; in flight, the white spotting on the upperwings is much less marked than in ad. **Habitat.** Extensive marshes and margins of perennial and ephemeral wetlands. **Status.** Common resident and local nomad. **Call.** A sucking sound when put to flight, more high-pitched and protracted than call of Great Snipe; drumming noise during aerial breeding display caused by air passing over the stiffened outertail feathers. (Afrikaanse Snip)

3. GREAT SNIPE *Gallinago media* (285)　　　　　　　　27-29 cm
Likely to be confused with African Snipe, which has a plain white belly, lacking the dark barring of this species. Great Snipe differs further in having a shorter, stouter bill and clear white spots on the upperwing coverts. At close quarters the white outertail feathers of ad. can be distinguished; those of African Snipe are barred. The flight is heavy and direct.
Juv. has the spots on the upperwing coverts less clearly defined and the outertail feathers barred. **Habitat.** Marshes and wetland margins, including river flood plains and seasonally inundated wetlands. **Status.** Rare summer visitor. Previously more abundant and widespread, now recorded regularly only in the north-central region. **Call.** Deep, short, single or double croak when flushed, lower in pitch than call of African Snipe. (Dubbelsnip)

4. RUDDY TURNSTONE *Arenaria interpres* (262)　　　　　　21-24 cm
This distinctive, stocky wader has a short, black bill and orange legs. In non-breeding plumage the upperparts are blackish and there are irregular dark markings on the front and sides of the breast. In breeding plumage, often seen before northward migration, the head and neck have a crisp black-and-white pattern and the inner wings and back take on a warm chestnut colouring. In flight in all plumages there is a distinct wing bar and parallel white lines running down the centre and sides of the back. The tail has a conspicuous subterminal black band. The underparts, including the underwings, are white in all plumages.
Juv. has the upperparts browner and more conspicuously scaled than in non-breeding ad. **Habitat.** Rocky and sandy shores, estuaries and coastal lagoons; rare inland. It flicks over small stones and weeds with its bill in search of food. Usually in small flocks. **Status.** Common summer visitor; regularly overwinters. **Call.** A hard 'kttuck', given especially in flight. (Steenloper)

See also pages 194, 200–201

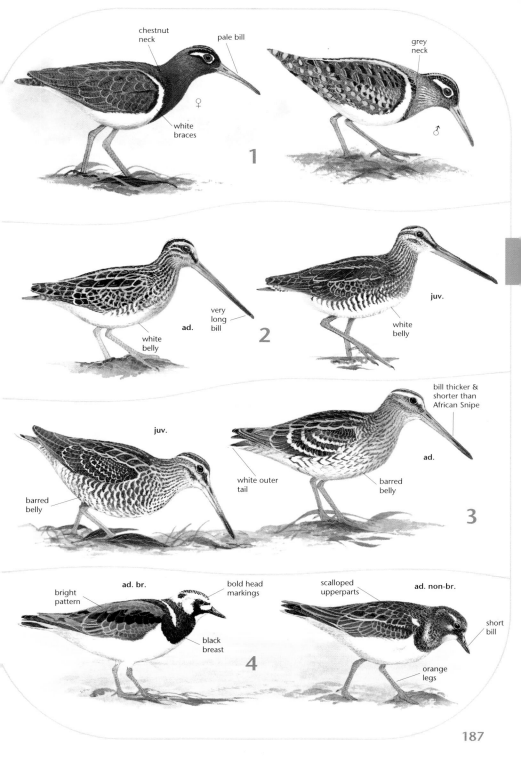

1

chestnut neck

pale bill

♀

white braces

grey neck

♂

2

ad.

very long bill

white belly

juv.

white belly

3

juv.

barred belly

white outer tail

bill thicker & shorter than African Snipe

ad.

barred belly

4

ad. br.

bright pattern

bold head markings

black breast

scalloped upperparts

ad. non-br.

short bill

orange legs

1. RED-NECKED PHALAROPE *Phalaropus lobatus* (292) 18-19 cm
Resembles Red Phalarope but has a darker grey back streaked with white, and a thinner, all-black bill; Red Phalarope's bill is wide along its entire length, while Red-necked Phalarope's bill is finely tapered. Non-br. Wilson's Phalarope has a much longer bill and yellow (not black) legs, and lacks a distinct black eye patch. In flight the upperparts are darker than Red Phalarope's. Red-necked Phalarope's rump is black, fringed with white, while Red Phalarope's rump is grey. Female is more brightly coloured than male in breeding plumage. Species is darker overall in breeding plumage, and acquires a small chestnut gorget; the chin is white.
Juv. resembles non-breeding ad. but may show some dark feathering on the upperparts. Habitat. Any quiet body of water, favouring coastal saltpans and sewage works. Status. Rare summer visitor, mainly to the west coast. Call. A low 'tchick' is given when put to flight. (Rooihalsfraiingpoot)

2. RED (GREY) PHALAROPE *Phalaropus fulicaria* (291) 20-22 cm
Similar to Red-necked Phalarope, but this species is more uniformly pale grey above and has a thicker, sometimes yellow-based bill. It may be distinguished from Red-necked Phalarope in flight by its rump, which is grey, not black fringed with white. Wilson's Phalarope has a longer, thinner bill and lacks the distinct black eye patch; in flight it has a square white (not dark) rump and lacks a wing bar. In breeding plumage the chestnut underparts, white face mask and black crown are diagnostic. Female in breeding plumage is more brightly coloured than male.
Juv. resembles non-breeding ad. but may show some dark feathering on the upperparts. Habitat. Usually in small flocks at sea; vagrants ashore. Status. Fairly common summer visitor to the west coast; vagrant elsewhere. Call. A soft, low 'wiit'. (Grysfraiingpoot)

3. WILSON'S PHALAROPE *Steganopus tricolor* (293) 22-24 cm
This species may be distinguished from the other, smaller phalaropes in non-breeding plumage by its longer bill, yellow (not dark) legs and the lack of a distinct black eye patch. In flight it differs in having a square, white rump, a grey tail and no wing bar. Rarely spins while foraging, preferring to lunge from side to side with the bill to retrieve food close to the surface. Sometimes forages by walking at the water's edge. In breeding plumage a distinct dark stripe runs through the eye and down the side of the neck, and the sides of the breast and mantle attain a rufous wash. Male in breeding plumage has a dark brown crown. Female in breeding plumage is brighter than male and shows a pale grey crown. Both sexes have blackish legs in breeding plumage.
Juv. has darker and more scalloped upperparts than ad. Habitat. Coastal wetlands. Status. Summer vagrant to coastal regions, most often in the west. Call. A short, grunting 'grrg'. (Bontfraiingpoot)

See also page 201

1

blackish rump, fringed white

ad. non-br.

thin bill

ad. non-br.

ad. non-br.

thin, pointed bill

from above

♂ br.

♀ br.

ads. worn (Sept–Oct)

2

broad, rounded bill

ad. non-br.

♂ br.

♀ br.

grey rump

ad. non-br.

thick bill

white rump

juv.

dark wings

♀ br.

3

long, thin bill

juv.

ad. non-br.

white rump

ad. transitional

189

1. COLLARED (REDWINGED) PRATINCOLE *Glareola pratincola* (304)   24-25 cm

Ad. in breeding plumage has a buffy yellow throat, edged with a thin black line. Tail extends beyond wing tips at rest. In non-breeding plumage, the collar is absent or reduced to a few speckles. Similar to Black-winged Pratincole but this species has dark rufous (not black) underwing coverts and appears generally paler. The flight is light and graceful, and the white rump and forked tail are conspicuous. Juv. lacks the clearly defined throat markings of ad. and has buff edges to the mantle feathers. The rufous underwing coverts and white trailing edge to the secondaries are diagnostic. **Habitat.** Wetland margins and open areas near water. **Status.** Locally common breeding summer visitor. **Call.** 'Kik-kik', given especially in flight. (Rooivlerksprinkaanvoël)

2. BLACK-WINGED PRATINCOLE *Glareola nordmanni* (305)   23-25 cm

At rest this species appears darker than Collared Pratincole. In flight, the white rump contrasts sharply with the rest of the upperparts. Its best distinguishing features are the black (not rufous) underwing coverts and the lack of a white trailing edge to the secondaries. It is seen in the region mainly in non-breeding plumage, when the throat collar is absent. Juv. is drabber and more scalloped on the upperparts, and lacks the black gorget of ad. It may have some rufous flecking on the underwing coverts. **Habitat.** Grassland, fallow lands and edges of wetlands. **Status.** Locally common to abundant summer visitor; nomadic. **Call.** An often-repeated, single- or double-noted 'pik'. (Swartvlerksprinkaanvoël)

3. ROCK PRATINCOLE *Glareola nuchalis* (306)   17-19,5 cm

Much smaller than Collared and Black-winged Pratincoles. A diagnostic white line extends from the eye down across the lower part of the nape to form a hind collar. The legs and the base of the bill are red. It appears very dark in flight, with a conspicuous white rump. Juv. is a dull and lightly buff-speckled version of ad. but lacks the white hind collar and has darker legs. **Habitat.** Large northern rivers, especially the Zambezi, where it frequents stretches of water with exposed, flat rocks or sandbars (less common on the Chobe and Okavango rivers). **Status.** Locally common breeding visitor, July to January. **Call.** A loud, repeated, plover-like 'kik-kik'. (Withalssprinkaanvoël)

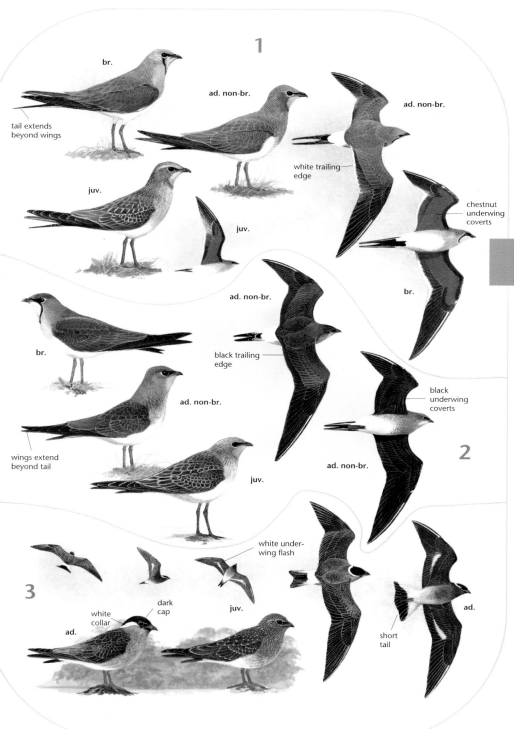

1

br.

tail extends
beyond wings

ad. non-br.

ad. non-br.

white trailing
edge

chestnut
underwing
coverts

juv.

juv.

br.

ad. non-br.

black trailing
edge

br.

black
underwing
coverts

ad. non-br.

wings extend
beyond tail

juv.

2

ad. non-br.

white under-
wing flash

3

dark
cap

juv.

ad.

white
collar

ad.

short
tail

See also pages 162–167, 202–203

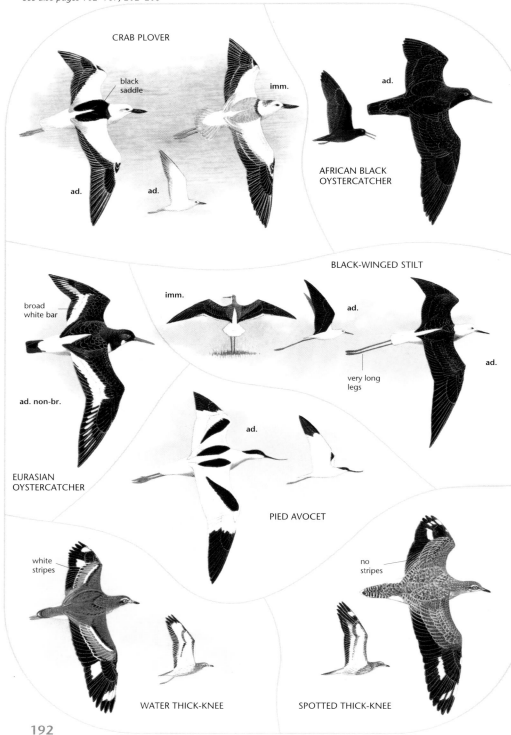

CRAB PLOVER

black saddle

imm.

ad.

ad. ad.

ad.

AFRICAN BLACK OYSTERCATCHER

BLACK-WINGED STILT

broad white bar

imm.

ad.

very long legs

ad.

ad. non-br.

EURASIAN OYSTERCATCHER

ad.

PIED AVOCET

white stripes

no stripes

WATER THICK-KNEE

SPOTTED THICK-KNEE

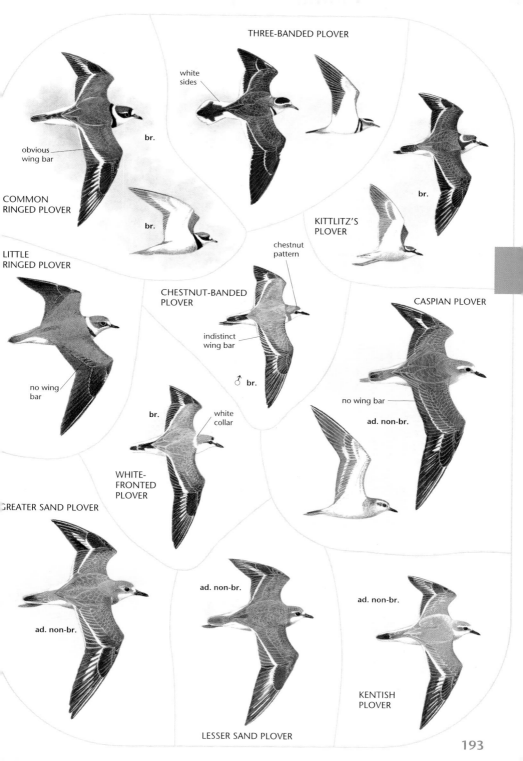

THREE-BANDED PLOVER

white sides

br.

COMMON
RINGED PLOVER

obvious wing bar

br.

KITTLITZ'S
PLOVER

br.

LITTLE
RINGED PLOVER

br.

CHESTNUT-BANDED
PLOVER

chestnut pattern

CASPIAN PLOVER

indistinct wing bar

♂ br.

no wing bar

ad. non-br.

no wing bar

br.

white collar

WHITE-
FRONTED
PLOVER

GREATER SAND PLOVER

ad. non-br.

ad. non-br.

ad. non-br.

ad. non-br.

KENTISH
PLOVER

LESSER SAND PLOVER

See also pages 176–179, 186–187

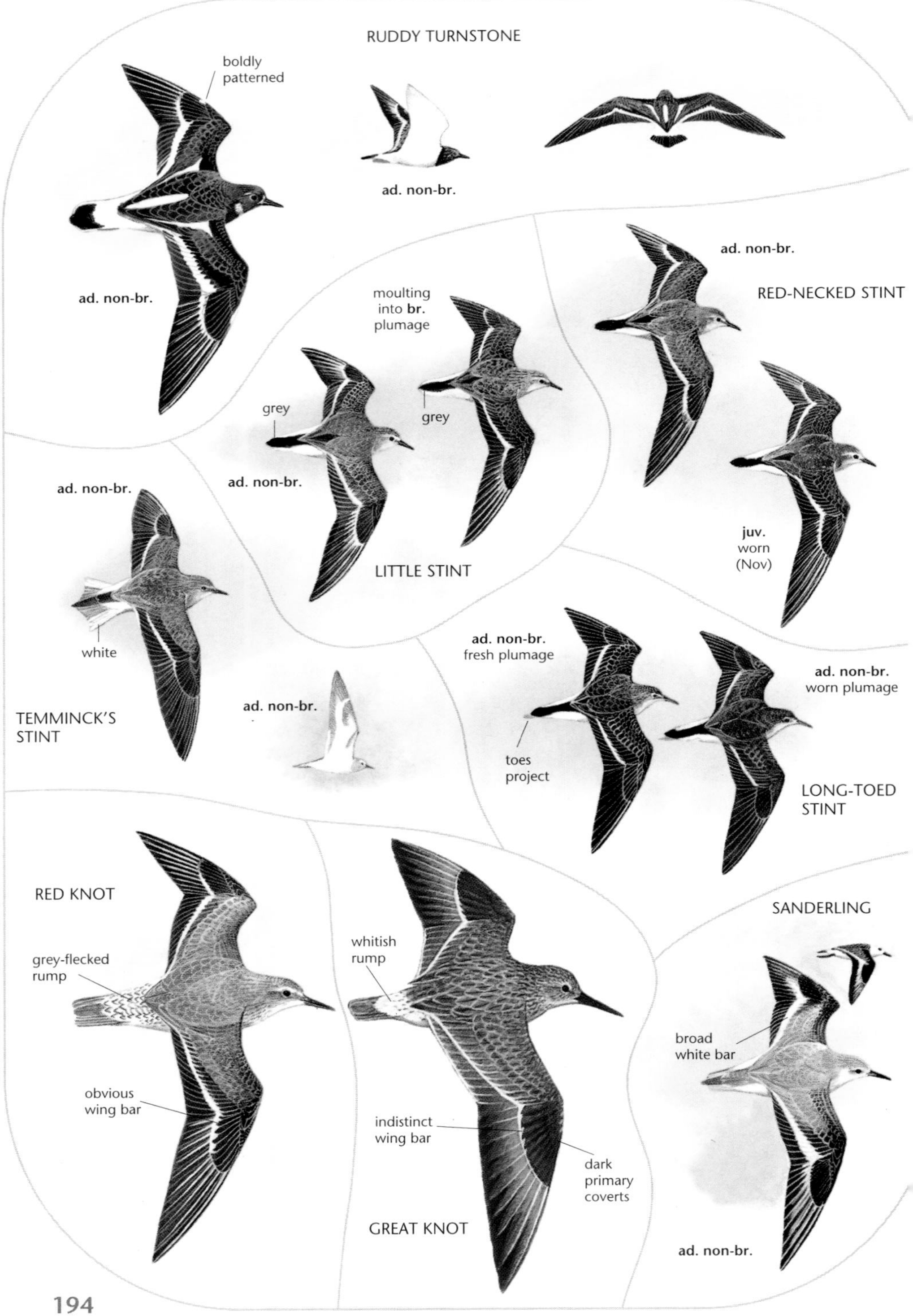

RUDDY TURNSTONE

boldly
patterned

ad. non-br.

ad. non-br.

ad. non-br.

RED-NECKED STINT

moulting
into **br.**
plumage

grey

grey

ad. non-br.

ad. non-br.

ad. non-br.

**juv.
worn
(Nov)**

LITTLE STINT

ad. non-br.
fresh plumage

ad. non-br.
worn plumage

white

toes
project

TEMMINCK'S
STINT

ad. non-br.

LONG-TOED
STINT

RED KNOT

SANDERLING

grey-flecked
rump

whitish
rump

obvious
wing bar

broad
white bar

indistinct
wing bar

dark
primary
coverts

GREAT KNOT

ad. non-br.

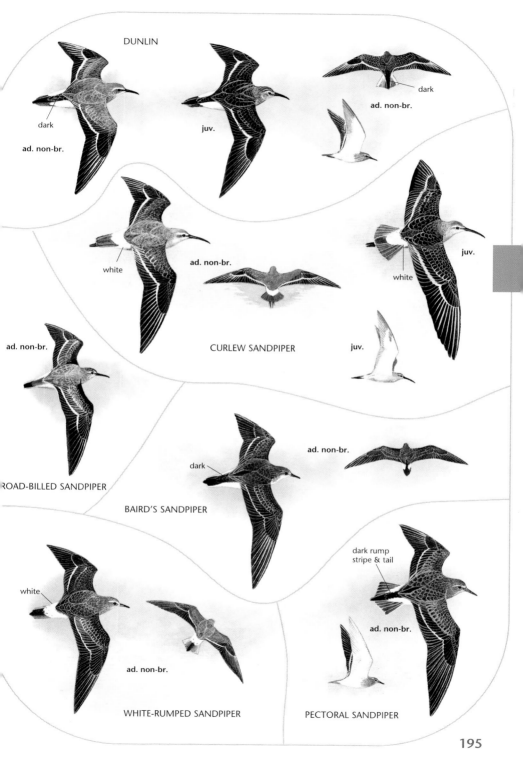

DUNLIN

dark

ad. non-br.

juv.

dark

ad. non-br.

white

ad. non-br.

CURLEW SANDPIPER

white

juv.

juv.

ad. non-br.

ROAD-BILLED SANDPIPER

dark

ad. non-br.

BAIRD'S SANDPIPER

white

ad. non-br.

WHITE-RUMPED SANDPIPER

dark rump
stripe & tail

ad. non-br.

PECTORAL SANDPIPER

See also pages 180–183

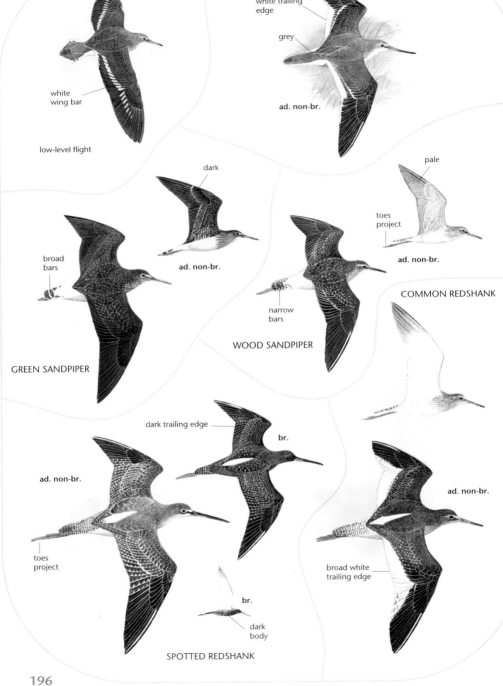

COMMON SANDPIPER

TEREK SANDPIPER

white trailing edge

grey

ad. non-br.

white wing bar

low-level flight

dark

pale

toes project

ad. non-br.

broad bars

ad. non-br.

narrow bars

COMMON REDSHANK

WOOD SANDPIPER

GREEN SANDPIPER

dark trailing edge

br.

ad. non-br.

ad. non-br.

toes project

broad white trailing edge

br.

dark body

SPOTTED REDSHANK

196

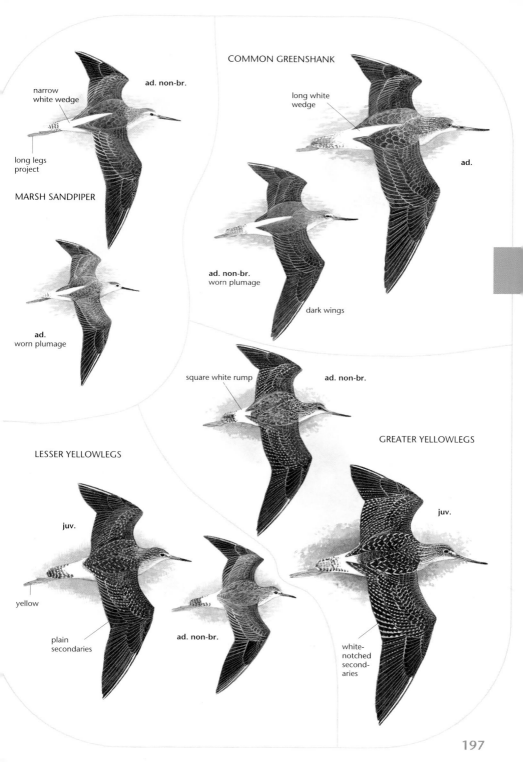

COMMON GREENSHANK

long white
wedge

ad.

narrow
white wedge

ad. non-br.

long legs
project

MARSH SANDPIPER

ad. non-br.
worn plumage

dark wings

ad.
worn plumage

square white rump

ad. non-br.

GREATER YELLOWLEGS

LESSER YELLOWLEGS

juv.

juv.

yellow

plain
secondaries

ad. non-br.

white-
notched
second-
aries

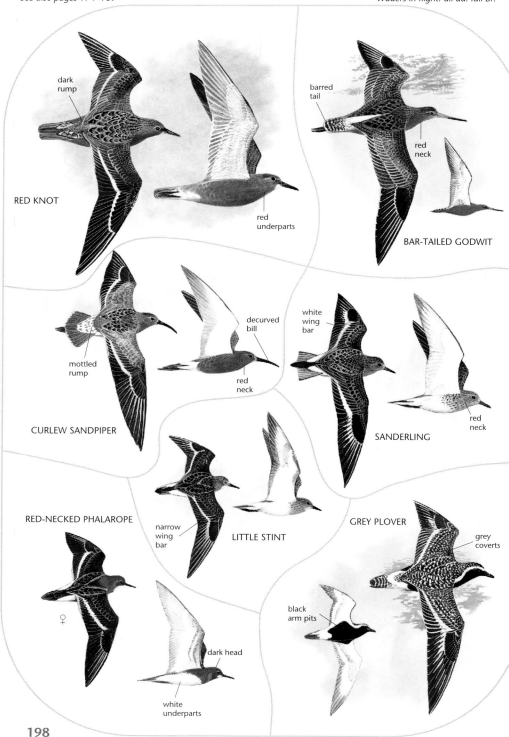

RED KNOT

dark rump

red underparts

BAR-TAILED GODWIT

barred tail

red neck

CURLEW SANDPIPER

mottled rump

decurved bill

red neck

SANDERLING

white wing bar

red neck

RED-NECKED PHALAROPE

♀

LITTLE STINT

narrow wing bar

dark head

white underparts

GREY PLOVER

grey coverts

black arm pits

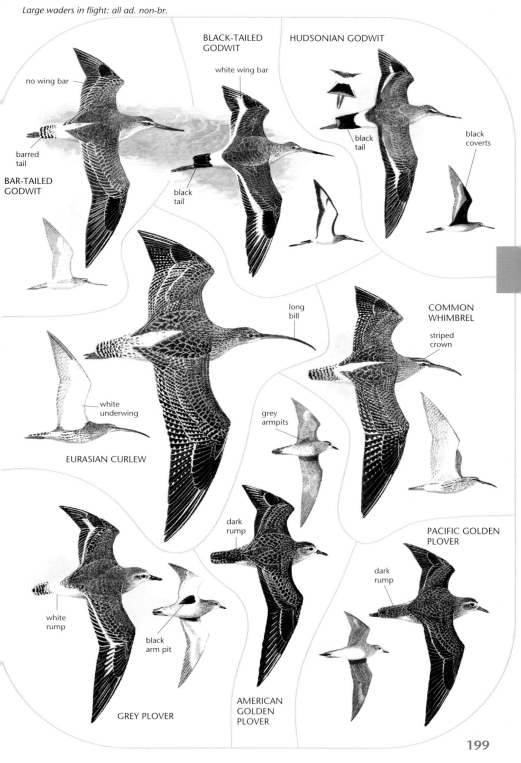

Large waders in flight: all ad. non-br.

BLACK-TAILED GODWIT

HUDSONIAN GODWIT

no wing bar

white wing bar

barred tail

black tail

black tail

black coverts

BAR-TAILED GODWIT

long bill

COMMON WHIMBREL

striped crown

white underwing

EURASIAN CURLEW

grey armpits

dark rump

PACIFIC GOLDEN PLOVER

white rump

black arm pit

dark rump

GREY PLOVER

AMERICAN GOLDEN PLOVER

199

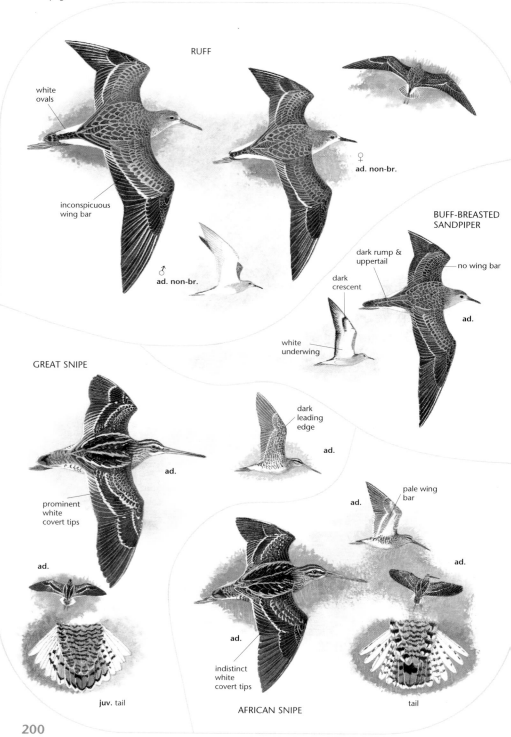

RUFF

white ovals

inconspicuous wing bar

♀ ad. non-br.

♂ ad. non-br.

BUFF-BREASTED SANDPIPER

dark rump & uppertail

no wing bar

dark crescent

white underwing

ad.

GREAT SNIPE

dark leading edge

ad.

ad.

pale wing bar

ad.

ad.

prominent white covert tips

ad.

ad.

indistinct white covert tips

juv. tail

AFRICAN SNIPE

tail

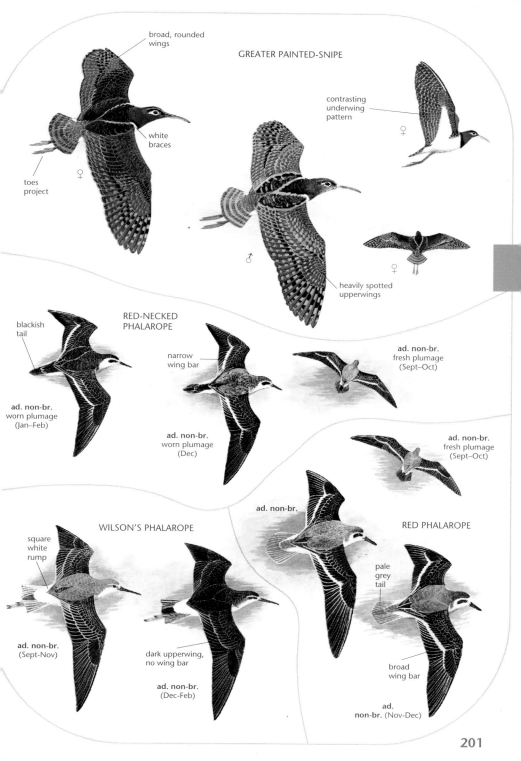

GREATER PAINTED-SNIPE

broad, rounded wings

contrasting underwing pattern

♀

white braces

toes project

♀

♂

heavily spotted upperwings

RED-NECKED PHALAROPE

blackish tail

narrow wing bar

ad. non-br. fresh plumage (Sept–Oct)

ad. non-br. worn plumage (Jan–Feb)

ad. non-br. worn plumage (Dec)

ad. non-br. fresh plumage (Sept–Oct)

ad. non-br.

WILSON'S PHALAROPE

square white rump

RED PHALAROPE

pale grey tail

ad. non-br. (Sept-Nov)

dark upperwing, no wing bar

ad. non-br. (Dec-Feb)

broad wing bar

ad. non-br. (Nov-Dec)

201

1. SPOTTED THICK-KNEE (DIKKOP) *Burhinus capensis* (297)   43 cm
Larger and darker than Water Thick-knee, with obviously spotted upperparts. It lacks a wing bar or panel but has two small, white patches on each upperwing, visible in flight. It is predominantly nocturnal.
Juv. like ad. **Habitat.** Grassland and savanna. **Status.** Common resident. **Call.** A rising then falling 'whiw-whiw-whiw', especially at night. (Gewone Dikkop)

2. WATER THICK-KNEE (DIKKOP) *Burhinus vermiculatus* (298)   38-41 cm
Smaller than Spotted Thick-knee. Has a large, grey wing panel, narrow, white wing bar, and streaked (not spotted) upperparts. The wing panel and wing bar distinguish it in flight. It is mainly nocturnal, but more active by day than Spotted Thick-knee.
Juv. resembles ad. **Habitat.** River edges and wetlands with suitable cover. Usually in pairs. **Status.** Common resident. **Call.** 'Ti-ti-tee-teee-tooo', slowing and dropping in pitch at the end; usually heard at night. (Waterdikkop)

3. TEMMINCK'S COURSER *Cursorius temminckii* (300)   19-21 cm
Confusion is likely only with Burchell's Courser, from which it differs in being more grey-brown above, and having a rufous (not grey) hind crown and a black patch (not a bar) on the belly. In flight the outertail and trailing edge of the secondaries are white; remainder of the underwing is black.
Juv. is duller than ad., with lightly speckled underparts and scalloped upperparts. **Habitat.** Dry, sparsely grassed and recently burned areas. **Status.** Locally common resident and nomad. **Call.** A grating 'keerkeer'. (Trekdrawwertjie)

4. BURCHELL'S COURSER *Cursorius rufus* (299)   23 cm
A plain buff-grey courser with a black-and-white line extending back from the eye and forming a hind collar. Distinguished from Temminck's Courser by its blue-grey hind crown and nape, and the black bar on the belly. In flight, there is a white trailing edge to the secondaries and a white tip to the outertail.
Juv. is mottled above; lower breast markings are less defined than in ad. **Habitat.** Dry, sparsely grassed areas. **Status.** Uncommon and decreasing, near-endemic; distribution erratic and unpredictable. **Call.** A harsh, repeated 'wark'. (Bloukopdrawwertjie)

5. DOUBLE-BANDED COURSER *Rhinoptilus africanus* (301)   20-24 cm
The two narrow, black bands ringing the upper breast are diagnostic. Its head is marked only with a creamy eyebrow stripe. The wing and back feathers are dark with contrasting, pale creamy buff edges. In flight the uppertail coverts are conspicuously white; the inner primaries and all the secondaries are chestnut.
Juv. has chestnut breast bands. **Habitat.** Dry, open areas, including deserts. **Status.** Common resident. **Call.** A thin, falling and rising 'teeu-wee' whistle and repeated 'kee-kee' notes. (Dubbelbanddrawwertjie)

6. THREE-BANDED COURSER *Rhinoptilus cinctus* (302)   25-28 cm
Three diagnostic bands, the upper and lower of which are rufous, ring the neck and breast. The white eye-stripe extends into a hind collar. In flight the white uppertail coverts contrast with the dark tail. It is largely nocturnal.
Habitat. Dry woodland, especially mopane. **Status.** Uncommon to locally common resident, confined to the extreme north. **Call.** A repeated 'kika-kika-kika'. (Driebanddrawwertjie)

7. BRONZE-WINGED COURSER *Rhinoptilus chalcopterus* (303)   25-28 cm
The broad, dusky band across the breast and lower neck is separated from the pale lower breast and belly by a black line. In flight the white uppertail coverts and narrow wing bars contrast with the dark upperparts. It is nocturnal.
Juv. has rufous-tipped feathers on the upperparts. **Habitat.** Woodland and savanna. **Status.** Fairly common resident and summer visitor; subject to local movements. **Call.** A ringing 'ki-kooi'. (Bronsvlerkdrawwertjie)

See also page 192

1 spotted above / spotted breast

2 streaked breast / pale panel

3 rufous hind crown / black edge

4 grey hind crown / white edge / black bar

5 chestnut wing / double bar

6 rufous ear coverts / rufous breast band

7 bold pattern / single bar

1. SUBANTARCTIC SKUA *Catharacta antarctica* (310)   60-66 cm

The largest skua, heavy-bodied and broad-winged with large white wing flashes. Its size and relatively short rump and tail distinguish it from juv. Pomarine Jaeger, which also has a less obvious white wing flash. Distinguished from South Polar Skua by the lack of contrast between the wing and underpart colours. **Habitat.** Open seas; regularly scavenges at trawlers. **Status.** Common visitor to all coasts, chiefly during winter. **Call.** A soft 'wek-wek' and a loud 'yap-yap'. (Bruinroofmeeu)

2. SOUTH POLAR SKUA *Catharacta maccormicki* (311)   53 cm

The plumage is variable, but the dark upperparts and underwing of ad. contrast with the paler head, nape and underbody. Both this species and Subantarctic Skua have a white flash in the primaries, but the latter species lacks the contrasting plumage and has a larger, heavier bill and chunkier body. Rare dark morph is smaller than Subantarctic Skua, more uniformly dark and, like all morphs, has a pale grey, grizzled area at base of bill. Sits more upright on the water with longer-necked appearance. **Juv.** is darker than ad. but also has the diagnostic pale collar and shows grey feathering at the base of the bill. **Habitat.** Open sea; scavenges at trawlers. **Status.** Rare passage migrant. **Call.** Not recorded in the region. (Suidpoolroofmeeu)

3. POMARINE JAEGER (SKUA) *Stercorarius pomarinus* (309)   65-78 cm

This species occurs most commonly in its pale form, when ad. may be identified by the spoon-shaped (not pointed) central tail feathers, although these are often worn or absent. In comparison with Parasitic and Long-tailed Jaegers it is more heavily built, is barrel-chested and has broader-based wings. **Juv.** is larger and heavier than juv. Parasitic Jaeger, is more heavily barred on the uppertail and undertail coverts, and has broader-based wings. **Habitat.** Open seas. **Status.** Fairly common summer visitor. **Call.** Usually silent in the region. (Knopstertroofmeeu)

4. PARASITIC JAEGER (ARCTIC SKUA) *Stercorarius parasiticus* (307)   46-67 cm

Pale, dark and intermediate morphs occur. Pomarine Jaeger is bulkier, broader-winged and larger-billed, and the central tail feathers, if present, are spoon-shaped (not pointed). Long-tailed Jaeger is greyer and slimmer, has narrower wings and much longer, pointed central tail feathers (if present), and lacks the white flash at the base of the primaries. **Juv.** closely resembles juv. Long-tailed Jaeger but is larger and bulkier and shows white primary flashes. **Habitat.** Prefers inshore waters, where it parasitises terns and gulls. **Status.** Common summer visitor; some overwinter. **Call.** Usually silent in the region. (Arktiese Roofmeeu)

5. LONG-TAILED JAEGER (SKUA) *Stercorarius longicaudus* (308)   35-58 cm

Ad. in breeding plumage has diagnostic, very long central tail feathers. It occurs in both pale and dark forms, the latter extremely rare. Compared to Parasitic and Pomarine jaegers the pale morph has a slimmer body, wings and bill and colder grey-brown plumage, and the white markings in the upperwings are confined to the outermost primaries. **Juv.** differs from juv. Parasitic Jaeger only by its smaller size and more tern-like proportions, the limited white in the upperwings and the paler legs. **Habitat.** Open oceans, where it attends trawlers. **Status.** Uncommon summer visitor and locally common passage migrant. **Call.** Silent in the region. (Langstertroofmeeu)

6. GREATER SHEATHBILL *Chionis albus* (912)   40 cm

A plump, white, pigeon-like bird with bare pink skin around the eyes and a yellow-ish base to the bill and sheath. **Juv.** has dark skin around the eyes and lacks the yellow base to the bill. **Habitat.** Oceanic islands and Antarctica. **Status.** Ship-assisted vagrant, mostly in winter. **Call.** Not recorded in the region. (Grootskedebek)

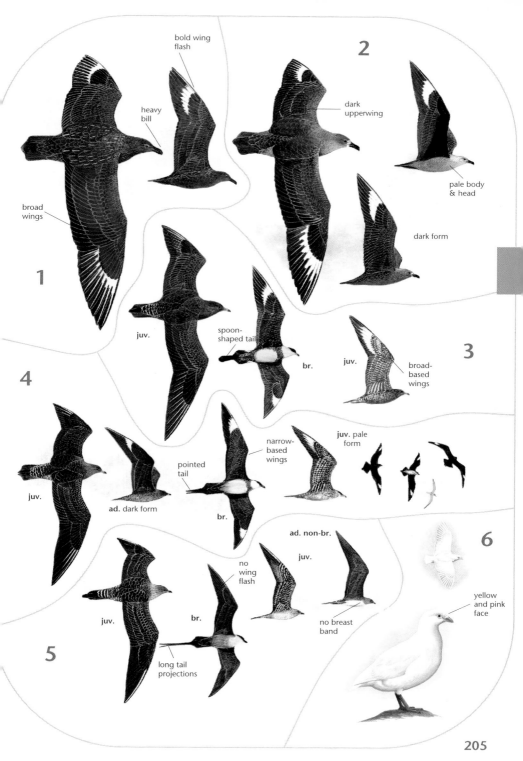

2

bold wing flash

heavy bill

dark upperwing

broad wings

pale body & head

dark form

1

4

juv.

spoon-shaped tail

br.

juv.

broad-based wings

3

juv.

ad. dark form

pointed tail

narrow-based wings

juv. pale form

br.

ad. non-br.

juv.

6

juv.

br.

no wing flash

no breast band

yellow and pink face

5

long tail projections

1. CAPE (KELP) GULL *Larus vetula* (312)   55-65 cm
The largest resident gull of the region. Bulkier than ad. Lesser Black-backed Gull and has a larger bill, steeper forehead, and olive (not yellow) legs. Sub-ad. is further distinguished from sub-ad. Lesser Black-backed Gull by its brownish (not pink) legs. At rest, the wings of Lesser Black-backed Gull project noticeably further beyond the tail. Cf. Kelp Gull below to distinguish it from this species.
Habitat. Inshore waters, open coast, estuaries, harbours and dumps. **Status.** Common resident. **Call.** A loud 'ki-ok' and a short, repeated alarm call, 'kwok'. (Grootswartrugmeeu)

2. KELP GULL *Larus dominicanus*   55-60 cm
Separable only at close range from Cape Gull by the pale, not dark eye. Other subtle differences include the neat, rounded head that differs from the flatly sloped, rakish and angular head of Cape Gull, and the smaller, shorter and more compact bill.
Juv. and imm. not reliably distinguishable from similarly aged Cape Gull. **Habitat.** Coastal areas. **Status.** Unclear; possibly regular winter visitor in small numbers. **Call.** Similar to Cape Gull. (Kelpmeeu)

3. LESSER BLACK-BACKED GULL *Larus fuscus* (313)   51-61 cm
At all ages this species may be distinguished from Cape and Kelp gulls by its more attenuated appearance, with the wings projecting well beyond tail at rest, and its less robust bill. Compared with Cape and Kelp gulls, ad. has rich yellow (not olive) legs.
Juv. may be distinguished from juv. Cape and Kelp gulls by having flesh-coloured (not brownish) legs and by its generally slender proportions and shape; it may be distinguished from juv. Herring Gull by the lack of pale windows in the inner primaries. **Habitat.** Estuaries and inland water bodies; the only large, dark-backed gull to be found far inland. **Status.** Uncommon summer visitor. **Call.** A typical, large-gull 'kow-kow' and a shorter 'kop'. (Kleinswartrugmeeu)

4. HERRING GULL *Larus argentatus* (314)   55-67 cm
A large, pale gull, similar in size and shape to Cape Gull and larger than Lesser Black-backed Gull. The very pale grey upperwings, with their black, white-spotted primary tips, make confusion with any local gull unlikely.
Juv. generally paler than juv. and imm. Lesser Black-backed, Cape and Kelp Gulls, with a pale window in the inner primaries. **Habitat.** In Africa, mainly open coast, estuaries and inshore waters. **Status.** Vagrant. **Call.** Loud, persistent 'kleeeuw kleeeuw'. (Haringmeeu)

5. CASPIAN TERN *Sterna caspia* (322)   47-54 cm
By far the largest tern of the region, this species has a black cap in breeding plumage and a streaked cap in non-breeding plumage, and a red or orange-red bill, usually black-tipped. The underwing tip is black. Royal Tern (p. 210) has a smaller, more orange bill and a more deeply forked tail.
Juv. has brown fringes to the wing coverts, more grey in the tail, and a paler base and more extensive black tip to the bill. **Habitat.** Islands, bays, estuaries, lagoons, inshore waters and large rivers. **Status.** Fairly common resident around the coast, uncommon inland. **Call.** A harsh, grating 'kraaak'. (Reusesterretjie)

6. AFRICAN SKIMMER *Rhynchops flavirostris* (343)   38-40 cm
The peculiarly shaped, yellow-tipped, red bill is diagnostic, the lower mandible being longer than the upper.
Juv. resembles ad. but the black upperparts are replaced by pale-fringed brown feathering and the bill is blackish, becoming brighter with age. **Habitat.** Large rivers, bays and lakes where there are open stretches of water for feeding and sandbanks for roosting. **Status.** Locally common resident in the far north; vagrant to South Africa. **Call.** A harsh 'rak-rak'. (Waterploeër)

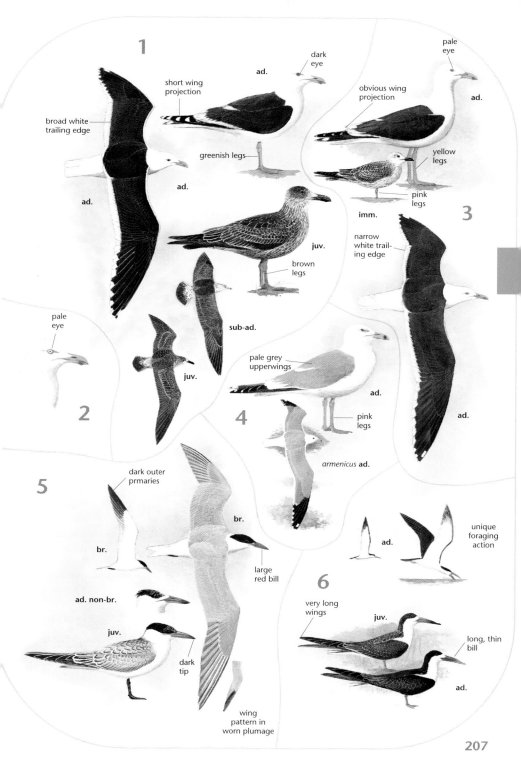

1

broad white trailing edge

short wing projection

dark eye

ad.

pale eye

obvious wing projection

ad.

yellow legs

greenish legs

pink legs

ad.

ad.

imm.

3

pale eye

brown legs

juv.

narrow white trailing edge

2

sub-ad.

juv.

pale grey upperwings

ad.

pink legs

ad.

4

armenicus ad.

5

dark outer primaries

br.

br.

large red bill

unique foraging action

ad.

6

ad. non-br.

very long wings

juv.

long, thin bill

juv.

dark tip

ad.

wing pattern in worn plumage

1. SABINE'S GULL *Larus sabini* (318)   27-32 cm
A small gull with a buoyant, tern-like flight. The boldly tricoloured upperwing and shallowly forked, white tail are diagnostic. In breeding plumage, it has a dark grey, almost black, hood and a yellow-tipped, black bill.
Habitat. Pelagic, but also frequents inshore waters, including large, sheltered bays. **Status.** Common summer visitor, often in flocks. **Call.** Silent in the region. (Mikstertmeeu)

2. FRANKLIN'S GULL *Larus pipixcan* (317)   32-36 cm
This species always has at least a partial black hood and whitish underwings. In breeding plumage it has a full black hood, a conspicuous white eye-ring and a pinkish breast. In flight the upperwing pattern is diagnostic: the black subterminal patches on the primaries are separated from the grey innerwing by a white band.
Juv. has a partial, black-streaked hood and relatively uniformly dark upperwings. **Habitat.** Open coast, estuaries and inland water bodies. **Status.** Vagrant. **Call.** A goose-like 'ha-ha-ha'. (Franklinse Meeu)

3. COMMON BLACK-HEADED GULL *Larus ridibundus* (319)   38-44 cm
Breeding ad. is paler grey above than Grey-headed Gull, with a dark brown-black hood and partial white eye-ring. In breeding plumage, the bill is dark red with a black tip. In non-breeding plumage it may be identified by the large, white wedge in the outerwing and the whitish (not grey) underwings.
Habitat. Coasts and inland waters. **Status.** Rare summer vagrant. **Call.** A typical, small-gull 'kraah'. (Swartkopmeeu)

4. BLACK-LEGGED KITTIWAKE *Rissa tridactyla* (320)   38-40 cm
May be confused with Sabine's Gull, but is larger and ad. has a diagnostic, all-yellow bill, squarish (not forked) tail, and black only on the tips of the outer primaries.
The upperwing of **imm.** has a distinct, black, open 'M' pattern. **Habitat.** Inshore and offshore waters. **Status.** Rare summer vagrant. **Call.** 'Kitt-e-wake'. (Swartpootbrandervoël)

5. GREY-HEADED GULL *Larus cirrocephalus* (315)   40-42 cm
Breeding ad. differs from the smaller Hartlaub's Gull in having a more extensive grey hood, a brighter red bill and legs, and pale silver-yellow (not dark) eyes. Both Common Black-headed and Franklin's Gulls are smaller, have very different upperwing patterns and lack the dark underwing of Grey-headed Gull.
Juv., compared with juv. Hartlaub's Gull, has more extensive smudges on the head, a dark-tipped, pinkish orange bill, darker upperwings and more black on its tail. **Habitat.** Open coast, and coastal and freshwater wetlands. **Status.** Locally common resident. **Call.** A typical 'karrh' and 'pok-pok'. (Gryskopmeeu)

6. HARTLAUB'S GULL *Larus hartlaubii* (316)   36-38 cm
Compared with breeding Grey-headed Gull this species is slightly smaller, has a thinner, darker bill, only a slight lavender hood, dark (not silver-yellow) eyes and deeper red legs. In non-breeding plumage it has a plain white head.
Juv., compared with juv. Grey-headed Gull, has darker legs, less black on the tail and only very faint smudges on the head, and lacks the two-tone bill. **Habitat.** Inshore waters, open coast, estuaries, harbours and dumps. **Status.** Common resident; endemic. **Call.** A drawn-out, rattling 'kaaarrh' and 'pok-pok'. (Hartlaubse Meeu)

7. SLENDER-BILLED GULL *Larus genei*   37-42 cm
Differs from non-br. Grey-headed and Hartlaub's Gulls by its different wing pattern and unusually shaped head. The bill appears long and drooped with shallow sloping forehead. Appears long-necked, long-legged and pigeon-breasted.
Habitat. Freshwater wetlands and coastal areas. **Status.** Rare vagrant. **Call.** Not recorded in the region. (Dunbekmeeu)

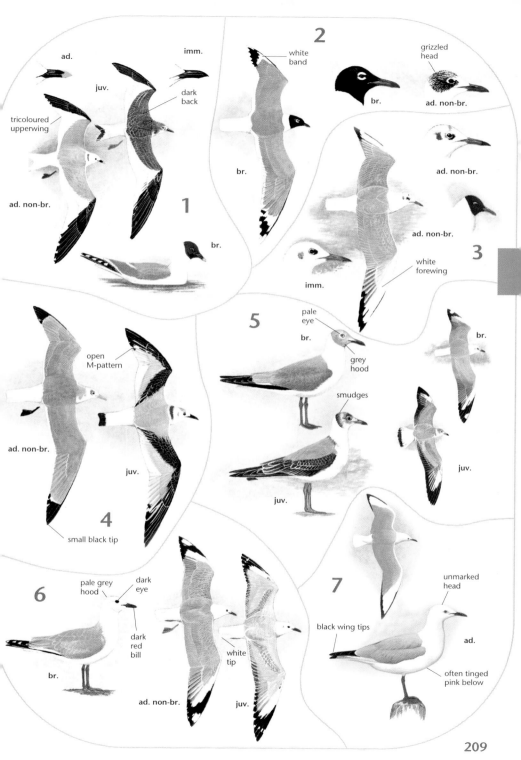

1

ad.

imm.

juv.

tricoloured upperwing

dark back

ad. non-br.

br.

2

white band

grizzled head

br.

ad. non-br.

br.

ad. non-br.

white forewing

imm.

3

ad. non-br.

4

open M-pattern

ad. non-br.

juv.

small black tip

5

pale eye

br.

grey hood

smudges

juv.

br.

juv.

6

pale grey hood

dark eye

dark red bill

br.

white tip

ad. non-br.

juv.

7

black wing tips

unmarked head

ad.

often tinged pink below

1. LESSER CRESTED TERN *Sterna bengalensis* (325) 35-37 cm

Smaller and more graceful than Swift Tern, from which it also differs in being paler above and in having a more slender and shorter orange (not yellow or greenish yellow) bill. Royal Tern is much larger, even paler above and has a larger, rich orange bill.

Juv., like juv. Swift Tern, has blackish brown on the wing coverts and saddle, but it can be distinguished by the orange-yellow bill. **Habitat.** Inshore waters, bays and estuaries. **Status.** Common summer visitor to Mozambique and KwaZulu-Natal, south to Durban; vagrant west to the Cape Peninsula. **Call.** A hoarse 'kreck'. (Kuifkopsterretjie)

2. SWIFT TERN *Sterna bergii* (324) 46-49 cm

Intermediate in size between Caspian (p. 206) and Sandwich Terns. It has a large yellow, greenish yellow or yellow-olive (not orange) bill; this distinguishes it from Lesser Crested Tern, which is also smaller and paler above. Royal Tern has much paler upperparts and a rich orange bill. In breeding plumage, Swift Tern has a white frons, whereas Royal Tern has a black cap reaching the base of the bill.

Juv. is barred dark blackish brown and has a dusky yellow-olive bill. **Habitat.** Inshore waters, islands, large bays and estuaries. **Status.** Common resident and local migrant. Breeds in the south and west of its range in late summer (occasionally winter) and then disperses to all coasts. **Call.** Ad.'s call is a harsh 'kree-eck'; juv. gives a thin, vibrating whistle. (Geelbeksterretjie)

3. ROYAL TERN *Sterna maxima* (323) 48 cm

A very pale tern with a rich orange bill, differing from the heavy red or black-tipped bill of the larger Caspian Tern (p. 206). In non-breeding plumage it has a very extensive white forehead and crown, never seen in Caspian Tern. Lesser Crested Tern is much smaller and has a brighter, more slender, orange bill. This species is paler above than similarly sized Swift Tern, and has an orange, not yellow, bill.

Juv. resembles juv. Swift Tern but shows an orange (not yellow-olive) bill. **Habitat.** Coasts, bays and estuaries. **Status.** Vagrant to northern Namibia. **Call.** A loud, harsh 'ree-ack'. (Koningsterretjie)

4. GULL-BILLED TERN *Sterna nilotica* (321) 35-38 cm

A very pale, relatively long-legged tern with a short, stubby, black bill resembling a gull's. It is similar in size to Sandwich Tern, but is heavier-bodied and broader-winged. It is seldom seen with the black cap of its breeding plumage; instead, it has a variable black smudge behind the eye. Sandwich Tern has a longer, yellow-tipped bill and a deeply forked white tail, as opposed to the shallowly forked, pale grey tail of Gull-billed Tern.

Juv. resembles non-breeding ad. **Habitat.** Variable, ranging from fields, marshes and vleis to the coast. **Status.** Summer vagrant **Call.** Variations on 'kek-kek'. (Oostelike Sterretjie)

5. SANDWICH TERN *Sterna sandvicensis* (326) 36-41 cm

A very pale tern, similar in size to Lesser Crested Tern. The black, yellow-tipped bill is diagnostic. This species could be confused with Gull-billed Tern, which has a short, stubby bill, but Sandwich Tern has a white (not grey) rump, and a more forked tail. In breeding plumage it has a black cap and the breast may have a faint pinkish hue.

Juv. resembles non-breeding ad. but has mottled upperparts; this plumage is rarely seen in the region. **Habitat.** Inshore waters, estuaries and bays, usually in association with other terns. **Status.** Common summer visitor to all coasts. **Call.** 'Kirik'. (Grootsterretjie)

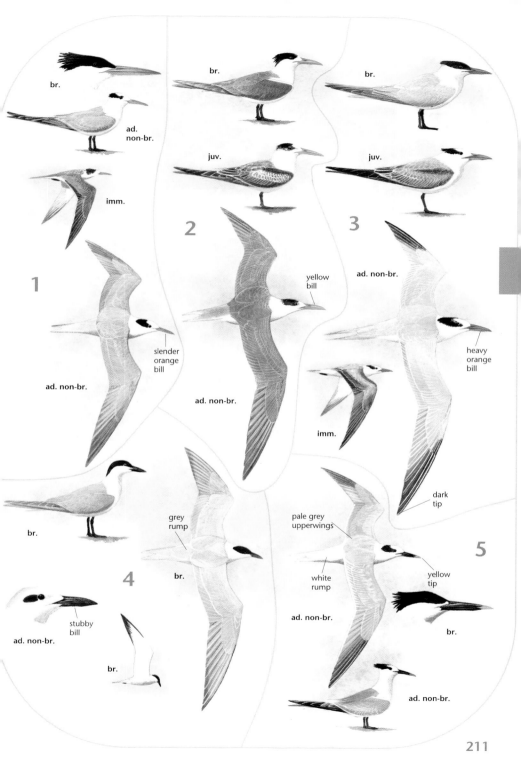

br.

ad.
non-br.

imm.

1

2

br.

juv.

yellow
bill

ad. non-br.

slender
orange
bill

ad. non-br.

br.

grey
rump

4

br.

stubby
bill

ad. non-br.

br.

3

br.

juv.

ad. non-br.

heavy
orange
bill

imm.

dark
tip

pale grey
upperwings

white
rump

yellow
tip

5

br.

ad. non-br.

ad. non-br.

211

1. COMMON TERN *Sterna hirundo* (327) 31-35 cm

It differs from Arctic and Antarctic terns by its longer bill and legs and, in non-breeding plumage, its greyish (not white) rump and tail. Rare variant has orange or orange-and-black bill in non-br. plumage. Compared with White-cheeked Tern it has a paler rump and tail, which contrast with the back. In breeding plumage it differs from Arctic Tern by its darker outerwing and black-tipped, red bill. Roseate Tern has a longer, heavier bill, paler grey upperparts and, early in the breeding season, conspicuously pinkish underparts. **Juv.** resembles non-breeding ad. but has dark carpal bars that are conspicuous at rest and in flight. **Habitat.** Open sea and coastal lakes. **Status.** Very common summer visitor to all coasts; regularly overwinters. **Call.** 'Kik-kik' and 'kee-arh'. (Gewone Sterretjie)

2. ARCTIC TERN *Sterna paradisaea* (328) 33-35 cm

Shorter-legged and shorter-billed than Common Tern, Arctic Tern also has a white (not pale grey) rump and tail, and paler wing tips in flight. In breeding plumage, the bill and legs are dark red. In non-breeding plumage, it most resembles Antarctic Tern but has a black (not dark red) bill and legs, and a shorter, more delicate bill. Antarctic Tern attains breeding plumage from October to April and Arctic Tern from April to September, so confusion is unlikely. **Juv.** differs from juv. Common Tern by its reduced carpal bar and pale secondaries, and by the marked contrast between the grey back and the white rump. **Habitat.** Pelagic; sometimes roosts ashore, usually with Common Terns. **Status.** Fairly uncommon but regular passage migrant and summer visitor. **Call.** A short 'kik-kik', given in flight. (Arktiese Sterretjie)

3. ANTARCTIC TERN *Sterna vittata* (329) 34-36 cm

More thickset than Arctic or Common terns, with a heavier coral red, dusky red or blackish bill. In breeding plumage it has a full black cap, dusky underparts and a white cheek stripe. In non-breeding plumage, it is white to pale grey below (depending on race), with a conspicuously grizzled crown. White-cheeked Tern has a grey (not white) rump. **Juv.** has chequered brown, grey and white upperparts and can be confused only with juv. Roseate Tern and Whiskered Tern (p. 216). Roseate Tern has paler upperparts. Whiskered Tern has a grey (not white) rump. **Habitat.** Coastal waters; roosts with other terns. **Status.** Fairly common winter visitor to Cape coastal waters, small numbers in summer on west coast. **Call.** A sharp, high-pitched 'kik-kik'. (Grysborssterretjie)

4. ROSEATE TERN *Sterna dougallii* (330) 33-38 cm

Distinguished by its pale upperparts, long, blackish bill with a red base and long, white outertail feathers projecting well beyond the wings at rest. Smaller Black-naped Tern (p. 214) lacks the black on the crown and has an all-black bill. In breeding plumage, has very long tail streamers, a pink flush to the breast, a black-tipped, red bill and crimson legs. **Juv.** differs from juv. Antarctic Tern in having a blacker cap, longer bill, greyer wings and more slender body. **Habitat.** Coastal waters; breeds on islands in Algoa Bay and Walker Bay. **Status.** Endangered resident and local migrant. Uncommon but regular in KwaZulu-Natal. **Call.** A grating 'aarh'. (Rooiborssterretjie)

5. WHITE-CHEEKED TERN *Sterna repressa* (336) 32-38 cm

The uniform colour of the back, rump and tail appears 'dirtier' grey than in Common or Arctic terns, in both of which the tail and rump are paler than the back. In breeding plumage it resembles Antarctic Tern, but has a grey (not white) rump, and Whiskered Tern (p. 216), from which it differs by its larger size, deeply forked tail and dusky grey (not white) vent. **Juv.** resembles non-breeding ad. **Habitat.** Inshore waters, estuaries. **Status.** Rare summer vagrant to the east coast. **Call.** A ringing 'kee-leck'. (Witwangsterretjie)

212

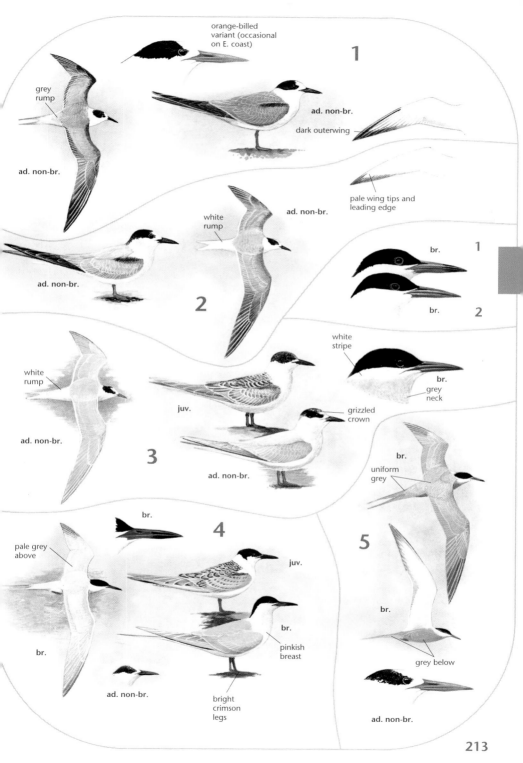

orange-billed variant (occasional on E. coast)

1

grey rump

ad. non-br.

ad. non-br.

dark outerwing

pale wing tips and leading edge

ad. non-br.

white rump

ad. non-br.

2

br. **1**

br. **2**

white stripe

br.
grey neck

white rump

juv.

grizzled crown

ad. non-br.

ad. non-br.

3

br.
uniform grey

pale grey above

br.

4

juv.

5

br.

br.
pinkish breast

br.

ad. non-br.

grey below

bright crimson legs

ad. non-br.

213

1. BRIDLED TERN *Sterna anaethetus* (333)   30-32 cm

This species can be confused only with Sooty Tern, but is smaller and has paler, brown-grey, not black upperparts. The white frons is narrower than in Sooty Tern and extends as an eyebrow stripe slightly behind the eye (Sooty Tern's frons patch ends at the eye). The crown is clearly darker than the back.

Juv. and imm. have the wing coverts finely edged with buffy white and the underparts white; the underparts of juv. Sooty Tern are partially or totally dirty grey. **Habitat.** Pelagic; occasionally roosts ashore. **Status.** Summer vagrant. **Call.** 'Wup-wup'. (Brilsterretjie)

2. SOOTY TERN *Sterna fuscata* (332)   40-44 cm

This species could be confused with Bridled Tern but it is larger, the white frons extends backwards only as far as the eye, and the black crown does not contrast with the blackish upperparts.

Juv. has largely or partially dirty grey underparts whereas juv. and imm. Bridled Tern are always white below. Imm. Sooty Tern has a white lower breast and belly. **Habitat.** Pelagic, but blown onto coast during severe storms. **Status.** Common summer visitor to Mozambican offshore waters, often foraging in large flocks. A summer vagrant to the KwaZulu-Natal and Cape coasts, with inland records from the northeastern parts of South Africa and southern Zimbabwe during and after cyclones. **Call.** Variations on 'wick-a-wick'. (Roetsterretjie)

3. BLACK-NAPED TERN *Sterna sumatrana* (331)   30 cm

Ad. has a black band extending backwards from the eye, broadening on the nape. The crown is pure white. The upperparts are pale, resembling those of Roseate Tern (p. 212), but the latter has black streaking on the crown and is larger. Black on the wing is restricted to the outer primary. Underparts are variably suffused with pink.

Juv. has the crown feathers tipped with black and the wings have a dusky carpal bar. **Habitat.** Coastal waters, sometimes roosting with other terns in estuaries. **Status.** Summer vagrant to Mozambique and KwaZulu-Natal. **Call.** A clipped, repeated 'ki-ki'. (Swartneksterretjie)

4. LITTLE TERN *Sterna albifrons* (335)   22-24 cm

This species differs from Damara Tern by its shorter, straight bill and white (not grey) tail. The dark outer primaries contrast with the remainder of the upperwing; the upperwing of Damara Tern is more uniform. It can also be distinguished by its call. The legs are brownish yellow and the bill shows varying amounts of yellow at the base, frequently appearing all dark; the legs and bill become yellower before the northward migration in March. Sometimes seen in breeding plumage, when frons is white (not black as in Damara Tern) and the bill is yellow with a black tip. **Habitat.** Shallow coastal waters, large bays and estuaries. **Status.** Fairly common summer visitor to the east coast, uncommon and patchily distributed in the west. **Call.** A rasping 'kek-kek'. (Kleinsterretjie)

5. DAMARA TERN *Sterna balaenarum* (334)   23 cm

This species differs from Little Tern by its longer, slightly decurved bill and by its more uniform upperparts; the rump and uppertail are pale grey (not white). In both breeding and non-breeding plumage the underparts are washed with very pale grey. In breeding plumage, it has a black bill, yellowish legs (with yellow feet) and a complete black cap. Frons white in non-breeding plumage.

Juv. has brown barring on the upperparts. **Habitat.** Sheltered coastlines, bays and lagoons. **Status.** Locally common resident; breeding summer visitor to southern parts of its range. Breeding endemic. **Call.** A high-pitched 'tsit-tsit' and a harsh, rapid 'kid-ick'. (Damarasterretjie)

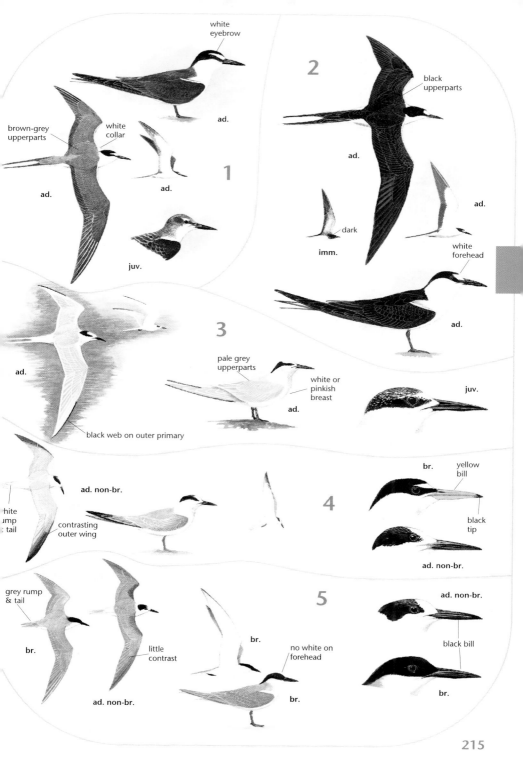

white
eyebrow

2

black
upperparts

ad.

ad.

brown-grey
upperparts

white
collar

ad.

1

ad.

ad.

dark

imm.

white
forehead

ad.

juv.

3

pale grey
upperparts

white or
pinkish
breast

ad.

juv.

ad.

black web on outer primary

hite
ump
tail

ad. non-br.

contrasting
outer wing

4

br.

yellow
bill

black
tip

ad. non-br.

grey rump
& tail

5

ad. non-br.

black bill

br.

little
contrast

br.

no white on
forehead

ad. non-br.

br.

br.

215

1. BROWN (COMMON) NODDY *Anous stolidus* (340) 36-45 cm
A brown tern with a wedge-shaped tail that is obviously notched only when fanned.
It may be confused with Lesser Noddy, which is smaller and has more uniformly dark
upperwings and underwings (upperwing coverts of Brown Noddy are obviously paler
than the flight feathers). The white forehead contrasts sharply with the brown lores.
The whitish grey cap does not extend onto the nape as in Lesser Noddy.
Juv. resembles ad. but the pale head markings may be confined to the forehead only.
Habitat. Pelagic, but occasionally roosts ashore. **Status.** Rare summer vagrant to the
coasts of Mozambique, KwaZulu-Natal and the Western Cape. **Call.** A hoarse 'kark'.
(Grootbruinsterretjie)

2. LESSER NODDY *Anous tenuirostris* (341) 30-34 cm
Smaller than Brown Noddy, with a proportionally longer and distinctly thinner bill.
The whitish forehead merges with the brown lores and the ashy grey crown extends
further back onto the nape than in Brown Noddy. The underwing is dark brown (not
pale and dark-rimmed as in Brown Noddy) and the upperwing is uniformly dark.
Juv. closely resembles ad. **Habitat.** Pelagic, but occasionally roosts ashore. **Status.**
Summer vagrant to KwaZulu-Natal and Mozambique following cyclones. **Call.** Not recorded in the region; reported elsewhere as a short, rattling 'churrr'. (Kleinbruinsterretjie)

3. BLACK TERN *Chlidonias niger* (337) 22-24 cm
In breeding plumage, it differs from White-winged Tern by its pale grey (not black)
underwing coverts, and the upperwings, which do not contrast with the back. In
non-breeding plumage it superficially resembles White-winged Tern, but the dark
shoulder smudge is diagnostic (could be confused with breast smudge of White-
winged Tern in transitional plumage). There is more black on the head than White-
winged Tern, and no colour contrast between the dusky grey back, rump and tail.
Whiskered Tern is paler, and has less black on the head and no shoulder smudge.
Juv. resembles non-breeding ad. **Habitat.** Usually forages at sea, often close inshore. Often
roosts at coastal wetlands. **Status.** Common summer visitor to the Namibian coast, uncommon to rare on the South African coast. Vagrant to Botswana and the northeastern interior
of South Africa. Call. Usually silent in the region; flight call a quiet 'kik-kik'. (Swartsterretjie)

4. WHITE-WINGED TERN *Chlidonias leucopterus* (339) 20-23 cm
When breeding this species resembles Black Tern, but has black underwing coverts,
predominantly white upperwings and a paler rump and tail. In non-breeding
plumage it resembles Whiskered Tern, but has a white (not grey) rump and
smudged head markings. Non-breeding Black Tern is much darker above, with more
black on the head, a dark rump and tail similar in colour to the back and upperwings, and a diagnostic black smudge on the breast at the base of the forewing.
Juv. resembles non-breeding ad. **Habitat.** Open water bodies, estuaries and marshes.
Occasionally forages at sea in sheltered bays and where large quantities of kelp are washed
ashore, also over open veld. **Status.** Common and widespread summer visitor. **Call.** A
short 'kek-kek'. (Witvlerksterretjie)

5. WHISKERED TERN *Chlidonias hybrida* (338) 25-26 cm
In breeding plumage this species resembles White-cheeked Tern (p. 212), but is
smaller and has a white vent and a less deeply forked tail. In non-breeding plumage
it is very similar to White-winged Tern, but has a pale grey rump and a grizzled
head pattern more closely resembling that of Antarctic Tern (p. 212). Black Tern is
darker, with more black on the head and a diagnostic dark shoulder smudge.
Juv. resembles juv. Antarctic Tern but the latter has a white (not grey) uppertail, and the
two species are unlikely to be seen in the same habitat. **Habitat.** Wide range of open,
freshwater bodies, from large lakes and river flood plains to small farm dams. **Status.** Fairly
common resident and local migrant. **Call.** A repeated, hard 'zizz'. (Witbaardsterretjie)

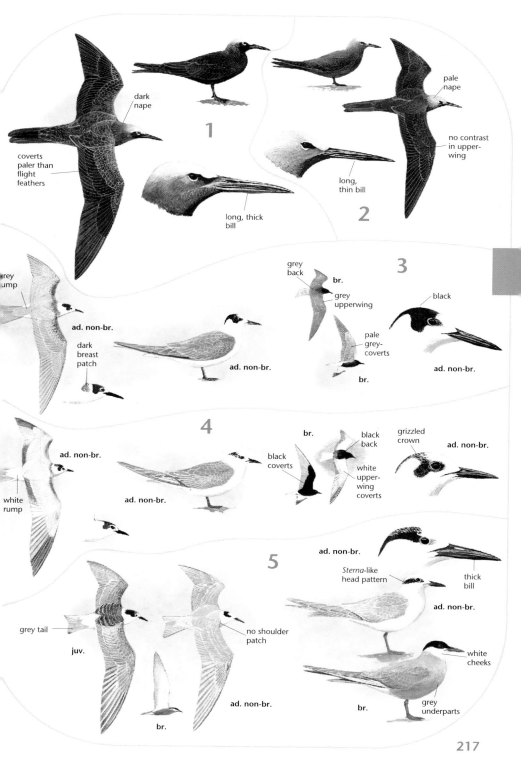

1

dark nape

coverts paler than flight feathers

long, thick bill

2

pale nape

no contrast in upper-wing

long, thin bill

3

grey rump

ad. non-br.

dark breast patch

ad. non-br.

grey back

br.

grey upperwing

pale grey-coverts

br.

black

ad. non-br.

4

ad. non-br.

white rump

ad. non-br.

br.

black coverts

black back

white upper-wing coverts

grizzled crown

ad. non-br.

5

ad. non-br.

Sterna-like head pattern

thick bill

ad. non-br.

grey tail

juv.

no shoulder patch

white cheeks

br.

grey underparts

ad. non-br.

br.

217

1. DOUBLE-BANDED SANDGROUSE *Pterocles bicinctus* (347)   25-28 cm
This species most resembles Namaqua Sandgrouse but male is easily identified by the black-and-white markings on the forehead, and the barring on the lower breast and belly. Male Double-banded and Namaqua Sandgrouse both have a thin, black-and-white breast band.
Female and juv. may be distinguished from female and juv. Namaqua Sandgrouse by their darker, streaked crown, barred (not streaked) upper breast, and rounded (not pointed) tail. **Habitat.** Woodland and savanna. Flocks gather at drinking sites at dusk. **Status.** Scarce to locally common resident. **Call.** A whistling 'chwee-chee-chee' and a soft 'wee-chee-choo-chip-chip' flight call. (Dubbelbandsandpatrys)

2. YELLOW-THROATED SANDGROUSE *Pterocles gutturalis* (346)   27-30 cm
The largest sandgrouse of the region; easily identified in flight by its dark brown belly and underwings.
Male has a creamy yellow throat and face, with a broad black neck band. Female and juv. also show the very dark belly and underwing, which eliminates confusion with any other female or juv. sandgrouse. Female lacks the black collar. **Habitat.** Open grassland to scrub savanna. Flocks gather at drinking sites during the morning. **Status.** Uncommon resident. **Call.** A deep, far-carrying bisyllabic 'aw-aw', the first higher pitched, given in flight; sometimes preceded by 'ipi'. (Geelkeelsandpatrys)

3. NAMAQUA SANDGROUSE Pterocles namaqua (344)   25 cm
This is the only sandgrouse in the region with a long, pointed tail. At rest or when walking, male most resembles Double-banded Sandgrouse but lacks the black and white bands on the forehead and has a plain (not barred) lower breast and belly.
Female and juv. differ from female and juv. Double-banded Sandgrouse in being more buffy yellow on the throat and breast, and in having a pointed (not rounded) tail. **Habitat.** Grassland, semi-desert and desert. Avoids mountainous and wet regions. **Status.** Common resident with local movements; near-endemic. **Call.** A nasal 'kalke-vein', given in flight. (Kelkiewyn)

4. BURCHELL'S SANDGROUSE *Pterocles burchelli* (345)   25 cm
The white-spotted, cinnamon breast and belly, combined with the white-spotted back and wing coverts, render this small sandgrouse unmistakable.
Female and juv. resemble male but have a yellowish, not blue-grey throat and face, and are generally drabber in colour. **Habitat.** Semi-arid savanna; particularly common on Kalahari sands. **Status.** Locally common to scarce resident; near-endemic. **Call.** A soft, mellow 'chup-chup, choop-choop', given in flight and around waterholes. (Gevlekte Sandpatrys)

1

white bar on head

short tail

♂

black & white breast band

♀

short tail

barred breast

♂

♂

2

black neck band

yellowish face & upper neck

♂

short tail

chestnut belly

♂

grey tail & back

♂

♀

plain, pale face

3

plain head & neck

♂

chestnut & white breast band

♀

♂

long tail

pointed tail

pointed tail

♂

4

spotted body

grey face, yellow orbital ring

♂

yellowish face

♀

♂

spotted body

chestnut coverts

♂

1. SPECKLED (ROCK) PIGEON *Columba guinea* (349) 30-34 cm

The reddish brown wing coverts spotted with white, the black bill and the bare red patches around the eyes are diagnostic; the legs are red. The only similar pigeon in the region is African Olive-Pigeon, which is larger and darker, and has bright yellow (not red) bare eye patches and legs.
Juv. lacks red on the face. **Habitat.** Mountain ranges, rocky terrain, coastal cliffs and cities. **Status.** Common resident. **Call.** A deep, booming 'hooo-hooo-hooo' and a softer 'coocoo-coocoo'. (Kransduif)

2. AFRICAN OLIVE-PIGEON (RAMERON PIGEON) *Columba arquatrix* (350) 37-42 cm

The largest pigeon in the region. Easily identified by its dark, purplish plumage, finely speckled with white, the conspicuous bare yellow patch surrounding the eyes, and the yellow bill, legs and feet. In flight it appears as a large, dark blue or black pigeon.
Sexes alike but female is duller. **Juv.** resembles ad. but has duller-coloured eye patches, bill, legs and feet. **Habitat.** Evergreen forests and exotic plantations, especially where stands of bugweed *Solanum mauritianum* occur; also mountain fynbos. **Status.** Common resident. **Call.** A low but raucous 'coo'. (Geelbekbosduif)

3. EASTERN BRONZE-NAPED (DELEGORGUE'S) PIGEON

Columba delegorguei (351) 24-30 cm

In the field this species appears as dark as African Olive-Pigeon but is much smaller. The iridescent patches on the sides of the neck are visible only at close range.
Male has a greyish head and a diagnostic, pale, half-moon patch on the hind collar. Female and juv. lack the pale hind collar and differ from the similar-sized Lemon Dove in having much darker upperparts and grey, not cinnamon, underparts. **Habitat.** Forest canopy. **Status.** Uncommon resident. **Call.** A frequently repeated hoot, rising and then falling in pitch. (Withalsbosduif)

4. LEMON (CINNAMON) DOVE *Aplopelia larvata* (360) 24-26 cm

When flushed from the forest floor, it 'explodes' and dashes off swiftly, giving the impression of a small, dark dove that lacks the pale, barred rump of the Blue-spotted and Emerald-spotted Wood-Doves (p. 224). When seen at rest on the forest floor, the pale greyish face and cinnamon underparts are diagnostic.
Sexes alike but female is duller. **Juv.** is similar to ad. but is drabber, with buff barring on the mantle. **Habitat.** Undergrowth of evergreen forests; rarely seen in the canopy. **Status.** Common resident. **Call.** A deep-based, somewhat raspy 'hooo-oooo', given from dense thickets. (Kaneelduifie)

5. ROCK DOVE (FERAL PIGEON) *Columba livia* (348) 33 cm

Feral; plumage is very variable, with black, blue, grey, white and reddish forms occurring. The blue form is identical to the ancestral Rock Dove of Europe: bluish grey, with black bars on the wings and tail, a white rump patch, and glossy green and purple on the sides of the neck.
Female is duller than male, with less gloss on the neck. **Juv.** is duller than female. **Habitat.** Urban areas; also breeds on coastal cliffs in the Eastern Cape. **Status.** Abundant resident. **Call.** Typical domestic pigeon 'coo-roo-coo'. (Tuinduif)

1
red facial skin
spotted wing coverts

2
yellow bill & facial skin
spotted underparts
yellow feet
yellow feet

3
♂ ♀
partial collar
grey below
red feet
♂ dark bill
dark red feet ♂

4
pale face
♂ ad.
chestnut below
dark primaries
imm.
♀
plain dark back & rump

5

1. AFRICAN MOURNING DOVE *Streptopelia decipiens* (353)   28-30 cm
This species may be distinguished from the similar Cape Turtle-Dove by the red skin around yellow eyes and the totally grey head. Confusion might arise with Red-eyed Dove, but that species is much larger, is overall very much darker and has a deep red (not pale) eye.
Juv. is browner than ad. **Habitat.** Thornveld, riverine forests, cultivated areas and gardens in bushveld. **Status.** Locally common resident. Particularly common at Satara and Letaba camps in the Kruger National Park. **Call.** A soft, dove-like 'coooc-currr'. (Rooioogtortelduif)

2. RED-EYED DOVE *Streptopelia semitorquata* (352)   30-33 cm
Larger and darker than the similar Cape Turtle-Dove, its all-pink head and red eye-ring are diagnostic. In flight, Red-eyed Dove shows grey (not white) outer tail feathers. The smaller and paler African Mourning Dove differs in having a grey head and a yellow (not red) eye.
Juv. lacks the half-collar and is generally browner than ad. **Habitat.** Diverse, from dry bushveld to coastal forests; has adapted to city gardens and open parks. **Status.** Common resident. **Call.** Alarm call is a 'chwaa'; other calls are variable but a very dove-like 'coo-coo, kook-co-co' is typical. (Grootringduif)

3. CAPE TURTLE-DOVE *Streptopelia capicola* (354)   25-28 cm
The white-tipped tail, which is conspicuous in flight, is diagnostic. It is much smaller and paler than Red-eyed Dove, which lacks the white tail tip. It may be distinguished from African Mourning Dove by having a paler grey head and a dark eye, and by lacking red skin around the eyes.
Juv. is duller than ad. and lacks the half-collar. **Habitat.** Found in virtually every habitat in the region, but avoids dense coastal forests. **Status.** Abundant resident. **Call.** A harsh 'kur-rrr' when alarmed; and the well-known dove call of Africa, 'kuk-cooo-kuk'. (Gewone Tortelduif)

4. LAUGHING DOVE *Streptopelia senegalensis* (355)   22-24 cm
This species may be distinguished from the larger Cape Turtle-Dove by the lack of a black hind collar, by the diagnostic, black-speckled necklace across its cinnamon breast, and by its cinnamon-coloured back. In flight, the blue-grey forewings contrast conspicuously with the cinnamon back, and the white tip and sides of the tail are obvious.
Sexes alike but female is smaller and paler. **Juv.** is duller than ad. **Habitat.** Found in a wide range of habitats but avoids true desert. **Status.** Abundant resident. The most common and best-known dove in the region, having adapted to gardens and city centres throughout. **Call.** Common call is a distinctive, rising and falling 'ooo-coooc-coooc-coo-coo'. (Rooiborsduifie)

5. EUROPEAN TURTLE-DOVE *Streptopelia turtur* (919)   26-28 cm
This species can be distinguished from Laughing Dove by its scaled upperparts and lacks that species' freckled breast band. It has an obvious and diagnostic oval, black-and-white striped patch on either side of the neck.
Juv. lacks the neck patch and has barred and mottled upperparts, which distinguish it from juv. Laughing Dove. **Habitat.** South African sightings have been made in thornveld, near water. **Status.** Vagrant. **Call.** Not recorded in the region. (Europese Tortelduif)

1

ad.

yellow eye, red eye-ring

uppertail

undertail

ad.

2

pale forehead

red eye & eye-ring

uppertail

undertail

3

narrow collar

dark eye, no bare skin

uppertail

4

no hind collar

cinnamon back

black-flecked necklace

5

striped hind-neck patches

no necklace

scaled upperparts

223

1. AFRICAN GREEN-PIGEON *Treron calvus* (361) 25-28 cm

When seen clambering about in a tree, the immediate impression is of a green, parrot-like bird. At closer range, this species is unmistakable with its green, grey and yellow plumage and chestnut vent. When feeding, it climbs about in fruiting trees, sometimes hanging upside-down on branches to obtain fruit.

Juv. has olive-yellow shoulder patches. **Habitat.** Forests, bushveld, savanna; always associated with fruiting trees, especially figs. **Status.** Common resident, subject to local movements. **Call.** Unlike that of any other pigeon in the region: a series of liquid whistles, 'thweeeloo, tleeeoo'. (Papegaaiduif)

2. EMERALD-SPOTTED (GREENSPOTTED) WOOD-DOVE
Turtur chalcospilos (358) 16-20 cm

At close range the dark bill and green wing spots distinguish this species from Blue-spotted Wood-Dove. It normally avoids the evergreen forests frequented by the latter.

Juv. is paler than ad. **Habitat.** Woodland and savanna. **Status.** Common resident. **Call.** One of the most characteristic calls of the bushveld: A series of low 'du-du-du-du' notes, which descend in scale and quicken towards the end; higher pitched than the calls of Blue-spotted Wood-Dove and Tambourine Dove. (Groenvlekduifie)

3. BLUE-SPOTTED WOOD-DOVE *Turtur afer* (357) 18-21 cm

Difficult to differentiate from Emerald-spotted Wood-Dove except at close range, when the yellow-tipped, red bill and blue wing spots are visible. In flight, its back and rump appear more rufous than those of Emerald-spotted Wood-Dove.

Juv. lacks the bill colouring and blue wing spots of ad. and is overall more rufous than juv. Emerald-spotted Wood-Dove. **Habitat.** Moist, broad-leaved woodland and along river courses in evergreen forests. **Status.** Uncommon resident. **Call.** A series of muffled 'du-du-du-du' call notes, like the calls of Emerald-spotted Wood-Dove and Tambourine Dove but more even-toned than the former and shorter than the latter. (Blouvlekduifie)

4. TAMBOURINE DOVE *Turtur tympanistria* (359) 20-22 cm

The white face and underparts of male are diagnostic. In flight, the chestnut underwings contrast strongly with the white belly, unlike Lemon Dove (p. 220), which has dark brown underwings and cinnamon underparts.

Female and **juv.** are slightly dusky below but still have paler faces and underparts than all other small doves. **Habitat.** Dense, evergreen, riverine and coastal forests. Usually flushed before it is seen; it flies fast, straight and low through the forest. **Status.** Common resident. **Call.** A series of 'du-du-du' notes, similar to call of Emerald-spotted Wood-Dove but lower pitched and not descending, and to that of Blue-spotted Wood-Dove but more prolonged. (Witborsduifie)

5. NAMAQUA DOVE *Oena capensis* (356) 28 cm

This is the smallest-bodied dove of the region and the only one to have a long, pointed tail and a black face and throat (in male). In flight the long tail, combined with the white underparts and chestnut flight feathers, renders this bird unmistakable.

Female and **juv.** lack the black face and throat of male and have slightly shorter tails. **Habitat.** Prefers drier regions such as thornveld, Karoo shrublands and sparse desert grassland. **Status.** Common resident, subject to local movements. **Call.** A distinctive, hollow sounding bisyllabic hoot, almost flufftail-like; the first note is sharp, the second longer. (Namakwaduifie)

1

green back

yellow eye

two-tone bill

yellow leggings

chestnut vent

2

dark bill

green wing spots

undertail

3

red & yellow bill

blue spots

4

♂

pale face

dusky breast

pale face

♂

♂

white breast & belly

♀

5

♀

black face, throat & foreneck

♂

chestnut flight feathers

long tail

juv.

1. CAPE PARROT *Poicephalus robustus* (362)   35-37 cm
This and Grey-headed Parrot are the largest parrots in the region, but confusion is unlikely as their ranges do not overlap. Differs from Grey-headed Parrot in having a brown head.
Female has red forehead. **Juv.** lacks the red shoulders and thighs but its size and massive bill should rule out confusion with other, smaller parrots in the region. **Habitat.** Evergreen mist forests dominated by yellowwoods, and adjacent farmlands and exotic plantations. **Status.** Endemic localised resident; endangered. Wild population probably fewer than 500. **Call.** Various loud, harsh screeches and squawks. (Woudpapegaai)

2. GREY-HEADED PARROT *Poicephalus fuscicollis*   36-38 cm
Confusion possible only with Cape Parrot, but ranges do not overlap. Slightly larger than Cape Parrot, with a distinctly grey, not brown head. The large size, massive bill and red shoulders and thighs rule out confusion with other, smaller parrots. **Habitat.** Both dry and moist woodland with large emergent trees and riverine forest. **Status.** Locally common; usually in pairs or small groups but gathers in large numbers at fruiting trees. **Call.** Typical parrot-like squawks and shrill screeches. (Savannepapegaai)

3. BROWN-HEADED PARROT *Poicephalus cryptoxanthus* (363)   24-25 cm
The greenest parrot in the region, this species has a uniformly dark brown head and bright yellow underwing coverts.
Juv. resembles ad. but is generally duller, with less vivid yellow underwings. **Habitat.** Thornveld, riverine forests and open woodland. **Status.** Locally common resident. **Call.** A typically parrot-like, raucous shriek. (Bruinkoppapegaai)

4. MEYER'S PARROT *Poicephalus meyeri* (364)   21-23 cm
Could be confused with female Rüppell's Parrot in north-central Namibia, where the ranges of the two abut. Meyer's Parrot differs in having a green or turquoise (not blue) rump and belly, and a brown (not grey) head, which sometimes shows a yellow bar across the crown.
Juv. resembles ad. but is duller in coloration and lacks the yellow bar across the crown. **Habitat.** Broad-leaved woodland and savanna. Flocks regularly congregate at waterholes. **Status.** Scarce to locally common. **Call.** A loud, piercing 'chee-chee-chee-chee', and various other screeches and squawks. (Bosveldpapegaai)

5. RÜPPELL'S PARROT *Poicephalus rueppellii* (365)   22-23 cm
At rest, male is best distinguished from Meyer's Parrot by its greyish (not brown) throat and head, red eyes, brown, not green, breast, and by its blue (not green or turquoise) belly. In flight, it is easily differentiated from Meyer's Parrot by its blue rump and more extensively yellow underwing coverts. Unlike Meyer's Parrot, this species never has a yellow bar on the crown.
Female is brighter than male, with more extensive blue on the vent and with a blue rump. **Juv.** resembles ad. but is duller. **Habitat.** Dry woodland, thornveld and dry river courses and, in the north, a preference for stands of baobab trees. **Status.** Uncommon to locally common resident. Near-endemic. **Call.** Screeches and squawks similar to those of Meyer's Parrot. (Bloupenspapegaai)

1

♀ ad.

♂ ad.

brown
head

pale bill

grey
head

ad.

2

3

ad.

green
back

no distinct
shoulder
patch

juv.

ad.

extensive
yellow
underwing

green
breast

4

brown
head

dark
back

ad.

green
breast

juv.

ad.

limited
yellow on
under-
wing

5

grey
head

dark
back

grey-brown
breast

blue
belly
& vent

♀

juv.

extensive
yellow
underwing

dark
breast

♀

1. ROSE-RINGED PARAKEET *Psittacula krameri* (366)   40 cm

The only parakeet in the region, this species has an extremely long, pointed tail. At close range the dark red bill and dark ring around the neck are diagnostic of this bright green species.

Female lacks the dark collar and the black chin. **Juv.** resembles female but has a shorter tail and is brighter green. **Habitat.** Urban and suburban parks and gardens. **Status.** Introduced resident. Uncommon and local, with small populations established in Durban and Johannesburg. **Call.** Various shrieks and screams, being particularly vocal at the roost. (Ringnekparkiet)

2. ROSY-FACED LOVEBIRD *Agapornis roseicollis* (367)   18 cm

Usually located by its screeching calls, and very difficult to detect when it sits motionless in a leafy tree or bush. The flight is rapid, and the blue rump shows up clearly against the green back. There is no range overlap with the similar Lilian's Lovebird, which has a green (not blue) rump.

Juv. is paler on the face and upper breast. **Habitat.** Dry, broad-leaved woodland, semi-desert and mountainous terrain. **Status.** Common near-endemic. **Call.** Typical parrot-like screeches and shrieks. (Rooiwangparkiet)

3. BLACK-CHEEKED LOVEBIRD *Agapornis nigrigenis* (369)   14 cm

The dark brown head contrasting with a bright red bill renders this small lovebird unmistakable. It is often considered a race of Rosy-faced Lovebird.

Juv. has a dark head, like ad., but its bill is dark grey (not red). It lacks the white eye-ring. **Habitat.** Riverine forests and open woodland. **Status.** Uncertain. Recent records from Victoria Falls may be of escaped cage birds, and records from north-central Namibia are almost certainly such. **Call.** Shrieking, identical to that of Lilian's Lovebird. (Swart-wangparkiet)

4. LILIAN'S LOVEBIRD *Agapornis lilianae* (368)   14 cm

Slightly smaller than the similar Rosy-faced Lovebird, this species differs in having a green (not blue) rump and a conspicuous white eye-ring. Range does not overlap with that of Rosy-faced Lovebird. Female has a paler pink head than male.

Juv. is similar to ad. but lacks the white eye-ring. **Habitat.** Broad-leaved woodland. **Status.** Uncommon resident. **Call.** A high-pitched, staccato shrieking. (Njassaparkiet)

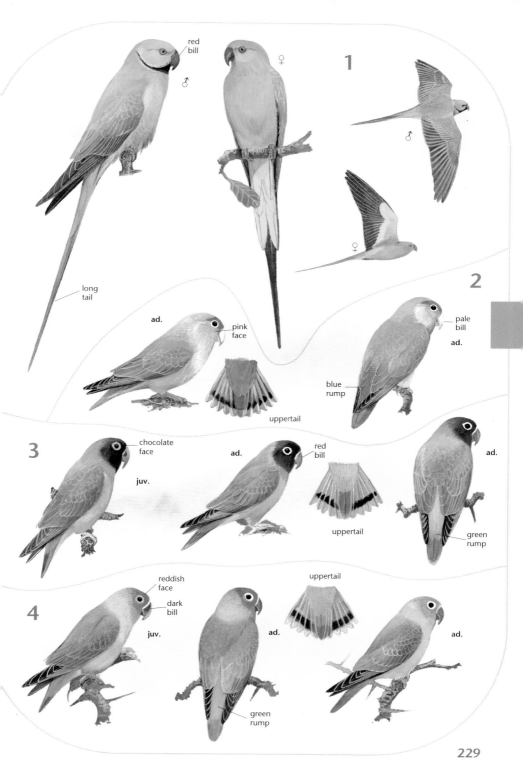

1

red
bill

♂

♀

long
tail

2

pale
bill

ad.

blue
rump

ad.

pink
face

uppertail

3

chocolate
face

juv.

ad.

red
bill

uppertail

ad.

green
rump

reddish
face

uppertail

dark
bill

4

juv.

ad.

ad.

green
rump

1. KNYSNA TURACO (LOURIE) *Tauraco corythaix* (370a)   40-42 cm
The all-green head, white stripe below the eye and white tips to the crest distinguish this species from Purple-crested Turaco. Livingstone's and Schalow's turacos differ in having elongated crests. Confusion is unlikely as their ranges do not overlap. In flight shows conspicuous crimson patches on the primaries.
Juv. has a shorter crest that lacks the white tips. **Habitat.** Evergreen mist and coastal forests. **Status.** Common resident; endemic. **Call.** A hoarse 'kow-kow-kow-kow', and a quieter 'krrr' alarm note. (Knysnaloerie)

2. SCHALOW'S TURACO (LOURIE) *Tauraco schalowi*   40 cm
Most closely resembles Livingstone's Turaco, but differs in that the crest is much longer and more elongated and the tail appears dark blue or purple rather than dark green. It is also slightly paler green below. The ranges of the two species do not overlap.
Juv. has a shorter crest than ad. **Habitat.** Riparian forest along the Zambezi River west of Victoria Falls, in Zimbabwe, and into eastern Caprivi. **Status.** Locally common resident. **Call.** A series of five to seven notes uttered at approximately one-second intervals and becoming increasingly raucous. (Langkuifloerie)

3. LIVINGSTONE'S TURACO (LOURIE) *Tauraco livingstonii* (370b)   40 cm
This species differs from Knysna Turaco in having a very long, pointed crest and a slightly darker back. Crest is shorter and less pointed than that of Schalow's Turaco. Confusion is unlikely between the green turacos because their ranges do not overlap.
Juv. has a shorter, less developed crest than ad. **Habitat.** Riverine, montane and coastal forests. **Status.** Common resident. **Call.** Similar to that of Knysna Turaco. (Mosambiekloerie)

4. PURPLE-CRESTED TURACO (LOURIE)
Musophaga porphyreolopha (371)   43 cm
Darker than the very green Knysna Turaco. It differs from that species mainly by its purple crest, which appears black unless it is seen in good light, and by the lack of white around the eyes and on the crest. Like Knysna Turaco, it is very furtive and is usually seen only as it leaps from tree to tree, when the red in its wings is conspicuous.
Juv. resembles ad. but is duller. **Habitat.** Coastal and riverine forests and broad-leaved woodland. **Status.** Common resident. **Call.** A loud 'kok-kok-kok-kok'. (Bloukuifloerie)

5. ROSS'S TURACO (LOURIE) *Musophaga rossae* (372)   51-54 cm
The only dark blue turaco of the region; unlikely to be confused with any other. The combination of the yellow face and red crest is diagnostic. Superficially similar Violet Turacos (*M. violacea*) are occasionally recorded as escaped cage birds: that species has red, not yellow skin around the eye and has a red-tipped, yellow bill.
Juv. is duller than ad., with a blackish bill. **Habitat.** Riverine forests. **Status.** Vagrant to northern Namibia, Botswana and Zimbabwe. **Call.** A loud cackling. (Rooikuifloerie)

6. GREY GO-AWAY-BIRD (LOURIE) *Corythaixoides concolor* (373)   48 cm
This ash-grey bird with its long tail and crest is one of the more obvious birds of the bushveld. Vocal and conspicuous, at times appearing like a giant mousebird, it is often seen in small groups perched high in thorn trees.
Juv. is buffier than ad. and has a shorter crest. **Habitat.** Thornveld and dry, open woodland. Adapted to wooded suburban gardens on the South African highveld. **Status.** Common resident. **Call.** A harsh, nasal 'waaaay' or 'kay-waaaay', from which it derives its name. (Kwêvoël)

1 fairly short, white-tipped crest

2 very long crest

purplish tail

long, dark-tipped crest

3 greenish tail

3

dark purple crest

no white around eye

red crest

4

dark blue neck & mantle

yellow bill & facial skin

5

long crest

6 uniform grey body

231

1. COMMON (EUROPEAN) CUCKOO *Cuculus canorus* (374)   32-34 cm

Virtually indistinguishable in appearance from African Cuckoo except on undertail pattern: African Cuckoo has a barred undertail whereas Common Cuckoo has a spotted undertail. Common Cuckoo is generally less yellow on the bill than African Cuckoo, but not consistently so.

Female occurs in a rare rufous colour form. **Juv.** may be brown, grey or chestnut; the upperparts are usually barred, with the feathers tipped with white; the underparts are heavily barred. **Habitat.** Diverse: woodland, savanna, riverine forests and plantations. **Status.** Scarce to locally common summer visitor. **Call.** Silent in the region. (Europese Koekoek)

2. AFRICAN CUCKOO *Cuculus gularis* (375)   32-34 cm

The call of this species is its most diagnostic feature. The barred (not spotted) undertail distinguishes it from Common Cuckoo. In Oct/Nov this species' plumage is fresh and migrant Common Cuckoo's plumage is worn and in heavy moult. The reverse is true in March/April.

Female resembles male but also occurs in a rare rufous form. **Juv.** has underparts and head entirely barred with black and white, and the upperparts blackish, scalloped with white. **Habitat.** Woodland and savanna. **Status.** Locally common summer visitor. **Call.** Similar to African Hoopoe's 'hoop-hoop' call but slower; female utters a fast 'kik-kik-kik'. (Afrikaanse Koekoek)

3. RED-CHESTED CUCKOO *Cuculus solitarius* (377)   28-31 cm

The characteristic three-note call during summer indicates this cuckoo's presence; otherwise it is very difficult to locate as it sits motionless in thick canopy foliage. The chestnut breast is diagnostic.

Juv. has black instead of rufous breast and is generally black above, with the white lower breast and belly heavily barred with black. Unlike juv. African and Common Cuckoos, the head, throat and upper breast are black, not barred. **Habitat.** Forests, exotic plantations, mature woodland and suburban gardens. **Status.** Common summer visitor. **Call.** Male utters a loud, often-repeated 'weet-weet-weeoo'; female gives a shrill 'pipipipipi'. (Piet-my-vrou)

4. LESSER CUCKOO *Cuculus poliocephalus* (376)   26-28 cm

Not readily distinguishable from African or Common cuckoos except at close quarters, when its smaller size, darker back, nape and crown, and more heavily barred underparts are visible. This species has a rare rufous form that is absent in Madagascar Cuckoo. In flight, the dark tail and rump contrast with the paler back, a feature not evident in either African or Common Cuckoo.

Female has a barred upper breast suffused with buff; upper breast of male is grey. **Juv.** resembles ad. **Habitat.** Savanna and riparian forests. **Status.** Summer vagrant. **Call.** Trisyllabic 'kook kook kook'. (Kleinkoekoek)

5. MADAGASCAR CUCKOO *Cuculus rochii* (925)   26-28 cm

Virtually indistinguishable in the field from Lesser Cuckoo except on call. However, this species visits Africa in the austral winter whereas Lesser Cuckoo is present in summer (although the only southern African record of this species was a singing male in summer).

Juv. is mottled with rufous on the upperparts. **Habitat.** Riverine forests and bushveld. **Status.** Regular winter visitor to East Africa but recorded only once in the region. **Call.** Reminiscent of Red-chested Cuckoo but deeper in tone, and has four (not three) notes, 'piet-my-vrou-vrou', the last note being lower. (Madagaskarkoekoek)

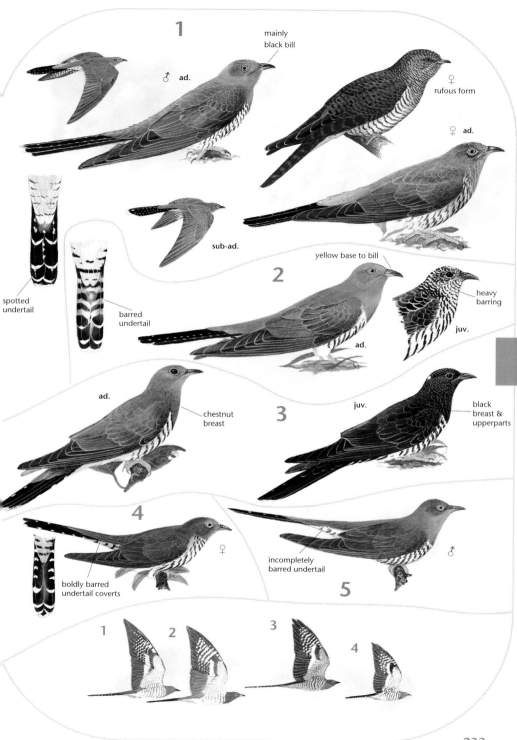

1

mainly
black bill

♂ ad.

♀
rufous form

♀ ad.

sub-ad.

spotted
undertail

barred
undertail

2

yellow base to bill

heavy
barring

juv.

ad.

3

ad.

chestnut
breast

juv.

black
breast &
upperparts

4

♀

boldly barred
undertail coverts

incompletely
barred undertail

♂

5

1   2   3   4

1. BLACK CUCKOO *Cuculus clamosus* (378) 28-31 cm
The only all-black cuckoo in the region. It is similar to the dark-form Jacobin Cuckoo but lacks the crest and white patches in the upperwings. There is a white flash present on the underwing and, at close range, indistinct pale tips to the tail feathers are noticeable.
Juv. is duller black than ad. **Habitat.** Woodland, forest, exotic plantations and suburban gardens. **Status.** Common summer visitor. **Call.** Male gives a droning, three- or four-syllabled 'whoo-wheee-whoo-whoo' ('I'm so siiiiiick'); female gives a fast 'yow-yow-yow-yow'. (Swartkoekoek)

2. LEVAILLANT'S (STRIPED) CUCKOO *Oxylophus levaillantii* (381) 38-40 cm
Unlikely to be confused with any other cuckoo except the light morph Jacobin Cuckoo, from which it differs by the diagnostic heavy, black striping on the throat and breast.
Juv. is browner above and very buff below, but still shows the diagnostic throat striping. **Habitat.** Savanna and woodland. **Status.** Locally common summer visitor. **Call.** A loud 'klee-klee-kleeuu', followed by a descending 'che-che-che-che'. (Gestreepte Nuwejaarsvoël)

3. JACOBIN CUCKOO *Oxylophus jacobinus* (382) 33-34 cm
Dark-form birds differ from the similar Black Cuckoo by the noticeable crest and the white patches on the primaries visible from above and below. Light morph birds resemble Levaillant's Cuckoo but are pure white below, lacking any stripes on the throat and breast.
Juv. is browner above. Dark morph juv. has dull black underparts; light morph juv. has creamy grey underparts. **Habitat.** Woodlands, especially thornveld. Dark morph is mainly coastal; pale morph is found mainly in the interior. **Status.** Common summer visitor. **Call.** A shrill, repeated 'klee-klee-kleeuu-kleeuu', indistinguishable from the start of Levaillant's Cuckoo's call. (Bontnuwejaarsvoël)

4. THICK-BILLED CUCKOO *Pachycoccyx audeberti* (383) 36 cm
Resembles Great Spotted Cuckoo but differs in having a uniformly dark grey (not white-spotted) back and wing coverts, and in lacking a crest. It has a noticeably thick, heavy bill.
Juv. is very striking with its white head flecked with black, and white-spotted upperparts. It differs from juv. Great Spotted Cuckoo by its lack of rufous wing patches and black cap. **Habitat.** Riparian forests and woodland. **Status.** Scarce summer visitor, with a few birds wintering on the northeast coast. **Call.** A repeated, ringing 'wee-yes-yes', and a harsh 'were-wick'. (Dikbekkoekoek)

5. GREAT SPOTTED CUCKOO *Clamator glandarius* (380) 36-41 cm
This large cuckoo is unmistakable, with its white-spotted dark back, elongated, wedge-shaped tail and grey crest.
Juv. is also heavily spotted on the back but has a small, black crest, buffy underparts and rufous patches on the primaries. **Habitat.** Woodland and savanna. **Status.** Common summer visitor. **Call.** A loud, far-carrying 'keeow-keeow-keeow', and a shorter, crow-like 'kark'. (Gevlekte Koekoek)

1

juv.

no crest

ad.

ad.

juv.

ad.

3

small crest

juv.

ad.

plain white
throat

white
flashes

ad.

streaked
throat

juv.

juv.

upperwings

ad. dark form

ad.

2

no crest

juv.

uniform
upperparts

ad.

juv.

4

ad.

grey cap

5

dark cap
and crest

buff
throat

juv.

rufous
primaries

ad.

ad.

ad.

juv.

1. BARRED LONG-TAILED CUCKOO *Cercococcyx montanus* (379) 32-33 cm
Much smaller-bodied than either African or Common Cuckoo (p. 232), with an exceptionally long, narrow tail. It is often located by its call, but when seen, the brownish, heavily barred upperparts and the broadly barred underparts, combined with the long tail and slender body, are diagnostic.
Juv. resembles ad. but has the underparts more dusky, with some streaking. **Habitat.** Lowland forests. **Status.** Uncertain; rare summer visitor probably decreasing in numbers due to deforestation. **Call.** A long series of 'cheee-phweew's, rising to a crescendo; also a shorter 'hwee-hooa' or 'hwee-hooo'. (Langstertkoekoek)

2. DIDERICK (DIEDERIK) CUCKOO *Chrysococcyx caprius* (386) 17-19 cm
Male is easily distinguished from similar male Klaas's Cuckoo by the broad, white stripe behind the eye, the white spots on the forewings and the red (not brown) eyes. Female differs from female Klaas's Cuckoo in having bolder but less extensive barring on the flanks, and in having white spots on the forewings.
Imm. resembles **female**. **Juv.** may be differentiated from juv. Klaas's Cuckoo by its conspicuous, red (not black) bill. **Habitat.** Woodland, savanna, grassland and suburban gardens. **Status.** Common summer visitor. **Call.** A clear, persistent 'dee-dee-deedereek'. (Diederikkie)

3. KLAAS'S CUCKOO *Chrysococcyx klaas* (385) 16-18 cm
Male differs from male Diderick Cuckoo in having only a small white patch behind the eye, no white markings on the wings, and a brown (not red) eye.
Female differs from female Diderick Cuckoo in having finer, more extensive barring on the flanks and breast, and in lacking white wing markings. **Juv.** resembles female but is browner, with less metallic coloration. **Habitat.** Forests, woodland, savanna, parks and gardens. **Status.** Common summer visitor; some birds overwinter. **Call.** A soft 'huee-jee', repeated five or six times. (Meitjie)

4. AFRICAN EMERALD CUCKOO *Chrysococcyx cupreus* (384) 21-23 cm
Male is unmistakable, with a brilliant, emerald-green throat, upper breast and upperparts, and sulphur-yellow lower breast and belly.
Female differs from female Klaas's and Diderick cuckoos in lacking the white behind the eye and in having a more brownish bronze cast to the upperparts and more heavily barred underparts. **Juv.** resembles female. **Habitat.** Evergreen forests, usually in the canopy. **Status.** Common summer visitor; some birds overwinter. **Call.** A loud, ringing whistle, 'wheet-huiee-wheet' ('pretty geor-gie'). (Mooimeisie)

1

ad.

ad.

ad.

long,
narrow tail

2

ad. ♀

white
wing
spots

♂ ad.

juv.

heavily
barred
flanks

♂ ad.

♀ ad.

juv.

no white
wing spots

♂ ad.

♀ ad.

finely
barred
flanks

♀ ad.

♂ ad.

no white
on head

♀ ad.

♂ ad.

3

4

♀ ad.

♂ ad.

♂ ad.

1

ad.

3

juv.

juv.

2

juv.

2

♀ ad.

2

♂ ad.

COUCALS

1. COPPERY-TAILED COUCAL *Centropus cupreicaudus* (389) 48 cm
The largest coucal of the region, this species most resembles Burchell's Coucal but has a longer, broader and floppier tail which, like the head, is black with a coppery sheen.
Juv. is the same size as ad. (thus ruling out confusion with other juv. coucals), and its long tail is barred with black and brown. **Habitat.** Marshlands, thick reedbeds and adjoining bush. **Status.** Common resident. **Call.** A louder, more resonant, bubbling call than those of other coucals. (Grootvleiloerie)

2. BURCHELL'S COUCAL *Centropus burchelli* (391) 40-41 cm
Very similar to the slightly smaller Senegal and White-browed Coucals but this species has fine, rufous barring on the rump and the base of the tail.
Juv. is indistinguishable in the field from juv. Senegal and White-browed Coucals. **Habitat.** Long grass, riverine scrub, reedbeds, woodland and suburban gardens. **Status.** Common resident; near-endemic. **Call.** A liquid, bubbling 'doo-doo-doo-doo', descending in scale, then rising towards the end of the phrase. (Gewone Vleiloerie)

3. WHITE-BROWED COUCAL *Centropus superciliosus* (391b) 40-41 cm
This species differs from Burchell's Coucal in having a clear, creamy eyebrow stripe and a white-flecked crown and nape. Ranges of the two do not overlap.
Juv. probably indistinguishable in the field from juv. Senegal and Burchell's Coucals. **Habitat.** Similar to that of Burchell's Coucal. **Status.** Common resident. **Call.** Bubbling song, similar to that of Burchell's Coucal. (Gestreepte Vleiloerie)

4. SENEGAL COUCAL *Centropus senegalensis* (390) 38-40 cm
Where the ranges of this species and Burchell's Coucal overlap, identification difficulties arise: Senegal Coucal lacks the fine barring on the rump and base of the tail. It differs from larger Coppery-tailed Coucal by its smaller size and by the brighter chestnut colouring on the wings and back.
Juv. of this species and juv. Coppery-tailed Coucal are indistinguishable in the field except on size. **Habitat.** Tangled vegetation and long grass, often near water. **Status.** Uncommon resident. **Call.** Bubbling song, very similar to that of Burchell's Coucal. (Senegalvleiloerie)

5. BLACK COUCAL *Centropus grillii* (388) 38 cm
A small coucal and the only one in the region to have a black head and body contrasting with a rich chestnut back and wings.
Sexes alike but female is larger. Non-breeding ad. and **juv.** birds differ from other coucals by their smaller size, small bill and clear, buff-streaked head and upperparts. **Habitat.** Moist grassland with rank vegetation. **Status.** Uncommon summer visitor. **Call.** A typical, bubbling coucal call, and a monotonous, repeated 'poopoop'. (Swartvleiloerie)

6. GREEN MALKOHA (COUCAL) *Ceuthmochares aereus* (387) 33 cm
This shy bird is very difficult to see in the thick, tangled undergrowth it frequents, and is usually located by its call. When flushed, the dull green upperparts and long tail, combined with the yellow bill, are diagnostic.
Juv. resembles ad. but has a duller, greenish bill. **Habitat.** Thick evergreen, riverine and coastal forests. **Status.** Scarce to locally common resident. **Call.** A clicking 'kik-kik-kik', winding up to a loud 'cher-cher-cher-cher'. (Groenvleiloerie)

1

coppery sheen

coppery sheen

2

ad.

juv.

barred tail base & rump

3

streaked foreparts, pale supercilium

ad.

ad.

4

unbarred tail base

buffy cap

lacks heavy streaking

juv.

5

all-black head

black body

ad.

grey below

green back & tail

yellow bill

6

239

1. VERREAUX'S (GIANT) EAGLE-OWL *Bubo lacteus* (402)   58-66 cm
The largest owl of the region. Its size and pale grey coloration make it easily identi-
fiable, and the pink eyelids are distinctive. The northern race of the Cape Eagle-
Owl approaches it in size but that species has rufous coloration and boldly
blotched and barred underparts.
Juv. is paler grey in colour than ad., and is finely barred. **Habitat.** Broad-leaved woodland,
savanna, thornveld and riverine forests. **Status.** Uncommon to locally common resident.
Call. A grunting, pig-like 'unnh-unnh-unnh'. (Reuse-ooruil)

2. PEL'S FISHING-OWL *Scotopelia peli* (403)   61-63 cm
The very large size and ginger coloration of this species render it unmistakable.
When alarmed, the bird fluffs up its head feathers, and this gives it a huge, round-
headed appearance. At rest, the large, dark brown eyes dominate the unmarked,
tawny facial disc. The unfeathered legs and feet are difficult to see in the field.
Juv. is paler and more buff coloured, with an almost white head. **Habitat.** Large trees
around lakes and slow-moving rivers. **Status.** Uncommon resident. **Call.** A deep, booming
'hoo-huuuum' and a jackal-like wailing. (Visuil)

3. CAPE EAGLE-OWL *Bubo capensis* (400)   48-54 cm
This species is not easily distinguished from the (rare) rufous form of the more
common Spotted Eagle-Owl unless it is heard calling; it is larger, and has black and
chestnut blotching on the breast, and bold (not fine) barring on the belly and
flanks. It also has much larger feet than does Spotted Eagle-Owl and orange (not
yellow) eyes. Rufous morph Spotted Eagle-Owl also has orange eyes. Birds in the
far north of the region are very much larger than those further south.
Juv. resembles ad. **Habitat.** Rocky and mountainous terrain. **Status.** Uncommon, localised
resident. **Call.** A loud, far-carrying 'hu-hooooo', the first syllable being sharp and penetrating; also a loud, dog-like yapping 'wak-wak-wak'. (Kaapse Ooruil)

4. SPOTTED EAGLE-OWL *Bubo africanus* (401)   43-50 cm
Grey and rufous colour forms occur. The grey form is the most common and is
distinguished from Cape Eagle-Owl by its smaller size, the lack of dark breast
blotches, the finely barred belly and flanks, the yellow (not orange) eyes, and
the smaller feet. The rare rufous colour form is more heavily blotched and has
orange eyes; it is best distinguished from Cape Eagle-Owl by its call, its smaller
size and its smaller feet.
Juv. resembles ad. **Habitat.** Diverse, from desert to mature woodland, savanna and wooded suburbia. **Status.** Resident; the most common eagle-owl of the region. **Call.** A hooting
'hu-hoo', similar to that of Cape Eagle-Owl but softer and less penetrating. (Gevlekte Ooruil)

5. BARN OWL *Tyto alba* (392)   33-36 cm
This golden buff and white owl could be confused with African Grass-Owl but is
much paler and has less contrast between the upperparts and the underparts. The
heart-shaped, white facial disc highlights the small, black eyes.
Juv. resembles ad. **Habitat.** Diverse; from deserts to moist savanna. Often found near
human habitation but also roosts in caves, hollow trees and mine shafts. **Status.** Common
resident. **Call.** Many and varied calls, the most usual being an eerie 'shreeee'. (Nonnetjie-uil)

6. AFRICAN GRASS-OWL *Tyto capensis* (393)   36-40 cm
Although it could be confused with Barn Owl, this species' much darker upperparts
contrast markedly with its whitish underparts. Marsh Owl (p. 242), found in the
same habitat, has a dusky (not plain white) face and underparts, and noticeably
rounded wings with buff patches at the base of the primaries.
Juv. has a rufous facial disc and darker underparts. **Habitat.** Marshes and tall grassland,
but not in reedbeds. **Status.** Uncommon resident. **Call.** A soft, cricket-like 'tk-tk-tk-tk ...',
uttered while on the wing. (Grasuil)

pink
eyelids

overall
grey
colour

1

plain face,
dark eyes

2

overall
ginger colour

3

orange
eyes

blotched
underparts

yellow
eyes

4

grey-barred
underparts

pale
below

6

pale back
& wings

dark brown
wings, back

5

1. AFRICAN WOOD-OWL *Strix woodfordii* (394)   33-35 cm

This medium-sized owl can be identified by its lack of ear tufts, its heavily barred, brown underparts and its pale, finely barred facial disc with large, dark brown eyes. The plumage coloration is variable, ranging from very dark brown to russet. **Juv.** resembles ad. **Habitat.** Evergreen and riverine forests, mature woodland and exotic plantations. **Status.** Common resident. **Call.** Close to the classic owl call, 'towhit-towhoo', but rendered as 'huoo-hoo-hoo', the female's call being higher pitched; also a high-pitched 'weooo'. Pairs regularly duet, the female calling first. (Bosuil)

2. MARSH OWL *Asio capensis* (395)   32-38 cm

A plain brown, medium-sized owl with a buff-coloured face, small ear tufts and dark brown eyes. In flight, it shows buff 'windows' in the primaries and dark marks on the underwing carpals. When flushed during the daytime, it invariably circles overhead before alighting. **Juv.** resembles ad. **Habitat.** Marshes and damp grassland; avoids thick reedbeds. Sometimes found in flocks. **Status.** Locally common resident. **Call.** A harsh, rasping 'krikkk-krikkk', likened to the sound of material being torn. (Vlei-uil)

3. SOUTHERN WHITE-FACED SCOPS-OWL *Ptilopsus granti* (397)   25-28 cm

The only other small owl with ear tufts is African Scops-Owl, from which this species differs by its conspicuous, white facial disc edged with black, and by its bright orange (not yellow) eyes. It is also larger and much paler grey than African Scops-Owl. **Juv.** is buffier than ad., with a greyish face and yellow eyes. **Habitat.** Thornveld and dry, broad-leaved woodland. **Status.** Common resident. **Call.** A fast, hooting 'doo-doo-doo-doo-hohoo' call. (Witwanguil)

4. AFRICAN BARRED OWLET *Glaucidium capense* (399)   20-21 cm

This species might be confused with Pearl-spotted Owlet, from which it differs in being larger and having barred head, upperparts and tail and conspicuous white edging to the scapulars. **Juv.** is less distinctly spotted below than ad. **Habitat.** Mature woodland and riparian gallery forests. **Status.** Locally common resident. **Call.** A soft, frequently repeated 'kerrr-kerrr-kerrr' and a 'trru-trrre'. (Gebande Uil)

5. PEARL-SPOTTED OWLET *Glaucidium perlatum* (398)   18-19 cm

The rounded head with no ear tufts and the white spotting on the back and tail distinguish this species from African and Southern White-faced Scops-Owls. It may be differentiated from African Barred Owlet by its smaller size and the lack of barring on the head and upperparts. It shows two black 'false eyes' on the nape. **Juv.** resembles ad. **Habitat.** Thornveld and broad-leaved woodland. **Status.** Common resident. **Call.** A series of 'tu-tu-tuee-tuee' whistles, rising and then descending in pitch. Often calls during the day. (Witkoluil)

6. AFRICAN SCOPS-OWL *Otus senegalensis* (396)   15-17 cm

The smallest owl of the region. Could be confused with Southern White-faced Scops-Owl because both have ear tufts, but this species has a grey (not white) face and is considerably smaller and slimmer and has yellow, not orange, eyes. Both grey and brown forms occur. Typically, it roosts on branches adjacent to a tree trunk; it is very inconspicuous by day. **Juv.** resembles ad. **Habitat.** Bushveld and dry, open woodland. Absent from forested regions. **Status.** Common resident. **Call.** A soft, frog-like 'prrrup', repeated at regular intervals. (Skopsuil)

1

brown form

dark 'spectacles'

no 'ears'

broadly barred front

rufous form

2

buffy facial disc

plain brown back & wings

dark below

3

white face, orange eyes

4

barred head

barred chest

blotched flanks

5

spotted head

streaked front

6

grey face, yellow eyes

243

1. EUROPEAN NIGHTJAR *Caprimulgus europaeus* (404) 25-28 cm
A large nightjar, paler than Freckled Nightjar and with more white in the wing and tail. The lack of rufous on the head and neck distinguishes it from Fiery-necked and Rufous-cheeked Nightjars. Distinguished from Swamp and Square-tailed Nightjars by the reduced white on the tail. Frequently roosts lengthwise on branches.
Female resembles female Pennant-winged Nightjar but is grey (not brown). **Juv.** resembles female. **Habitat.** Woodland, savanna, plantations and suburban areas. **Status.** Scarce to common summer visitor. **Call.** Silent in Africa. (Europese Naguil)

2. PENNANT-WINGED NIGHTJAR *Macrodipteryx vexillarius* (410) 23-26 cm
Breeding male has unmistakable broad white stripe across the primaries, and predominantly white elongated inner primaries that trail well behind the bird. Female lacks white on the wings or tail and has rufous-and-black-barred flight feathers.
Juv. resembles female. **Habitat.** Mature broad-leaved woodland. **Status.** Locally common summer visitor. **Call.** A continuous, high-pitched twittering. (Wimpelvlerknaguil)

3. FRECKLED NIGHTJAR *Caprimulgus tristigma* (408) 23-26 cm
Differs from both European and Pennant-winged Nightjars by its greyish upperparts, which blend well with the rocky terrain it frequents. In flight it may be distinguished from European Nightjar by the outer tail feathers, the tips of which show less white. Female lacks the white tail patches of male.
Juv. resembles female. **Habitat.** Rocky outcrops in woodland and hilly terrain; also found roosting on buildings in towns and cities. **Status.** Locally common resident. **Call.** A yapping, double-noted 'kow-kow', sometimes extending to four syllables. (Donkernaguil)

4. FIERY-NECKED NIGHTJAR *Caprimulgus pectoralis* (405) 22-24 cm
At rest this species may be distinguished from Rufous-cheeked Nightjar by its rich rufous (not orange-buff) collar. Male in flight may be distinguished from Rufous-cheeked and Square-tailed Nightjars by the extent of white in the outer tail feathers.
Female and **juv.** have the white areas in the wing and tail replaced by buff. **Habitat.** Woodland, savanna and plantations. **Status.** Common resident. **Call.** A plaintive, descending, six-syllabled 'good Lord, deliiiiiver us'. (Afrikaanse Naguil)

5. RUFOUS-CHEEKED NIGHTJAR *Caprimulgus rufigena* (406) 24 cm
This species differs from Fiery-necked Nightjar in having an orange-buff (not rufous) collar and in lacking the rufous on the breast. Female differs from female Fiery-necked Nightjar in having less buff on the tail.
Juv. resembles female. **Habitat.** Dry thornveld, woodland and scrub desert. **Status.** Locally common summer visitor. **Call.** A prolonged churring, usually preceded by a choking 'chukoo, chukoo'. (Rooiwangnaguil)

6. SQUARE-TAILED (MOZAMBIQUE) NIGHTJAR *Caprimulgus fossii* (409) 21-24 cm
This species resembles Swamp Nightjar in having the outer tail feathers white, but differs in being larger and darker brown and less buff above. Female is larger than female Swamp Nightjar and has less white on the tail.
Juv. resembles female. **Habitat.** Coastal dune scrub and sandy woodland, often near water. **Status.** Common resident. **Call.** A prolonged churring, changing at intervals in pitch ('changing gears'). (Laeveldnaguil)

7. SWAMP (NATAL) NIGHTJAR *Caprimulgus natalensis* (407) 21-22 cm
This species resembles Square-tailed Nightjar in having almost entirely white outer tail feathers (buff in female), but Swamp Nightjar is smaller and paler. Female lacks the white in the wings.
Juv. resembles female. **Habitat.** Palm savanna and open grassland. **Status.** Rare to locally common resident. **Call.** 'Chow-chow-chow' or 'chop-chop-chop'. (Natalse Naguil)

244

See also pages 246–247

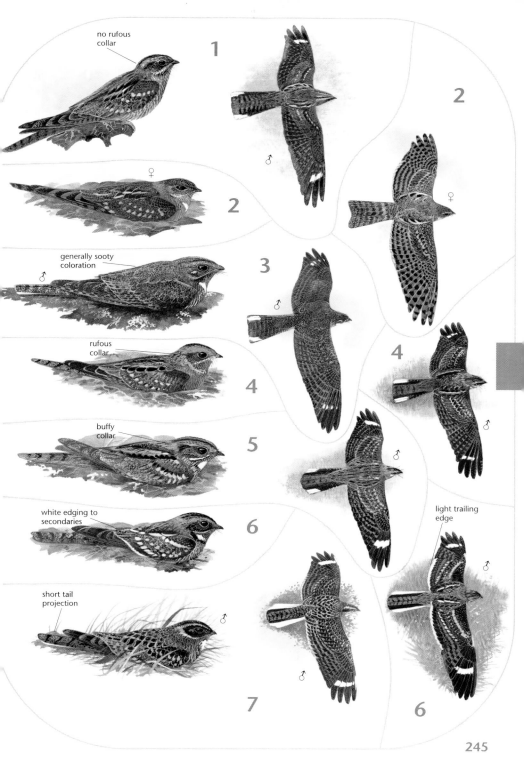

no rufous collar

1

2

generally sooty coloration

3

rufous collar

4

buffy collar

5

white edging to secondaries

6

short tail projection

7

light trailing edge

See also pages 244–245

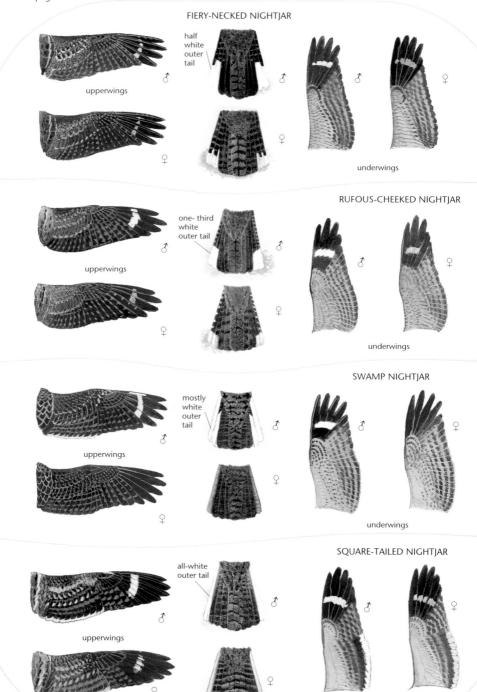

FIERY-NECKED NIGHTJAR

half white outer tail

upperwings

♂

♀

♂

♀

underwings

RUFOUS-CHEEKED NIGHTJAR

one-third white outer tail

upperwings

♂

♀

♂

♀

underwings

SWAMP NIGHTJAR

mostly white outer tail

upperwings

♂

♀

♂

♀

underwings

SQUARE-TAILED NIGHTJAR

all-white outer tail

upperwings

♂

♀

♂

♀

underwings

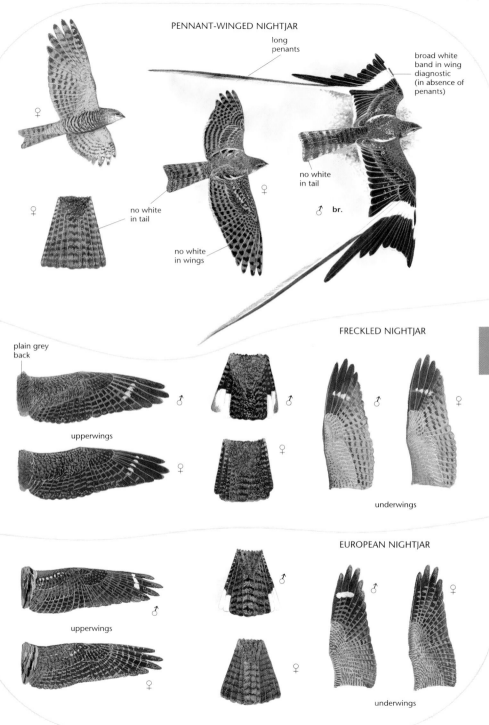

PENNANT-WINGED NIGHTJAR

long penants

broad white band in wing diagnostic (in absence of penants)

no white in tail

♂ br.

♀

♀

♀

no white in tail

no white in wings

FRECKLED NIGHTJAR

plain grey back

upperwings

♂

♀

♂

♀

♂

♀

underwings

EUROPEAN NIGHTJAR

upperwings

♂

♀

♂

♀

♂

♀

underwings

247

1. ALPINE SWIFT *Tachymarptis melba* (418)   21-22 cm
A very large, fast-flying swift and the only one to show white underparts and a dark breast band. It is often seen in mixed flocks with other swift species.
Habitat. Aerial and wide ranging. Breeds on high, inland cliffs with vertical cracks. **Status.** Common resident and summer visitor. **Call.** A shrill scream. (Witpenswindswael)

2. MOTTLED SWIFT *Tachymarptis aequatorialis* (419)   20 cm
Much the same size and shape as Alpine Swift but lacks the white underparts of that species. It has scaled and mottled underparts like Bradfield's Swift but is darker and much larger.
Habitat. Aerial and wide ranging. Breeds in vertical cracks on inland cliffs. **Status.** Uncommon resident, found in granite koppie country of Zimbabwe and Mozambique. **Call.** A typical swift scream. (Bontwindswael)

3. BRADFIELD'S SWIFT *Apus bradfieldi* (413)   18 cm
Paler than both Common and African Black swifts. At close range and in good light, a scaled, mottled effect is discernible on the underparts. In the field it is unlikely to be distinguished from Pallid Swift unless both are seen together.
Habitat. Aerial and wide ranging. Breeds in crevices on inland cliffs. **Status.** Locally common resident. **Call.** A high-pitched screaming at breeding sites. (Muiskleurwindswael)

4. PALLID SWIFT *Apus pallidus* (414)   17 cm
Very difficult to tell from African Black, Common and Bradfield's Swifts unless they are seen together. It differs from African Black and Common Swifts in being paler, with a more extensive white throat patch and a paler forehead. It may be distinguished from Bradfield's Swift by being slightly paler and lacking the scaled effect on the underparts. A direct field comparison is probably required for certain identification. In comparison with all three species, Pallid Swift has a more robust body and a slower flight action.
Habitat. Aerial. **Status.** Vagrant: one specimen recorded from the Northern Cape. **Call.** Silent in Africa. (Bruinwindswael)

5. COMMON (EUROPEAN) SWIFT *Apus apus* (411)   16-18 cm
This species is difficult to distinguish from Pallid and African Black Swifts. It may be distinguished from the former only under optimum viewing conditions and when both species are present: Common Swift has less white on its throat and a more slender body. It differs from African Black Swift in having the secondaries and back uniformly dark.
Habitat. Aerial and wide ranging; sometimes in flocks numbering hundreds. **Status.** Common summer visitor, less common in the south. **Call.** Seldom heard in the region; a shrill scream. (Europese Windswael)

6. AFRICAN BLACK SWIFT *Apus barbatus* (412)   16-18 cm
This species can be distinguished (with difficulty) from Common Swift if the upperparts are seen clearly. The secondaries, especially the inner secondaries, are paler than the rest of the wing and back, and show up as contrasting, pale greyish brown patches.
Habitat. Aerial. Breeds in crevices on inland cliffs. **Status.** Common resident and partial migrant. **Call.** A high-pitched screaming at breeding sites. (Swartwindswael)

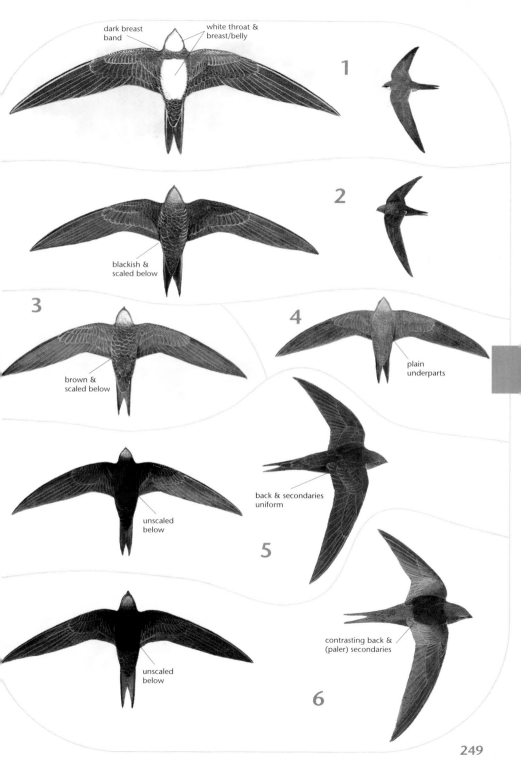

dark breast band

white throat & breast/belly

1

blackish & scaled below

2

3

brown & scaled below

4

plain underparts

unscaled below

back & secondaries uniform

5

unscaled below

contrasting back & (paler) secondaries

6

1. BÖHM'S SPINETAIL *Neafrapus boehmi* (423)   9 cm
The smallest swift of the region. The white belly, square white rump and very short tail are diagnostic. Flight is very fast and erratic, almost bat-like. Differs from pale-bellied form of Brown-throated Martin (p. 298) in flight action and rump colour.
Habitat. Thornveld and open, broad-leaved woodland; often in the vicinity of baobab trees. Nests inside a hollow baobab. Status. Uncommon and localised resident. Call. Recorded as a high-pitched 'tri-tri-tri-peep'. (Witpensstekelstert)

2. MOTTLED SPINETAIL *Telacanthura ussheri* (422)   14 cm
Differs from Little Swift by the white throat extending onto the upper breast, where it appears mottled, and in having a small, white patch on the undertail coverts.
Habitat. Along forested rivers, often near baobab trees. Status. Uncommon and localised resident. Call. Recorded as a soft twittering. (Gevlekte Stekelstert)

3. LITTLE SWIFT *Apus affinis* (417)   12-14 cm
The combination of its small size, large, square, white rump patch that wraps around the flanks, and square tail is diagnostic. In flight it seems squat and dumpy, and the wing tips appear rounded.
Habitat. Aerial. The most common swift over towns, often seen wheeling in tight flocks during display flights. Usually nests in colonies, with adjacent nests touching, under the eaves of buildings and rocky overhangs. Status. Common resident. Call. A soft twittering and high-pitched screeching. (Kleinwindswael)

4. HORUS SWIFT *Apus horus* (416)   13-15 cm
May be confused with Little Swift, as both show a broad, white rump that wraps around the flanks, but this is a more robust bird. It is also distinguished by its forked tail, which may appear square-ended when it is closed. It differs from White-rumped Swift in having more white on the rump and a less deeply forked tail.
Habitat. Aerial; frequently found over mountainous terrain, sandbanks and road cuttings. Breeds in holes in vertical sandbanks. Status. Summer visitor; resident in low-lying north-eastern areas. Uncommon and localised. Call. Normally silent but does scream at breeding sites. (Horuswindswael)

5. WHITE-RUMPED SWIFT *Apus caffer* (415)   14-15 cm
The long, deeply forked tail of this swift is diagnostic. The tail is frequently held closed, appearing long and pointed. The thin, white, U-shaped band across the rump is less obvious than in either Little or Horus Swifts.
Habitat. Aerial, over open country, mountainous terrain and in towns and cities. Usually occupies swallows' nests, and sometimes holes in buildings. Status. Common summer visitor. Call. A typically swift scream, given at breeding sites. (Witkruiswindswael)

6. SCARCE SWIFT *Schoutedenapus myoptilus* (420)   17 cm
A nondescript, dull, grey-brown swift that has the body outline and tail shape of White-rumped Swift but lacks the white rump of that species. It may be distinguished from African Black and Common Swifts (p. 248) by its duller brown plumage and the longer, more deeply forked tail, and by its smaller size.
Habitat. Aerial, over cliffs and rocky bluffs in forested mountain areas. Status. Rare resident in eastern Zimbabwe. Call. Nasal twittering and a trill. (Skaarswindswael)

7. AFRICAN PALM-SWIFT *Cypsiurus parvus* (421)   17 cm
A slender, streamlined swift; long, thin wings, deeply forked tail, and grey-brown coloration are diagnostic. Occurs in small groups or in flocks with other swifts.
Habitat. Usually found in the vicinity of palm trees, including those growing in towns and cities. Status. Common resident and local migrant. Call. A soft, high-pitched scream. (Palmwindswael)

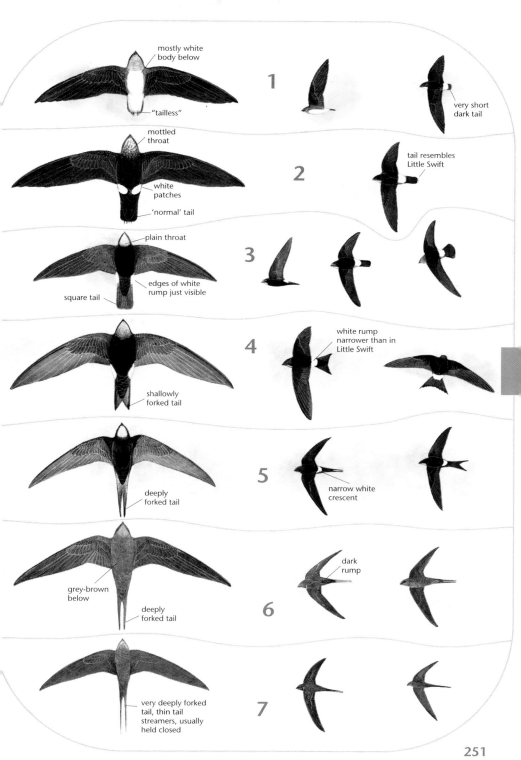

mostly white
body below

"tailless"

very short
dark tail

1

mottled
throat

white
patches

'normal' tail

tail resembles
Little Swift

2

plain throat

edges of white
rump just visible

square tail

3

white rump
narrower than in
Little Swift

shallowly
forked tail

4

deeply
forked tail

narrow white
crescent

5

grey-brown
below

deeply
forked tail

dark
rump

6

very deeply forked
tail, thin tail
streamers, usually
held closed

7

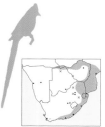

1. NARINA TROGON *Apaloderma narina* (427) 30-34 cm
Although brightly coloured, this furtive species is difficult to see as it normally sits with its back to the observer, well camouflaged by its leafy, green surroundings. The combination of its crimson lower breast and belly and bright, emerald-green upper breast and back is diagnostic.
Female has a brown face and throat and a duller crimson breast. **Juv.** resembles female. **Habitat.** Riverine and evergreen forests, and dense, broad-leaved woodland. **Status.** Locally common resident, with local movements. **Call.** A soft, hoarse hoot, repeated six to ten times. (Bosloerie)

2. AFRICAN BROADBILL *Smithornis capensis* (490) 13 cm
Easily overlooked; usually detected only when displaying. The broad, flattened bill is not easily seen in the field except at close range and at certain angles. Only during the short, circular display flight is the white 'puffball' on the lower back fluffed out and visible.
Male has a black cap and heavily streaked underparts. **Female** and **juv.** are dowdier and lack an obvious black cap. **Habitat.** Coastal forests and thickets, and the understorey of riverine forests. **Status.** Uncommon and localised resident. **Call.** At dawn and dusk, a frog-like 'prrrrrrruup' is given during display flight. (Breëbek)

3. AFRICAN (ANGOLA) PITTA *Pitta angolensis* (491) 18-20 cm
This brilliantly coloured bird is unmistakable but difficult to see in the dark under-storey of the forests it frequents; it is usually glimpsed as it rises off the forest floor in a bright flash of colour. When disturbed it often remains motionless for long periods.
Juv. is drabber than ad. **Habitat.** Thick riverine forests and sandy coastal forests. **Status.** Rare and localised summer visitor; vagrants as far south as Port Elizabeth. **Call.** A frog-like 'quoort', given in display. (Angolapitta)

4. RED-FACED MOUSEBIRD *Urocolius indicus* (426) 34 cm
The red facial patch is diagnostic. In flight, the grey rump contrasts slightly with the back and tail, which appear to be slightly suffused with green. Head and breast are pale cinnamon. The birds usually fly in small parties, and have a fast, powerful and direct flight action.
Juv. has a yellowish green face. **Habitat.** Thornveld, open broad-leaved woodland, low-land fynbos and suburban gardens, avoiding forests and extremely dry regions. **Status.** Common resident. **Call.** A clear whistle, 'tsee-tee-tee', the first note being the highest in pitch. (Rooiwangmuisvoël)

5. SPECKLED MOUSEBIRD *Colius striatus* (424) 35 cm
Distinguished from White-backed and Red-faced Mousebirds by its drabber brown coloration, black facial patch, and black-and-white bill. The flight action is weaker and floppier than that of the other mousebird species. Often seen in groups, dash-ing from one bush to the next in 'follow-my-leader' fashion.
Juv. resembles ad. but lacks the black on the face. **Habitat.** Thick, tangled bush and fruit-ing trees; common in urban and suburban parks and gardens. **Status.** Common resident. **Call.** A harsh 'zhrrik-zhrrik'. (Gevlekte Muisvoël)

6. WHITE-BACKED MOUSEBIRD *Colius colius* (425) 34 cm
In flight the back, with its white stripe bordered by black, is diagnostic. At rest it differs from Speckled and Red-faced Mousebirds by its whitish bill, grey head and upperparts and red feet.
Juv. resembles ad. **Habitat.** Thornveld, fynbos scrub and semi-desert. **Status.** Common resident; near-endemic. **Call.** A whistling 'zwee-wewit'. (Witkruismuisvoël)

♂

♀

♂

♂

black cap

dark cap

♂

♀

2

streaked below

juv.

red mask & mainly red bill

3

blue rump

buffy supercilium & dark crown

blue on wings

4

red belly

black & white bill

purplish brown legs & feet

5

white back

mainly white bill

coral-red legs & feet

6

1. GIANT KINGFISHER *Megaceryle maximus* (429)   38-43 cm
The largest kingfisher in the region. It is unmistakable, with its long, heavy bill, dark, white-spotted back and rufous breast (male) or belly (female). It rarely hovers.
Juv. male has a black-speckled, chestnut breast; juv. female has a white breast. **Habitat.** Wooded streams and dams, fast-flowing rivers in mountains, and coastal lagoons. **Status.** Common resident. **Call.** A loud, harsh 'kahk-kah-kahk'. (Reusevisvanger)

2. PIED KINGFISHER *Ceryle rudis* (428)   23-25 cm
The only wholly black-and-white kingfisher in the region. It frequently hovers over water before diving to seize a fish.
Male has a double breast band. Female has a single, incomplete breast band. **Juv.** resembles female. **Habitat.** Any open stretch of fresh water, coastal lagoons and tidal rock pools. **Status.** Common resident. **Call.** A rattling twitter and a sharp, high-pitched 'chik-chik'. (Bontvisvanger)

3. HALF-COLLARED KINGFISHER *Alcedo semitorquata* (430)   18-20 cm
The black bill is diagnostic and is not seen on any other small ad. 'blue' kingfisher in the region. It is larger than Malachite Kingfisher, with which it overlaps in distribution, but lacks the turquoise crest and can be differentiated by the black bill and blue cheeks. It may be distinguished from juv. Malachite Kingfisher (which also has a dark bill) by its larger size, blue, not chestnut cheeks and the lack of the turquoise crest.
Juv. has black-tipped breast feathers and appears barred. **Habitat.** Wooded streams and, less often, coastal lagoons. **Status.** Uncommon resident. **Call.** A high-pitched 'chreep' or a softer 'peeek-peek'. (Blouvisvanger)

4. MALACHITE KINGFISHER *Alcedo cristata* (431)   13-14 cm
This species differs from the similar but smaller African Pygmy Kingfisher in having the turquoise-and-black barred crown extending down to the eye, and in lacking the violet wash on the sides of the head. In northeastern Namibia, on the Okavango River and Panhandle, a white-breasted form occurs that has a much paler blue back and crest.
Juv. has a black bill, which might lead to confusion with Half-collared Kingfisher, but Malachite Kingfisher is smaller, and has a dark back, chestnut, not blue, cheeks and reddish brown underparts. **Habitat.** Lakes and dams, and along streams and lagoons. **Status.** Common resident. **Call.** A high-pitched 'peep-peep', given in flight. (Kuifkopvisvanger)

5. AFRICAN PYGMY-KINGFISHER *Ispidina picta* (432)   12-13 cm
The smallest kingfisher in the region. It may be differentiated from the similar Malachite Kingfisher by its smaller size, its broad orange supercilium and the violet wash around the ear coverts.
Juv. resembles ad. but has a blackish bill. **Habitat.** Non-aquatic; frequents woodland, savanna and coastal forests. **Status.** Common summer visitor. **Call.** A high-pitched 'chip-chip' flight note. (Dwergvisvanger)

1

♂ juv.

large size

checkered
upperparts

chestnut
breast

♂ ad.

♂ ad.

♀ ad.

2

♂

hovers

♀

ad.

♂   ♀

3

black
bill

very blue
upperparts

blue
cheeks

4

red bill

ad.

juv.

black bill

blue

orange
cheeks

5

ad.

small size

orange
super-
cilium

juv.

KINGFISHERS

1. WOODLAND KINGFISHER *Halcyon senegalensis* (433)   20-22 cm
Very similar to Mangrove Kingfisher, but unlikely to be found in the same habitat.
It differs in having a black lower mandible (not an all-red bill) and a much paler
head with a black stripe extending from the base of the bill, through and slightly
behind the eye. Rarely has an all-red bill, but these birds can be distinguished by
the predominantly blue, not grey, head.
Juv. has a dusky, reddish brown bill. **Habitat.** Non-aquatic; woodland and savanna with
tall trees. **Status.** Common summer visitor. **Call.** A loud, piercing 'trrp-trrrrrrrrr', the latter
part descending. (Bosveldvisvanger)

2. MANGROVE KINGFISHER *Halcyon senegaloides* (434)   21-23 cm
Closely resembles Woodland Kingfisher but is easily distinguished by its all-red (not
red-and-black) bill, and darker grey, not blue, head. Rarely, Woodland Kingfishers
have all-red bills – see above.) It differs from Grey-headed Kingfisher in having a
blue back and in lacking the chestnut belly, and can be distinguished from Brown-
hooded Kingfisher as that species has a dark brown back, a streaked head and
rufous patches on the sides of the breast.
Juv. resembles ad. but has a brownish bill and dark scaling on the breast. **Habitat.**
Mangrove swamps and well-wooded coastal rivers. **Status.** Uncommon resident. **Call.** A
noisy species in the mangroves, giving a loud, ringing 'cheet choo-che che che', the latter
part of which ends in a trill. (Manglietvisvanger)

3. BROWN-HOODED KINGFISHER *Halcyon albiventris* (435)   .   19-20 cm
Distinguished from other similar red-billed kingfishers by its brownish head
streaked with black, the rufous patches on the sides of the breast and the well-
streaked flanks. It differs from Striped Kingfisher by its all-red (not black-and-red)
bill and by the lack of white in the upper- or underwing.
Male has a black back and female a brown back. **Juv.** resembles female. **Habitat.** Non-
aquatic; thornveld, open, broad-leaved woodland and coastal forests. Has adapted to
suburbia and is common in gardens and parks. **Status.** Common resident. **Call.** A whistled
'tyi-ti-ti-ti' and a harsher 'klee-klee-klee' alarm note. (Bruinkopvisvanger)

4. GREY-HEADED (GREYHOODED) KINGFISHER
Halcyon leucocephala (436)   20-21 cm
The combination of a grey head and chestnut belly is diagnostic. It may be distinguished from Brown-hooded Kingfisher by the lack of any streaking on the head
and flanks. Mangrove Kingfisher has a heavier red bill, a blue back, and lacks the
chestnut belly.
Juv. has a blackish bill, and dark barring on the breast and neck. **Habitat.** Non-aquatic;
broad-leaved woodland and savanna. **Status.** Scarce to locally common summer visitor.
Call. A whistled 'cheeo cheeo weecho-trrrrr', similar in pitch to, but much slower than,
that of Brown-hooded Kingfisher. (Gryskopvisvanger)

5. STRIPED KINGFISHER *Halcyon chelicuti* (437)   16-18 cm
The dark cap lightly streaked with grey, the black-and-red bill and the white collar
are diagnostic. It may be distinguished from Brown-hooded Kingfisher, which
often occurs in the same habitat, by its smaller size, darker cap and white collar.
The blue rump is evident only in flight. In flight it shows extensive white on the
underwing and a white flash in the upperwing (Brown-hooded Kingfisher has no
white in the wings).
Sexes differ in their underwing pattern: male has a black band across the remiges, which
female lacks. **Juv.** has a dusky bill and a blackish, scaled breast and flanks. **Habitat.**
Thornveld, and riverine and coastal forests. **Status.** Common resident. **Call.** A high-
pitched, piercing 'cheer-cherrrrrr', the last notes running together. (Gestreepte Visvanger)

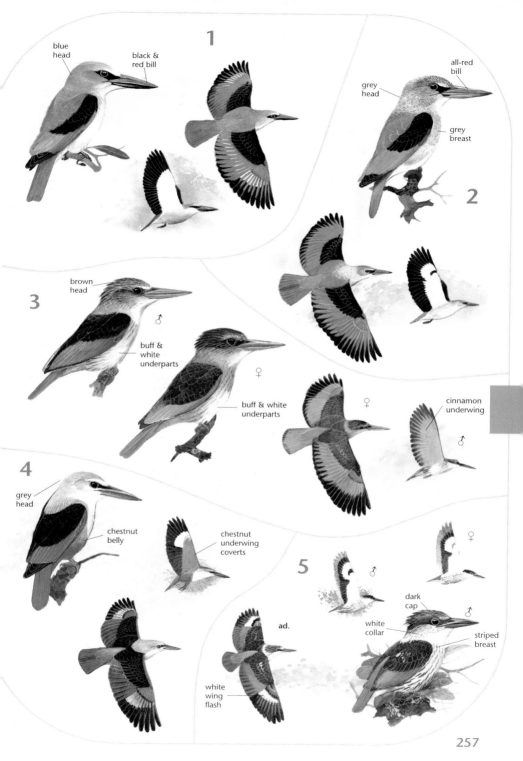

1
blue head
black & red bill

2
all-red bill
grey head
grey breast

3
brown head
buff & white underparts ♂
buff & white underparts ♀
cinnamon underwing ♂
♀

4
grey head
chestnut belly
chestnut underwing coverts

5
♀
♂
dark cap
white collar ♂
white wing flash
striped breast
ad.

257

1. EUROPEAN BEE-EATER *Merops apiaster* (438) 26-28 cm

In the region, the only bee-eater with a chestnut crown and mantle, and a yellow back. Juv. has a green back but its pale blue underparts should eliminate confusion with other bee-eaters in the region. **Habitat.** Thornveld, open broad-leaved woodland, fynbos and adjacent grassy areas. **Status.** Common summer visitor; some breed. **Call.** A far-carrying flight call: a frog-like 'prrrup' and 'krroop-krroop'. (Europese Byvreter)

2. BLUE-CHEEKED BEE-EATER *Merops persicus* (440) 23-31 cm

This species differs from Madagascar Bee-eater in having a green (not brown) crown, a blue forehead, eyebrow stripe and cheeks, and a yellow chin. In worn plumage the blue facial colour can appear white, causing potential confusion with Madagascar Bee-eater. In such birds, crown colour (green vs brown) is the key to separation.

Juv. is duller than ad. and lacks tail streamers. **Habitat.** Flood plains and adjacent broad-leaved woodland. **Status.** Localised summer visitor. **Call.** A liquid 'prrrup' and 'prrreo', less mellow than that of European Bee-eater. (Blouwangbyvreter)

3. MADAGASCAR (OLIVE) BEE-EATER *Merops superciliosus* (439) 23-31 cm

This species differs from Blue-cheeked Bee-eater by its brown (not green) crown, dark rufous throat and paler green underparts. It vaguely resembles Böhm's Bee-eater (p. 260) but has a dull brown (not chestnut) cap, brown, not green, mantle, and is much larger.

Juv. lacks tail streamers. **Habitat.** Open broad-leaved woodland near lakes, rivers and swamps. **Status.** Common but localised summer visitor. **Call.** 'Prrrup'. (Olyfbyvreter)

4. WHITE-FRONTED BEE-EATER *Merops bullockoides* (443) 22-24 cm

The crimson-and-white throat, white forehead and lack of pointed tail projections are diagnostic.

Juv. resembles ad. but is duller. **Habitat.** Margins of wide, slow-flowing rivers with steep sandbanks, and other freshwater expanses; also in woodland far from water. **Status.** Common resident. **Call.** 'Qerrr', and twittering noises when roosting. (Rooikeelbyvreter)

1

blue breast

yellow back

chestnut crown & mantle

green cap

green cap

2

brown cap

brown cap

3

4

white forehead

red & white throat

no tail projections

1. SOUTHERN CARMINE BEE-EATER *Merops nubicoides* (441) 26-36 cm
A long-tailed, pinkish red bee-eater with a dark turquoise crown and pale blue vent and rump.
Juv. lacks the elongated central tail feathers, and has a brown (not carmine) back and less brightly coloured underparts. Rarely, juvs have pale blue chin, throat and cheeks that could cause confusion with Northern Carmine Bee-eater. **Habitat.** Woodland, savanna and flood plains. Colonial breeder in river banks. **Status.** Common summer visitor. **Call.** A deep 'terk, terk'. (Rooiborsbyvreter)

2. WHITE-THROATED BEE-EATER *Merops albicollis* (917) 20-30 cm
Unmistakable, with its diagnostic black-and-white striped head, black breast band and green upperparts.
Juv. is duller green and lightly scalloped above. **Habitat.** Forest and woodland margins in equatorial Africa. In South Africa recorded in Kalahari riverbed, thornveld, fynbos and south-coast thicket. **Status.** Vagrant. **Call.** Similar to but higher-pitched and more repetitive than that of European Bee-eater (p. 258). (Witkeelbyvreter)

3. SWALLOW-TAILED BEE-EATER *Merops hirundineus* (445) 19-22 cm
The only bee-eater in the region to have a forked tail. It is most likely to be confused with Little Bee-eater but has a blue (not black) collar, blue-green underparts and a blue, forked tail.
Juv. shows the diagnostic forked tail but lacks the yellow throat and blue collar. **Habitat.** Diverse: from semi-desert scrub to forest margins. **Status.** Common resident with local movements. **Call.** A 'kwit-kwit' or a soft twittering. (Swaelstertbyvreter)

4. BÖHM'S BEE-EATER *Merops boehmi* (442) 18-22 cm
This species differs from Madagascar Bee-eater (p. 258) in that it is much smaller, has a chestnut (not dull brown) cap, a green, not brown, mantle, lacks the pale eyebrow stripe and has a russet throat extending to the breast.
Juv. resembles ad. but is duller and has shorter central tail feathers. **Habitat.** Open areas in broad-leaved woodland along rivers and streams. **Status.** Uncertain; no recent information. **Call.** A soft 'swee'. (Roeskopbyvreter)

5. LITTLE BEE-EATER *Merops pusillus* (444) 14-17 cm
The smallest bee-eater in the region. It is easily identified by its combination of small size, yellow throat, black collar, buff-yellow belly and square-ended, dark-tipped tail. In flight, it shows conspicuous, russet underwings.
Juv. lacks the black collar of ad. **Habitat.** Savanna, woodland, riverine reedbeds and forest margins. **Status.** Common resident. **Call.** A 'zeet-zeet' or 'chip-chip'. (Kleinbyvreter)

Adult bee-eaters

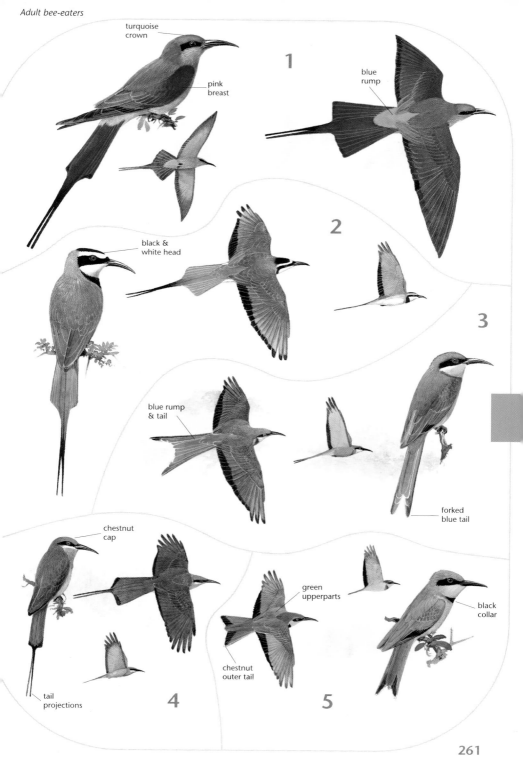

turquoise crown

pink breast

1

blue rump

2

black & white head

3

blue rump & tail

forked blue tail

chestnut cap

green upperparts

black collar

chestnut outer tail

tail projections

4

5

1. LILAC-BREASTED ROLLER *Coracias caudatus* (447)   32-36 cm
Distinguished from similar Racket-tailed Roller by its obviously lilac (not blue) breast, generally paler coloration, turquoise, not brown, crown and pointed, elongated outer tail feathers (that are absent during moult).
Juv. lacks the elongated tail feathers but the lilac-coloured breast differentiates it from juv. European and Racket-tailed Rollers. **Habitat.** Savanna. Perches conspicuously, often along telephone lines. **Status.** Common resident. **Call.** Harsh squawks and screams given when displaying. (Gewone Troupant)

2. RACKET-TAILED ROLLER *Coracias spatulatus* (448)   36 cm
Appears bluer overall than Lilac-breasted Roller, but has less blue in the upper-wings, no lilac on the breast, and elongated outer tail feathers with spatulate tips (which are absent during moult).
Juv. lacks the diagnostic tail, and differs from juv. Lilac-breasted Roller in having violet-and-brown wing coverts and a blue-green (not lilac-tinged) breast. **Habitat.** Tall woodland; does not perch openly as does Lilac-breasted Roller, favouring perch sites just below the tree canopy. **Status.** Uncommon resident. **Call.** Similar to that of Lilac-breasted Roller but higher pitched and more cackling. (Knopsterttroupant)

3. EUROPEAN ROLLER *Coracias garrulus* (446)   30-31 cm
Differs from Lilac-breasted and Racket-tailed rollers in having an all-blue head and a square-ended tail. **Juv.** Racket-tailed Roller appears similar but that species is slimmer, has a distinctive, white-streaked forehead and a green (not blue) crown and nape.
Juv. is more olive-green in colour. **Habitat.** Savanna. **Status.** Common summer visitor. **Call.** Normally silent in the region but when alarmed gives a 'krack-krack' call. (Europese Troupant)

4. PURPLE ROLLER *Coracias naevius* (449)   33-38 cm
The largest roller of the region and easily identified by its broad, pale eyebrow stripe and lilac-brown underparts streaked with white.
Juv. resembles ad. but is duller. **Habitat.** Dry thornveld and open, broad-leaved woodland. **Status.** Scarce to common resident with local movements. **Call.** In display flight repeatedly utters a harsh 'karaa-karaa' while flying with an exaggerated, side-to-side, rocking motion. (Groottroupant)

5. BROAD-BILLED ROLLER *Eurystomus glaucurus* (450)   27-28 cm
The smallest roller in the region and the only one that appears dark with a bright yellow bill. In flight, it shows a blue tail with a dark central stripe and purple underwing coverts.
Juv. resembles ad. but is duller and has greenish underparts streaked with black; bill is bright yellow, as in ad. **Habitat.** Riverine forests and adjacent savanna, with a preference for perching and breeding in dead trees. **Status.** Locally common summer visitor. **Call.** Harsh screams and cackles. (Geelbektroupant)

1

turquoise crown

lilac breast

pointed outer feathers

2

brown cap

racket tail

3

blue head

no tail projections

4

pale eyebrow stripe

heavily streaked front

5

blue tail, vent & underwing

very dark overall

yellow bill

short tail

1. SOUTHERN GROUND-HORNBILL *Bucorvus leadbeateri* (463)   90-100 cm
An unmistakable, turkey-sized, black bird with conspicuous red facial and throat patches and a large, black, decurved bill. The toes are distinctively arched. In flight, it shows broad white outer wings.
Female is distinguished from male by having a blue throat patch. **Juv.** differs from ad. in having yellow (not red) facial and throat patches. **Habitat.** Savanna, woodland and grassland with adjoining forests. **Status.** Resident; mainly confined to large reserves and national parks. Threatened in many parts of its range. **Call.** A loud, booming duet 'ooomph ooomph', given early in the morning. (Bromvoël)

2. SILVERY-CHEEKED HORNBILL *Bycanistes brevis* (456)   75 cm
The male has a huge, creamy casque on the bill. The black of the underparts extends well down the belly, giving the impression of a much darker bird than Trumpeter Hornbill. In flight, it may be distinguished from Trumpeter Hornbill by the lack of white leading and trailing edges to the wing (white only at carpal joint of underwing) and by the whole back being white.
Female and **juv.** have much reduced, darker casques. **Habitat.** Tall evergreen and riverine forests. **Status.** Uncommon, localised resident, nomadic within its range. **Call.** A deep wail, a harsh 'quark-quark' and nasal calls. (Kuifkopboskraai)

3. TRUMPETER HORNBILL *Bycanistes bucinator* (455)   58-60 cm
Similar to Silvery-cheeked Hornbill but smaller, and with a reduced, dark casque on top of the dark bill, a black throat and upper breast and a white lower breast and belly. At close range, it can be seen that the bare skin around the eye is pinkish red. In flight, it shows white tips to the secondaries, white underwing coverts and a white rump. The back is black.
Female has a smaller bill than male, and much reduced casque. **Juv.** has almost no casque. **Habitat.** Lowland, coastal and riverine evergreen forests. **Status.** Common resident, nomadic within its range. **Call.** A wailing, infantile 'waaaaa-weeeee-waaaaa'. (Gewone Boskraai)

1

♂

very large
serrated bill

♀

juv.

white outer
wings

2

pale
casque

♂

black breast
& belly

♀

black body,
white vent

3

red facial skin

grey
bill

♀

♂

white lower
breast & belly

white trailing edge

1. BRADFIELD'S HORNBILL *Tockus bradfieldi* (461)   56 cm
Differs from Monteiro's Hornbill in having no white in the wings and in lacking white outer tail feathers. It may be distinguished from Crowned Hornbill by the paler brown coloration on the head and back, and by its smaller, orange-red bill.
Female has a smaller bill, and the facial skin is turquoise, not black as in male. **Juv.** resembles ad. **Habitat.** Open mopane woodland and mixed thornveld. **Status.** Common resident. **Call.** A rapidly repeated, whistling 'chleeoo' note; in calling display the bill is raised vertically. (Bradfieldse Neushoringvoël)

2. MONTEIRO'S HORNBILL *Tockus monteiri* (462)   56 cm
The large expanse of white on the outer tail feathers, the white-spotted upperwing coverts and the white secondaries are diagnostic. The similar Bradfield's Hornbill has no white in the wings and has a white-tipped tail.
Habitat. Dry thornveld and broad-leaved woodland. **Status.** Common resident; local movements in winter flocks. **Call.** A hollow-sounding 'tooaak tooaak'; in display, the head is lowered and the wings are held closed. (Monteirose Neushoringvoël)

3. CROWNED HORNBILL *Tockus alboterminatus* (460)   54 cm
Differs from Bradfield's Hornbill in having a shorter, deeper red bill with a yellow line at the base and with an obvious casque, and by having a darker head, back and tail and a pale yellow eye.
Habitat. Inland, coastal and riverine forests. **Status.** Common resident; nomadic in the dry season. Often in flocks. **Call.** A whistling 'chleeoo chleeoo'. (Gekroonde Neushoringvoël)

4. AFRICAN GREY HORNBILL *Tockus nasutus* (457)   46-51 cm
Male is the only small hornbill in the region to have a dark bill with a creamy stripe at the base and a casque. The top of female's bill is pale yellow and the tip maroon.
Habitat. Thornveld and dry, broad-leaved woodland. **Status.** Common resident. **Call.** A soft, plaintive whistling, 'phee pheeoo phee pheeoo'; in calling display the bill is held vertically and the wings are flicked open on each note. (Grysneushoringvoël)

5. SOUTHERN YELLOW-BILLED HORNBILL *Tockus leucomelas* (459)   55 cm
The large, yellow bill is diagnostic. This hornbill is very similar to Red-billed Hornbill in plumage coloration but has smaller white primary spots, visible only in flight. Female has a shorter, predominantly dark bill and a dark head and throat.
Habitat. Thornveld and dry, broad-leaved woodland. **Status.** Common resident. **Call.** A rapid, hollow-sounding 'tok tok tok tok tok tokatokatoka'; in calling display the head is lowered and the wings are fanned. (Geelbekneushoringvoël)

6. RED-BILLED HORNBILL *Tockus erythrorhynchus* (458)   40-51 cm
Confusable with Damara Hornbill but is smaller and darker overall, has obvious dark streaking on the face, neck and throat, and has a pale, not dark eye. Speckled upperparts should obviate confusion with other, larger, red-billed hornbills.
Habitat. Thornveld and savanna. **Status.** Common resident. **Call.** A series of rapid 'wha wha wha' calls, followed by a 'kuk-we kuk-we'; in calling display the head is lowered but the wings are held closed. (Rooibekneushoringvoël)

7. DAMARA HORNBILL *Tockus damarensis*   55-57 cm
The almost totally white head and dark eye are diagnostic. Black on the head is confined to a dark crown stripe extending to the nape. Slightly larger than Red-billed Hornbill; ranges overlap slightly but the white head and dark eye should rule out confusion.
Habitat. Semi-arid scrub and woodland. **Status.** Locally common resident, endemic to central and northern Namibia and southern Angola. **Call.** Similar to Red-billed Hornbill. (Damararooibekneushoringvoël)

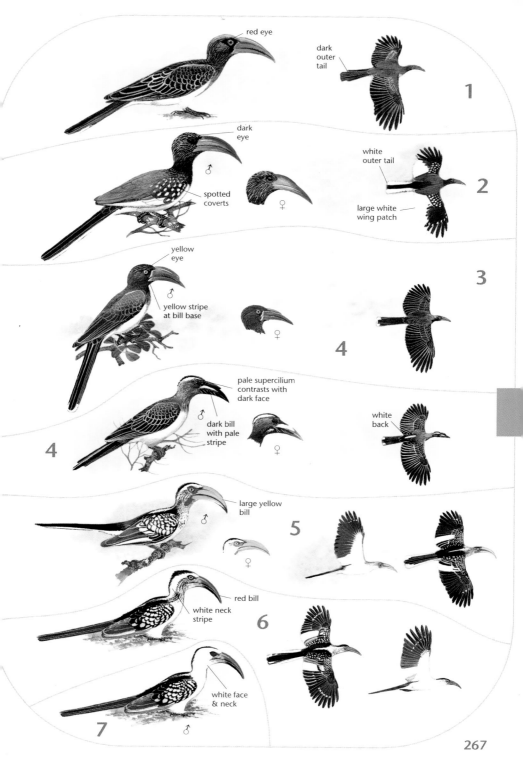

red eye

dark outer tail

1

dark eye

♂

spotted coverts

♀

white outer tail

large white wing patch

2

yellow eye

♂

yellow stripe at bill base

♀

3

4

pale supercilium contrasts with dark face

♂

dark bill with pale stripe

♀

white back

4

large yellow bill

♂

♀

5

red bill

white neck stripe

6

white face & neck

♂

7

1. GREEN (REDBILLED) WOOD-HOOPOE *Phoeniculus purpureus* (452)   32-36 cm
Larger than Common Scimitarbill, this species has a long, decurved, red bill, red legs, white wing bars and a long tail. In good light, the bottle-green head and back of this species distinguish it from Violet Wood-Hoopoe.
Female has the bill less decurved and shorter than that of male. **Juv.** has a black bill but it is far less decurved than that of Common Scimitarbill. Juv. male has a brown throat patch; juv. female has a black throat patch. **Habitat.** A wide variety of woodland and thornveld habitats. **Status.** Common resident. **Call.** Harsh chattering and cackling, usually uttered by groups of birds. (Rooibekkakelaar)

2. VIOLET WOOD-HOOPOE *Phoeniculus damarensis* (453)   36-40 cm
Easily confused with Green Wood-Hoopoe, but in good light this species' violet (not bottle-green) head, mantle and back can be seen. It is also noticeably larger, and has a floppier flight action.
Female has the bill less decurved and noticeably shorter than that of male. **Juv.** male has a brown throat patch and juv. female has a black throat patch; juvs are very difficult to distinguish from juv. Green Wood-Hoopoe in the field. **Habitat.** Dry thornveld, wooded, dry watercourses and mopane woodland. **Status.** Uncommon resident. **Call.** Harsh cackling, similar to that given by Green Wood-Hoopoe but slower. (Perskakelaar)

3. COMMON (GREATER) SCIMITARBILL *Rhinopomastus cyanomelas* (454)   28-30 cm
Smaller and more slender than Green and Violet wood-hoopoes, this species differs from juvs of those species (which, like this species, have black bills) by its long, extremely decurved bill and black (not red) legs and feet. In the field it appears black, except in direct sunlight when a purple sheen is noticeable. The white bar on the primaries is visible in flight. Some individuals, probably juveniles, lack the white primary bar.
Female has a brownish (not glossy black) head and a shorter bill. **Juv.** resembles female. **Habitat.** Dry thornveld and open, broad-leaved woodland. **Status.** Common resident. **Call.** A high-pitched, whistling 'sweep-sweep-sweep', and a harsher chattering. (Swartbekkakelaar)

4. AFRICAN HOOPOE *Upupa africana* (451)   25-28 cm
Unmistakable, with its long, slightly decurved bill and long, black-tipped crest that is held erect when the bird is alarmed. Its cinnamon-coloured body and the black-and-white barring on the wings and tail are conspicuous in flight.
Female has secondaries barred black and white. **Juv.** is duller than female. **Habitat.** Thornveld, open broad-leaved woodland, parks and gardens. **Status.** Common resident. **Call.** A frequently uttered 'hoop-hoop-hoop'. (Hoephoep)

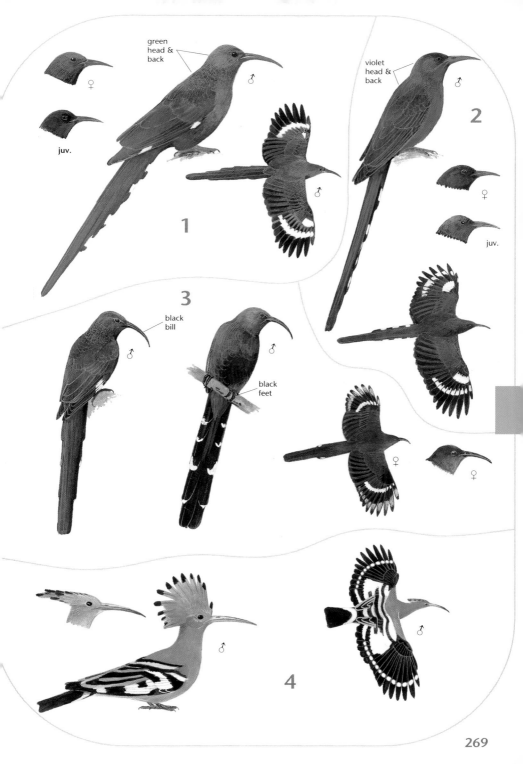

green
head &
back

♀

juv.

♂

1

violet
head &
back

♂

2

♀

juv.

♂

3

black
bill

♂

♂

black
feet

♀

♀

♂

4

1. GREATER HONEYGUIDE *Indicator indicator* (474)   18-20 cm
The male's pink bill, dark crown, black throat and white ear patches are diagnostic.
Female lacks the facial characteristics of male, and differs from similar-sized Scaly-
throated Honeyguide in having an unmarked throat and breast.
Juv. has the underparts washed with yellow and a dark brown back. **Habitat.** Woodland,
savanna and plantations; avoids forests. **Status.** Scarce to locally common resident. **Call.** A
ringing 'whit-purr' or 'vic-tor', repeated at intervals; call is uttered from regularly used site
high in tree. Guiding call is a harsh, rattling chatter. (Grootheuningwyser)

2. SCALY-THROATED HONEYGUIDE *Indicator variegatus* (475)   18-19 cm
The only honeyguide in the region to have the head, throat and breast mottled
and speckled. When seen in the forest canopy it could be confused with
Lesser Honeyguide, but the latter has moustachial stripes and lacks the mottled
head and breast.
Sexes alike but male is larger than female. **Juv.** has the front washed with green and
spotted with black. **Habitat.** Forests. **Status.** Scarce to locally common resident. **Call.** A
drawn-out, insect-like, ventriloquistic trill, 'trrrrrrrr', rising at the end, repeated at one- to two-
minute intervals. The same call-site is used for months or years. (Gevlekte Heuningwyser)

3. LESSER HONEYGUIDE *Indicator minor* (476)   13-15 cm
Usually located by its far-carrying call, this species is the size of and has the jizz of
Southern Grey-headed Sparrow (p. 394), from which it is easily distinguished by its
white outer tail and streaked, olive-coloured wings. It is smaller than Greater and
Scaly-throated Honeyguides, and is differently marked and coloured. The short,
stocky bill readily distinguishes it from Green-backed Honeybird.
Juv. lacks the moustachial stripe of ad. **Habitat.** Woodland, forests and thornveld; has
adapted to urban and suburban gardens. **Status.** Common resident. **Call.** Characteristic
'frip', repeated at short intervals, 15-40 times. The same call-site is used for months or
years. (Kleinheuningwyser)

4. PALLID (EASTERN) HONEYGUIDE *Indicator meliphilus* (477)   11-13 cm
Resembles Lesser Honeyguide but is smaller, greenish on the head and nape, and
faintly streaked on the throat. The short, thick bill eliminates confusion with
Green-backed and Brown-backed Honeybirds.
Juv. resembles ad. **Habitat.** Lowland riparian forests. **Status.** Uncommon, localised resi-
dent. **Call.** Repeated, high-pitched whistle. (Oostelike Heuningwyser)

5. GREEN-BACKED HONEYBIRD (SLENDERBILLED HONEYGUIDE)
Prodotiscus zambesiae (479)   12 cm
May be distinguished from Brown-backed Honeybird by its stockier build, shorter tail
and the greenish wash across its back and rump. Similar in shape to the larger Pallid
Honeyguide but have a very small, thin bill and a grey (not greenish) crown and nape.
Juv. is paler and greyer than ad. **Habitat.** Restricted to miombo and other broad-leaved
woodland. **Status.** Uncommon to locally common resident. **Call.** A repeated 'skeea',
uttered in display flight. (Dunbekheuningvoël)

6. BROWN-BACKED HONEYBIRD (SHARPBILLED HONEYGUIDE)
Prodotiscus regulus (478)   13 cm
Resembles Spotted Flycatcher (p. 354) in appearance and jizz but may be dis-
tinguished by the lack of streaking and by the white outer tail feathers. The lack of
a green wash distinguishes it from Green-backed Honeybird, and its sharp, thin
beak distinguishes it from Pallid Honeyguide.
Juv. resembles ad. **Habitat.** Woodland, savanna, edges of forests and plantations. **Status.**
Uncommon to locally common resident; range has expanded westwards in recent years.
Call. A rapid churring when perched; a metallic 'zwick' given during the dipping display
flight. (Skerpbekheuningvoël)

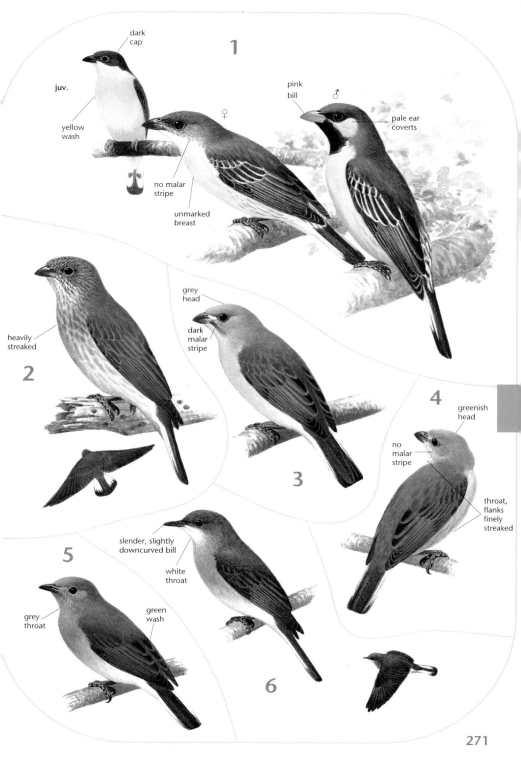

1

dark cap

juv.

yellow wash

♀

pink bill ♂

pale ear coverts

no malar stripe

unmarked breast

2

heavily streaked

grey head

dark malar stripe

3

4

greenish head

no malar stripe

throat, flanks finely streaked

5

slender, slightly downcurved bill

white throat

grey throat

green wash

6

1. GREEN (WOODWARD'S) BARBET *Stactolaema olivacea* (468)   15-17 cm

A drab green barbet with a dark crown and pale, greenish yellow ear patches. In flight, it shows pale green areas at the base of the primaries. Green Tinkerbird (p. 274) is vaguely similar but confusion is unlikely as their ranges never overlap; furthermore, Green Barbet is much larger and lacks a yellow rump.
Juv. is duller than ad. **Habitat.** Coastal forests. **Status.** Common but highly localised resident; restricted to Ngoye forest, KwaZulu-Natal. **Call.** A hollow-sounding 'kwop-kwop-kwop', repeated many times. (Groenhoutkapper)

2. WHYTE'S BARBET *Stactolaema whytii* (467)   18 cm

Paler than White-eared Barbet, it also lacks the white ear patches of that species. The pale yellow forehead, white stripe below the eye and whitish patches on the wings eliminate confusion with any other barbet in the region.
Juv. has no yellow on the forehead and has a paler head and throat than ad. **Habitat.** Miombo woodland and riverine forests, showing a preference for fig trees. **Status.** Locally common resident. **Call.** A soft 'coo', repeated several times. (Geelbleshoutkapper)

3. BLACK-COLLARED BARBET *Lybius torquatus* (464)   18-20 cm

The bright red face and throat, broadly bordered with black, are diagnostic. A very rare colour variant has a yellow face and throat.
Juv's head and throat are dark brown, streaked with orange and red. **Habitat.** Forests, woodland, savanna and wooded suburbs. **Status.** Common resident. Often found in groups. **Call.** Ringing duet starting with a harsh 'krrr-krrrr' and exploding into a 'tooo puudly tooo puudly', the 'tooo' being higher pitched. (Rooikophoutkapper)

4. WHITE-EARED BARBET *Stactolaema leucotis* (466)   17-18 cm

The white ear-stripes and belly of this species contrast with the dark brown to black head, throat and back.
Juv. has a paler base to the bill and a slightly paler back and throat. **Habitat.** Coastal forests and bush, especially alongside rivers. **Status.** Common resident. Often found in groups. **Call.** A loud, twittering 'treee-treeetee-teeetree', and various harsher 'waa waa' notes. (Witoorhoutkapper)

5. CRESTED BARBET *Trachyphonus vaillantii* (473)   23-24 cm

The shaggy crest, yellow face speckled with red, and yellow underparts with a broad black breast band are diagnostic.
Sexes alike but female is usually less vividly coloured. **Juv.** resembles ad. **Habitat.** Woodland, savanna, riverine forests and suburban gardens. **Status.** Common resident. **Call.** Male utters a sustained trilling 'trrrrrrrr.....'; female responds with a repeated 'puka-puka'. (Kuifkophoutkapper)

1

black cap

yellow
ear-patch

2

yellow
forehead

white wing
patches

3

rare yellow-
headed form

4

broad
white
ear-stripe

5

shaggy
crest

1. ACACIA PIED BARBET *Tricholaema leucomelas* (465) 16-18 cm

The larger size, black throat and white underparts distinguish this species from the smaller, similarly patterned Red-fronted Tinkerbird.
Juv. lacks the red forehead. **Habitat.** Woodland and savanna, especially arid thornveld; also suburbs, parks and orchards. **Status.** Common resident. **Call.** A nasal 'nehh, nehh, nehh', repeated at intervals, and a low-pitched 'poop-oop-oop-oop...'. (Bonthoutkapper)

2. GREEN TINKERBIRD (TINKER BARBET) *Pogoniulus simplex* (472) 9-10 cm

This species is uniformly drab green with a bright yellow rump and a pale yellow panel on the folded wing.
Juv. resembles ad. **Habitat.** Canopy of coastal forests. **Status.** Uncertain; occurrence in the region based on one old record that may be suspect. **Call.** A ringing 'pop-op-op-op-op-op', not unlike the calls of other tinkerbirds. (Groentinker)

3. YELLOW-FRONTED TINKERBIRD (TINKER BARBET)
Pogoniulus chrysoconus (470) 11 cm

The yellow forehead colour is the feature that best distinguishes this species from Red-fronted Tinkerbird. Considerable variation occurs in the forehead colour: It ranges from pale yellow to bright orange but never attains the bright red of Red-fronted Tinkerbird. Overall, it is paler in colour than Red-fronted Tinkerbird.
Juv. lacks the yellow forehead. **Habitat.** Woodland and savanna. **Status.** Common resident. **Call.** A continuous 'pop-pop-pop...' or 'tink tink tink...', almost indistinguishable from that of Red-fronted Tinkerbird, but slightly slower and lower pitched. (Geelblestinker)

4. YELLOW-RUMPED TINKERBIRD (GOLDENRUMPED TINKER BARBET)
Pogoniulus bilineatus (471) 9-11 cm

The black back and the black crown with white stripes on the sides of the head are diagnostic. The small, yellow rump patch is not easy to see in the field.
Juv. has the black upperparts narrowly barred and spotted with yellow. **Habitat.** Lowland riverine and coastal forests. **Status.** Common resident. **Call.** 'Doo-doo-doo-doo'; a lower-pitched, more ringing note than that of Red-fronted Tinkerbird, repeated in phrases of four to six notes, not continuously. (Swartblestinker)

5. RED-FRONTED TINKERBIRD (TINKER BARBET) *Pogoniulus pusillus* (469) 9-10,5 cm

Differs from Yellow-fronted Tinkerbird in having a bright red forehead. It is also darker overall than Yellow-fronted Tinkerbird.
Juv. lacks the red forehead. **Habitat.** Coastal and lowland riparian forests. **Status.** Common resident. **Call.** A continuous, monotonous 'pop-pop-pop...', almost indistinguishable from that of Yellow-fronted Tinkerbird, but slightly faster and higher pitched. (Rooiblestinker)

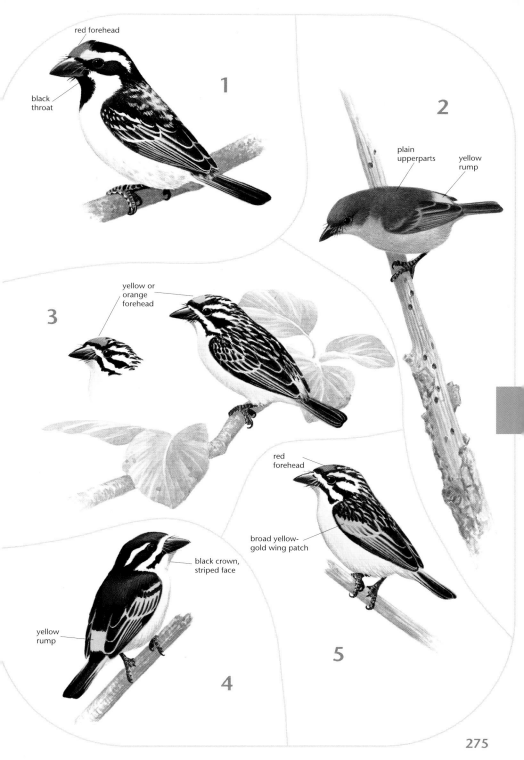

1 red forehead

black throat

2 plain upperparts

yellow rump

3 yellow or orange forehead

4 black crown, striped face

yellow rump

5 red forehead

broad yellow-gold wing patch

1. GROUND WOODPECKER *Geocolaptes olivaceus* (480) 25 cm
The only entirely terrestrial woodpecker in the region. It is easily identified by its diagnostic pinkish red breast and rump.
Female and **juv.** are very similar to male but have much reduced and duller pinkish red on the breast and rump, and lack the reddish moustachial stripes. **Habitat.** Boulder-strewn, grassy slopes of hills and mountains, to sea level in the southwest of its range. Usually in small family parties. **Status.** Common resident; endemic. **Call.** A far-carrying 'pee-aargh', and a ringing 'ree-chick'. (Grondspeg)

2. RED-THROATED WRYNECK *Jynx ruficollis* (489) 19 cm
The brown barred and mottled plumage should eliminate confusion with any woodpecker. It might be mistaken for Spotted Creeper (p. 306) but is much larger and has a dark chestnut throat and upper breast. It moves jerkily, similarly to the woodpeckers. It feeds on the ground.
Juv. is paler than ad. **Habitat.** Grassland and open savanna; has adapted well to suburban gardens and stands of eucalyptus. **Status.** Common resident. **Call.** A series of two to ten squeaky 'kweek' notes; also a repeated, scolding 'peegh'. (Draaihals)

3. GREEN-BACKED (LITTLE SPOTTED) WOODPECKER
Campethera cailliautii (485) 15-16 cm
Male can be distinguished from similar-sized male Cardinal Woodpecker by its red forehead and crown, yellow-spotted (not barred) back, spotted (not streaked) front, and the lack of moustachial stripes.
Female differs from female Cardinal Woodpecker by its red hind crown and by the lack of black moustachial stripes. **Juv.** resembles female but the red on the crown is reduced or absent. **Habitat.** Riparian forests and tall, broad-leaved woodland. **Status.** Uncommon resident. **Call.** A high-pitched, whining 'whleeee'. (Gevlekte Speg)

4. OLIVE WOODPECKER *Dendropicos griseocephalus* (488) 16-18 cm
The greyish head, unmarked, dull green body and red rump are diagnostic.
Male has a bright red crown and nape. Female has a uniformly grey head. **Juv.** male has a reduced red crown, variably mottled with black. **Habitat.** Montane, coastal and riverine evergreen forests. **Status.** Common resident. **Call.** A cheerful, disyllabic note, 'wir-rit', repeated at intervals. (Gryskopspeg)

5. CARDINAL WOODPECKER *Dendropicos fuscescens* (486) 14-15 cm
In size it could be confused with Green-backed Woodpecker. It differs in that it has bold, black moustachial stripes and appears black and white (not green and white) all over. Male can further be distinguished from male Green-backed Woodpecker by its brown (not red) forehead.
Female has a black nape. **Juv.** male has a red crown and a black nape. **Habitat.** Diverse; from thick forests to dry thornveld. **Status.** Common resident; in general, the most common woodpecker in the subregion. **Call.** A high-pitched 'krrrek krrrek krrrek'; also makes a soft, drumming sound. (Kardinaalspeg)

1

reddish-pink rump

pink breast

2

rufous throat

4

♀

♂

no spotting or streaking

♂ juv.

3

♀

no malar stripe

spotted underparts

juv.

♂

no malar stripe

spotted underparts

5

brown frons

black malar stripe

♀

streaked underparts

♂

♂ juv.

1. GOLDEN-TAILED WOODPECKER *Campethera abingoni* (483)   18-20 cm
Similar to Knysna Woodpecker but this species is paler below and much less heavily streaked and blotched with brown on the breast and belly. Male has heavy streaking on the cheeks and throat, eliminating confusion with male Bennett's Woodpecker. Female lacks the red moustachial stripe, and the red is restricted to the nape.
Juv. resembles female. **Habitat.** Thornveld, dry, open, broad-leaved woodland and coastal forests. **Status.** Common resident. **Call.** A loud, nasal 'wheeeeeaa' shriek. (Goudstertspeg)

2. BENNETT'S WOODPECKER *Campethera bennettii* (481)   18-20 cm
Male differs from all other woodpeckers in the region by having an all-red forehead, crown and moustachial stripes. Male of north-western race *buysi* has mostly unmarked, pale peach-coloured underparts.
Female is readily identifiable by the brown throat and ear coverts. **Juv.** resembles female. **Habitat.** Broad-leaved woodland and savanna. Often feeds on the ground. **Status.** Scarce to common resident. **Call.** A high-pitched, chattering 'whirrr-itt-whrrr-itt', often uttered in duet. (Bennettse Speg)

3. SPECKLE-THROATED WOODPECKER *Campethera scriptoricauda* (482)   22 cm
Male may be confused only with the very similar male Bennett's Woodpecker but differs by its speckled (not plain, creamy white) throat.
Female differs from female Bennett's Woodpecker by its spotted (not brown) throat and ear coverts. It is doubtful if **juvs** of these two species could be told apart in the field. **Habitat.** Mixed broad-leaved woodland between Beira and the lower Zambezi River in Mozambique, especially where there is a tall grass understorey. **Status.** Uncertain, probably a fairly common resident. **Call.** Not known to differ from calls of Bennett's Woodpecker. (Tanzaniese Speg)

4. BEARDED WOODPECKER *Dendropicos namaquus* (487)   23-25 cm
The white face with its bold, black moustachial stripes and ear coverts is diagnostic. Both sexes have very dark underparts finely barred with black and white.
Male has a red mid-crown. Female has a black crown and nape with the forehead speckled white. **Juv.** male has a red crown and nape and a black forehead lightly speckled white. **Habitat.** Broad-leaved woodland, thornveld and riverine forests, especially in areas where there are tall, dead trees. **Status.** Common resident. **Call.** A loud, rapid 'wik-wik-wik-wik'; drums very loudly. (Baardspeg)

5. KNYSNA WOODPECKER *Campethera notata* (484)   18-20 cm
Both male and female are very much darker than Golden-tailed Woodpecker, and are heavily blotched (not streaked) with dark brown on the underparts.
Male's dark red forehead, crown and moustachial stripes are heavily blotched with black and less obvious than those of male Golden-tailed Woodpecker. Female has indistinct moustachial stripes. **Juv.** resembles female. **Habitat.** Coastal evergreen forests, euphorbia scrub and mature thicket including coastal milkwood thickets. **Status.** Locally common resident; endemic. **Call.** A higher-pitched shriek than that of Golden-tailed Woodpecker. (Knysnaspeg)

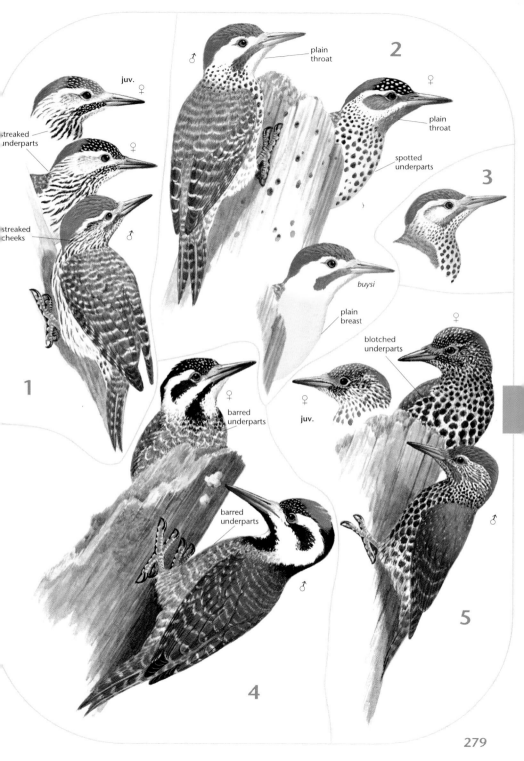

juv. ♀

streaked
underparts

♀

streaked
cheeks

♂

1

2

♂

plain
throat

♀

plain
throat

spotted
underparts

3

buysi

plain
breast

♀

juv.

blotched
underparts

♀

♂

♀
barred
underparts

barred
underparts

♂

4

5

1. DUSKY LARK *Pinarocorys nigricans* (505) 19-20 cm
The bold, black-and-white face pattern and the heavy spotting on the underparts impart a thrush-like appearance. It has pale (almost white) legs and a dark back. When foraging it slowly raises and opens its wings.
Habitat. Open grassy areas in thornveld and broad-leaved woodland; frequently found in newly burnt grassland and woodland. **Status.** Uncommon non-breeding summer visitor. **Call.** A soft 'chrrp, chrrp', uttered when flushed. (Donkerlewerik)

2. FLAPPET LARK *Mirafra rufocinnamomea* (496) 14-15 cm
Very similar to Eastern Clapper Lark but longer tailed, darker plumaged and with darker outer tail feathers. The aerial display is also different: it flies high, rattling its wings in a series of short bursts, but is otherwise silent in display.
Juv. is duller than ad. **Habitat.** Lowland grassland, open thornveld and broad-leaved woodland. **Status.** Common resident. **Call.** A short 'tuee', given when perched. (Laeveldklappertjie)

3. EASTERN CLAPPER LARK *Mirafra fasciolata* 15 cm
Differs from Cape and Agulhas Clapper Larks in display and range. Plumage variable, with southern birds being rich rufous above and northern birds grey. Differs from Flappet Lark in having a slightly shorter tail with paler outer feathers. When displaying, climbs steeply while clapping its wings, then parachutes down with legs trailing.
Habitat. Grassland and open savanna. **Status.** Locally common, near-endemic. **Call.** A long, ascending whistle 'poooooeeee', similar to Cape Clapper Lark but rising less in pitch and preceded by slower wing-clapping. (Hoëveldklappertjie)

4. CAPE CLAPPER LARK *Mirafra apiata* (495) 15 cm
Differs from other clapper larks in display and range. Appears dark overall at long range, with richly marked greyish upperparts. Underparts are rich rufous with dark streaking. Shy and skulking when not displaying and difficult to flush.
Habitat. Karoo scrub and coastal fynbos, especially in areas with many restios. **Status.** Common endemic. **Call.** Long, ascending whistle 'pooooooeeeeee', preceded by faster wing-clapping than Eastern Clapper Lark. (Kaapse Klappertjie)

5. AGULHAS CLAPPER LARK *Mirafra marjoriae* 15 cm
Averages darker and less rufous above than Cape Clapper Lark, but individual variation is considerable, so identification in the northwest of its range, where it may come into contact with Cape Clapper Lark, is problematic.
Habitat. Coastal fynbos and fallow lands. **Status.** Common endemic. **Call.** Display typically comprises rapid wing clapping accompanied by two descending, not ascending, whistled 'peeeoo' notes, which start earlier in display than Cape Clapper Lark's. (Overbergklappertjie)

6. MELODIOUS LARK *Mirafra cheniana* (492) 12 cm
Confusion is unlikely between this and similar Monotonous Lark because of their vastly different habitats. In display the bird rises to a great height and circles on whirring wings, singing constantly.
Juv. is more mottled above and duller below than ad. **Habitat.** Gentle slopes in upland grassland. **Status.** Common but localised resident; endemic. Nomadic within its range. **Call.** A 'chuk chuk chuer' call-note with a jumbled, melodious song comprising mimicked notes of other birds. (Spotlewerik)

7. MONOTONOUS LARK *Mirafra passerina* (493) 14 cm
Distinguished from Stark's Lark (p. 288) in flight by its chestnut wing patches. Display flight is short, with the bird launching itself from a perch and rising to 15-20 metres, calling all the time. Usually sings from a perch on a bush or tree, by day and night.
Juv. is more mottled than ad. **Habitat.** Thornveld and mopane woodland with sparse grass cover. **Status.** Common resident and nomad; near-endemic. Summer visitor to the south of its range. **Call.** Frequently repeated 'trrp-chup-chip-choop'. (Bosveldlewerik)

1

thrush-like face

very pale legs

2

western form

eastern form

dark underparts

3

brown crown

brown back

4

brown crown

grey back

5

brown crown

heavily marked brown back

6

white throat & eyebrow stripe

7

plain face

puffy white throat

1. DUNE LARK *Certhilauda erythrochlamys* (503)   17 cm

Distinguished from Karoo Lark by its paler coloration, plain or only slightly streaked, sandy-brown back, and lightly streaked underparts; the flanks and belly are plain, not streaked. Differs from Barlow's Lark and Red Lark by its longer bill, less bold spotting on the underparts and much paler, sandy-coloured upperparts. Some Barlow's Larks around Lüderitz, Namibia, are very similar, but their ranges do not overlap.

Habitat. Scrub growth on gravel plains between sand dunes in the Namib Desert. **Status.** Fairly common, localised resident; endemic. **Call.** Similar to that of Karoo Lark but preceded by a series of 'tip-ip-ip-ip' notes. (Duinlewerik)

2. BARLOW'S LARK *Certhilauda barlowi* (947)   19 cm

Differs from Karoo Lark in having plain, not streaked flanks, being slightly larger and longer-billed, and in appearing bull-necked. Coastal birds are pale sandy brown above, inland birds reddish. Coastal birds closely resemble Dune Lark but are more streaked below and their ranges do not overlap.

Habitat. Arid scrublands and vegetated dunes. **Status.** Has a restricted range in southern Namibia and the extreme northwest of South Africa, and is common within this area; endemic. **Call.** A series of simple lead-in notes followed by a long, uniform trill. Most similar to Dune Lark but has fewer lead-in notes and a shorter trill. (Barlowse Lewerik)

3. KAROO LARK *Certhilauda albescens* (502)   17 cm

Upperpart coloration varies regionally. Has a noticeable white eye-stripe, dark ear coverts and boldly streaked underparts, including the belly and flanks. In flight it shows a very dark-coloured tail. In the north it differs from Barlow's Lark by having streaked flanks and Red Lark by its shorter, more slender bill, and by the dark brown streaking on the upperparts. It may be distinguished from Dune Lark by its darker, rufous-streaked upperparts and darker streaking on the underparts.

Juv. is more mottled above than ad. **Habitat.** Karoo shrublands and coastal shrublands on the west coast. **Status.** Common resident; endemic. **Call.** Short 'chleeep-chleeep-chrrr-chrrrp' song, given in display flight or from the top of a bush. (Karoolewerik)

4. RED LARK *Certhilauda burra* (504)   19 cm

Differs from Dune and Barlow's larks by its rich rufous upperparts, and differs further from Dune Lark by its boldly streaked breast. It is similar to the red form of Karoo Lark but is larger, and has a much heavier bill and plain rufous upperparts. Two colour forms occur: birds occurring on dunes are red above, while those on the plains are browner wih darker centres to the upperpart feathers. The plains form is most likely to be confused with Karoo Lark, although range overlap is slight.

Juv. has slightly mottled upperparts. **Habitat.** Scrub-covered red sand dunes and surrounding karroid shrublands. **Status.** Fairly common but highly localised resident; endemic. **Call.** A short 'chrrk', given when flushed. The song is similar to that of Karoo Lark but is slower and lower-pitched; sings in the air or from a bush. (Rooilewerik)

1

pale
back

faint
streaking

2

chestnut
back

barlowi

pinkish
back

white,
unstreaked
flanks

cavei

patae

3

Karoo form

southwestern
Cape race

grey
above

Namaqualand race

streaked
flanks

4

dune form

rufous upperparts

heavy thrush-like streaking

streaked
back

plains form

1. SABOTA LARK *Calendulauda sabota* (498) 15 cm
Colour varies regionally, but this species is consistently boldly marked above and below and lacks rufous in the outer wing. The bill is short and dark (the lower mandible being paler), and a straight, white eye-stripe runs from the base of the bill to the nape, giving the head a capped appearance. The bill size decreases from west to east. Large-billed race *naevia* in west treated by some as a full species (Bradfield's Lark).
Habitat. Thornveld and arid savanna. Status. Common resident, near-endemic. Call. A jumbled song of rich, melodious 'chips' and twitterings; mimics other birds. Often calls from an elevated perch. (Sabotalewerik)

2. FAWN-COLOURED LARK *Mirafra africanoides* (497) 14-16 cm
Upperpart coloration varies regionally, but the white underparts and slightly streaked breast are diagnostic.
Juv. is more mottled than ad. Habitat. Kalahari scrub, broad-leaved savanna and thornveld; on sandy soils. The southwestern edge of its range overlaps with the range of Red Lark (p. 282). Status. Common resident. Call. A jumble of harsh 'chips' and twitterings, ending in a buzzy slur, given from treetops or during the short aerial flight. (Vaalbruinlewerik)

3. LARGE-BILLED (SOUTHERN THICKBILLED) LARK *Galerida magnirostris* (512) 18 cm
The thick-based, heavy bill, with yellow at the base of the lower mandible, is diagnostic. This is a robust, heavily built lark with a relatively short, dark tail and boldly streaked underparts. It has a crest which is raised when the bird is alarmed or singing.
Juv. is spotted white above. Habitat. Lowland and montane fynbos, montane grassland, Karoo shrublands, and cultivated and fallow fields. Status. Common resident; endemic. Call. A soft but far-carrying 'treeeleeeleee', sounding like a rusty gate being opened. Highly vocal. (Dikbeklewerik)

4. RUFOUS-NAPED LARK *Mirafra africana* (494) 15-18 cm
Colour varies regionally, but the rufous outer wings and nape are consistent features. It has a small, erectile crest.
Juv. has a blotched breast, not clearly spotted as in ad. Habitat. Diverse: from open grassland with stunted bushes to thornveld and cultivated areas. Status. Common resident. Call. A frequently repeated, trisyllabic 'tree, tree-loo' when perched; the wings are often flapped during the perched song. A jumbled mixture of imitated calls given during display flight. (Rooineklewerik)

5. RED-CAPPED LARK *Calandrella cinerea* (507) 14-15 cm
Upperpart coloration is very variable but the rufous cap, unmarked, white underparts and russet smudges on the sides of the breast are diagnostic.
Male is redder than female and has a longer crest. Juv. has dark brown upperparts, spotted with white, and is pale below with a heavily spotted breast; it lacks the red cap and epaulettes of the ad. Habitat. Open country with very short grass cover. Status. Common resident. In the dry season often found in flocks. Call. A sparrow-like 'tchweerp', given in flight; song a sustained jumble of melodious phrases, given during display flight. (Rooikoplewerik)

1

bold white
eyebrow stripe

small-billed
eastern form

thick
bill

streaked
necklace

large-billed
western form

2

pale form

faint
streaking

white
below

yellow
bill base

heavy
streaking

crest

3

eastern form

rusty
nape

western
form

4

red
cap

red
shoulder

white, unmarked
underparts

♂ ad.

5

1. SHORT-CLAWED LARK *Certhilauda chuana* (501)   19 cm
Differs from Rufous-naped Lark in lacking any rufous on the nape or wings, but in flight shows a rufous rump. The buff-white eyebrow stripe runs directly from the base of the straight, slender bill to the nape, giving a capped effect.
Habitat. Dry, open thornveld and open, grassy areas with scattered trees. **Status.** Uncommon resident; endemic. **Call.** A short 'chreep-chuu-chree', given when perched in a tree. The display flight is similar to that of the long-billed larks; the flight is a steep ascent and descent, with the bird whistling on the descent. (Kortkloulewerik)

2. CAPE LONG-BILLED LARK *Certhilauda curvirostris* (500)   20-24 cm
A large, long-bodied lark with a long decurved bill. Grey-brown above with prominent dark streaking. White underparts are densely streaked, streaking extending onto flanks and belly.
Female is smaller than male with a noticeably shorter bill. Northern form larger and greyer than southern birds, with a spectacularly long, decurved bill. **Habitat.** Coastal dunes and croplands. **Status.** Locally common endemic. **Call.** Querulous 'whir-irry' contact call. Song is a far-carrying descending whistle 'seeeooo' given in display or from the ground. Display flight common to all long-billed larks; bird flies close to the ground then swings up vertically to 10–15 metres above ground, closes its wings just before the top of its climb, calls and then drops, opening its wings just above the ground. (Weskuslangbeklewerik)

3. AGULHAS LONG-BILLED LARK *Certhilauda brevirostris*   18-20 cm
Most similar to southern form of Cape Long-billed Lark, but differs by being more buff overall with a shorter bill and tail. Differs from Karoo Long-billed Lark by having underpart streaking extending onto the flanks and belly.
Habitat. Farmlands, coastal fynbos and semi-arid Karoo shrub. **Status.** Locally common endemic. **Call.** Display song is a two-note 'seeoo seeoo' whistle. (Overberglangbeklewerik)

4. KAROO LONG-BILLED LARK *Certhilauda subcoronata*   18-22 cm
Upperpart coloration varies from dark chocolate brown in the south to reddish, with a noticeably grey hind neck, in the north. From north to south the amount of streaking reduces, especially in Bushmanland where the belly and flanks are always unstreaked. In areas of overlap with Cape Long-billed Lark near the Gariep (Orange) River it is easily differentiated by its reddish upperparts and unmarked belly and flanks.
Habitat. Karoo scrub and grasslands west of 25°E, typically in rocky areas. **Status.** Common endemic. **Call.** At close range a soft inhalation is audible before the long, descending whistle 'uh-seeeeooooo'. (Karoolangbeklewerik)

5. BENGUELA LONG-BILLED LARK *Certhilauda benguelensis*   18-20 cm
Identification criteria not fully resolved; species status recognised on the basis of significant genetic difference from other long-billed larks. Most closely resembles northern form of Karoo Long-billed Lark but is variable and tends to be slightly more streaked on the crown, back and breast.
Habitat. Arid rocky hill slopes and plains north of the Brandberg, Namibia (southern limit to range uncertain). **Status.** Common endemic to northern Namibia and southern Angola. **Call.** A slightly quavering, long, descending whistle 'seeooeeeooo'. (Kaokolangbeklewerik)

6. EASTERN LONG-BILLED LARK *Certhilauda semitorquata*   16-20 cm
Smaller and less streaked than all other long-billed larks with the upperparts reddish, slightly streaked brown in the west and virtually unstreaked in the east. Underparts buff with diffuse streaking restricted to the breast. Bill is the shortest, slimmest and straightest of all long-billed larks; this, combined with a longish tail, imparts a pipit-like appearance.
Habitat. Grassland, generally on rocky slopes. **Status.** Common endemic. **Call.** A long, descending, whistled 'seeeeoooo'. (Grasveldlangbeklewerik)

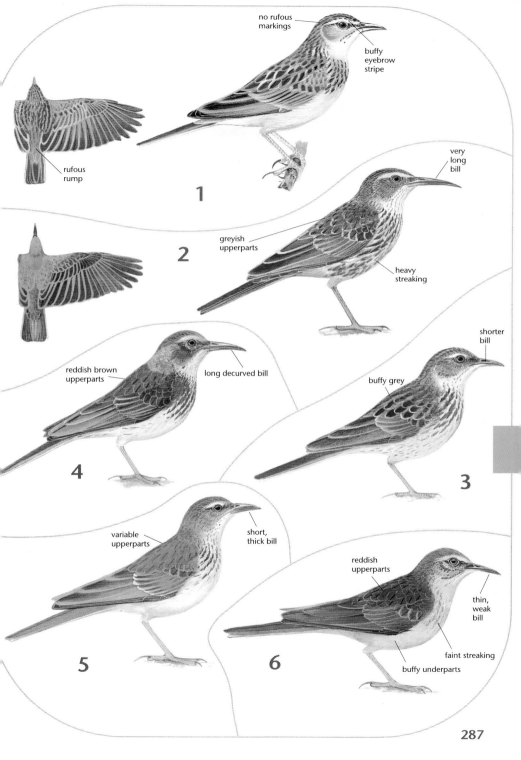

no rufous markings

buffy eyebrow stripe

rufous rump

1

very long bill

greyish upperparts

heavy streaking

2

reddish brown upperparts

long decurved bill

shorter bill

buffy grey

4

3

variable upperparts

short, thick bill

reddish upperparts

thin, weak bill

faint streaking

buffy underparts

5

6

1. RUDD'S LARK *Heteromirafra ruddi* (499)   14 cm
A very small lark that appears large-headed and long-legged, with a very thin tail.
If clearly seen, the buff stripe down the centre of the crown is diagnostic. The display flight is high, and can last up to 30 minutes.
Juv. resembles ad. **Habitat.** Short upland grassland, usually near damp depressions.
Status. Rare, localised resident; critically endangered; endemic. **Call.** A clear, whistled song, 'pee-witt-weerr', given in display flight. (Drakensberglewerik)

2. BOTHA'S LARK *Spizocorys fringillaris* (509)   12-13 cm
A small, pink-billed lark with heavily streaked upperparts. It may be distinguished
from Pink-billed Lark by its white (not brown) underparts, white, not buff, outer
tail feathers, streaked flanks and thinner bill.
Juv. is paler than ad. **Habitat.** Heavily grazed, upland grassland. **Status.** Uncommon,
localised resident; endemic. **Call.** A cheerful, repeated 'chiree'; a 'chuk, chuk', uttered in
flight. (Vaalrivierlewerik)

3. PINK-BILLED LARK *Spizocorys conirostris* (508)   12-13 cm
The short, conical, pink bill distinguishes this from most other larks. It differs from
Botha's Lark by its dark underparts, which contrast boldly with the white throat
and unstreaked flanks. Western forms are paler below, but these do not overlap in
range with Botha's Lark. Where their ranges overlap, it can be differentiated from
Stark's Lark by its less grey coloration and lack of an obvious crest.
Juv. has a dark bill and is duller and more speckled than ad. **Habitat.** Upland grassland,
farmlands and desert scrub. **Status.** A common but nomadic resident; near-endemic. **Call.**
When flushed, small flocks utter a soft 'si-si-si'. (Pienkbeklewerik)

4. SCLATER'S LARK *Spizocorys sclateri* (510)   13-14 cm
When seen at close range, a dark brown, teardrop-shaped mark below the eye is
both obvious and diagnostic. In flight it differs from Stark's and Pink-billed larks by
its bold, white outer tail feathers that broaden towards the tail base and that, in
profile, suggest a pale rump.
Juv. is paler than ad. and has more spotting than streaking above. **Habitat.** Stony quartzite
plains and ridges in arid shrublands. **Status.** Uncommon and nomadic resident; endemic.
Call. A repeated 'tchweet-tchweet', given in flight. (Namakwalewerik)

5. STARK'S LARK *Spizocorys starki* (511)   13-14 cm
Much paler than Sclater's and Pink-billed Larks, this species lacks the teardrop mark
of the former and differs from both in having an erectile crest.
Juv. is spotted with white on the upperparts. **Habitat.** Stony desert scrub to gravel plains
of the Namib Desert; also grassy areas on Namib and Kalahari sands, especially when
breeding. **Status.** Common but localised resident; near-endemic. Nomadic, sometimes in
large flocks. **Call.** A short 'chree-chree', given in flight; song a melodious jumble of notes,
given in display flight. (Woestynlewerik)

large
head

buff crown
stripe

1

thin
pinkish
bill

white outer
feathers

2

pale
underparts

no crest

pink,
conical
bill

dark
underparts

buffy
outer
feathers

3

pale base
to tail

4

dark tear
drop

pale eye-
ring

erectile crest

dark form

pale form

5

289

1. CHESTNUT-BACKED SPARROWLARK (FINCHLARK)
Eremopterix leucotis (515)   12-13 cm
Differs from Grey-backed Sparrowlark in having a chestnut back and forewings and a wholly black crown. Female is mottled with buff and brown above, and has a black lower breast and belly; it differs from female Grey-backed Sparrowlark in having chestnut wing coverts.
Juv. resembles **female** but is paler below. **Habitat.** Road verges and cultivated lands, sparsely grassed parts of thornveld, and lightly wooded areas. **Status.** Common but nomadic resident; usually in flocks, sometimes mixed with Grey-backed Sparrowlarks. **Call.** A short 'chip-chwep', uttered in flight. (Rooiruglewerik)

2. GREY-BACKED SPARROWLARK (FINCHLARK) *Eremopterix verticalis* (516) 12-13 cm
The greyish back and wings of this species distinguish it from Chestnut-backed Sparrowlark.
Male is further distinguished from male Chestnut-backed Sparrowlark by the white patch on the hind crown. Female is very much greyer in appearance than female Chestnut-backed Sparrowlark, lacking the latter's chestnut wing coverts. **Juv.** is more mottled than female. **Habitat.** Karoo shrublands, desert, grassland and cultivated lands. **Status.** Common but nomadic resident; near-endemic. Usually in flocks, sometimes mixed with Chestnut-backed Sparrowlarks. **Call.** A sharp 'chruk, chruk', given in flight. (Grysruglewerik)

3. BLACK-EARED SPARROWLARK (FINCHLARK) *Eremopterix australis* (517) 12-13 cm
The all-black head and underparts are diagnostic in male. In flight male appears all black and therefore might be confused with an indigobird, but the dark chestnut back and relatively broad, all-black underwings are diagnostic.
Female differs from female Chestnut-backed and Grey-backed Sparrowlarks by being dark chestnut above, heavily streaked with black below, and in lacking a dark belly patch. **Juv.** resembles female. **Habitat.** Karoo shrublands and grassland, Kalahari sandveld, gravel plains and, occasionally, cultivated lands. **Status.** Uncommon and highly nomadic resident; endemic. Usually in flocks. **Call.** A short 'preep' or 'chip-chip', given in flight; male has a butterfly-like display. (Swartoorlewerik)

4. GRAY'S LARK *Ammomanes grayi* (514)   13-14 cm
This small lark is the palest and least marked lark in the region, and is unlikely to be confused with any other lark. The pale desert form of Tractrac Chat (p. 318) is similar in colour but has an obvious white base to its tail, a thin, dark bill and a very upright stance on long legs, and flicks its wings when landing. Gray's Lark does not flick its wings.
Juv. is more mottled above than ad. **Habitat.** Sparsely vegetated gravel plains along the coastal desert strip of Namibia. **Status.** Resident. Uncommon and nomadic within its range; near-endemic. **Call.** Song is a very high-pitched, un-larklike mixture of descending, metallic-sounding 'tinks' and whistles, normally given before dawn; a short 'tseet' or 'tew-tew', given in flight. (Namiblewerik)

5. SPIKE-HEELED LARK *Chersomanes albofasciata* (506)   13-15 cm
Colour varies considerably, but the long, slightly decurved bill, white throat contrasting strongly with the darker breast and belly, and the short, dark tail tipped with white are diagnostic. It has a very upright stance.
Sexes alike but male larger than female. **Juv.** is mottled with white above and below. **Habitat.** Grassland, Karoo shrublands and desert grassland on gravel plains. **Status.** Common resident; usually in small groups. **Call.** A trilling 'trrrep, trrrep' flight call. (Vlaktelewerik)

1

pale bird

chestnut back

♀

chestnut back

♂

pale nuchal collar

chestnut back

♀

♀

2

dark form

♂

pale form

♂

grey back

♀

heavy streaking

♂

♀

3

♀

all black below

♂

♀

♂

no belly patch

♀

4

very pale back

plain face

pale form

short legs

dark form

5

southeastern form

long, decurved bill

central form

northwestern form

short, white-tipped tail

291

SWALLOWS

1. RED-BREASTED SWALLOW *Hirundo semirufa* (524)　　　　　19-24 cm
This very dark swallow could be confused with Mosque Swallow, from which it differs by its red throat and breast and dark buff, not white, underwing coverts. Smaller and shorter-tailed Red-rumped Swallow is much paler and streaked below, has a blue cap that does not extend below the eye, a complete rusty nuchal collar and the flight feathers appear pale grey, not black, from below.
Juv. has a creamy white throat and breast but differs from ad. Mosque Swallow by its buffy, not white, underwing coverts. **Habitat.** Grassland and savanna. **Status.** Common summer visitor. **Call.** A soft, warbling song; twittering notes are uttered in flight. (Rooiborsswael)

2. MOSQUE SWALLOW *Hirundo senegalensis* (525)　　　　　20-24 cm
Likely to be confused only with Red-breasted Swallow from which it differs in being much paler and having white (not buff) underwing coverts and a white throat.
Juv. Red-breasted Swallow has variable amounts of white on the throat and breast but always has buff (not white) wing coverts, and has the blue on its head extending well below the eye. Juv. is paler below and less glossed above. **Habitat.** Open woodland, often near rivers, and especially near baobabs. **Status.** Uncommon and localised resident. **Call.** A nasal 'harrrrp', and a guttural chuckling. (Moskeeswael)

3. RED-RUMPED SWALLOW *Hirundo daurica* (904)　　　　　17-18 cm
Most similar to Greater Striped Swallow but has a dark blue (not reddish) cap and less pronounced streaking on the underparts. It might be confused with the slightly larger Mosque and Red-breasted Swallows but is overall very much paler and has an obvious rusty nape. The flight feathers appear pale grey, not black, from below. **Habitat.** Chiefly in highland and mountainous areas. **Status.** Rare visitor, both old and recent records from northeastern Zimbabwe. **Call.** A single-note 'djuit' and a twittering song, softer and shorter than that of Barn Swallow (p. 294). (Rooinekswael)

4. SOUTH AFRICAN CLIFF-SWALLOW *Hirundo spilodera* (528)　　　　　15 cm
Differs from the striped swallows in having only a slight notch in a square-ended tail, dark mottling, not streaking on the throat and breast, heavier build and chunkier proportions. It can be distinguished from Barn Swallow (p. 294) by the pale rump and mottled breast. The crown is dark brown, slightly glossed in front.
Juv. lacks the blue-black gloss of ad. above. **Habitat.** Upland grassland and Karoo scrub, usually in the vicinity of road bridges. **Status.** Common summer visitor; breeding endemic. **Call.** A twittering 'chooerp-chooerp'. (Familieswael)

5. GREATER STRIPED SWALLOW *Hirundo cucullata* (526)　　　　　20 cm
Larger than Lesser Striped Swallow, this species appears very much paler, with the striping on the buffy underparts discernible only at close range. The orange on the crown is slightly paler, and on the rump it is much paler. There is no rufous on the vent, and the ear coverts are white.
Juv. has a little blue-black gloss above, a reddish brown crown, and a partial brown band on the breast. **Habitat.** Grassland and vleis. **Status.** Common summer visitor; breeding endemic. **Call.** A twittering 'chissick'. (Grootstreepswael)

6. LESSER STRIPED SWALLOW *Hirundo abyssinica* (527)　　　　　15-17 cm
Darker than Greater Striped Swallow, with heavy black striping on the white underparts. The rufous rump extends onto the sides of the vent and the ear coverts are orange.
Female has shorter outer tail feathers. **Juv.** has less blue-black gloss above than ad., and a brown (not rufous) crown. **Habitat.** Usually near water; frequently perches. **Status.** Common resident and summer visitor. **Call.** A descending series of squeaky, nasal 'zeh-zeh-zeh-zeh' notes. (Kleinstreepswael)

Adult swallows

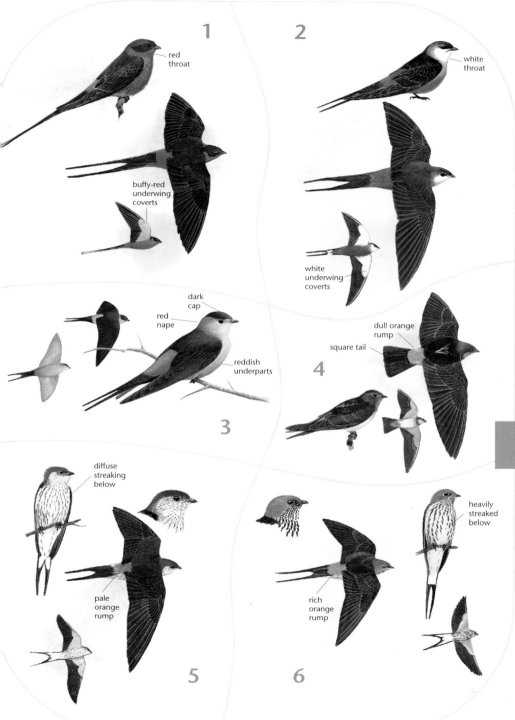

1
red throat
buffy-red underwing coverts

2
white throat
white underwing coverts

3
dark cap
red nape
reddish underparts

4
dull orange rump
square tail

5
diffuse streaking below
pale orange rump

6
rich orange rump
heavily streaked below

1. BARN (EUROPEAN) SWALLOW *Hirundo rustica* (518) 15-18 cm

The red throat and forehead, blue-black breast band and deeply forked tail are diagnostic. Differs from similar Angola Swallow in being creamy or deep buff on the lower breast and belly, but never grey.

Male has longer tail streamers than female. **Juv.** is browner and has shorter outer tail feathers than ads. **Habitat.** Cosmopolitan, except in closed forest. **Status.** Abundant non-breeding summer visitor. **Call.** A soft, high-pitched twittering. (Europese Swael)

2. ANGOLA SWALLOW *Hirundo angolensis* (519) 14-15 cm

Less agile in flight than similar Barn Swallow. Red on the throat extends onto the breast and is bordered by a narrow, incomplete black band. Underparts are pale grey, not creamy or deep buff. Outer tail streamers are much shorter than those of Barn Swallow and the tail is less deeply forked.

Juv. has the red of ad. replaced by pale rufous, and is less glossy above. **Habitat.** Rivers and bridges, and in association with man. **Status.** Vagrant. **Call.** A weak twittering. (Angolaswael)

3. WIRE-TAILED SWALLOW *Hirundo smithii* (522) 13-17 cm

Smaller than White-throated Swallow, this species differs in lacking a black breast band, and having a bright chestnut cap and a black streak across the vent. It is very fast and agile in flight. The very thin tail streamers are often difficult to see.

Juv. has the chestnut of ad. replaced largely by brown and is less glossy blue above. **Habitat.** Usually found near water, often breeding under bridges. **Status.** Common resident. **Call.** A sharp, metallic 'tchik'. (Draadstertswael)

4. WHITE-THROATED SWALLOW *Hirundo albigularis* (520) 14-17 cm

The white throat and blue-black breast band are diagnostic. Sand and Banded Martins (p. 298) also have a white throat and dark breast band, but the breast bands are brown and both species have brown upperparts.

Juv. is less glossy than ad. above, and has a reddish brown forehead. **Habitat.** Closely associated with water. **Status.** Common breeding summer visitor. **Call.** Soft warbles and twitters. (Witkeelswael)

5. PEARL-BREASTED SWALLOW *Hirundo dimidiata* (523) 14 cm

May be distinguished from Wire-tailed Swallow by its lack of both tail streamers and a vent band, and by its blue cap. When seen from below, it differs from Grey-rumped Swallow and Common House-Martin (p. 296) in having white (not dark) underwing coverts and, when seen from above, a dark rump. It lacks white spots in the tail and the blue gloss is not well developed.

Juv. is less glossy above than ad. **Habitat.** Over bushveld and fresh water, and in association with man. **Status.** Locally common resident with seasonal movements in parts of its range. **Call.** A subdued chipping note, uttered in flight. (Pêrelborsswael)

Adult swallows

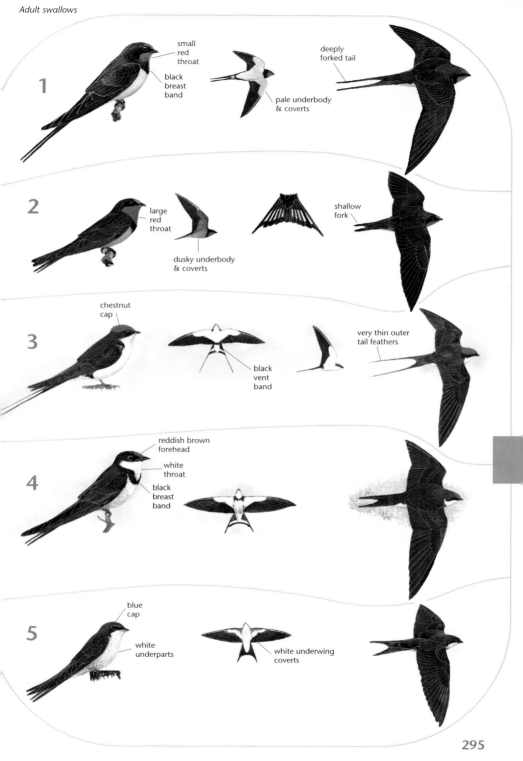

1
small red throat
black breast band
deeply forked tail
pale underbody & coverts

2
large red throat
dusky underbody & coverts
shallow fork

3
chestnut cap
black vent band
very thin outer tail feathers

4
reddish brown forehead
white throat
black breast band

5
blue cap
white underparts
white underwing coverts

1. WHITE-HEADED SAW-WING (SWALLOW)
Psalidoprocne albiceps (913)   12-15 cm

The snowy white head of this species is bisected by a black line running through the eye to the nape (sunglasses). The rest of the plumage is black with a slight greenish sheen.
Female and **juv.** have the white on the crown partly grizzled. **Habitat.** Open forest glades and wooded slopes. **Status.** Vagrant. **Call.** Recorded elsewhere as a weak twittering. (Witkopsaagvlerkswael)

2. EASTERN SAW-WING (SWALLOW) *Psalidoprocne orientalis* (537)   13-15 cm

Differs from Black Saw-wing in having conspicuous white underwing coverts and in being overall more slender and longer tailed.
Juv. is very dark brown and lacks the gloss of ad. **Habitat.** Over evergreen forests and miombo woodland, and around rivers in these habitats. **Status.** Locally common resident. **Call.** Soft twittering and a short 'chip'. (Tropiese Saagvlerkswael)

3. BLACK SAW-WING (SWALLOW) *Psalidoprocne holomelaena* (536)   13-15 cm

An all-black saw-wing that differs from Blue Swallow in having only slightly glossy, greenish black plumage and a less deeply forked tail with shorter tail streamers. It may be distinguished from Eastern Saw-wing by its black (not white) underwing coverts and shorter tail. The smaller size and slow, fluttering flight should eliminate confusion with any of the dark swifts in the region.
Juv. is very dark brown and lacks the gloss of ad. **Habitat.** Fringes and clearings in forests and plantations. **Status.** Locally common resident; summer visitor to south of range. **Call.** A soft 'chrrp' alarm call. (Swartsaagvlerkswael)

4. BLUE SWALLOW *Hirundo atrocaerulea* (521)   18-25 cm

The glossy, dark blue plumage and long outer tail feathers are diagnostic. It differs from the similar Black Saw-wing in having blue (not slightly glossed greenish black) plumage, by the long tail streamers (in male) and by its much more dynamic flight action.
Female lacks long tail streamers. **Juv.** has a brown throat and generally much less glossy plumage than ad. **Habitat.** Upland grassland, often bordering forests. **Status.** Breeding summer visitor. Rare and highly localised; endangered through loss of habitat. **Call.** A musical 'bee-bee-bee-bee', uttered in flight. (Blouswael)

5. COMMON HOUSE-MARTIN *Delichon urbicum* (530)   14 cm

Swallow-like; the only martin in the region to have pure white underparts and a white rump (in ad.). In flight it is easily confused from below with Grey-rumped Swallow, but has a less deeply forked tail, broader-based, shorter wings and a noticeably shorter, less deeply forked tail.
Juv. has a pale grey rump and is less glossy above than ad. **Habitat.** Over dry, broad-leaved woodland and thornveld, mountainous terrain, and coastal habitats in the south. **Status.** Common summer visitor; has bred in the Western Cape. **Call.** A single 'chirrp'. (Huisswael)

6. GREY-RUMPED SWALLOW *Pseudhirundo griseopyga* (531)   13-14 cm

The combination of greyish brown crown and dull grey rump contrasting slightly with blue-black upperparts is diagnostic. In flight it could be confused from below with Common House-Martin, but it has a longer, more deeply forked tail and the underparts are off-white, not white.
Juv. has a reddish brown rump. **Habitat.** Over rivers in thornveld, and open grassland adjacent to lakes and vleis. **Status.** Locally common resident; summer visitor to the south. **Call.** Flight call-note recorded as 'chraa'. (Gryskruisswael)

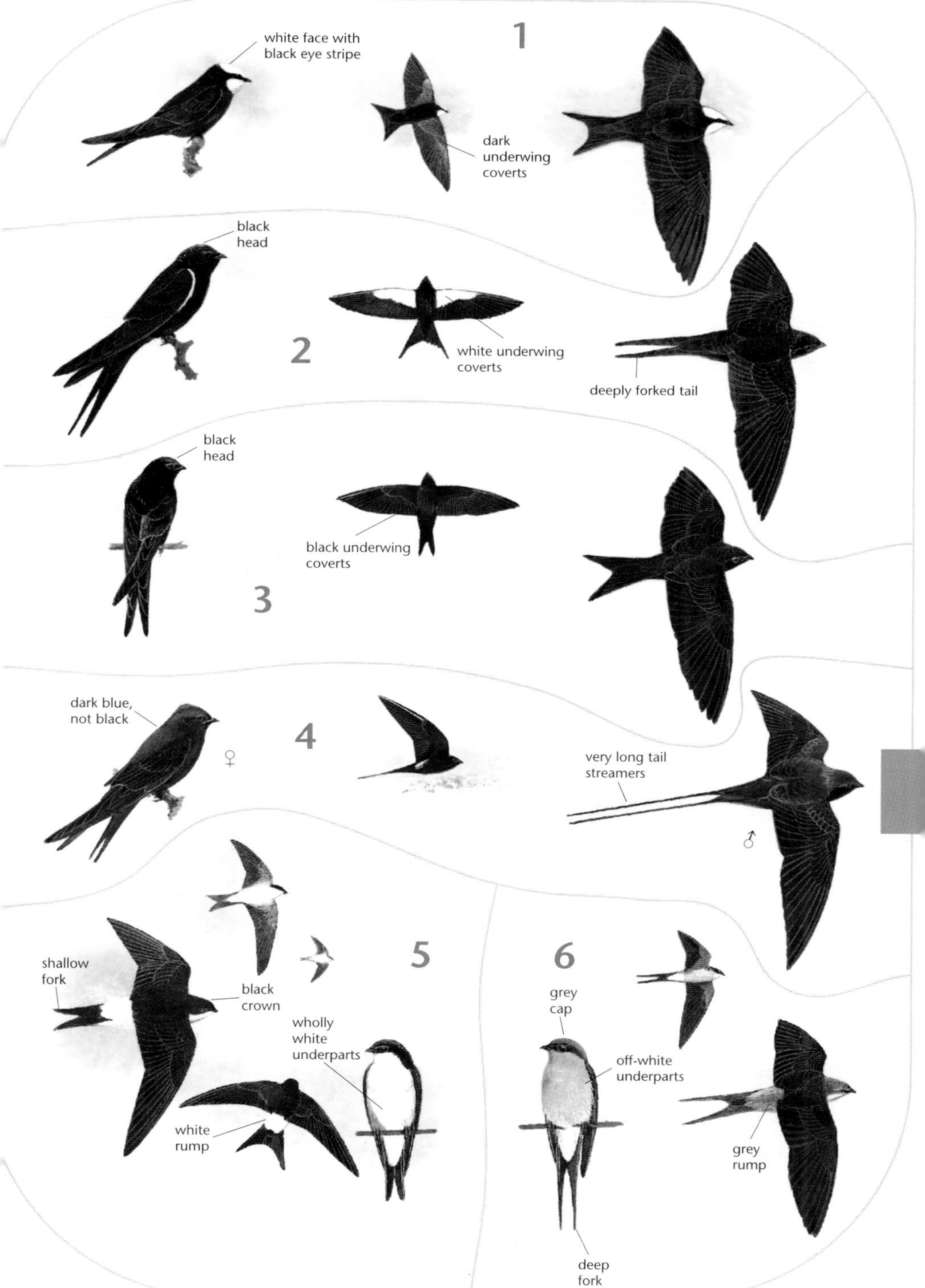

1

white face with
black eye stripe

dark
underwing
coverts

2

black
head

white underwing
coverts

deeply forked tail

3

black
head

black underwing
coverts

4

dark blue,
not black

♀

very long tail
streamers

♂

5

shallow
fork

black
crown

wholly
white
underparts

white
rump

6

grey
cap

off-white
underparts

grey
rump

deep
fork

1. BANDED MARTIN *Riparia cincta* (534)   15-17 cm
Larger than Sand Martin, this species has white underwing coverts, a small, white eyebrow and a square-ended tail. It often has a thin, brown line across the vent.
Juv. has the upperparts scaled with pale buff, and lacks most of the white eyebrow. **Habitat.** Frequents areas of low vegetation or grassland. **Status.** Locally common breeding summer visitor. **Call.** Flight call is a 'che-che-che'; song is a jumble of harsh 'chip-choops'. (Gebande Oewerswael)

2. SAND MARTIN *Riparia riparia* (532)   11-12 cm
May be distinguished from Brown-throated Martin by its white throat and brown breast band. It differs from the larger Banded Martin in having all-dark underwings and a forked tail, and in lacking the white eyebrow.
Juv. resembles ad. **Habitat.** Usually over or near fresh water. **Status.** Locally common summer visitor. **Call.** A grating 'chrrr'. (Europese Oewerswael)

3. BROWN-THROATED MARTIN *Riparia paludicola* (533)   11-12 cm
Occurs in two colour forms, one dark brown with a small amount of white on the vent, the other having a brown throat and breast with the rest of the underparts white. May be told from Sand Martin by its brown throat. The dark form could be confused with Rock Martin but is smaller and darker brown below, and lacks white tail spots. Differs from Böhm's Spinetail (p. 250) in flight action and rump colour.
Juv. resembles ad. but has pale fringes to the secondaries. **Habitat.** Over freshwater lakes, streams and rivers, especially near sandbanks. **Status.** Common resident; the brown-bellied form is found chiefly in the south and southeast of the range. **Call.** A soft twittering. (Afrikaanse Oewerswael)

4. MASCARENE MARTIN *Phedina borbonica* (535)   12-14 cm
In the region, the only brown martin with heavily striped underparts and a white vent. It might be mistaken for juv. Lesser Striped Swallow (p. 292) but that species has a chestnut crown and rump. At a distance it resembles the dark form of Brown-throated Martin, but the white on its vent and its heavier and chunkier proportions should eliminate confusion.
Juv. has pale fringes to the secondaries. **Habitat.** Chiefly over dense miombo woodland and forests. **Status.** Uncommon and localised non-breeding winter visitor to Mozambican coastal regions. **Call.** Usually silent in Africa. (Gestreepte Kransswael)

5. ROCK MARTIN *Hirundo fuligula* (529)   12-15 cm
This brown martin differs from all-brown form of Brown-throated Martin in being larger, paler on the throat, breast and underwing coverts, and having white tail spots (visible in the spread tail).
Juv. has pale edges to the upperwing coverts and secondaries. **Habitat.** Cliffs, quarries, rocky terrain and around buildings. **Status.** Common resident with local movements. **Call.** Soft, indistinct twitterings. (Kransswael)

Adult birds

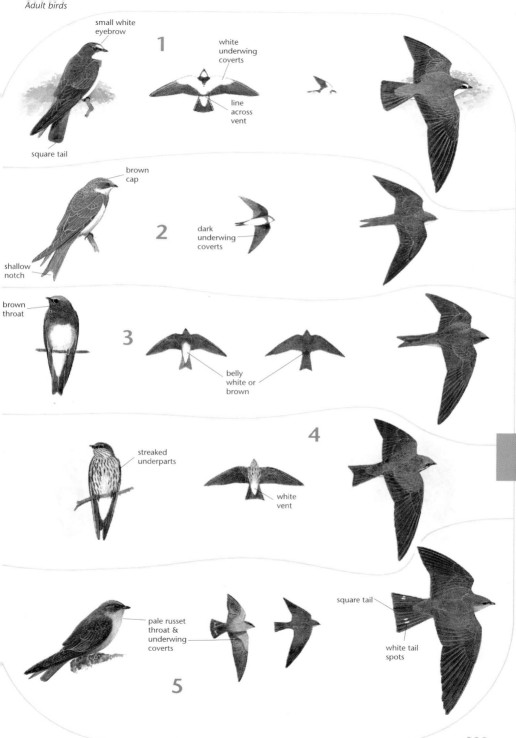

1 small white eyebrow

white underwing coverts

line across vent

square tail

2 brown cap

shallow notch

dark underwing coverts

3 brown throat

belly white or brown

4 streaked underparts

white vent

5 pale russet throat & underwing coverts

square tail

white tail spots

299

1. FORK-TAILED DRONGO *Dicrurus adsimilis* (541)   23-26 cm
The only all-black perching bird in the region to have a deeply forked tail. Square-tailed Drongo and Southern Black Flycatcher (p. 354) are similar, but are smaller and have only a slight fork in the tail.
Juv. has buff-tipped feathers on the underparts and forewing, and a yellow gape. **Habitat.** Woodland, savanna and exotic plantations. **Status.** Common resident. **Call.** A variety of grating or shrill notes; mimics birds of prey, especially Pearl-spotted Owlet (p. 242). (Mikstertbyvanger)

2. SQUARE-TAILED DRONGO *Dicrurus ludwigii* (542)   18 cm
Smaller than Fork-tailed Drongo, and the tail is only slightly notched. It differs from Southern Black Flycatcher (p. 354) by its smaller, rounder head, and red (not dark brown) eye that can be seen at close range. It also flicks its wings, especially when agitated. It may be distinguished from larger male Black Cuckooshrike by its slightly notched tail and the lack of both a yellow shoulder and an orange-yellow gape.
Female is duller black than male. **Juv.** resembles female but has pale tips to the feathers. **Habitat.** Evergreen forests. **Status.** Scarce to locally common resident. **Call.** A strident 'cheweet-weet-weet' and other phrases. (Kleinbyvanger)

3. BLACK CUCKOOSHRIKE *Campephaga flava* (538)   18-21 cm
Male differs from Southern Black Flycatcher (p. 354) and Square-tailed Drongo in having a rounded tail, and by its habit of quietly creeping through the tree canopy (not dashing after insects in flight).
Male has a yellow shoulder (this is sometimes absent), but the orange-yellow gape is diagnostic. Female resembles a female *Chrysococcyx* cuckoo (p. 236) but is larger and more barred below, and has bright yellow outer tail feathers. **Juv.** resembles female. **Habitat.** Mature woodland and forest margins. **Status.** Locally common resident and summer visitor. **Call.** A high-pitched, prolonged 'trrrrrrrr'. (Swartkatakoeroe)

4. GREY CUCKOOSHRIKE *Coracina caesia* (540)   21-23 cm
The combination of all-grey plumage, white orbital ring, and black patch between the base of the bill and the eye is diagnostic.
Female is paler than male and lacks the black patch at the base of the bill. **Juv.** has flight and tail feathers tipped with white, and a barred black rump. **Habitat.** Evergreen forests. **Status.** Uncommon resident. **Call.** A soft, thin 'seeeeeeeep'. (Bloukatakoeroe)

5. WHITE-BREASTED CUCKOOSHRIKE *Coracina pectoralis* (539)   25-27 cm
Confusable only with Grey Cuckooshrike, from which it differs in having a white breast and belly.
Female is paler than male, and usually has a white chin and throat. **Juv.** is even paler than either male or female, with spotted underparts, and upperparts barred with white. **Habitat.** Tall woodland, especially miombo and riverine forests. **Status.** Uncommon resident. **Call.** A 'duid-duid', given by male; a 'tchee-ee-ee-ee', given by female. (Witborskatakoeroe)

1

♂

red eye

deep notch

juv.

tail during moult

2

♂

red eye

shallow notch

juv.

3

♂

some have yellow shoulders

♂

yellow gape

rounded tail

♀

yellow-edged wing feathers

barred below

yellow outer tail

♂

♀

mostly yellow underwings

4

♂

grey breast & belly

grey underwing coverts

♂

♀

white underwing coverts

♂

white breast & belly

5

1. AFRICAN GOLDEN ORIOLE *Oriolus auratus* (544)   20-21 cm
A brighter yellow bird than Eurasian Golden Oriole, from which it differs mainly by its yellow wing coverts, the black eye-stripe extending behind the eye and in having wholly yellow outer tail feathers.
Female may be distinguished from female Eurasian Golden Oriole by its yellower coloration and yellowish green (not olive-green) wing coverts. Underparts almost entirely unstreaked. **Juv.** resembles female. **Habitat.** Tall woodland (especially miombo) and riverine forest. **Status.** Uncommon summer visitor. **Call.** A liquid whistle, 'fee-yoo-fee-yoo'. (Afrikaanse Wielewaal)

2. EURASIAN (EUROPEAN) GOLDEN ORIOLE *Oriolus oriolus* (543)   22-25 cm
Male differs from male African Golden Oriole by its black, not yellow, upperwing coverts and the black eye-stripe that extends only marginally behind the eye.
Female is very similar to female African Golden Oriole but is less yellow and lightly streaked below, and has olive-green upperwing coverts and green upperparts. **Juv.** resembles female but is more streaked. **Habitat.** Tall woodland, savanna and exotic plantations. **Status.** Fairly common non-breeding summer visitor. **Call.** A liquid 'chleeooop', seldom heard in southern Africa. (Europese Wielewaal)

3. (EASTERN) BLACK-HEADED ORIOLE *Oriolus larvatus* (545)   20-22 cm
The black head is diagnostic in all plumages. If seen from a distance, it might be confused with the rare Green-headed Oriole but it has a yellow (not green) back.
Juv. has a dark bill, its head is dark brown, flecked with black and the bib is streaked. **Habitat.** Mature woodland, especially broad-leaved; also forest edge, exotic plantations and mature gardens. **Status.** Common resident. **Call.** A whistle, 'pooodleeoo', and a harsher 'kweeer' note. (Swartkopwielewaal)

4. GREEN-HEADED ORIOLE *Oriolus chlorocephalus* (546)   21-23 cm
The green head, yellow collar and green back are diagnostic. From a distance the head appears black, and this might lead to confusion with Black-headed Oriole; however, the back also appears black, not yellow as in Black-headed Oriole.
Juv. has dull yellow underparts, the breast slightly streaked with olive, and an olive wash on the head and throat. **Habitat.** Evergreen montane forest. **Status.** Rare resident; in the region, found only on Mt. Gorongoza, Mozambique. **Call.** Liquid call, typical of orioles. (Groenkopwielewaal)

1

all-yellow outer tail

♂

yellow wing coverts

yellow mantle ♀

yellow below

♂

♀

2

♂

black wing coverts

greenish mantle ♀

pale, lightly streaked below

♀

♂

juv.

3

ad.

yellow back

black head & throat

juv.

ad.

ad.

4

green head & throat

yellow collar

dark green back

ad.

juv.

ad.

ad.

303

1. WHITE-NECKED RAVEN *Corvus albicollis* (550)   54-56 cm
The massive, black, white-tipped bill and the white crescent on the back of the neck are diagnostic. In flight and from a distance it may be distinguished from Cape and Pied Crows by its much broader wings, larger, heavier head and short, broad tail.
Juv. is less glossy black than ad. **Habitat.** Mountainous and hilly areas, coastal cliffs and coastal towns (in the southwest of its range). **Status.** Locally common resident. **Call.** A deep, throaty 'kwook'. (Withalskraai)

2. PIED CROW *Corvus albus* (548)   46-50 cm
The only white-bellied crow in the region. From a distance it may be distinguished from White-necked Raven by its longer tail, smaller head and white breast.
Juv. resembles ad. but there is less contrast in the black-and-white plumage. **Habitat.** Cosmopolitan. **Status.** Common resident; often in flocks. **Call.** A loud 'kwaaa' or 'kwooork' cawing. (Witborskraai)

3. CAPE (BLACK) CROW *Corvus capensis* (547)   43-45 cm
Larger than House Crow, and differs in being uniformly glossy black with a long, slender, slightly decurved bill.
Juv. is duller, lacking the glossy, blue-black plumage of ad. **Habitat.** Upland grassland, open country, cultivated fields and dry, desert regions. **Status.** Common resident; sometimes in flocks. **Call.** A crow-like 'kah-kah', lower in pitch than that of Pied Crow; song is a complex repertoire of bubbling notes. (Swartkraai)

4. HOUSE CROW *Corvus splendens* (549)   34-38 cm
The smallest and only grey-bodied crow in the region. The head, wings and tail are a glossy blue-black.
Juv. body colour is greyish brown, but in other respects juv. resembles ad. **Habitat.** Not often seen away from human habitation, as it scavenges food or forages on open fields. **Status.** Resident. Populations have been established in Durban since 1972 and on the Cape Flats since the late 1980s. Also in Mozambique. **Call.** A higher-pitched 'kaah, kaah' than that of other crows. (Huiskraai)

1
white nape
huge bill, white tip
short tail

2
white collar
white lower breast & belly

3
uniformly black
thin bill

4
greyish breast, nape & mantle

1. ASHY TIT *Parus cinerascens* (552)   13 cm
Differs from Grey Tit by its blue-grey (not brownish grey) back, and blue-grey (not buff) flanks and belly. It is darker than Miombo Tit, with less white in the wings. **Juv.** is a duller version of ad. **Habitat.** Thornveld and arid savanna. **Status.** Common resident; endemic. **Call.** Harsher and more scolding than that of Grey Tit. (Akasiagrysmees)

2. (SOUTHERN) GREY TIT *Parus afer* (551)   13 cm
Distinguished from Ashy Tit and Miombo Tit by having a distinctive brownish grey (not blue-grey) back, a buff belly and flanks, and a proportionally shorter tail. **Juv.** is browner than ad. **Habitat.** Fynbos and Karoo scrub. **Status.** Common resident; endemic. **Call.** Song a cheery 'klee-klee-klee-cheree-cheree'; alarm note a harsh 'chrrr'. (Piet-tjou-tjougrysmees)

3. MIOMBO (NORTHEN GREY) TIT *Parus griseiventris* (553)   13 cm
Range overlaps marginally with that of Ashy Tit. Distinguished from this species by being thinner billed, paler, and having a buff (not white) cheek stripe and outer tail. **Juv.** is a duller version of ad. **Habitat.** Miombo woodland. **Status.** Common resident. **Call.** Scolding 'tjou-tjou-tjou-tjou' notes. (Miombogrysmees)

4. CINNAMON-BREASTED TIT *Parus pallidiventris*   14-15 cm
Resembles a washed-out Rufous-bellied Tit (ranges non-overlapping). Differs mainly in having a much paler (buff or buff grey) belly and a dark eye. **Habitat.** Miombo woodland. **Status.** Fairly common resident. **Call.** Similar to Rufous-bellied Tit. (Swartkopmees)

5. RUFOUS-BELLIED TIT *Parus rufiventris* (556)   14-15 cm
The dark head and breast, lack of white cheek patches, and the rufous belly, flanks and vent are diagnostic. The bright yellow eye is conspicuous. **Juv.** is duller than ad., and has a brown eye and buff edges to its wing feathers. **Habitat.** Miombo and teak woodland. **Status.** Uncommon resident. **Call.** A harsh, tit-like 'chrrr chrrr' and a clear 'chick-wee, chick-wee' song. (Rooipensmees)

6. SOUTHERN BLACK TIT *Parus niger* (554)   14-16 cm
Male Southern Black Tit has less white in the wings than Carp's Tit. **Female** differs from female Carp's Tit in being paler grey below and having less white in the wings. **Juv.** resembles female. **Habitat.** Forests and broad-leaved woodland. **Status.** Common resident. **Call.** A harsh, chattering 'chrr-chrr-chrr' and a musical 'phee-cher-phee-cher'. (Gewone Swartmees)

7. CARP'S TIT *Parus carpi* (555)   14-15 cm
Smaller than Southern Black Tit, this species has more white in the wings and has uniformly black, not grey-barred, undertail coverts. **Female** is duller than male, and has more white in the wings than female Southern Black Tit. **Juv.** resembles female. **Habitat.** Thornveld and arid savanna. **Status.** Common; near-endemic. **Call.** Similar to that of Southern Black Tit. (Ovamboswartmees).

8. SPOTTED CREEPER *Salpornis spilonotus* (559)   14-15 cm
Smaller than any woodpecker in the region. The sunbird-like, curved bill and brown upperparts, heavily spotted with white, are diagnostic. It creeps jerkily up tree trunks. **Juv.** is duller than ad. **Habitat.** Confined to miombo woodland. **Status.** Locally common to uncommon resident. **Call.** A fast, thin 'sweepy-swip-swip-swip' and a harsher 'keck-keck'. Note: It is uncertain whether the Spotted Creeper of Africa is specifically distinct from the race occurring in India. (Boomkruiper)

1
grey underparts

2
brownish back
pale buff underparts

3
broad white cheeks
white underparts

4
dark eye

5
pale eye
rich underparts

6
barred undertail
black primaries
grey underparts
♂
♀

7
♂
♀
blackish underparts
white edging to primaries

8

1. ARROW-MARKED BABBLER *Turdoides jardineii* (560)   21-24 cm
The white-streaked ('arrow-marked') head and breast, red-rimmed, yellow eye and uniform, brown rump are diagnostic.
Juv. has a brown eye and much less white streaking than ad. **Habitat.** Woodland and savanna. **Status.** Common resident. Lives in groups of up to 12 birds. **Call.** A loud 'chow-chow-chow-chow...', with several birds often calling simultaneously. (Pylvlekkatlagter)

2. BLACK-FACED BABBLER *Turdoides melanops* (561)   21-25 cm
Differs from Hartlaub's Babbler in having a dark, not white rump and from Arrow-marked Babbler by the obvious scalloping (not streaking) on the breast. A small black patch at the base of the bill and the bright yellow eye are diagnostic. It is considerably more furtive than the other babblers.
Juv. resembles ad. but has a brown eye. **Habitat.** Broad-leaved woodland. Forages in scattered groups amongst leaf litter. **Status.** Uncommon resident. **Call.** A nasal 'wha-wha-wha' and a harsh, fast 'papapapa'. (Swartwangkatlagter)

3. HARTLAUB'S BABBLER *Turdoides hartlaubii* (562)   22-24 cm
Superficially resembles Arrow-marked Babbler but has a diagnostic white rump and vent, and has white scalloping (not streaking) on its head and body.
Juv. resembles ad. but is much paler, especially on the throat and breast. **Habitat.** Reedbeds and surrounding woodland. **Status.** Common resident. Lives in groups. **Call.** Noisy; a loud 'kwekkwekkwek' or 'papapapapapa', with several birds calling simultaneously. (Witkruiskatlagter)

4. BARE-CHEEKED BABBLER *Turdoides gymnogenys* (564)   24 cm
This species may be distinguished from Southern Pied Babbler by its dark back, chestnut nape and the lack of white on its wing coverts. It has a small area of bare, black skin below and behind the eye.
Juv. could be confused with juv. Southern Pied Babbler but is much darker, especially on the back and nape, and is usually seen in the company of ads of its own species. **Habitat.** Dry, broad-leaved woodland, frequenting river courses and wooded koppies. **Status.** Locally common resident; near-endemic. Lives in groups. **Call.** Typical babbler 'kerrrakerrra-kek-kek-kek'. (Kaalwangkatlagter)

5. SOUTHERN PIED BABBLER *Turdoides bicolor* (563)   22-24 cm
The only babbler in the region with an all-white head, back and underparts.
Juv. is initially wholly pale brown, but whitens with age. **Habitat.** Arid savanna, especially thornveld. **Status.** Common resident; near-endemic. Lives in groups. **Call.** A higher-pitched 'kwee kwee kwee kweer' babbling than that of the other species. (Witkatlagter)

6. BOULDER CHAT *Pinarornis plumosus* (610)   25 cm
The brownish black plumage and the white-tipped outer tail feathers are diagnostic. In flight a row of small, white spots are visible on the edge of the primary and secondary coverts. It runs and bounds over large boulders, occasionally raising its tail well over its back when landing.
Female is duller than male. **Juv.** resembles ad. **Habitat.** Well-wooded terrain with large, granite boulders. **Status.** Locally common resident. **Call.** A clear, sharp whistle and a softer 'wink, wink'. (Swartberglyster)

1

juv.

reddish eye

ad.

streaked
breast

dark
rump

2

yellow eye

dark rump

scalloped
breast

3

red eye

scalloped
breast

white
rump

black face
markings

rufous
nape

dark
back

imm.

plain
head

ad.

white
back

4

5

6

white outer
tail tips

white
covert
spots

1. CAPE BULBUL *Pycnonotus capensis* (566) 19-21 cm
Overall much darker in appearance than African Red-eyed and Dark-capped Bulbuls, with the dark brown on the underparts extending onto the lower belly. The white eye-ring is diagnostic.
Juv. lacks the white eye-ring and is darker below than Dark-capped and African Red-eyed Bulbuls. **Habitat.** Fynbos, coastal scrub, riverine forests, exotic plantations and gardens. **Status.** Common resident; endemic. **Call.** A sharp, liquid whistle, 'peet-peet-patata'. (Kaapse Tiptol)

2. AFRICAN RED-EYED BULBUL *Pycnonotus nigricans* (567) 19-21 cm
The red eye-ring is diagnostic and distinguishes this species from Dark-capped and Cape Bulbuls. The head colour is darker than that of Dark-capped Bulbul and contrasts with the greyish buff collar and upper breast.
Juv. may be distinguished from juv Dark-capped Bulbul by its pale pink eye-ring. **Habitat.** Thornveld, riverine bush and suburban gardens. **Status.** Common resident; near-endemic. **Call.** Liquid whistles similar to those of Dark-capped Bulbul. (Rooioogtiptol)

3. DARK-CAPPED (BLACKEYED) BULBUL *Pycnonotus tricolor* (568) 19-22 cm
This species lacks the red eye-ring of African Red-eyed Bulbul, and further differs in having less contrast between the dark head and the breast.
Juv. resembles ad. **Habitat.** Frequents a wide variety of habitats, from thornveld to forest edges, parks and gardens. **Status.** Abundant resident. **Call.** A harsh, sharp 'kwit, kwit, kwit', given when alarmed or when going to roost; song is a liquid 'cheloop chreep choop'. (Swartoogtiptol)

4. TERRESTRIAL BROWNBUL (BULBUL) *Phyllastrephus terrestris* (569) 17-19 cm
A dull brown bird with greyish underparts. The white throat contrasting with the dark brown head is the best field characteristic. In its search for food it forms small, noisy flocks, the birds scuffling around on the forest floor, scattering earth and leaf litter with their feet and bills.
Sexes alike but male is larger. **Juv.** resembles ad. **Habitat.** Thick thornveld, and evergreen and riverine forests. **Status.** Common resident. **Call.** A soft, chattering 'trrup cherrup trrup', given by small foraging groups. (Boskrapper)

5. BUSH BLACKCAP *Lioptilus nigricapillus* (565) 15-17 cm
A small, unmistakable bulbul with a black cap and a bright, coral-pink bill and legs. Shy and unobtrusive, it is usually found in dense foliage.
Juv. is duller than ad. and has a dusky pink bill. **Habitat.** Montane evergreen forests, mainly at forest margins and in small isolated forest patches. **Status.** Uncommon resident; endemic. Altitudinal migrant, breeding at higher altitudes, wintering at lower. **Call.** Not unlike that of Dark-capped Bulbul but more varied and melodious. (Rooibektiptol)

1

white
eye-ring

2

red
eye-ring

3

dark
eye-ring

4

uniform brown
upperparts

white
throat

5

pink
bill

ad.

juv.

1. SOMBRE GREENBUL (BULBUL) *Andropadus importunus* (572)   15-18 cm
This species is generally a drab olive-green, and lacks diagnostic field characteristics except the white eye. The northeastern race *hypoxanthus* is very yellow below, and could be confused with Yellow-bellied Greenbul, except for its white (not dark red) eye. This is an inconspicuous, but vocal, canopy-dwelling species.
Juv. is even duller than ad. **Habitat.** Evergreen forests, coastal bush and thick thornveld. **Status.** Common resident. **Call.** Normal call is a piercing 'weeewee', followed by a liquid chortle. (Gewone Willie)

2. TINY GREENBUL (SLENDER BULBUL) *Phyllastrephus debilis* (571)   12-14 cm
This is the smallest greenbul of the region. It resembles Sombre Greenbul, but can be distinguished from that species by its smaller size, paler underparts, and grey crown and cheeks.
Juv. has a greenish crown. **Habitat.** Lowland forests. **Status.** Common resident. **Call.** A shrill 'shriiip' and a bubbling song. (Kleinboskruiper)

3. STRIPE-CHEEKED GREENBUL (BULBUL) *Andropadus milanjensis* (573)   19-21 cm
Distinguished from the similar Sombre Greenbul by its grey head, dark eye with a pale eye-ring, and the faint white streaks on the cheeks. A shy forest inhabitant, it is often difficult to locate in the forest canopy.
Juv. has a greener crown than ad. **Habitat.** Montane evergreen forests and forest margins. **Status.** Locally common resident. **Call.** A throaty 'chrrup-chip-chrup-chrup'. (Streepwangwillie)

4. YELLOW-STREAKED GREENBUL (BULBUL)
Phyllastrephus flavostriatus (570)   18-20 cm
This species is small and slim in build. The back is dull olive, and the underparts off-white, with faint yellow streaks visible only at close range and in good light. The bill is thin and the eye brown. It is best identified by its unusual, woodpecker-like action of creeping about tree trunks, continually flicking open one wing at a time.
Sexes alike but male is noticeably larger. **Juv.** resembles ad. **Habitat.** Mid-stratum and canopy of moist, evergreen forests. **Status.** Locally common resident. **Call.** A 'weet-weet-weet' and a sharp 'kleeet-kleeat'. (Geelstreepboskruiper)

5. (AFRICAN) YELLOW-BELLIED GREENBUL (BULBUL)
Chlorocichla flaviventris (574)   20-23 cm
Distinguished from Sombre Greenbul by its yellow underparts and dark red (not white) eye. The thin white eyebrow is prominent. The race *hypoxanthus* of Sombre Greenbul also has a very yellow breast and belly but differs in having a greenish (not brown) crown, and a white eye. The bright yellow underwing coverts are conspicuous in flight.
Juv. is duller than ad. **Habitat.** Evergreen and riverine forests, thornveld and coastal scrub. It is not often found in the canopy, preferring thick tangles at a lower level. **Status.** Common resident. **Call.** A loud, monotonous, nasal 'neh-neh-neh-neh'. (Geelborswillie)

6. EASTERN (YELLOWSPOTTED) NICATOR *Nicator gularis* (575)   20-23 cm
The bright yellow spots on the wing coverts are diagnostic of this greenish bird. It could be confused with female Black Cuckooshrike (p. 300) but that species is heavily barred below. Its behaviour is like that of a bush shrike, as it moves slowly through thick tangles, and it is very difficult to see. The yellow tips to the tail feathers are obvious when the bird is flying away.
Juv. is duller than ad. **Habitat.** Dense riverine and coastal forests and scrub, particularly on sandy soil. **Status.** Common resident. **Call.** A short, rich, liquid jumble of notes. (Geelvleknikator)

1

white eye

2

pale eye

grey cap

pale throat

dark eye with pale eye-ring

faintly streaked cheeks

3

dark eye

pale throat

yellow underwing

4

5

dark red eye

bright yellow underparts

juv.

shrike-like bill

ad.

6

yellow spotting on wings

yellow tail tip

1. ORANGE GROUND-THRUSH *Zoothera gurneyi* (579) 18-21 cm
Differs from both Olive and Kurrichane thrushes by the dark bill, bright orange throat and breast and conspicuous white tips to the wing coverts that form two white bars on the folded wing.
Juv. is spotted with buff on the upperparts and mottled with black and orange below, but it still shows the diagnostic white bars on the wing coverts. **Habitat.** Montane evergreen forests; there is some altitudinal movement in winter to coastal forests. **Status.** Uncommon resident. **Call.** A sibilant 'tseeep'; a melodious song of clear, whistled phrases, such as 'chee-cheeleeroo-chruup'. (Oranjelyster)

2. KAROO THRUSH *Turdus smithi* 20-22 cm
Confusable only with Olive Thrush but is greyer above, especially on the head, and is much darker below, with orange confined to lower belly only and a grey, not white vent.
Habitat. Prefers drier areas to Olive Thrush but has adapted to suburbia. **Status.** Common endemic. **Call.** Similar to Olive Thrush but with different phrasing in song. (Bruinlyster)

3. OLIVE THRUSH *Turdus olivaceus* 20-22 cm
Much more orange on underparts than Karoo Thrush and has a white, not grey vent. Differs from Orange Ground-Thrush by lacking white wing bars and from Kurrichane Thrush by lacking malar stripes.
Habitat. Montane forests, coastal forests and scrub. It has adapted to suburbia. **Status.** Common resident. **Call.** A sharp 'chink' and drawn out 'tseeep'. Song is a fluty 'whet-tooo-wheetoo' and variations of this. (Olyflyster)

4. KURRICHANE THRUSH *Turdus libonyanus* (576) 18-22 cm
The white, faintly speckled throat, broad black malar stripes, orange eye-ring and bright orange bill are diagnostic. Olive Thrush has a yellower bill, a dark throat and lacks the malar stripes.
Juv. resembles juv. Olive Thrush but is paler. **Habitat.** Thornveld, open woodland, and parks and gardens, where it may occur alongside Olive Thrush. **Status.** Common resident. **Call.** A loud, whistling 'peet-peeoo'. (Rooibeklyster)

5. GROUNDSCRAPER THRUSH *Psophocichla litsitsirupa* (580) 22-24 cm
Distinguished from Spotted Ground-Thrush by the lack of white bars on its wing coverts and by the bolder, more contrasting black face markings; its habitat is also quite different. In flight, it shows a chestnut panel in the wing. It differs from the much smaller Dusky Lark (p. 280) by its bolder face markings and pale grey upperparts.
Juv. is speckled off-white on the underparts, with conspicuous white tips to the wing coverts; the spots on the underside are smaller than in ad. **Habitat.** Dry thornveld, open broad-leaved woodland, parks and gardens. **Status.** Common resident. **Call.** Specific name (*litsitsirupa*) is onomatopoeic of its song: a loud, clear and varied, whistling phrase. (Gevlekte Lyster)

6. SPOTTED GROUND-THRUSH *Zoothera guttata* (578) 19-21 cm
Distinguished from Groundscraper Thrush by the bold white bars on the wing coverts; also frequents entirely different habitats. This and Groundscraper Thrush superficially resemble Dusky Lark (p. 280) but both are larger, have paler backs, and are unlikely to be found in flocks.
Juv. is spotted with buff on the upperparts and wing coverts; the spotting on the underparts is finer than in ad. **Habitat.** Understorey of coastal evergreen forests. **Status.** Uncommon resident and partial local migrant; predominantly a winter visitor to northern and eastern coastal forests. **Call.** A quiet 'tseeeep'; a whistled, fluty song of short phrases of four or five notes. (Natallyster)

1

white wing bars

2

grey vent

3

juv.

brown eye-ring

speckled throat

white vent

4

orange eye-ring

black malar stripe

5

no wing bars

grey above

6

white wing bars

1. CAPE ROCK-THRUSH *Monticola rupestris* (581) 19-21 cm
The largest rock thrush in the region. Male differs from male Sentinel Rock-Thrush in having a brown (not blue) back and forewing, and by the blue on its throat not extending onto the upper breast.
Female has much richer red underparts than other female rock-thrushes. **Juv.** resembles female but the upperparts are spotted with buff and the feathers of the underside edged with black, giving a scaled appearance. **Habitat.** Mountainous and rocky terrain, both coastally and inland. **Status.** Common resident; endemic. **Call.** Song a whistling 'tsee-tsee-tseet-chee-chweeeoo'; alarm a harsh grating. (Kaapse Kliplyster)

2. SENTINEL ROCK-THRUSH *Monticola explorator* (582) 16-18 cm
Male differs from male Cape Rock-Thrush by its blue (not brown) back and forewing, with the blue of the throat extending onto the upper breast. Could be confused with Short-toed Rock-Thrush, but it lacks the conspicuous pale forehead, crown and nape of that species.
Female differs from female Cape Rock-Thrush in being smaller, and in having a paler, mottled (not uniformly red-brown) breast. **Juv.** resembles female but has the upperparts spotted with buffy white; the throat, breast and flanks are scaled with brown. **Habitat.** Mountainous and rocky terrain, often in association with Cape Rock-Thrush. **Status.** Locally common resident (decreasing in west of its range) and partial altitudinal migrant; endemic. **Call.** Whistled song similar to that of Cape Rock-Thrush but not as loud. (Langtoonkliplyster)

3. SHORT-TOED ROCK-THRUSH *Monticola brevipes* (583) 16-18 cm
The pale blue or white forehead, crown and nape of the male are diagnostic. Birds in the east (*pretoriae*) are considered by some as a distinct species, Transvaal Rock-Thrush. They have darker heads and females have heavily spotted throat and breast.
Female has a large white throat patch streaked with brown, and a rufous breast and belly. **Juv.** is spotted with buff on the upperparts and with black below. **Habitat.** Wooded koppies and rocky slopes. **Status.** Common resident; near-endemic. **Call.** A thin 'tseeep'; song of whistled phrases like those of other rock thrushes; includes mimicry. (Korttoonkliplyster)

4. MIOMBO ROCK-THRUSH *Monticola angolensis* (584) 16-18 cm
The pale blue-grey crown and back of male are mottled with black, preventing confusion with any other rock-thrush.
Female has distinctly mottled upperparts and bold malar stripes that differentiate this species from other female rock-thrushes. **Juv.** resembles female but has black and whitish mottling on the underparts. **Habitat.** Miombo woodland, usually in hilly terrain. **Status.** Locally common resident; unobtrusive. **Call.** A two-noted whistle; song a high-pitched variety of melodic phrases. (Angolakliplyster)

5. CAPE ROCK-JUMPER *Chaetops frenatus* (611) 23-25 cm
Male is similar to Drakensberg Rock-jumper but is slightly larger and has a dark rufous-red (not orange-buff) breast and belly. Ranges are non-overlapping.
Female and juv. are darker buff below than female Drakensberg Rock-jumper and have a more boldly marked head pattern. **Habitat.** Rocky mountain slopes and scree; down to sea level in southwest of range. **Status.** Common but localised resident; endemic. Found in pairs or small groups. **Call.** A loud, clear 'wheeoo'. (Kaapse Berglyster)

6. DRAKENSBERG (ORANGEBREASTED) ROCK-JUMPER
Chaetops aurantius (612) 23-25 cm
Differs from slightly larger Cape Rock-jumper in having an orange-buff breast and belly. Ranges are non-overlapping.
Female and juv. are pale buff below and have less distinctly marked heads. **Habitat.** Usually found above 2 000 m on rocky mountain slopes and grassy hillsides with scattered boulders. **Status.** Common resident; endemic. **Call.** Like Cape Rock-jumper's, a rapidly repeated, piping whistle. (Oranjeborsberglyster)

1

mottled brown back

warm brown underparts

♂   ♀

2

pale, mottled underparts

blue extends to chest

blue-back

♀   ♂

3

dark spotting

grey head & back

pretoriae

white throat, slightly streaked

white cap (variable)

bold malar stripes

♀   ♂   ♀   ♂   ♀

4

5

♀   ♀

6

♂

1. FAMILIAR CHAT *Cercomela familiaris* (589)   14-15 cm
Differs from Tractrac and Sickle-winged Chats in being darker grey-brown below, with a richer chestnut rump and outer tail feathers. Like other chats, it flicks its wings when at rest, but this species also 'trembles' its tail.
Juv. is spotted with buff above, and scaled below. **Habitat.** Rocky and mountainous terrain, also miombo woodland and regularly around human habitation. **Status.** Common resident. **Call.** A soft 'shek-shek' alarm call and a warbling trill. (Gewone Spekvreter)

2. SICKLE-WINGED CHAT *Cercomela sinuata* (591)   14-15 cm
The dark upperparts contrasting with the paler underparts distinguish this species from the more uniformly coloured Familiar Chat. It further differs in having the (paler) salmon-buff on the rump confined to the tail base, and by its longer legged, more upright stance. In comparison with Familiar Chat it spends more time on the ground and runs more swiftly.
Juv. has buff-tipped feathers. **Habitat.** Short lowland and montane grassland, Karoo scrub vegetation, and barren, sandy or stony areas; agricultural lands on the west coast. **Status.** Common resident; endemic. **Call.** A very soft, typically chat-like 'chak-chak', and a warbled song. (Vlaktespekvreter)

3. ARNOTT'S CHAT *Myrmecocichla arnotti* (594)   16-18 cm
Male distinguished from all colour morphs of male Mountain Wheatear by its entirely black rump and tail.
Female lacks the white cap but has a conspicuous white throat and upper breast, finely speckled with black. **Juv.** has a black head and a white shoulder patch. **Habitat.** Miombo and mopane woodland. **Status.** Common resident. **Call.** A quiet, whistled 'fick' or 'feee'. (Bontpiek)

4. KAROO CHAT *Cercomela schlegelii* (592)   16-18 cm
Paler than the similar, grey form of female Mountain Wheatear, it also differs in having a grey (not white) rump and completely white outer tail feathers. Its larger size and all-white outer tail feathers prevent confusion with Tractrac or Sickle-winged Chats.
Juv. is buff-spotted above and scaled below. **Habitat.** Karoo and desert scrub in the south; extending to escarpment zone in the north. **Status.** Common resident; near-endemic. **Call.** A typically chat-like 'chak-chak' or 'trrat-trrat'. (Karoospekvreter)

5. TRACTRAC CHAT *Cercomela tractrac* (590)   14-15 cm
Smaller than Karoo Chat and lacks the all-white outer tail feathers of that species. Paler and greyer than both Familiar and Sickle-winged chats, it has a white or pale buff rump. The Namib form found on hummock dunes and at the coast is almost white, with darker wings and tail, whereas the gravel plains bird, found to the southeast, is darker.
Juv. is more mottled than ad. **Habitat.** Karoo and desert scrub, hummock dunes and gravel plains. **Status.** Common resident; near-endemic. **Call.** A soft, fast 'tactac'; song a quiet, musical bubbling; territorial defence call a loud chattering. (Woestynspekvreter)

6. MOUNTAIN WHEATEAR (CHAT) *Oenanthe monticola* (586)   18-20 cm
Males show very variable plumage coloration, but all have a white rump, white sides to the tail and a white shoulder patch. The white cap may or may not be present. It differs from male Arnott's Chat in having a white (not black) rump and white outer tail feathers.
Female is a uniform sooty brown except for the white rump and outer tail feathers. **Juv.** resembles female. **Habitat.** Mountainous and rocky terrain. **Status.** Common resident; near-endemic. **Call.** A clear, thrush-like, whistling song, interspersed with harsh chatters. (Bergwagter)

1

juv.

pale form
wing-flicking

grey-brown below

dark form

chestnut rump
& outer tail

2

off-white
below

dull salmon rump
& outer tail base

♀

3

dark form

grey
rump

white
outer
tail

black rump
& tail

♂

4

pale form

white or
near-
white
rump

white
outers
do not
reach
tip

Namib
form

♂

white
shoulder
patch

♀

dark form

white rump &
outer tail

5

6

1. PIED WHEATEAR *Oenanthe pleschanka* (907)　　　　　　　14-15 cm

Male superficially resembles Mountain Wheatear (p. 318) but is smaller, has a black face and throat and clear white underparts; lacks white shoulder patches. In transitional plumage, the black areas are flecked with buff.

Female is virtually indistinguishable from female Northern Wheatear. **Juv.** resembles female. **Habitat.** Usually dry, stony regions with scattered scrub. **Status.** Vagrant, with one summer record from KwaZulu-Natal. **Call.** Not recorded in the region; described elsewhere as a harsh 'zack-zack'. (Bontskaapwagter)

2. ISABELLINE WHEATEAR *Oenanthe isabellina* (915)　　　　　　15-17 cm

Difficult to distinguish from Northern Wheatear in non-breeding plumage, but it is larger, has longer legs and less white on the rump, and has white or whitish buff (not grey) underwing coverts. The contrasting black alula is diagnostic.

Juv. resembles ad. **Habitat.** Bush and scrub. **Status.** Vagrant, with one summer record from Botswana. **Call.** Not recorded in the region. (Isabellaskaapwagter)

3. CAPPED WHEATEAR *Oenanthe pileata* (587)　　　　　　　　17-18 cm

With its conspicuous white forehead, eyebrow stripe and black cap, ad. is unmistakable.

Juv. differs from similar non-breeding ad. and juv. Northern Wheatear by its larger size, small patch of white at the base of its outer tail feathers, buff tipping to the feathers on the upperparts and the presence of a diffuse, speckled breast band. Juv. could also be confused with female Buff-streaked Chat (p. 322) but has a white (not buff) rump, and is found in quite different habitat. **Habitat.** Barren, sandy or stony areas and short grassland in flat country. **Status.** Common resident with local movements. **Call.** A 'chik-chik' alarm note; song a loud warbling with slurred chattering. (Hoëveldskaapwagter)

4. NORTHERN (EUROPEAN) WHEATEAR *Oenanthe oenanthe* (585)　　14-15 cm

Breeding male of this species is unmistakable with its blue-grey crown and back, and black ear patches.

Female, non-breeding male and **juv.** could be confused with juv. Capped Wheatear, but differ in having a white rump and more extensive white on the outer tail feathers, which lends a distinct T pattern to the black area of the tail. Grey underwing coverts aid differentiation from Isabelline Wheatear. Female and juv. Pied Wheatears are longer tailed, paler breasted and have light scalloping on the mantle. **Habitat.** Dry, stony or sandy areas with stunted scrub growth. **Status.** Very rare summer visitor. **Call.** A harsh 'chak-chak'; song not recorded in the region. (Europese Skaapwagter)

5. WHINCHAT *Saxicola rubetra* (597)　　　　　　　　　　　13-14 cm

Breeding male differentiated from female African Stonechat by its well-defined white eyebrow stripe, more extensive white bar on the upperwing coverts, the white patch at the base of its primaries, and the white sides to the base of its tail.

Female, non-breeding male and juv. differ from female African Stonechat by the broad, creamy eyebrow stripe, white wing bar and diagnostic white base to the outer tail feathers. **Habitat.** Open grassland with patches of stunted scrub. **Status.** Rare summer visitor to the extreme north. **Call.** Described elsewhere as a scolding 'tick-tick'. (Europese Bontrokkie)

6. AFRICAN (COMMON) STONECHAT *Saxicola torquatus* (596)　　13-14 cm

In all plumages, both sexes of this species are distinguishable from Whinchat as neither shows a conspicuous pale eyebrow stripe.

Male is unmistakable with its black head, the white on the neck, wings and rump, and its rufous breast. Female is duller but retains the white in the wings and has a buff rump. **Juv.** is mottled with dark buff above and is paler below than ad. **Habitat.** Upland grassland and open, treeless areas with short scrub; also wetland areas of Namibia. **Status.** Common resident with local movements. **Call.** A 'weet-weet' followed by a harsh 'chak'. (Gewone Bontrokkie)

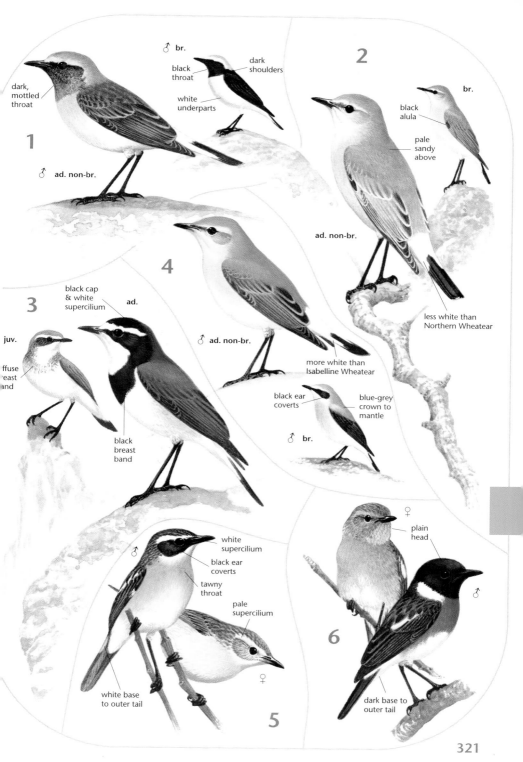

1

dark, mottled throat

♂ br.

black throat

dark shoulders

white underparts

♂ ad. non-br.

2

br.

black alula

pale sandy above

ad. non-br.

less white than Northern Wheatear

3

black cap & white supercilium

ad.

juv.

diffuse breast band

black breast band

4

♂ ad. non-br.

more white than Isabelline Wheatear

black ear coverts

blue-grey crown to mantle

♂ br.

5

white supercilium

black ear coverts

tawny throat

pale supercilium

white base to outer tail

♀

♂

6

♀

plain head

♂

dark base to outer tail

1. BUFF-STREAKED CHAT *Oenanthe bifasciata* (588)   16-17 cm

The male's black face, throat and wings and buffy underparts are diagnostic. The white eye-stripe extends down the side on the neck and into a characteristic 'V' on the mantle.
Female differs from juv. Capped Wheatear (p. 320) in having a buff (not white) rump. **Juv.** is mottled with black and buff above and below, and has a rufous rump. **Habitat.** Rock-strewn, grassy hill slopes. **Status.** Common but localised resident; endemic. **Call.** Loud, rich warbling, including mimicry of other birds' songs. (Bergklipwagter)

2. (SOUTHERN) ANTEATING CHAT *Myrmecocichla formicivora* (595)   17-18cm

In flight this species is easily distinguished from other dark chats by the conspicuous white patches on the primaries. At rest it appears very plump and short tailed, and has an upright stance.
Male is very dark brown and has a white shoulder patch. Female is paler brown than male. **Juv.** resembles female but is more mottled. **Habitat.** Grassland dotted with termite mounds, and open, sandy or stony areas. **Status.** Common resident; endemic. **Call.** A short, sharp 'peek' or 'piek'. (Swartpiek)

3. MOCKING CLIFF-CHAT *Thamnolaea cinnamomeiventris* (593)   19-21 cm

The male's black plumage, bright chestnut belly, vent and rump, and white shoulder patch are diagnostic.
Female is dark grey above and chestnut below, lacking any white in the plumage. **Juv.** resembles female. **Habitat.** Bases of cliffs and wooded, rocky slopes. **Status.** Common but localised resident. **Call.** Song a loud, melodious mixture of mimicked bird song. (Dassievoël)

4. COMMON (EUROPEAN) REDSTART *Phoenicurus phoenicurus* (916)   13-1cm

Breeding male is unmistakable with its black throat, white forehead and red breast and tail.
Female and non-breeding male might be confused with Familiar or Sickle-winged chats (p. 318) but can be distinguished from these species by the brighter rufous tail that is continuously 'trembled' and by the lack of continual wing-flicking. **Juv.** resembles female but is faintly mottled on the back and breast. **Habitat.** Wooded areas. **Status.** Vagrant, with one record from the Northwest Province. **Call.** Loud 'hooeeet', resembling that of Willow Warbler (p. 330). (Europese Rooistert)

5. HERERO CHAT *Namibornis herero* (618)   17 cm

The black patch that runs through the eye and onto the ear coverts contrasts with the clear white eyebrow stripe and white throat, creating a superficial resemblance to female Red-backed Shrike (p. 372). The outer tail feathers and rump are rufous and, at close range, faint streaking is visible on the breast.
Juv. resembles ad. but is more mottled. **Habitat.** Dry scrub and thornveld at the base of hills and in boulder-strewn country. Spends much time perched in trees and bushes. **Status.** Uncommon and localised resident; near-endemic. **Call.** Mostly silent except during the breeding season when a melodious, warbling 'twi-tedeelee-doo' song is uttered; also has a soft, warbling repertoire. (Hererospekvreter)

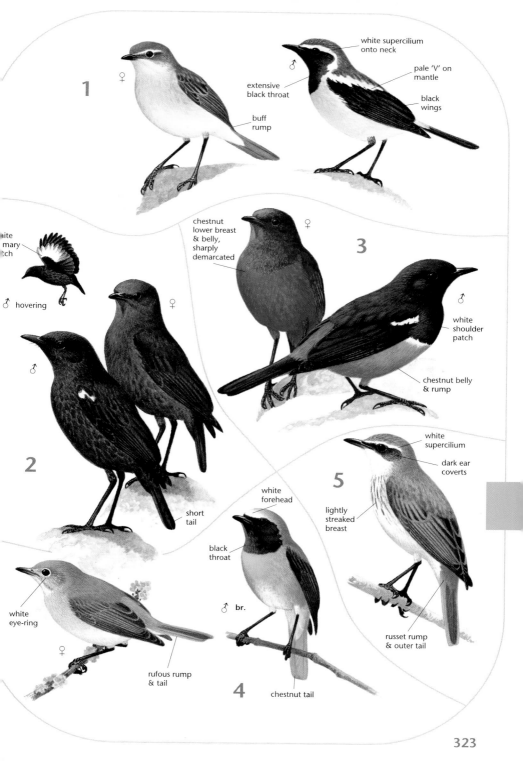

1
♀
white supercilium onto neck
♂
extensive black throat
pale 'V' on mantle
black wings
buff rump

white primary patch
♂ hovering

chestnut lower breast & belly, sharply demarcated
♀
3
♂
white shoulder patch
chestnut belly & rump

2
♂
♀
short tail

white eye-ring
♀
rufous rump & tail

white forehead
black throat
♂ br.
4
chestnut tail

5
white supercilium
dark ear coverts
lightly streaked breast
russet rump & outer tail

1. CHORISTER ROBIN-CHAT (ROBIN) *Cossypha dichroa* (598) 20 cm
The dark upperparts, yellow-orange underparts and lack of a white eye-stripe render this large robin-chat distinctive. Superficially it resembles Red-capped Robin-Chat, but it lacks the powder-blue forewings and the orange face of that species.
Juv. is a sooty, mottled tawny-buff above and below, and the tail is red-orange with a dark centre. **Habitat.** Evergreen forests. **Status.** Common resident with local movements (from interior to coastal forests in winter); endemic. **Call.** Contact call a plaintive 'toy-toy, toy-toy'; song loud and bubbly, including much mimicry of other forest birds. (Lawaaimakerjanfrederik)

2. RED-CAPPED ROBIN-CHAT (NATAL ROBIN) *Cossypha natalensis* (600) 16-18 cm
This species may be distinguished from all other robin-chats by its powder-blue back and wings, russet-brown crown and nape and bright red-orange face and underparts.
Juv. is sooty, and mottled above and below with buff and brown; the tail is red-orange with a black centre as in ad. **Habitat.** Dense thickets and tangles in evergreen forests, also mature suburban gardens. **Status.** Common resident. **Call.** Contact call a soft 'seee-saw, seee-saw'; song like that of Chorister Robin-Chat but a more slurred, rambling series of melodious phrases, including much mimicry. (Nataljanfrederik)

3. CAPE ROBIN-CHAT (ROBIN) *Cossypha caffra* (601) 16-17 cm
Best distinguished from White-browed Robin-Chat by its shorter white eyebrow stripe, and by the orange on the underparts being confined to the throat and upper breast; the rest of the breast is grey, and the belly and undertail coverts are tawny orange.
Juv. is brownish and heavily mottled with buff and black; it has a red tail with a dark centre. **Habitat.** Forest edge, bushveld, scrub and fynbos, gardens and parks. **Status.** Common resident (except on the KwaZulu-Natal coast where it is mainly a winter visitor). **Call.** Alarm call a guttural 'wur-da-durrr'; song a series of melodious phrases, often starting 'cherooo-weet-weet-weeeet'. (Gewone Janfrederik)

4. WHITE-BROWED ROBIN-CHAT (HEUGLIN'S ROBIN)
Cossypha heuglini (599) 19-20 cm
May be distinguished from the similarly sized and coloured Chorister Robin-Chat by the paler back and broad, conspicuous white eyebrow stripe.
Juv. is sooty coloured, with heavy buff and brown spotting on the upperparts and underparts; the tail is red-orange with a dark centre as in ad. **Habitat.** Dense riverine thickets and tangles, gardens and parks. **Status.** Common resident. **Call.** A characteristic, loud, crescendo song of repeated phrases. (Heuglinse Janfrederik)

5. (AFRICAN) WHITE-THROATED ROBIN-CHAT (ROBIN)
Cossypha humeralis (602) 17 cm
The only robin in the region with a white wing bar, throat and breast. The rufous tail with a dark centre also differs from the tails of other robin-chatss in having black tips to all the feathers. Usually seen as it dashes for cover, it gives the impression of being a small, black-and-white bird with a red tail.
Juv. is sooty coloured, heavily mottled with buff and brown above and below; it lacks the white wingbar but has a rufous-and-black tail like that of ad. **Habitat.** Dry thornveld, thickets and riverine scrub. **Status.** Common, endemic. **Call.** Alarm call a repeated 'seet-cher, seet-cher'; song an attractive medley of whistled phrases incorporating much mimicry of other birds' calls. (Witkeeljanfrederik)

6. WHITE-CHESTED (WHITEBREASTED) ALETHE *Alethe fuelleborni* (605) 17-18 cm
The only robin-like bird in the region to have completely white underparts. The upperparts and the tail are a rich russet colour and the cap is grey.
Juv. is mottled with buff above and has a buffy breast and rust-coloured rump and tail. **Habitat.** Understorey of lowland, evergreen forests. **Status.** Rare and localised resident. **Call.** A lively, whistling 'fweer-her-hee-her-hee-her'. (Witborswoudlyster)

1

no white eyebrow

uniform black upperparts

2

blue-grey back

orange face

4

white supercilium

juv.

3

plain wings

ad.

pale grey lower breast

white chin to breast

white wing bar

5

6

russet wings

russet tail

dark grey cap

pale legs

underparts wholly white

325

1. BROWN SCRUB-ROBIN (ROBIN) *Cercotrichas signata* (616) 14-17 cm

Likely to be confused with Bearded Scrub-Robin; it differs in lacking the buff-coloured flanks of that species, and has less distinct white eyebrow and malar stripes. A shy, skulking bird that enters open forest glades at dawn and dusk.
Juv. resembles ad. but is spotted with buff on the upperparts and scaled with sooty black on the chest. **Habitat.** Thick tangles of coastal and evergreen forests. **Status.** Locally common resident; endemic. **Call.** A melodious 'twee-choo-sree-sree' introduces a varied song; alarm note a sibilant 'zeeeeet'. (Bruinwipstert)

2. (EASTERN) BEARDED SCRUB-ROBIN (ROBIN)
Cercotrichas quadrivirgata (617) 14-17 cm

The broad, white eyebrow stripe finely edged with black, the black malar stripes, the buff to orange flanks and upper breast and the rufous rump are diagnostic. This species differs from the duller Brown Scrub-Robin in having bolder head markings and more brightly coloured flanks. The northwestern race *ovamboensis* of White-browed Scrub-Robin lacks distinct streaking on the breast and vaguely resembles this species, but retains the two white bars on the upperwing coverts.
Juv. is mottled with tawny buff above and below; the tail is the same as that of ad. **Habitat.** Prefers drier forest than Brown Scrub-Robin; also frequents broad-leaved woodland and thornveld. **Status.** Common resident; easily overlooked. **Call.** Alarm call of one or two sharp notes followed by a 'churr, chek-chek kwezzzzz'; a clear, penetrating song of often-repeated, mixed phrases. (Baardwipstert)

3. WHITE-BROWED SCRUB-ROBIN (ROBIN) *Cercotrichas leucophrys* (613) 14-16 cm

Resembles Kalahari Scrub-Robin but differs in having a heavily streaked (not unmarked) breast, and white bars on the wing coverts. The breast streaking eliminates confusion with Brown and Bearded Scrub-Robins. The northwestern race *ovamboensis* lacks breast streaking, but its distribution does not overlap with either Brown or Bearded Scrub-Robins.
Juv. is speckled with buff and brown above; it is whitish below, heavily scaled with brown on the breast; the tail is brown with all except the central feathers broadly tipped with white, as in ad. **Habitat.** Woodland and savanna. **Status.** Common resident. **Call.** A harsh 'trrrrrr' alarm note and a fluty but repetitive song; the characteristic call at dawn and dusk is a whistled 'seeep po go'. (Gestreepte Wipstert)

4. KALAHARI SCRUB-ROBIN (ROBIN) *Cercotrichas paena* (615) 14-16 cm

A sandy brown bird with a pale eyebrow, a rufous rump and uppertail, and a broad, black subterminal bar to the narrowly white-tipped tail. It lacks the breast streaks and white wing bar of White-browed Scrub-Robin and in flight shows more rufous on the tail.
Juv. is mottled with sooty black and buff above and below; tail like ad.'s **Habitat.** Dry thornveld, thicket and tangled growth around waterholes and dry riverbeds. **Status.** Common near-endemic. **Call.** Alarm note a harsh 'zzeee'; contact call a whistled 'seeeup'; a musical song of whistles and chirps, more varied than those of Karoo or White-browed Scrub-Robins. (Kalahariwipstert)

5. KAROO SCRUB-ROBIN (ROBIN) *Cercotrichas coryphoeus* (614) 14-17 cm

This species lacks the breast streaking of White-browed Scrub-Robin; it is much darker than Kalahari Scrub-Robin and lacks rufous in the tail. The distinctive features of this species are the dull, grey-brown plumage, the white throat patch, the small white eyebrow stripe, and the white tips to the dark tail feathers.
Juv. is sooty brown, mottled with buff; the eyebrow is indistinct. **Habitat.** Karoo scrub and fynbos. **Status.** Common resident; endemic. **Call.** A harsh, chittering 'tchik, tchik, tcheet'; song a mixture of whistles and grating notes. (Slangverklikker)

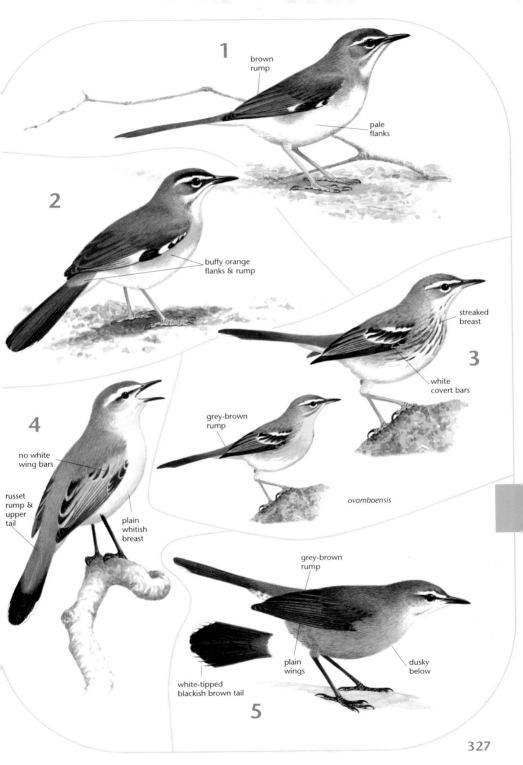

1

brown rump

pale flanks

2

buffy orange flanks & rump

3

streaked breast

white covert bars

4

grey-brown rump

no white wing bars

russet rump & upper tail

plain whitish breast

ovamboensis

5

grey-brown rump

plain wings

dusky below

white-tipped blackish brown tail

327

1. WHITE-STARRED (STARRED) ROBIN *Pogonocichla stellata* (606)　　15-16 cm
Ad. of this small, dark blue and yellow robin is unmistakable; the white 'stars' on the throat and forehead are usually concealed, but the bright yellow 'windows' of the tail are conspicuous as the bird flits through the forest undergrowth.
Juv. is sooty coloured, heavily spangled with yellowish buff above and below; imm. is dull olive above and greyish yellow below; the tail of both has the same pattern as that of ad. but is dull yellow and dusky. **Habitat.** Coastal and inland evergreen forests; winter visitor to coastal KwaZulu-Natal plain. **Status.** Common but localised and easily overlooked resident. **Call.** A soft 'chuk' or 'zit' note; a whistled 'too-twee' contact call, frequently repeated; a quiet, warbling song. (Witkoljanfrederik)

2. SWYNNERTON'S ROBIN *Swynnertonia swynnertoni* (607)　　13-14 cm
May be distinguished from similar White-starred Robin by having an orange (not yellow) breast, and a diagnostic black-and-white bib. It also has an all-black (not yellow-and-black) tail.
Female has a greenish crown and face (not dark grey as in male). **Juv.** is brown above, spotted with buffy yellow; the underparts are duller than in ad., with the throat crescent a drab greyish brown; the breast and belly are mottled with brown and grey. **Habitat.** Evergreen montane forests and ravines. **Status.** Uncommon resident. **Call.** Song, given by male, a subdued, three-syllabled 'zitt, zitt, slurr', the last syllable lower pitched; alarm a monotonous, quiet purring. (Bandkeeljanfrederik)

3. EAST COAST AKALAT (GUNNING'S ROBIN) *Sheppardia gunningi* (608)　　11-12 cm
A small, dull forest robin, brown above, and with an orange-yellow throat, olive-yellow flanks and white belly. The diagnostic field characteristics are difficult to see: powder-blue forewings and an indistinct small, white patch on the lores. It is furtive and infrequently seen.
Juv. is olive-brown above, spotted with buff; the underparts are buff, scaled with russet-brown. **Habitat.** Lowland forests. **Status.** Common, localised resident. **Call.** Alarm a series of piping 'seeep' notes; a fast, high-pitched but not loud song of several short phrases, frequently repeated. (Gunningse Janfrederik)

4. THRUSH NIGHTINGALE *Luscinia luscinia* (609)　　16 cm
This large, drab, skulking warbler is usually located by its song. The dull russet tail and slightly mottled breast, flanks and undertail coverts aid identification.
Juv. is more mottled on the head, back and breast than ad. **Habitat.** Tangled thickets along rivers and in damp areas. **Status.** Uncommon (and easily overlooked) summer visitor, mainly in the north. **Call.** A rich, warbling song interspersed with harsh, grating notes. (Lysternagtegaal)

5. RUFOUS-TAILED PALM-THRUSH *Cichladusa ruficauda* (604)　　17-18 cm
Similar to Collared Palm-Thrush but lacks the black border on the breast, has a richer rufous crown and back, and a darker eye.
Juv. resembles ad., with dark mottling on the underparts. **Habitat.** Riverine thickets and Borassus palm savanna. **Status.** Locally common resident on the Cunene River, west of Ruacana in Namibia. **Call.** A melodious and sustained whistling, including imitations of other birds' songs. (Rooistertmôrelyster)

6. COLLARED PALM-THRUSH *Cichladusa arquata* (603)　　17-19 cm
The buff throat and breast with a narrow black collar and pale eye are both diagnostic. The black line encircling the breast is often incomplete, and the sides of the neck and the flanks are extensively washed with grey.
Juv. is a mottled buff-brown. **Habitat.** Hyphaene or Borassus palm savanna. **Status.** Scarce to locally common resident. **Call.** An explosive, whistled song, consisting of 'weet-chuk' or 'cur-lee chuk-chuk' phrases. (Palmmôrelyster)

1
slate-grey head
bright yellow below
ad.
extensive yellow in tail
imm.

2
juv.
small white bib, bordered black
orange breast
ad.
dark tail

3
white spot
orange breast
blue forewing
white belly

4
dull russet rump & tail
mottled undertail coverts
diffuse streaking

5
plain below
rufous tail

6
pale eye
ad.
necklace
imm.

1. YELLOW-THROATED WOODLAND-WARBLER *Phylloscopus ruficapilla* (644)   11 cm
This small, active warbler has a rufous crown and areas of bright yellow on the throat, breast and undertail that contrast with the greyish belly and olive-grey back. A noticeable yellow eyebrow stripe contrasts with the darker crown.
Juv. has a greener wash on the breast than ad. **Habitat.** Evergreen forests and wooded gullies. **Status.** Locally common resident. **Call.** A 'seee suuu seee suuu' song, with variations in phrasing. (Geelkeelsanger)

2. WILLOW WARBLER *Phylloscopus trochilus* (643)   11 cm
Most individuals are either olive above and yellow below or brown above and white below, but intermediates do occur. The bill is thin and weak in comparison with that of Icterine Warbler. The distinct yellow on the underparts is restricted to the throat and breast, with the belly mainly dull white. The bill is markedly shorter than that of Icterine Warbler and the legs are brownish rather than bluish grey.
Juv. has the underparts yellow; the eyebrow stripe and face are much brighter yellow than those of ad. **Habitat.** Wide range of broad-leaved woodland and dry thornveld habitats. **Status.** Abundant summer visitor. **Call.** A soft 'hoeet hoeet' and a short, melodious song, descending in scale. (Hofsanger)

3. ICTERINE WARBLER *Hippolais icterina* (625)   13-14 cm
Larger than Willow Warbler and normally a brighter yellow below. Some are whitish below and greyish brown above. It is best distinguished by the large bill and head with a more angular, sloping forehead, the bluish grey (not brown) legs and the pale wing panel. A short, yellow eyebrow stripe and a pale eye-ring may be evident.
Juv. can appear greyer than ad., with much paler yellow underparts. **Habitat.** Thornveld, dry broad-leaved woodland, exotic plantations, gardens and riverine thickets. **Status.** Common summer visitor. **Call.** Varied, jumbled notes, including a harsh 'tac, tac'. (Spotsanger)

4. OLIVE-TREE WARBLER *Hippolais olivetorum* (626)   15-16 cm
This large, grey warbler might be confused with Grey Tit-Flycatcher (p. 354) but it lacks the conspicuous white outer tail feathers and the tail-spreading action of that species. The bill is long and heavy, and a pale grey panel is noticeable in the wings.
Juv. resembles ad. **Habitat.** Dense clumps of thicket in thornveld. **Status.** Uncommon summer visitor. **Call.** Most easily located by its chattering song, which sounds like that of Great Reed-Warbler (p. 338). (Olyfboomsanger)

5. GARDEN WARBLER *Sylvia borin* (619)   13-15 cm
A small, greyish or olive-brown warbler, paler below but without marked contrasts or distinctive features. The head is rounded, with an indistinct, pale eyebrow stripe.
Juv. resembles ad. **Habitat.** Prefers thick tangles in a range of forest, bush and riverine habitats. **Status.** Common summer visitor. **Call.** Often located by its subdued, monotonous song, interspersed with soft, grating phrases and a harsh 'tec'. (Tuinsanger)

6. COMMON WHITETHROAT *Sylvia communis* (620)   13-15 cm
Grey head of male contrasts with the silvery white throat and rufous wing panel.
Female has a brown head. Juv. lacks the white outer tail feathers of ad. **Habitat.** Dry thornveld thickets, often near water. **Status.** Locally common summer visitor. **Call.** Soft 'whit' and grating 'tchack' and 'tchurr' alarm calls; song a harsh, snappy mixture of grating and melodious notes. (Witkeelsanger)

7. (EUROPEAN) BLACKCAP *Sylvia atricapilla* (911)   13-15 cm
Male not likely to be confused with Bush Blackcap (p. 310) because of its much smaller size and its black (not pink) bill and feet.
Female and juv. have a brown or blackish brown cap. **Habitat.** Thick bush and forest edge. **Status.** Very rare summer vagrant. **Call.** Similar to Garden Warbler's but more varied and less subdued. (Swartkroonsanger)

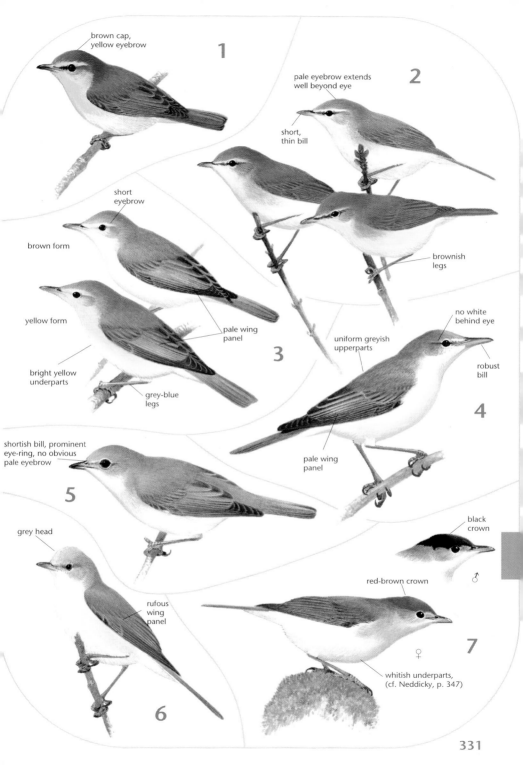

1 brown cap, yellow eyebrow

2 pale eyebrow extends well beyond eye

short, thin bill

brownish legs

3

short eyebrow

brown form

yellow form

bright yellow underparts

pale wing panel

grey-blue legs

4 uniform greyish upperparts

no white behind eye

robust bill

pale wing panel

5 shortish bill, prominent eye-ring, no obvious pale eyebrow

6 grey head

rufous wing panel

7 black crown

♂

red-brown crown

♀

whitish underparts, (cf. Neddicky, p. 347)

1. BURNT-NECKED EREMOMELA *Eremomela usticollis* (656)　　　　10 cm
This small warbler is a dark bluish grey above and pale buff below. The main distinguishing marks are around the head and throat, where the combination of pale yellow eyes plus rufous cheeks and ear coverts is reliable, with the small, rusty throat bar often inconspicuous or absent, but diagnostic when seen.
Female lacks brown on cap and has fainter brown throat bar. **Juv.** lacks the rufous patches on the face and the rusty throat bar of ad. **Habitat.** Mainly thornveld but also found in mixed, dry broad-leaved woodland and dry river courses. Usually in small groups. **Status.** Common resident. **Call.** A high-pitched 'chii-cheee-cheee', followed by a sibilant 'trrrrrrrrr'. (Bruinkeelbossanger)

2. GREEN-CAPPED EREMOMELA *Eremomela scotops* (655)　　　　12 cm
The bright yellow underparts, greenish upperparts and greenish yellow crown are diagnostic, and distinguish this species from other eremomelas and similarly coloured warblers. The pale yellow eye is discernible at close range. It resembles a white-eye in jizz and habits.
Juv. is paler and a fresher green above than ad. **Habitat.** Open, broad-leaved woodland and riverine forests. Usually in small groups. **Status.** Uncommon and localised resident. **Call.** A repeated 'tweer-tweer-tweer' and a rasping alarm note. (Donkerwangbossanger)

3. YELLOW-BELLIED EREMOMELA *Eremomela icteropygialis* (653)　　　　10 cm
May be distinguished from other eremomelas by the combination of olive-grey to grey upperparts and greyish white throat and breast contrasting with the pale yellow flanks and belly. The intensity and extent of yellow on the underparts varies geographically. The dark eye-stripe through the brown eye contrasts with the whitish throat and narrow, pale eyebrow stripe. It could be confused with Cape Penduline-Tit but is larger and longer billed, and lacks the black forehead of that species.
Juv. has duller yellow underparts than ad. **Habitat.** Thornveld, open broad-leaved woodland and scrub. Usually solitary or in pairs. **Status.** Common resident. **Call.** Song is crombec-like: a high-pitched, frequently repeated 'tchee-tchee-tchuu'. (Geelpensbossanger)

4. KAROO EREMOMELA *Eremomela gregalis* (654)　　　　12 cm
A long-tailed eremomela distinguished by its olive-green upperparts, shading to greyer on the face and neck and contrasting with silvery white underparts. The conspicuous pale eye, yellow flanks and undertail coverts distinguish it from the camaropteras (p. 340) (but ranges do not overlap); it does not cock its tail.
Juv. is browner than ad. **Habitat.** Karoo and semi-desert scrub, especially along dry river courses. Often in small groups. **Status.** Uncommon and localised resident; endemic. **Call.** A wailing 'quee, quee-quee' song. (Groenbossanger)

5. GREY PENDULINE-TIT *Anthoscopus caroli* (558)　　　　8 cm
This species lacks the distinctive black forehead, eye-stripe and speckled throat of Cape Penduline-Tit and is generally much greyer, with buff flanks and belly, whitish on the breast and buff on the face and forehead. It occurs in small groups of three to five.
Juv. resembles ad. **Habitat.** Broad-leaved and miombo woodlands. **Status.** Common resident. **Call.** A soft 'chissick' or 'tseeep'. (Gryskapokvoël)

6. CAPE PENDULINE-TIT *Anthoscopus minutus* (557)　　　　8 cm
May be distinguished from the eremomelas by its tiny size, short, more conical bill, rotund body and very short tail. It could be confused with Grey Penduline-Tit, but differs in having a black forehead extending as an eye-stripe, a yellowish (not buff) belly and flanks, and a speckled throat. The black forehead differentiates it from Yellow-bellied Eremomela.
Juv. has paler yellow underparts than ad. **Habitat.** Fynbos, Karoo scrub, semi-desert and dry thornveld. **Status.** Common resident; near-endemic. **Call.** A soft 'tseep'. (Kaapse Kapokvoël)

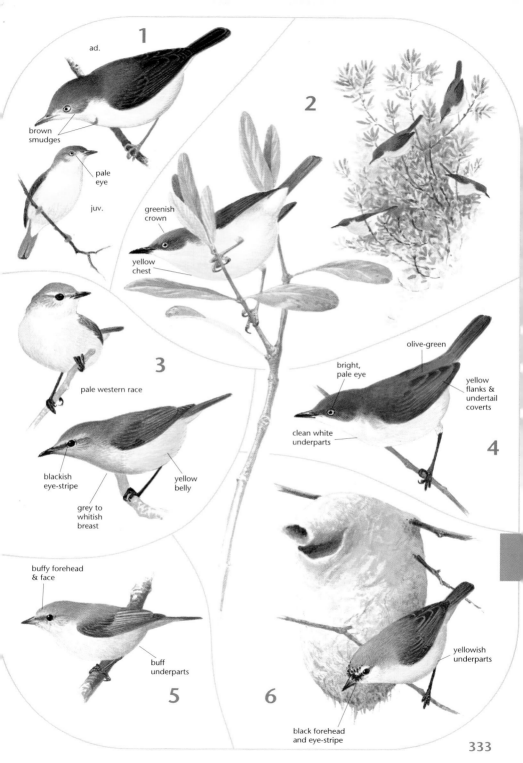

1

ad.

brown
smudges

pale
eye

juv.

2

greenish
crown

yellow
chest

3

pale western race

blackish
eye-stripe

grey to
whitish
breast

yellow
belly

4

olive-green

bright,
pale eye

yellow
flanks &
undertail
coverts

clean white
underparts

5

buffy forehead
& face

buff
underparts

6

yellowish
underparts

black forehead
and eye-stripe

1. KNYSNA WARBLER *Bradypterus sylvaticus* (640)   14-15 cm
This secretive warbler is best located and identified by its song. It is largely olive-brown, and paler below. It is smaller than the more widespread Barratt's Warbler and the spotting is restricted to the throat and upper breast. The tail is broad and graduated, but shorter and squarer than that of Barratt's Warbler. Male has a dark, triangular loral spot.
Female has a paler throat and lacks the dark loral spot. **Juv.** resembles female. **Habitat.** Well-wooded gullies, and bracken and briar thickets. **Status.** Uncommon, localised resident; decreasing; endemic. **Call.** A loud, clear song that begins with a 'tseep tseep tseep' and accelerates to a rattling trill towards the end. (Knysnaruigtesanger)

2. BARRATT'S WARBLER *Bradypterus barratti* (639)   15 cm
Very similar to Little Rush-Warbler in appearance, but never frequents reedbeds. Its song, more heavily spotted breast, larger size and longer, heavy, rounded tail distinguish Barratt's Warbler from Knysna Warbler. This secretive species keeps close to, and often feeds and runs on, the ground.
Juv. has slightly warmer coloration than ad., being more olive above and yellowish below. **Habitat.** Thick, tangled growth on the edges of evergreen forests and plantations. **Status.** Locally common resident; endemic; altitudinal migrant. **Call.** A harsh 'chrrrrr' alarm note; an explosive 'seee-pllip-pllip' song. (Ruigtesanger)

3. VICTORIN'S WARBLER *Bradypterus victorini* (641)   16 cm
The most colourful of the *Bradypterus* warblers (and almost certainly incorrectly classified as a *Bradypterus*), this species may be distinguished by its reddish brown cap and grey ear coverts contrasting with the yellow eyes, paler throat and buff-red underparts.
Juv. is paler below and slightly more rufous above than ad. **Habitat.** Montane fynbos, especially in thick tangles alongside streams, gullies and damp areas; to sea level in several places. **Status.** Common and localised resident; endemic. **Call.** Diagnostic: a clear, repeated 'weet-weet-weeeo', accelerating towards the end; superficially similar to Cape Grassbird (p. 340) song, but more repetitive with less inflection. (Rooiborsruigtesanger)

4. BROAD-TAILED WARBLER *Schoenicola brevirostris* (642)   14-16 cm
The most conspicuous feature is the long, broad, black tail. Both the underside of the tail feathers and the undertail coverts are tipped with buff. This feature is most conspicuous in flight or after heavy rains, when the bird is often seen perched on grass stems drying out its tail and wings. The shape of the head is also distinctive, with the flattened forehead and culmen forming an almost straight line.
Juv. has yellowish rather than buffy white underparts. **Habitat.** Long, rank grass adjoining rivers, dams and damp areas. **Status.** Resident at low altitudes; summer visitor to higher areas. Locally common but easily overlooked, especially outside the breeding season. **Call.** A soft, metallic 'zeenk', repeated at intervals of a few seconds, and a clear, high-pitched 'peee, peee'. (Breëstertsanger)

5. (AFRICAN SEDGE) LITTLE RUSH-WARBLER *Bradypterus baboecala* (638)   13-16 cm
Distinguished from all other reed-dwelling warblers by its very dark, dusky brown upperpart coloration, dappled throat and breast and long, rounded tail. It tends to skulk but performs a distinctive display flight over reedbeds with rapidly beating wings.
Juv. resembles ad. **Habitat.** Reed and sedge beds. **Status.** Locally common resident with local movements. **Call.** A harsh, ratchet-like 'brrrup... brrrup... trrp...trrp...trrp' song that speeds up towards the end, and a nasal 'nneeeuu' resembling Cape Longclaw (p. 370). (Kaapse Vleisanger)

1

♀

dark
underparts

shortish tail

2

pale underparts

3

pale
eye

grey
cheeks

warm buff
underparts

longish tail

4

dark undertail
coverts

dark, broad tail with
buff feather tips

5

dark brown
upperparts

buff
undertail

1. (CAPE REED) LESSER SWAMP-WARBLER *Acrocephalus gracilirostris* (635) 14-16 cm
Larger than African Reed-Warbler and much whiter below and around the face, with a distinct white eyebrow stripe. The bill is long and heavy and the legs dark brown. There is a distinct rufous wash on the flanks. It is the most easily seen of the reed warblers.
Juv. resembles ad. **Habitat.** Reedbeds adjoining wetlands. **Status.** Locally common resident. **Call.** A rich, fluty 'cheerup-chee-trrrree' song. (Kaapse Rietsanger)

2. RIVER WARBLER *Locustella fluviatilis* (627)   13-14 cm
May be distinguished from other water-associated warblers by its browner upperparts and its graduated, rounded tail, which is usually a warmer brown than the back. The underparts are buff, with the throat whiter and with dark streaking on the throat and breast. The sides of the breast and the flanks have a darker wash, and the long undertail coverts are brown with broad white tips. It is very secretive.
Juv. tends to be a warmer rufous colour above than ad., and creamy buff below. **Habitat.** Thickets in woodland and riverine scrub, usually close to water. **Status.** Rare summer visitor; readily located only during March, when it starts to sing. **Call.** Usually detected only by its buzzy, insect-like 'derr-derr-zerr-zerr' song, heard mainly in the morning; call is a sharp, weaver-like 'chick', accompanied by wing and tail flicking. (Sprinkaansanger)

3. AFRICAN (MARSH) REED-WARBLER *Acrocephalus baeticatus* (631)   12-13 cm
Difficult to distinguish from Marsh-Warbler in the field. It is smaller, warmer brown above, and shorter winged (the folded wing does not extend beyond the rump as it does in Marsh-Warbler), and is usually found in different habitat. The profile of the forehead is not as steep as in Marsh-Warbler.
Juv. resembles ad. but has a rufous rump. **Habitat.** Over or close to marshy ground, in reed or sedge beds, or in rank, reedy areas; non-breeding birds may range into gardens. **Status.** Common summer visitor. **Call.** A harsher, more churring and repetitive song than that of Marsh Warbler, including mimicked phrases of other birds; repeats notes of song two to four times. Song probably indistinguishable from that of Eurasian Reed-Warbler, except on the basis of the species mimicked. (Kleinrietsanger)

4. EURASIAN (EUROPEAN) REED-WARBLER *Acrocephalus scirpaceus* (630)   12-13 cm
In the field, can be distinguished from Marsh-Warbler only by song and habitat; distinguishable from African Reed-Warbler with certainty only in the hand.
Juv. resembles ad. **Habitat.** Although there is some overlap, this species is more aquatic in habitat than Marsh-Warbler, frequenting reedbeds and rank vegetation close to water; may occur side-by-side with African Reed-Warbler. **Status.** Rare but possibly regular summer visitor to the extreme north and northwest; vagrant elsewhere. **Call.** Song a typical *Acrocephalus* mixture of musical and harsh notes, 'tchak, tchak, tchak...churr, churr, churr', probably distinguishable from that of African Reed-Warbler only on the basis of the species mimicked. Call notes include a low 'churrr'. (Hermanse Rietsanger)

5. (EUROPEAN) MARSH-WARBLER *Acrocephalus palustris* (633)   12-13 cm
Similar to African Reed-Warbler but larger, less rufous and longer winged (the folded wing extends beyond the rump). It has a rounder forehead profile. It also frequents different habitats.
Juv. resembles ad. **Habitat.** Non-aquatic: bracken and briar on mountain slopes, forest edges, woodland and riverine thickets and garden shrubberies. **Status.** Common summer visitor. **Call.** Song distinguishable from songs of African and Eurasian Reed-Warblers by its clear, melodious phrases; often mimics other birds. Call notes include a sharp 'chuck'. (Europese Rietsanger)

1

bold white
eyebrow

streaked
throat

2

long,
scalloped
undertail
coverts

3

short
primaries

4

long
primaries

5

long
primaries

⁘ wing formulae to show differences
in primary feather emargination

1. (AFRICAN) MOUSTACHED GRASS-WARBLER *Melocichla mentalis* (663)   18-19 cm
Might be mistaken for Cape Grassbird (p. 340) but distinguished by its broad, rounded tail, pale, unstreaked breast, single, black malar stripe and uniform, unstreaked, rufous back and crown. Broad-tailed Warbler (p. 334) lacks the malar stripe and has broad buff tips to otherwise dark undertail coverts and feathers.
Juv. lacks the chestnut forehead of ad. **Habitat.** Long, rank grass adjoining forests and in open glades, often near damp areas. **Status.** Rare, localised resident. **Call.** A bubbling 'tip-tiptwiddle-iddle-see'. (Breëstertgrasvoël)

2. GREATER SWAMP-WARBLER *Acrocephalus rufescens* (636)   16-18 cm
Differs from Great Reed-Warbler by its smaller size, the greyish brown sides to the breast, belly and flanks, and by its darker brown upperparts. It has no white eyebrow stripe. It is larger and darker than Lesser Swamp-Warbler (p. 336).
Juv. resembles ad. **Habitat.** Papyrus swamps. **Status.** Locally common resident in the Okavango region. **Call.** A loud 'churrup, churr-churr', interspersed with harsher notes. (Rooibruinrietsanger)

3. GREAT REED-WARBLER *Acrocephalus arundinaceus* (628)   18-20 cm
A large and robust reed-warbler, often located by its harsh, guttural song. It resembles a large African Reed-Warbler (p. 336) with a long, heavy bill and a well-defined pale eyebrow stripe. It is larger and darker than Basra Reed-Warbler.
Juv. has warmer coloration than ad. and the underparts are washed buffy orange. **Habitat.** Reedbeds and bush thickets; often near water. **Status.** Common summer visitor. **Call.** A prolonged 'chee-chee-chaak-chaak'. (Grootrietsanger)

4. BASRA REED-WARBLER *Acrocephalus griseldis* (629)   14-16 cm
A large, slim reed-warbler with a dark tail and a long bill accentuated by the flat forehead. In comparison with Great Reed-Warbler, the plumage is colder with the upperparts olive-grey and underparts whiter, and the build is less robust, closer to that of smaller reed-warblers. Look for the narrow, white eyebrow stripe with a contrasting dark line through the eye, as well as the unstreaked, white throat and the greyish legs.
Juv. resembles ad. **Habitat.** Reedbeds, thickets and rank vegetation, invariably near water. **Status.** Summer vagrant to the east. **Call.** A nasal and subdued 'chuc-chuc-churruc-churruc-chuc', similar to contact call of Terrestrial Brownbul (p. 310). (Basrarietsanger)

5. DARK-CAPPED (AFRICAN) YELLOW WARBLER *Chloropeta natalensis* (637)   14 cm
Superficially resembles Icterine Warbler (p. 330), but has darker olive-green upperparts, a yellower rump, brighter yellow underparts and dark grey legs. The two species also occupy quite different habitats. Often inconspicuous, but it sings, and may hawk insects, from an exposed perch.
Female is duller, with less contrast between the back and the underparts. Juv. resembles female but with a buff wash. **Habitat.** Bracken, sedges and tangled vegetation at forest edge. **Status.** Locally common resident with some seasonal movement. **Call.** A soft 'chip-chip-cheezee-cheeze'. (Geelsanger)

6. (EUROPEAN) SEDGE WARBLER *Acrocephalus schoenobaenus* (634)   12-13 cm
The only 'streaked' *Acrocephalus* warbler in the region, it has an olive-brown mantle streaked with blackish brown, a short, brown tail and a contrasting, unstreaked, rufous rump. The head shows a striking broad, creamy eyebrow stripe and a darker, streaked crown. These characteristics distinguish it from some of the superficially similar cisticolas, which have longer tails with black-and-white tips.
Juv. is yellower and more distinctly marked than ad. **Habitat.** Reedbeds and rank weedy areas bordering wetlands, and thickets sometimes far from water. **Status.** Common summer visitor. **Call.** A harsh chattering interspersed with sharp, melodious phrases and a 'tuk' call. (Europese Vleisanger)

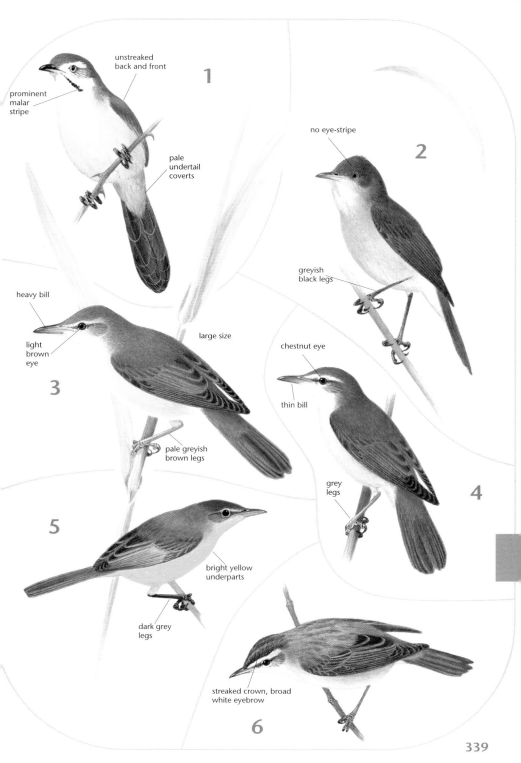

1

prominent malar stripe

unstreaked back and front

pale undertail coverts

2

no eye-stripe

greyish black legs

3

heavy bill

light brown eye

large size

pale greyish brown legs

4

chestnut eye

thin bill

grey legs

5

bright yellow underparts

dark grey legs

6

streaked crown, broad white eyebrow

1. ROCKRUNNER *Achaetops pycnopygius* (662)   16-17 cm
This large, ground-dwelling warbler can be identified by its heavily streaked, dark back, white breast spotted with black at the sides, and bright rufous belly and undertail.
Juv. is less distinctly marked than ad. **Habitat.** Boulder-strewn, grassy hillsides and the bases of small hills. **Status.** Common, easily overlooked resident; endemic. **Call.** A hollow, melodious warbling, 'rooodle-trrooodlee'. (Rotsvoël)

2. CAPE GRASSBIRD *Sphenoeacus afer* (661)   17-19 cm
The long, pointed, straggly tail, chestnut cap and black malar and moustachial stripes are diagnostic. The heavily streaked back and the pointed tail eliminate confusion with Moustached Grass-Warbler (p. 338). It is much larger than any cisticola.
Juv. has a streaked cap and is duller than ad. **Habitat.** Coastal and mountain fynbos; long, rank grass on mountain slopes and in river valleys. **Status.** Common resident, endemic. **Call.** A nasal 'pheeeoo' and a jangled, musical song. (Grasvoël)

3. CINNAMON-BREASTED WARBLER *Euryptila subcinnamomea* (660)   14 cm
The rufous breast band, flanks and rump and the black tail are diagnostic.
Juv. is more rufous above than ad. **Habitat.** Scrub-covered, rocky hillsides, in dry river gullies and gorges. **Status.** Uncommon, localised and easily overlooked resident; endemic. **Call.** A shrill, whistled 'peeeee' or 'chreeee'; song is a short burst of melodious phrases. (Kaneelborssanger)

4. STIERLING'S (BARRED) WREN-WARBLER *Calamonastes stierlingi* (659)   13 cm
Differs from African Wren-Warbler in having white underparts more distinctly barred with black, orange-brown eyes, and flesh-coloured (not brown) legs.
Juv. resembles ad. **Habitat.** Mixed thornveld, broad-leaved, miombo and mopane woodland. **Status.** Common resident. **Call.** A repeated, fast, three-syllabled 'plip-lip-lip'. (Stierlingse Sanger)

5. (AFRICAN) BARRED WREN-WARBLER *Calamonastes fasciolatus* (658)   14 cm
A medium-sized warbler with a long tail that is often held cocked or fanned over its back. The throat and breast are plain brown in breeding male, with the rest of the underparts buff with dusky barring, but the undertail coverts are plain and unbarred. Non-breeding males are barred from chin to belly. The eyes and legs are brown.
Female resembles non-breeding male. **Juv.** is more rufous, with a yellowish wash on the breast. **Habitat.** Dry thornveld and broad-leaved woodland. **Status.** Common resident. **Call.** A thin 'trrrreee' and 'pleelip-pleelip'. (Gebande Sanger)

6. GREEN-BACKED CAMAROPTERA (BLEATING WARBLER)
Camaroptera brachyura (657a)   10-11 cm
Identical to Grey-backed Camaroptera except that the mantle is green (not grey). It might be confused with Karoo Eremomela (p. 332), which frequents much drier habitats, but the eremomela has a much longer tail, yellow-washed flanks and a pale (not dark) eye. It characteristically cocks its tail.
Juv. is slightly streaked below. **Habitat.** Moist evergreen forests and scrub. **Status.** Common resident. **Call.** A nasal 'neeehhh' and a loud, snapping 'bidup-bidup-bidup'. (Groenrugkwêkwêvoël)

7. GREY-BACKED CAMAROPTERA (BLEATING WARBLER)
Camaroptera brevicaudata (657b)   10-11 cm
A small, rotund warbler with a short tail that is often held cocked over its back. It differs from Green-backed Camaroptera in having a grey (not green) mantle when breeding, and an ashy brown mantle when not breeding.
Juv. streaked below. **Habitat.** Dry woodland, thornveld. **Status.** Common resident. **Call.** Similar to that of Green-backed Camaroptera. (Grysrugkwêkwêvoël)

1

black spotting

rufous belly to undertail

2

black malar and moustachial stripes

rufous crown

streaked back

long tail (usually appears 'tatty')

3

black tail

rufous flanks

grey throat to upper breast

rufous band

4

pale eye

white, barred underparts

5

dark eye

brown-barred throat & breast

br.

ad. non-br.

6

green back

7

grey back

341

1. FAIRY FLYCATCHER *Stenostira scita* (706)   12 cm
Warbler-like in habits. The pinkish grey wash across the breast, black stripe through the eye broadening onto black ear coverts, a broad white eyebrow stripe, white stripe in the wing and white outer tail feathers are diagnostic.
Juv. is browner than ad. **Habitat.** Karoo scrub and montane fynbos in summer, thornveld in winter. **Status.** Seasonal migrant, breeding in the south of its range in summer, moving to the north of its range in winter; endemic. **Call.** A repeated, wispy 'tisee-tchee-tchee' and a descending 'cher cher cher'. (Feevlieëvanger)

2. LAYARD'S TIT-BABBLER *Parisoma layardi* (622)   14-15 cm
Paler than Chestnut-vented Tit-Babbler. Its best distinguishing character is the white (not chestnut) vent. The silvery white eye contrasts with the dark head, and the throat streaking is less pronounced than in Chestnut-vented Tit-Babbler. Superficially, it resembles Grey Tit-Flycatcher (p. 354), but it lacks the tail-spreading action of that species and has streaking on the throat.
Juv. resembles ad. but lacks the streaking on the throat. **Habitat.** Thornveld, coastal fynbos and Karoo scrub, especially in rocky, hilly areas. **Status.** Common resident; endemic. **Call.** A clear 'pee-pee-cheeri-cheeri', similar in quality to that of Chestnut-vented Tit-Babbler but with different phrasing. (Grystjeriktik)

3. CHESTNUT-VENTED TIT-BABBLER *Parisoma subcaeruleum* (621)   14-15 cm
Darker grey than the very similar Layard's Tit-Babbler, with a chestnut vent, and the white on the tail confined to the tip. The streaking on the throat is bolder and more extensive than in Layard's Tit-Babbler.
Juv. resembles ad. but lacks the streaking on the throat. **Habitat.** Diverse: from thornveld, especially thickets, to lowland fynbos and scrub and dry river beds in semi-desert. **Status.** Common resident. **Call.** A loud, fluty 'cheruuup-chee-chee' or 'tjerik-tik-tik', hence the Afrikaans name; also imitates calls of other birds. (Bosveldtjeriktik)

4. LONG-BILLED CROMBEC *Sylvietta rufescens* (651)   12 cm
Almost tailless, it lacks the chestnut breast band and ear patches of Red-capped Crombec and differs from Red-faced Crombec in having a longer bill, thin grey eye-stripe, brownish grey (not ashy grey) upperparts, and in lacking the russet tinge to the face.
Juv. resembles ad. **Habitat.** Woodland, savanna, fynbos and arid scrublands. **Status.** Common resident. **Call.** A repeated 'trree-rriit, trree-rriit' and a harsher 'ptttt'. (Bosveldstompstert)

5. RED-CAPPED CROMBEC *Sylvietta ruficapilla* (652)   10-12 cm
This species appears almost tailless. It may be distinguished from the other two crombec species in the region by its rufous ear patches and breast band. The forehead and crown are racially variable from chestnut to grey. The one southern African specimen has a grey forehead and crown. The back is paler grey than in Red-faced Crombec.
Juv. is buffier above than ad., with buff flecking on the wings. **Habitat.** Miombo woodland. **Status.** Very rare vagrant, with one old specimen record west of Victoria Falls in Zimbabwe. **Call.** A ringing, repeated 'richi-chichi-chichir'. (Rooikroonstompstert)

6. RED-FACED CROMBEC *Sylvietta whytii* (650)   9-10 cm
Appears almost tailless. It may be distinguished from Long-billed Crombec by its pale, ashy grey upperparts, noticeably shorter bill, pale chestnut face without a dark eye-stripe and richer, buffier underparts. It differs from Red-capped Crombec in lacking that species' distinctive chestnut ear patches and breast band.
Juv. is brownish grey above. **Habitat.** Miombo woodland and riparian forests. **Status.** Locally common resident. **Call.** A trilling, repeated 'wit-wit-wit-wit...' and a thin 'si-si-si-see'. (Rooiwangstompstert)

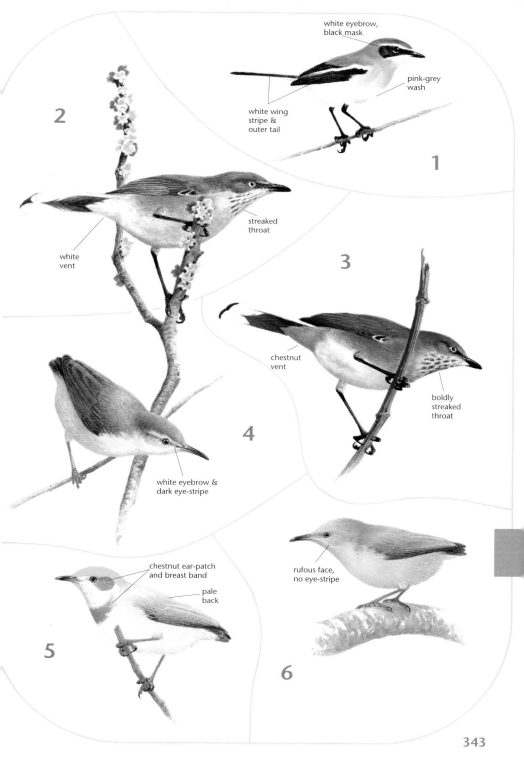

1

white eyebrow, black mask

white wing stripe & outer tail

pink-grey wash

2

streaked throat

white vent

3

chestnut vent

boldly streaked throat

4

white eyebrow & dark eye-stripe

5

chestnut ear-patch and breast band

pale back

6

rufous face, no eye-stripe

1. CHIRINDA APALIS *Apalis chirindensis* (646) 11-13 cm
Could be confused with White-tailed Crested Flycatcher (p. 356), which occurs in the same area, but has a slender (not broad, fan-shaped and white-tipped) tail and completely different habits. A restless bird, it creeps and flits through the canopy when foraging and does not fan its tail or swing from side to side on a perch. No other apalis in the region is uniformly grey in colour.
Juv. resembles ad. but is tinged yellow or green and has a paler bill. **Habitat.** Evergreen montane forests. **Status.** Uncommon resident; endemic to the highland forests of eastern Zimbabwe and western Mozambique. **Call.** A repeated 'chipip chipip'. (Gryskleinjantjie)

2. BLACK-HEADED APALIS *Apalis melanocephala* (647) 11-13 cm
The only apalis in the region to have black upperparts and white underparts. At close range the white eye, which contrasts strongly with the black cap and ear coverts, is visible.
Juv. is paler than ad. and resembles Chirinda Apalis. **Habitat.** Canopy of evergreen, coastal and riverine forests. **Status.** Locally common resident. **Call.** A piercing 'wiii-tiiit-wiii-tiiit', repeated many times. (Swartkopkleinjantjie)

3. YELLOW-BREASTED APALIS *Apalis flavida* (648) 11-12 cm
The combination of grey head, white throat, yellow breast (sometimes with a small, black, lower bar in males from the south), red eye and white belly is diagnostic.
Sexes alike but female always lacks the black breast bar. **Juv.** is paler yellow on the breast than ad. **Habitat.** Frequents a wide range of woodland habitats but avoids montane evergreen forests. **Status.** Common resident. **Call.** A fast, buzzy 'chizzick-chizzick-chizzick', like that of Lesser Honeyguide (p. 270) but more rapid. Pairs often call in duet. (Geelborskleinjantjie)

4. RUDD'S APALIS *Apalis ruddi* (649) 11-12 cm
Could be confused with Bar-throated Apalis but lacks the white outer tail feathers, and has a small, white stripe in front of and above the eye, and a dark (not pale) eye. The lime-green back contrasts strongly with the grey head, and the bird looks 'neater' than Bar-throated Apalis.
Sexes similar but female has a narrower throat band. **Juv.** resembles female but is buffier below. **Habitat.** Thornveld and coastal forests. **Status.** Common resident; endemic. **Call.** Similar to Bar-throated Apalis, but slower. Male calls a fast 'tuttuttuttut', answered by female with a slower 'clink-clink-clink'. (Ruddse Kleinjantjie)

5. BAR-THROATED APALIS *Apalis thoracica* (645) 11-12 cm
The only apalis in the region to have both white outer tail feathers and a pale eye. It is racially very variable in colour, and may best be distinguished from similar Rudd's Apalis by the white outer tail feathers, the pale eye and the lack of a small, white eyebrow stripe.
Male has a broader breast band than female. **Juv.** resembles female but is buffier below. **Habitat.** Montane forests, wooded kloofs, scrub and fynbos. **Status.** Common resident. **Call.** A sharp, rapidly repeated 'pilllip-pilllip-pilllip'; often in duet. (Bandkeelkleinjantjie)

6. LIVINGSTONE'S FLYCATCHER *Erythrocercus livingstonei* (707) 12 cm
An unmistakable small flycatcher which has a long, rufous tail with a black sub-terminal band (not easily seen), sulphur-yellow underparts and a blue-grey cap. Constantly in motion, it flicks and fans its tail sideways. It is usually found in small groups.
Juv. lacks the tail bar of ad. **Habitat.** Riverine and coastal forests. **Status.** Locally common resident. **Call.** A sharp 'chip-chip' and a clear, warbled song. (Rooistertvlieëvanger)

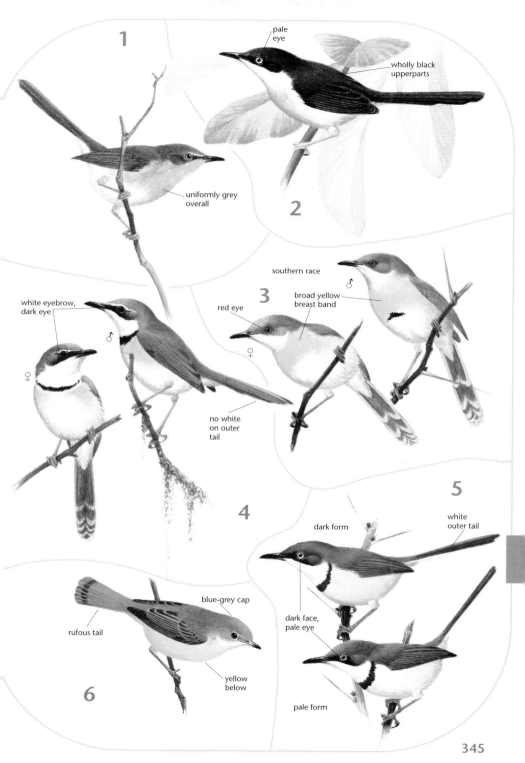

1

2
pale eye
wholly black upperparts

uniformly grey overall

white eyebrow, dark eye
♂
♀

3
southern race
♂
broad yellow breast band
red eye
♀
no white on outer tail

4

5
dark form
white outer tail
dark face, pale eye
pale form

6
blue-grey cap
rufous tail
yellow below

345

1. ZITTING (FANTAILED) CISTICOLA *Cisticola juncidis* (664)   10 cm

The tail is more boldly marked than in other small cisticolas: dark grey above and below, with a black subterminal band and conspicuously tipped with white. Tail appears larger than in other small, short-tailed cisticolas.
Female is duller than male. **Juv.** is pale yellow below (although some are white below). **Habitat.** Areas of thick grass, especially in damp situations. **Status.** Common resident. **Call.** A 'zit', repeated at the crest of each undulation during display flight; a faster 'chit-chit-chit', given in flight. It does not snap its wings. (Landeryklopkloppie)

2. DESERT CISTICOLA *Cisticola aridulus* (665)   10 cm

Similar to Zitting Cisticola, but paler and lacking the black subterminal bar on the tail. It also differs in habitat, display and song.
Sexes alike but female has a shorter tail. **Juv.** is paler below. **Habitat.** Arid grassland and old fields. **Status.** Common resident. **Call.** Song a fast 'zink zink zink' or 'sii sii sii sii', uttered in swooping display flight; when alarmed, a 'tuc tuc tuc tuc' is given and the wings are snapped. (Woestynklopkloppie)

3. CLOUD CISTICOLA *Cisticola textrix* (666)   10 cm

Birds in the southwest of the range are easily recognised by the conspicuous streaking on the breast; these birds may constitute an undescribed species. Elsewhere, it is almost indistinguishable from Wing-snapping and Desert Cisticolas except that it has a stocky body and unusually long legs and toes and a different display and song.
Juv. is bright yellow below. **Habitat.** Grassland. **Status.** Common resident. **Call.** A 'see-see-see-see-chick-chick-chick' uttered by displaying male while cruising at great height; it does not snap its wings before landing. (Gevlekte Klopkloppie)

4. WING-SNAPPING (AYRES') CISTICOLA *Cisticola ayresii* (667)   10 cm

Almost indistinguishable from Cloud Cisticola except when heard and seen in display flight. Neater and slimmer than Cloud Cisticola, it has shorter legs.
Juv. is paler than ad. **Habitat.** Upland grassland and occasionally near the coast. **Status.** Common resident. **Call.** Song a 'soo-see-see-see', uttered while cruising at a great height. On descending and just before it jinks, it loudly snaps its wings many times. (Kleinste Klopkloppie)

5. PALE-CROWNED CISTICOLA *Cisticola cinnamomeus* (668)   10 cm

Male in breeding plumage is easily distinguished from other very small cisticolas by the black lores, which contrast with the pale, buff crown. In non-breeding plumage it is virtually indistinguishable from Cloud and Wing-snapping cisticolas.
Female resembles non-breeding male. **Juv.** is yellow below. **Habitat.** Damp or marshy areas in upland grassland. **Status.** Uncommon, localised resident; near-endemic. **Call.** Display flight performed at both high and low levels. Song a soft, hardly discernible 'tsee-tsee-tsee-itititititi'. Does not snap its wing. (Bleekkopklopkloppie)

6. SHORT-WINGED CISTICOLA *Cisticola brachypterus* (680)   10-11 cm

Resembles Neddicky but has a shorter tail and clear buff underparts, and lacks the rufous crown.
Juv. has a yellowish wash to the underparts. **Habitat.** Areas of rank grass in miombo woodland. **Status.** Uncommon, localised resident. **Call.** A soft, repeated 'see-see-sippi-ippi', uttered from a tree top. (Kortvlerktinktinkie)

7. NEDDICKY *Cisticola fulvicapilla* (681)   11 cm

The greyish underparts, uniform brownish upperparts and chestnut cap render the southern form one of the easiest cisticolas to identify. The northern form is similar to Short-winged Cisticola but has buffier underparts, a chestnut cap and a longer tail.
Juv. is yellower than ad. **Habitat.** Grassy understorey of woodland, savanna and plantations. **Status.** Common resident. **Call.** Song a monotonous, frequently repeated 'weep' or 'tseep'; alarm call a fast 'tictictictic'. (Neddikkie)

1

ad. non-br.

1,2 very similar; best
distinguished by call

br.

white-tipped tail

ad. non-br.

ad. non-br.

3

o subterminal bar

br.

2

br.

spotted
breast

3,4 very similar; best
distinguished by call

southern
Cape form

br.

4

short legs

back & crown plain brown

ad. non-br.

br.

black
lores

5

br.

6

ad. non-br.

rufous
cap

rufous cap

ad. non-br.
northern race

dusky
underparts

br. southern race

7

1. GREY-BACKED CISTICOLA *Cisticola subruficapilla* (669)   13-14 cm

The southern form has a diagnostic grey back streaked with black; the northern form closely resembles Wailing Cisticola, differing in having cold greyish buff underparts (warm buff in Wailing Cisticola). Range of northern form does not overlap with that of Wailing Cisticola.
Juv. is duller than ad., with a yellowish face. **Habitat.** Fynbos and Karoo scrub. **Status.** Very common resident; near-endemic. **Call.** A muffled 'prrrrrrt' followed by sharp 'hweee phweee' notes, less strident than similar call of Chestnut-vented Tit-Babbler (p. 342). (Grysrugtinktinkie)

2. WAILING CISTICOLA *Cisticola lais* (670)   13-14 cm

Differs from the northern form of Grey-backed Cisticola in having much warmer buff (not cold grey-buff) belly and flanks. The calls and songs of these two species are very similar.
Juv. is washed with yellow below. **Habitat.** Grassland and bracken on hilly slopes, especially in rocky areas. **Status.** Common resident. **Call.** Similar to that of Grey-backed Cisticola: a plaintive, drawn-out 'wheee', often accompanied by other, shorter notes. (Huiltinktinkie)

3. TINKLING CISTICOLA *Cisticola rufilatus* (671)   12-13 cm

The long, rufous tail, rufous crown, and ear patch separated by a white eyebrow are diagnostic. Confusion is likely only with Rattling Cisticola, which has a duller crown and tail and a different call.
Sexes alike but female has a shorter tail. **Juv.** resembles ad. **Habitat.** Dry, broad-leaved savanna and scrub. **Status.** Scarce to locally common resident. **Call.** A series of tinkling, bell-like notes. (Rooitinktinkie)

4. CROAKING CISTICOLA *Cisticola natalensis* (678)   13-17 cm

This large cisticola is unlikely to be confused with any other because of its size, bulky body shape, short tail (when breeding), and unusually thick bill. The upperparts are well mottled with dark brown and there is no rufous in the streaked crown.
Sexes alike but female is smaller than male. **Juv.** is a warmer brown than ad., with a yellowish wash below. **Habitat.** Grassland in bush clearings, and grassy hillsides and valleys. **Status.** Common resident. **Call.** A deep 'trrrrp' or 'chee-fro', given during bounding display flight or from an exposed perch. (Groottinktinkie)

5. RATTLING CISTICOLA *Cisticola chiniana* (672)   11-14 cm

Easily confused with Tinkling Cisticola because of its plumage coloration, but has much less red on the head, and the rufous on the tail is not as bright.
Juv. is yellower than ad. **Habitat.** Woodland, savanna and scrub. **Status.** Common resident; the most obvious and abundant cisticola of the bushveld areas. **Call.** Lower-pitched rattle at end of short song is diagnostic; may be rendered as 'cher-cher-cher, tooitooitooi'; uttered from top of bush. Alarm a repeated, scolding 'chee-chee'. (Bosveldtinktinkie)

6. LAZY CISTICOLA *Cisticola aberrans* (679)   13-14 cm

In shape and habits, the most prinia-like cisticola of the region (including its habit of jerking the tail), but it differs from all prinias by its rufous crown and warm buff underparts. It may be distinguished from Neddicky (p. 346) by its long, thin tail, which is often held cocked.
Juv. resembles ad. **Habitat.** Grass- and bush-covered hillsides strewn with rocks and boulders. **Status.** Common, localised resident. **Call.** Song a scolding 'tzeeee-tzeeeh-cheee-cheee'. (Luitinktinkie)

1

northern form

southern form

streaked below

greyish white underparts

2

buffy underparts

tail ad. non-br.

3

rufous head with pale eyebrow

ad. non-br.

rufous tail with black tip

br.

br.

4

♂ ad. non-br.

large size

♂ br.

♂ br.

large bill

♀ br.

♂ ad. non-br.

♂ non-br.

5

streaked back

br.

plain back

buff underparts

brown tail

no terminal bar on long tail

br.

6

1. RUFOUS-WINGED (BLACKBACKED) CISTICOLA *Cisticola galactotes* (675)   11-13 cm
Most easily confused with Levaillant's Cisticola, which also has a black-streaked back. However, this species can readily be distinguished by its call, and by its back, which is more boldly streaked with black. When breeding it shows a greyish (not red) tail. Range does not overlap with that of the very similar Luapula Cisticola.
Habitat. Reedbeds, long grass and sedges near water. **Status.** Common resident. **Call.** A long, harsh 'tzzzzzzrp' and a louder, whistled alarm, 'prrrrt'. (Swartrugtinktinkie)

2 LUAPULA (BLACKBACKED) CISTICOLA *Cisticola luapula*   11-13 cm
Most likely to be confused with longer-tailed Chirping Cisticola but differs in having less buffy underparts and a more boldly marked back. Best differentiated through calls and song. Range does not overlap with that of similar Rufous-winged Cisticola.
Habitat. Swamps and marshes, preferring *Phragmites* reed stands to dense papyrus. **Status.** Locally common in pairs. **Call.** Various `cherup', 'tic tic', and `zrrtttt' trills, sometimes given in display flight. (Luapulatinktinkie)

3. CHIRPING CISTICOLA *Cisticola pipiens* (676)   15 cm
This species could be confused with the similar Luapula Cisticola: Their ranges overlap and the two species often co-occur. However, it is longer tailed and further differs by its call, by the back being less boldly streaked with black, and by having a buff wash on the breast and belly.
Habitat. Reedbeds and papyrus swamps in the Okavango region. **Status.** Common, localised resident. **Call.** A loud 'cheet-cheet-zrrrrr' and 'chwer-chwer-chwer'. (Piepende Tinktinkie)

4. LEVAILLANT'S CISTICOLA *Cisticola tinniens* (677)   14 cm
Could be confused with Rufous-winged Cisticola but is normally distinguished by its reddish (not grey) tail; at close range it can be seen that the black feathers of its back are edged with brown (not grey). The song and call of this species differ from those of Rufous-winged Cisticola. Ranges overlap marginally in southern KwaZulu-Natal.
Juv. resembles ad. but is yellower below. **Habitat.** Reedbeds, sedges and long grass adjacent to rivers and dams. **Status.** Common resident. **Call.** A warbling, musical 'chrip-trrrup-trreee' and a wailing 'cheee-weee-weee'. (Vleitinktinkie)

5. RED-FACED CISTICOLA *Cisticola erythrops* (674)   13-14 cm
Differs from other reed-dwelling cisticolas in having a uniformly coloured (not black-streaked) back. The face, sides of the breast and flanks are washed with rufous in non-breeding plumage.
Habitat. Reedbeds and rank vegetation bordering streams. **Status.** Common resident. **Call.** A series of piercing whistles, 'weee, cheee, cheee, cheer, cheer', rising and falling in scale, uttered from a perch. (Rooiwangtinktinkie)

6. SINGING CISTICOLA *Cisticola cantans* (673)   13-14 cm
Most closely resembles Red-faced Cisticola, but is greyer above and below, is found in different habitats and has a marked rufous cap.
Habitat. Long grass in clearings in open woodlands. **Status.** Uncommon, localised resident. **Call.** A disyllabic 'jhu-jee' or 'wheecho', very different from the piercing whistles of Red-faced Cisticola. (Singende Tinktinkie)

7. RED-WINGED WARBLER *Heliolais erythropterus* (682)   12-14 cm
This long-tailed warbler resembles Tawny-flanked Prinia (p. 352) but may be distinguished by its bright rufous wings, which contrast with the dark brown upperparts, and by the lack of a prominent white eye-stripe. In non-breeding plumage, the upperparts assume a rusty colour, blending with the rufous wings.
Juv. is paler than ad. **Habitat.** Long grass in woodland clearings and alongside streams. **Status.** Uncommon, localised resident. **Call.** A musical 'pseep-pseep-pseep'. (Rooivlerksanger)

br.

greyish
brown tail

ad. non-br.

3

very similar;
best distinguished
on voice

russet tail

greyish brown
long tail

ad. non-br.

4

br.

ad. non-br.

uniform
upperparts

5

br.

ad. non-br.

6

grey
breast

ad. non-br.

br.

grey
breast

wing feathers
edged with russet

wing feathers
edged with russet

grey head
& mantle

7

br.

bright
rufous
wings

bright
rufous
wings

ad. non-br.

1. NAMAQUA WARBLER *Phragmacia substriata* (687)   13-14 cm
Likely to be confused only with Karoo Prinia, but differs in having a richer, russet brown back, a longer, more wispy tail, and very faint streaking on the underside confined to the breast. Unlike Karoo Prinia, it lacks buff tips to its undertail feathers.
Juv. is duller than ad. **Habitat.** Thick bush in dry river gullies, and reedbeds adjoining rivers and dams. **Status.** Common resident; endemic to the Karoo. **Call.** A high-pitched 'trreep-trreep-trrrrrrrr' song. (Namakwalangstertjie)

2. RUFOUS-EARED WARBLER *Malcorus pectoralis* (688)   14-15 cm
The reddish ear coverts and narrow, black breast band are diagnostic. It is prinia-like in appearance and habits, although it forages freely on the ground and often runs swiftly from bush to bush with its tail half cocked.
Sexes alike but male has a broader breast band. **Juv.** lacks the breast band and has pale brown ear coverts. **Habitat.** Karoo and semi-desert scrub. **Status.** Common resident; endemic. **Call.** A scolding 'chweeo, chweeo, chweeo...'. (Rooioorlangstertjie)

3. DRAKENSBERG PRINIA *Prinia hypoxantha* (686b)   12-14 cm
Can be confused only with Karoo Prinia, from which it differs in having a less densely streaked breast, washed with yellow.
Juv. is paler below than ad. **Habitat.** Forest edge, wooded gullies and bracken-briar tangles, normally at higher elevations than Karoo Prinia. **Status.** Common resident; endemic. **Call.** Similar to Karoo Prinia's. (Drakensberglangstertjie)

4. KAROO (SPOTTED) PRINIA *Prinia maculosa* (686a)   12-14 cm
Could be confused with Drakensberg Prinia, but is less yellow below and more heavily streaked on the breast. May be distinguished from Namaqua Warbler by its buff-tipped (not plain) undertail and by the more heavily streaked front.
Juv. is yellower below. **Habitat.** Fynbos, Karoo scrub and bracken-covered slopes in mountainous terrain. **Status.** Common resident; endemic. **Call.** A sharp 'chleet-chleet-chleet' and a faster 'tit-tit-tit-tit'. (Karoolangstertjie)

5. TAWNY-FLANKED PRINIA *Prinia subflava* (683)   11-12 cm
May be distinguished from the non-breeding Black-chested Prinia by its clear white (not yellowish) throat and breast, warm buff flanks and belly, and russet edges to the wings. Non-breeding Roberts' Warbler is similar but is much darker and lacks the strongly contrasting head markings and the russet edges to the wing feathers.
Juv. resembles ad. **Habitat.** Understorey of broad-leaved woodland and thick, rank vegetation adjoining water. **Status.** Common resident. **Call.** A rapidly repeated 'przzt-przzt-przzt' and a harsh 'chrzzzt'. (Bruinsylangstertjie)

6. BLACK-CHESTED PRINIA *Prinia flavicans* (685)   14-15 cm
The only prinia in the region with a broad, black breast band in breeding plumage. In non-breeding plumage the bird might be mistaken for Tawny-flanked Prinia, but it lacks the russet edges to the wing feathers and is usually washed yellow below.
Female has a narrower breast band than male. **Juv.** resembles non-breeding ad. but is yellower below. **Habitat.** Arid scrub, thornveld, exotic plantations and suburban gardens. **Status.** Common resident. **Call.** A loud, repetitive 'zzzrt-zzzzrt-zzzrt-zzzrt' note. (Swartbandlangstertjie)

7. ROBERTS' WARBLER (PRINIA) *Oreophilais robertsi* (684)   13-14 cm
Unmistakable in breeding plumage, when the throat and breast are washed with grey and upperparts appear very dark. Otherwise, it is paler below and differs from Tawny-flanked Prinia by the pale eye and lack of russet edges to the wing feathers.
Juv. has a dark eye. **Habitat.** Thick bracken and briar adjoining forests. **Status.** Common, localised resident; endemic to eastern Zimbabwe and western Mozambique highlands. **Call.** A strident 'cha-cha-cha-cha'. (Woudlangstertjie)

1

russet back

faintly streaked breast

2

rufous cheeks

ad.

juv.

ad.

dark eye

dark brown back

streaked throat

heavily streaked breast

juv.

3

pale eye

unstreaked throat

lightly streaked breast

yellow wash

4

russet edges to wing feathers

buff flanks

5

uff form **non-br.**

no russet on wing

br.

no russet on wing

yellow wash below

non-br.

unstreaked

6

pale yellow eye

uniformly dark head

grey throat

no russet on wing

br.

7

1. AFRICAN DUSKY FLYCATCHER *Muscicapa adusta* (690)   12 cm
This species is smaller and darker than Spotted Flycatcher. At close range the lack of forehead streaking, which differentiates these two species, is obvious. The chin is pale and unmarked and the underparts are washed grey-brown with ill-defined streaking.
Juv. is spotted with buff above, and is whitish spotted with brown below. **Habitat.** Evergreen forest edges and glades, riverine forests and well-wooded suburban gardens. **Status.** Common resident. **Call.** A soft, high-pitched 'tzzeet' and 'tsirit'. (Donkervlieëvanger)

2. SPOTTED FLYCATCHER *Muscicapa striata* (689)   13-14 cm
Larger than the similar African Dusky Flycatcher, this species is also paler below with a streaked forehead (diagnostic) and more clearly streaked underparts. It often flicks its wings on alighting.
Juv. is mottled with brown and buff, but is not likely to be seen in the region. **Habitat.** A wide range of wooded habitats, from the edges of evergreen forests to semi-arid bush. **Status.** Common summer visitor. **Call.** A soft 'tzee' and 'zeck, chick-chick'. (Europese Vlieëvanger)

3. ASHY (BLUEGREY) FLYCATCHER *Muscicapa caerulescens* (691)   14-15 cm
In comparison with Grey Tit-Flycatcher this species is bluer above and greyer below, has a black loral stripe bordered white above and a plain, pale grey tail (not a dark tail with white outer tail feathers). Its habits differ from those of Grey Tit-Flycatcher in that it hawks insects from branches and frequently flies to the ground for food.
Juv. is speckled with dark brown and buff, both above and below. **Habitat.** Riverine forests and moist, open broad-leaved woodland. **Status.** Common resident. **Call.** Song a soft 'sszzit-sszzit-sreee-sreee', descending in scale. (Blougrysvlieëvanger)

4. GREY TIT-FLYCATCHER (FANTAILED FLYCATCHER)
Myioparus plumbeus (693)   14 cm
The dark tail with white outer tail feathers and lack of a black loral stripe distinguish it from the otherwise similar Ashy Flycatcher. The habits of the two species also differ: Grey Tit-Flycatcher is found within foliage of trees, frequently fanning its tail as it moves.
Juv. is spotted with brown and buff above and below. **Habitat.** Riverine forests, mature woodland and savanna. **Status.** Uncommon resident. **Call.** A soft, tremulous, whistled 'treee-trooo'. (Waaierstertvlieëvanger)

5. SOUTHERN BLACK FLYCATCHER *Melaenornis pammelaina* (694)   20-22 cm
May be distinguished from male Black Cuckooshrike (p. 300) by lacking the yellow gape and by having a square (not rounded) tail. It differs from Square tailed Drongo (p. 300) by the square (not notched) tail and brown (not red) eye. It hawks from perches, taking food from the ground.
Juv. is dull black, scalloped with brown. **Habitat.** Woodland, savanna and forest edges. **Status.** Common resident. **Call.** Song a wheezy 'tzzit-terra-loora-loo'. (Swartvlieëvanger)

6. FISCAL FLYCATCHER *Sigelus silens* (698)   17-20 cm
Often mistaken for Common Fiscal (p. 372), but is easily recognised in flight as it has a shorter tail with conspicuous white patches on the sides; its bill is thin and flat (not stubby and hooked), and the white in the wings is confined to the secondaries (not on the shoulders). It is larger than male Collared Flycatcher (p. 358), which has a white collar and lacks the white tail panels.
Female is brown (not black) above. **Juv.** is a dull version of female, spotted and scalloped above and below with brown. **Habitat.** Bush, scrub, suburban gardens and exotic plantations. **Status.** Common resident; endemic. **Call.** A weak, soft, chittering song; a 'tssisk' alarm call. (Fiskaalvlieëvanger)

1

plain forehead

grey-brown below

all-grey tail

2

streaked forehead

pale below

3

black & white loral stripes

4

dark tail with white outers

plain face

5

dark brown eye

square tail

white shoulder patch

long tail

Common Fiscal (not to scale) (p. 372)

6

♀

bill not hooked

♂

white secondary patch

white tail patches

fairly short tail

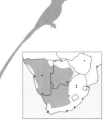

1. CHAT FLYCATCHER *Bradornis infuscatus* (697)   20 cm
A large flycatcher of thrush-like proportions. It is uniformly brownish above, with paler underparts and a pale brown panel on the folded secondaries.
Juv. is spotted with buff above and below. **Habitat.** Dry fynbos; Karoo and desert scrub. **Status.** Common resident. **Call.** Song a rich, warbled 'cher-cher-cherrip', with squeaky, hissing notes. (Grootvlieëvanger)

2. MARICO FLYCATCHER *Bradornis mariquensis* (695)   18 cm
The contrasting pure white underparts and brown upperparts differentiate this species from Pale Flycatcher. It is conspicuous, often perching on fences and phone lines along roadsides.
Juv. is spotted above and streaked below. **Habitat.** Thornveld. **Status.** Common resident. **Call.** Song a soft 'tsii-cheruk-tukk'. (Maricovlieëvanger)

3. PALE (MOUSECOLOURED) FLYCATCHER *Bradornis pallidus* (696)   17 cm
Differs from Marico Flycatcher in having buffy brown underparts and being grey-brown rather than russet brown above.
Juv. is paler than ad. and mottled with brown and grey. **Habitat.** Moist, broad-leaved woodland. **Status.** Scarce to common resident. **Call.** Song consists of a melodious warbling interspersed with harsh chitters; alarm call is a soft 'churr'. (Muiskleurvlieëvanger)

4. BLUE-MANTLED CRESTED FLYCATCHER *Trochocercus cyanomelas* (708)   13-14 cm
The glossy, black head and shaggy crest render the male unmistakable.
Female could be confused with White-tailed Crested Flycatcher but is paler grey on the head and throat, has a white wing stripe, and lacks white in the tail. **Juv.** resembles female but is duller buff. **Habitat.** Montane, coastal and riverine forests. **Status.** Common resident. **Call.** Alarm is a harsh 'zweet-zwa', similar to that of African Paradise-Flycatcher; song is a fluty whistle. (Bloukuifvlieëvanger)

5. AFRICAN PARADISE-FLYCATCHER
Terpsiphone viridis (710)   17-20 cm (plus 18 cm tail in br. male)
The dark head and breast, bright blue bill and eye-ring, and chestnut back and tail are diagnostic. The male loses its long tail in the non-breeding season.
Female has a shorter tail and a duller blue eye-ring and bill. **Juv.** is duller than female. **Habitat.** Evergreen, coastal and riverine forests and bush; suburban gardens. **Status.** Summer visitor; resident in the northeast. **Call.** Alarm a harsh 'zweet-zweet-zwayt', similar to that of Blue-mantled Crested Flycatcher; song a loud 'twee-tiddly-te-te'. (Paradysvlieëvanger)

6. (AFRICAN) WHITE-TAILED CRESTED FLYCATCHER
Elminia albonotata (709)   13-14 cm
Easily recognised by its habit of fanning and closing its tail (thereby displaying the white outer tail feathers and white spots on tips of tail feathers) while moving from side to side. Blue-mantled Crested Flycatcher has a white wing bar and lacks white in the tail.
Juv. is duller than ad. **Habitat.** Montane forests. **Status.** Locally common resident. **Call.** Song a fast 'tsee-tsee-teuu-choo' and other jumbled notes, including mimicked calls of other birds. (Witstertvlieëvanger)

7. BLACK-AND-WHITE (VANGA) FLYCATCHER *Bias musicus* (699)   14-15 cm
Male is unmistakable with its diagnostic black crest, black throat and bib, small white wing patch (cf. Blue-mantled Crested Flycatcher) and bright yellow legs and eyes. It is the shortest tailed of the region's flycatchers.
Female has a black cap with a slight crest, and a bright chestnut back, wings and tail. **Juv.** resembles female but is duller, and is streaked on the head. **Habitat.** Lowland riverine forests. **Status.** Uncommon resident. **Call.** Song a loud, whistled 'whitu-whitu-whitu'; alarm note a sharp 'we-chip'. (Witpensvlieëvanger)

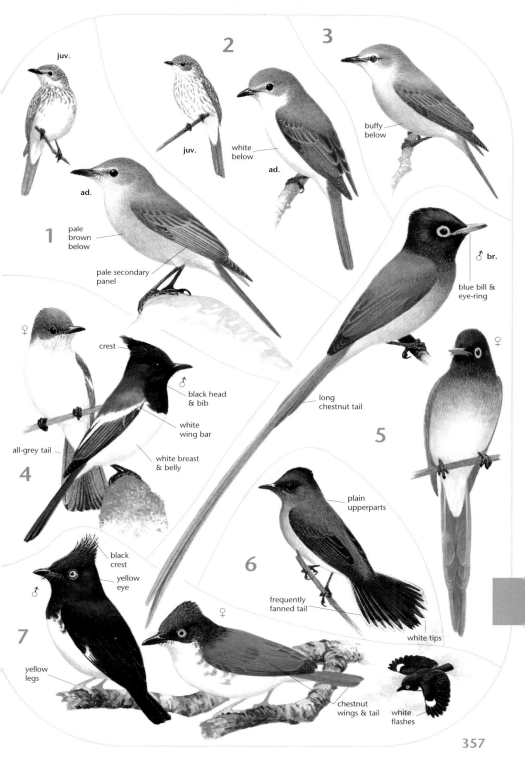

1

juv.

ad.

pale brown below

pale secondary panel

2

juv.

white below

ad.

3

buffy below

♂ br.

blue bill & eye-ring

long chestnut tail

5

♀

4

♀

crest

all-grey tail

black head & bib

white wing bar

white breast & belly

6

plain upperparts

frequently fanned tail

white tips

7

black crest

yellow eye

♂

yellow legs

♀

chestnut wings & tail

white flashes

1. COLLARED FLYCATCHER *Ficedula albicollis* (692)   12-13 cm
Male in its pied breeding plumage is unmistakable. It superficially resembles male
Fiscal Flycatcher (p. 354), but that species is much larger and has a longer tail and
no white collar.
Female and non-breeding male superficially resemble female Southern Hyliota but may be
distinguished by the greyer upperparts and slight grey (not yellow) wash below. Unlike the
hyliotas they display typical flycatcher habits. **Juv.** resembles female but lacks the collar.
Habitat. Miombo and other broad-leaved woodland. **Status.** Rare summer visitor. **Call.** A
'zip' or soft 'whit-whit-whit'. (Withalsvlieëvanger)

2. SOUTHERN (MASHONA) HYLIOTA *Hyliota australis* (624)   14 cm
This species is distinguished from the very similar Yellow-bellied Hyliota by its matt
blue-black upperparts, by the small white panel on the secondary coverts not
extending onto the tertials, and by the pale yellow underparts. Both hyliota species
are distinguished from Collared Flycatcher by their shorter tails, lack of a complete
or partial collar, and their habit of foraging (not aerial sallying) in the leafy canopy.
Female has warm brown upperparts, not grey-brown as in female Yellow-bellied Hyliota.
Juv. resembles female but is duller. **Habitat.** Miombo and other broad-leaved woodland.
Status. Locally common resident. **Call.** A high-pitched trilling similar to that of Yellow-bellied Hyliota. (Mashonahyliota)

3. YELLOW-BELLIED (-BREASTED) HYLIOTA *Hyliota flavigaster* (623)   14 cm
Male distinguished from male Southern Hyliota by having distinctly glossy blue-
black upperparts, more white in the wings, and richer yellow underparts.
Female is difficult to distinguish from female Southern Hyliota but has grey-brown (not
warm brown) upperparts. **Juv.** is barred with buff above. **Habitat.** Miombo and mopane
woodland. **Status.** Uncommon and highly localised resident. **Call.** A high-pitched 'trreet
trreet'. (Geelborshyliota)

4. AFRICAN YELLOW WHITE-EYE *Zosterops senegalensis* (797)   11 cm
The bright, sulphur-yellow underparts and very pale green, almost yellow upperparts differentiate this species from Cape White-eye. The head is almost completely
yellow whereas that of Cape White-eye is green. Cape White-eyes in the east of
the range are brighter yellow than elsewhere, but have predominantly green, not
yellow heads.
Juv. is a very much paler yellow and green than juv. Cape White-eye. **Habitat.** A variety of
woodlands, from thornveld to montane forests. **Status.** Common resident. **Call.** Similar to
that of Cape White-eye. (Geelglasogie)

5. CAPE WHITE-EYE *Zosterops capensis* (796)   12 cm
Usually distinguished from African Yellow White-eye by its greyish underparts and
green (not yellow) upperparts. However, birds in Mpumalanga have pale green,
almost yellow backs; here, only the gryeish green vent and greenish (not yellow)
head differentiates this species from African Yellow White-eye. Lacks the obvious
buff sides to the breast and flanks of Orange River White-eye.
Juv. is duller than ad. **Habitat.** Forests, woodland, savanna, exotic plantations and suburban gardens. **Status.** Common resident; endemic. **Call.** A soft, sweet 'tweee-tuuu-twee-
twee', often repeated. (Kaapse Glasogie)

6. ORANGE RIVER WHITE-EYE *Zosterops pallidus*   12 cm
Differs from Cape White-eye by having a very obvious peachy buff wash across the
sides of the breast and flanks that contrasts with yellow throat and vent. Range
does not overlap with that of African Yellow White-eye.
Habitat. Arid to semi-arid scrub, dry river beds and riverine woodland and reed beds.
Status. Locally common endemic. **Call.** Higher pitched and more trilling than Cape White-
eye. (Gariepglasogie)

2

no collar

matt upperparts

short wing bar

♀

♂

1

white frons

white collar

extensive white on wings

♂ **non-br.**

partial collar

off-white below (not tinged yellow)

extensive wing bar

♂ **br.**

3

glossy upperparts

extended wing bar

♂

♀

4

yellow-green back

yellow crown

bright yellow below

green crown

southern and western Cape

grey breast & belly

5

green back & crown

green wash

eastern forests

6

peachy-buffy flanks

arid west

359

1. PRIRIT BATIS *Batis pririt* (703)   12 cm

Although male is very similar to male Chinspot Batis, their calls differ and their ranges do not overlap.

Female differs from female Chinspot Batis in having a buffy yellow to rufous wash over the throat and breast instead of the clearly defined chestnut chin patch. **Juv.** resembles female. **Habitat.** Dry thornveld, broad-leaved woodland and dry riverine bush. **Status.** Common resident; near-endemic. **Call.** A series of numerous, slow 'teuu, teuu, teuu, teuu' notes, descending in scale. (Priritbosbontrokkie)

2. CAPE BATIS *Batis capensis* (700)   13 cm

Male of this species is the only batis in the region with completely russet-washed wings and flanks.

Female lacks the black breast band of male and has a rufous throat spot. Differs from the smaller female Woodwards' Batis in lacking the complete, white eyebrow stripe. **Juv.** resembles female. **Habitat.** Moist evergreen forests and heavily wooded gorges in mountain ranges. **Status.** Common resident; endemic. **Call.** A soft 'chewrra-warrra-warrra' and 'foo-foo-foo'. (Kaapse Bosbontrokkie)

3. WOODWARDS' BATIS *Batis fratrum* (704)   11 cm

Male lacks a black breast band and, although it resembles female Pririt Batis, their ranges do not overlap.

Female is very similar to female Chinspot Batis, but lacks the obvious chestnut chin patch and has rufous wing panels. **Juv.** resembles female. **Habitat.** Coastal forests and scrub. **Status.** Locally common resident. **Call.** A clear, penetrating whistle, 'tch-tch-pheeeoooo'. (Woodwardse Bosbontrokkie)

4. CHINSPOT BATIS *Batis molitor* (701)   13 cm

Male is very similar to male Pririt and Pale Batises; the latter has a narrower breast band and the former has indistinct, black markings on the flanks, lacking in Chinspot Batis. The calls of these species are, however, easily distinguishable.

Female has a distinctive, clearly defined, rufous spot on the chin, unlike the diffuse chestnut on other female batises' throats. **Juv.** resembles female but has a mottled head and breast. **Habitat.** Dry, broad-leaved woodland and dry thornveld. **Status.** Common resident. **Call.** A clear, descending 'teuu-teuu-teuu' ('three blind mice'), and harsh 'chrr-chrr' notes. (Witliesbosbontrokkie)

5. PALE (MOZAMBIQUE) BATIS *Batis soror* (702)   10 cm

The smallest batis in the region. Male is distinguished from male Chinspot Batis by the narrower black breast band and dappled, black-and-white back.

Female is much smaller than female Chinspot Batis, and the chestnut chin patch is ill defined. **Juv.** is undescribed. **Habitat.** Miombo woodland and lowland forests. **Status.** Common resident in northern Mozambique, localised in eastern Zimbabwe. **Call.** Soft, frequently repeated 'tcheeo, tcheeo, tcheeo'. (Mosambiekbosbontrokkie)

6. BLACK-THROATED WATTLE-EYE (WATTLE-EYED FLYCATCHER)
Platysteira peltata (705)   13 cm

The conspicuous, bright red wattle over the eye, black cap and narrow, black breast band of the male are diagnostic.

Female is distinguished from male Black-and-white Flycatcher (p. 356) by its much smaller size, its red eye wattles and pale rump, and by the lack of a crest. **Juv.** resembles female. **Habitat.** Coastal and riverine forests and, occasionally, mangrove stands. **Status.** Uncommon and localised resident. **Call.** A repeated 'wichee-wichee-wichee-wichee'. (Beloogbosbontrokkie)

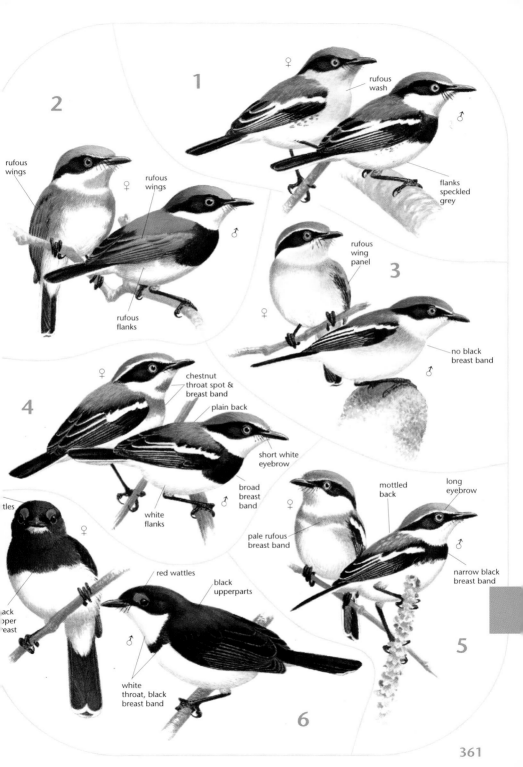

1

♀

rufous
wash

♂

flanks
speckled
grey

2

rufous
wings

rufous
wings

♀

♂

rufous
flanks

3

rufous
wing
panel

♀

♂

no black
breast band

4

♀

chestnut
throat spot &
breast band

plain back

short white
eyebrow

broad
breast
band

white
flanks

♂

...tles

♀

...ack
...pper
...east

red wattles

black
upperparts

♂

white
throat, black
breast band

6

mottled
back

long
eyebrow

♀

pale rufous
breast band

♂

narrow black
breast band

5

1. CAPE WAGTAIL *Motacilla capensis* (713) 19-20 cm

The unmarked, greyish brown upperparts, combined with the narrow, dark grey breast band, are diagnostic. This wagtail may be distinguished from Mountain Wagtail by the shorter tail and buffy (not white) belly and flanks, and by the reduced amount of white in the wings.

Juv. is a duller version of ad. and has a buff-yellow wash over the belly. **Habitat.** Usually near fresh water or coastal lagoons but also in city parks and gardens. **Status.** Common resident. **Call.** A clear, ringing 'tseee-chee-chee' call; a whistled, trilling song. (Gewone Kwikkie)

2. AFRICAN PIED WAGTAIL *Motacilla aguimp* (711) 20 cm

An unmistakable, large wagtail with black-and-white pied plumage.

Juv. might be confused with ad. or juv. Cape Wagtail but can be distinguished by its white wing coverts. **Habitat.** Along larger rivers and at coastal lagoons. **Status.** Locally common resident. **Call.** A loud, shrill 'chee-chee-cheree-cheeroo'. (Bontkwikkie)

3. GREY WAGTAIL *Motacilla cinerea* (715) 17-19 cm

This species might be mistaken for Yellow Wagtail but has a blue-grey (not green) back that contrasts with its greenish yellow rump. The flanks and vent are a bright sulphur-yellow. It also has a noticeably longer tail.

Breeding male has a black throat but in non-breeding plumage this is reduced to a speckled area. Female has a white throat. **Juv.** resembles female but is duller, and has a bright yellow vent. **Habitat.** Verges of fast-flowing streams and ponds. **Status.** Rare summer vagrant. **Call.** A single, sharp 'tit'. (Gryskwikkie)

4. MOUNTAIN (LONGTAILED) WAGTAIL *Motacilla clara* (712) 18-20 cm

Its unusually long tail, pale grey upperparts and white (not buff) underparts differentiate this species from Cape Wagtail. It also shows more extensive white in the wings and is a more slender bird.

Juv. is browner than ad. **Habitat.** Confined to fast-flowing streams in evergreen and coastal forests. **Status.** Locally common resident. **Call.** A sharp, high-pitched 'cheeerip' or 'chissik'. (Bergkwikkie)

5. CITRINE WAGTAIL *Motacilla citreola* (714) 15-17 cm

Breeding male or female could be confused with br. *lutea* race of Yellow Wagtail but has a grey, not olive back, two noticeable white wing bars and a longer tail. Non-breeding and imm. birds told from similar-plumaged Yellow Wagtail by their longer tails, lack of any yellow on the vent and greyer, less olive upperparts.

Habitat. Usually associated with freshwater areas. **Status.** Vagrant; one record from the Eastern Cape. **Call.** Similar to Yellow Wagtail. (Sitrienkwikkie)

6. YELLOW WAGTAIL *Motacilla flava* (714) 16-18cm

Can be confused only with Grey Wagtail, but this species is smaller and has a much shorter tail and a green (not blue-grey) back. The head colour is variable, according to race.

Female and non-breeding male, which are normally seen in the region, differ widely in the amount of yellow on the underparts as a result of racial variation. **Juv.** is yellowish brown above and pale buff below, with a blackish breast band. **Habitat.** Short, cropped, grassy verges of coastal lagoons, sewage ponds and wetlands. **Status.** Uncommon to locally common summer visitor. Sometimes in flocks. **Call.** A weak, thin 'tseeep'. (Geelkwikkie)

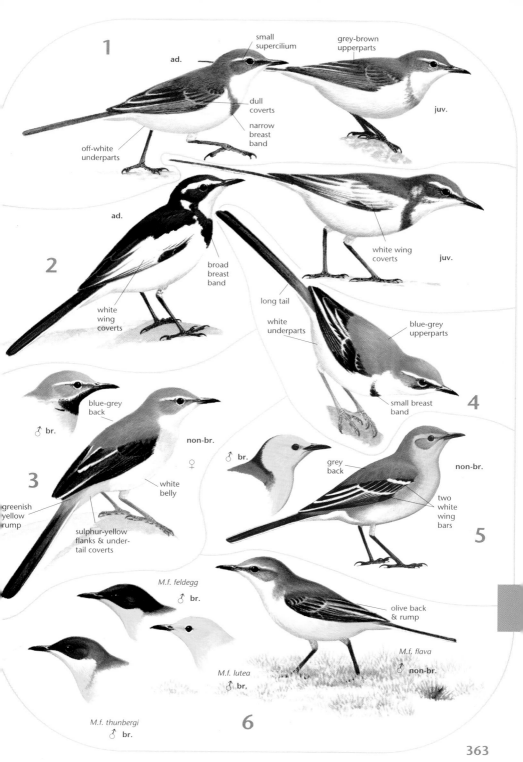

1

ad.

small
supercilium

grey-brown
upperparts

juv.

dull
coverts

narrow
breast
band

off-white
underparts

2

ad.

broad
breast
band

white wing
coverts

juv.

white
wing
coverts

long tail

white
underparts

blue-grey
upperparts

4

small breast
band

♂ br.

blue-grey
back

non-br.

♀

white
belly

♂ br.

grey
back

non-br.

two
white
wing
bars

5

3

greenish
yellow
rump

sulphur-yellow
flanks & under-
tail coverts

M.f. feldegg
♂ br.

olive back
& rump

M.f. lutea
♂ br.

M.f. flava
♂ non-br.

M.f. thunbergi
♂ br.

6

PIPITS

1. WOOD PIPIT *Anthus nyassae* (909)   16-18 cm

Closely resembles Long-billed Pipit, but occurs in woodland rather than open grassland. It has a shorter tail and bill than Long-billed Pipit, and more extensive pale areas in the base of the outer tail feathers. The ranges of the two species do not overlap.

Juv. is spotted above, and more heavily streaked below than ad. **Habitat.** Confined to miombo and teak woodland where it forages in rocky clearings on the ground. **Status.** Locally common resident. **Call.** Song similar to that of Long-billed Pipit, but more variable and slightly higher pitched. (Boskoester)

2. LONG-BILLED PIPIT *Anthus similis* (717)   18 cm

May be told from African Pipit (p. 366) by this species' buff (not white) outer tail feathers, less distinct facial markings and streaking on the breast, and by the song and call. It is difficult to distinguish from Mountain Pipit but has a less boldly streaked breast and a different call and display. The well-marked back differentiates it from Buffy and Plain-backed Pipits (p. 366).

Juv. is paler and more heavily spotted than ad. **Habitat.** Prefers boulder-strewn hillsides with scant bush cover, also found in agricultural lowlands in west of range. **Status.** Locally common resident. **Call.** A high-pitched, three-noted 'tchreep-tritit-churup'. (Nicholsonse Koester)

3. AFRICAN ROCK PIPIT *Anthus crenatus* (721)   *17 cm*

This is a drab, uniformly coloured pipit with a stout, heavy bill. At a distance the pale eye-stripe is the only plumage feature evident. Only at close range can the very faint, narrow streaking on the breast and the greenish edges to the secondary coverts be seen. Usually located by its distinctive song, it is fairly secretive when not calling.

Juv. resembles ad. but is mottled above. **Habitat.** Boulder-strewn, steep, grassy hillsides; Karoo koppies. **Status.** Locally common resident; endemic. **Call.** A carrying 'tseeet-tser-rroooo', the second note descending; calls with typical erect stance, bill pointed upwards, from a low perch. (Klipkoester)

4. MOUNTAIN PIPIT *Anthus hoeschi* (901)   18 cm

Difficult to distinguish from African Pipit (p. 366), with which it often associates, but this pipit is larger, has bold streaking on the breast and a pink (not yellow) base to the lower mandible; in flight it shows buff (not white) outer tail feathers. It may be distinguished from Long-billed and Buffy pipits (this page and p. 366) by its behaviour, display song and heavily marked breast.

Juv. is more heavily streaked on the underparts than ad. **Habitat.** Montane grassland, usually above 2 000 m. **Status.** Common summer visitor; breeding endemic. **Call.** Display song, given in flight, closely resembles that of African Pipit (p. 366), but is deeper in pitch and slower in tempo. (Bergkoester)

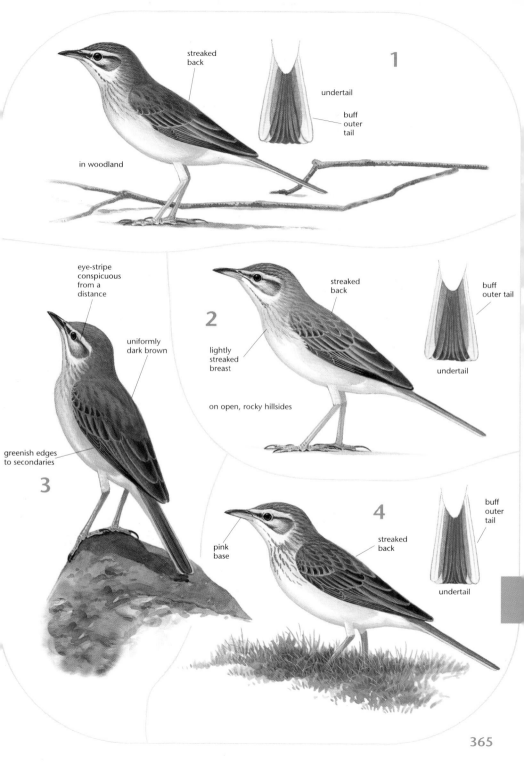

1

streaked back

in woodland

undertail

buff outer tail

2

eye-stripe conspicuous from a distance

uniformly dark brown

greenish edges to secondaries

streaked back

lightly streaked breast

on open, rocky hillsides

buff outer tail

undertail

3

4

pink base

streaked back

buff outer tail

undertail

1. LONG-TAILED PIPIT *Anthus longicaudatus*   19 cm

Could be confused with other large, plain-backed pipits, and most closely resembles Buffy Pipit. It differs in being larger and darker overall, with a long, heavy, square-ended tail. The bill is also shorter and is a yellowish horn colour at the base. It is even more horizontal in stance than Buffy Pipit, wags its tail continually, and does not stand as upright as Buffy Pipit occasionally does. When foraging, its head is often held below the horizontal.

Habitat. Short-grassed open areas. **Status.** Recently described species, of which little is known. **Status.** Occurs in the Kimberley region during the winter, where it is fairly common. Breeding grounds unknown. **Call.** A single thin, short note. (Langstertkoester)

2. AFRICAN (GRASSVELD) PIPIT *Anthus cinnamomeus* (716)   16-17 cm

Display flight and song distinguish it from all species except Mountain Pipit (p. 364), from which it differs by its call, its white (not buffy) outer tail feathers and the yellow (not pink) base to its lower mandible. It may be told from Long-billed Pipit (p. 364) by its bolder facial markings and breast streaking, and the white (not buff) outer tail feathers.

Juv. is darker above, and has more heavily streaked underparts. **Habitat.** Virtually any type of open grassland. **Status.** Common resident. **Call.** Song a repeated, three- to five-noted 'trrit-trrit-trrit', uttered while performing an undulating display flight 30–100 m above the ground. (Gewone Koester)

3. PLAIN-BACKED PIPIT *Anthus leucophrys* (718)   16-17 cm

Differs from African and Long-billed Pipits (this page and p. 364) by its uniform, unstreaked back and narrow, buff outer tail feathers, and by the lack of distinct breast markings. It is very difficult to distinguish from Buffy Pipit; Plain-backed Pipit has a yellowish (not pink) base to the lower mandible, darker upperparts and stronger breast markings, although the latter characteristic varies in both species.

Juv. is heavily mottled above. **Habitat.** Hillsides covered with short grass and, when not breeding, forms flocks in stubble grain fields. Also favours recently burnt areas and occasionally forages along the high-water drift line. **Status.** Locally common resident, subject to local movements. **Call.** A loud, clear 'chrrrup-chereeoo'; also single calls, often given in flight, but does not have a display flight. (Donkerkoester)

4. BUFFY PIPIT *Anthus vaalensis* (719)   16-18 cm

Difficult to distinguish from Plain-backed Pipit but the breast markings are often faint, with a rich, buffy belly and flanks. The base of the bill is pink (not yellow). On the ground it stops often, generally remaining horizontal, but does occasionally stand bold and upright. Moves its tail up and down, wagtail-like, more frequently than other pipits.

Juv. resembles ad. but is mottled above. **Habitat.** Similar to that of Plain-backed Pipit (hillsides covered with short grass) but usually at lower altitudes. **Status.** Uncommon resident. **Call.** A repeated, two-noted song, 'tchreep-churup'. When flushed, it gives a short 'sshik'. (Vaalkoester)

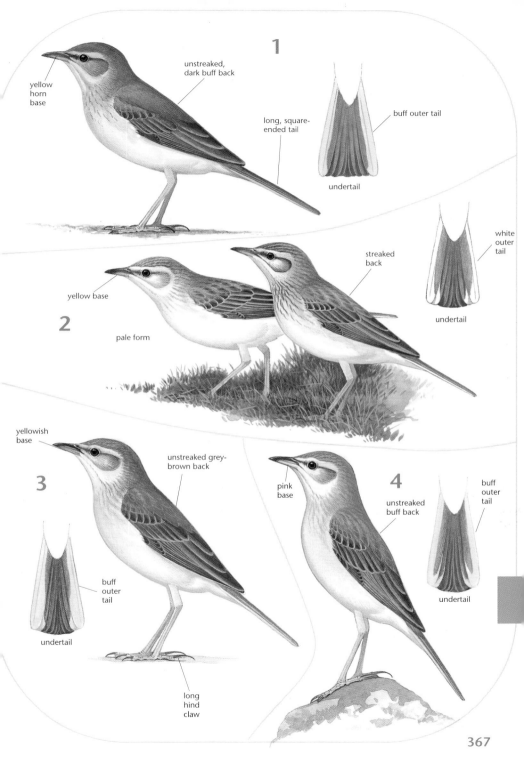

1

yellow horn base

unstreaked, dark buff back

long, square-ended tail

buff outer tail

undertail

white outer tail

undertail

2

yellow base

pale form

streaked back

3

yellowish base

unstreaked grey-brown back

buff outer tail

undertail

long hind claw

4

pink base

unstreaked buff back

buff outer tail

undertail

1. BUSHVELD PIPIT *Anthus caffer* (723)   13-14 cm

Distinguished from Tree Pipit by its smaller size, and by the shorter tail, paler plumage and diffuse, less distinct streaking on its breast. The throat is washed with brown, with faint streaking (not almost white as in Tree Pipit). In comparison with Short-tailed Pipit, it is larger, has a longer, broader tail and is less heavily streaked below.

Juv. is paler than ad. and is speckled above. **Habitat.** Thornveld and open broad-leaved woodland. **Status.** Fairly common but localised resident. **Call.** A characteristic 'zeet', given as it flies from the ground to a tree; song a treble note, 'zrrrt-zrree-chreee', uttered from a perch in a tree. (Bosveldkoester)

2. SHORT-TAILED PIPIT *Anthus brachyurus* (724)   12 cm

A small, squat pipit, very much darker and more heavily streaked above and below than either Tree or Bushveld Pipits. In flight, it shows a noticeably shorter, thinner tail than other small pipits. When flushed, it flies off speedily, resembling a large cisticola, with the white outer tail feathers showing clearly.

Juv. resembles ad. **Habitat.** Grassy hillsides, scantily covered with protea scrub, and grassy glades in miombo woodland. KwaZulu-Natal population winters on the coastal plain. **Status.** Resident and local migrant. **Call.** Calls from perches or during circling display flights; similar to Bushveld Pipit, a buzzy, bubbling 'chrrrrt-zhrrrreet-zzeeep'. (Kortstertkoester)

3. TREE PIPIT *Anthus trivialis* (722)   15 cm

Longer tailed and larger than either Bushveld or Short-tailed Pipit. It has a short bill. It shows much more contrast between the pale throat and dark upperparts than do the other two species. It may be differentiated with difficulty from non-br. Red-throated Pipit, but has less clearly streaked underparts and lacks dark brown streaking on the rump.

Juv. is buffier than ad. **Habitat.** Grassy areas in open broad-leaved woodland. **Status.** Uncommon summer visitor. **Call.** A soft, nasal 'teeez', given in flight or when flushed; song melodic and canary-like. (Boomkoester)

4. RED-THROATED PIPIT *Anthus cervinus* (903)   15 cm

Most likely to be confused with Tree Pipit but is darker, and has clear white underparts heavily streaked with black, and a streaked (not uniformly coloured) rump. In breeding plumage, the dull, brick-red throat and breast are diagnostic.

Juv. does not occur in the region. **Habitat.** Damp grassland, usually near water. **Status.** Vagrant, with two records from KwaZulu-Natal and one from Namibia. **Call.** A clear, penetrating 'chup', and a buzzy 'skeeeaz'. (Rooikeelkoester)

5. STRIPED PIPIT *Anthus lineiventris* (720)   17-18 cm

A fairly plump, heavily built pipit that differs from all others by its boldly striped underparts with the dark stripes extending onto the belly. The dark upperparts have variably yellow-edged wing feathers, and the tail is very dark with conspicuous white outer tail feathers.

Juv. is paler than ad. and is speckled above. **Habitat.** Thickly wooded, boulder-strewn hillslopes. **Status.** Locally common resident. **Call.** A loud, penetrating, thrush-like song, uttered from a rock or tree perch. (Gestreepte Koester)

1

heavily streaked above

diffuse streaking

short tail

2

dark, heavily streaked above and below

very short, thin tail

white outer tail

3

unstreaked rump

br.

4

heavy streaking below

streaked rump

ad. non-br.

5

heavily streaked underparts extending to belly

wing feathers edged with yellow

white outer tail feathers

1. YELLOW-BREASTED PIPIT *Anthus chloris* (725)　　　　17 cm
The only pipit in the region to show an all-yellow throat and breast. The upper-parts are heavily scaled and are similar to those of a longclaw. In flight, the yellow underparts and underwing coverts are diagnostic. Lacks the broad yellow eyebrow stripe and black breast band of Golden Pipit, but the two are very unlikely to be encountered in the same habitat. In non-breeding plumage it lacks the yellow underparts and is identified by its boldly scaled upperparts and plain, buff under-parts, lightly streaked on the breast.
Juv. is buff below and paler above than ad. **Habitat.** Short, dense grassland at altitudes above 1 500 m. **Status.** Uncommon resident; endemic. **Call.** A rapid, repeated 'chip, chip, chip', like the call of a displaying male Long-tailed Widowbird (p. 404); also a subdued 'suwiep'. (Geelborskoester)

2. GOLDEN PIPIT *Tmetothylacus tenellus* (726)　　　　13-15 cm
Although this species resembles a diminutive, bright golden Yellow-throated Longclaw, the predominantly bright yellow upperwings and underwings render it unmistakable.
Female and **juv.** are duller than male on the breast and lack the black breast band. **Habitat.** Open, dry broad-leaved woodland and thornveld. **Status.** Rare summer vagrant, with records from Zimbabwe and northeastern South Africa. **Call.** A short burst of scratchy notes. (Goudkoester)

3. YELLOW-THROATED LONGCLAW *Macronyx croceus* (728)　　　　20-22 cm
Could be confused with Golden Pipit (which is smaller, much brighter and more extensively yellow) and with juv. Cape Longclaw (which has a browner, more uni-form back and a greatly reduced collar).
Sexes alike but female is duller. **Juv.** may be differentiated from juv. Cape Longclaw by the buff-yellow coloration below and by the bright yellow edging to the wing feathers. **Habitat.** Grassland adjoining freshwater areas, coastal estuaries and lagoons; also in well-grassed savanna woodland away from water. **Status.** Common resident. **Call.** A loud, whistled 'phooooeeet' or series of loud whistles, frequently uttered from a perch on top of a bush or small tree; also calls in flight. (Geelkeelkalkoentjie)

4. CAPE (ORANGETHROATED) LONGCLAW *Macronyx capensis* (727)　　　　20 cm
Could be confused with Yellow-throated Longclaw but has deeper yellow under-parts and a diagnostic orange throat encircled with black. Unlike Yellow-throated Longclaw it seldom lands in trees when it is disturbed.
Female is duller than male. **Juv.** has a yellow throat with a vestigial collar; it differs from juv. Yellow-throated Longclaw in having buffish to orange underparts and wing feathers edged with buff (not yellow). **Habitat.** Wide range of coastal and upland grasslands. **Status.** Common resident; the most widespread longclaw; endemic. **Call.** A fairly melodi-ous song, 'cheewit-cheewit', often given in flight; also a cat-like mewing alarm call and a loud, high-pitched 'tsweet' contact call. (Oranjekeelkalkoentjie)

5. ROSY-THROATED (PINKTHROATED) LONGCLAW
Macronyx ameliae (730)　　　　19-20 cm
Being slender and long tailed, this species is much more pipit-like in shape than either Yellow-throated or Cape Longclaws. The pink throat and breast are diagnos-tic. The white outer tail feathers, extending right up to the base of the tail, show clearly in flight.
Female and **juv.** lack the black breast band and are less pink but still show a rosy hue over the belly and flanks. **Habitat.** Moist grassland surrounding open areas of fresh water. **Status.** Uncommon and patchily distributed resident. **Call.** A sharp, pipit-like 'chiteeet'. (Rooskeelkalkoentjie)

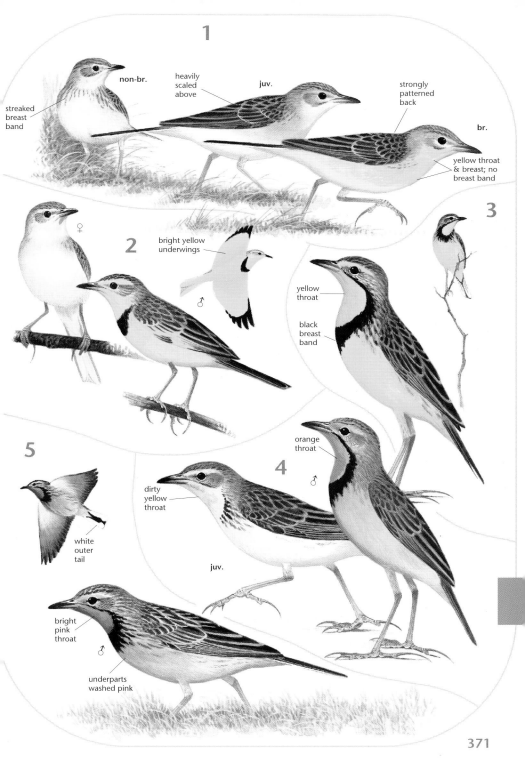

1

non-br.

streaked breast band

heavily scaled above

juv.

strongly patterned back

br.

yellow throat & breast; no breast band

2

♀

bright yellow underwings

♂

3

yellow throat

black breast band

4

orange throat

♂

dirty yellow throat

juv.

5

white outer tail

bright pink throat

♂

underparts washed pink

1. CRIMSON-BREASTED SHRIKE *Laniarius atrococcineus* (739)　　　23 cm
The striking combination of bright crimson underparts and black upperparts with a white wing bar renders this species unmistakable. A rare form occurs in which the crimson is replaced with yellow.
Juv. is barred with greyish brown, with varying amounts of crimson below; above, it is finely barred with black, with buff edges to the feathers. **Habitat.** Thornveld, dry river courses and semi-arid scrub. **Status.** Common resident; near-endemic. **Call.** A harsh 'trrrrr' and a whistled 'qwip-qwip' duet. (Rooiborslaksman)

2. MAGPIE (AFRICAN LONGTAILED) SHRIKE *Corvinella melanoleuca* (735)　40-50 cm
The combination of the black-and-white plumage and very long, wispy tail is diagnostic. Gregarious, it typically occurs in groups of four to eight birds.
Female has a shorter tail and whiter flanks than male. **Juv.** is shorter tailed than ad., and is dull black with fine barring. **Habitat.** Thornveld. **Status.** Common resident. **Call.** A liquid, whistled 'peeleeo'. (Langstertlaksman)

3. SOUZA'S SHRIKE *Lanius souzae* (734)　　　17 cm
Resembles a very pale female Red-backed Shrike but is easily distinguished by its white shoulder patches, brown, not black, tail and very pale grey head contrasting with the black mask. It may be distinguished from juv. Common Fiscal by its smaller size and by the lack of crescentic barring below.
Female resembles male but may be distinguished by its pale rufous flanks. **Juv.** lacks the grey on the head and is barred below. **Habitat.** Miombo and mopane woodlands. **Status.** Uncertain; possibly a very rare resident in the extreme north-central region. **Call.** Soft, grating sounds. (Souzase Laksman)

4. RED-BACKED SHRIKE *Lanius collurio* (733)　　　16-18 cm
In the region, the only shrike with a combination of a chestnut-coloured back and a grey crown.
Male has a blue-grey head and rump, and light underparts contrasting with the chestnut back; these are diagnostic. Female and **juv.** are duller reddish brown above, and have greyish brown crescentic barring below. **Habitat.** Thornveld and savanna. **Status.** Common summer visitor. **Call.** A harsh 'chak, chak' and a soft, warbler-like song. (Rooiruglaksman)

5. LESSER GREY SHRIKE *Lanius minor* (731)　　　20-22 cm
In comparison with Red-backed Shrike, this species is larger, has a more extensive black mask that encompasses the forehead, a grey, not chestnut, back and predominantly black, not brown, wings.
Female is duller, often with less black on the forehead. **Juv.** differs from juv. and female Red-backed Shrike by its much larger size and buffier, less barred underparts. **Habitat.** Mixed, dry thornveld and semi-desert scrub. **Status.** Common summer visitor. **Call.** A soft 'chuk'; a warbled song, heard before migration. (Gryslaksman)

6. COMMON FISCAL (FISCAL SHRIKE) *Lanius collaris* (732)　　　21-23 cm
One of the most common shrikes of the region, hunting from exposed perches along roadsides and in suburbia. Black-backed Puffback (p. 378) and boubous (p. 374) are also black and white but are shy, skulking birds. Shorter-tailed Fiscal Flycatcher (p. 354) male is similar but lacks the white shoulder patches and white outer tail feathers. Races of the arid west have a conspicuous white eyebrow stripe and are sometimes considered a different species, Latakoo Fiscal.
Male is black above and white below, with prominent white shoulder patches. Female resembles male but shows a rufous patch on the flanks. **Juv.** is greyish brown, with grey crescentic barring below. **Habitat.** Virtually every habitat except dense forest. **Status.** Common resident. **Call.** A harsh grating; a melodious, whistled song jumbled with harsher notes; and mimicry of other birds' calls. (Fiskaallaksman)

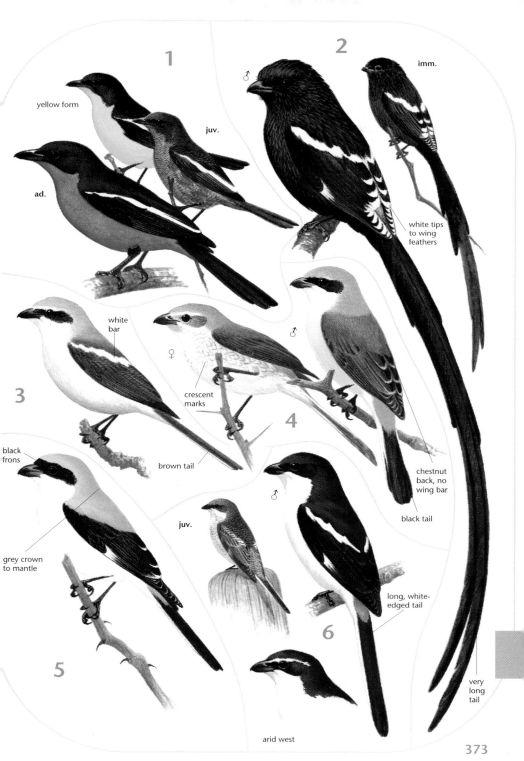

1

yellow form

ad.

juv.

2

♂

imm.

white tips
to wing
feathers

3

white
bar

♀

crescent
marks

♂

brown tail

chestnut
back, no
wing bar

black tail

4

black
frons

grey crown
to mantle

juv.

♂

long, white-
edged tail

5

6

arid west

very
long
tail

1. SOUTHERN BOUBOU *Laniarius ferrugineus* (736)　　20-22 cm

Similar to Common Fiscal (p. 372) but has a shorter tail and the white on the wing extends onto the secondaries; it is also shy and skulking in its habits. Distinguished from Tropical and Swamp Boubous by its rufous flanks, undertail and belly.
Female is slightly greyer above, with a rufous wash on the breast. **Juv.** is mottled buff-brown above and barred below. **Habitat.** Thickets in riverine and evergreen forests. **Status.** Common resident; endemic. **Call.** A variable duet with basic notes of 'boo-boo' followed by a whistled 'whee-ooo'. (Suidelike Waterfiskaal)

2. TROPICAL BOUBOU *Laniarius aethiopicus* (737)　　19-22 cm

Easily confused with Southern Boubou but paler below, showing a more marked contrast between its black upperparts and pinkish white underparts. The pink-tinged underparts differentiate this species from Swamp Boubou, which is pure white below. **Juv.** is duller than ad. and spotted with buff above and below. **Habitat.** Thickets, riverine and evergreen forests, gardens. **Status.** Common resident. **Call.** Duet, unlike that of Southern Boubou; also whistles, a croaking 'haw' and a tearing 'weer-weer' calls. (Tropiese Waterfiskaal)

3. SWAMP BOUBOU *Laniarius bicolor* (738)　　22-23 cm

Distinguished from both Southern and Tropical boubous by having pure white underparts with no trace of rufous or pink coloration.
Juv. is spotted with buff above and barred below. **Habitat.** Thickets alongside rivers, and papyrus swamps. **Status.** Common resident. **Call.** Duets of whistled 'hoouu' and harsh rattling sounds. (Moeraswaterfiskaal)

4. BLACK-CROWNED TCHAGRA *Tchagra senegalus* (744)　　19-22 cm

The black forehead and crown and the paler underparts differentiate it from other tchagras. It is also a larger, bolder bird and is more conspicuous in its behaviour.
Juv. has a mottled crown and a horn-coloured bill. **Habitat.** Mixed thornveld and riverine scrub. **Status.** Common resident. **Call.** Song consists of a loud, whistled 'whee-cheree, cherooo, cheree-cherooo' on a descending scale, becoming slurred towards the end. (Swartkroontjagra)

5. ANCHIETA'S (MARSH) TCHAGRA *Antichromus anchietae* (745)　　15-19 cm

This marsh-dwelling shrike is easily identified by its black cap, russet upperparts and creamy to buff underparts.
Female has a broad, white eyebrow stripe. **Juv.** resembles female but has an off-white crown. **Habitat.** Rank bracken and sedges growing in damp hollows, and marshy areas with long grass. **Status.** Uncommon, localised resident. **Call.** A shrill, trilling song, given in display flight. (Vleitjagra)

6. BROWN-CROWNED (THREESTREAKED) TCHAGRA
Tchagra australis (743)　　17-19 cm

Very similar in appearance to Southern Tchagra, but this species has a paler crown and forehead, and its broad, white eyebrow stripe is bordered by black stripes. It is also smaller and paler, and has a less massive bill.
Juv. is duller than ad. **Habitat.** Thick tangles and undergrowth in thornveld. **Status.** Common resident. **Call.** Aerial display flight and song very similar to those of Southern Tchagra. (Rooivlerktjagra)

7. SOUTHERN TCHAGRA *Tchagra tchagra* (742)　　17-21 cm

Differs from the similar Brown-crowned Tchagra by its longer, heavier bill and by the lack of conspicuous black stripes bordering its buff eyebrow stripe. It is also slightly larger and darker in appearance.
Juv. is duller than ad. **Habitat.** Coastal scrub, forest edges and thickets. **Status.** Common resident; endemic. **Call.** Song, given in aerial display, a 'wee-chee-chee-cheee', descending in pitch. (Grysborstjagra)

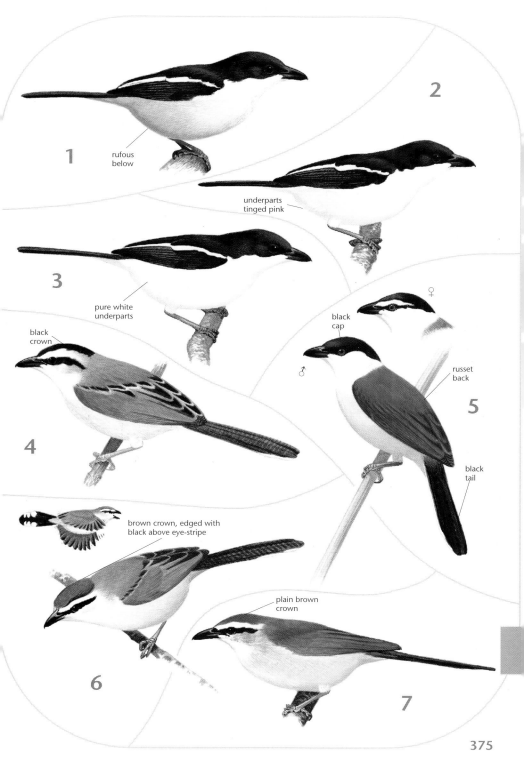

1
rufous below

2
underparts tinged pink

3
pure white underparts

4
black crown

5
♀
black cap
♂
russet back
black tail

6
brown crown, edged with black above eye-stripe

7
plain brown crown

1. GREY-HEADED BUSH-SHRIKE *Malaconotus blanchoti* (751)   24-26 cm
Its large size and heavy, hooked bill prevent confusion with Orange-breasted and Black-fronted Bush-Shrikes. The bright yellow underparts sometimes have a faint orange wash across the breast.
Juv. has a greyish, barred head and is pale yellow below. **Habitat.** Thornveld and mixed, broad-leaved woodland. **Status.** Common resident. **Call.** A drawn-out 'oooooop' (hence colloquial name 'Ghostbird') and a 'tic-tic-oooop'. (Spookvoël)

2. BOKMAKIERIE *Telophorus zeylonus* (746)   22-23 cm
The bright lemon-yellow underparts and broad, black breast band are diagnostic. The vivid yellow tip to the dark green tail is conspicuous in flight.
Juv. lacks the breast band of ad. and is greyish green below. **Habitat.** Fynbos, Karoo scrub and suburban gardens. **Status.** Common resident; endemic. **Call.** Very varied, but usually a 'bok-bok-kik'. (Bokmakierie)

3. GORGEOUS BUSH-SHRIKE *Telophorus quadricolor* (747)   18 cm
More often heard than seen, but the bright red throat, black breast band and yellow-orange belly are diagnostic.
Female is duller than male. **Juv.** has a yellow throat, lacks the black breast band of ad., and is distinguished from juv. Orange-breasted and Black-fronted Bush-Shrikes by its green (not grey) crown and mantle. **Habitat.** Dense tangled thickets. **Status.** Common resident. **Call.** An often-repeated 'kong-kong-kooit', and variations of this. (Konkoit)

4. BLACK-FRONTED BUSH-SHRIKE *Telophorus nigrifrons* (749)   18-19 cm
Can be confused with Orange-breasted Bush-Shrike (which lacks the broad, black face mask and forehead and has a yellow eyebrow), and the olive form of Olive Bush-Shrike (which has a green, not black, forehead).
Female has reduced black on the forehead and is duller than male. **Juv.** has buff-yellow, barred underparts. **Habitat.** A less skulking species than other bush-shrikes, it frequents the canopy of evergreen forests. **Status.** Uncommon, localised resident. **Call.** A harsh 'tic-chrrrrr' and a ringing 'oo-pooo' **Call.** (Swartoogboslaksman)

5. OLIVE BUSH-SHRIKE *Telophorus olivaceus* (750)   17-18 cm
Occurs in two colour forms. The ruddy form has a blue-grey head and, unlike any other bush-shrike, has a white eyebrow stripe. The olive form is duller: the bird has a green (not blue-grey) crown and nape and lacks the white eyebrow stripe.
Female of both forms lacks black on the cheeks. **Juv.** of both forms lacks head markings of ad. and is faintly barred below. **Habitat.** Evergreen and riverine forests. **Status.** Common resident. **Call.** Varied; includes a whistled 'cheeoo-cheeoo-cheeoo-cheeoo' and a call similar to Orange-breasted Bush-Shrike's 'poo-poo-poo-poooo'. (Olyfboslaksman)

6. ORANGE-BREASTED BUSH-SHRIKE *Telophorus sulfureopectus* (748)   16-18 cm
Differs from all other similar bush-shrikes by its conspicuous yellow forehead and eyebrow stripe. It superficially resembles a diminutive Grey-headed Bush-Shrike.
Female is duller than male. **Juv.** is distinguished from juv. Black-fronted Bush-Shrike by being paler grey on the head and paler yellow below. It resembles juv. Olive Bush-Shrike (ruddy form). **Habitat.** Thornveld and riverine forests. **Status.** Common resident. **Call.** Frequently repeated 'poo-poo-poo-pooooo' and a 'titit-eeezz'. (Oranjeborsboslaksman)

plain grey head, pale orange eye

juv.

juv.

1

ad.

2

juv.

yellow throat

black breast band

3

juv.

red throat

black band

ad.

ad.

juv.

5

♀

black forehead

♀

♂

4

black eyebrow ends before bill

juv.

olive form

yellow forehead & eyebrow

ad.

ruddy form

6

juv.

1. CHESTNUT-FRONTED HELMET-SHRIKE *Prionops scopifrons* (755)   16-18 cm
The chestnut-coloured forehead and blue, not red, eye-ring differentiate this species from Retz's Helmet-Shrike. It differs further in having a dark grey (not jet-black) body. It is a gregarious species.
Juv. is uniform grey, and lacks the bristly, chestnut forehead. **Habitat.** Lowland forests. **Status.** Uncommon, localised resident. **Call.** A repeated 'churee', with bill-snapping and other notes. (Stekelkophelmlaksman)

2. RETZ'S (REDBILLED) HELMET-SHRIKE *Prionops retzii* (754)   19-21 cm
Larger than Chestnut-fronted Helmet-Shrike, lacks the chestnut forehead, and has a red eye-ring and jet-black (not dark grey) plumage. It is a gregarious species.
Juv. is paler than ad., with a brown eye-ring, bill and legs. **Habitat.** Mostly mopane and miombo woodlands. **Status.** Common resident. **Call.** Harsh grating calls, much like those of White-crested Helmet-Shrike. (Swarthelmlaksman)

3. WHITE-CRESTED (WHITE) HELMET-SHRIKE *Prionops plumatus* (753)   17-20 cm
The grey crown, white collar, white flashes in the wings and white outer tail feathers are diagnostic. It is a gregarious and conspicuous species.
Juv. is duller than ad., with a brown eye; it lacks the yellow eye-ring and black ear coverts. **Habitat.** Mixed woodland and thornveld. **Status.** Common resident with local movements and occasional 'invasions' beyond its normal range. **Call.** A repeated 'cherow', often taken up by the group in chorus. (Withelmlaksman)

4. WHITE-TAILED SHRIKE *Lanioturdus torquatus* (752)   15 cm
The striking black, white and grey plumage, long legs and very short, white tail are diagnostic. It is often seen on the ground or hopping over rocks; with its very upright posture it appears almost tailless. Found in pairs and small groups.
Juv. resembles ad. but has a mottled crown. **Habitat.** Dry thornveld and scrub desert. **Status.** Common resident; near-endemic. **Call.** Clear, drawn-out whistles and harsh cackling. (Kortstertlaksman)

5. SOUTHERN WHITE-CROWNED SHRIKE *Eurocephalus anguitimens* (756)   24 cm
This large, robust bird is the only shrike in the region to have a white crown and forehead. The throat and breast are also white, while the belly and flanks are washed with buff. Extensive black ear coverts, grey-brown nape and back, and dark eye separate it from Southern Pied and Bare-cheeked Babblers (p. 308). Gregarious, it usually occurs in groups of five or six birds.
Juv. is paler than ad., with a mottled crown. **Habitat.** Mixed dry woodland and thornveld. **Status.** Common resident; near-endemic. **Call.** A shrill, whistling 'kree, kree, kree', bleating and harsh chattering. (Kremetartlaksman)

6. BRUBRU *Nilaus afer* (741)   12-13,5 cm
Size, thick bill and broad, straight white eyebrow stripe should prevent confusion with batises (p. 360). The combination of chequered back, broad white eyebrow stripe and russet flank stripe is diagnostic.
Female is duller than male. Juv. is mottled with buff and brown above and below. **Habitat.** Dry thornveld and open broad-leaved woodland. **Status.** Common resident. **Call.** A soft, trilling 'prrrrr', given by male, often answered by 'eeeu' from female. (Bontroklaksman)

7. BLACK-BACKED PUFFBACK *Dryoscopus cubla* (740)   16-18 cm
The only shrike in the region to have a large, white rump, which is conspicuous (in male) when it is spread and puffed up during display. At other times the bird resembles a small boubou but has a shorter tail, white wing coverts and a bright red eye.
Male is glossy black above. Female is duller than male, and has a white eyebrow. Juv. resembles female but has a brown eye. **Habitat.** A wide variety of woodland and forests. **Status.** Common resident. **Call.** A sharp, repeated 'chick, weeo'. (Sneeubal)

1

blue eye-ring,
chestnut forehead

2

red eye-ring,
black forehead

3

4

yellow
eye

short,
white
tail

black
breast
band

7

red eye

white
rump

♀

white
flanks

dark cap
& red eye

♂

white
crown

dark
ear
coverts

broad
supercilium

dark
crown

♀

russet
flanks

♂ display

5

♂

6

379

1. GREATER BLUE-EARED STARLING *Lamprotornis chalybaeus* (765)   23-24 cm
Distinguished from Cape Glossy Starling by its broad, dark blue (not green) ear patch and blue (not green) belly and flanks. Larger than Miombo Blue-eared Starling, it also has a broader ear patch and blue (not magenta) belly and flanks. **Juv.** is less glossy than ad. **Habitat.** Thornveld and mopane woodland. **Status.** Common resident. **Call.** A distinctive, nasal 'squee-aar' (unlike any call of Cape Glossy Starling) and a warbled song. (Grootblouoorglansspreeu)

2. CAPE GLOSSY STARLING *Lamprotornis nitens* (764)   25 cm
The short-tailed 'glossy' starlings are difficult to distinguish in the field unless seen at close range. This species differs from Greater Blue-eared and Miombo Blue-eared Starlings by its uniformly glossy green ear patches and head and glossy green belly and flanks. It may be distinguished from the smaller Black-bellied Starling by its generally brighter, shinier plumage and by the belly being green, not dull black. **Juv.** is duller than ad., with dull straw-yellow (not bright orange-yellow) eyes. **Habitat.** Thornveld, mixed woodland and suburbia. **Status.** Common, widespread resident. **Call.** Song a slurred 'trrr-chree-chrrrr'. (Kleinglansspreeu)

3. MIOMBO (SOUTHERN LESSER) BLUE-EARED STARLING
Lamprotornis elisabeth (766)   18-20 cm
Although it could be confused with Greater Blue-eared Starling, this is a smaller bird with a more compact head and a finer bill. The dark blue ear patch is less extensive and appears as a black line through and behind the eye. The belly and flanks are magenta (not blue). **Juv.** has distinctive chestnut underparts or mottled blue-and-brown plumage. **Habitat.** Confined to miombo woodland. **Status.** Common, localised resident. **Call.** Higher pitched than that of Greater Blue-eared Starling, and with a 'wirri-girri' flight call. (Kleinblouoorglansspreeu)

4. VIOLET-BACKED (PLUMCOLOURED) STARLING
Cinnyricinclus leucogaster (761)   15-17 cm
Male's upperparts and throat are an unusual, glossy amethyst colour; this colour may vary with wear from bluish to coppery. **Female** and **juv.** birds are very different in appearance, with brown, thrush-like plumage. Juv. resembles female, with dark eyes. **Habitat.** Most woodland, but avoids thick, evergreen forests. **Status.** Common summer visitor. **Call.** A soft but sharp 'tip, tip'; song a short series of buzzy whistles. (Witborsspreeu)

5. BLACK-BELLIED STARLING *Lamprotornis corruscus* (768)   18-21 cm
The smallest and least glossy of all the starlings in this group, having a black belly and flanks.
Male has a bronze gloss on the belly that is visible at close range, and has red, not yellow-orange, eyes for a short period during the breeding season. Female and juv. are duller than male and appear black in the field. **Habitat.** Coastal and riverine forests. **Status.** Locally common resident; irregular visitor in the extreme south of its range. **Call.** Harsh, chippering notes interspersed with shrill whistles. (Swartpensglansspreeu)

1

dark, broad mask

sturdy bill

blue belly & flanks

juv.

blackish below

2

no facial mask

3

dark, narrow mask

ad.

juv.

magenta belly & flanks

dark chestnut below

4

♀

juv.

♂

5

black belly and flanks

1. BURCHELL'S STARLING *Lamprotornis australis* (762)　　　　32-34 cm
Larger and more heavily built than Meves's Starling. This species has broader, more rounded wings and a shorter, broader tail, although the tail is proportionally longer than that of other, smaller, glossy starlings.
Juv. is duller than ad. **Habitat.** Thornveld and dry broad-leaved woodland. **Status.** Common resident, near endemic. **Call.** Song a jumble of throaty chortles and chuckles. (Grootglansspreeu)

2. MEVES'S (LONGTAILED) STARLING *Lamprotornis mevesii* (763)　　　34-36 cm
The long, pointed tail is diagnostic. Although similar, this species is a smaller bodied, more compact bird than Burchell's Starling. These are the only two glossy starlings with dark eyes (in ad.). Usually in groups.
Sexes are similar but female is smaller. **Juv.** is duller in colour than ad. but the long, pointed tail is evident. **Habitat.** Tall mopane woodland and riverine forests. **Status.** Common but localised resident. **Call.** A harsh 'keeeaaaa' and churring notes. (Langstertglansspreeu)

3. SHARP-TAILED STARLING *Lamprotornis acuticaudus* (767)　　　　26 cm
Difficult to distinguish from the other short-tailed, glossy starlings unless the diagnostic wedge-shaped tail is seen. In flight, the underside of the primaries appears pale (not black as in other similar starlings).
Sexes differ in eye colour; red in male, orange in female. **Juv.** is duller than ad., and is greyish below, with buff-edged feathers. **Habitat.** Dry, broad-leaved woodland and dry rivercourses. **Status.** Uncommon resident. **Call.** A reedy 'chwee-chwee-chwee' when in a flock. (Spitsstertglansspreeu)

4. PALE-WINGED STARLING *Onychognathus nabouroup* (770)　　　26-28 cm
Could be confused with Red-winged Starling but has a predominantly cream-coloured (not chestnut) patch in the primaries, visible only in flight. It shows a bright orange (not dark) eye.
Juv. is duller than ad. **Habitat.** Rocky ravines and cliffs in dry and desert regions. **Status.** Common resident and local nomad; near-endemic. **Call.** In flight, a ringing 'preeoo'; warbling calls like those of Cape Glossy Starling (p. 380), quite unlike the whistles of Red-winged Starling. (Bleekvlerkspreeu)

5. RED-WINGED STARLING *Onychognathus morio* (769)　　　27-30 cm
The bright chestnut flight feathers with dark tips and dark (not orange) eyes differentiate this species from Pale-winged Starling.
Female has an ash-grey head and upper breast. **Juv.** resembles male. **Habitat.** Rocky ravines, cliffs and suburbia. **Status.** Common resident. **Call.** A clear, whistled 'cher-leeeeoo', and a variety of other, musical whistles. (Rooivlerkspreeu)

dark brown eye

heavy build

1

long, rounded tail

slim build

long, pointed tail

3

juv.

2

bright orange eye

dark red eye

♂

4

long, wedge-shaped tail

cream

♀

dark red eye

chestnut flight feathers

♂

5

1. COMMON (INDIAN) MYNA *Acridotheres tristis* (758) 25 cm
The only myna of the region and unlikely to be confused with any starling because of its white wing patches, white tips to the tail feathers and bare yellow skin around the eyes. Moulting ads sometimes lose most of their head feathers and the head then appears yellow.
Juv. is paler than ad. **Habitat.** Urban and suburban regions. **Status.** Locally abundant introduced resident. **Call.** Jumbled titters and chattering. (Indiese Spreeu)

2. COMMON (EUROPEAN) STARLING *Sturnus vulgaris* (757) 20-22 cm
Breeding male is easily identified by its yellow beak and glossy black plumage speckled with white. Non-breeding male has a dark bill.
Female has a paler abdomen and is more speckled. **Juv.** resembles female Wattled Starling but is uniformly grey, lacks the pale rump, and has a dark bill. **Habitat.** A wide range of habitats, from cities to open farmland, but always close to human habitation. **Status.** Common to abundant introduced resident. **Call.** Song includes mimicry, whistles and chattering. (Europese Spreeu)

3. WATTLED STARLING *Creatophora cinerea* (760) 19-21 cm
This species has a short tail and pointed wings like Common Starling, but always shows a greyish white rump in flight.
Breeding male is distinctive with its pale grey body, black-and-yellow head and black wattles; all ad. males have black wings and tail. Female is grey with a whitish rump. **Juv.** resembles female but is browner. **Habitat.** Grassland and open, broad-leaved woodland. Often in large flocks. **Status.** Common, nomadic resident. **Call.** Various hisses and cackles, and a 'ssreeeeo' note. (Lelspreeu)

4. (AFRICAN) PIED STARLING *Spreo bicolor* (759) 27-28 cm
This large, dark brownish black starling is distinguished by its conspicuous white vent and undertail coverts. At close range the diagnostic yellow base to the lower mandible and the bright creamy white eyes can be seen.
Juv. is matt black, with a dark eye and a paler base to the bill. **Habitat.** Grassland and Karoo scrub, often around farmyards and stock. Usually in flocks. **Status.** Common resident; endemic. **Call.** A loud 'skeer-kerrra-kerrra'; also a warbling song. (Witgatspreeu)

5. RED-BILLED OXPECKER *Buphagus erythrorhynchus* (772) 19-21 cm
Distinguished from Yellow-billed Oxpecker by its all-red bill, the bare yellow skin around the eyes and the dark (not pale) rump.
Juv. has a predominantly black bill, is overall darker than juv. Yellow-billed Oxpecker, and has a dark (not pale) rump. **Habitat.** Savanna, in association with game and cattle. Usually in flocks. **Status.** Common resident in game reserves; scarce elsewhere. Formerly more widespread. **Call.** A scolding 'churrrr' and a hissing 'zzzzzzist'. (Rooibekrenostervoël)

6. YELLOW-BILLED OXPECKER *Buphagus africanus* (771) 19-22 cm
Paler than Red-billed Oxpecker and easily identified by its bright yellow bill with a red tip, as well as by the pale lower back and rump.
Juv. has a brown (not black) bill and is paler than juv. Red-billed Oxpecker. The pale back and rump contrast with rest of upperparts. **Habitat.** Thornveld and broad-leaved woodland, often near water. Frequently found in association with buffalo, rhino and hippo. Usually in flocks. **Status.** Locally common resident, formerly more widespread. **Call.** A short, hissing 'kriss, kriss'. (Geelbekrenostervoël)

1

bare yellow skin

white wing patch

white tip

2

juv.

ad. non-br.

ad. br.

3

white rump

♂ br.

ad. non-br.

white rump

4

pale eye

white vent

5

yellow eye-ring

red base

ad.

dark rump

juv.

lacks eye-ring

yellow base

ad.

pale rump

6

juv.

1. GURNEY'S SUGARBIRD *Promerops gurneyi* (774)   m=29 cm; f=23 cm
Unlikely to be confused with Cape Sugarbird because of its smaller size, shorter tail, and conspicuous russet breast and crown. Ranges of the two do not overlap. **Sexes** often indistinguishable; male usually has a marginally longer tail. **Juv.** resembles female. **Habitat.** Stands of flowering proteas and aloes in mountainous regions. **Status.** Common but localised resident; some movement to lower altitudes in winter. Endemic. **Call.** A higher pitched, more melodious, rattling song than that of Cape Sugarbird. (Rooiborssuikervoël)

2. CAPE SUGARBIRD *Promerops cafer* (773)   m=34-44 cm; f=25-29 cm
Cape Sugarbird is easily distinguished from Gurney's Sugarbird by its exceptionally long, wispy tail; it has a brown, not russet, breast and crown and has distinct malar stripes.
Male's tail constitutes 65% or more of the total body length. Female's constitutes only 50% of the total body length. Female's bill is shorter and the breast is less heavily marked. **Juv.** resembles female. **Habitat.** Stands of flowering proteas at all altitudes and in commercial protea nurseries. **Status.** Common resident; endemic. **Call.** A complex song, including starling-like chirps and whistles, as well as harsh, grating noises. (Kaapse Suikervoël)

3. MALACHITE SUNBIRD *Nectarinia famosa* (775)   m=25 cm; f=15 cm
Breeding male has metallic green plumage with yellow pectoral tufts and elongated central tail feathers. Bronzy Sunbird also has tail projections but that species appears black in the field.
Male in eclipse plumage resembles female. With its brown back, female is very similar to female Bronzy Sunbird, but is larger, paler yellow below and lacks distinct streaking below. **Juv.** resembles female. **Habitat.** Fynbos, protea- and aloe-covered hills and in montane and coastal scrub; also gardens and parks. **Status.** Common resident; some movement to lower altitudes in winter. **Call.** A loud 'tseep-tseep'; song a series of twittering notes. (Jangroentjie)

4. BRONZY (BRONZE) SUNBIRD *Nectarinia kilimensis* (776)   m=22 cm; f=13 cm
Slightly smaller than the similarly shaped Malachite Sunbird with a more sharply decurved bill.
Male has metallic bronze plumage appearing black unless seen in good light; it has no eclipse plumage. Female resembles female Malachite Sunbird but is smaller, has a shorter, more decurved bill, and has brighter yellow underparts that are distinctly streaked with brown. It has slightly elongated central tail feathers (tail of female Malachite Sunbird is square ended). **Juv.** resembles female. **Habitat.** Evergreen forest edges, bracken and adjoining grassland. **Status.** Common but localised resident. **Call.** A loud, piercing 'chee-wit', repeated at half-second intervals; also high-pitched twittering. (Bronssuikerbekkie)

5. ORANGE-BREASTED SUNBIRD *Anthobaphes violacea* (777)   m=15 cm; f=12 cm
The dark head, orange-yellow breast and belly, and elongated central tail feathers of male are diagnostic.
Female is larger than female Southern Double-collared Sunbird (p. 392) and is more uniformly olive-green above and below. **Juv.** resembles female. **Habitat.** Fynbos, and flowering montane protea and aloe stands. **Status.** Common resident; endemic. **Call.** A metallic twanging; rapid 'ticks', given in pursuit flight and a jumbled, twittering song that includes mimicry of other species. (Oranjeborssuikerbekkie)

1

russet
crown

♀

russet
breast ♂

2

brown
crown

♂

♀

malar
stripe

very
long tail

eclipse
plumage ♂

♀

square-
ended
tail

♂ br.

3

4

♂

♀

5

♂ sub-ad.

♀

yellow-
olive
above

♂

slightly
pointed
tail

SUNBIRDS

1. SCARLET-CHESTED SUNBIRD *Chalcomitra senegalensis* (791)   15 cm
Male's black body and scarlet chest are diagnostic. There is no eclipse plumage.
Female is greyish olive above and may be distinguished from female Amethyst Sunbird by the very heavily mottled underparts. **Juv.** resembles female. **Habitat.** Woodland, savanna and suburban gardens. **Status.** Common, widespread resident. **Call.** A loud, whistled 'cheeup, chup, toop, toop, toop' song. (Rooiborssuikerbekkie)

2. AMETHYST (AFRICAN BLACK) SUNBIRD *Chalcomitra amethystina* (792)   15 cm
At a distance male appears all black, but at close range has a greenish iridescence on the forehead and a metallic purple throat. Species has no eclipse plumage.
Female could be confused with female Scarlet-chested Sunbird but has paler underparts, which are streaked rather than mottled. **Habitat.** Forest edge, woodland, savanna and suburban gardens. **Status.** Common resident. **Call.** A fast, twittering song. (Swartsuikerbekkie)

3. COPPER (COPPERY) SUNBIRD *Cinnyris cuprea* (778)   13 cm
Male resembles a small Bronzy Sunbird (p. 386) but lacks elongated tail feathers.
Female is much smaller than female Malachite and Bronzy Sunbirds (p. 386), and is brighter yellow below with faint speckling on the throat and breast. **Juv.** resembles female, but juv. male's throat is dark. **Habitat.** Diverse; usually woodland, forest edges and clearings, and riverine forests. **Status.** Uncommon, localised breeding summer visitor. **Call.** A harsh 'chit-chat'; a soft, warbling song. (Kopersuikerbekkie)

4. SHELLEY'S SUNBIRD *Cinnyris shelleyi* (781)   12 cm
Occurs in association with the similar Miombo Double-collared Sunbird (p. 392), but male can be distinguished by its black (not pale olive) belly and green (not blue) rump.
Female differs from female Miombo Double-collared Sunbird in having the yellow underparts lightly streaked with brown. **Juv.** resembles female. **Habitat.** Miombo and riverine scrub. **Status.** Uncertain: recently reported from south bank of the Zambezi River, east of Lake Kariba and west of Victoria Falls. **Call.** A 'didi-didi'; a nasal 'chibbee-cheeu-cheeu' song. (Swartpenssuikerbekkie)

5. GREY SUNBIRD *Cyanomitra veroxii* (789)   14 cm
A dull-coloured sunbird with uniformly pale grey underparts and darker grey upperparts. It differs from Eastern Olive Sunbird by its call, its grey coloration and red pectoral tufts. Forehead and shoulder faintly washed with green.
Juv. resembles ad. but is more olive below. **Habitat.** Coastal and riverine forests. **Status.** Common but localised resident. **Call.** A harsh, grating 'tzzik, tzzik'; a short 'chrep, chreep, peepy' song. (Gryssuikerbekkie)

6. WESTERN OLIVE SUNBIRD *Cyanomitra obscura* (953)   11-15 cm
Male indistinguishable in the field from Eastern Olive Sunbird, but ranges of the two species do not overlap.
Female lacks the yellow pectoral tufts of female Eastern Olive Sunbird. **Juv.** has a paler throat than ad. **Habitat.** Montane forest. **Status.** Common resident in the eastern highlands of Zimbabwe. **Call.** Song resembles that of Eastern Olive Sunbird, but is slightly slower and less variable in pitch. (Hoogland-olyfsuikerbekkie)

7. EASTERN OLIVE SUNBIRD *Cyanomitra olivacea* (790)   11-15 cm
Generally dull olive, darker above and paler below. The yellow pectoral tufts of males and females are concealed when the bird is perched. It is likely to be confused only with Grey Sunbird, which occurs in the same habitat, and with Western Olive Sunbird, although their ranges do not overlap. .
Juv. has a rust-coloured throat. **Habitat.** Coastal, riverine and mist-belt forests; moist, broad-leaved woodland. **Status.** Common resident. **Call.** A sharp 'tuk, tuk, tuk'; an accelerating, descending, piping song. (Olyfsuikerbekkie)

1
♂
♀
dark, mottled
underparts

2
♀
pale, streaked
underparts
♂

3
♀
♂
dark
overall
short
tail

4
♀
streaked
underparts
♂
broad
red band
black
belly
green
rump

5
uniform
pale grey
underparts

6
7
yellow
tufts
♀
unstreaked
dull olive
underparts
no yellow
tufts
♀

1. COLLARED SUNBIRD *Hedydipna collaris* (793)　　　　　10 cm
Smaller than similarly coloured Variable Sunbird, with a much shorter bill and a green (not blue) throat extending only to the upper breast.
Female is metallic green above and uniformly yellow below, and resembles a small warbler. **Juv.** resembles female. **Habitat.** Mist-belt, coastal and riverine forests, and dense woodland. **Status.** Common resident. **Call.** A soft 'tswee'; a harsh, chirpy song. (Kortbeksuikerbekkie)

2. PLAIN-BACKED (BLUETHROATED) SUNBIRD
Anthreptes reichenowi (794)　　　　　10 cm
Warbler-like in appearance. The size of Collared Sunbird, but slimmer bodied, and bright yellow below with dull, brownish green upperparts.
Male has a blue-black forehead and large throat patch ; may be confused with juv. male Variable and White-bellied Sunbirds moulting into full ad. plumage. Female's dull green upperparts distinguish her from female Collared Sunbird. **Juv.** resembles female. **Habitat.** Mixed moist woodland and coastal forests. **Status.** Uncommon to locally common resident. **Call.** A sharp 'tik-tik'. (Bloukeelsuikerbekkie)

3. VARIABLE (YELLOWBELLIED) SUNBIRD *Cinnyris venustus* (786)　　　　　11 cm
Male superficially resembles smaller Collared Sunbird but has a much longer bill, more blue than green on the back and head, and a broad, purple breast band.
Female resembles female White-bellied Sunbird but differs in having a pale yellow belly and flanks. **Juv.** resembles female. Juv. male can resemble ad. male Plain-backed Sunbird, but has a small, metallic green wrist patch and lacks the blue forehead. **Habitat.** Miombo and broad-leaved riverine woodland. **Status.** Locally common resident in Zimbabwe and Mozambique, with vagrants farther south. **Call.** A 'tsui-tse-tse'; a trilling song. (Geelpenssuikerbekkie)

4. WHITE-BELLIED SUNBIRD *Cinnyris talatala* (787)　　　　　11 cm
Male is the only sunbird in the region to have a bottle-green head and breast and a white belly.
Female is very similar to females of several other species, being uniformly dull brown above and off-white below, with a few indistinct streaks. **Juv.** resembles female. Juv. male may resemble ad. male Plain-backed Sunbird, but has a small, metallic green wrist patch and lacks the blue forehead. **Habitat.** Dry woodland and savanna; parks and gardens. **Status.** Common and widespread resident. **Call.** A loud 'pichee, pichee', followed by a rapid tinkle of notes. (Witpenssuikerbekkie)

5. WESTERN VIOLET-BACKED SUNBIRD *Anthreptes longuemarei* (795)　　　　　13 cm
Male's dark violet head, back and tail are diagnostic, and are most obvious when seen in sunlight.
Female is brown above and white below, with a violet tail and a conspicuous white eyebrow stripe. **Juv.** lacks the violet on the tail and resembles juv. White-bellied or Variable Sunbirds, but has a very much shorter bill. **Habitat.** Miombo woodland. **Status.** Uncommon, localised resident. **Call.** A sharp 'chit-chit' or 'skee'. (Blousuikerbekkie)

6. DUSKY SUNBIRD *Cinnyris fuscus* (788)　　　　　10 cm
The slightly metallic, black head, throat, upper breast and back and contrasting white belly are diagnostic in male. However, male plumage is variable and sometimes there is only a black line running from the throat onto the breast. The pectoral tufts are orange.
Female is a light grey-brown above and off-white below. It resembles female Southern Double-collared (p. 392) and White-bellied sunbirds, but is paler and more uniformly coloured below. **Juv.** resembles female but has a blackish throat. **Habitat.** Dry thornveld, dry, wooded, rocky valleys and scrub desert. **Status.** Common resident and nomad; near-endemic. **Call.** A 'chrrrr-chrrrr'; a short, warbling song. (Namakwasuikerbekkie)

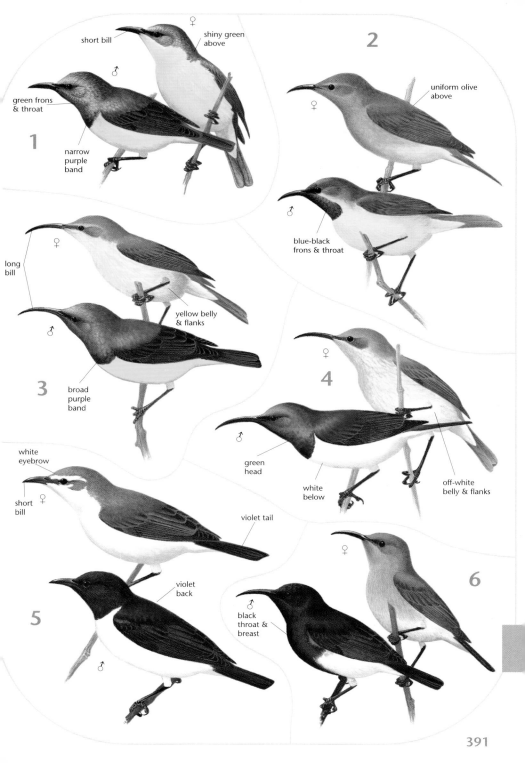

1
♀ shiny green above
short bill
♂
green frons & throat
narrow purple band

2
uniform olive above
♀
♂
blue-black frons & throat

3
long bill
♀
yellow belly & flanks
♂
broad purple band

4
♀
♂
green head
white below
off-white belly & flanks

5
white eyebrow
short bill
♀
violet tail
violet back
♂

6
♀
♂
black throat & breast

391

1. GREATER DOUBLE-COLLARED SUNBIRD *Cinnyris afer* (785)　　　　14 cm
This species is larger than Southern Double-collared Sunbird and with a longer, heavier bill; male has a much broader red breast band.
Female has grey-brown upperparts and yellow-grey underparts. It differs from female Southern Double-collared Sunbird by its larger size and longer, heavier bill. **Juv.** resembles female. **Habitat.** Fynbos, evergreen scrub, forest fringes and suburbia. **Status.** Common resident; endemic. **Call.** A harsh, frequently repeated 'tchut-tchut-tchut'; a fast, twittering song. (Groot-rooibandsuikerbekkie)

2. SOUTHERN (LESSER) DOUBLE-COLLARED SUNBIRD *Cinnyris chalybeus* (783) 12 cm
Male is very similar to but smaller than Greater Double-collared Sunbird, and may be distinguished from that species by its shorter bill and narrower red breast band.
Female is most similar to female Orange-breasted Sunbird (p. 386), but is greyer below; not as pale as female Dusky Sunbird (p. 390). **Juv.** resembles female. **Habitat.** Coastal scrub, fynbos, forests. **Status.** Common resident, endemic. **Call.** A harsh 'chee-chee'; a fast, rising and falling song. (Klein-rooibandsuikerbekkie)

3. MIOMBO DOUBLE-COLLARED SUNBIRD *Cinnyris manoensis* (784)　　　13 cm
Occurring in the same habitats as the very similar Shelley's Sunbird (p. 388), this species is distinguished by its pale olive (not black) belly and blue, not green, rump. In the field, male of this species – apart from its grey upper rump and lower back – is virtually indistinguishable from Southern Double-collared Sunbird, but their ranges do not overlap.
Female is buffy green above and pale yellowish grey below. **Juv.** resembles female. **Habitat.** Miombo woodland and edges of montane forest. **Status.** Common resident. **Call.** Similar to that of Southern Double-collared Sunbird. (Miombo-rooibandsuikerbekkie)

4. MARICO SUNBIRD *Cinnyris mariquensis* (779)　　　　11-13,5 cm
May be distinguished from the very similar Purple-banded Sunbird by its larger size, longer, thicker bill and broader purple breast band. It differs from the double-collared sunbirds by its black (not grey) belly and from Shelley's (p. 388) and Neergaard's Sunbirds by its purple (not red) breast band.
Female has grey-brown upperparts and pale yellow, dusky-streaked underparts. It may be distinguished from female Purple-banded Sunbird by its larger size and longer, thicker bill. **Juv.** resembles female. **Habitat.** Thornveld and dry, broad-leaved woodland. **Status.** Common resident. **Call.** A long series of closely spaced 'tsip's; a fast, warbling song. (Maricosuikerbekkie)

5. NEERGAARD'S SUNBIRD *Cinnyris neergaardi* (782)　　　　10 cm
Within its restricted range, male of this green-and-black sunbird cannot be confused with any other sunbird. It is small, with a thin, short, decurved bill, a black belly and a narrow red breast band.
Female's upperparts are greyish brown and the underparts a pale, dull yellow. It differs from female Purple-banded Sunbird (with which it coexists) by its paler, unstreaked underparts. **Juv.** resembles female. **Habitat.** Thornveld and sand forests. **Status.** Common but very localised resident; endemic. **Call.** A thin, wispy 'weesi-weesi-weesi'; a short, chippy song. (Bloukruissuikerbekkie)

6. PURPLE-BANDED SUNBIRD *Cinnyris bifasciatus* (780)　　　　9-11 cm
Smaller than Marico Sunbird, with a thinner, shorter and less decurved bill. Male differs from male Neergaard's Sunbird in having a purple (not red) breast band.
Female is less yellow below and has a shorter bill than does female Marico Sunbird. **Juv.** resembles female but has a dark throat. **Habitat.** Thornveld, moist broad-leaved woodland and coastal forest and scrub. **Status.** Common resident. **Call.** A high-pitched 'teeet-teeet-tit-tit' song, accelerating at the end, never sustained as is the song of Marico Sunbird. (Purperbandsuikerbekkie)

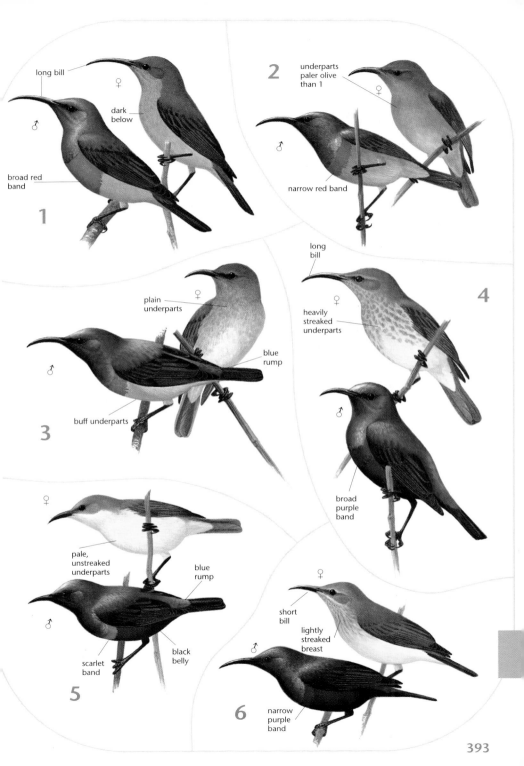

1
long bill
♀
dark below
♂
broad red band

2
underparts paler olive than 1
♀
♂
narrow red band

3
plain underparts
♀
blue rump
♂
buff underparts

4
long bill
♀
heavily streaked underparts
♂
broad purple band

5
♀
pale, unstreaked underparts
blue rump
♂
scarlet band
black belly

6
♀
short bill
lightly streaked breast
♂
narrow purple band

1. GREAT SPARROW *Passer motitensis* (802) 15 cm

A larger and brighter, more colourful version of House Sparrow. Differs from House Sparrow by its larger size, bright chestnut back and sides of the head, and chestnut (not grey) rump.

Female is larger and much redder on the back and shoulders than female House Sparrow. **Juv.** resembles female. **Habitat.** Dry thornveld; not usually associated with human habitation. **Status.** Locally common resident. **Call.** A 'cheereep, cheereeu', very similar to that of House Sparrow. (Grootmossie)

2. HOUSE SPARROW *Passer domesticus* (801) 14 cm

Male is easily recognised by its grey crown and rump, reddish brown back, black throat and white cheeks. It may be distinguished from larger Great Sparrow by having overall duller plumage and having a grey, not bright chestnut rump.

Female and juv. are a dull grey-brown and show a narrow, off-white eye-stripe that differentiates them from ad. and juv. Yellow-throated Petronia. **Habitat.** Towns, cities and gardens; rarely away from human habitation. **Status.** Common to abundant resident. **Call.** Various chirps, chips and a 'chissick'. (Huismossie)

3. CAPE SPARROW *Passer melanurus* (803) 15 cm

Male is unmistakable: it is the only sparrow in the region to have a pied head.

Female is distinguished from female House and Great sparrows by its plain chestnut back, and by its grey head and faint shadow markings of the male's pied head pattern. **Juv.** resembles female. **Habitat.** Grassland, grain fields and human habitation. **Status.** Common resident; near-endemic. **Call.** A series of musical cheeps. (Gewone Mossie)

4. (AFRICAN) YELLOW-THROATED PETRONIA (SPARROW)

Petronia superciliaris (805) 15 cm

The dark head with its broad, creamy white eyebrow stripe is the best field characteristic. The yellow throat spot is not often seen except at close range. It may be distinguished from the much larger White-browed Sparrow-Weaver (p. 396) by the lack of white on the rump.

Juv. lacks the yellow on the throat. **Habitat.** Thornveld, broad-leaved woodland and riverine bush. **Status.** Locally common resident. **Call.** A loud, sparrow-like chipping and liquid 'cheroop'. (Geelvlekmossie)

5. NORTHERN GREY-HEADED SPARROW *Passer griseus* 15-16 cm

Very similar to Southern Grey-headed Sparrow but has a purer grey (lacking brownish hues) head and whiter throat, with the grey colour extending further onto the underparts. The mantle is brighter chestnut and the bill more bulky and robust.

Habitat. Lightly wooded areas and very often around human habitation. **Status.** Within the region, restricted to a small area near Kazungula, Botswana and around the Victoria Falls, Zimbabwe. **Call.** Similar to Southern Grey-headed Sparrow. (Witkeelmossie)

6. SOUTHERN GREY-HEADED SPARROW *Passer diffusus* (804) 15 cm

The chestnut rump, back and wings, combined with the unmarked grey head, should prevent confusion with any other sparrow except Northern Grey-headed Sparrow. Female House, Great and Cape Sparrows superficially resemble this species but all have white or buff head markings. The bill is black in breeding season, and dull yellow in winter. Slightly smaller and less robust than Northern Grey-headed Sparrow; more greyish brown on the head and has a smaller bill.

Juv. is duller than ad. **Habitat.** Mixed woodlands and, in some regions, suburbia. **Status.** Common resident. **Call.** Various chirping notes. (Gryskopmossie)

1

♀

♂

chestnut
rump

2

♂

grey rump

♀

plain
back

black &
white
head

♂

3

6

juv.

ad.

chestnut back with
white shoulder streak

broad white
eye-stripe

ad.

large bill

whitish
throat

4

juv.

5

1. RED-BILLED BUFFALO-WEAVER *Bubalornis niger* (798)   21-24 cm
The robust red bill, black plumage and white wing patches are diagnostic of this large weaver. In flight, it might be mistaken for Pale-winged Starling (p. 382) but the chunky red bill should eliminate confusion.
Female and **juv.** are brown versions of male. **Habitat.** Dry thornveld and broad-leaved woodland. Breeds communally, making untidy masses of sticks in large trees or on electricity pylons. **Status.** Common, nomadic resident. **Call.** Song a 'chip-chip-doodley-doodley-dooo'. (Buffelwewer)

2. WHITE-BROWED SPARROW-WEAVER *Plocepasser mahali* (799)   17-19 cm
This large, plump, short-tailed weaver is distinctive with its broad, white eyebrow stripe and conspicuous white rump. The smaller Yellow-throated Petronia (p. 394) has a buff (not white) eyebrow stripe and lacks the white rump. Birds in the north show faint speckling across the breast.
Male has a black bill. Female has a horn-coloured bill. **Juv.** resembles ad. but has a pinkish brown bill. **Habitat.** Thornveld and dry, scrubby river courses. Makes an untidy nest of dry grass in the outside branches of a tree. **Status.** Common resident. **Call.** A harsh 'chik-chik'; a loud, liquid 'cheeoop-preeoo-chop' whistle. (Koringvoël)

3. THICK-BILLED WEAVER *Amblyospiza albifrons* (807)   15-17 cm
The only dark weaver to have a massive, thick black bill, white wing patches and a white forehead.
Female and **juv.** are heavily streaked below but still show the diagnostic heavy (horn-coloured) bill. **Habitat.** Reedbeds (when breeding), and coastal and evergreen forests. **Status.** Common resident. **Call.** A 'tweek, tweek' flight call; chattering, given when breeding. (Dikbekwewer)

4. DARK-BACKED (FOREST) WEAVER *Ploceus bicolor* (808)   13-15 cm
In the region, this is the only weaver with black upperparts and bright yellow underparts.
Juv. has dark brown upperparts, a grizzled forehead and throat, and yellow underparts. **Habitat.** Evergreen, riverine and coastal forests. **Status.** Locally common resident. **Call.** Song a 'cooee-cooee-squizzzz', and variations of this. (Bosmusikant)

5. SOCIABLE WEAVER *Philetairus socius* (800)   14 cm
The black chin, black buff-edged flank features and scaly back render this species unmistakable. Gregarious birds, they build huge, communal nests that appear to 'thatch' the trees or telephone poles in which they are built.
Juv. lacks the black face mask of ad. and has reduced flank markings. **Habitat.** Dry thornveld and broad-leaved woodland. **Status.** Common resident; endemic. **Call.** A chattering 'chicker-chicker', given in flight. (Versamelvoël)

1

heavy
red bill

♂

♀

2

white eye-brow
& rump

♂

3

heavy
bill

♀

♂

4

♀

yellow
underparts

♂

5

juv.

black
chin

ad.

black
flank
marks

1. VILLAGE (SPOTTEDBACKED) WEAVER *Ploceus cucullatus* (811)   14-16 cm
Larger than Southern and Lesser Masked-Weavers. Breeding male has a mottled black-and-yellow back, and the mask does not extend above the bill except in northern Zimbabwean race, which has a wholly black head.
Female has a yellowish throat that contrasts with a whitish breast and belly, and a dull, mottled, greyish back. The eye may be red. Non-breeding male and juv. resemble female. **Habitat.** Savanna. Colonial nester in reedbeds, trees overhanging water and, in thornveld, sometimes away from water. Forms large flocks and frequents grassland when not breeding. **Status.** Common resident. **Call.** A throaty 'chuck-chuk', and buzzy, swizzling notes. (Bontrugwewer)

2. SOUTHERN MASKED-WEAVER *Ploceus velatus* (814)   11-14,5 cm
Breeding male is distinguished from Lesser Masked-Weaver by its brown (not grey) legs, red (not white) eyes, and the black mask that terminates on the forehead, not the mid-crown; the mask forms a point on the throat. It differs from Village Weaver in having a uniformly dull green (not yellow-spotted) back.
Female has a greenish back with some streaking, and is buffy on the breast and belly. The eye is brown. Non-breeding male resembles female but has red eyes. **Juv.** resembles female. **Habitat.** Savanna and grassland. Breeds colonially in trees overhanging water; sometimes nests far from water in thornveld and suburbia. **Status.** Common resident. **Call.** A sharp 'zik, zik', and the usual swizzling weaver notes. (Swartkeelgeelvink)

3. LESSER MASKED-WEAVER *Ploceus intermedius* (815)   13-14 cm
In breeding plumage the shape of the black mask distinguishes male from the similar Southern Masked-Weaver: the mask extends well onto the crown and comes to a rounded (not pointed) end on the throat. This species also has a white (not red) eye and grey (not brown) legs.
Female and non-breeding male lack the mask and are yellower below than Southern Masked-Weaver. Female has a dark eye. **Juv.** resembles female. **Habitat.** Savanna. Breeds colonially in trees overhanging water, and in reeds. **Status.** Locally common resident. **Call.** Typical swizzling sounds. (Kleingeelvink)

4. SPECTACLED WEAVER *Ploceus ocularis* (810)   14-15 cm
Diagnostic features of both sexes are the sharp, pointed dark bill, the black line through the very pale yellow eye, and the chestnut brown wash over the head.
Male has a black bib. Female resembles male but lacks the black bib; it has a yellow eye and a black bill throughout the year. **Juv.** initially lacks the black facial markings; the black line through the eye develops during the first year. **Habitat.** Coastal, evergreen and riverine forests, and moister areas in thornveld. A shy weaver that is more often heard than seen. **Status.** Common resident. **Call.** A descending 'dee-dee-dee-dee-dee'; also a swizzling song. (Brilwewer)

5. RED-HEADED WEAVER *Anaplectes rubriceps* (819)   13-14 cm
Breeding male's scarlet head, breast and mantle are diagnostic.
Female and non-breeding male both have a lemon-yellow head, show a diagnostic pinkish orange bill, and have a clear white belly and flanks. **Juv.** resembles female. **Habitat.** Thornveld, and mopane and miombo woodland. **Status.** Locally common resident. **Call.** 'Cherrra-cherrra' and a high-pitched swizzling. (Rooikopwewer)

6. CHESTNUT WEAVER *Ploceus rubiginosus* (812)   15 cm
With its black head and chestnut back and underparts, breeding male is unmistakable.
Female and non-breeding male are drab, sparrow-like birds with a chestnut tinge to the lower back and rump and a well-defined, yellowish throat that ends in a brownish breast band. **Juv.** resembles female but has streaking on the breast. **Habitat.** Thornveld and dry broad-leaved woodland. **Status.** Locally common nomad in Namibia and northwestern Botswana. **Call.** Usual 'chuk, chuk' and swizzling weaver notes. (Bruinwewer)

1
yellow forehead
mottled back
♀
mottled back
black crown
♂ br. northern race
♂ br.

2
brown eye, streaked back
♀
narrow black forehead
red eye
plain back
brown legs
♂ br.

3
white eye
♀
yellow breast
broad black forehead, white eye
♂ br.
grey legs

4
♀
black line through pale eye
♂ br.

5
♀
sharply pointed, pink bill
♂ br.

6
♀
brownish band
♂ br.

1. CAPE WEAVER *Ploceus capensis* (813)   17 cm

Breeding male may be distinguished from the smaller Yellow Weaver by its heavier bill, less brilliant yellow plumage, white eye and the brown or orange wash over its face. It differs from both Southern Brown-throated and Golden Weavers by its greener back and by the orange wash over the face and forehead. It lacks the well-defined chestnut bib of Southern Brown-throated Weaver, from which it differs further by its pale (not dark) eye.

Male has a pale eye. Female and non-breeding male are olive above. Female and **juv.** have brown eyes. The large size and long, pointed bill help to differentiate them from other species. **Juv.** resembles female. **Habitat.** Grassland and fynbos, often along river courses. Nests communally in reedbeds and trees. **Status.** Common resident; endemic. **Call.** A harsh 'azwit, azwit' and swizzling noises. (Kaapse Wewer)

2. SOUTHERN BROWN-THROATED WEAVER *Ploceus xanthopterus* (818)   15 cm

Breeding male is the brightest of all the 'yellow' weavers and with its chestnut bib is unmistakable. It may be distinguished from Cape Weaver by its more brilliant yellow coloration, by the lack of orange wash over the face and crown, and by its brown (not pale) eye.

Breeding female has yellow underparts and brown eyes. Non-breeding male and female have horn-coloured bill and legs, olive-green head and nape, olive mantle, rust-coloured rump, buff throat, breast and flanks, and white on the remainder of the underparts. **Juv.** resembles non-breeding male. **Habitat.** Forest and scrub. Breeds over water in reedbeds. **Status.** Uncommon, localised resident. **Call.** A soft 'zweek, zweek' and swizzling notes. (Bruinkeelwewer)

3. GOLDEN WEAVER *Ploceus xanthops* (816)   15-17 cm

May be distinguished from the smaller Yellow Weaver by its large, heavy, black bill and yellow (not red) eye in both sexes.

Male is brightest yellow in the non-breeding season and has a green back in the breeding season. Female is a duller version of breeding male. **Juv.** resembles female, but is greener and has a brown eye. **Habitat.** Woodland and savanna. Breeds in reedbeds and trees. **Status.** Uncommon resident in the southeast, becoming locally more common in the extreme north and east. **Call.** A typical weaver-like 'chuk' and swizzling calls. (Goudwewer)

4. OLIVE-HEADED WEAVER *Ploceus olivaceiceps* (809)   14 cm

The golden crown, olive cheeks and orange breast of male are diagnostic.

Female has an olive head and back, and bright yellow underparts. **Juv.** resembles female but is paler, especially above. **Habitat.** Miombo woodland. **Status.** Uncommon and patchily distributed resident in southern Mozambique. **Call.** A loud chattering. (Olyfkopwewer)

5. YELLOW WEAVER *Ploceus subaureus* (817)   11-14 cm

Smaller and a brighter yellow than Golden Weaver, this species has a smaller, shorter bill and a red (not yellow) eye. Male may be distinguished from the larger, pale-eyed Cape Weaver by its more vivid yellow plumage and more rounded head. Some have an orange wash on the face.

Female and non-breeding male have greenish backs with some streaking, and are yellowish below. **Juv.** resembles female. **Habitat.** Breeds in reedbeds, and trees near water, mostly in savanna during winter. **Status.** Locally common resident. **Call.** Softer 'chuks' and swizzling than other, larger weavers. (Geelwewer)

1

♀

long, pointed bill

white eye

♂ br.

2

♀

brown eye

♂ br.

chestnut bib

white eye

♀

white eye

♂ br.

heavy black bill

3

5

red eye

♀

4

red eye

gold crown, olive cheeks

♀

olive head

olive back

yellow below

♂

♂ br.

1. RED-BILLED QUELEA *Quelea quelea* (821) 11-13 cm

Breeding male has a black or white mask, ringed with pink or dull yellow, and a bright red bill and legs.

Non-breeding male and female are drab, but show red bills and legs. Breeding female has a waxy yellow bill. **Juv.** resembles female, but has a pale brown bill. **Habitat.** Savanna, especially thornveld, and croplands. **Status.** Nomadic; at times very abundant. **Call.** Flocks make a chittering noise. Song a jumble of harsh and melodious notes. (Rooibekkwelea)

2. RED-HEADED QUELEA *Quelea erythrops* (822) 10-12 cm

Breeding male differs from male Red-billed Quelea by its red head and dark grey (not red) bill, and by the lack of a black mask. The red head markings do not extend as far onto the nape and upper breast as they do in Cardinal Quelea and there is some black grizzling on the throat that Cardinal Quelea lacks.

Female and non-breeding male have a much more yellow wash across the face and breast than Red-billed Quelea; they have a brown bill and legs. Breeding female has the face and throat washed with pale orange. **Juv.** resembles non-breeding female. **Habitat.** Damp grassland and adjoining woodland. **Status.** Locally common and nomadic migrant. May flock with Southern Red Bishops. **Call.** A soft twittering. (Rooikopkwelea)

3. CARDINAL QUELEA *Quelea cardinalis* (823) 10-11 cm

Breeding male could be confused only with Red-headed Quelea, but the red coloration of the head extends onto the upper breast, and the bill is black (not brownish); lacks any black on the throat.

Non-breeding male has the head narrowly streaked with tawny and black, usually with some red markings, and has a buff supercilium; the throat and breast are yellowish, and bill is horn-coloured. Female resembles non-breeding male but lacks any red facial markings. **Juv.** is buffier below than female, with dusky streaking on the breast. **Habitat.** Grassland and cultivated areas. **Status.** Vagrant to extreme north-central regions. **Call.** A sizzling chatter. (Kardinaalkwelea)

4. SOUTHERN RED BISHOP *Euplectes orix* (824) 10-11 cm

Breeding male is similar to Black-winged Bishop but differs in having a black forehead and brown (not black) primaries.

Female, non-breeding male and **juv.** are difficult to distinguish from similar plumage stages of Yellow-crowned Bishop, but Southern Red Bishop has more heavily streaked underparts with a buff (not white) background colour. **Habitat.** Grassland and savanna, usually associated with water. Breeds in reedbeds, sometimes in crops. **Status.** Common and widespread resident. Highly gregarious. **Call.** In display, males give a buzzing, chirping song; normal flight call is a 'cheet-cheet'. (Rooivink)

5. BLACK-WINGED (FIRECROWNED) BISHOP *Euplectes hordeaceus* (825) 11-13 cm

May be distinguished from Southern Red Bishop in breeding plumage by its darker mantle, black primaries and red (not black) forehead.

Female and non-breeding male resemble Southern Red Bishop at similar plumage stages, but both have a heavier bill and male retains the black primaries. **Juv.** resembles female. **Habitat.** Damp grassy areas and reedbeds in miombo woodland. **Status.** Uncommon, localised resident. **Call.** A buzzing chatter, similar to that of Southern Red Bishop. (Vuurkopvink)

6. YELLOW-CROWNED (GOLDEN) BISHOP *Euplectes afer* (826) 9,5-10,5 cm

Breeding male differs from breeding male Yellow Bishop (p. 404) by its smaller size and yellow crown. It is difficult to distinguish from Southern Red Bishop when not breeding, but is smaller, whitish (not buff) below, with faint streaking confined to the sides of the breast and flanks, and has a prominent buffy yellow eye-stripe.

Female and juv. resemble non-breeding male. **Habitat.** Grassland and vleis. Breeds in wet areas, often low down in grass or reeds. **Status.** Locally common resident; gregarious. **Call.** Buzzing and chirping notes. (Goudgeelvink)

♂ transitional

2

black or
white mask

♂ br.

♂ br.

♂ non-br.

♂ br.

♀ br.

grey bill

brown-
streaked
nape

fine dark
streaking

♂ br.

♀ br.

1

3

♀

♂ transitional

black
forehead

brown
wing

red
nape

♀

♂ transitional

4

♂ br.

♂

yellow
crown

♂ br.

♀

red
forehead

♂ non-br.

white
below

♀

5

black wing

♂ br.

♂ non-br.

6

1. LONG-TAILED WIDOWBIRD (WIDOW)

Euplectes progne (832)   m=19 cm (plus 40 cm tail); f=16 cm

The largest widowbird of the region. Breeding male is unmistakable with its long, heavy tail, and the bright red shoulder bordered by a whitish or buffy stripe.

Non-breeding male has black wing feathers and is distinguished from non-breeding male Fan-tailed Widowbird by its larger size, broad, rounded wings and the buff stripe below the red shoulder. Female, sub-ad. male and **juv.** are far larger than all other similarly coloured widowbirds. **Habitat.** Open grassland, especially in valleys and damp areas. **Status.** Common resident. **Call.** Male gives a 'cheet, cheet' and a harsher 'zzit, zzit'. (Langstertflap)

2. RED-COLLARED WIDOWBIRD (WIDOW)

Euplectes ardens (831)   15 cm (plus 25 cm tail in br. male)

Breeding male's long, wispy tail and red throat collar are diagnostic.

Female, non-breeding male and **juv.** show a bold, black-and-buff-striped head pattern, and have unstreaked, buffy underparts; male retains the black primaries. **Habitat.** Grassy and bracken-covered mountain slopes and, frequently, in sugarcane in KwaZulu-Natal. **Status.** Locally common resident. **Call.** A fast, high-pitched 'tee-tee-tee-tee-tee', given by displaying males. (Rooikeelflap)

3. WHITE-WINGED WIDOWBIRD (WIDOW) *Euplectes albonotatus* (829)   15-19 cm

Male is the only short-tailed widowbird in the region with white on the primary coverts.

Breeding male may be told from Yellow-mantled Widowbird by its shorter tail, white in the wings, pale bill, and lack of yellow on the back. In non-breeding plumage it shows yellow shoulders and a white patch at the base of the primaries. Female is pale below and less streaked than other widowbirds. **Juv.** resembles female. **Habitat.** Rank grass in savanna. **Status.** Common resident. Gregarious. **Call.** A 'zeh-zeh-zeh' and a repetitive 'witz-witz-witz'. (Witvlerkflap)

4. FAN-TAILED WIDOWBIRD (REDSHOULDERED WIDOW) *Euplectes axillaris* (828) 15-17 cm

Breeding male is the only small, short-tailed widowbird with a red shoulder.

Female and non-breeding male are heavily streaked above, often with a chestnut-brown wash below. Male retains the black primaries and red epaulettes in non-breeding plumage. **Juv.** resembles female. **Habitat.** Reedbeds, damp grassland and stands of sugarcane. **Status.** Common resident. **Call.** Various twittering and chirping sounds, given by male during display. (Kortstertflap)

5. YELLOW BISHOP (YELLOWRUMPED WIDOW) *Euplectes capensis* (827)   15 cm

In comparison with Yellow-mantled Widowbird, breeding male has a much shorter tail, and a yellow rump and lower back (not a yellow mantle).

Non-breeding male is streaked greyish brown above, and is pale below. Breast and flanks are heavily streaked with brown, but retains a bright yellow rump and shoulder. Some show a white lower mandible. Female differs from female Yellow-mantled Widowbird in being more heavily streaked below and having a dull yellow rump. **Juv.** resembles female. **Habitat.** Damp grassy areas, bracken-covered mountain valleys, and fynbos. **Status.** Common resident. **Call.** A 'zeet, zeet, zeet' and a harsh 'zzzzzzzzt', given by male in flight. (Kaapse Flap)

6. YELLOW-MANTLED WIDOWBIRD (YELLOWBACKED WIDOW)

Euplectes macrourus (830)   13,5-20 cm

Breeding male is the only widowbird with a long black tail and a yellow mantle. It differs from Yellow Bishop by its longer tail and the lack of yellow on the lower back, and from White-winged Widowbird by the lack of white in the wings.

Female and non-breeding male are less heavily streaked on the breast and lack the dull yellow rump of female Yellow Bishop. Female has no yellow in the wings; male has black wings with small yellow epaulettes. **Juv.** resembles female. **Habitat.** Damp grassland and marshy areas. **Status.** Locally common resident. **Call.** A buzzing twitter. (Geelrugflap)

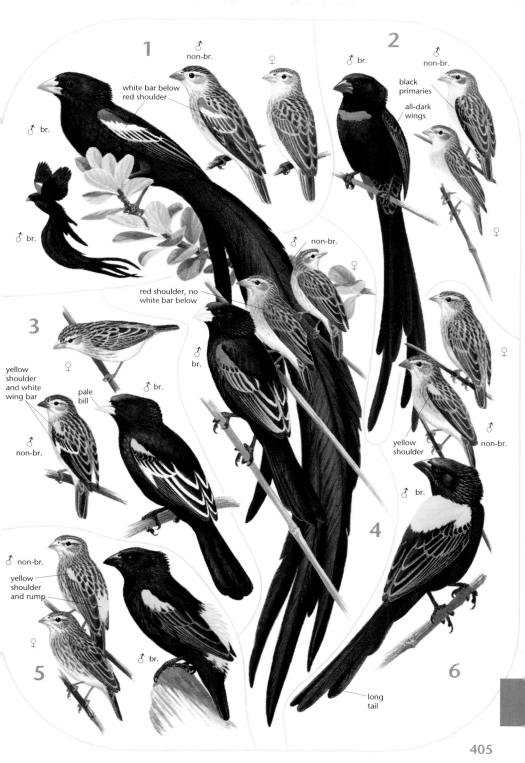

1

♂ non-br.

white bar below
red shoulder

♀

♂ br.

♂ br.

2

♂ br.

black primaries

all-dark wings

♂ non-br.

♀

♀

♂ non-br.

♀

red shoulder, no
white bar below

♂ br.

3

yellow
shoulder
and white
wing bar

♀

pale
bill

♂ br.

♂
non-br.

♀

♂
non-br.

yellow
shoulder

♂
non-br.

♂ br.

♂ non-br.

yellow
shoulder
and rump

♀

♂ br.

5

4

6

long
tail

1. PIN-TAILED WHYDAH *Vidua macroura* (860)   12 cm (plus 22 cm tail in br. male)
Breeding male is unmistakable, being black above with a broad white nuchal collar and underparts, a red bill and long 'pintails'. It may be told from breeding male Shaft-tailed Whydah by its white (not buff) underparts and by the lack of spatulate tips to the tail feathers.
Female and non-breeding male are buff above and pale below, and have a boldly striped, black-and-buff head. The bill is red in male, brownish in female. **Juv.** is plain brown and paler below. **Habitat.** Savanna, grassland, scrub, parks and gardens. Parasitises mainly waxbills, but also cisticolas, mannikins and prinias. **Status.** Common resident. **Call.** 'Tseet-tseet-tseet', given by displaying males. (Koningrooibekkie)

2. SHAFT-TAILED WHYDAH *Vidua regia* (861)   12 cm (plus 22 cm tail in br. male)
Breeding male of this species has black and buff plumage (not black and white as in breeding male Pin-tailed Whydah) and has diagnostic spatulate tips to its elongate tail feathers.
Female and non-breeding male have streaked head markings, not the bold black stripes of the similarly plumaged Pin-tailed Whydah. **Juv.** is dull brown with dark streaking on the back. **Habitat.** Grassy areas in thornveld. Parasitises Violet-eared Waxbill (p. 412). **Status.** Common resident. **Call.** Similar to but harsher than that of Pin-tailed Whydah. (Pylstertrooibekkie)

3. LONG-TAILED (EASTERN) PARADISE-WHYDAH
Vidua paradisaea (862)   11-13 cm (plus 23 cm tail in br. male)
Breeding male has black upperparts and head, a yellow hind collar and belly, and a reddish chestnut breast. The elongate tail feathers of breeding male are stiff, curve downward and taper gradually to a point; tail tips of Broad-tailed Paradise-Whydah are broader and taper very rapidly to a point at the tip.
Female, non-breeding male and **juv.** are grey-brown above, with an off-white head striped with black. The bill is black. They are virtually indistinguishable from the similarly plumaged Broad-tailed Paradise-Whydah. **Habitat.** Mixed woodland, especially thornveld. Parasitises Green-winged Pytilia (p. 416). **Status.** Common resident with local movements. **Call.** A sharp 'chip-chip' and a short 'cheroop-cherrup' song. (Gewone Paradysvink)

4. BROAD-TAILED PARADISE-WHYDAH
Vidua obtusa (863)   11-13 cm (plus 15 cm tail in br. male)
Breeding male is virtually identical in coloration to breeding male Long-tailed Paradise-Whydah, but has a shorter tail, which is broad at the tip, tapering rapidly to a point; the nape is orange (not yellow-orange).
Female, non-breeding male and **juv.** are virtually indistinguishable in the field from the similarly plumaged Long-tailed Paradise-Whydah. **Habitat.** Miombo and other broad-leaved woodland. Parasitises Orange-winged Pytilia (p. 416). **Status.** Uncommon resident. **Call.** Similar to that of Long-tailed Paradise-Whydah. (Breëstertparadysvink)

1

♂ display flight

juv.

pale bill

striped head

♀

white collar & underparts

♂ br.

♂ whydah x indigobird hybrid

♂

2

♂ transitional

3

juv.

red bill

♀

dark bill

♀

♂ br.

♂ br.

orange collar & underparts

♂ br.

4

♀

broad, tapering tail tip

pointed tail tip

spatulate tips

1. DUSKY INDIGOBIRD (BLACK WIDOWFINCH) *Vidua funerea* (864)   11 cm

Breeding male is jet-black, with a white bill and red or orange-red legs and feet. **Female**, non-breeding male and **juv.** are mottled with black and buff above, and have an off-white head striped with black. The bill is off-white and the legs are red. **Habitat.** Forest edge, thornveld, riverine scrub, and suburbia. Parasitises African Firefinch (p. 410). **Status.** Common resident. **Call.** A short, canary-like jingle, and a scolding 'chit-chit-chit'. (Gewone Blouvinkie)

2. PURPLE INDIGOBIRD (WIDOWFINCH) *Vidua purpurascens* (865)   11 cm

In breeding plumage the combination of white or pale pink bill and whitish or pale pink legs and feet distinguish both male and female from other indigobirds. It may be distinguished from other indigobirds when in non-breeding and juv. plumages only by leg and bill colour.

Habitat. Savanna, especially thornveld. Parasitises Jameson's Firefinch (p. 410). **Status.** Locally common resident in the south of its range, becoming more common in the north-east. **Call.** A rapid chattering that includes mimicked calls and song of Jameson's Firefinch. (Witpootblouvinkie)

3. CUCKOO FINCH *Anomalospiza imberbis* (820)   10-14 cm

Male is similar to a small female 'yellow' weaver but its yellow colouring is brighter, especially below, and it has a diagnostic short, conical, black bill. **Female** is a streaky brown, resembling a female bishop, but the heavy bill is characteristic. **Juv.** resembles female. **Habitat.** Open grassland, especially near damp areas. **Status.** Uncommon local migrant. **Call.** A swizzling noise, uttered during display. (Koekoekvink)

4. VILLAGE INDIGOBIRD (STEELBLUE WIDOWFINCH) *Vidua chalybeata* (867)   11 cm

Breeding male is jet-black; over most of its range the red bill, legs and feet differentiate both male and female from other indigobirds. West of Victoria Falls the bill is white. The white-billed form does not co-occur with white-billed Dusky Indigobird.

Female, non-breeding male and **juv.** resemble other indigobirds except for their red bills and legs. **Habitat.** Woodland, tall grassveld, and old cultivated lands. Parasitises Red-billed Firefinch (p. 410). **Status.** Common resident. **Call.** A canary-like song which includes clear, whistled 'wheeet-wheeet-wheeetoo' notes, and mimicked notes of Red-billed Firefinch. (Staalblouvinkie)

5. ZAMBEZI INDIGOBIRD (TWINSPOT WIDOWFINCH) *Vidua codringtoni*   11 cm

Breeding male most closely resembles Dusky Indigobird, from which it may be told by the much brighter greenish or bluish wash to the plumage and by its more orange (not red) legs.

Female is very similar to other female indigobirds but the grey breast and white belly are distinctly demarcated. It is best identified when heard mimicking the song of its host, Red-throated Twinspot (p. 418). **Habitat.** Occurs in a variety of wooded habitats alongside Red-throated Twinspot in Zimbabwe. **Status.** Uncertain. **Call.** Mimics the song of Red-throated Twinspot. [Note: The common name of this species may change in future given that it does not occur along the Zambezi River.] (Groenblouvinkie)

1

white bill ♀

white bill ♂

red legs

red legs

♂ non-br.

3

2

white bill ♂

white bill

white legs

♂

white legs

white bill ♀

short, stubby bill ♀

short black bill

♂

white legs

4

♂ transitional

red bill ♀

bill red in east, white in west

♂

red legs

red legs

5

body washed green/blue

♂

orange legs

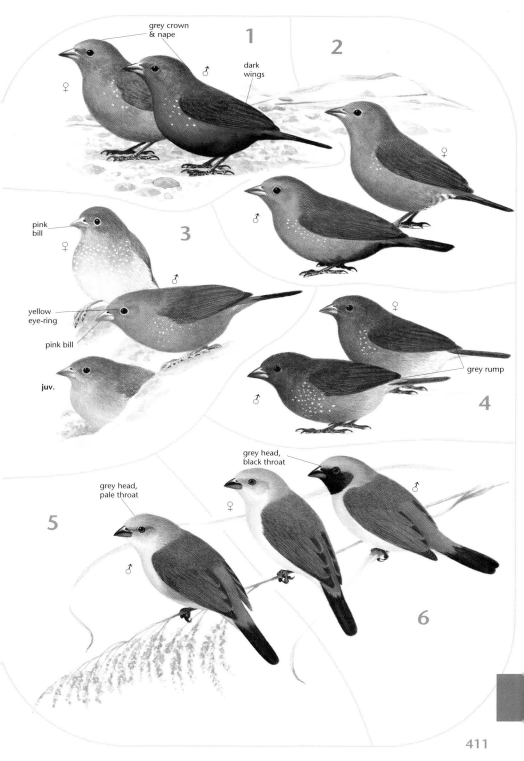

1

grey crown & nape

dark wings

♀

♂

2

♀

♂

3

pink bill

♀

♂

yellow eye-ring

pink bill

juv.

4

♀

grey rump

♂

5

grey head, pale throat

♂

6

grey head, black throat

♀

♂

1. VIOLET-EARED WAXBILL *Granatina granatina* (845)　　　15 cm
The red bill, violet cheeks, brilliant blue rump and black tail are diagnostic.
Male has chestnut head and body plumage and a black chin. Female has biscuit-coloured head and body with a blue rump; the violet on the cheeks is less extensive than on male. **Juv.** resembles female but lacks the violet on the face. **Habitat.** Woodland and savanna, especially thornveld. **Status.** Common resident. **Call.** A soft, whistled 'tiu-woowee'. (Koningblousysie)

2. BLACK-FACED (BLACKCHEEKED) WAXBILL *Estrilda erythronotos* (847)　　　12 cm
The greyish brown body and head, conspicuous black face patch, barred wings and dark red rump and flanks render this species unmistakable.
Female and juv. are duller versions of male. **Habitat.** Grassy areas and thick tangles in dry thornveld. **Status.** Common resident. Gregarious. **Call.** A high-pitched 'chuloweee'. (Swartwangsysie)

3. COMMON WAXBILL *Estrilda astrild* (846)　　　11-12 cm
This small, brownish, long-tailed finch is best identified by its red bill and eye-stripe, and by the small, pinkish red patch on the belly.
Juv. resembles ad. but is duller, and has a black bill. **Habitat.** Long grass in damp areas, alongside rivers and in reedbeds. **Status.** Common resident. Gregarious. **Call.** A nasal 'cher-cher-cher' and a 'ping, ping' flight note. (Rooibeksysie)

4. GREY WAXBILL *Estrilda perreini* (848)　　　11 cm
Could be confused with Cinderella Waxbill, but their distributions do not overlap. This species differs in having the red confined to the rump and uppertail coverts. Yellow-bellied and Swee Waxbills (p. 410) also show the red rump, but have green, not grey backs.
Juv. is duller and lacks the black eye-stripe. **Habitat.** Edges of evergreen forests, and thick coastal and riverine forests. **Status.** Locally common resident. **Call.** A soft, whistled 'pseeu, pseeu'. (Gryssysie)

5. CINDERELLA WAXBILL *Estrilda thomensis* (849)　　　11 cm
The western counterpart of Grey Waxbill. It is distinguished from that species by its generally paler grey coloration, by the red base of the bill, and by the red on the rump extending to the lower belly and flanks.
Juv. lacks the red on the flanks. **Habitat.** Riverine scrub and forests, and adjacent mopane woodland. **Status.** Uncommon resident, restricted to northwestern Namibia from Oshikango westwards. **Call.** A thin but penetrating, reedy 'sweee-sweee-sweeeooo-swoooo' with the emphasis on the third note, and a short, repeated 'trrt-tsoo'. (Angolasysie)

6. BLUE WAXBILL *Uraeginthus angolensis* (844)　　　13 cm
The powder-blue face, breast and tail render this species unmistakable.
Female has the blue confined to the face and breast. **Juv.** resembles female but is paler. **Habitat.** Drier areas of mixed woodland, and suburbia in some regions. **Status.** Common resident. **Call.** A soft 'kway-kway-sree-seee-seee-seee'. (Gewone Blousysie)

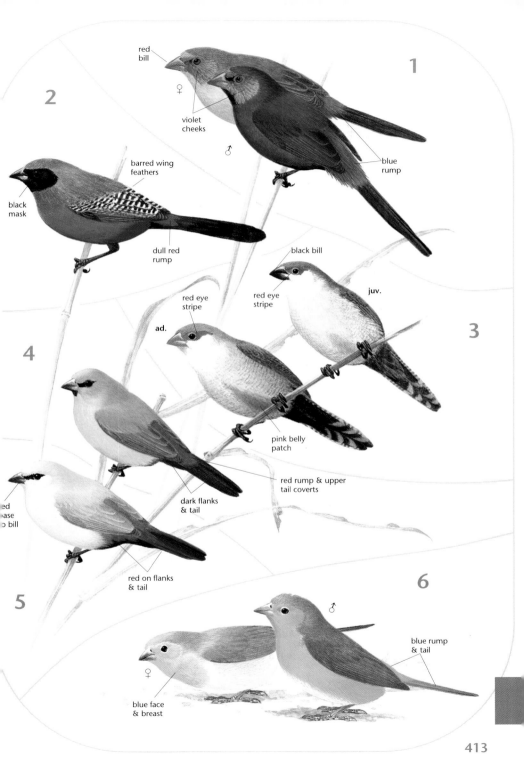

1

red bill

violet cheeks

blue rump

♀

♂

2

barred wing feathers

black mask

dull red rump

3

black bill

red eye stripe

red eye stripe

juv.

ad.

4

pink belly patch

red rump & upper tail coverts

dark flanks & tail

red base o bill

red on flanks & tail

5

6

blue rump & tail

♂

blue face & breast

♀

1. BRONZE MANNIKIN *Lonchura cucullata* (857)   9 cm
Has less black on the head than does Red-backed Mannikin, and further differs by
having a brown (not chestnut) back. Can be distinguished from Magpie Mannikin
by its smaller size and less massive, bicoloured bill.
Juv. is uniformly dun brown, unlike juv. Red-backed Mannikin, which has a reddish brown
back and paler underparts. **Habitat.** A wide variety of grassy areas in woodland, forest
edges, damp regions and suburbia. **Status.** Very common resident. Gregarious. **Call.** A
soft, buzzy 'chizza, chizza'. (Gewone Fret)

2. RED-BACKED MANNIKIN *Lonchura nigriceps* (858)   9 cm
The conspicuous chestnut back, black-and-white spangles on the wings and flanks,
and pale grey bill distinguish this species from both Bronze and Magpie mannikins.
Juv. differs from juv. Bronze Mannikin by its chestnut-tinged back and paler underparts.
Habitat. Moist, broad-leaved woodland and forests. **Status.** Common resident.
Gregarious. **Call.** A thin, soft 'seeet-seeet', uttered when flushed from grass. (Rooirugfret)

3. MAGPIE (PIED) MANNIKIN *Lonchura fringilloides* (859)   11-12 cm
The largest mannikin of the region, it is easily distinguished from Bronze and Red-
backed mannikins by its markedly black-and-white appearance, its large, heavy bill,
and the broad dark bars on its flanks.
Juv. is grey-brown above and off-white below. **Habitat.** Bamboo stands, and riverine and
coastal forests. **Status.** Uncommon, localised resident. **Call.** A chirruping 'peeoo-peeoo'.
(Dikbekfret)

4. CUT-THROAT FINCH *Amadina fasciata* (855)   10-11 cm
The pinkish red band across the throat is diagnostic in male. The plumage is generally brown, heavily barred and mottled with black and white.
Female is smaller than female Red-headed Finch, is boldly barred on the head, and has the
back distinctly streaked and mottled. **Juv.** resembles female, but juv. male shows a pale
throat band. **Habitat.** Dry thornveld. **Status.** Locally common resident. **Call.** An 'eee-eee-
eee' flight call. (Bandkeelvink)

5. RED-HEADED FINCH *Amadina erythrocephala* (856)   13 cm
The upperparts of this species are generally brown, and the underparts are pale
and heavily scalloped.
Male has a bright red head. Red-headed Quelea (p. 402) is similar but has plain underparts. Female differs from the smaller female Cut-throat Finch in having a uniformly pale
brown head, and less heavily barred and streaked underparts and upperparts. **Juv.** is duller
than ad. **Habitat.** Dry grassland, thornveld and broad-leaved woodland. **Status.** Common
resident and nomad; near-endemic. **Call.** A soft 'chuk-chuk', and a 'zree, zree' flight call.
(Rooikopvink)

6. SCALY-FEATHERED FINCH *Sporopipes squamifrons* (806)   10 cm
An unmistakable small finch with a black-and-white freckled forehead, black malar
stripes, and white-fringed wing and tail feathers.
Juv. resembles ad. but lacks the black malar stripes and the freckling on the forehead.
Habitat. Dry thornveld, bushy desert watercourses, cattle kraals and around farm buildings. **Status.** Common resident and nomad; near-endemic. Gregarious. **Call.** A soft 'chizz,
chizz, chizz', given by small groups in flight. (Baardmannetjie)

1
dark bill
two-toned bill
brown back
brown back
juv.
ad.

2
pale bill
reddish-brown back
juv.
pale bill
chestnut back
ad.

3
juv.
brown back
ad.
large, dark bill
heavy flank bars

4
♀
barred head
♂
red throat band
widely barred below

5
plain brown head
♀
red head
barred below
♂
pale scalloping below

6
speckled forehead
black malar stripe

415

1. GREEN-WINGED PYTILIA (MELBA FINCH) *Pytilia melba* (834)   12 cm

Could be confused with Orange-winged Pytilia but is much more brightly coloured, male showing a crimson bill, forehead and throat, a blue-grey nape, and boldly barred belly and flanks. It lacks the orange wing panel of Orange-winged Pytilia.

Female has an all-grey head and upper breast, and differs from female Orange-winged Pytilia in being brighter, barred dark grey on white below, and lacking the orange wing panels. **Juv.** resembles female but is more olive above and plain greyish below. **Habitat.** Thornveld and dry broad-leaved woodland. **Status.** Common resident. **Call.** A pretty, trilling song that rises and falls in pitch; also a short 'wick'. (Gewone Melba)

2. ORANGE-WINGED (GOLDENBACKED) PYTILIA *Pytilia afra* (833)   11 cm

Male could be confused with male Green-winged Pytilia, but has the red face markings extending behind the eye, is less distinctly barred (whitish on olive) on the belly and flanks, and has an orange wing panel.

Female can be distinguished from female Green-winged Pytilia by its drabber coloration, olive green breast and belly finely barred with white, and the orange wing panel. **Juv.** resembles female but is more orange on the rump. **Habitat.** Thick, tangled scrub, usually near water and often in miombo woodland. **Status.** Uncommon, localised resident. **Call.** A 'seee', and a piping whistle of two widely spaced notes. (Oranjevlerkmelba)

3. LOCUSTFINCH *Ortygospiza locustella* (853)   9 cm

Although the habits of the Locustfinch are similar to those of African Quailfinch, the calls of the two species are very different.

Male is easily told by its red face, throat and breast, rufous wings, black back spotted with white, and black belly. Female is distinguished from female African Quailfinch by its rufous wings and the lack of white facial markings. **Juv.** is streaked with black and brown above; it is browner below than female. **Habitat.** Grassland, especially in damper areas. **Status.** Uncommon, localised resident. **Call.** A fast 'tinka-tinka-tinka', given in flight. (Rooivlerkkwartelvinkie)

4. AFRICAN QUAILFINCH *Ortygospiza atricollis* (852)   9 cm

Rarely seen on the ground, but when flushed from the grass it has a diagnostic jerky flight and a distinctive call. The black-and-white face pattern, barred black-and-white breast and flanks, and lack of red on the rump differentiate it from Orange-breasted Waxbill.

Sexes are similar, but may be distinguished by the forehead, cheeks and throat being black in male and grey in female. **Juv.** is plain buff below. **Habitat.** Open grassland. **Status.** Common resident. **Call.** A continual, tinny 'skreaky-skreak', given in flight. (Gewone Kwartelvinkie)

5. ORANGE-BREASTED WAXBILL *Amandava subflava* (854)   10 cm

Superficially resembles the Swee and Yellow-bellied Waxbills (p. 410) but lacks the grey on the head and has a bright yellow-orange belly and barred flanks. It may be distinguished from African Quailfinch by its red (not dark) rump, as well as by its call.

Female has a yellow belly and lacks the red eyebrow. **Juv.** resembles female but is plain buff below. **Habitat.** Grassland and weedy areas, especially near water. **Status.** Common resident, sometimes in large flocks. **Call.** A soft, clinking 'zink zink zink' flight call; a rapid 'trip-trip' on take-off. (Rooiassie)

1

red frons
& throat

green
wings

♀

♂

barred black &
white below

2

red
mask

♂

orange
wing panel

♀

4

'spectacled' face

♀

red
wings

♀

dark rump
& wings

barred breast
& flanks

♂

3

red sides
to rump

♂

red
wings

red face &
breast

5

red
eyebrow

red
rump

♂

♀

barred
flanks

1. PINK-THROATED TWINSPOT *Hypargos margaritatus* (838)   12 cm

Male is much paler than male Red-throated Twinspot, has a pinkish face and lacks the deep red throat and breast.

Female has a light grey-brown throat, breast and belly; it differs from female Red-throated Twinspot in having no trace of red or pink or russet on the throat and breast. **Juv.** resembles female but is plain buff below. **Habitat.** Thick tangles in thornveld and coastal scrub. **Status.** Locally common resident; endemic. **Call.** A soft, reedy trill. (Rooskeelkolpensie)

2. RED-THROATED TWINSPOT *Hypargos niveoguttatus* (839)   12 cm

Male may be distinguished from Pink-throated Twinspot by its grey crown and deep red (not pink) face, throat and breast.

Female differs from female Pink-throated Twinspot by its grey crown and the pinkish red wash across the breast. **Juv.** resembles female but is duller above. **Habitat.** Prefers moister situations than Pink-throated Twinspot, and the edges of evergreen forests. Host of the recently described Zambezi Indigobird (p. 408). **Status.** Locally common resident. **Call.** A trill, similar to that of Pink-throated Twinspot. (Rooikeelkolpensie)

3. GREEN TWINSPOT *Mandingoa nitidula* (835)   10 cm

The combination of a red face, predominantly dull green upperparts, and black lower breast, belly and flanks boldly spotted with white is diagnostic.

Female has a buffy face. **Juv.** is duller than female, and lacks the black-and-white belly and flank markings. **Habitat.** Mist-belt, coastal and riverine forests, usually adjacent to small clearings. **Status.** Locally common resident; easily overlooked because of its secretive habits. **Call.** A soft, rolling, insect-like 'zrrreet'. (Groenkolpensie)

4. RED-FACED CRIMSONWING *Cryptospiza reichenovii* (836)   10-11 cm

Superficially resembles Lesser Seedcracker but has a black (not red) tail and dull red (not dark brown) back and wings; red on the head is confined to eye patches.

Female lacks the male's red eye patches and differs from female Lesser Seedcracker in having red in the wings. **Juv.** has less red on the upperparts than ad. **Habitat.** Understorey and thick tangles of evergreen forests. **Status.** Uncommon, localised resident. **Call.** A soft, repeated 'zeet'. (Rooiwangwoudsysie)

5. LESSER (NYASA) SEEDCRACKER *Pyrenestes minor* (837)   13 cm

Differs from Red-faced Crimsonwing by its bright red face and throat and red (not black) tail; lacks any red in the wings.

Female closely resembles male but has a reduced red face patch. **Juv.** lacks red on the head. **Habitat.** Thickets along small streams, and near water in forest clearings and miombo woodland. **Status.** Uncommon to locally common resident. **Call.** A 'tzeet', and a sharp, clipped 'quap'. (Oostelike Saadbrekertjie)

1

brown crown

♂

pale, greyish upper breast

♀

2

grey crown

♂

russet upper breast

♀

3

green upperparts & wings

♀

♂

4

♀

red eye patch

♂

reddish back & wings

black tail

5

brown back & wings

♀

red tail

♂

all-red head

1. YELLOW CANARY *Serinus flaviventris* (878)   13 cm
Males grade in colour from uniform bright yellow in the northwest to streaked, olive-backed birds in the southeast. The bill is always slighter than that of Brimstone Canary, and the head is less marked than that of Yellow-fronted Canary. **Female** is drab grey-brown above and paler below, and streaked darker brown on both the upperparts and the underparts. **Juv.** resembles female but is more heavily streaked. **Habitat.** Karoo and coastal scrub, and scrubby mountain valleys. **Status.** Common resident; near-endemic. **Call.** A fast, jumbled series of 'chissick' and 'cheree' notes. (Geelkanarie)

2. BRIMSTONE (BULLY) CANARY *Serinus sulphuratus* (877)   13-15 cm
Has a more massive bill than any other yellow canary. The birds found in the Western and Eastern Cape provinces are greener than other forms.
Female is duller than male. **Juv.** is greyer than ad. **Habitat.** A wide range of woodland and grassland, but prefers coastal scrub. **Status.** Common resident. **Call.** Lower in pitch and slower than that of other canaries. (Dikbekkanarie)

3. LEMON-BREASTED CANARY *Serinus citrinipectus* (871)   11 cm
Resembles Yellow-fronted Canary, with which it sometimes flocks.
Male has a pale lemon throat and upper breast, well demarcated from the remainder of its underparts, which are a pale buff. It lacks the bold head markings of Yellow-fronted Canary but has a short, black malar stripe and a small white patch below the eye. Female resembles Black-throated Canary but is buff below and lacks the black-speckled throat. **Juv.** resembles female. **Habitat.** Palm savanna and adjoining thornveld, and open grassland. **Status.** Locally common resident; near-endemic. **Call.** Similar to that of Black-throated Canary, but higher pitched and shorter. (Geelborskanarie)

4. YELLOW-FRONTED (YELLOWEYED) CANARY *Serinus mozambicus* (869)   10-12 cm
Colour varies regionally (brightest in east). Facial pattern diagnostic. Differs from Brimstone Canary by its smaller size, less robust bill, yellow rump and white tail tips. **Juv.** has buffy yellow, lightly streaked underparts. **Habitat.** Thornveld, and mixed woodland and savanna. **Status.** Common to abundant resident. Gregarious. **Call.** A 'zeee-zereee-chereeo'. (Geeloogkanarie)

5. BLACK-THROATED CANARY *Serinus atrogularis* (870)   11 cm
A pale grey-brown canary, heavily streaked with dark brown on the upperparts, with a diagnostic bright lemon-yellow rump and white tail tips that contrast with the otherwise drab plumage. The black throat is most obvious during the breeding season.
Female has less black on the throat. **Juv.** is spotted on the throat. **Habitat.** Thornveld, dry, broad-leaved woodland, and near waterholes in dry regions. **Status.** Common resident, subject to local movements. Gregarious. **Call.** A prolonged series of wheezy whistles and chirrups. (Bergkanarie)

6. FOREST CANARY *Serinus scotops* (873)   13 cm
A very dark, heavily streaked canary with a small black chin, greyish cheeks and a yellow eye-stripe. The pale base to the bill contrasts with the dark face.
Female and juv. have a less prominent black bib. **Habitat.** Evergreen forests, forest edges and clearings. **Status.** Common but localised resident; endemic. **Call.** A single, high-pitched 'tseeek' contact call and a quiet, jumbled song. (Gestreepte Kanarie)

7. CAPE CANARY *Serinus canicollis* (872)   11-13 cm
May be told from Yellow-fronted Canary by the lack of bold facial markings, the yellow forehead and crown, and the greater amount of grey on the nape.
Female has less grey on the nape. **Juv.** has greenish yellow underparts overlaid with heavy brown streaking. **Habitat.** Fynbos, grassland and suburban gardens; prefers mountainous terrain. **Status.** Common resident. Gregarious. **Call.** Flight call usually a three-note 'tsit-it-it'. A typical canary song is given from a perch and during display flight. (Kaapse Kanarie)

1

small bill

♀

♂

damarensis

2

heavy bill

ad. yellow form

3

♂

white face patches

lemon yellow throat

whitish below

♀

white tip

4

dark malar stripe

yellow supercilium

yellow belly

white tip

5

♀

♂

streaked uppers

♂

bright yellow rump

6

grey cheek

white tip

heavily streaked

7

grey nape

two-toned face

♂

♀

1. PROTEA SEED-EATER (CANARY) *Serinus leucopterus* (880)   15 cm
A dark canary, distinguishable from White-throated Canary (p. 424) by having a brown, not greenish yellow rump and by its small, black chin. The pale bill contrasts with the dark face. The narrow white edgings to the secondary coverts, creating two pale bars on the folded wing, are diagnostic.
Juv. resembles ad. **Habitat.** Thick, tangled valley scrub and dense stands of mature proteas on hillsides. **Status.** Uncommon and localised resident; endemic. **Call.** Contact call a 'tree-lee-loo'; song loud and varied. (Witvlerkkanarie)

2. STREAKY-HEADED SEED-EATER (CANARY) *Serinus gularis* (881)   13-14 cm
The broad, whitish eyebrow stripe is the most distinctive feature. Distinguished from White-throated Canary (p. 424) by its finely streaked, grey-and-white crown and by the brown-streaked, not plain greenish yellow rump. Differs from Black-eared Seed-eater in lacking the streaked breast and distinct black ear patches.
Juv. resembles ad. but is heavily streaked with brown below. **Habitat.** Mixed woodland and scrub. **Status.** Common resident. **Call.** A soft, weak 'trrreet', and a short song. (Streepkopkanarie)

3. BLACK-EARED SEED-EATER (CANARY) *Serinus mennelli* (882)   14 cm
Differs from Streaky-headed Seed-eater by distinct black cheeks and streaked breast.
Female and **juv.** have dark grey cheeks, but still show a streaked breast. **Habitat.** Miombo and mopane woodland. **Status.** Uncommon, localised resident. **Call.** A twittering whistle, 'teeu-twee-teeu, twiddy-twee-twee'. (Swartoorkanarie)

4. BLACK-HEADED CANARY *Alario alario* (876)   12 cm
Male has a chestnut back and tail, and black stripes down the sides of the breast forming an inverted 'V'. The all-black head distinguishes it from Damara Canary.
Female lacks black markings but does show the diagnostic chestnut back and tail. (see Damara Canary). **Habitat.** Karoo scrub and adjacent mountainous terrain, especially bushy vegetation; cultivated lands. **Status.** Endemic; locally common. Gregarious. **Call.** A soft 'sweea' or 'tweet'. (Swartkopkanarie)

5. DAMARA CANARY *Alario leucolaema*   12 cm
Differs from Black-headed Canary in having a pied, not all black head.
Female has a slightly paler head and breast than female Black-headed Canary. **Habitat.** Arid to semi-arid scrub on rocky hills and open plains. **Status.** Locally common endemic in small groups but sometimes in large mixed flocks with Black-headed Canaries. **Call.** Very similar to that of Black-headed Canary. [Note: Although there is no evidence in captivity or the wild for hybridisation between Black-headed and Damara Canaries, their specific status requires confirmation.] (Bontkopkanarie)

6. DRAKENSBERG SISKIN *Pseudochloroptila symonsi* (875)   13 cm
Resembles only Cape Siskin, but their ranges do not overlap. It lacks the white-tipped primaries and tail feathers of Cape Siskin, but has diagnostic white outer tail feathers.
Female lacks yellow in its plumage. **Juv.** is heavily streaked on the head and breast. **Habitat.** Montane scrub and grassland. **Status.** Locally common resident; endemic. **Call.** Similar to that of Cape Siskin. (Bergpietjiekanarie)

7. CAPE SISKIN *Pseudochloroptila totta* (874)   12 cm
Resembles Drakensberg Siskin but has white tips to the flight and tail feathers (not white outer tail feathers). The ranges of these two species do not overlap.
Female is less richly coloured than male, and has less extensive white tips to the flight feathers (often not visible in the field). **Juv.** is heavily streaked on the head and breast. **Habitat.** Montane fynbos, forest margins, and sometimes along the coast; also frequents exotic pine plantations. **Status.** Common, localised resident; endemic. **Call.** Diagnostic contact call, 'voyp-veeyr', often given in flight; also a typically canary-like song. (Kaapse Pietjiekanarie)

1

black throat

white wing bars

brown rump

dark-cheeked race

2

white supercilium

grey cheeks

plain underparts

3

black cheeks

♂

streaked breast

4

uniform head

all-black head

♂

chestnut back, rump and tail

♀

5

pied head

♂

6

♂

♂

♀

♂

♀

7

♂

white primary and tail tips

white outer tail

1. WHITE-THROATED CANARY *Serinus albogularis* (879)　　　　　15 cm
Differs from other drab-coloured canaries by the combination of its small, white throat patch and greenish yellow rump. In similar habitat, it is distinguishable from female Yellow Canary (p. 420) by the massive bill and the absence of breast streaking. Juv. resembles ad. **Habitat.** Fynbos, Karoo scrub and scrub-filled mountain valleys. **Status.** Common resident; near-endemic. **Call.** A mixture of canary- and sparrow-like notes, given from a perch. (Witkeelkanarie)

2. COMMON CHAFFINCH *Fringilla coelebs* (868)　　　　　14,5-16 cm
Male is the only finch of the region to have a pinkish face and breast, a blue-grey head, and conspicuous white wing bars.
Female is a dowdy, grey-brown, sparrow-like bird but still shows clear white wing bars. Juv. resembles females. **Habitat.** Exotic pine and oak plantations, and well-wooded gardens. **Status.** Introduced from Europe; uncommon, localised resident on the eastern slopes of Table Mountain. **Call.** A clear 'pink, pink, pink'; a short, rattling song, falling in pitch, typically uttered from high in a tree. (Gryskoppie)

3. CABANIS'S BUNTING *Emberiza cabanisi* (883)　　　　　16-17 cm
May be distinguished from Golden-breasted Bunting by its greyish (not chestnut) mantle, streaked black, and by the black cheeks without a white stripe below the eye. **Female** and **juv.** are duller versions of male. **Habitat.** Miombo woodland. **Status.** Uncommon, localised resident. **Call.** A clear 'tsseeoo' contact note; song described as a 'wee-chidder-chidder-wee'. (Geelstreepkoppie)

4. CINNAMON-BREASTED (ROCK) BUNTING *Emberiza tahapisi* (886)　　14-15 cm
In comparison with Cape Bunting, this species has cinnamon (not grey) underparts and a black (not white) throat; it also lacks the contrasting chestnut wing coverts. **Female** and **juv.** have less bold black-and-white head markings than male but still show the diagnostic cinnamon underparts. **Habitat.** Rocky slopes in mountainous terrain, and mixed woodland in the north. **Status.** Common resident; nomadic when not breeding. **Call.** A grating, rattling song; a soft 'pee-pee-wee'. (Klipstreepkoppie)

5. GOLDEN-BREASTED BUNTING *Emberiza flaviventris* (884)　　　15-16 cm
Although very similar to Cabanis's Bunting, this species differs in having a white stripe below the eye, a chestnut (not greyish) mantle, and a richer yellow breast, washed with orange. The white wing bars are conspicuous in flight. **Female** and **juv.** are duller versions of male. **Habitat.** Thornveld, broad-leaved woodland and exotic plantations. **Status.** Common resident. **Call.** A nasal, buzzy 'zzhrrrr'; song a varied 'weechee, weechee, weechee'. (Rooirugstreepkoppie)

6. LARK-LIKE BUNTING *Emberiza impetuani* (887)　　　　　14 cm
A dowdy, nondescript bird that looks like a lark but behaves in typical bunting fashion. It lacks any diagnostic field characteristics apart from the pale cinnamon wash over the breast and the rufous edging to the wing feathers. **Female** and **juv.** are paler than male. **Habitat.** Karoo scrub, dry rocky valleys and open plains, thornveld and dry broad-leaved woodland. Gathers in large numbers at waterholes. **Status.** Common resident and nomadic; near-endemic. **Call.** A soft, nasal 'tuc-tuc'; a short, rapid buzzy song. (Vaalstreepkoppie)

7. CAPE BUNTING *Emberiza capensis* (885)　　　　　16 cm
The greyish breast, chestnut wing coverts, and lack of black on the throat differentiate this species from Cinnamon-breasted Bunting. **Juv.** has less definite head markings and duller chestnut wings than ad. **Habitat.** Sandy coastal scrub in the south, and mountainous terrain farther north. **Status.** Common resident. **Call.** A nasal, ascending three- to four-note 'zzoo-zeh-zee-zee'; a loud, chirping song. (Rooivlerkstreepkoppie)

2

pink face, grey crown and nape

♀

♂

white wing & shoulder patches

1

heavy bill

white throat

♂

plain breast

greenish-yellow rump

dark tip

3

♀ grey mantle, streaked back

♂

4

♀

dark throat

chestnut mantle

♀

5

white stripe below the eye

♂

♂

dark chestnut below

7

pale throat

grey-brown below

6

pale bill

chestnut wing coverts

rufous-edged wing features

Brown, L.H., Urban, E.K. & Newman, K.B. (eds). 1982. *The Birds of Africa,* Vol 1. Academic Press, London.

Chantler, P. & Driessens, G. 1995. Swifts: *a Guide to the Swifts and Treeswifts of the World.* Pica Press, Sussex.

Chittenden, H. (ed). 1992. *Top Birding Spots in Southern Africa.* Southern Book Publishers, Johannesburg.

Clancey, P.A. (ed). 1980. *SAOS Checklist of Southern African Birds.* Southern African Ornithological Society, Johannesburg.

Clancey, P.A.1967. *Gamebirds of Southern Africa.* Purnell, Cape Town.

Clancey, P.A. 1971. *A Handlist of the Birds of Southern Moçambique.* Instituto de Investigaiao Cientifica de Moçmbique, Lourenço Marques (Maputo).

Clancey, P.A. 1985. *The Rare Birds of Southern Africa.* Winchester Press, Johannesburg.

Clement, P., Harris, A. & Davis, J. 1993. *Finches and Sparrows: An Identification Guide.* Christopher Helm, London.

Clinning, C. & Butchart, D. 1989. *Southern African Bird Names Explained.* Southern African Ornithological Society, Johannesburg.

Cyrus, D. & Robson, N. 1980. *Bird Atlas of Natal.* University of Natal Press, Pietermaritzburg.

Del Hoyo, I., Elliott, A. & Sargatal, I. (eds). 1992, 1994, 1996. *Handbook of the Birds of the World,* Vols I, II and III. Lynx Edicions, Barcelona.

Earle, R. & Grobler, N. 1987. *First Atlas of Bird Distribution in the Orange Free State.* National Museum, Bloemfontein.

Fry, C.H., Fry, K. & Harris, A. 1992. *Kingfishers, Bee-eaters and Rollers: A Handbook.* Christopher Helm, London.

Fry, C.H., Keith, S. & Urban, E.K. (eds). 1988. *The Birds of Africa,* Vol 3. Academic Press, London.

Ginn, P.J., McIlleron, W.G. & Milstein, P. le S. 1989. *The Complete Book of Southern African Birds.* Struik Winchester, Cape Town.

Harrap, S. & Quinn, D. 1996. *Tits, Nuthatches and Treecreepers.* Christopher Helm, London.

Harrison, P. 1983. Seabirds: *An Identification Guide.* Croom Helm, London.

Harrison, P. 1987. *Seabirds of the World: A Photographic Guide.* Christopher Helm, London.

Hockey, P.A.R. 1996. *Sasol Birds of Southern Africa:* Checklist and Alternative Names (2nd ed.). Struik Publishers, Cape Town.

Hockey, P.A.R. & Douie, C. 1995. *Waders of Southern Africa.* Struik Winchester, Cape Town.

Hockey, P.A.R., Underhill, L.G., Neatherway, M. & Ryan, P.G. 1989. *Atlas of the Birds of the Southwestern Cape.* Cape Bird Club, Cape Town.

Irwin, M.P.S. 1981. *The Birds of Zimbabwe.* Quest Publishing, Salisbury (Harare).

Johnson, D.N. & Horner, R.F. 1986. 'Identifying Widows, Bishops and Queleas in female plumage'. *Bokmakierie* 38:13-17.

Keith, S., Urban, E.K. & Fry, C.H. (eds). 1992. *The Birds of Africa,* Vol IV. Academic Press, London.

Kemp, A.C. 1995. *The Horn bills.* Oxford University Press, Oxford.

Komen, J. 1988. 'Identity crisis: African Marsh, European Reed and European Marsh Warblers'. *Bokmakierie* 40:106-110.

Maclean, G.L. 1993. *Roberts' Birds of Southern Africa.* John Voelcker Bird Book Fund, Cape Town.

Maclean, G.L. & Darroll, G. 1986. *Ducks of Sub-Saharan Africa.* Acorn Books, Randburg.

Madge, S. & Burn, H. 1988. *Wildfowl: an Identification Guide to the Ducks, Geese and*

Swans of the World. Christopher Helm, London.

Madge, S. & Burn, H. 1994. *Crows and jays: a Guide to the Crows, Jays and Magpies of the World.* Christopher Helm, London.

Newman, K.B. 1987. *Birds of the Kruger National Park.* Southern Book Publishers, Johannesburg.

Newman, K. 1989. *Birds of Botswana.* Southern Book Publishers, Johannesburg.

Newman, K.B. 1993. *Birds of Southern Africa.* Southern Book Publishers, Johannesburg.

Newman, K. & Holtshausen, G. 1990. 'Identifying White Egrets'. *Birding in Southern Africa* 42:111-113.

Olsen, K.M. & Larsson, H. 1995. *Terns of Europe and North America.* Christopher Helm, London.

Penry, H. 1994. *Bird Atlas of Botswana.* University of Natal Press, Pietermaritzburg.

Pickford, P., Pickford, B. & Tarboton, W. 1989. *Southern African Birds of Prey.* Struik Publishers, Cape Town.

Quickelberge, C.D. 1989. *Birds of the Transkei.* Durban Natural History Museum, Durban.

Rowan, M.K. 1983. *The Doves, Parrots, Louries and Cuckoos of Southern Africa.* David Philip Publishers, Cape Town.

Sibley, C.G & Ahlquist, E. 1990. *Phylogeny and Classification of Birds.* Yale University Press, New Haven.

Sibley, C.G. & Monroe, B.L. jr. 1990. *Distribution and Taxonomy of Birds of the World.* Yale University Press, New Haven.

Sinclair, J.C. 1990. *South African Birds: A Photographic Guide.* Struik Publishers, Cape Town.

Sinclair, J.C. 1994. *Field Guide to the Birds of Southern Africa.* Struik Publishers, Cape Town.

Sinclair, J.C. & Davidson, I. 1995. *Southern African Birds: A Photographic Guide.* Struik Publishers, Cape Town.

Sinclair, J.C. & Goode, D. 1986. *Birds of Prey. Struik Publishers,* Cape Town.

Sinclair, J.C. & Goode, D. 1987. *Highveld Birds. Struik Publishers,* Cape Town.

Sinclair, J.C. & Mendelsohn, J. 1981. *Everyone's Guide to South African Birds.* Struik Publishers, Cape Town.

Sinclair, J.C. & Sinclair, J. 1995. *Birds of Namibia: A Photographic Guide.* Struik Publishers,Cape Town.

Sinclair, J.C. & Whyte, I. 1991. *Field Guide to the Birds of the Kruger National Park.* Struik Publishers, Cape Town.

Sinclair, J.C., Meakin, P. & Goode, D. 1990. *Common Birds.* Struik Publishers, Cape Town.

Skead, C.J. (ed.). 1960. *The Canaries, Seedeaters and Buntings of Southern Africa.* South African Bird Book Fund.

Skead, C.J. 1967. *The Sunbirds of Southern Africa.* AA Balkema, Cape Town.

Solomon, D. & Williams, I. 1992. *Birdwatch Zimbabwe.* Birds of a Feather, Harare.

Steyn, P. 1982. *Birds of Prey of Southern Africa.* David Philip Publishers, Cape Town.

Steyn, P. 1996. *Nesting Birds: the Breeding Habits of Southern African Birds.* Fernwood Press, Cape Town.

Turner, A. & Rose, C. 1989. *A Handbook to the Swallows and Martins of the World.* Christopher Helm, London.

Urban, E.K., Fry, C.H. & Keith, S. 1986. *The Birds of Africa,* Vol 2. Academic Press, London.

Van Perlo, B. 1995. *Birds of Eastern Africa.* HarperCollins, Hong Kong.

Winkler, H., Christie, D.A. & Nurney, D. 1995. *Woodpeckers: a Guide to the Woodpeckers, Piculets and Wrynecks of the World.* Pica Press, Sussex.

Zimmerman, D.A., Turner, D.A. & Nurney, D. 1995. *Birds of Kenya and Northern Tanzania.* Russel Friedman Books, Halfway House.

CHECKLIST

- 1 Common Ostrich
- 2 King Penguin
- 3 African Penguin
- 4 Rockhopper Penguin
- 5 Macaroni Penguin
- Gentoo Penguin
- Magellanic Penguin
- 6 Great Crested Grebe
- 7 Blacknecked Grebe
- 8 Little Grebe
- 9 Southern Royal Albatross
- Northern Royal Albatross
- 10 Wandering Albatross
- 11 Shy Albatross
- 12 Black-browed Albatross
- 13 Grey-headed Albatross
- 14 Atlantic Yellow-nosed Albatross
- Indian Yellow-nosed Albatross
- Buller's Albatross
- 905 Laysan Albatross
- 15 Dark-mantled Sooty Albatross
- 16 Light-mantled Sooty Albatross
- Tristan Albatross
- Salvin's Albatross
- Chatham Albatross
- 17 Southern Giant-Petrel
- 18 Northern Giant-Petrel
- 19 Southern Fulmar
- 20 Antarctic Petrel
- 21 Pintado Petrel
- 22 Bulwer's Petrel
- Jouanin's Petrel
- 23 Great-winged Petrel
- 24 Soft-plumaged Petrel
- 25 White-headed Petrel
- 26 Atlantic Petrel
- 27 Kerguelen Petrel
- 28 Blue Petrel
- 29 Broad-billed Prion
- Antarctic Prion
- Salvin's Prion
- Spectacled Petrel
- 30 Slenderbilled Prion
- 31 Fairy Prion
- 32 White-chinned Petrel
- 33 Grey Petrel
- 34 Cory's Shearwater
- Streaked Shearwater
- 35 Great Shearwater
- 36 Flesh-footed Shearwater
- 37 Sooty Shearwater
- Balearic Shearwater
- 38 Manx Shearwater
- 39 Little Shearwater
- 40 Audubon's Shearwater
- Mascarene Shearwater
- 41 Wedge-tailed Shearwater
- 42 European Storm-Petrel
- 43 Leach's Storm-Petrel
- 918 Matsudaira's Storm-Petrel
- 44 Wilson's Storm-Petrel
- 45 White-bellied Storm-Petrel
- 46 Black-bellied Storm-Petrel
- White-faced Storm-Petrel
- 47 Red-tailed Tropicbird
- 48 White-tailed Tropicbird
- 910 Red-billed Tropicbird
- 49 Great White Pelican
- 50 Pink-backed Pelican
- 52 Brown Booby
- 921 Red-footed Booby
- 53 Cape Gannet
- 54 Australian Gannet
- 55 White-breasted Cormorant
- 56 Cape Cormorant
- 57 Bank Cormorant
- 58 Reed Cormorant
- 59 Crowned Cormorant
- 60 African Darter
- 61 Greater Frigatebird
- 922 Lesser Frigatebird
- 62 Grey Heron
- 63 Black-headed Heron
- 64 Goliath Heron
- 65 Purple Heron
- Western Reef Heron
- 66 Great Egret
- 67 Little Egret
- 68 Yellow-billed Egret
- 69 Black Heron
- 70 Slaty Egret
- Little Blue Heron
- 71 Cattle Egret
- 72 Squacco Heron
- 73 Malagasy Pond-Heron
- 74 Green-backed Heron
- 75 Rufous-bellied Heron
- 76 Black-crowned Night-Heron
- 77 White-backed Night-Heron
- 78 Little Bittern
- 79 Dwarf Bittern
- 80 Eurasian Bittern
- 81 Hamerkop
- 83 White Stork
- 84 Black Stork
- 85 Abdim's Stork
- 86 Woolly-necked Stork
- 87 African Openbill
- 88 Saddle-billed Stork
- 89 Marabou Stork
- 90 Yellow-billed Stork
- 91 African Sacred Ibis
- 92 Southern Bald Ibis
- 93 Glossy Ibis
- 94 Hadeda Ibis
- 95 African Spoonbill
- 96 Greater Flamingo
- 97 Lesser Flamingo
- 99 White-faced Duck
- 100 Fulvous Duck
- 101 White-backed Duck
- 102 Egyptian Goose
- 103 South African Shelduck
- 104 Yellow-billed Duck
- 105 African Black Duck
- 923 Mallard
- 106 Cape Teal
- 107 Hottentot Teal
- 108 Red-billed Teal
- 109 Northern Pintail
- 110 Garganey
- 111 Northern Shoveler
- 112 Cape Shoveler
- 113 Southern Pochard
- 114 African Pygmy Goose
- 115 Comb Duck
- 116 Spur-winged Goose
- 117 Maccoa Duck
- 118 Secretarybird
- 119 Lammergeier
- 120 Egyptian Vulture
- 121 Hooded Vulture
- 122 Cape Vulture
- 123 White-backed Vulture
- Rüppell's Vulture
- 124 Lappet-faced Vulture
- 125 White-headed Vulture
- 126a Black Kite
- Yellow-billed Kite
- 127 Black-shouldered Kite
- 128 African Cuckoo Hawk
- 129 Bat Hawk

- 130 European Honey-Buzzard
- 131 Verreaux's Eagle
- 132 Tawny Eagle
- 133 Steppe Eagle
- 134 Lesser Spotted Eagle
- 135 Wahlberg's Eagle
- 136 Booted Eagle
- 137 African Hawk-Eagle
- 138 Ayres' Hawk-Eagle
- 139 Long-crested Eagle
- 140 Martial Eagle
- 141 African Crowned Eagle
- 142 Brown Snake-Eagle
- 143 Black-chested Snake-Eagle
- 144 Southern Banded Snake-Eagle
- 145 Western Banded Snake-Eagle
- 146 Bateleur
- 147 Palm-nut Vulture
- 148 African Fish-Eagle
- 149 Steppe Buzzard
- 150 Forest Buzzard
- 151 Long-legged Buzzard
- 152 Jackal Buzzard
- 153 Augur Buzzard
- 154 Lizard Buzzard
- 155 Rufous-chested Sparrowhawk
- 156 Ovambo Sparrowhawk
- 157 Little Sparrowhawk
- 158 Black Sparrowhawk
- 159 Shikra
- 160 African Goshawk
- 161 Gabar Goshawk
- 162 Southern Pale Chanting Goshawk
- 163 Dark Chanting Goshawk
- 164 Western Marsh-Harrier
- 165 African Marsh-Harrier
- 166 Montagu's Harrier
- 167 Pallid Harrier
- 168 Black Harrier
- 169 African Harrier-Hawk
- 170 Osprey
- 171 Peregrine Falcon
- 172 Lanner Falcon
- 173 Eurasian Hobby
- 174 African Hobby
- 175 Sooty Falcon
- 176 Taita Falcon
- 177 Eleonora's Falcon
- 178 Red-necked Falcon
- 179 Redfooted Falcon
- 180 Amur Falcon
- 181 Rock Kestrel

- 182 Greater Kestrel
- 183 Lesser Kestrel
- 184 Grey Kestrel
- 185 Dickinson's Kestrel
- 186 Pygmy Falcon
- 187 Chukar Partridge
- 188 Coqui Francolin
- 189 Crested Francolin
- 190 Grey-winged Francolin
- 191 Shelley's Francolin
- 192 Red-winged Francolin
- 193 Orange River Francolin
- 194 Red-billed Francolin
- 195 Cape Francolin
- 196 Natal Francolin
- 197 Hartlaub's Francolin
- 198 Red-necked Spurfowl
- 199 Swainson's Spurfowl
- 200 Common Quail
- 201 Harlequin Quail
- 202 Blue Quail
- 203 Helmeted Guineafowl
- 204 Crested Guineafowl
- 924 Common Peacock
- 205 Small Buttonquail
- 206 Hottentot Buttonquail
- Black-rumped Buttonquail
- 207 Wattled Crane
- 208 Blue Crane
- 209 Grey Crowned Crane
- 210 African Rail
- 211 Corn Crake
- 212 African Crake
- 213 Black Crake
- 214 Spotted Crake
- 215 Baillon's Crake
- 216 Striped Crake
- 217 Red-chested Flufftail
- 218 Buff-spotted Flufftail
- 219 Streaky-breasted Flufftail
- 221 Striped Flufftail
- 222 White-winged Flufftail
- 223 African Purple Swamphen
- 224 Allen's Gallinule
- 225 American Purple Gallinule
- 226 Common Moorhen
- 227 Lesser Moorhen
- 228 Red-knobbed Coot
- 229 African Finfoot
- 230 Kori Bustard
- 231 Denham's Bustard
- 232 Ludwig's Bustard
- 233 Barrow's Korhaan
- 234 Blue Korhaan
- 235 Karoo Korhaan

- 236 Rüppell's Korhaan
- 237 Red-crested Korhaan
- 238 Black-bellied Bustard
- 239a Southern Black Korhaan
- 239b Northern Black Korhaan
- 240 African Jacana
- 241 Lesser Jacana
- 242 Greater Painted-Snipe
- 243 Eurasian Oystercatcher
- 244 African Black Oystercatcher
- 245 Common Ringed Plover
- Little Ringed Plover
- 246 White-fronted Plover
- 908 Kentish Plover
- 247 Chestnut-banded Plover
- 248 Kittlitz's Plover
- 249 Three-banded Plover
- 250 Lesser Sand Plover
- 251 Greater Sand Plover
- 252 Caspian Plover
- 253a American Golden Plover
- 253 Pacific Golden Plover
- 254 Grey Plover
- 255 Crowned Lapwing
- 256 Senegal Lapwing
- 257 Black-winged Lapwing
- 258 Blacksmith Lapwing
- 920 Spur-winged Lapwing
- 259 White-crowned Lapwing
- 260 African Wattled Lapwing
- 261 Long-toed Lapwing
- 262 Ruddy Turnstone
- 263 Terek Sandpiper
- 264 Common Sandpiper
- 265 Green Sandpiper
- 266 Wood Sandpiper
- 267 Spotted Redshank
- 268 Common Redshank
- 269 Marsh Sandpiper
- 270 Common Greenshank
- 902 Lesser Yellowlegs
- 906 Greater Yellowlegs
- 271 Red Knot
- Great Knot
- 272 Curlew Sandpiper
- 273 Dunlin
- 274 Little Stint
- 275 Long-toed Stint
- 276 Red-necked Stint
- 277 White-rumped Sandpiper
- 278 Baird's Sandpiper
- 279 Pectoral Sandpiper
- 280 Temminck's Stint
- 281 Sanderling
- 282 Buff-breasted Sandpiper

- ❏ 283 Broad-billed Sandpiper
- ❏ 284 Ruff
- ❏ 285 Great Snipe
- ❏ 286 African Snipe
- ❏ 287 Black-tailed Godwit
- ❏ 288 Bar-tailed Godwit
- ❏ 914 Hudsonian Godwit
- ❏ 289 Eurasian Curlew
- ❏ 290 Common Whimbrel
- ❏ 291 Red Phalarope
- ❏ 292 Red-necked Phalarope
- ❏ 293 Wilson's Phalarope
- ❏ 294 Pied Avocet
- ❏ 295 Black-winged Stilt
- ❏ 296 Crab Plover
- ❏ 297 Spotted Thick-knee
- ❏ 298 Water Thick-knee
- ❏ 299 Burchell's Courser
- ❏ 300 Temminck's Courser
- ❏ 301 Double-banded Courser
- ❏ 302 Three-banded Courser
- ❏ 303 Bronze-winged Courser
- ❏ 304 Collared Pratincole
- ❏ 305 Black-winged Pratincole
- ❏ 306 Rock Pratincole
- ❏ 912 Greater Sheathbill
- ❏ 307 Parasitic Jaeger
- ❏ 308 Long-tailed Jaeger
- ❏ 309 Pomarine Jaeger
- ❏ 310 Subantarctic Skua
- ❏ 311 South Polar Skua
- ❏ Kelp Gull
- ❏ 313 Lesser Black-backed Gull
- ❏ 314 Herring Gull
- ❏ 315 Grey-headed Gull
- ❏ 316 Hartlaub's Gull
- ❏ 317 Franklin's Gull
- ❏ 318 Sabine's Gull
- ❏ 319 Common Black-headed Gull
- ❏ 312 Cape Gull
- ❏ Slender-billed Gull
- ❏ 320 Black-legged Kittiwake
- ❏ 321 Gull-billed Tern
- ❏ 322 Caspian Tern
- ❏ 323 Royal Tern
- ❏ 324 Swift Tern
- ❏ 325 Lesser Crested Tern
- ❏ 326 Sandwich Tern
- ❏ 327 Common Tern
- ❏ 328 Arctic Tern
- ❏ 329 Antarctic Tern
- ❏ 330 Roseate Tern
- ❏ 331 Black-naped Tern
- ❏ 332 Sooty Tern
- ❏ 333 Bridled Tern

- ❏ 334 Damara Tern
- ❏ 335 Little Tern
- ❏ 336 White-cheeked Tern
- ❏ 337 Black Tern
- ❏ 338 Whiskered Tern
- ❏ 339 White-winged Tern
- ❏ 340 Brown Noddy
- ❏ 341 Lesser Noddy
- ❏ 343 African Skimmer
- ❏ 344 Namaqua Sandgrouse
- ❏ 345 Burchell's Sandgrouse
- ❏ 346 Yellow-throated Sandgrouse
- ❏ 347 Double-banded Sandgrouse
- ❏ 348 Rock Dove
- ❏ 349 Speckled Pigeon
- ❏ 350 African Olive-Pigeon
- ❏ 351 Eastern Bronze-naped Pigeon
- ❏ 352 Red-eyed Dove
- ❏ 353 African Mourning Dove
- ❏ 354 Cape Turtle-Dove
- ❏ 919 European Turtle-Dove
- ❏ 355 Laughing Dove
- ❏ 356 Namaqua Dove
- ❏ 357 Blue-spotted Wood-Dove
- ❏ 358 Emerald-spotted Wood- Dove
- ❏ 359 Tambourine Dove
- ❏ 360 Lemon Dove
- ❏ 361 African Green-Pigeon
- ❏ 362 Cape Parrot
- ❏ 363 Brown-headed Parrot
- ❏ 364 Meyer's Parrot
- ❏ 365 Rüppell's Parrot
- ❏ Grey-headed Parrot
- ❏ 366 Rose-ringed Parakeet
- ❏ 367 Rosy-faced Lovebird
- ❏ 368 Lilian's Lovebird
- ❏ 369 Black-cheeked Lovebird
- ❏ 370a Knysna Turaco
- ❏ 370b Livingstone's Turaco
- ❏ Schalow's Turaco
- ❏ 371 Purple-crested Turaco
- ❏ 372 Ross's Turaco
- ❏ 373 Grey Go-away-bird
- ❏ 374 Common Cuckoo
- ❏ 375 African Cuckoo
- ❏ 376 Lesser Cuckoo
- ❏ 925 Madagascar Cuckoo
- ❏ 377 Red-chested Cuckoo
- ❏ 378 Black Cuckoo
- ❏ 379 Barred Long-tailed Cuckoo
- ❏ 380 Great Spotted Cuckoo
- ❏ 381 Levaillant's Cuckoo
- ❏ 382 Jacobin Cuckoo
- ❏ 383 Thick-billed Cuckoo
- ❏ 384 African Emerald Cuckoo

- ❏ 385 Klaas's Cuckoo
- ❏ 386 Diderick Cuckoo
- ❏ 387 Green Malkoha
- ❏ 388 Black Coucal
- ❏ 389 Coppery-tailed Coucal
- ❏ 390 Senegal Coucal
- ❏ 391a Burchell's Coucal
- ❏ 391b White-browed Coucal
- ❏ 392 Barn Owl
- ❏ 393 African Grass-Owl
- ❏ 394 African Wood-Owl
- ❏ 395 Marsh Owl
- ❏ 396 African Scops-Owl
- ❏ 397 Southern White-faced
      Scops Owl
- ❏ 398 Pearl-spotted Owlet
- ❏ 399 African Barred Owlet
- ❏ 400 Cape Eagle-Owl
- ❏ 401 Spotted Eagle-Owl
- ❏ 402 Giant Eagle-Owl
- ❏ 403 Pel's Fishing-Owl
- ❏ 404 European Nightjar
- ❏ 405 Fiery-necked Nightjar
- ❏ 406 Rufous-cheeked Nightjar
- ❏ 407 Swamp Nightjar
- ❏ 408 Freckled Nightjar
- ❏ 409 Square-tailed Nightjar
- ❏ 410 Pennant-winged Nightjar
- ❏ 411 Common Swift
- ❏ 412 African Black Swift
- ❏ 413 Bradfield's Swift
- ❏ 414 Pallid Swift
- ❏ 415 White-rumped Swift
- ❏ 416 Horus Swift
- ❏ 417 Little Swift
- ❏ 418 Alpine Swift
- ❏ 419 Mottled Swift
- ❏ 420 Scarce Swift
- ❏ 421 African Palm-Swift
- ❏ 422 Mottled Spinetail
- ❏ 423 Böhm's Spinetail
- ❏ 424 Speckled Mousebird
- ❏ 425 White-backed Mousebird
- ❏ 426 Red-faced Mousebird
- ❏ 427 Narina Trogon
- ❏ 428 Pied Kingfisher
- ❏ 429 Giant Kingfisher
- ❏ 430 Half-collared Kingfisher
- ❏ 431 Malachite Kingfisher
- ❏ 432 African Pygmy-Kingfisher
- ❏ 433 Woodland Kingfisher
- ❏ 434 Mangrove Kingfisher
- ❏ 435 Brown-hooded Kingfisher
- ❏ 436 Grey-headed Kingfisher
- ❏ 437 Striped Kingfisher

- 438 European Bee-eater
- 439 Madagascar Bee-eater
- 440 Blue-cheeked Bee-eater
- 441 Southern Carmine Bee-eater
- 442 Böhm's Bee-eater
- 443 White-fronted Bee-eater
- 444 Little Bee-eater
- 445 Swallow-tailed Bee-eater
- 917 White-throated Bee-eater
- 446 European Roller
- 447 Lilac-breasted Roller
- 448 Racket-tailed Roller
- 449 Purple Roller
- 450 Broad-billed Roller
- 451 African Hoopoe
- 452 Green Wood-Hoopoe
- 453 Violet Wood-Hoopoe
- 454 Common Scimitarbill
- 455 Trumpeter Hornbill
- 456 Silvery-cheeked Hornbill
- 457 African Grey Hornbill
- 458 Red-billed Hornbill
- 459 Southern Yellow-billed Hornbill
- 460 Crowned Hornbill
- 461 Bradfield's Hornbill
- 462 Monteiro's Hornbill
- 463 Southern Ground-Hornbill
- Damara Hornbill
- 464 Black-collared Barbet
- 465 Acacia Pied Barbet
- 466 White-eared Barbet
- 467 Whyte's Barbet
- 468 Green Barbet
- 469 Red-fronted Tinkerbird
- 470 Yellow-fronted Tinkerbird
- 471 Yellow-rumped Tinkerbird
- 472 Green Tinkerbird
- 473 Crested Barbet
- 474 Greater Honeyguide
- 475 Scaly-throated Honeyguide
- 476 Lesser Honeyguide
- 477 Pallid Honeyguide
- 478 Brown-backed Honeybird
- 479 Green-backed Honeybird
- 480 Ground Woodpecker
- 481 Bennett's Woodpecker
- 482 Speckle-throated Woodpecker
- 483 Golden-tailed Woodpecker
- 484 Knysna Woodpecker
- 485 Green-backed Woodpecker
- 486 Cardinal Woodpecker
- 487 Bearded Woodpecker
- 488 Olive Woodpecker
- 489 Red-throated Wryneck

- 490 African Broadbill
- 491 African Pitta
- 492 Melodious Lark
- 493 Monotonous Lark
- 494 Rufous-naped Lark
- 495 Cape Clapper Lark
- Eastern Clapper Lark
- Agulhas Clapper Lark
- 496 Flappet Lark
- 497 Fawn-coloured Lark
- 498 Sabota Lark
- 499 Rudd's Lark
- 500 Cape Long-billed Lark
- Agulhas Long-billed Lark
- Eastern Long-billed Lark
- Karoo Long-billed Lark
- Benguela Long-billed Lark
- 501 Short-clawed Lark
- 502 Karoo Lark
- Barlow's Lark
- 503 Dune Lark
- 504 Red Lark
- 505 Dusky Lark
- 506 Spike-heeled Lark
- 507 Red-capped Lark
- 508 Pink-billed Lark
- 509 Botha's Lark
- 510 Sclater's Lark
- 511 Stark's Lark
- 512 Large-billed Lark
- 514 Gray's Lark
- 515 Chestnut-backed Sparrowlark
- 516 Grey-backed Sparrowlark
- 517 Black-eared Sparrowlark
- 518 Barn Swallow
- 519 Angola Swallow
- 520 White-throated Swallow
- 521 Blue Swallow
- 522 Wire-tailed Swallow
- 523 Pearl-breasted Swallow
- 524 Red-breasted Swallow
- 904 Red-rumped Swallow
- 525 Mosque Swallow
- 526 Greater Striped Swallow
- 527 Lesser Striped Swallow
- 528 South African Cliff-Swallow
- 529 Rock Martin
- 530 Common House-Martin
- 531 Grey-rumped Swallow
- 532 Sand Martin
- 533 Brown-throated Martin
- 534 Banded Martin
- 535 Mascarene Martin
- 536 Black Saw-wing
- 537 Eastern Saw-wing

- 913 White-headed Saw-wing
- 538 Black Cuckooshrike
- 539 White-breasted Cuckooshrike
- 540 Grey Cuckooshrike
- 541 Fork-tailed Drongo
- 542 Square-tailed Drongo
- 543 Eurasian Golden Oriole
- 544 African Golden Oriole
- 545 Black-headed Oriole
- 546 Green-headed Oriole
- 547 Cape Crow
- 548 Pied Crow
- 549 House Crow
- 550 White-necked Raven
- 551 Grey Tit
- 552 Ashy Tit
- 553 Miombo Tit
- 554 Southern Black Tit
- 555 Carp's Tit
- 556 Rufous-bellied Tit
- Cinnamon-breasted Tit
- 557 Cape Penduline-Tit
- 558 Grey Penduline-Tit
- 559 Spotted Creeper
- 560 Arrow-marked Babbler
- 561 Black-faced Babbler
- 562 Hartlaub's Babbler
- 563 Southern Pied Babbler
- 564 Bare-cheeked Babbler
- 565 Bush Blackcap
- 566 Cape Bulbul
- 567 African Red-eyed Bulbul
- 568 Dark-capped Bulbul
- 569 Terrestrial Brownbul
- 570 Yellow-streaked Greenbul
- 571 Tiny Greenbul
- 572 Sombre Greenbul
- 573 Stripe-cheeked Greenbul
- 574 Yellow-bellied Greenbul
- 575 Eastern Nicator
- 576 Kurrichane Thrush
- 577 Olive Thrush
- Karoo Thrush
- 578 Spotted Ground-Thrush
- 579 Orange Ground-Thrush
- 580 Groundscraper Thrush
- 581 Cape Rock-Thrush
- 582 Sentinel Rock-Thrush
- 583 Short-toed Rock-Thrush
- 584 Miombo Rock-Thrush
- 916 Common Redstart
- 586 Mountain Wheatear
- 587 Capped Wheatear
- 585 Northern Wheatear
- 915 Isabelline Wheatear

- 907 Pied Wheatear
- 588 Buff-streaked Chat
- 589 Familiar Chat
- 590 Tractrac Chat
- 591 Sickle-winged Chat
- 592 Karoo Chat
- 593 Mocking Cliff-Chat
- 594 Arnott's Chat
- 595 Anteating Chat
- 596 African Stonechat
- 597 Whinchat
- 598 Chorister Robin-Chat
- 599 White-browed Robin-Chat
- 600 Red-capped Robin-Chat
- 601 Cape Robin-Chat
- 602 White-throated Robin-Chat
- 603 Collared Palm-Thrush
- 604 Rufous-tailed Palm-Thrush
- 605 White-chested Alethe
- 606 White-starred Robin
- 607 Swynnerton's Robin
- 608 East Coast Akalat
- 609 Thrush Nightingale
- 610 Boulder Chat
- 611 Cape Rock-jumper
- 612 Drakensberg Rock-jumper
- 613 White-browed Scrub-Robin
- 614 Karoo Scrub-Robin
- 615 Kalahari Scrub-Robin
- 616 Brown Scrub-Robin
- 617 Bearded Robin
- 618 Herero Chat
- 619 Garden Warbler
- 620 Common Whitethroat
- 911 Blackcap
- 621 Chestnut-vented Tit-babbler
- 622 Layard's Tit-babbler
- 623 Yellow-bellied Hyliota
- 624 Southern Hyliota
- 625 Icterine Warbler
- 626 Olive-tree Warbler
- 627 River Warbler
- 628 Great Reed-Warbler
- 629 Basra Reed-Warbler
- 630 Eurasian Reed-Warbler
- 631 African Reed-Warbler
- 633 Marsh Warbler
- 634 Sedge Warbler
- 635 Lesser Swamp-Warbler
- 636 Greater Swamp-Warbler
- 637 Dark-capped Yellow Warbler
- 638 Little Rush-Warbler
- 639 Barratt's Warbler
- 640 Knysna Warbler
- 641 Victorin's Warbler

- 642 Broad-tailed Warbler
- 643 Willow Warbler
- 644 Yellow-throated Woodland Warbler
- 645 Bar-throated Apalis
- 646 Chirinda Apalis
- 647 Black-headed Apalis
- 648 Yellow-breasted Apalis
- 649 Rudd's Apalis
- 650 Red-faced Crombec
- 651 Long-billed Crombec
- 652 Red-capped Crombec
- 653 Yellow-bellied Eremomela
- 654 Karoo Eremomela
- 655 Green-capped Eremomela
- 656 Burnt-necked Eremomela
- 657 Green-backed Camaroptera
- Grey-backed Camaroptera
- 658 African Wren-Warbler
- 659 Stierling's Wren-Warbler
- 660 Cinnamon-breasted Warbler
- 661 Cape Grassbird
- 662 Rockrunner
- 663 Moustached Grass-Warbler
- 664 Zitting Cisticola
- 665 Desert Cisticola
- 666 Cloud Cisticola
- 667 Wing-snapping Cisticola
- 668 Pale-crowned Cisticola
- 669 Grey-backed Cisticola
- 670 Wailing Cisticola
- 671 Tinkling Cisticola
- 672 Rattling Cisticola
- 673 Singing Cisticola
- 674 Red-faced Cisticola
- 675 Rufous-winged Cisticola
- 676 Chirping Cisticola
- 677 Levaillant's Cisticola
- 678 Croaking Cisticola
- 679 Lazy Cisticola
- 680 Short-winged Cisticola
- Luapula Cisticola
- 681 Neddicky
- 682 Red-winged Warbler
- 683 Tawny-flanked Prinia
- 684 Roberts' Warbler
- 685 Black-chested Prinia
- 686a Karoo Prinia
- 686b Drakensberg Prinia
- 687 Namaqua Warbler
- 688 Rufous-eared Warbler
- 689 Spotted Flycatcher
- 690 African Dusky Flycatcher
- 691 Ashy Flycatcher
- 692 Collared Flycatcher

- 693 Grey Tit-Flycatcher
- 694 Southern Black Flycatcher
- 695 Marico Flycatcher
- 696 Pale Flycatcher
- 697 Chat Flycatcher
- 698 Fiscal Flycatcher
- 699 Black-and-white Flycatcher
- 700 Cape Batis
- 701 Chinspot Batis
- 702 Pale Batis
- 703 Pririt Batis
- 704 Woodward's Batis
- 705 Black-throated Wattle-eye
- 706 Fairy Flycatcher
- 707 Livingstone's Flycatcher
- 708 Blue-mantled Crested Flycatcher
- 709 White-tailed Crested Flycatcher
- 710 African Paradise-Flycatcher
- 711 African Pied Wagtail
- 712 Mountain Wagtail
- 713 Cape Wagtail
- 714 Yellow Wagtail
- 715 Grey Wagtail
- Citrine Wagtail
- 716 African Pipit
- 717 Long-billed Pipit
- 718 Plain-backed Pipit
- 719 Buffy Pipit
- Long-tailed Pipit
- 720 Striped Pipit
- 721 African Rock Pipit
- 722 Tree Pipit
- 723 Bushveld Pipit
- 901 Mountain Pipit
- 909 Wood Pipit
- 903 Red-throated Pipit
- 724 Short-tailed Pipit
- 725 Yellow-breasted Pipit
- 726 Golden Pipit
- 727 Cape Longclaw
- 728 Yellow-throated Longclaw
- 730 Rosy-throated Longclaw
- 731 Lesser Grey Shrike
- 732 Common Fiscal Shrike
- 733 Red-backed Shrike
- 734 Souza's Shrike
- 735 Magpie Shrike
- 736 Southern Boubou
- 737 Tropical Boubou
- 738 Swamp Boubou
- 739 Crimson-breasted Shrike
- 740 Black-backed Puffback
- 741 Brubru

- ☐ 742 Southern Tchagra
- ☐ 743 Brown-crowned Tchagra
- ☐ 744 Black-crowned Tchagra
- ☐ 745 Anchieta's Tchagra
- ☐ 746 Bokmakierie
- ☐ 747 Gorgeous Bush-Shrike
- ☐ 748 Orange-breasted Bush-Shrike
- ☐ 749 Black-fronted Bush-Shrike
- ☐ 750 Olive Bush-Shrike
- ☐ 751 Grey-headed Bush-Shrike
- ☐ 752 White-tailed Shrike
- ☐ 753 White-crested Helmet-Shrike
- ☐ 754 Retz's Helmet-Shrike
- ☐ 755 Chestnut-fronted Helmet-Shrike
- ☐ 756 Southern White-crowned Shrike
- ☐ 757 Common Starling
- ☐ 758 Common Myna
- ☐ 759 Pied Starling
- ☐ 760 Wattled Starling
- ☐ 761 Violet-backed Starling
- ☐ 762 Burchell's Starling
- ☐ 763 Meves' Starling
- ☐ 764 Cape Glossy Starling
- ☐ 765 Greater Blue-eared Starling
- ☐ 766 Miombo Blue-eared Starling
- ☐ 767 Sharp-tailed Starling
- ☐ 768 Black-bellied Starling
- ☐ 769 Red-winged Starling
- ☐ 770 Pale-winged Starling
- ☐ 771 Yellow-billed Oxpecker
- ☐ 772 Red-billed Oxpecker
- ☐ 773 Cape Sugarbird
- ☐ 774 Gurney's Sugarbird
- ☐ 775 Malachite Sunbird
- ☐ 776 Bronzy Sunbird
- ☐ 777 Orange-breasted Sunbird
- ☐ 778 Copper Sunbird
- ☐ 779 Marico Sunbird
- ☐ 780 Purple-banded Sunbird
- ☐ 781 Shelley's Sunbird
- ☐ 782 Neergaard's Sunbird
- ☐ 783 Southern Double-collared Sunbird
- ☐ 784 Miombo Double-collared Sunbird
- ☐ 785 Greater Double-collared Sunbird
- ☐ 786 Variable Sunbird
- ☐ 787 White-bellied Sunbird
- ☐ 788 Dusky Sunbird
- ☐ 789 Grey Sunbird
- ☐ Western Olive Sunbird

- ☐ 790 Eastern Olive Sunbird
- ☐ 791 Scarlet-chested Sunbird
- ☐ 792 Amethyst Sunbird
- ☐ 793 Collared Sunbird
- ☐ 794 Plain-backed Sunbird
- ☐ 795 Western Violet-backed Sunbird
- ☐ 796 Cape White-eye
- ☐ 797 African Yellow White-eye
- ☐ Orange River White-eye
- ☐ 798 Red-billed Buffalo-Weaver
- ☐ 799 White-browed Sparrow-weaver
- ☐ 800 Sociable Weaver
- ☐ 801 House Sparrow
- ☐ 802 Great Sparrow
- ☐ 803 Cape Sparrow
- ☐ 804 Southern Grey-headed Sparrow
- ☐ Northern Grey-headed Sparrow
- ☐ 805 Yellow-throated Petronia
- ☐ 806 Scaly-feathered Finch
- ☐ 807 Thick-billed Weaver
- ☐ 808 Dark-backed Weaver
- ☐ 809 Olive-headed Weaver
- ☐ 810 Spectacled Weaver
- ☐ 811 Village Weaver
- ☐ 812 Chestnut Weaver
- ☐ 813 Cape Weaver
- ☐ 814 Southern Masked-Weaver
- ☐ 815 Lesser Masked-Weaver
- ☐ 816 Golden Weaver
- ☐ 817 Yellow Weaver
- ☐ 818 Southern Brown-throated Weaver
- ☐ 819 Red-headed Weaver
- ☐ 820 Cuckoo Finch
- ☐ 821 Red-billed Quelea
- ☐ 822 Red-headed Quelea
- ☐ 823 Cardinal Quelea
- ☐ 824 Southern Red Bishop
- ☐ 825 Black-winged Bishop
- ☐ 826 Yellow-crowned Bishop
- ☐ 827 Yellow Bishop
- ☐ 828 Fan-tailed Widowbird
- ☐ 829 White-winged Widowbird
- ☐ 830 Yellow-mantled Widow
- ☐ 831 Red-collared Widowbird
- ☐ 832 Long-tailed Widowbird
- ☐ 833 Orange-winged Pytilia
- ☐ 834 Green-winged Pytilia
- ☐ 835 Green Twinspot
- ☐ 836 Red-faced Crimsonwing
- ☐ 837 Lesser Seedcracker

- ☐ 838 Pink-throated Twinspot
- ☐ 839 Red-throated Twinspot
- ☐ 840 African Firefinch
- ☐ 841 Jameson's Firefinch
- ☐ 842 Red-billed Firefinch
- ☐ 843 Brown Firefinch
- ☐ 844 Blue Waxbill
- ☐ 845 Violet-eared Waxbill
- ☐ 846 Common Waxbill
- ☐ 847 Black-faced Waxbill
- ☐ 848 Grey Waxbill
- ☐ 849 Cinderella Waxbill
- ☐ 850 Swee Waxbill
- ☐ 851 Yellow-bellied Waxbill
- ☐ 852 African Quail Finch
- ☐ 853 Locust Finch
- ☐ 854 Orange-breasted Waxbill
- ☐ 855 Cut-throat Finch
- ☐ 856 Red-headed Finch
- ☐ 857 Bronze Mannikin
- ☐ 858 Red-backed Mannikin
- ☐ 859 Magpie Mannikin
- ☐ 860 Pin-tailed Whydah
- ☐ 861 Shaft-tailed Whydah
- ☐ 862 Long-tailed Paradise-Whydah
- ☐ 863 Broad-tailed Paradise-Whydah
- ☐ 864 Dusky Indigobird
- ☐ 865 Purple Indigobird
- ☐ Zambezi Indigobird
- ☐ 867 Village Indigobird
- ☐ 868 Common Chaffinch
- ☐ 869 Yellow-fronted Canary
- ☐ 870 Black-throated Canary
- ☐ 871 Lemon-breasted Canary
- ☐ 872 Cape Canary
- ☐ 873 Forest Canary
- ☐ 874 Cape Siskin
- ☐ 875 Drakensberg Siskin
- ☐ 876 Black-headed Canary
- ☐ 877 Brimstone Canary
- ☐ 878 Yellow Canary
- ☐ 879 White-throated Canary
- ☐ Damara Canary
- ☐ 880 Protea Seed-eater
- ☐ 881 Streaky-headed Seed-eater
- ☐ 882 Black-eared Seed-eater
- ☐ 883 Cabanis's Bunting
- ☐ 884 Golden-breasted Bunting
- ☐ 885 Cape Bunting
- ☐ 886 Cinnamon-breasted Bunting
- ☐ 887 Lark-like Bunting

CHECKLIST

433

INDEX TO AFRIKAANS NAMES

INDEX TO COMMON NAMES